Learning to Use
WINDOWS APPLICATIONS

LOTUS 1-2-3 Release 5
FOR WINDOWS

SHELLY
CASHMAN
SERIES

Learning to Use

WINDOWS APPLICATIONS

LOTUS 1-2-3 Release 5 FOR WINDOWS

Gary B. Shelly
Thomas J. Cashman
Kathleen Shelly

Contributing Author

Steven G. Forsythe

boyd & fraser
publishing company

An International Thomson Publishing Company

Danvers • Albany • Bonn • Boston • Cincinnati • Detroit • London • Madrid • Melbourne
Mexico City • New York • Paris • San Francisco • Singapore • Tokyo • Toronto • Washington

Special thanks go to the following reviewers of the Shelly Cashman Series Windows Applications textbooks:

Susan Conners, Purdue University Calumet; **William Dorin**, Indiana University Northwest; **Robert Erickson**, University of Vermont; **Deborah Fansler**, Purdue University Calumet; **Roger Franklin**, The College of William and Mary; **Roy O. Foreman**, Purdue University Calumet; **Patricia Harris**, Mesa Community College; **Cynthia Kachik**, Santa Fe Community College; **Suzanne Lambert**, Broward Community College; **Anne McCoy**, Miami-Dade Community College/Kendall Campus; **Karen Meyer**, Wright State University; **Mike Michaelson**, Palomar College; **Michael Mick**, Purdue University Calumet; **Cathy Paprocki**, Harper College; **Jeffrey Quasney**, Educational Consultant; **Denise Rall**, Purdue University; **Sorel Reisman**, California State University, Fullerton; **John Ross**, Fox Valley Technical College; **Lorie Szalapski**, St. Paul Technical College; **Susan Sebok**, South Suburban College; **Betty Svendsen**, Oakton Community College; **Jeanie Thibault**, Educational Dynamics Institute; **Margaret Thomas**, Ohio University; **Carole Turner**, University of Wisconsin; **Diane Vaught**, National Business College; **Dwight Watt**, Swainsboro Technical Institute; **Melinda White**, Santa Fe Community College; **Eileen Zisk**, Community College of Rhode Island; and **Sue Zulauf**, Sinclair Community College.

© 1995 boyd & fraser publishing company
One Corporate Place • Ferncroft Village
Danvers, Massachusetts 01923

International Thomson Publishing
boyd & fraser publishing company is an ITP company
The ITP trademark is used under license.

Printed in the United States of America

For more information, contact boyd & fraser publishing company:

boyd & fraser publishing company
One Corporate Place • Ferncroft Village
Danvers, Massachusetts 01923, USA

International Thomson Publishing Europe
Berkshire House 168-173
High Holborn
London, WC1V 7AA, England

Thomas Nelson Australia
102 Dodds Street
South Melbourne 3205
Victoria, Australia

Nelson Canada
1120 Birchmont Road
Scarborough, Ontario
Canada M1K 5G4

International Thomson Editores
Campose Eliseos 385, Piso 7
Col. Polanco
11560 Mexico D.F. Mexico

International Thomson Publishing GmbH
Konigswinterer Strasse 418
53227 Bonn, Germany

International Thomson Publishing Asia
221 Henderson Road
#05-10 Henderson Building
Singapore 0315

International Thomson Publishing Japan
Hirakawacho Kyowa Building, 3F
2-2-1 Hirakawacho
Chiyoda-ku, Tokyo 102, Japan

ISBN 0-87709-991-X

1 2 3 4 5 6 7 8 9 10   BC   9 8 7 6 5

This book was designed using Windows 3.11, QuarkXpress 3.31 for Windows, and CorelDraw 3.0 for Windows.

CONTENTS

INTRODUCTION TO COMPUTERS COM1

OBJECTIVES	COM1
WHY STUDY COMPUTERS AND APPLICATION SOFTWARE?	COM2
WHAT IS A COMPUTER?	COM3
WHAT DOES A COMPUTER DO?	COM3
HOW DOES A COMPUTER KNOW WHAT TO DO?	COM4
WHAT ARE THE COMPONENTS OF A COMPUTER?	COM4
Input Devices	COM4
The Processor Unit	COM7
Output Devices	COM7
AUXILIARY STORAGE	COM10
COMPUTER SOFTWARE	COM14
System Software	COM14
Application Software	COM14
PERSONAL COMPUTER APPLICATION SOFTWARE PACKAGES	COM15

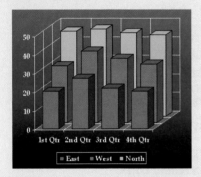

WHAT IS COMMUNICATIONS?	COM18
Communications Channels	COM19
Communications Equipment	COM19
COMMUNICATIONS NETWORKS	COM20
Local Area Networks (LANs)	COM20
Wide Area Networks (WANs)	COM22
HOW TO PURCHASE A COMPUTER SYSTEM	COM22
HOW TO INSTALL A COMPUTER SYSTEM	COM26
HOW TO MAINTAIN YOUR COMPUTER SYSTEM	COM28
SUMMARY OF INTRODUCTION TO COMPUTERS	COM30
STUDENT ASSIGNMENTS	COM30
Student Assignment 1: True/False	COM30
Student Assignment 2: Multiple Choice	COM31
Student Assignment 3: Comparing Personal Computer Advertisements	COM32
Student Assignment 4: Evaluating On-Line Information Services	COM32
Student Assignment 5: Visiting Local Computer Retail Stores	COM32
INDEX	COM32

USING MICROSOFT WINDOWS 3.1 WIN1

PROJECT ONE
An Introduction to Windows **WIN2**

OBJECTIVES	WIN2
INTRODUCTION	WIN2
What Is a User Interface?	WIN3
MICROSOFT WINDOWS	WIN3
Starting Microsoft Windows	WIN4
COMMUNICATING WITH MICROSOFT WINDOWS	WIN5
The Mouse and Mouse Pointer	WIN5
Mouse Operations	WIN6
The Keyboard and Keyboard Shortcuts	WIN9
Menus and Commands	WIN10
Selecting a Menu	WIN11
Choosing a Command	WIN11
Dialog Boxes	WIN12
USING MICROSOFT WINDOWS	WIN14
Opening a Group Window	WIN14
Correcting an Error While Double-Clicking a Group Icon	WIN16
Starting an Application	WIN16
Correcting an Error While Double-Clicking a Program-Item Icon	WIN18
Maximizing an Application Window	WIN18
Creating a Document	WIN19
Printing a Document by Choosing a Command from a Menu	WIN20
Quitting an Application	WIN21
FILE AND DISK CONCEPTS	WIN22
Naming a File	WIN23
Directory Structures and Directory Paths	WIN23
Saving a Document on Disk	WIN24
Correcting Errors Encountered While Saving a Document File	WIN27
Quitting an Application	WIN28
OPENING A DOCUMENT FILE	WIN28
Starting the Notepad Application and Maximizing the Notepad Window	WIN28
Opening a Document File	WIN29
Editing the Document File	WIN31
Saving the Modified Document File	WIN31
USING WINDOWS HELP	WIN32
Choosing a Help Topic	WIN33
Exiting the Online Help and Paintbrush Applications	WIN35
QUITTING WINDOWS	WIN36
Verify Changes to the Desktop Will Not be Saved	WIN36
Quitting Windows Without Saving Changes	WIN37
PROJECT SUMMARY	WIN38
KEY TERMS	WIN38
QUICK REFERENCE	WIN39
STUDENT ASSIGNMENTS	WIN40
COMPUTER LABORATORY EXERCISES	WIN43

PROJECT TWO
Disk and File Management **WIN47**

OBJECTIVES	WIN47
INTRODUCTION	WIN47
STARTING WINDOWS	WIN48
Starting File Manager and Maximizing the File Manager Window	WIN48

FILE MANAGER	**WIN49**
FORMATTING A DISKETTE	**WIN50**
Diskette Size and Capacity	WIN50
Formatting a Diskette	WIN51
Correcting Errors Encountered While	
Formatting a Diskette	WIN54
COPYING FILES TO A DISKETTE	**WIN54**
Maximizing the Directory Window	WIN55
Selecting a Group of Files	WIN55
Copying a Group of Files	WIN57
Correcting Erros Encountered While	
Copying Files	WIN59
Replacing a File on Disk	WIN60
Changing the Current Drive	WIN61
Correcting Errors Encountered While	
Changing the Current Drive	WIN62
RENAMING A FILE	**WIN63**
DELETING A FILE	**WIN65**
CREATING A BACKUP DISKETTE	**WIN67**
Correcting Errors Encountered While	
Copying a Diskette	WIN71
SEARCHING FOR HELP USING	
ONLINE HELP	**WIN71**
Searching for a Help Topic	WIN72
Searching for Help Using a Word or Phrase	WIN75
Quitting File Manager and Online Help	WIN77
SWITCHING BETWEEN APPLICATIONS	**WIN77**
Verify Changes to the File Manager Window	
Will Not be Saved	WIN79
Quitting File Manager	WIN79
ADDITIONAL COMMANDS AND CONCEPTS	**WIN80**
Activating a Group Window	WIN81
Closing a Group Window	WIN82
Resizing a Group Window	WIN83
Arranging Icons	WIN85
Minimizing an Application Window to an Icon	WIN86
PROJECT SUMMARY	**WIN86**
KEY TERMS	**WIN87**
QUICK REFERENCE	**WIN87**
STUDENT ASSIGNMENTS	**WIN88**
COMPUTER LABORATORY EXERCISES	**WIN92**
INDEX	**WIN96**

SPREADSHEETS USING LOTUS 1-2-3 RELEASE 5 FOR WINDOWS L1

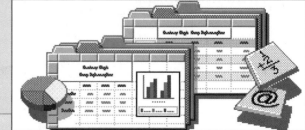

▶ PROJECT ONE
Building a Worksheet L2

OBJECTIVES	**L2**
WHAT IS LOTUS 1-2-3 FOR WINDOWS?	**L2**
INTRODUCTION	**L3**
PROJECT ONE	**L3**
Worksheet Preparation Steps L4	
STARTING LOTUS 1-2-3 RELEASE 5	
FOR WINDOWS	**L4**
THE 1-2-3 WINDOW	**L6**
Control Panel	L6
Work Area	L7
SELECTING A CELL	**L10**
ENTERING LABELS	**L10**
Entering the Worksheet Titles	L10
Correcting a Mistake While Typing	L13
Entering Column Titles	L13
Entering Row Titles	L15

ENTERING VALUES	**L16**
CALCULATING A SUM	**L18**
COPYING A CELL TO ADJACENT CELLS	**L19**
Summing a Row Total	L22
Copying Adjacent Cells in a Column	L23
SAVING A WORKSHEET	**L24**
USING FORMATTING TEMPLATES TO	
FORMAT THE WORKSHEET	**L26**
CHARTING A WORKSHEET	**L30**
PRINTING A WORKSHEET	**L37**
CLOSING THE WORKSHEET	**L39**
EXITING 1-2-3	**L39**
OPENING A WORKSHEET FILE	**L40**
CORRECTING ERRORS	**L42**
Correcting Errors Prior to Confirming a Data	
Entry Into a Cell	L42
Editing Data in a Cell	L42
Undoing Most Recent Actions	L44
Clearing a Cell or Range of Cells	L44
Clearing the Entire Worksheet	L45
1-2-3 ONLINE HELP	**L46**
1-2-3 Tutorial	L47
1-2-3 CLASSIC MENU	**L48**
PROJECT SUMMARY	**L49**
KEY TERMS AND INDEX	**L49**
QUICK REFERENCE	**L50**
STUDENT ASSIGNMENTS	**L51**
COMPUTER LABORATORY EXERCISES	**L56**
COMPUTER LABORATORY ASSIGNMENTS	**L58**

▶ PROJECT TWO
Formulas and Worksheet Enhancement L62

OBJECTIVES	**L62**
INTRODUCTION	**L62**
PROJECT TWO	**L63**
Spreadsheet Preparation Steps	L64
STARTING LOTUS 1-2-3 RELEASE 5	
FOR WINDOWS	**L65**
ENTERING WORKSHEET TITLES	**L65**
ENTERING DATA	**L66**
Entering Formulas	L67
Entering the Worksheet Data	L73
Entering Portfolio Summary Data	L77
SAVING THE WORKSHEET	**L84**
UNDERSTANDING FONTS AND FONT	
ATTRIBUTES	**L84**
FORMATTING LABELS	**L85**
Formatting the Worksheet Title	L85
Formatting the Column and Row Titles	L88
FORMATTING VALUES	**L90**
Currency Format	L90
Comma Format	L91
Percent Format	L92
Centering Values	L93
CHANGING THE WIDTHS OF COLUMNS	
AND HEIGHTS OF ROWS	**L93**
Changing the Widths of Columns	L94
Changing the Heights of Rows	L97

ADDING COLOR TO THE WORKSHEET **L98**
Changing the Color of the Worksheet Title L99
Changing the Color of the Worksheet L101
CHARTING THE WORKSHEET **L102**
Adding Titles to a Chart L105
Formatting the Chart Titles L106
CHECKING SPELLING **L108**
PRINT PREVIEW AND PRINTING THE WORKSHEET DATA SEPARATELY FROM THE CHART **L112**
PRINTING THE CHART SEPARATELY FROM THE WORKSHEET **L115**
DISPLAYING AND PRINTING THE FORMULAS IN THE WORKSHEET **L116**
PROJECT SUMMARY **L117**
KEY TERMS AND INDEX **L118**
QUICK REFERENCE **L118**
STUDENT ASSIGNMENTS **L119**
COMPUTER LABORATORY EXERCISES **L124**
COMPUTER LABORATORY ASSIGNMENTS **L127**

▶ **PROJECT THREE**
What-If Analysis **L134**
OBJECTIVES **L134**
INTRODUCTION **L134**
PROJECT THREE **L134**
Worksheet Preparation Steps L136
STARTING LOTUS 1-2-3 RELEASE 5 FOR WINDOWS **L137**
CHANGING WORKSHEET STYLE DEFAULTS **L137**
CREATING TEXT BLOCKS **L139**
USING DRAG-AND-FILL TO ENTER A DATA SEQUENCE IN A RANGE **L142**
Entering the Row Titles L144
USING DRAG AND DROP TO COPY CELLS **L144**
Completing the Entries in the Projected Percentages Section L146
ENTERING THE REVENUE VALUES **L148**
ROUNDING **L148**
ABSOLUTE CELL REFERENCES **L149**
Entering and Copying a Formula L153
Entering Additional Functions and Formulas L153
Completing the Entries L157
SAVING THE FILE **L158**
FORMATTING TEXT BLOCKS **L158**
Changing the Font Size and Attributes in a Text Block L158
Resizing Text Blocks L160
Aligning Text in a Text Block L162
Moving the Text Block L163
FORMATTING THE WORKSHEET **L164**
Adding a Pattern and Designer Frame to a Text Block L164
Formatting the Column and Row Titles L167
Formatting Values in the Worksheet L167
Adding Borders to Cells L168
Changing the Widths of Columns and Heights of Rows L171
Formatting the Projected Percentages Section L172
MULTIPLE WORKSHEETS **L172**
Inserting a Worksheet L172
Naming Worksheets L174
CREATING A STACKED BAR CHART **L175**
Adding X-Axis Labels L179
Adding Chart and Axis Titles L181

ENHANCING A STACKED BAR CHART **L182**
Resizing the Chart Title Frame L182
Adding Grid Lines to the Chart L183
Changing Font Size, Font Color, and Font Style L184
Adding a Designer Frame to the Chart L185
CHECKING THE SPELLING OF A WORKSHEET **L186**
PRINT PREVIEW AND PRINTING A WORKSHEET IN LANDSCAPE **L186**
Printing Landscape Reports L187
Printing a Chart L189
CHANGING VALUES IN CELLS REFERENCED IN A FORMULA **L190**
Splitting the Window into Panes L190
PROJECT SUMMARY **L192**
KEY TERMS AND INDEX **L193**
QUICK REFERENCE **L193**
SMARTICON REFERENCE **L195**
STUDENT ASSIGNMENTS **L195**
COMPUTER LABORATORY EXERCISES **L199**
COMPUTER LABORATORY ASSIGNMENTS **L201**

▶ **PROJECT FOUR**
Multiple Worksheets **L209**
OBJECTIVES **L209**
INTRODUCTION **L209**
PROJECT FOUR **L209**
Worksheet Preparation Steps L211
STARTING LOTUS 1-2-3 RELEASE 5 FOR WINDOWS **L212**
CREATING MULTIPLE WORKSHEETS **L212**
Copying Data Between Worksheets Using Drag-and-Drop L214
Entering the Worksheet Title and Data for the Universal Electronics Balance Sheet L217
Naming the Worksheets L218
CREATING A CONSOLIDATED WORKSHEET **L218**
Inserting a Worksheet Before the Current Worksheet L218
Copying Data Between Worksheets Using the Copy and Paste Icons L220
Creating Three-Dimensional Formulas L222
Completing the Worksheet L226
FORMATTING MULTIPLE WORKSHEETS **L226**
Grouping Worksheets L227
Formatting the Worksheet Titles L228
Formatting the Row Titles L228
Formatting the Values in US Dollar Format and Comma Format L229
Increasing the Widths of Columns and Heights of Rows L230
Adding Color, Underlining, and Designer Frames to the Worksheet L231
Changing the Color of the Worksheet Tabs L232
Viewing Multiple Worksheets L233
SAVING THE FILE **L237**
CREATING A PIE CHART **L237**
Adding a Title, Subtitle, and Note to a Chart L239
Adding Data Labels to a Chart L240
Exploding a Pie Slice L242
Adding a Text Block and an Arrow to a Chart L243
Formatting the Pie Chart L245
PRINTING MULTIPLE WORKSHEETS **L246**
Adding Page Breaks L246
Adding Headers and Footers L248
Printing the Multiple Worksheets L250
PROJECT SUMMARY **L254**
KEY TERMS AND INDEX **L254**
QUICK REFERENCE **L254**

STUDENT ASSIGNMENTS	**L255**
COMPUTER LABORATORY EXERCISES	**L260**
COMPUTER LABORATORY ASSIGNMENTS	**L261**

▶ PROJECT FIVE
Charts and Maps · **L269**

OBJECTIVES	**L269**
INTRODUCTION	**L269**
TYPES OF CHARTS	**L269**
Line Charts	L270
Mixed Charts	L270
HLCO Charts	L271
CREATING A CHART	**L271**
LINE CHARTS	**L272**
Understanding Charting Terms	L272
Understanding the Rules for Automatic Charting	L273
Creating a Line Chart	L274
Changing the Line Style, Width, Color, and Symbol	L275
Adding X-Axis and Y-Axis Grid Lines	L276
Changing the Format of Values	L278
Changing the Axes Titles and Background Color	L279
Renaming a Chart	L280
Saving a Chart	L282
Printing a Chart	L282
MIXED CHARTS	**L284**
Rotating Data in a Cell	L284
Creating a Mixed Chart	L286
Changing the Second Y-Axis Scale and Adding a Title	L288
Moving the Chart Legend and Plot	L290
Drawing an Ellipse and an Arrow	L292
Changing the Pattern and Edge Color of Bars	L293
HIGH-LOW-CLOSE-OPEN CHARTS	**L295**
Creating the HLCO Chart	L296
CHART SUMMARY	**L299**
MAPS	**L299**
Creating a Map	L300
Changing the Map Title	L302
Changing Bin Colors	L303
PROJECT SUMMARY	**L305**
KEY TERMS AND INDEX	**L306**
QUICK REFERENCE	**L306**
STUDENT ASSIGNMENTS	**L308**
COMPUTER LABORATORY EXERCISES	**L312**
COMPUTER LABORATORY ASSIGNMENTS	**L313**

▶ PROJECT SIX
Data Analysis · **L318**

OBJECTIVES	L318
INTRODUCTION	**L318**
PROJECT SIX	**L319**
Changing the Font of the Worksheet	L321
CREATING THE SEMINAR VARIABLES SECTION	**L321**
Naming a Range Using Adjacent Labels	L322
CREATING THE MANAGEMENT SEMINARS SECTION	**L324**
Displaying the System Date	L324
Entering the Row Titles	L326
Using Range Names in Formulas	L327
Completing the Management Seminars Section	L332
FORMATTING THE WORKSHEET	**L334**
SAVING THE FILE	**L336**
USING BACKSOLVER TO ANALYZE WORKSHEET DATA	**L336**

USING A 1-VARIABLE WHAT-IF TABLE TO ANALYZE WORKSHEET DATA	**L338**
Entering the What-if Table Title and Column Headings	L340
Using Drag-and-Fill to Create a Data Sequence	L340
Entering a Formula in a 1-Variable What-if Table	L341
Calculating the 1-Variable What-if Table	L342
Entering New Seminar Variables and Recalculating the What-if Table	L344
Formatting the 1-Variable What-if Table and Naming the Worksheet Tab	L345
CREATING A MACRO TO AUTOMATE DATA ENTRY	**L346**
Macro Commands	L347
Planning a Macro Command	L348
Entering Macro Commands in the Worksheet	L348
Naming the Macro	L351
WORKING WITH A MACRO BUTTON	**L352**
RUNNING A MACRO WITH A BUTTON	**L355**
DOCUMENTING THE MACRO	**L358**
CREATING A MACRO TO PRINT THE WORKSHEET	**L358**
FORMATTING THE MACROS WORKSHEET	**L363**
USING VERSION MANAGER TO ANALYZE DATA	**L363**
Creating a Version	L364
Displaying Versions	L369
PROTECTING DATA	**L370**
PROJECT SUMMARY	**L374**
KEY TERMS AND INDEX	**L374**
QUICK REFERENCE	**L375**
STUDENT ASSIGNMENTS	**L375**
COMPUTER LABORATORY EXERCISES	**L380**
COMPUTER LABORATORY ASSIGNMENTS	**L383**

▶ PROJECT SEVEN
Working with Database Tables · **L391**

OBJECTIVES	**L391**
INTRODUCTION	**L391**
PROJECT SEVEN	**L391**
STARTING LOTUS 1-2-3 RELEASE 5 FOR WINDOWS	**L393**
CREATING A DATABASE TABLE	**L393**
FORMATTING A DATABASE TABLE	**L395**
SAVING THE FILE	**L397**
SORTING A DATABASE TABLE	**L397**
Sorting a Database Table on a Single Sort Key	L397
Sorting a Database Table on Multiple Sort Keys	L400
FINDING RECORDS USING CRITERIA	**L402**
Finding Records Using a Single Criterion	L402
Finding Records Using Multiple Criteria	L407
QUERY TABLES	**L410**
Creating a Query Table	L410
Formatting Query Tables	L416
Changing Field Names in a Query Table	L417
Printing the Query_Table Worksheet	L420
CREATING A CROSSTAB TABLE TO SUMMARIZE DATABASE TABLE INFORMATION	**L421**
Printing the Summary Worksheet	L426
PROJECT SUMMARY	**L427**
KEY TERMS AND INDEX	**L427**
QUICK REFERENCE	**L427**
STUDENT ASSIGNMENTS	**L428**
COMPUTER LABORATORY EXERCISES	**L432**
COMPUTER LABORATORY ASSIGNMENTS	**L434**

INDEX	**L442**

PREFACE

▶ THE WINDOWS ENVIRONMENT

S ince the introduction of Microsoft Windows version 3.1, the personal computing industry has moved rapidly toward establishing Windows as the de facto user interface. The majority of software development funds in software vendor companies are devoted to Windows applications. Virtually all PCs purchased today, at any price, come preloaded with Windows and often with one or more Windows applications packages. With an enormous installed base, it is clear that Windows is the operating environment for both now and the future.

The Windows environment places the novice as well as the experienced user in the world of the mouse and a common graphical user interface between all applications. An up-to-date educational institution that teaches applications software to students for their immediate use and as a skill to be used within industry must teach Windows-based applications software.

▶ OBJECTIVES OF THIS TEXTBOOK

L *earning to Use Windows Applications: Lotus 1-2-3 Release 5 for Windows* was specifically developed for an introductory spreadsheet course. No previous experience with a computer is assumed, and no mathematics beyond the high school freshman level is required. The objectives of this book are as follows:

- ▶ To teach the fundamentals of Windows and Lotus 1-2-3 for Windows
- ▶ To acquaint the student with the proper way to solve spreadsheet problems
- ▶ To use practical problems to illustrate spreadsheet applications
- ▶ To take advantage of the many new capabilities of spreadsheets in a windows environment (see Figure P-1).

The textbook covers all essential aspects of Lotus 1-2-3 for Windows. When students complete a course using this book, they will have a firm knowledge of Windows and will be able to solve a variety of spreadsheet problems. Further, because they will be learning Windows, students will find the migration to other Windows applications software to be relatively simple and straightforward.

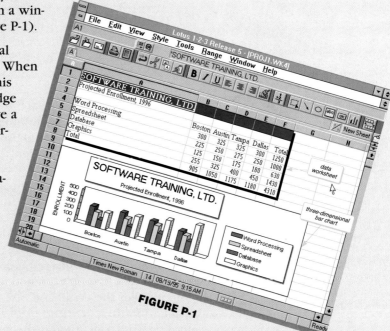

FIGURE P-1

▶ THE SHELLY CASHMAN APPROACH

The Shelly Cashman Series Windows Applications books present word processing, spreadsheet, database, programming, presentation graphics, and Windows itself by showing the actual screens displayed by Windows and the applications software. Because the student interacts with pictorial displays when using Windows, written words in a textbook do not suffice. For this reason, the Shelly Cashman Series emphasizes screen displays as the primary means of teaching Windows applications software. Every screen shown in the Shelly Cashman Series Windows Applications books appears in color, because the student views color on the screen. In addition, the screens display exactly as the student will see them. The screens in this book were captured while using the software. Nothing has been altered or changed except to highlight portions of the screen when appropriate (see the screens in Figure P-2).

The Shelly Cashman Series Windows Applications books present the material using a unique pedagogy designed specifically for the graphical environment of Windows. The textbooks are primarily designed for a lecture/lab method of presentation, although they are equally suited for a tutorial/hands-on approach wherein the student learns by actually completing each project following the step-by-step instructions. Features of this pedagogy include the following:

▶ **Project Orientation:** Each project in the book solves a complete problem, meaning that the student is introduced to a problem to be solved and is then given the step-by-step process to solve the problem.

▶ **Step-by-Step Instructions:** Each of the tasks required to complete a project is identified throughout the development of the project. For example, a task might be to change the second y-axis scale and add a title to a mixed chart. Then, each step to accomplish the task is specified. The steps are accompanied by screens (see Figure P-2). The student is not told to perform a step without seeing the result of the step on a color screen. Hence, students learn from this book the same as if they were using the computer. This attention to detail in accomplishing a task and showing the resulting screen makes the Shelly Cashman Series Windows Applications textbooks unique.

▶ **Multiple Ways to Use the Book:** Because each step to accomplish a task is illustrated with a screen, the book can be used in a number of ways, including: (a) Lecture and textbook approach — The instructor lectures on the material in the book. The student reads and studies the material and then applies the knowledge to an application on a computer; (b) Tutorial approach — The student performs each specified step on a computer. At the end of the project, the student has solved the problem and is ready to solve comparable student assignments; (c) Reference — Each task in a project is clearly identified. Therefore, the material serves as a complete reference because the student can refer to any task to determine how to accomplish it.

▶ **Windows/Graphical User Interface Approach:** Windows provides a graphical user interface. All of the examples in the book use this interface. Thus, the mouse is used for the majority of control functions and is the preferred user communication tool. When specifying a command to be executed, the sequence is as follows: (a) If a button invokes the command, use the button; (b) If a button is not available, use the command from a menu; (c) If a button or a menu cannot be used, only then is the keyboard used to implement a Windows command.

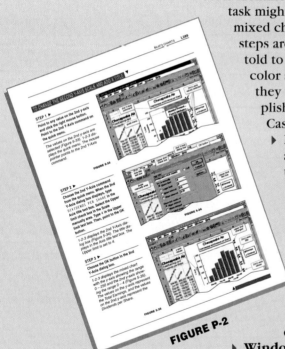

FIGURE P-2

▶ **Emphasis on Windows Techniques:** The most general techniques to implement commands, enter information, and generally interface with Windows are presented. This approach allows the student to move from one application software package to another under Windows with a minimum amount of relearning with respect to interfacing with the software. An application-specific method is taught only when no other option is available.

▶ **Reference for All Techniques:** Even though general Windows techniques are used in all examples, a Quick Reference chart (see Figure P-3) at the end of each project details not only the mouse and menu methods for implementing a command, but also contains the keyboard shortcuts for the commands presented in the project. Therefore, students are exposed to all means for implementing a command.

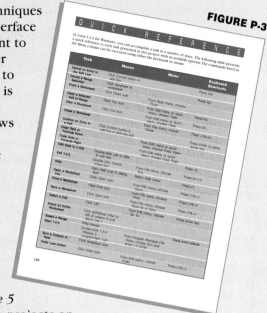

FIGURE P-3

▶ ORGANIZATION OF THIS TEXTBOOK

L *earning to Use Windows Applications: Lotus 1-2-3 Release 5 for Windows* consists of an introduction to computers, two projects on Microsoft Windows 3.1, and seven projects on Lotus 1-2-3 Release 5 for Windows.

An Introduction to Computers

Many students taking a course in the use of spreadsheet software will have little previous experience using computers. For this reason, the textbook begins with a section titled *Introduction to Computers* that covers computer hardware and software concepts important to first-time computer users.

Using Microsoft Windows 3.1

To effectively use Lotus 1-2-3 Release 5 for Windows, students need a practical knowledge of the Microsoft Windows graphical user interface. Thus, two Microsoft Windows projects are included prior to the spreadsheet projects.

Project 1 – An Introduction to Windows   The first project introduces the students to Windows concepts, Windows terminology, and how to communicate with Windows using the mouse and keyboard. Topics include starting and exiting Windows; opening group windows; maximizing windows; scrolling; selecting menus; choosing a command from a menu; starting and exiting Windows applications; obtaining online Help; and responding to dialog boxes.

Project 2 – Disk and File Management   The second project introduces the students to File Manager. Topics include formatting a diskette; copying a group of files; renaming and deleting files; searching for help topics; activating, resizing, and closing a group window; switching between applications; and minimizing an application window to an application icon.

Spreadsheets Using Lotus 1-2-3 Release 5 for Windows

After presenting the basic computer and Windows concepts, this textbook provides detailed instruction on how to use Lotus 1-2-3 Release 5 for Windows. The material is divided into seven projects as follows:

Project 1 – Building a Worksheet   In Project 1, students are introduced to the 1-2-3 window and the basic characteristics of a worksheet. Topics include starting 1-2-3; selecting a range; entering labels and values; using the SmartSum icon to calculate a sum; copying an @function to adjacent cells; saving a worksheet; using formatting templates; charting a worksheet; printing a worksheet; closing and opening a worksheet; correcting errors; and using online Help.

FIGURE P-4

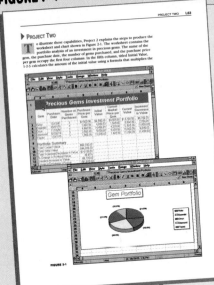

Project 2 – Formulas and Worksheet Enhancement   In Project 2, students use formulas to build a worksheet and learn more about formatting and charting a worksheet. Topics include entering and copying formulas; using the @MAX and @MIN functions; formatting labels and values; changing the widths of columns and heights of rows; adding color to a worksheet (Figure P-4); charting worksheet data in a pie chart; checking spelling; printing worksheet data and charts separately; and displaying and printing the formulas in a worksheet.

Project 3 – What-If Analysis   In Project 3, students use worksheets for management-decision making by learning the what-if capabilities of worksheets. Topics include changing worksheet style defaults; creating text blocks; using Drag-and-Fill to create a sequence; using drag and drop to copy cells; rounding and the @ROUND function; relative and absolute cell references; formatting text blocks; creating a stacked bar chart on a second worksheet; adding grid lines to a chart; adding a designer frame to a chart; and printing a worksheet in landscape.

Project 4 – Multiple Worksheets   In Project 4, students learn to work with multiple worksheets. Topics include using the Copy and Paste commands and drag-and-drop to copy data between worksheets; inserting worksheets before a current worksheet; naming a worksheet tab; creating a three-dimensional formula; formatting multiple worksheets using Group mode; viewing multiple worksheets in perspective; exploding a pie slice; adding a text block and an arrow to a chart; adding page breaks and headers and footers to multiple worksheets; and printing multiple worksheets.

Project 5 – Charts and Maps   In Project 5, students learn in-depth explanations of charting worksheet data, building on the charting skills taught in the first four projects. Emphasis is placed on choosing the correct chart type for the data to be charted. Charts include line charts, mixed charts, and HLCO charts. Topics include understanding the rules 1-2-3 follows for creating charts; changing the line style, width, color and symbol; adding x-axis and y-axis grid lines; changing the format of values; changing the axes titles and background colors; renaming a chart; rotating data in a cell; changing the second y-axis scale; drawing an ellipse and an arrow; and changing the pattern and edge color of bars. Students are also introduced to the mapping capabilities of 1-2-3. Topics include creating a map, editing the map title, and changing the bin colors.

Project 6 – Data Analysis   In Project 6, students learn more about analyzing data in a worksheet and how to use macros. Topics include naming ranges using adjacent labels; displaying the system date; using range names in formulas; analyzing worksheet data using Backsolver; creating a what-if table; using macros to automate data entry and print worksheet data; creating a macro button to run a macro; using Version Manager to analyze data; and protecting a worksheet.

Project 7 – Working with Database Tables   In Project 7, students learn to create, sort, and query a database table. Topics include creating and formatting a database table; sorting a database table on a single sort key; sorting a database table on multiple sort keys; finding records using a single criterion; finding records using multiple criteria; creating a query table; and creating a crosstab table to summarize database table information.

FIGURE P-5

▶ END-OF-PROJECT STUDENT ACTIVITIES

ach project ends with a wealth of student activities including these notable features:

▶ A list of Key Terms for review
▶ A Quick Reference that lists the ways to carry out a task using the mouse, menu, or keyboard shortcuts
▶ Six Student Assignments for homework and classroom discussion
▶ Three Computer Laboratory Exercises that usually require the student to load and manipulate a Lotus 1-2-3 file from the Student Diskette that accompanies this book
▶ Four Computer Laboratory Assignments (see Figure P-5) that require the student to develop a complete project assignment; the assignments increase in difficulty from a relatively easy assignment to a case study

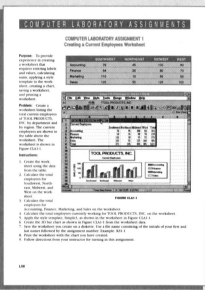

▶ ANCILLARY MATERIALS FOR TEACHING FROM THE SHELLY CASHMAN SERIES WINDOWS APPLICATIONS TEXTBOOKS

FIGURE P-6

 comprehensive instructor's support package accompanies all textbooks in the Shelly Cashman Series.

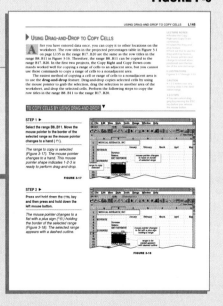

Annotated Instructor's Edition (AIE)   The AIE is designed to assist you with your lectures by suggesting transparencies to use, summarizing key points, proposing pertinent questions, offering important tips, alerting you to pitfalls, and incorporating the answers to the Student Assignments. There are several hundred annotations throughout the textbook (see Figure P-6).

Computer-Based LCD Lecture Success System   The Shelly Cashman Series proudly presents the finest LCD learning material available in textbook publishing. The Lecture Success System diskette, together with a personal computer and LCD technology, are used in lieu of transparencies. The system enables you to explain and illustrate the step-by-step, screen-by-screen development of a project in the textbook without entering large amounts of data, thereby improving your students' grasp of the material. The Lecture Success System leads to a smooth, easy error-free lecture.

The Lecture Success System diskette comes with files that correspond to key figures in the book. You load the files that pertain to a project and display them as needed. If the students want to see a series of steps a second time, simply reopen the file you want to start with and redo the steps. This presentation system is available to adopters without charge.

FIGURE P-7

Instructor's Materials   This instructor's ancillary (Figure P-7) contains the following:

▶ Detailed lesson plans including project objectives, project overview, and a three-column outline of each project that includes page references and transparency references
▶ Answers to all student assignments at the end of the projects
▶ A text bank of more than 600 True/False, Multiple Choice, and Fill-In questions
▶ Transparency masters for every screen, diagram, and table in the textbook
▶ An Instructor's Diskette that includes the projects and solutions to the Computer Laboratory Assignments at the end of each project

MicroExam IV   MicroExam IV, a computerized test-generating system, is available free to adopters of any Shelly Cashman Series textbooks. It includes all of the questions from the test bank just described. MicroExam IV is an easy-to-use, menu-driven software package that provides instructors with testing flexibility and allows customizing of testing documents.

▶ ACKNOWLEDGMENTS

The Shelly Cashman Series would not be the success it is without the contributions of outstanding publishing professionals. First, and foremost, among them is Becky Herrington, director of production and designer. She is the heart and soul of the Shelly Cashman Series, and it is only through her leadership, dedication, and untiring efforts that superior products are produced.

Under Becky's direction, the following individuals made significant contributions to these books: Ginny Harvey, series administrator and manuscript editor; Peter Schiller, production manager; Ken Russo, senior illustrator and cover art; Mike Bodnar, Greg Herrington, Dave Bonnewitz, and Dave Wyer, illustrators; Jeanne Black, Betty Hopkins, and Rebecca Evans, typographers; Tracy Murphy, series coordinator; Sue Sebok and Melissa Dowling LaRoe, copy editors; Marilyn Martin and Nancy Lamm, proofreaders; Henry Blackham, cover and opener photography; and Dennis Woelky, glass etchings.

Special recognition for a job well done must go to James Quasney, who, together with writing, assumed the responsibilities as series editor. Particular thanks go to Thomas Walker, president and CEO of boyd & fraser publishing company, who recognized the need, and provided the support, to produce the full-color Shelly Cashman Series Windows Applications textbooks.

We hope you will find using the book an enriching and rewarding experience.

Gary B. Shelly
Thomas J. Cashman

▶ Shelly Cashman Series – Traditionally Bound Textbooks

T he Shelly Cashman Series presents both Windows- and DOS-based personal computer applications in a variety of traditionally bound textbooks, as shown in the table below. For more information, see your ITP representative or call 1-800-423-0563.

COMPUTERS	
Computers	Using Computers: A Gateway to Information
	Using Computers: A Gateway to Information Brief Edition
Computers and Windows Applications	Using Computers and Microsoft Office: Introductory Concepts and Techniques (also available in spiral bound)
	Using Computers and Microsoft Office: Advanced Concepts and Techniques (also available in spiral bound)
	Using Computers and Works 3.0 (also available in spiral bound)
	Complete Computer Concepts and Microsoft Works 2.0 (also available in spiral bound)
Computers and DOS Applications	Complete Computer Concepts and WordPerfect 5.1, Lotus 1-2-3 Release 2.2, and dBASE IV Version 1.1 (also available in spiral bound)
	Complete Computer Concepts and WordPerfect 5.1, Lotus 1-2-3 Release 2.2, and dBASE III PLUS (also available in spiral bound)
Computers and Programming	Using Computers and Programming in QuickBASIC
	Using Computers and Programming in Microsoft BASIC

WINDOWS APPLICATIONS	
Integrated Packages	Microsoft Office: Introductory Concepts and Techniques (also available in spiral bound)
	Microsoft Office: Advanced Concepts and Techniques (also available in spiral bound)
	Microsoft Works 3.0 (also available in spiral bound)
	Microsoft Works 2.0 (also available in spiral bound)
Graphical User Interface	Microsoft Windows 3.1 Introductory Concepts and Techniques
	Microsoft Windows 3.1 Complete Concepts and Techniques
Windows Applications	Microsoft Word 2.0, Microsoft Excel 4, and Paradox 1.0 (also available in spiral bound)
Word Processing	Microsoft Word 6* • Microsoft Word 2.0
	WordPerfect 6* • WordPerfect 5.2
Spreadsheets	Microsoft Excel 5* • Microsoft Excel 4
	Lotus 1-2-3 Release 5* • Lotus 1-2-3 Release 4*
	Quattro Pro 5*
Database Management	Paradox 5* • Paradox 4.5 • Paradox 1.0
	Microsoft Access 2*
Presentation Graphics	Microsoft PowerPoint 4*

DOS APPLICATIONS	
Operating Systems	DOS 6 Introductory Concepts and Techniques
	DOS 6 and Microsoft Windows 3.1 Introductory Concepts and Techniques
Integrated Package	Microsoft Works 3.0 (also available in spiral bound)
DOS Applications	WordPerfect 5.1, Lotus 1-2-3 Release 2.2, and dBASE IV Version 1.1 (also available in spiral bound)
	WordPerfect 5.1, Lotus 1-2-3 Release 2.2, and dBASE III PLUS (also available in spiral bound)
Word Processing	WordPerfect 6.0
	WordPerfect 5.1 Step-by-Step Function Key Edition
	WordPerfect 5.1
	WordPerfect 5.1 Function Key Edition
	WordPerfect 4.2 (with Educational Software)
	WordStar 6.0 (with Educational Software)
Spreadsheets	Lotus 1-2-3 Release 4 • Lotus 1-2-3 Release 2.4 • Lotus 1-2-3 Release 2.3
	Lotus 1-2-3 Release 2.2 • Lotus 1-2-3 Release 2.01
	Quattro Pro 3.0
	Quattro with 1-2-3 Menus (with Educational Software)
Database Management	dBASE 5
	dBASE IV Version 1.1
	dBASE III PLUS (with Educational Software)
	Paradox 4.5
	Paradox 3.5 (with Educational Software)

PROGRAMMING AND NETWORKING	
Programming	Microsoft BASIC
	QuickBASIC
	Microsoft Visual Basic 3.0 for Windows*
Networking	Novell Netware for Users
Internet	The Internet: Introductory Concepts and Techniques

*Also available as a mini-book in the Double Diamond Edition

▶ SHELLY CASHMAN SERIES – Custom Edition PROGRAM

I f you do not find a Shelly Cashman Series traditionally bound textbook to fit your needs, boyd & fraser's unique **Custom Edition** program allows you to choose from a number of options and create a textbook perfectly suited to your course. The customized materials are available in a variety of binding styles, including boyd & fraser's patented **Custom Edition** kit, spiral bound, and notebook bound. Features of the **Custom Edition** program are:

▶ Textbooks that match the content of your course
▶ Windows- and DOS-based materials for the latest versions of personal computer applications software
▶ Shelly Cashman Series quality, with the same full-color materials and Shelly Cashman Series pedagogy found in the traditionally bound books
▶ Affordable pricing so your students receive the **Custom Edition** at a cost similar to that of traditionally bound books

The table on the right summarizes the available materials. For more information, see your ITP representative or call 1-800-423-0563.

COMPUTERS	
Computers	Using Computers: A Gateway to Information
	Using Computers: A Gateway to Information Brief Edition
	Introduction to Computers (32-page)
OPERATING SYSTEMS	
Graphical User Interface	Microsoft Windows 3.1 Introductory Concepts and Techniques
	Microsoft Windows 3.1 Complete Concepts and Techniques
Operating Systems	Introduction to DOS 6 (using DOS prompt)
	Introduction to DOS 5.0 (using DOS shell)
	Introduction to DOS 5.0 or earlier (using DOS prompt)
WINDOWS APPLICATIONS	
Integrated Packages	Microsoft Works 3.0
	Microsoft Works 2.0
Microsoft Office	Microsoft Office (16-page)
	Object Linking and Embedding (OLE) (32-page)
Word Processing	Microsoft Word 6*
	Microsoft Word 2.0
	WordPerfect 6*
	WordPerfect 5.2
Spreadsheets	Microsoft Excel 5*
	Microsoft Excel 4
	Lotus 1-2-3 Release 5*
	Lotus 1-2-3 Release 4*
	Quattro Pro 5*
Database Management	Paradox 5*
	Paradox 4.5
	Paradox 1.0
	Microsoft Access 2*
Presentation Graphics	Microsoft PowerPoint 4*
DOS APPLICATIONS	
Integrated Package	Microsoft Works 3.0
Word Processing	WordPerfect 6.0
	WordPerfect 5.1 Step-by-Step Function Key Edition
	WordPerfect 5.1
	WordPerfect 5.1 Function Key Edition
	Microsoft Word 5.0
	WordPerfect 4.2
	WordStar 6.0
Spreadsheets	Lotus 1-2-3 Release 4
	Lotus 1-2-3 Release 2.4
	Lotus 1-2-3 Release 2.3
	Lotus 1-2-3 Release 2.2
	Lotus 1-2-3 Release 2.01
	Quattro Pro 3.0
	Quattro with 1-2-3 Menus
Database Management	dBASE 5
	dBASE IV Version 1.1
	dBASE III PLUS
	Paradox 4.5
	Paradox 3.5
PROGRAMMING AND NETWORKING	
Programming	Microsoft BASIC
	QuickBASIC
	Microsoft Visual Basic 3.0 for Windows*
Networking	Novell Netware for Users
Internet	The Internet: Introductory Concepts and Techniques

* Also available as a mini-module

Introduction to Computers

Objectives

After completing this chapter, you will be able to:

▶ Define the term computer and discuss the four basic computer operations: input, processing, output, and storage

▶ Define data and information

▶ Explain the principal components of the computer and their use

▶ Describe the use and handling of diskettes and hard disks

▶ Discuss computer software and explain the difference between system software and application software

▶ Describe several types of personal computer applications software

▶ Discuss computer communications channels and equipment and LAN and WAN computer networks

▶ Explain how to purchase, install, and maintain a personal computer system

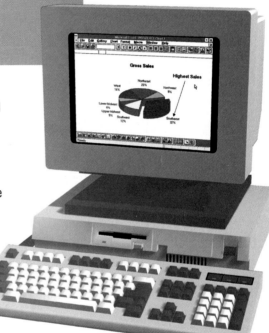

Every day, computers impact how individuals work and how they live. The use of small computers, called personal computers or microcomputers , continues to increase and has made computing available to almost anyone. In addition, advances in communication technology allow people to use personal computer systems to easily and quickly access and send information to other computers and computer users. At home, at work, and in the field, computers are helping people to do their work faster, more accurately, and in some cases, in ways that previously would not have been possible.

Why Study Computers and Application Software?

*T*oday, many people believe that knowing how to use a computer, especially a personal computer, is a basic skill necessary to succeed in business or to function effectively in society. As you can see in Figure 1, the use of computer technology is widespread in the world. It is important to understand that while computers are used in many different ways, there are certain types of common applications computer users need to know. It is this type of software that you will learn as you use this book. Given the widespread use and availability of computer systems, knowing how to use common application software on a computer system is an essential skill for practically everyone.

FIGURE 1
Computers in use in a wide variety of applications and professions. New applications are being developed every day.

Before you learn about application software, however, it will help if you understand what a computer is, the components of a computer, and the types of software used on computers. These topics are explained in this introduction. Also included is information that describes computer networks and a list of guidelines for purchasing, installing, and maintaining a personal computer.

What Is a Computer?

T he most obvious question related to understanding computers is, "What is a computer?" A computer is an electronic device, operating under the control of instructions stored in its own memory unit, that can accept data (input), process data arithmetically and logically, produce output from the processing, and store the results for future use. Generally the term is used to describe a collection of devices that function together as a system. An example of the devices that make up a personal computer, or microcomputer, is shown in Figure 2.

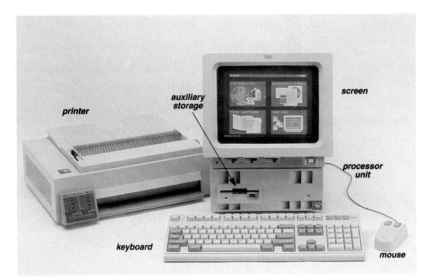

FIGURE 2
Devices that comprise a personal computer.

printer

auxiliary storage

screen

processor unit

keyboard

mouse

What Does a Computer Do?

W hether small or large, computers can perform four general operations. These operations comprise the information processing cycle and are: input, process, output, and storage. Collectively, these operations describe the procedures a computer performs to process data into information and store it for future use.

All computer processing requires data. Data refers to the raw facts, including numbers, words, images, and sounds, given to a computer during the input operation. In the processing phase, the computer manipulates the data to create information. Information refers to data processed into a form that has meaning and is useful. During the output operation, the information that has been created is put into some form, such as a printed report, that people can use. The information can also be placed in computer storage for future use.

These operations occur through the use of electronic circuits contained on small silicon chips inside the computer (Figure 3). Because these electronic circuits rarely fail and the data flows along these circuits at close to the speed of light, processing can be accomplished in billionths of a second. Thus, the computer is a powerful tool because it can perform these four operations reliably and quickly.

The people who either use the computer directly or use the information it provides are called computer users, end users, or sometimes, just users.

FIGURE 3
Inside a computer are chips and other electronic components that process data in billionths of a second.

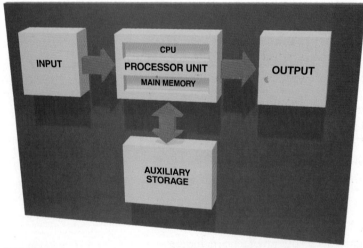

FIGURE 4
A computer is composed of input devices through which data is entered into the computer; the processor that processes data stored in main memory; output devices on which the results of the processing are made available; and auxiliary storage units that store data for future processing.

How Does a Computer Know What to Do?

For a computer to perform the operations in the information processing cycle, it must be given a detailed set of instructions that tell it exactly what to do. These instructions are called a computer program, or software. Before processing for a specific job begins, the computer program corresponding to that job is stored in the computer. Once the program is stored, the computer can begin to operate by executing the program's first instruction. The computer executes one program instruction after another until the job is complete.

What Are the Components of a Computer?

To understand how computers process data into information, you need to examine the primary components of the computer. The four primary components of a computer are: input devices, the processor unit, output devices, and auxiliary storage units (Figure 4).

Input Devices

Input devices enter data into main memory. Many input devices exist. The two most commonly used are the keyboard and the mouse.

The Keyboard The most commonly used input device is the keyboard, on which data is entered by manually keying in or typing. The keyboard on most computers is laid out in much the same manner as the one shown in Figure 5. The alphabetic keys are arranged like those on a typewriter.

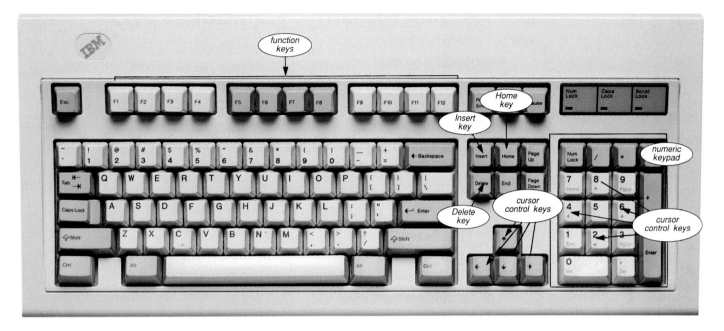

FIGURE 5
This keyboard represents most desktop personal computer keyboards.

A **numeric keypad** is located on the right side of most keyboards. This arrangement of keys allows you to enter numeric data rapidly. To activate the numeric keypad you press and engage the NUMLOCK key located above the numeric keypad. The NUMLOCK key activates the numeric keypad so when the keys are pressed, numeric characters are entered into the computer memory and appear on the screen. A light turns on at the top right of the keyboard to indicate that the numeric keys are in use.

The **cursor** is a symbol, such as an underline character, which indicates where you are working on the screen. The **cursor control keys**, or **arrow keys**, allow you to move the cursor around the screen. Pressing the UP ARROW (↑) key causes the cursor to move upward on the screen. The DOWN ARROW (↓) key causes the cursor to move down; the LEFT ARROW (←) and RIGHT ARROW (→) keys cause the cursor to move left and right on the screen. On the keyboard in Figure 5, there are two sets of cursor control keys. One set is included as part of the numeric keypad. The second set of cursor control keys is located between the typewriter keys and the numeric keypad. To use the numeric keypad for cursor control, the NUMLOCK key must be disengaged. If the NUMLOCK key is engaged (indicated by the fact that as you press any numeric keypad key, a number appears on the screen), you can return to the cursor mode by pressing the NUMLOCK key. On most keyboards, a NUMLOCK light will indicate when the numeric keypad is in the numeric mode or the cursor mode.

The other keys on the keypad—PAGE UP, PAGE DOWN, HOME, and END—have various functions depending on the software you use. Some programs make no use of these keys; others use the PAGE UP and PAGE DOWN keys, for example, to display previous or following pages of data on the screen. Some software uses the HOME key to move the cursor to the upper left corner of the screen. Likewise, the END key may be used to move the cursor to the end of a line of text or to the bottom of the screen, depending on the software.

Function keys on many keyboards can be programmed to accomplish specific tasks. For example, a function key might be used as a help key. Whenever that key is pressed, messages display that give instructions to help the user. The keyboard in Figure 5 has twelve function keys located across the top of the keyboard.

Other keys have special uses in some applications. The SHIFT keys have several functions. They work as they do on a typewriter, allowing you to type capital letters. The SHIFT key is always used to type the symbol on the upper portion of any key on the keyboard. Also, to temporarily use the cursor control keys on the numeric keypad as numeric entry keys, you can press the SHIFT key to switch into numeric mode. If you have instead pressed the NUMLOCK key to use the numeric keys, you can press the SHIFT key to shift temporarily back to the cursor mode.

The keyboard has a BACKSPACE key, a TAB key, an INSERT key and a DELETE key that perform the functions their names indicate.

The ESCAPE (ESC) key is generally used by computer software to cancel an instruction or exit from a situation. The use of the ESC key varies between software packages.

As with the ESC key, many keys are assigned special meaning by the computer software. Certain keys may be used more frequently than others by one piece of software but rarely used by another. It is this flexibility that allows you to use the computer in so many different applications.

The Mouse   A mouse (Figure 6) is a pointing device you can use instead of the cursor control keys. You lay the palm of your hand over the mouse and move it across the surface of a pad that provides traction for a rolling ball on the bottom of the mouse. The mouse detects the direction of the ball movement and sends this information to the screen to move the cursor. You push buttons on top of the mouse to indicate your choices of actions from lists or icons displayed on the screen.

FIGURE 6
The mouse input device is used to move the cursor and choose selections on the computer screen.

The Processor Unit

The **processor unit** is composed of the central processing unit and main memory. The **central processing unit (CPU)** contains the electronic circuits that cause processing to occur. The CPU interprets instructions to the computer, performs the logical and arithmetic processing operations, and causes the input and output operations to occur. On personal computers, the CPU is designed into a chip called a **microprocessor** (Figure 7).

Main memory, also called **random access memory**, or **RAM**, consists of electronic components that store data including numbers, letters of the alphabet, graphics, and sound. Any data to be processed must be stored in main memory. The amount of main memory in computers is typically measured in kilobytes or megabytes. One **kilobyte (K or KB)** equals 1,024 memory locations and one **megabyte (M or MB)** equals approximately 1 million memory locations. A memory location, or **byte**, usually stores one character. Therefore, a computer with 4MB can store approximately 4 million characters. One megabyte of memory can hold approximately 500 pages of text information.

FIGURE 7
A Pentium microprocessor from Intel Corporation. The microprocessor circuits are located in the center. Small gold wires lead from the circuits to the pins that fit in the microprocessor socket on the main circuit board of the computer. The pins provide an electronic connection to different parts of the computer.

Output Devices

Output devices make the information resulting from processing available for use. The output from computers can be presented in many forms, such as a printed report or color graphics. When a computer is used for processing tasks, such as word processing, spreadsheets, or database management, the two output devices most commonly used are the printer and the television-like display device called a screen, monitor, or CRT (cathode ray tube).

Printers   Printers used with computers can be either impact printers or nonimpact printers. An **impact printer** prints by striking an inked ribbon against the paper. One type of impact printer often used with personal computers is the dot matrix printer (Figure 8).

FIGURE 8
Dot matrix are the least expensive of the personal computer printers. Some can be purchased for less than $200. Advantages of dot matrix printers include the capability to handle wide paper and to print multipart forms.

FIGURE 9
On a dot matrix printer with a nine-pin print head, the letter E is formed with seven vertical and five horizontal dots. As the nine-pin print head moves from left to right, it fires one or more pins into the ribbon, making a dot on the paper. At the first print position, it fires pins 1 through 7. At print positions 2 through 4, it fires pins 1,4, and 7. At print position 5, it fires pins 1 and 7. Pins 8 and 9 are used for lowercase characters such as g, j, p, q, and y that extend below the line.

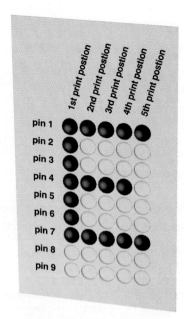

To print a character, a **dot matrix printer** generates a dot pattern representing a particular character. The printer then activates wires in a print head contained on the printer, so selected wires press against the ribbon and paper, creating a character. As you see in Figure 9, the character consists of a series of dots produced by the print head wires. In the actual size created by the printer, the characters are clear and easy to read.

Dot matrix printers vary in the speed with which they can print characters. These speeds range from 50 to more than 300 characters per second. Generally, the higher the speed, the higher the cost of the printer. Compared to other printers, dot matrix offer the lowest initial cost and the lowest per-page operating costs. Other advantages of dot matrix printers are that they can print on multipart forms and they can be purchased with wide carriages that can handle paper larger than 8 1/2 by 11 inches.

Nonimpact printers, such as ink jet printers and laser printers, form characters by means other than striking a ribbon against paper (Figure 10). Advantages of using a nonimpact printer are that it can print graphics and it can print in varying type sizes and styles called **fonts** (Figure 11). An **ink jet printer** forms a character by using a nozzle that sprays drops of ink onto the page. Ink jet printers produce relatively high-quality images and print between 30 and 150 characters per second in text mode and one to two pages per minute in graphics mode.

FIGURE 10 ▲
Two types of nonimpact printers are the laser printer (top) and the ink jet printer. Nonimpact printers are excellent for printing work that includes graphics.

FIGURE 11 ▶
Nonimpact printers do an excellent job of printing text in different typefaces, usually referred to as fonts. Technically, a font is a typeface in a particular size. It is common, however, to refer to the different typefaces as fonts. Dot matrix printers can print some fonts but usually at a slower rate and quality than nonimpact printers. The names of four different typefaces (fonts) are shown.

Laser printers work similar to a copying machine by converting data from the computer into a beam of light that is focused on a photoconductor drum, forming the images to be printed. The photoconductor attracts particles of toner that are fused by heat and pressure onto paper to produce an image. Laser printers produce high-quality output and are used for applications that combine text and graphics such as **desktop publishing** (Figure 12). Laser printers for personal computers can cost from $500 to more than $10,000. They can print four to sixteen pages of text and graphics per minute.

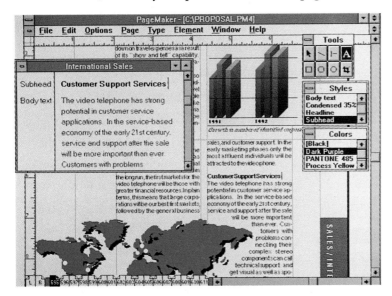

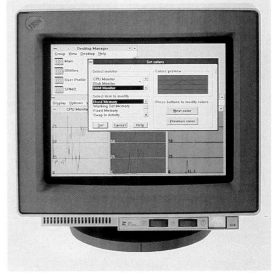

FIGURE 12
High-quality printed documents can be produced with laser printers and desktop publishing software.

Computer Screens Most full-size personal computers use a TV-like display device called a **screen, monitor,** or **CRT** (cathode ray tube) (Figure 13). Portable computers use a flat panel display that uses **liquid crystal display (LCD)** technology similar to a digital watch. The surface of the screen is made up of individual picture elements called **pixels.** Each pixel can be illuminated to form characters and graphic shapes (Figure 14). Color screens have three colored dots (red, green, and blue) for each pixel. These dots can be turned on to display different colors. Most color monitors today use super VGA (video graphics array) technology that can display 800 × 600 (width × height) pixels.

FIGURE 13
Many personal computer systems now come with color screens. Color can be used to enhance the information displayed so the user can understand it more quickly.

FIGURE 14
Pixel is an abreviation of the words picture element, one of thousands of spots on a computer screen that can be turned on and off to form text and graphics.

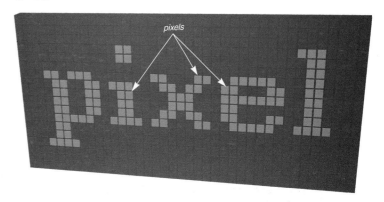

Auxiliary Storage

Auxiliary storage devices are used to store instructions and data when they are not being used in main memory. Two types of auxiliary storage most often used on personal computers are diskettes and hard disks. CD-ROM disk drives are also becoming common.

Diskettes   A diskette is a circular piece of oxide-coated plastic that stores data as magnetic spots. Diskettes are available in various sizes and storage capacities. Personal computers most commonly use diskettes that are 5 1/4 inches or 3 1/2 inches in diameter (Figure 15).

FIGURE 15
The most commonly used diskettes for personal computers are the 5 1/4-inch size on the left and the 3 1/2-inch size on the right. Although they are smaller in size, the 3 1/2-inch diskettes can store more data.

To read data stored on a diskette or to store data on a diskette, you insert the diskette in a disk drive (Figure 16). You can tell that the computer is reading data on the diskette or writing data on it because a light on the disk drive will come on while read/write operations are taking place. Do not try to insert or remove a diskette when the light is on as you could cause permanent damage to the data stored on it.

The storage capacities of disk drives and the related diskettes can vary widely (Figure 17). The number of characters that can be stored on a diskette by a disk drive depends on two factors: (1) the recording density of the bits on a track; and (2) the number of tracks on the diskette.

FIGURE 16
A user inserts a 3 1/2-inch diskette into the disk drive of a personal computer.

DIAMETER (INCHES)	DESCRIPTION	CAPACITY (BYTES)
5.25	Double-sided, double-density	360KB
5.25	Double-sided high-density	1.25MB
3.5	Double-sided double-density	720KB
3.5	Double-sided high-density	1.44MB

FIGURE 17
Storage capacities of different size and type diskettes.

Disk drives found on many personal computers are 5 1/4-inch, double-sided disk drives that can store from 360,000 bytes to 1.25 million bytes on the diskette. Another popular type is the 3 1/2-inch diskette, which, although physically smaller, stores from 720,000 bytes to 1.44 million bytes. An added benefit of the 3 1/2-inch diskette is its rigid plastic housing that protects the magnetic surface of the diskette.

The recording density is stated in bits per inch (bpi)—the number of magnetic spots that can be recorded on a diskette in a one-inch circumference of the innermost track on the diskette. Diskettes and disk drives used today are identified as being double-density or high-density. You need to be aware of the density of diskettes used by your system because data stored on high-density diskettes, for example, cannot be processed by a computer that has only double-density disk drives.

The second factor that influences the number of characters that can be stored on a diskette is the number of tracks on the diskette. A track is a very narrow recording band forming a full circle around the diskette (Figure 18).

FIGURE 18
Each track on a diskette is a narrow, circular band. On a diskette containing 80 tracks, the outside track is called track 0 and the inside track is called track 79. The disk surface is divided into sectors.

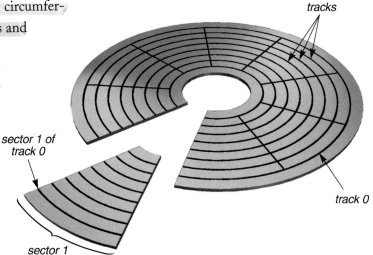

tracks

sector 1 of track 0

track 0

sector 1

The tracks are separated from each other by a very narrow blank gap. Each track on a diskette is divided into sectors. The term sector is used to refer to a pie-shaped section of the disk. It is also used to refer to a section of track. Sectors are the basic units for diskette storage. When data is read from a diskette, it reads a minimum of one full sector from a track. When data is stored on a diskette, it writes one full sector on a track at a time. The tracks and sectors on the diskette and the number of characters that can be stored in each sector are defined by a special formatting program that is used with the computer.

Data stored in sectors on a diskette must be retrieved and placed into main memory to be processed. The time required to access and retrieve data, called the **access time,** can be important in some applications. The access time for diskettes varies from about 175 milliseconds (one millisecond equals 1/1000 of a second) to approximately 300 milliseconds. On average, data stored in a single sector on a diskette can be retrieved in approximately 1/15 to 1/3 of a second.

Diskette care is important to preserve stored data. Properly handled, diskettes can store data indefinitely. However, the surface of the diskette can be damaged and the data stored can be lost if the diskette is handled improperly.

A diskette will give you very good service if you follow a few simple procedures:

1. Keep diskettes in their original box or in a special diskette storage box to protect them from dirt and dust and prevent them from being accidentally bent. Store 5 1/4-inch diskettes in their protective envelopes. Store the container away from heat and direct sunlight. Magnetic and electrical equipment, including telephones, radios, and televisions, can erase the data on a diskette, so do not place diskettes near such devices. Do not place heavy objects on a diskette, because the weight can pinch the covering, causing damage when the disk drive attempts to rotate.

2. To affix one of the self-adhesive labels supplied with most diskettes, it is best to write or type the information on the label before you place the label on the diskette. If the label is already on the diskette, use only a felt-tip pen to write on the label, and press lightly. Do not use ball point pens, pencils, or erasers on lables that are already on diskettes.

3. To use the diskette, grasp the diskette on the side away from the side to be inserted into the disk drive. Slide the diskette carefully into the slot on the disk drive. If the disk drive has a latch or door, close it. If it is difficult to close the disk drive door, do not force it—the diskette may not be inserted fully, and forcing the door closed may damage the diskette. Reinsert the diskette if necessary, and try again to close the door.

The diskette write-protect feature (Figure 19) prevents the accidental erasure of the data stored on a diskette by preventing the disk drive from writing new data or erasing existing data. On a 5 1/4-inch diskette, a write-protect notch is located on the side of the diskette. A special write-protect label is placed over this notch whenever you want to protect the data. On the 3 1/2-inch diskette, a small switch can slide to cover and uncover the write-protection window. On a 3 1/2-inch diskette, when the window is uncovered the data is protected.

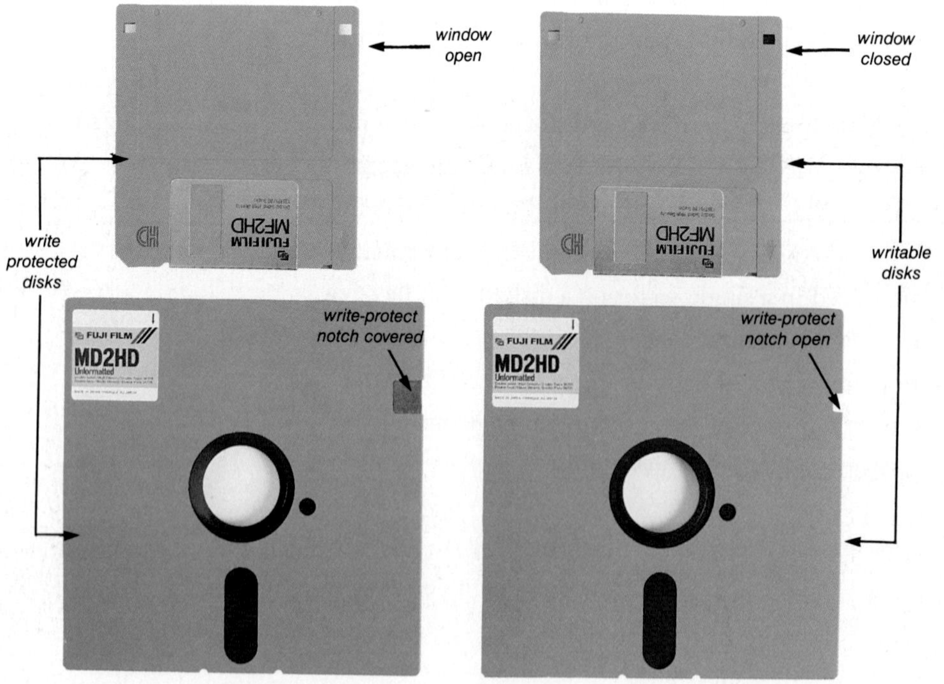

FIGURE 19
Data cannot be written on the 3 1/2-inch diskette on the top left because the window in the corner of the diskette is open. A small piece of plastic covers the window of the 3 1/2-inch diskette on the top right, so data can be written on this diskette. The reverse situation is true for the 5 1/4-inch diskettes. The write-protect notch of the 5 1/4-inch diskette on the bottom left is covered and, therefore, data cannot be written to the diskette. The notch of the 5 1/4-inch diskette on the bottom right, however, is open. Data can be written to this diskette.

Hard Disk   Another form of auxiliary storage is a hard disk. A hard disk consists of one or more rigid metal platters coated with a metal oxide material that allows data to be magnetically recorded on the surface of the platters (Figure 20). Although hard disks are available in removable cartridge form, most disks cannot be removed from the computer. As with diskettes, the data is recorded on hard disks on a series of tracks. The tracks are divided into sectors when the disk is formatted

The hard disk platters spin at a high rate of speed, typically 3,600 revolutions per minute. When reading data from the disk, the read head senses the magnetic spots that are recorded on the disk along the various tracks and transfers that data to main memory. When writing, the data is transferred from main memory and is stored as magnetic spots on the tracks on the recording surface of one or more of the disk platters. Unlike diskette drives, the read/write heads on a hard disk drive do not actually touch the surface of the disk.

The number of platters permanently mounted on the spindle of a hard disk varies. On most drives, each surface of the platter can be used to store data. Thus, if a hard disk drive uses one platter, two surfaces are available for data. If the drive uses two platters, four sets of read/write heads read and record data from the four surfaces. Storage capacities of internally mounted fixed disks for personal computers range from 80 million characters to more than 500 million characters. Larger capacity, stand-alone hard disk units are also available that can store more than one billion bytes of information. One billion bytes is called a gigabyte.

The amount of effective storage on both hard disks and diskettes can be increased by the use of compression programs. Compression programs use sophisticated formulas to replace spaces and repeated text and graphics patterns with codes that can later be used to recreate the compressed data. Text files can be compressed the most; as much as an eighth of their original volume. Graphics files can be compressed the least. Overall, a 2-to-1 compression ratio is average.

CD-ROM   Compact disk read-only memory (CD-ROM) disks are increasingly used to store large amounts of prerecorded information (Figure 21). Each CD-ROM disk can store more than 600 million bytes of data—the equivalent of 300,000 pages of text. Because of their large storage capacity, CD-ROM is often used for multimedia material. Multimedia combines text, graphics, video (pictures), and audio (sound) (Figure 22 on the next page).

spindle
disk surface
read/write head
access arm

FIGURE 20
The protective cover of this hard disk drive has been removed. A read/write head is at the end of the access arm that extends over the recording surface, called a platter.

FIGURE 21
CD-ROM disk drives allow the user to access tremendous amounts of prerecorded information — more than 600MB of data can be stored on one CD-ROM disk.

Computer Software

C omputer software is the key to productive use of computers. With the correct software, a computer can become a valuable tool. Software can be categorized into two types: system software and application software.

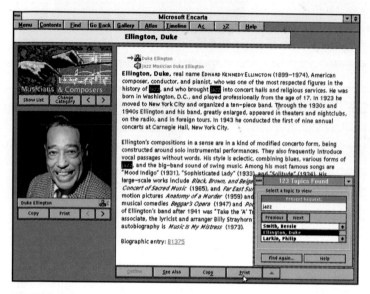

FIGURE 22
Microsoft Encarta is a multimedia encyclopedia available on a CD-ROM disk. Text, graphics, sound, and animation are all available. The camera-shaped icon at the top of the text indicates that a photograph is available for viewing. The speaker-shaped icon just below the camera indicates that a sound item is available. In this topic, if the user chooses the speaker icon with the mouse, a portion of Duke Ellington's music is played.

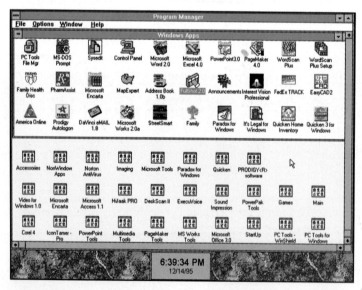

FIGURE 23
Microsoft Windows is a graphical user interface that works with the DOS operating system to make the computer easier to use. The small pictures or symbols on the main part of the screen are called icons. The icons represent different processing options, such as word pro-cessing or electronic spreadsheet applications, the user can choose.

System Software

System software consists of programs to con-trol the operations of computer equipment. An important part of system software is a set of programs called the **operating system**. Instruc-tions in the operating system tell the computer how to perform the functions of loading, stor-ing, and executing an application and how to transfer data. For a computer to operate, an operating system must be stored in the comput-er's main memory. When a computer is started, the operating system is loaded into the com-puter and stored in main memory. This process is called **booting**. The most commonly used operating system on personal computers is **DOS (Disk Operating System)**.

Many computers use an **operating envi-ronment** that works with the operating system to make the computer system easier to use. Operating environments have a **graphical user interface (GUI)** displaying visual clues such as icon symbols to help the user. Each **icon** repre-sents an application software package, such as word processing or a file or document where data is stored. **Microsoft Windows** (Figure 23) is a graphical user interface that works with DOS. Apple Macintosh computers also have a built in graphical user interface in the operating system.

Application Software

Application software consists of programs that tell a computer how to produce information. The different ways people use computers in their careers or in their personal lives, are examples of types of application software. Business, scientific, and educational programs are all examples of application software.

Personal Computer Application Software Packages

P ersonal computer users often use application software packages. Some of the most commonly used packages are: word processing, electronic spreadsheet, presentation graphics, database, communications, and electronic mail software.

Word processing software (Figure 24) is used to create and print documents. A key advantage of word processing software is its capability to make changes easily in documents, such as correcting spelling, changing margins, and adding, deleting, or relocating entire paragraphs. These changes would be difficult and time consuming to make using manual methods such as a typewriter. With a word processor, documents can be printed quickly and accurately and easily stored on a disk for future use. Word processing software is oriented toward working with text, but most word processing packages can also include numeric and graphic information.

Electronic spreadsheet software (Figure 25) allows the user to add, subtract, and perform user-defined calculations on rows and columns of numbers. These numbers can be changed and the spreadsheet quickly recalculates the new results. Electronic spreadsheet software eliminates the tedious recalculations required with manual methods. Spreadsheet information is frequently converted into a graphic form. Graphics capabilities are now included in most spreadsheet packages.

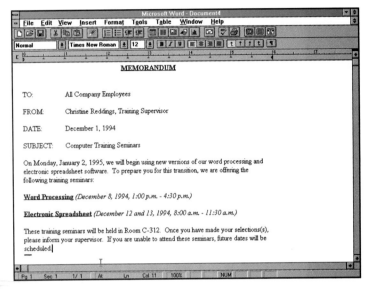

FIGURE 24

Word processing software is used to write letters, memos, and other documents. As the user types words and letters, they display on the screen. The user can easily add, delete, and change any text entered until the document looks exactly as desired. The user can then save the document on auxiliary storage and can also print it on a printer.

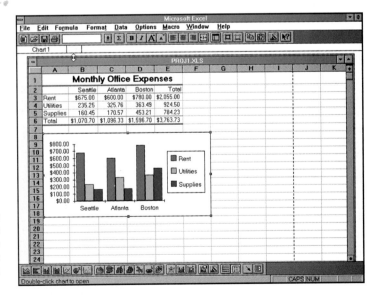

FIGURE 25

Electronic spreadsheet software is frequently used by people who work with numbers. The user enters the data and the formulas to be used on the data and calculates the results. Most spreadsheet programs have the capability to use numeric data to generate charts, such as the bar chart.

Database software (Figure 26) allows the user to enter, retrieve, and update data in an organized and efficient manner. These software packages have flexible inquiry and reporting capabilities that allow users to access the data in different ways and create custom reports that include some or all of the information in the database.

FIGURE 26
Database software allows the user to enter, retrieve, and update data in an organized and efficient manner. This database table illustrates how a business organized customer information. Once the table is defined, the user can add, delete, change, display, print, or reorganize the database records.

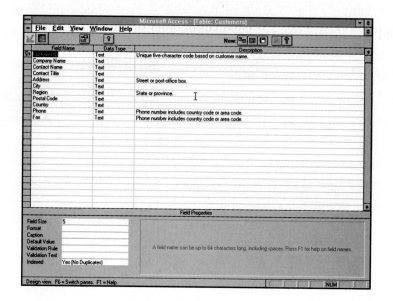

Presentation graphics software (Figure 27) allows the user to create documents called slides to be used in making presentations. Using special projection devices, the slides are projected directly from the computer. In addition, the slides can be printed and used as handouts, or converted into transparencies and displayed on overhead projectors. Presentation graphics software includes many special effects, color, and art that enhance information presented on a slide. Because slides frequently include numeric data, presentation graphics software includes the capability to convert the numeric data into many forms of charts.

FIGURE 27
Presentation graphics software allows the user to create documents called slides for use in presentations. Using special projection devices, the slides display as they appear on the computer screen. The slides can also be printed and used as handouts or converted into transparencies to be used with overhead projectors.

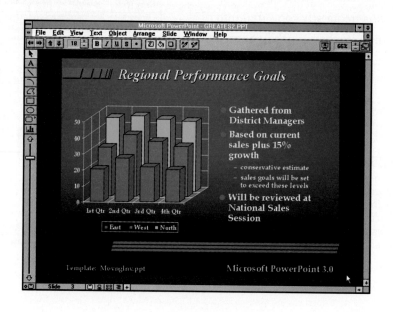

Communications software (Figure 28) is used to transmit data and information from one computer to another. For the transfer to take place, each computer must have communications software. Organizations use communications software to transfer information from one location to another. Many individuals use communications software to access on-line databases that provide information on current events, airline schedules, finances, weather, and hundreds of other subjects.

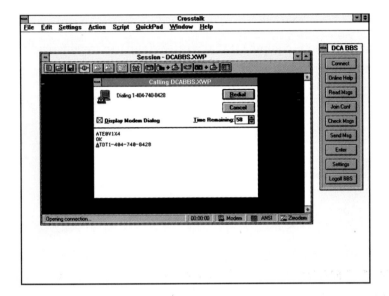

FIGURE 28
Communications software allows users to transmit data from one computer to another. This software enables the user to choose a previously entered phone number of another computer. Once the number is chosen, the communications software dials the number and establishes a communication link. The user can then transfer data or run programs on the remote computer.

Electronic mail software, also called **e-mail** (Figure 29), allows users to send messages to and receive messages from other computer users. The other users may be on the same computer network or on a separate computer system reached through the use of communications equipment and software.

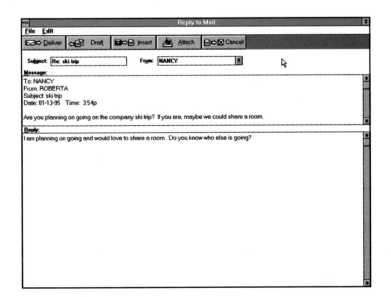

FIGURE 29
Electronic mail software allows users to send and receive messages with other computer users. Each user has an electronic mail box to which messages are sent. This software enables a user to add a reply to a received message and then send the reply back to the person who sent the original message.

What Is Communications?

Communications refers to the transmission of data and information over a communications channel, such as a standard telephone line, between one computer and another computer. Figure 30 shows the basic model for a communications system. This model consists of the following equipment:

1. A computer.
2. Communications equipment that sends (and can usually receive) data.
3. The communications channel over which the data is sent.
4. Communications equipment that receives (and can usually send) data.
5. Another computer.

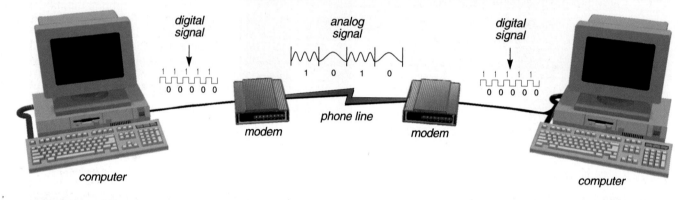

FIGURE 30
The basic model of a communications system. Individual electrical pulses of the digital signal from the computer are converted into analog (electrical wave) signals for transmission over voice telephone lines. At the main computer receiving end, another modem converts the analog signals back into digital signals that can be processed by the computer.

The basic model also includes communications software. When two computers are communicating with each other, compatible communications software is required on each system.

Communications is important to understand because of on-line services and the trend to network computers. With communications equipment and software, access is available to an increasing amount and variety of information and services. **On-line information services** such as Prodigy (Figure 31) and America On-Line offer the latest news, weather, sports, and financial information along with shopping, entertainment, and electronic mail.

International networks such as the Internet allow users to access information at thousands of Internet member organizations around the world. Electronic bulletin boards can be found in most cities with hundreds available in large metropolitan areas. An electronic **bulletin board system (BBS)** is a computer and at least one phone line that allows users to *chat* with the computer operator, called the **system operator (sys op)** or, if more than one phone line is available, with other BBS users. BBS users can also leave messages for other users. BBSs are often devoted to a specific subject area such as games, hobbies, or a specific type of computer or software. Many computer hardware and software companies operate BBSs so users of their products can share information.

Communications Channels

A **communications channel** is the path the data follows as it is transmitted from the sending equipment to the receiving equipment in a communications system. These channels are made up of one or more **transmission media**, including twisted pair wire, coaxial cable, fiber optics, microwave transmission, satellite transmission, and wireless transmission.

Communications Equipment

If a personal computer is within approximately 1,000 feet of another computer, the two devices can usually be directly connected by a cable. If the devices are more than 1,000 feet, however, the electrical signal weakens to the point that some type of special communications equipment is required to increase or change the signal to transmit it farther. A variety of communications equipment exists to perform this task, but the equipment most often used is a modem.

Computer equipment is designed to process data as **digital signals**, individual electrical pulses grouped together to represent characters. Telephone equipment was originally designed to carry only voice transmission, which is com-

FIGURE 31
Prodigy is one of several on-line service providers offering information on a number of general-interest subjects. The topic areas display on the right. Users access Prodigy and other on-line services by using a modem and special communications software.

prised of a continuous electrical wave called an **analog signal** (see Figure 30). Thus, a special piece of equipment called a modem converts between the digital signals and analog signals so telephone lines can carry data. A **modem** converts the digital signals of a computer to analog signals that are transmitted over a communications channel. A modem also converts analog signals it receives into digital signals used by a computer. The word modem comes from a combination of the words *mo*dulate, which means to change into a sound or analog signal, and *dem*odulate, which means to convert an analog signal into a digital signal. A modem is needed at both the sending and receiving ends of a communications channel. A modem may be an external stand-alone device that is connected to the computer and phone line or an internal circuit board that is installed inside the computer.

Modems can transmit data at rates from 300 to 38,400 bits per second (bps). Most personal computers use a 2,400 bps or higher modem. Business or heavier volume users would use faster and more expensive modems.

Communication Networks

A communication **network** is a collection of computers and other equipment using communications channels to share hardware, software, data, and information. Networks are classified as either local area networks or wide area networks.

Local Area Networks (LANs)

A **local area network**, or LAN, is a privately owned communications network and covers a limited geographic area, such as a school computer laboratory, an office, a building, or a group of buildings.

The LAN consists of a communications channel connecting a group of personal computers to one another. Very sophisticated LANs are capable of connecting a variety of office devices, such as word processing equipment, computer terminals, video equipment, and personal computers.

Three common applications of local area networks are hardware, software, and information resource sharing. **Hardware resource sharing** allows each personal computer in the network to access and use devices that would be too expensive to provide for each user or would not be justified for each user because of only occasional use. For example, when a number of personal computers are used on the network, each may need to use a laser printer. Using a LAN, the purchase of one laser printer serves the entire network. Whenever a personal computer user on the network needs the laser printer, it is accessed over the network. Figure 32 depicts a simple local area network consisting of four personal computers linked together by a cable. Three of the personal computers (computer 1 in the sales and marketing department, computer 2 in the accounting department, and computer 3 in the personnel department) are available for use at all times. Computer 4 is used as a **server**, which is dedicated to handling the communications needs of the other computers in the network. The users of this LAN have connected the laser printer to the server. Using the LAN, all computers and the server can use the printer.

FIGURE 32
A local area network (LAN) consists of multiple personal computers connected to one another. The LAN allows users to share softwre, hardware, and information.

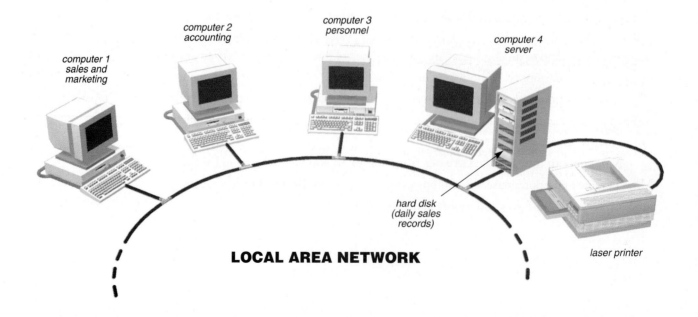

computer 1
sales and
marketing

computer 2
accounting

computer 3
personnel

computer 4
server

hard disk
(daily sales
records)

laser printer

LOCAL AREA NETWORK

Frequently used software is another type of resource sharing that often occurs on a local area network. For example, if all users need access to word processing software, the software can be stored on the hard disk of the server and accessed by all users as needed. This is more convenient and faster than having the software stored on a diskette and available at each computer.

Information resource sharing allows anyone using a personal computer on the local area network to access data stored on any other computer in the network. In actual practice, hardware resource sharing and information resource sharing are often combined. The capability to access and store data on common auxiliary storage is an important feature of many local area networks.

Information resource sharing is usually provided by using either the file-server or client-server method. Using the **file-server** method, the server sends an entire file at a time. The requesting computer then performs the processing. With the **client-server** method, processing tasks are divided between the server computer

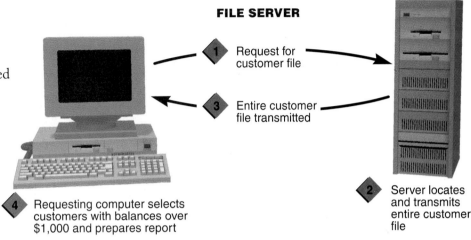

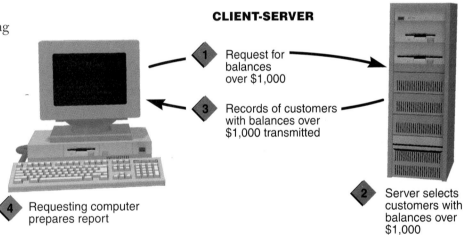

and the *client* computer requesting the information. Figure 33 illustrates how the two methods would process a request for information stored on the server system for customers with balances over $1,000. With the file-server method, all customer records would be transferred to the requesting computer. The requesting computer would then process the records to identify the customers with balances over $1,000. With the client-server method, the server system would review the customers' records and only transfer records of customers meeting the criteria. The client-server method greatly reduces the amount of data sent over a network but requires a more powerful server system.

FIGURE 33

A request for information about customers with balances over $1,000 would be processed differently by the file-server and client-server networks.

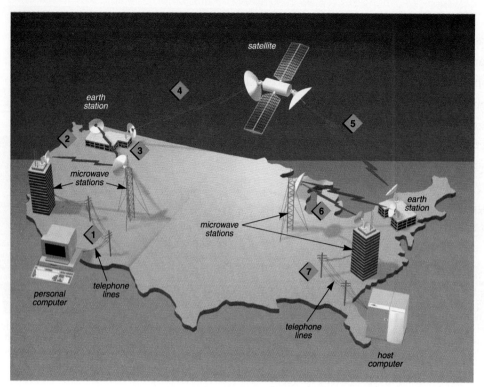

Wide Area Networks (WANs)

A wide area network, or WAN, is geographic in scope (as opposed to local) and uses telephone lines, microwaves, satellites, or a combination of communications channels (Figure 34). Public wide area network companies include common carriers such as the telephone companies. Telephone company deregulation has encouraged a number of companies to build their own wide area networks. Communications companies, such as MCI, have built WANs to compete with other communications companies.

FIGURE 34
A wide area network (WAN) may use a number of different communications channels such as telephone lines, microwaves, and satellites.

How to Purchase a Computer System

*T*he desktop personal computer (PC) is the most widely purchased type of system. The following guidelines assume you are purchasing a desktop IBM-compatible PC, to be used for home or light business use. That is not meant to imply that Macintosh or other non DOS or Windows operating system computers are not worth considering. Software requirements and the need to be compatible with other systems you may work with should determine the type of system you purchase. A portable computer would be an appropriate choice if your situation requires that you have a computer with you when you travel.

1. Determine what applications you will use on your computer. This decision will guide you as to the type and size of computer.

2. Choose your software first. Some packages only run on Macintosh computers, others only on a PC. Some packages only run under the Windows operating system. In addition, some software requires more memory and disk space than other packages.

3. Be aware of hidden costs. Realize that there will be some additional costs associated with buying a computer. Such costs might include; an additional phone line or outlet to use the modem, computer furniture, consumable supplies such as diskettes and paper, diskette holders, reference manuals on specific software packages, and special training classes you may want to take. Depending on where you buy your computer, the seller may be willing to include some or all of these in the system purchase price.

4. **Buy equipment that meets the *Energy Star* power consumption guidelines.** These guidelines require that computer systems, monitors, and printers, reduce electrical consumption if they have not been used for some period of time, usually several minutes. Equipment meeting the guidelines can display the *Energy Star* logo.

5. **Use a spreadsheet like the one shown in Figure 35 to compare purchase alternatives.** Use a separate sheet of paper to take notes on each vendor's system and then summarize the information on the spreadsheet.

6. **Consider buying from local computer dealers and direct mail companies.** Each has certain advantages. The local dealer can more easily provide hands-on support, if necessary. With a mail order company, you are usually limited to speaking to someone over the phone. Mail order companies usually, but not always, offer the lowest prices. The important thing to do when shopping for a system is to make sure you are comparing identical or similar configurations.

System Cost Comparison Worksheet		Desired	#1	#2	#3	#4
Base System	Mfr	—	Delway			
	Model		4500X			
	Processor	486DX	486DX			
	Speed	50MHz	50			
	Pwr Supply	200watts	220			
	Exp Slots	5	5			
	Price		$995			
Memory	8MB Ram		incl			
Disk	Mfr		Conner			
	Size	>300MB	340			
	Price		incl			
Diskette	3 1/2					
	5 1/4					
	Combination		$50			
Monitor	Mfr		NEC			
	Model		5FG			
	Size	15in	15			
	Price		$300			
Sound	Mfr		Media Labs			
	Model		Pro			
	Price		$75			
CDROM	Mfr		NEC			
	Speed		450/200			
	Price		$100			
Mouse	Mfr		Logitech			
	Price		incl			
Modem	Mfr		Boca			
	Mod/fax Speeds	14.4/14.4	14.4/14.4			
	Price		$125			
Printer	Mfr		HP			
	Model		4Z			
	Type		laser			
	Speed	6ppm	8ppm			
	Price		$675			
Surge Protector	Mfr		Brooks			
	Price		$35			
Options	Tape Backup					
	UPS					
Other	Sales Tax		0			
	Shipping		$30			
	1 YR Warranty		incl			
	1 YR On-Site Svc		incl			
	3 YR On-Site Svc		$150			
Software	List free software		Windows			
			MS Works			
			diagnostics			
	TOTAL		$2,535			

FIGURE 35
A spreadsheet is an effective way to summarize and compare the prices and equipment offered by different system vendors.

7. **Consider more than just price.** Don't necessarily buy the lowest cost system. Consider intangibles such as how long the vendor has been in business, its reputation for quality, and reputation for support.

8. **Look for free software.** Many system vendors now include free software with their systems. Some even let you choose which software you want. Such software only has value, however, if you would have purchased it if it had not come with the computer.

9. **Buy a system compatible with the one you use elsewhere.** If you use a personal computer at work or at some other organization, make sure the computer you buy is compatible. That way, if you need or want to, you can work on projects at home.

10. **Consider purchasing an on-site service agreement.** If you use your system for business or otherwise can't afford to be without your computer, consider purchasing an on-site service agreement. Many of the mail order vendors offer such support through third-party companies. Such agreements usually state that a technician will be on-site within 24 hours. Some systems include on-site service for only the first year. It is usually less expensive to extend the service for two or three years when you buy the computer rather than waiting to buy the service agreement later.

11. **Use a credit card to purchase your system.** Many credit cards now have purchase protection benefits that cover you in case of loss or damage to purchased goods. Some also extend the warranty of any products purchased with the card. Paying by credit card also gives you time to install and use the system before you have to pay for it. Finally, if you're dissatisfied with the system and can't reach an agreement with the seller, paying by credit card gives you certain rights regarding withholding payment until the dispute is resolved. Check your credit card agreement for specific details.

12. **Buy a system that will last you for at least three years.** Studies show that many users become dissatisfied because they didn't buy a powerful enough system. Consider the following system configuration guidelines. Each of the components will be discussed separately:

Base System Components:	Optional Equipment:
486SX or 486DX processor, 33 megahertz	5 1/4" diskette drive
150 watt power supply	14.4K fax modem
160 to 300MB hard disk	laser printer
4 to 8MB RAM	sound card and speakers
3 to 5 expansion slots	CD-ROM drive
3 1/2" diskette drive	tape backup
14" or 15" color monitor	uninterruptable power supply (UPS)
mouse or other pointing device	
enhanced keyboard	
ink jet or bubble jet printer	
surge protector	

Processor: A 486SX or 486DX processor with a speed rating of at least 33 mega-hertz is needed for today's more sophisticated software, even word processing soft-ware. Buy a system that can be upgraded to the Pentium processor.

Power Supply: 150 watts. If the power supply is too small, it won't be able to support additional expansion cards that you might want to add in the future.

Hard Disk: 160 to 300 megabytes (MB). Each new release of software requires more hard disk space. Even with disk compression programs, disk space is used up fast. Start with more disk than you ever think you'll need.

Memory (RAM): 4 to 8 megabytes (MB). Like disk space, the new applications are demanding more memory. It's easier and less expensive to obtain the memory when you buy the system than if you wait until later.

Expansion Slots: 3 to 5 open slots on the base system. Expansion slots are needed for scanners, tape drives, video boards, and other equipment you may want to add in the future as your needs change and the price of this equipment becomes lower.

Diskette Drives: Most software is now distributed on 3 1/2-inch disks. Consider adding a 5 1/4-inch diskette to read data and programs that may have been stored on that format. The best way to achieve this is to buy a combination diskette drive which is only slightly more expensive than a single 3 1/2-inch diskette drive. The combination device has both 3 1/2- and 5 1/4-inch diskette drives in a single unit.

Color Monitor: 14 to 15 inch. This is one device where it pays to spend a little more money. A 15-inch super VGA monitor will display graphics better than a 14-inch model. For health reasons, make sure you pick a low radiation model.

Pointing Device: Most systems include a mouse as part of the base package.

Enhanced Keyboard: The keyboard is usually included with the system. Check to make sure the keyboard is the *enhanced* and not the older *standard* model. The enhanced keyboard is sometimes called the *101* keyboard because it has 101 keys.

Printer: The price of nonimpact printers has come within several hundred dollars of the lowest cost dot matrix printers. Unless you need the wide carriage or multi-part form capabilities of a dot matrix, purchase a nonimpact printer.

Surge Protector: A voltage spike can literally destroy your system. It is low-cost insurance to protect yourself with a surge protector. Don't merely buy a fused multi-plug outlet from the local hardware store. Buy a surge protector designed for com-puters with a separate protected jack for your phone (modem) line.

Fax Modem: Volumes of information are available via on-line databases. In addition, many software vendors provide assistance and free software upgrades via bulletin boards. For the speed they provide, 14.4K modems are worth the extra money. Facsimile (fax) capability only costs a few dollars more and gives you more communication options.

Sound Card and Speakers: More and more software and support materials are incorporating sound.

CD-ROM Drive: Multimedia is the wave of the future and it requires a CD-ROM drive. Get a double- or triple-speed model.

Tape Backup: Larger hard disks make backing up data on diskettes impractical. Internal or external tape backup systems are the most common solution. Some portable units, great if you have more than one system, are designed to connect to your printer port. The small cassette tapes can store the equivalent of hundreds of diskettes.

Uninterruptable Power Supply (UPS): A UPS uses batteries to start or keep your system running if the main electrical power is turned off. The length of time they provide depends on the size of the batteries and the electrical requirements of your system but is usually at least 10 minutes. The idea of a UPS is to give you enough time to save your work. Get a UPS that is rated for your size system.

Remember that the types of applications you want to use on your system will guide you as to the type and size of computer that is right for you. The ideal computer system you choose may differ from the general recommendation that is presented here. Determine your needs and buy the best system your budget will allow.

How to Install a Computer System

1. **Allow for adequate workspace around the computer.** A workspace of at least two feet by four feet is recommended.

2. **Install bookshelves.** Bookshelves above and/or to the side of the computer area are useful for keeping manuals and other reference materials handy.

3. **Install your computer in a well-designed work area.** The height of your chair, keyboard, monitor, and work surface is important and can affect your health. See Figure 36 for specific guidelines.

4. **Use a document holder.** To minimize neck and eye strain, obtain a document holder that holds documents at the same height and distance as your computer screen.

5. Provide adequate lighting.

6. While working at your computer, be aware of health issues. See Figure 37 for a list of computer user health guidelines.

7. Install or move a phone near the computer. Having a phone near the computer really helps if you need to call a vendor about a hardware or software problem. Oftentimes the vendor support person can talk you through the correction while you're on the phone. To avoid data loss, however, don't place diskettes on the phone or any other electrical or electronic equipment.

8. Obtain a computer tool set. Computer tool sets are available from computer dealers, office supply stores, and mail order companies. These sets will have the right-sized screwdrivers and other tools to work on your system. Get one that comes in a zippered carrying case to keep all the tools together.

9. Save all the paperwork that comes with your system. Keep it in an accessible place with the paperwork from your other computer-related purchases. To keep different-sized documents together, consider putting them in a plastic zip-lock bag.

10. Record the serial numbers of all your equipment and software. Write the serial numbers on the outside of the manuals that came with the equipment as well as in a single list that contains the serial numbers of all your equipment and software.

11. Keep the shipping containers and packing materials for all your equipment. This material will come in handy if you have to return your equipment for servicing or have to move it to another location.

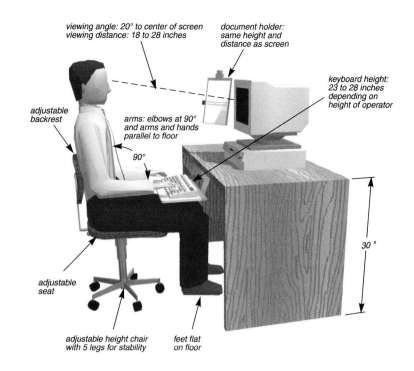

FIGURE 36
More than anything else, a well-designed work area should be flexible to allow adjustment to the height and build of different individuals. Good lighting and air quality should also be considered.

COMPUTER USER HEALTH GUIDELINES
1. Work in a well-designed work area. Figure 36 illustrates the guidelines.
2. Alternate work activities to prevent physical and mental fatigue. If possible, change the order of your work to provide some variety.
3. Take frequent breaks. At least once per hour, get out of your chair and move around. Every two hours, take at least a 15 minute break.
4. Incorporate hand, arm, and body stretching exercises into your breaks. At lunch, try to get outside and walk.
5. Make sure your computer monitor is designed to minimize electromagnetic radiation
6. Try to eliminate or minimize surrounding noise. Noisy environments contribute to stress and tension.
7. If you frequently have to use the phone and the computer at the same time, consider using a telephone headset. Cradling the phone between your head and shoulder can cause muscle strain.
8. Be aware of symptoms of repetitive strain injuries; soreness, pain, numbness, or weakness in neck, shoulders, arms, wrists, and hands. Don't ignore early signs; seek medical advice.

FIGURE 37
All computer users should follow the Computer User Health Guidelines to maintain their health.

12. **Look at the inside of your computer.** Before you connect power to your system, remove the computer case cover and visually inspect the internal components. The user manual usually identifies what each component does. Look for any disconnected wires, loose screws or washers, or any other obvious signs of trouble. Be careful not to touch anything inside the case unless you are grounded. Static electricity can permanently damage the microprocessor chips on the circuit boards. Before you replace the cover, take several photographs of the computer showing the location of the circuit boards. These photos may save you from taking the cover off in the future if you or a vendor has a question about what equipment controller card is installed in what expansion slot.

13. **Identify device connectors.** At the back of your system there are a number of connectors for the printer, the monitor, the mouse, a phone line, etc. If they aren't already identified by the manufacturer, use a marking pen to write the purpose of each connector on the back of the computer case.

14. **Complete and send in your equipment and software registration cards right away.** If you're already entered in the vendors user database, it can save you time when you call in with a support question. Being a registered user also makes you eligible for special pricing on software upgrades.

15. **Install your system in an area where the temperature and humidity can be maintained.** Try to maintain a constant temperature between 60 and 80 degrees farenheight when the computer is operating. High temperatures and humidity can damage electronic components. Be careful when using space heaters; their hot, dry air has been known to cause disk problems.

16. **Keep your computer area clean.** Avoid eating and drinking around the computer. Smoking should be avoided also. Cigarette smoke can quickly cause damage to the diskette drives and diskette surfaces.

17. **Check your insurance.** Some policies have limits on the amount of computer equipment they cover. Other policies don't cover computer equipment at all if it is used for a business (a separate policy is required).

How to Maintain Your Computer System

1. **Learn to use system diagnostic programs.** If a set didn't come with your system, obtain one. These programs help you identify and possibly solve problems before you call for technical assistance. Some system manufacturers now include diagnostic programs with their systems and ask that you run the programs before you call for help.

2. **Start a notebook that includes information on your system.** This notebook should be a single source of information about your entire system, both hardware and software. Each time you make a change to your system, adding or removing hardware or software, or when you change system parameters, you should record the change in the notebook. Items to include in the notebook are the following:

✓ Serial numbers of all equipment and software.

✓ Vendor support phone numbers. These numbers are often buried in user manuals. Look up these numbers once and record all of them on a single sheet of paper at the front of your notebook.

✓ Date and vendor for each equipment and software purchase.

✓ File listings for key system files (e.g., autoexec.bat and config.sys).

✓ Notes on discussions with vendor support personnel.

✓ A chronological history of any equipment or software problems. This history can be helpful if the problem persists and you have to call several times.

3. **Periodically review disk directories and delete unneeded files.** Files have a way of building up and can quickly use up your disk space. If you think you may need a file in the future, back it up to a diskette.

4. **Any time you work inside your computer turn the power off and disconnect the equipment from the power source.** In addition, before you touch anything inside the computer, touch an unpainted metal surface such as the power supply. This will discharge any static electricity that could damage internal components.

5. **Reduce the need to clean the inside of your system by keeping the surrounding area dirt and dust free.** Diskette cleaners are available but should be used sparingly (some owners never use them unless they experience diskette problems). If dust builds up inside the computer it should be carefully removed with compressed air and a small vacuum. Don't touch the components with the vacuum.

FIGURE 38
How a virus program can be transmitted from one computer to another.

6. **Back up key files and data.** At a minimum, you should have a diskette with your **command.com**, **autoexec.bat**, and **config.sys** files. If your system crashes, these files will help you get going again. In addition, backup any files with a file extension of **.sys**. For Windows systems, all files with a file extension of **.ini** and **.grp** should be backed up.

7. **Protect your system from computer viruses.** Computer viruses are programs designed to *infect* computer systems by copying themselves into other computer files (Figure 38). The virus program spreads when the infected files are used by or copied to another system.

A COMPUTER VIRUS: WHAT IT IS AND HOW IT SPREADS

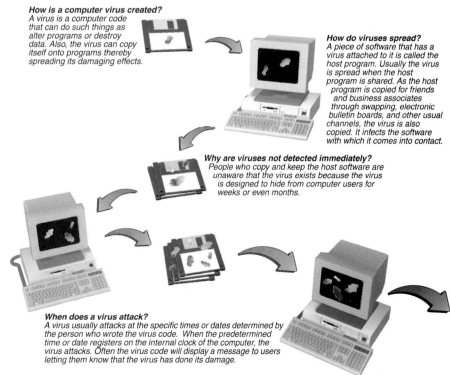

How is a computer virus created?
A virus is a computer code that can do such things as alter programs or destroy data. Also, the virus can copy itself onto programs thereby spreading its damaging effects.

How do viruses spread?
A piece of software that has a virus attached to it is called the host program. Usually the virus is spread when the host program is shared. As the host program is copied for friends and business associates through swapping, electronic bulletin boards, and other usual channels, the virus is also copied. It infects the software with which it comes into contact.

Why are viruses not detected immediately?
People who copy and keep the host software are unaware that the virus exists because the virus is designed to hide from computer users for weeks or even months.

When does a virus attack?
A virus usually attacks at the specific times or dates determined by the person who wrote the virus code. When the predetermined time or date registers on the internal clock of the computer, the virus attacks. Often the virus code will display a message to users letting them know that the virus has done its damage.

Virus programs are dangerous because they are often designed to damage the files of the infected system. Protect yourself from viruses by installing an anti-virus program on your computer.

Summary of Introduction to Computers

*A*s you learn to use the software taught in this book, you will also become familiar with the components and operation of your computer system. When you need help understanding how the components of your system function, refer to this introduction. You can also refer to this section for information on computer communications and for guidelines when you decide to purchase a computer system of your own.

Student Assignments

Student Assignment 1: True/False

Instructions: Circle T if the statement is true or F if the statement is false.

T F   1. A computer is an electronic device, operating under the control of instructions stored in its own memory unit, that can accept data (input), process data arithmetically and logically, produce output from the processing, and store the results for future use.

T F   2. Information refers to data processed into a form that has meaning and is useful.

T F   3. A computer program is a detailed set of instructions that tells a computer exactly what to do.

T F   4. A mouse is a communications device used to convert between digital and analog signals so telephone lines can carry data.

T F   5. The central processing unit contains the processor unit and main memory.

T F   6. A laser printer is an impact printer that provides high-quality output.

T F   7. Auxiliary storage is used to store instructions and data when they are not being used in main memory.

T F   8. A diskette is considered to be a form of main memory.

T F   9. CD-ROM is often used for multimedia material that combines text, graphics, video, and sound.

T F   10. The operating system tells the computer how to perform functions such as how to load, store, and execute an application program and how to transfer data between the input/output devices and main memory.

T F   11. Programs such as database management, spreadsheet, and word processing software are called system software.

T F   12. For data to be transferred from one computer to another over communications lines, communications software is required only on the sending computer.

T F   13. A communications network is a collection of computers and other equipment that use communications channels to share hardware, software, data, and information.

T F 14. Determining what applications you will use on your computer will help you to purchase a computer that is the type and size that meets your needs.

T F 15. The path the data follows as it is transmitted from the sending equipment to the receiving equipment in a communications system is called a modem.

T F 16. Computer equipment that meets the power consumption guidelines can display the *Energy Star* logo.

T F 17. An on-site maintenance agreement is important if you cannot be without the use of your computer.

T F 18. An anit-virus program is used to protect your computer equipment and software.

T F 19. When purchasing a computer, consider only the price because one computer is no different from another.

T F 20. A LAN allows you to share software but not hardware.

Student Assignment 2: Multiple Choice

Instructions: Circle the correct response.

1. The four operations performed by a computer include _____ .
   a. input, control, output, and storage
   b. interface, processing, output, and memory
   c. input, output, processing, and storage
   d. input, logical/rational, arithmetic, and output

2. A hand-held input device that controls the cursor location is _____ .
   a. the cursor control keyboard
   b. a mouse
   c. a modem
   d. the CRT

3. A printer that forms images without striking the paper is _____ .
   a. an impact printer   b. a nonimpact printer   c. an ink jet printer   d. both b and c

4. The amount of storage provided by a diskette is a function of _____ .
   a. the thickness of the disk
   b. the recording density of bits on the track
   c. the number of recording tracks on the diskette
   d. both b and c

5. Portable computers use a flat panel screen called a _____ .
   a. a multichrome monitor
   b. a cathode ray tube
   c. a liquid crystal display
   d. a monochrome monitor

6. When not in use, diskettes should be _____ .
   a. stored away from magnetic fields
   b. stored away from heat and direct sunlight
   c. stored in a diskette box or cabinet
   d. all of the above

7. CD-ROM is a type of _____ .
   a. main memory
   b. auxiliary storage
   c. communications equipment
   d. system software

8. An operating system is considered part of _____ .
   a. word processing software
   b. database software
   c. system software
   d. spreadsheet software

9. The type of application software most commonly used to create and print documents is _____ .
   a. word processing   b. electronic spreadsheet   c. database   d. none of the above

10. The type of application software most commonly used to send messages to and receive messages from other computer users is _____ .
    a. electronic mail   b. database   c. presentation graphics   d. none of the above

Student Assignment 3: Comparing Personal Computer Advertisements

Instructions: Obtain a copy of a recent computer magazine and review the advertisements for desktop personal computer systems. Compare ads for the least and most expensive desktop systems you can find. Discuss the differences.

Student Assignment 4: Evaluating On-Line Information Services

Instructions: Prodigy and America On-Line both offer consumer oriented on-line information services. Contact each company and request each to send you information on the specific services it offers. Try to talk to someone who actually uses one or both of the services. Discuss how each service is priced and the differences between the two on-line services.

Student Assignment 5: Visiting Local Computer Retail Stores

Instructions: Visit local computer retail stores and compare the various types of computers and support equipment available. Ask about warranties, repair services, hardware setup, training, and related issues. Report on the knowledge of the sales staff assisting you and their willingness to answer your questions. Does the store have standard hardware packages, or are they willing to configure a system to your specific needs? Would you feel confident buying a computer from this store?

Index

America On-Line, COM18
Application software, COM2-3, **COM14-17**
Auxiliary storage, COM10-14

BACKSPACE key, COM6
Backup, COM29
Bits per inch (bpi), COM11
Booting the computer system, **COM14**

CD-ROM (compact disk read-only memory), **COM13**, COM25
Central processing unit (CPU), **COM7**
Chips, COM4
Client-server method, **COM21**
Color screens, COM9, COM25
Communications, **COM18-22**
Communications channel, COM18, **COM19**
Communications software, **COM17**, COM18
Compression programs, **COM13**
Computer(s), COM3, COM4
  communications system and, COM18
  compatibility of, COM24
  components of, COM4-14
Computer screens, COM9
Computer system, COM22-30
Computer users, COM4
Computer viruses, COM29-30
Controller card, COM28
CRT (cathode ray tube), **COM9**
Cursor, **COM5**
Cursor control keys, **COM5-6**

Data, COM3
  transmission over communications channel, COM18
Database software, **COM16**
Data entry, COM5-6
DELETE key, COM6
Desktop publishing, **COM9**
Diagnostic programs, COM28
Digital signals, **COM19**
Disk directories, COM29
Disk drives, COM10, COM11
Diskette, **COM10-12**
Diskette drives, COM25

DOS (Disk Operating System), COM14
Dot matrix printers, COM7-8, COM26
Double-density diskettes, COM11
DOWN ARROW key, COM5

Electronic bulletin board system (BBS), **COM18**
Electronic mail (e-mail) software, **COM17**
Electronic spreadsheet software, **COM15**
END key, COM6
End users, COM4
Energy Star power consumption guide, COM23
ESCAPE (ESC) key, **COM6**
Expansion slots, COM25, COM28

File-server method, **COM21**
Fonts, COM8
Function keys, **COM6**

Gigabyte, **COM13**
Graphics, spreadsheet packages and, COM15
Graphics files, compression of, COM13

Hard disk, COM13
Hardware, registration cards for, COM28
Hardware resource sharing, COM20-21
Health guidelines, COM27
High-density diskettes, COM11
HOME key, COM6

Impact printer, **COM7**
Information, COM3, COM18
Information processing cycle, **COM3**
Information resource sharing, **COM21**
Ink jet printer, **COM8**
Input, COM3
Input devices, **COM4-6**
INSERT key, COM6
Intel Corporation, COM7

Keyboard, COM5-6
Kilobyte (K or KB), **COM7**

Laser printer, COM8-9
LEFT ARROW key, COM5
Liquid crystal display (LCD) technology, **COM9**
Local area network (LAN), **COM20-22**

Macintosh, COM22
Main memory, **COM7**
Megabyte (M or MB), **COM7**
Memory, COM7, COM25
Microprocessor, **COM7**
Modem (*mo*dulate *dem*odulate), **COM19**
Monitor, **COM9**
Mouse, **COM6**, COM25
Multimedia material, COM13-14

Network(s), COM18, COM20-22
Nonimpact printers, **COM8**, COM26
Numeric keypad, **COM5**
NUMLOCK key, COM5

On-line information services, COM17, **COM18**
Operating system, **COM14**
Output devices, **COM7-9**
Output operation, **COM3**

PAGE DOWN key, COM6
PAGE UP key, COM6
Pentium microprocessor, COM7, COM25
Pixels, **COM9**
Pointing device, COM6, COM25
Portable computers, COM9, COM22
Power consumption, COM23
Power supply, COM25, COM26, COM29
Presentation graphics software, **COM16**
Printers
  local area network and, COM20
  purchasing, COM26
  types of, COM7-8
Processing, COM3
Processor unit, **COM7**, COM25
Prodigy, COM18

Read/write operations, COM10, COM13
Recording density, COM11
RIGHT ARROW key, COM5

Screen, **COM9**
Sectors, disk, COM11
Server, **COM20**
SHIFT keys, COM6
Silicon chips, COM4
Slides, **COM16**
Software, **COM4**
  application, COM2-3, COM14-17
  bulletin board systems and, COM26
  free, COM24
  purchasing, COM23
  registration of, COM28
  system, COM14
Storage, COM3-4, COM10-14
  disk drives, COM10
  diskettes, COM10-11
  hard disk, COM13
  sectors, COM11
  tape, COM26
Super VGA (video graphics array), COM9
System operator (sysop), **COM18**
System software, **COM14**

TAB key, COM6
Tape backup, COM26
Text files, compression of, COM13
Tracks, disk, COM11
Transmission media, **COM19**
Typefaces, COM8

Uninterruptable Power Supply (UPS), COM26
UP ARROW key, COM5

Vendors, COM23-24
Viruses, COM29-30

Wide area network (WAN), **COM22**
Windows operating system, COM22, COM23
Word processing software, **COM15**
Write/protect notch, COM12

Photo Credits

Figure 1, (1) Compaq Computer Corp. All rights reserved.; (2) International Business Machines Corp.; (3) UNISYS Corp.; (4) Compaq Computer Corp. All rights reserved.; (5) International Business Machines Corp.; (6) Zenith Data Systems; (7) International Business Machines Corp.; (8) International Business Machines Corp.; (9) Hewlett-Packard Co.; Figure 2, International Business Machines Corp.; Figure 3, Compaq Computer Corp. All rights reserved.; Figure 5, International Business Machines Corp.; Figure 6, Logitech, Inc.; Figure 7, Intel Corp.; Figure 8, Epson America, Inc.; Figure 10 (top), Hewlett-Packard Co.; Figure 10 (bottom), Epson America, Inc.; Figure 12, Aldus Corp.; Figure 13, International Business Machines Corp.; Figure 15, Jerry Spagnoli; Figure 16, Greg Hadel; Figure 19, Jerry Spagnoli; Figure 20, Microscience International Corp.; Figure 21, 3M Corp.; Illustrations, Dave Wyer.

W I N D O W S

USING *M*ICROSOFT *W*INDOWS 3.1

▶ PROJECT ONE

AN INTRODUCTION TO WINDOWS

Objectives **WIN2**
Introduction **WIN2**
Microsoft Windows **WIN3**
Communicating with Microsoft
 Windows **WIN5**
Using Microsoft
 Windows **WIN14**
File and Disk Concepts **WIN22**
Opening a Document
 File **WIN28**
Using Windows Help **WIN32**
Quitting Windows **WIN36**
Project Summary **WIN38**
Key Terms **WIN38**
Quick Reference **WIN39**
Student Assignments **WIN40**
Computer Laboratory
 Exercises **WIN43**

▶ PROJECT TWO

FILE AND DISK OPERATIONS

Objectives **WIN47**
Introduction **WIN47**
Starting Windows **WIN48**
File Manager **WIN49**
Formatting a Diskette **WIN50**
Copying Files to a
 Diskette **WIN54**
Renaming a File **WIN63**
Deleting a File **WIN65**
Creating a Backup
 Diskette **WIN67**
Searching for Help Using Online
 Help **WIN71**
Additional Commands and
 Concepts **WIN80**
Project Summary **WIN86**
Key Terms **WIN87**
Quick Reference **WIN87**
Student Assignments **WIN88**
Computer Laboratory
 Exercises **WIN92**

INDEX **WIN96**

AN INTRODUCTION TO WINDOWS

OBJECTIVES   You will have mastered the material in this project when you can:

▸ Describe a user interface
▸ Describe Microsoft Windows
▸ Identify the elements of a window
▸ Perform the four basic mouse operations of pointing, clicking, double-clicking, and dragging
▸ Correct errors made while performing mouse operations
▸ Understand the keyboard shortcut notation
▸ Select a menu
▸ Choose a command from a menu

▸ Respond to dialog boxes
▸ Start and exit an application
▸ Name a file
▸ Understand directories and subdirectories
▸ Understand directory structures and directory paths
▸ Create, save, open, and print a document
▸ Open, enlarge, and scroll a window
▸ Obtain online Help while using an application

▸ INTRODUCTION

T he most popular and widely used graphical user interface available today is **Microsoft Windows**, or **Windows**. Microsoft Windows allows you to easily communicate with and control your computer. In addition, Microsoft Windows makes it easy to learn the application software installed on your computer, transfer data between the applications, and manage the data created while using an application.

In this project, you learn about user interfaces, the computer hardware and computer software that comprise a user interface, and Microsoft Windows. You use Microsoft Windows to perform the operations of opening a group window, starting and exiting an application, enlarging an application window, entering and editing data within an application, printing a document on the printer, saving a document on disk, opening a document, and obtaining online Help while using an application.

What Is a User Interface?

A **user interface** is the combination of hardware and software that allows the computer user to communicate with and control the computer. Through the user interface, you are able to control the computer, request information from the computer, and respond to messages displayed by the computer. Thus, a user interface provides the means for dialogue between you and the computer.

Hardware and software together form the user interface. Among the hardware associated with a user interface are the CRT screen, keyboard, and mouse (Figure 1-1). The CRT screen displays messages and provides information. You respond by entering data in the form of a command or other response using the keyboard or mouse. Among the responses available to you are responses that specify what application software to run, when to print, and where to store the data for future use.

USER INTERFACE   **FIGURE 1-1**

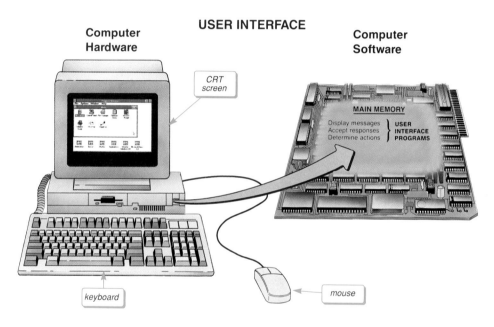

The computer software associated with the user interface are the programs that engage you in dialogue (Figure 1-1). The computer software determines the messages you receive, the manner in which you should respond, and the actions that occur based on your responses. The goal of an effective user interface is to be **user friendly**, meaning the software can be easily used by individuals with limited training. Research studies have indicated that the use of graphics can play an important role in aiding users to effectively interact with a computer. A **graphical user interface**, or **GUI**, is a user interface that displays graphics in addition to text when it communicates with the user.

▶ MICROSOFT WINDOWS

Microsoft Windows, or Windows, the most popular graphical user interface, makes it easy to learn and work with **application software**, which is software that performs an application-related function, such as word processing. Numerous application software packages are available for purchase from retail computer stores, and several applications are included with the Windows interface software. In Windows terminology, these application software packages are referred to as **applications**.

Starting Microsoft Windows

When you turn on the computer, an introductory screen consisting of the Windows logo, Windows name, version number (3.1), and copyright notices displays momentarily (Figure 1-2). Next, a blank screen containing an hourglass icon ( ) displays (Figure 1-3). The **hourglass icon** indicates that Windows requires a brief interval of time to change the display on the screen, and you should wait until the hourglass icon disappears.

FIGURE 1-2

FIGURE 1-3

FIGURE 1-4

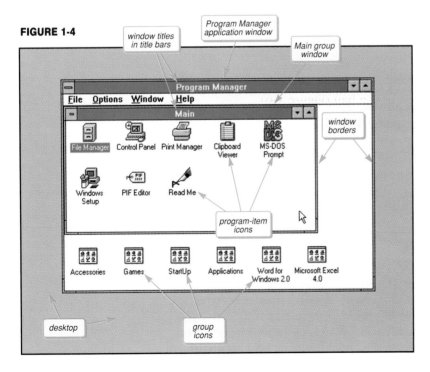

Finally, two rectangular areas, or **windows**, display (Figure 1-4). The double-line, or **window border**, surrounding each window determines their shape and size. The horizontal bar at the top of each window, called the **title bar**, contains a **window title** that identifies each window. In Figure 1-4, the Program Manager and Main titles identify each window.

The screen background on which the windows display is called the **desktop**. If your desktop does not look similar to the desktop in Figure 1-4, your instructor will inform you of the modifications necessary to change your desktop.

The Program Manager window represents the **Program Manager** application. The Program Manager application starts when you start Windows and is central to the operation of Windows. Program Manager organizes related applications into groups and displays the groups in the Program Manager window. A window that represents an application, such as the Program Manager window, is called an **application window**.

Small pictures, or **icons**, represent an individual application or groups of applications. In Figure 1-4 on the previous page, the Main window contains a group of eight icons (File Manager, Control Panel, Print Manager, Clipboard Viewer, MS-DOS Prompt, Windows Setup, PIF Editor, and Read Me). A window that contains a group of icons, such as the Main window, is called a **group window**. The icons in a group window, called **program-item icons**, each represent an individual application. A name below each program-item icon identifies the application. The program-item icons are unique and, therefore, easily distinguished from each other.

The six icons at the bottom of the Program Manager window in Figure 1-4 on the previous page, (Accessories, Games, StartUp, Applications, Word for Windows 2.0, and Microsoft Excel 4.0), called **group icons**, each represent a group of applications. Group icons are similar in appearance and only the name below the icon distinguishes one icon from another icon. Although the program-item icons of the individual applications in these groups are not visible in Figure 1-4, a method to view these icons will be demonstrated later in this project.

▶ COMMUNICATING WITH MICROSOFT WINDOWS

The Windows interface software provides the means for dialogue between you and the computer. Part of this dialogue involves requesting information from the computer and responding to messages displayed by the computer. You can request information and respond to messages using either the mouse or keyboard.

The Mouse and Mouse Pointer

A **mouse** is a pointing device commonly used with Windows that is attached to the computer by a cable and contains one or more buttons. The mouse in Figure 1-5 contains two buttons, the left mouse button and the right mouse button. On the bottom of this mouse is a ball (Figure 1-6).

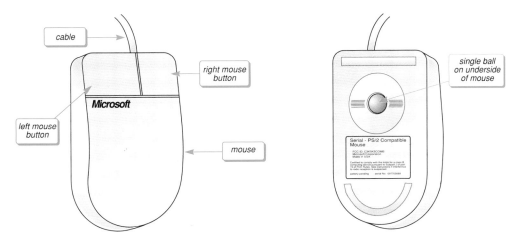

FIGURE 1-5   **FIGURE 1-6**

As you move the mouse across a flat surface (Figure 1-7), the movement of the ball is electronically sensed, and a **mouse pointer** in the shape of a block arrow (⤢) moves across the desktop in the same direction.

Mouse moves diagonally across flat surface

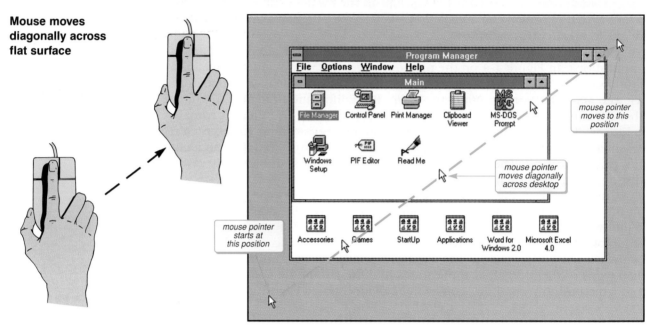

FIGURE 1-7

Mouse Operations

You use the mouse to perform four basic operations: (1) pointing; (2) clicking; (3) double-clicking; and (4) dragging. **Pointing** means moving the mouse across a flat surface until the mouse pointer rests on the item of choice on the desktop. In Figure 1-8, you move the mouse diagonally across a flat surface until the tip of the mouse pointer rests on the Print Manager icon.

Mouse moves diagonally

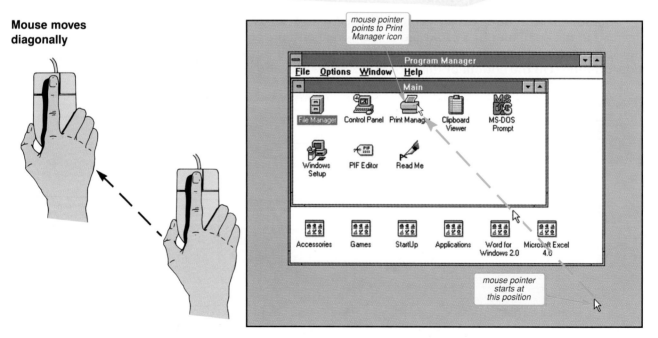

FIGURE 1-8

Clicking means pressing and releasing a mouse button. In most cases, you must point to an item before pressing and releasing a mouse button. In Figure 1-9, you highlight the Print Manager icon by pointing to the Print Manager icon (Step 1) and pressing and releasing the left mouse button (Step 2). These steps are commonly referred to as clicking the Print Manager icon. When you click the Print Manager icon, Windows highlights, or places color behind, the name below the Print Manager icon (Step 3).

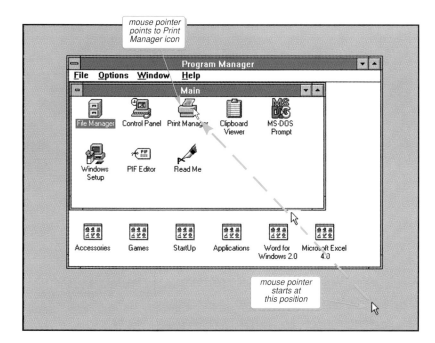

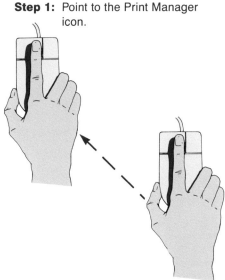

Step 1: Point to the Print Manager icon.

Step 2: Press and release the left mouse button.

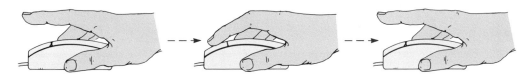

Step 3: Windows highlights the Print Manager name.

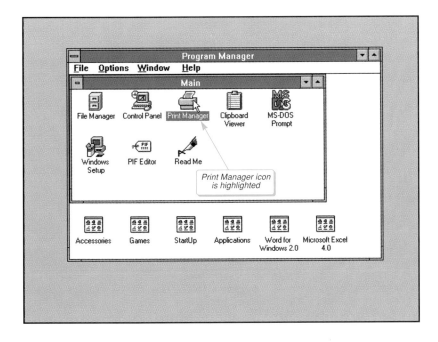

FIGURE 1-9

Double-clicking means quickly pressing and releasing a mouse button twice without moving the mouse. In most cases, you must point to an item before quickly pressing and releasing a mouse button twice. In Figure 1-10, to open the Accessories group window, point to the Accessories icon (Step 1), and quickly press and release the left mouse button twice (Step 2). These steps are commonly referred to as double-clicking the Accessories icon. When you double-click the Accessories icon, Windows opens a group window with the same name (Step 3).

Step 1: Point to the Accessories icon.

Step 2: Quickly press and release the left mouse button twice.

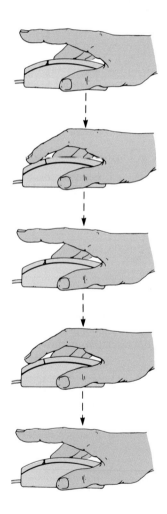

Step 3: Windows opens the Accessories group window.

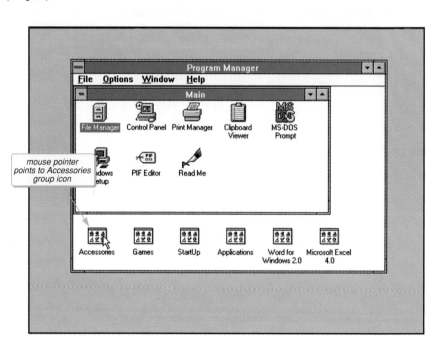

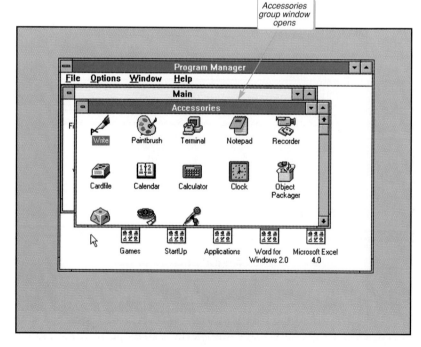

FIGURE 1-10

Dragging means holding down the left mouse button, moving an item to the desired location, and then releasing the left mouse button. In most cases, you must point to an item before doing this. In Figure 1-11, you move the Control Panel program-item icon by pointing to the Control Panel icon (Step 1), holding down the left mouse button while moving the icon to its new location (Step 2), and releasing the left mouse button (Step 3). These steps are commonly referred to as dragging the Control Panel icon.

In Figure 1-11, the location of the Control Panel program-item icon was moved to rearrange the icons in the Main group window. Dragging has many uses in Windows, as you will see in subsequent examples.

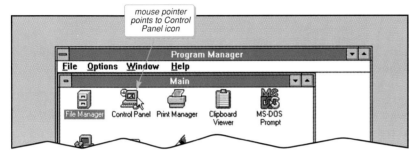

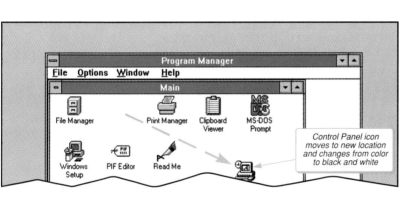

Step 1: Point to the Control Panel icon.

Step 2: Hold down the left mouse button and move the icon to its new location.

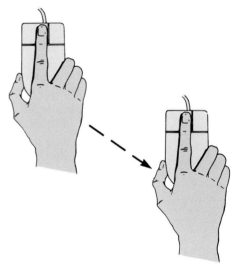

Step 3: Release the left mouse button.

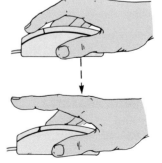

FIGURE 1-11

The Keyboard and Keyboard Shortcuts

The **keyboard** is an input device on which you manually key, or type, data. Figure 1-12 on the next page shows the enhanced IBM PS/2 keyboard. Any task you accomplish with a mouse you can also accomplish with the keyboard. Although the choice of whether you use the mouse or keyboard is a matter of personal preference, the mouse is strongly recommended.

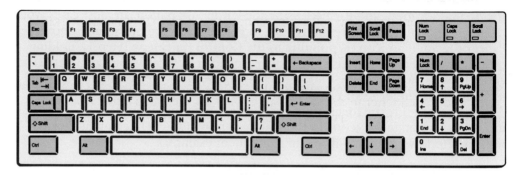

FIGURE 1-12

The Quick Reference at the end of each project provides a list of tasks presented and the manner in which to complete them using a mouse, menu, or keyboard.

To perform tasks using the keyboard, you must understand the notation used to identify which keys to press. This notation is used throughout Windows to identify **keyboard shortcuts** and in the Quick Reference at the end of each project. Keyboard shortcuts can consist of pressing a single key (RIGHT ARROW), pressing two keys simultaneously as shown by two key names separated by a plus sign (CTRL + F6), or pressing three keys simultaneously as shown by three key names separated by plus signs (CTRL + SHIFT + LEFT ARROW).

For example, to move the highlight from one program-item icon to the next you can press the RIGHT ARROW key (RIGHT ARROW). To move the highlight from the Main window to a group icon, hold down the CTRL key and press the F6 key (CTRL + F6). To move to the previous word in certain Windows applications, hold down the CTRL and SHIFT keys and press the LEFT ARROW key (CTRL + SHIFT + LEFT ARROW).

Menus and Commands

A **command** directs the software to perform a specific action, such as printing on the printer or saving data for use at a future time. One method in which you carry out a command is by choosing the command from a list of available commands, called a menu.

Windows organizes related groups of commands into **menus** and assigns a menu name to each menu. The **menu bar**, a horizontal bar below the title bar of an application window, contains a list of the menu names for that application. The menu bar for the Program Manager window in Figure 1-13 contains the following menu names: File, Options, Window, and Help. One letter in each name is underlined.

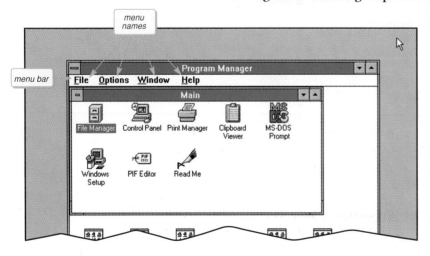

FIGURE 1-13

Selecting a Menu

To display a menu, you select the menu name. **Selecting** means marking an item. In some cases, when you select an item, Windows marks the item with a highlight by placing color behind the item. You select a menu name by pointing to the menu name in the menu bar and pressing the left mouse button (called clicking) or by using the keyboard to press the ALT key and then the keyboard key of the underlined letter in the menu name. Clicking the menu name File in the menu bar or pressing the ALT key and then the F key opens the File menu (Figure 1-14).

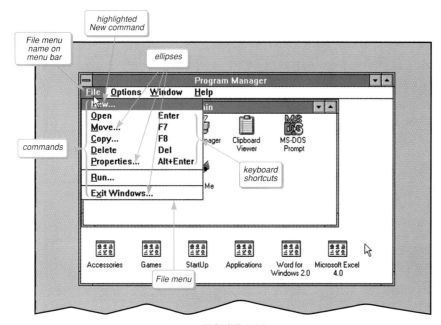

FIGURE 1-14

The File menu in Figure 1-14 contains the following commands: New, Open, Move, Copy, Delete, Properties, Run, and Exit Windows. The first command in the menu (New) is highlighted and a single character in each command is underlined. Some commands (New, Move, Copy, Properties, Run, and Exit Windows) are followed by an ellipsis (...). An **ellipsis** indicates Windows requires more information before executing the command. Commands without an ellipsis, such as the Open command, execute immediately.

Choosing a Command

You **choose** an item to carry out an action. You can choose using a mouse or keyboard. For example, to choose a command using a mouse, either click the command name in the menu or drag the highlight to the command name. To choose a command using the keyboard, either press the keyboard key of the underlined character in the command name or use the Arrow keys to move the highlight to the command name and press the ENTER key.

Some command names are followed by a keyboard shortcut. In Figure 1-14, the Open, Move, Copy, Delete, and Properties command names have keyboard shortcuts. The keyboard shortcut for the Properties command is ALT + ENTER. Holding down the ALT key and then pressing the ENTER key chooses the Properties command without selecting the File menu.

Dialog Boxes

When you choose a command whose command name is followed by an ellipsis (...), Windows opens a dialog box. A **dialog box** is a window that appears when Windows needs to supply information to you or wants you to enter information or select among options.

For example, Windows may inform you that a document is printing on the printer through the use of dialog box; or Windows may ask you whether you want to print all the pages in a printed report or just certain pages in the report.

A dialog box contains a title bar that identifies the name of the dialog box. In Figure 1-15, the name of the dialog box is Print.

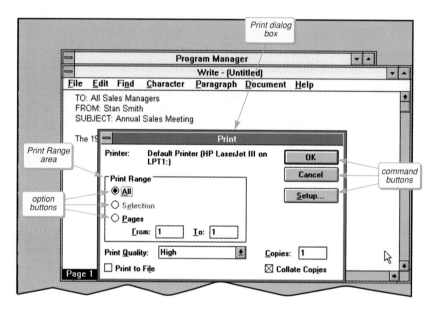

FIGURE 1-15

The types of responses Windows will ask for when working with dialog boxes fall into five categories: (1) Selecting mutually exclusive options; (2) Selecting one or more multiple options; (3) Entering specific information from the keyboard; (4) Selecting one item from a list of items; (5) Choosing a command to be implemented from the dialog box.

Each of these types of responses is discussed in the following paragraphs, together with the method for specifying them.

The Print dialog box in Figure 1-15 opens when you choose the Print command from the File menu of some windows. The Print Range area, defined by the name Print Range and a rectangular box, contains three option buttons.

The **option buttons** give you the choice of printing all pages of a report (All), selected parts of a report (Selection), or certain pages of a report (Pages). The option button containing the black dot (All) is the **selected button**. You can select only one option button at a time. A dimmed option, such as the Selection button, cannot be selected. To select an option button, use the mouse to click the option button or press the TAB key until the area containing the option button is selected and press the Arrow keys to highlight the option button.

The Print dialog box in Figure 1-15 on the previous page also contains the OK, Cancel, and Setup command buttons. **Command buttons** execute an action. The OK button executes the Print command, and the Cancel button cancels the Print command. The Setup button changes the setup of the printer by allowing you to select a printer from a list of printers, select the paper size, etc.

Figure 1-16 illustrates text boxes and check boxes. A **text box** is a rectangular area in which Windows displays text or you enter text. In the Print dialog box in Figure 1-16, the Pages option button is selected, which means only certain pages of a report are to print. You select which pages by entering the first page in the From text box (1) and the last page in the To text box (4). To enter text into a text box, select the text box by clicking it or by pressing the TAB key until the text in the text box is highlighted, and then type the text using the keyboard. The Copies text box in Figure 1-16 contains the number of copies to be printed (3).

FIGURE 1-16

Check boxes represent options you can turn on or off. An X in a check box indicates the option is turned on. To place an X in the box, click the box, or press the TAB key until the Print To File check box is highlighted, and then press SPACEBAR. In Figure 1-16, the Print to File check box, which does not contain an X, indicates the Print to File option is turned off and the pages will print on the printer. The Collate Copies check box, which contains an X, indicates the Collate Copies feature is turned on and the pages will print in collated order.

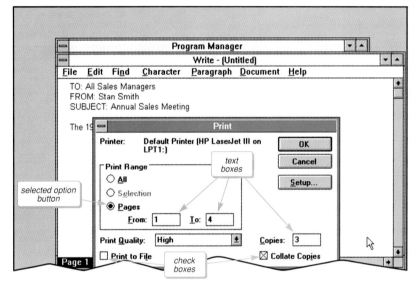

The Print dialog boxes in Figure 1-17 and Figure 1-18 on the next page, illustrate the Print Quality drop-down list box. When first selected, a **drop-down list box** is a rectangular box containing highlighted text and a down arrow box on the right. In Figure 1-17, the highlighted text, or **current selection**, is High.

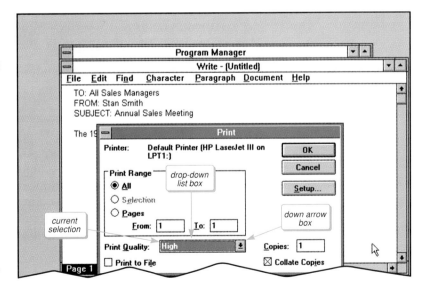

FIGURE 1-17

When you click the down arrow button, the drop-down list in Figure 1-18 appears. The list contains three choices (High, Medium, and Low). The current selection, High, is highlighted. To select from the list, use the mouse to click the selection or press the TAB key until the Print Quality drop-down list box is highlighted, press the DOWN ARROW key to highlight the selection, and then press ALT + UP ARROW or ALT + DOWN ARROW to make the selection.

Windows uses drop-down list boxes when a list of options must be presented but the dialog box is too crowded to contain the entire list. After you make your selection, the list disappears and only the current selection displays.

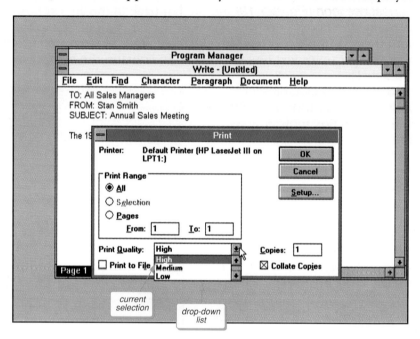

FIGURE 1-18

▶ USING MICROSOFT WINDOWS

T he remainder of this project illustrates how to use Windows to perform the operations of starting and quitting an application, creating a document, saving a document on disk, opening a document, editing a document, printing a document and using the Windows help facility. Understanding how to perform these operations will make completing the remainder of the projects in this book easier. These operations are illustrated by the use of the Notepad and Paintbrush applications.

One of the many applications included with Windows is the Notepad application. **Notepad** allows you to enter, edit, save, and print notes. Items that you create while using an application, such as a note, are called **documents**. In the following section, you will use the Notepad application to learn to (1) open a group window, (2) start an application from a group window, (3) maximize an application window, (4) create a document, (5) select a menu, (6) choose a command from a menu, (7) print a document, and (8) quit an application. In the process, you will enter and print a note.

Opening a Group Window

Each group icon at the bottom of the Program Manager window represents a group window that may contain program-item icons. To open the group window and view the program-item icons in that window use the mouse to point to the group icon and then double-click the left mouse button, as shown in the steps on the next page.

TO OPEN A GROUP WINDOW ▼

STEP 1 ▶

Point to the Accessories group icon at the bottom of the Program Manager window.

The mouse pointer points to the Accessories icon (Figure 1-19).

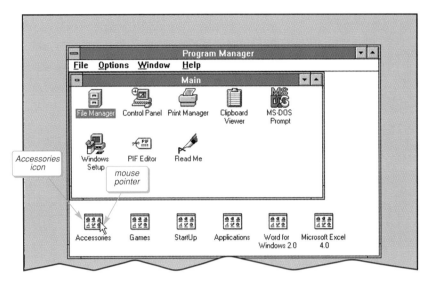

FIGURE 1-19

STEP 2 ▶

Double-click the left mouse button.

Windows removes the Accessories icon from the Program Manager window and opens the Accessories group window on top of the Program Manager and Main windows (Figure 1-20). The Accessories window contains the Notepad icon.

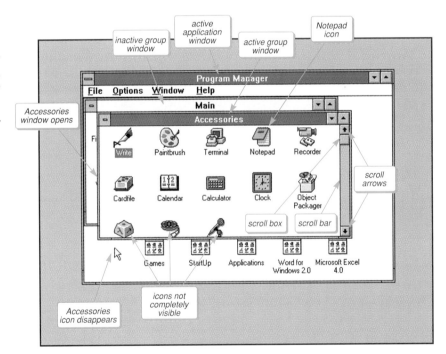

FIGURE 1-20

Opening a group window when one or more group windows are already open in the Program Manager window causes the new group window to display on top of the other group windows. The title bar of the newly opened group window is a different color or intensity than the title bars of the other group windows. This indicates the new group window is the active window. The **active window** is the window currently being used. Only one application window and one group window can be active at the same time. In Figure 1-20 on the previous page, the colors of the title bars indicate that Program Manager is the active application window (green title bar) and the Accessories group window is the active group window (green title bar). The color of the Main window title bar (yellow) indicates the Main window is inactive. The colors may not be the same on the computer you use.

A scroll bar appears on the right edge of the Accessories window. A **scroll bar** is a bar that appears at the right and/or bottom edge of a window whose contents are not completely visible. In Figure 1-20 on the previous page, the third row of program-item icons in the Accessories window is not completely visible. A scroll bar contains two **scroll arrows** and a **scroll box** which enable you to view areas of the window not currently visible. To view areas of the Accessories window not currently visible, you can click the down scroll arrow repeatedly, click the scroll bar between the down scroll arrow and the scroll box, or drag the scroll box toward the down scroll arrow until the area you want to view is visible in the window.

Correcting an Error While Double-Clicking a Group Icon

While double-clicking, it is easy to mistakenly click once instead of double-clicking. When you click a group icon such as the Accessories icon once, the **Control menu** for that icon opens (Figure 1-21). The Control menu contains the following seven commands: Restore, Move, Size, Minimize, Maximize, Close, and Next. You choose one of these commands to carry out an action associated with the Accessories icon. To remove the Control menu and open the Accessories window after clicking the Accessories icon once, you can choose the Restore command; or click any open area outside the menu to remove the Control menu and then double-click the Accessories icon; or simply double-click the Accessories icon as if you had not clicked the icon at all.

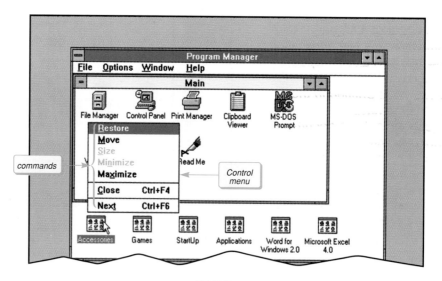

FIGURE 1-21

Starting an Application

Each program-item icon in a group window represents an application. To start an application, double-click the program-item icon. In this project, you want to start the Notepad application. To start the Notepad application, perform the steps on the next page.

TO START AN APPLICATION ▼

STEP 1 ▶

Point to the Notepad icon (Figure 1-22).

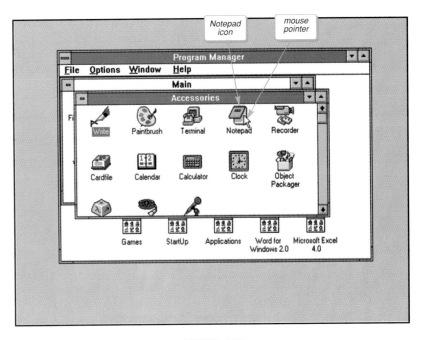

FIGURE 1-22

STEP 2 ▶

Double-click the left mouse button.

*Windows opens the Notepad window on the desktop (Figure 1-23). Program Manager becomes the inactive application (yellow title bar) and Notepad is the active application (green title bar). The word Untitled in the window title (Notepad — [Untitled]) indicates a document has not been created and saved on disk. The menu bar contains the following menus: File, Edit, Search, and Help. The area below the menu bar contains an insertion point, mouse pointer, and two scroll bars. The **insertion point** is a flashing vertical line that indicates the point at which text entered from the keyboard will be displayed. When you point to the interior of the Notepad window, the mouse pointer changes from a block arrow to an I-beam (I).*

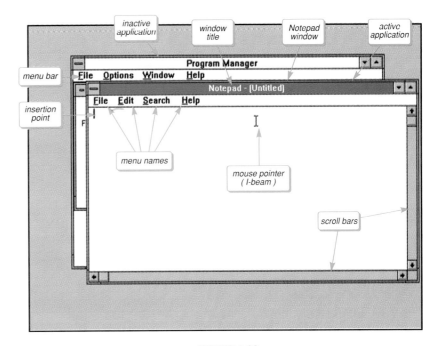

FIGURE 1-23

Correcting an Error While Double-Clicking a Program-Item Icon

While double-clicking a program-item icon you can easily click once instead. When you click a program-item icon such as the Notepad icon once, the icon becomes the **active icon** and Windows highlights the icon name (Figure 1-24). To start the Notepad application after clicking the Notepad icon once, double-click the Notepad icon as if you had not clicked the icon at all.

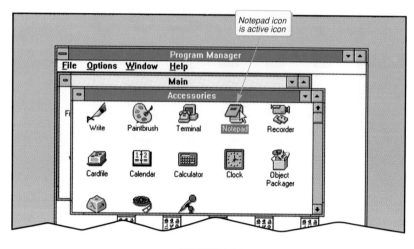

FIGURE 1-24

Maximizing an Application Window

Before you work with an application, maximizing the application window makes it easier to see the contents of the window. You can maximize an application window so the window fills the entire desktop. To maximize an application window to its maximum size, choose the **Maximize button** (▲) by pointing to the Maximize button and clicking the left mouse button. Complete the following steps to maximize the Notepad window.

TO MAXIMIZE AN APPLICATION WINDOW ▼

STEP 1 ►

Point to the Maximize button in the upper right corner of the Notepad window.

The mouse pointer becomes a block arrow and points to the Maximize button (Figure 1-25).

FIGURE 1-25

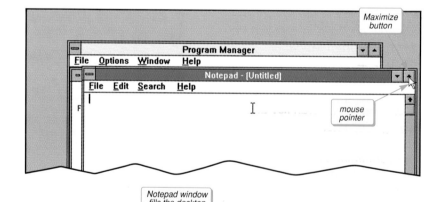

STEP 2 ►

Click the left mouse button.

The Notepad window fills the desktop (Figure 1-26). The **Restore button** (♦) replaces the Maximize button at the right side of the title bar. Clicking the Restore button will return the window to its size before maximizing.

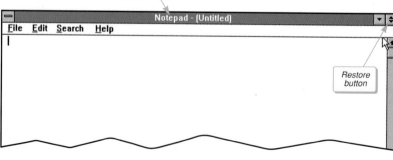

FIGURE 1-26

Creating a Document

To create a document in Notepad, type the text you want to display in the document. After typing a line of text, press the ENTER key to terminate the entry of the line. To create a document, enter the note to the right by performing the steps below.

> Things to do today —
> 1) Take fax\phone to Conway Service Center
> 2) Pick up payroll checks from ADM
> 3) Order 3 boxes of copier paper

TO CREATE A NOTEPAD DOCUMENT ▼

STEP 1 ▶

Type Things to do today – **and press the** ENTER **key.**

The first line of the note is entered and the insertion point appears at the beginning of the next line (Figure 1-27).

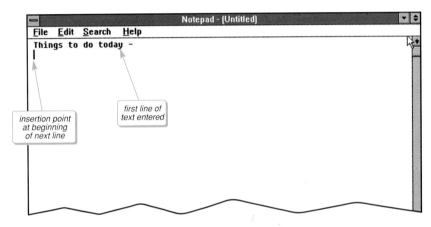

FIGURE 1-27

STEP 2 ▶

Type the remaining lines of the note. Press the ENTER **key after typing each line.**

The remaining lines in the note are entered and the insertion point is located at the beginning of the line following the note (Figure 1-28).

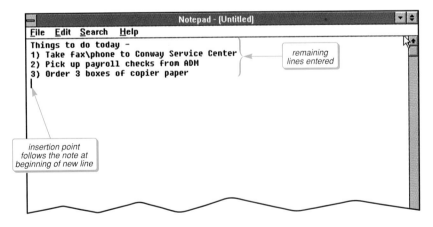

FIGURE 1-28

Printing a Document by Choosing a Command from a Menu

After creating a document, you often print the document on the printer. To print the note, complete the following steps.

TO PRINT A DOCUMENT ▼

STEP 1 ▶

Point to File on the Notepad menu bar (Figure 1-29).

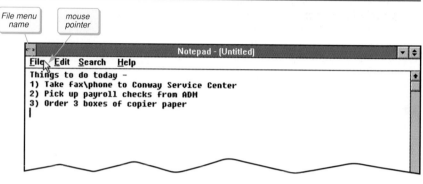

FIGURE 1-29

STEP 2 ▶

Select File by clicking the left mouse button.

Windows opens the File menu in the Notepad window (Figure 1-30). The File menu name is high-lighted and the File menu con-tains the following commands: New, Open, Save, Save As, Print, Page Setup, Print Setup, and Exit. Windows highlights the first command in the menu (New). Notice the commands in the Notepad File menu are different than those in the Program Man-ager File menu (see Figure 1-14 on page WIN11). The commands in the File menu will vary depend-ing on the application you are using.

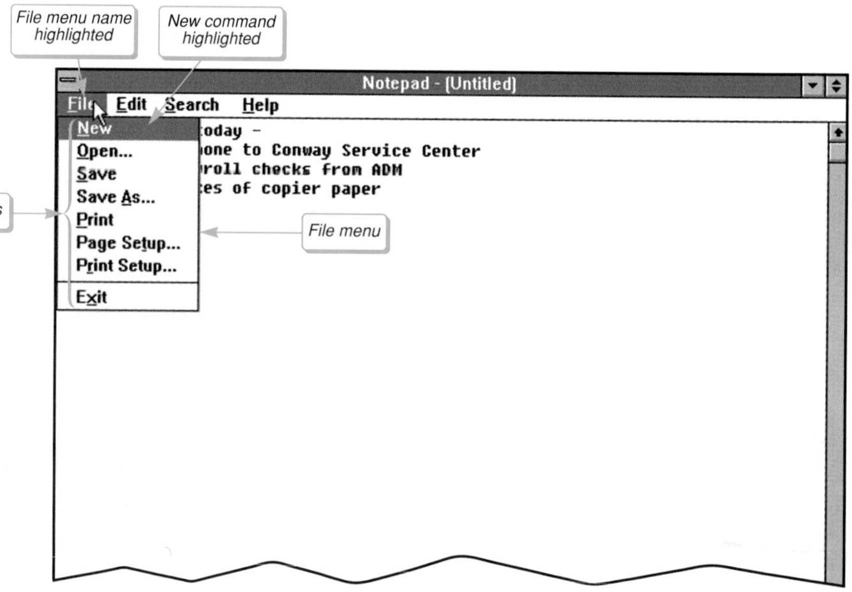

FIGURE 1-30

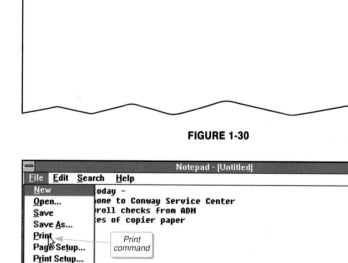

STEP 3 ▶

Point to the Print command.

The mouse pointer points to the Print command (Figure 1-31).

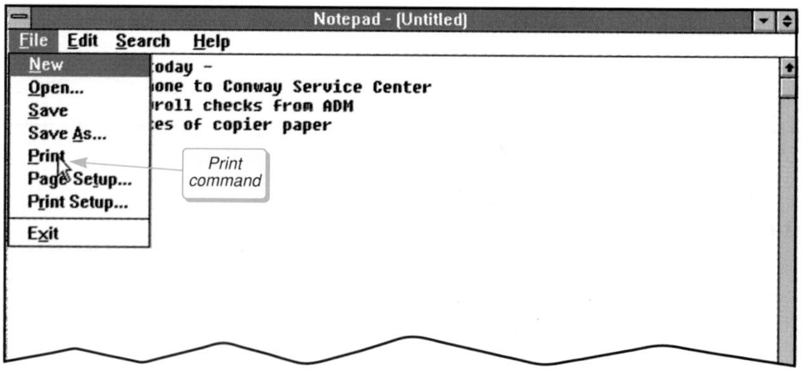

FIGURE 1-31

STEP 4 ▶

Choose the Print command from the File menu by clicking the left mouse button.

Windows momentarily opens the Notepad dialog box (Figure 1-32). The dialog box contains the Now Printing text message and the Cancel command button (Cancel). When the Notepad dialog box closes, Windows prints the document on the printer (Figure 1-33).

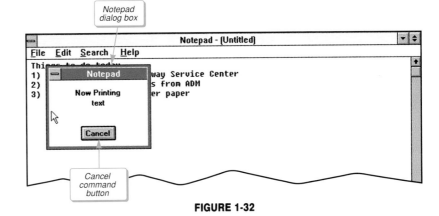

FIGURE 1-32

```
                        (Untitled)



    Things to do today —
    1) Take fax\phone to Conway Service Center
    2) Pick up payroll checks from ADM
    3) Order 3 boxes of copier paper
```

FIGURE 1-33

Quitting an Application

When you have finished creating and printing the document, quit the application by following the steps below and on the next page.

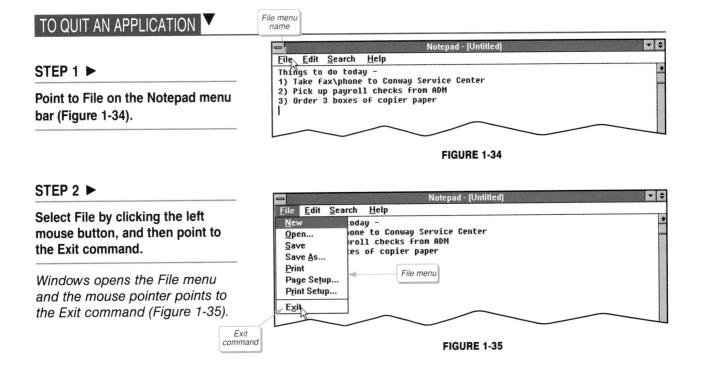

TO QUIT AN APPLICATION ▼

STEP 1 ▶

Point to File on the Notepad menu bar (Figure 1-34).

FIGURE 1-34

STEP 2 ▶

Select File by clicking the left mouse button, and then point to the Exit command.

Windows opens the File menu and the mouse pointer points to the Exit command (Figure 1-35).

FIGURE 1-35

STEP 3 ▶

Choose the Exit command from the File menu by clicking the left mouse button, and then point to the No button.

Windows opens the Notepad dialog box (Figure 1-36). The dialog box contains the following: The message, The text in the [Untitled] file has changed., the question, Do you want to save the changes?, and the Yes, No, and Cancel command buttons. The mouse pointer points to the No button ( ). You choose the Yes button (No) to save the document on disk and exit Notepad. You choose the No button if you do not want to save the document and want to exit Notepad. You choose the Cancel button to cancel the Exit command.

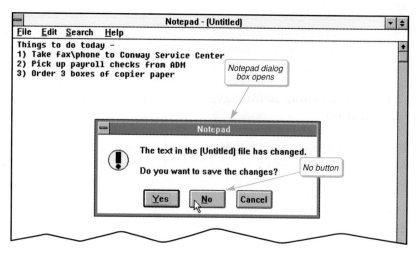

FIGURE 1-36

STEP 4 ▶

Choose the No button by clicking the left mouse button.

Windows closes the Notepad dialog box and Notepad window and exits the Notepad application (Figure 1-37).

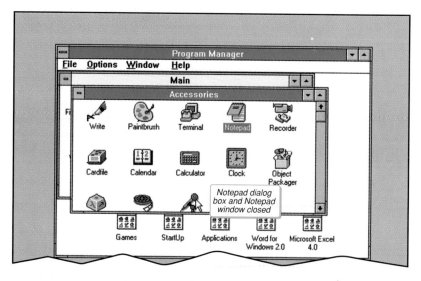

FIGURE 1-37

In the preceding example, you used the Microsoft Windows graphical user interface to accomplish the tasks of opening the Accessories group window, starting the Notepad application from the Accessories group window, maximizing the Notepad application window, creating a document in the Notepad application window, printing the document on the printer, and quitting the Notepad application.

▶ FILE AND DISK CONCEPTS

To protect against the accidental loss of a document and to save a document for use in the future, you should save a document on disk. Before saving a document on disk, however, you must understand the concepts of naming a file, directories, subdirectories, directory structures, and directory paths. The following section explains these concepts.

Naming a File

When you create a document using an application, the document is stored in main memory. If you quit the application without saving the document on disk, the document is lost. To save the document for future use, you must store the document in a **document file** on the hard disk or on a diskette before quitting the application. Before saving a document, you must assign a name to the document file.

All files are identified on disk by a **filename** and an **extension**. For example, the name SALES.TXT consists of a filename (SALES) and an extension (.TXT). A filename can contain from one to eight characters and the extension begins with a period and can contain from one to three characters. Filenames must start with a letter or number. Any uppercase or lowercase character is valid except a period (.), quotation mark (''), slash (/), backslash (\), brackets ([]), colon (:), semicolon (;), vertical bar (|), equal sign (=), comma (,), or blank space. Filenames cannot be CON, AUX, COM1, COM2, COM3, COM4, LPT1, LPT2, LPT3, PRN, and NUL.

To more easily identify document files on disk, it is convenient to assign the same extension to document files you create with a given application. The Notepad application, for instance, automatically uses the .TXT extension for each document file saved on disk. Typical filenames and extensions of document files saved using Notepad are: SHOPPING.TXT, MECHANIC.TXT, and 1994.TXT.

You can use the asterisk character (*) in place of a filename or extension to refer to a group of files. For example, the asterisk in the expression *.TXT tells Windows to reference any file that contains the .TXT extension, regardless of the filename. This group of files might consist of the HOME.TXT, AUTOPART-.TXT, MARKET.TXT, JONES.TXT, and FRANK.TXT files.

The asterisk in MONTHLY.* tells Windows to reference any file that contains the filename MONTHLY, regardless of the extension. Files in this group might consist of the MONTHLY.TXT, MONTHLY.CAL, and MONTHLY.CRD files.

Directory Structures and Directory Paths

After selecting a name and extension for a file, you must decide which auxiliary storage device (hard disk or diskette) to use and in which directory you want to save the file. A **directory** is an area of a disk created to store related groups of files. When you first prepare a disk for use on a computer, a single directory, called the **root directory**, is created on the disk. You can create **subdirectories** in the root directory to store additional groups of related files. The hard disk in Figure 1-38 contains the root directory and the WINDOWS, MSAPPS, and SYSTEM subdirectories. The WINDOWS, MSAPPS, and SYSTEM subdirectories are created when Windows is installed and contain files related to Windows.

HARD DISK

FIGURE 1-38

Directory Structure	Directory Path
🗁 c:\	C:\
🗁 windows	C:\WINDOWS
🗀 msapps	C:\WINDOWS\MSAPPS
🗀 system	C:\WINDOWS\SYSTEM

▶ **TABLE 1-1**

The relationship between the root directory and any subdirectories is called the **directory structure**. Each directory or subdirectory in the directory structure has an associated directory path. The **directory path** is the path Windows follows to find a file in a directory. Table 1-1 contains a graphic representation of the directory structure and the associated paths of drive C.

Each directory and subdirectory on drive C is represented by a file folder icon in the directory structure. The first file folder icon, an unshaded open file folder (🗁), represents the root directory of the current drive (drive C). The c:\ entry to the right of the icon symbolizes the root directory (identified by the \ character) of drive C (c:). The path is C:\. Thus, to find a file in this directory, Windows locates drive C (C:) and the root directory (\) on drive C.

The second icon, a shaded open file folder (🗁), represents the current subdirectory. This icon is indented below the first file folder icon because it is a subdirectory. The name of the subdirectory (windows) appears to the right of the shaded file folder icon. Because the WINDOWS subdirectory was created in the root directory, the path for the WINDOWS subdirectory is C:\WINDOWS. To find a file in this subdirectory, Windows locates drive C, locates the root directory on drive C, and then locates the WINDOWS subdirectory in the root directory.

Because the current path is C:\WINDOWS, the file folder icons for both the root directory and WINDOWS subdirectory are open file folders. An open file folder indicates the directory or subdirectory is in the current path. Unopened file folders represent subdirectories not in the current path.

The third and fourth icons in Table 1-1, unopened file folders (🗀), represent the MSAPPS and SYSTEM subdirectories. The unopened file folders indicate these subdirectories are not part of the current path. These file folder icons are indented below the file folder for the WINDOWS subdirectory which means they were created in the WINDOWS subdirectory. The subdirectory names (msapps and system) appear to the right of the file folder icons.

Since the MSAPPS and SYSTEM subdirectories were created in the WINDOWS subdirectory, the paths for these subdirectories are C:\WINDOWS\MSAPPS and C:\WINDOWS\SYSTEM. The second backslash (\) in these paths separates the two subdirectory names. To find a file in these subdirectories, Windows locates drive C, locates the root directory on drive C, then locates the WINDOWS subdirectory in the root directory, and finally locates the MSAPPS or SYSTEM subdirectory in the WINDOWS subdirectory.

Saving a Document on Disk

After entering data into a document, you will often save it on the hard disk or a diskette to protect against accidental loss and to make the document available for use later. In the previous example using the Notepad application, the note was not saved prior to exiting Notepad. Instead of exiting, assume you want to save the document you created. The screen before you begin to save the document is shown in Figure 1-39. To save the document on a diskette in drive A using the filename, agenda, perform the steps that begin at the top of the next page.

FIGURE 1-39

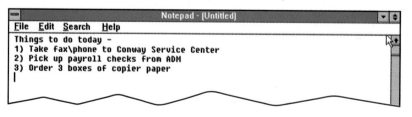

TO SAVE A FILE ▼

STEP 1 ►

Insert a formatted diskette into drive A (Figure 1-40).

The diskette must be properly formatted before being used to save data. To learn the technique for formatting a diskette see Project 2.

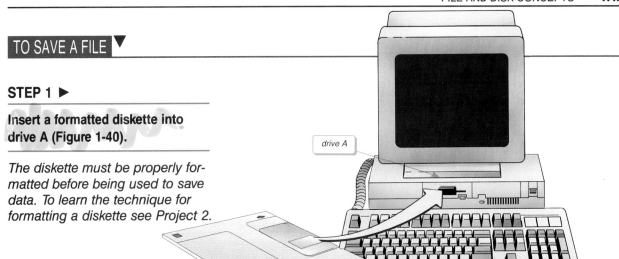

drive A

diskette

FIGURE 1-40

STEP 2 ►

Select File on the Notepad menu bar, and then point to the Save As command.

Windows opens the File menu in the Notepad window and the mouse pointer points to the Save As command (Figure 1-41). The ellipsis (...) following the Save As command indicates Windows will open a dialog box when you choose this command.

```
Notepad - [Untitled]
File  Edit  Search  Help
New        oday -
Open...     one to Conway Service Center
Save        roll checks from ADM
Save As...  es of copier paper
Print
Page Setup...
Print Setup...
Exit
```
ellipsis

File menu

Save As command

FIGURE 1-41

STEP 3 ►

Choose the Save As command from the File menu by clicking the left mouse button.

The Save As dialog box opens (Figure 1-42). The File Name text box contains the highlighted *.txt entry. Typing a filename from the keyboard will replace the entire *.txt entry with the filename entered from the keyboard. The current path is c:\windows and the Directories list box contains the directory structure of the current subdirectory (windows). The drive selection in the Drives drop-down list box is c:. The dialog box contains the OK (OK) and Cancel (Cancel) command buttons.

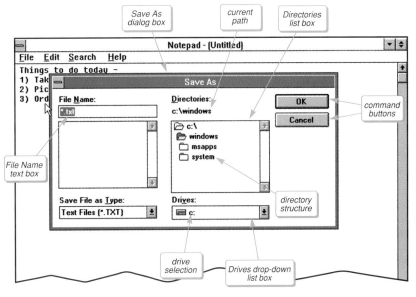

Save As dialog box / current path / Directories list box / command buttons / File Name text box / directory structure / drive selection / Drives drop-down list box

FIGURE 1-42

STEP 4 ▶

Type agenda **in the File Name text box, and then point to the Drives drop-down list box arrow.**

The filename, agenda, and an insertion point display in the File Name text box (Figure 1-43). When you save this document, Notepad will automatically add the .TXT extension to the agenda filename and save the file on disk using the name AGENDA.TXT. The mouse pointer points to the Drives drop-down list box arrow.

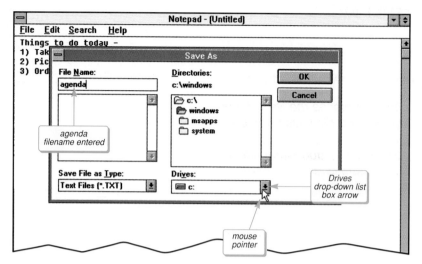

FIGURE 1-43

STEP 5 ▶

Choose the Drives drop-down list box arrow by clicking the left mouse button, and then point to the drive a: icon (🖫) in the Drives drop-down list.

Windows displays the Drives drop-down list (Figure 1-44). The drive a: icon and drive c: icon appear in the drop-down list. The mouse pointer points to the drive a: icon.

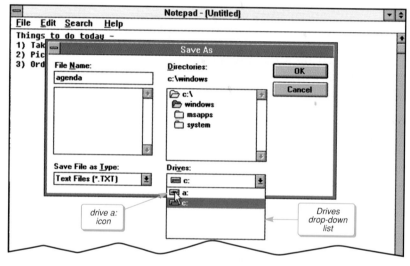

FIGURE 1-44

STEP 6 ▶

Select the drive a: icon by clicking the left mouse button, and then point to the OK button.

The selection is highlighted and the light on drive A turns on while Windows checks for a diskette in drive A (Figure 1-45). The current path changes to a:\ and the Directories list box contains the directory structure of the diskette in drive A.

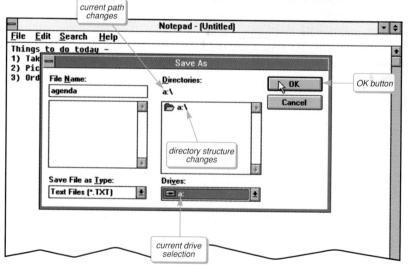

FIGURE 1-45

STEP 7 ►

Choose the OK button in the Save As dialog box by clicking the left mouse button.

Windows closes the Save As dialog box and displays an hourglass icon while saving the AGENDA.TXT document file on the diskette in drive A. After the file is saved, Windows changes the window title of the Notepad window to reflect the name of the AGENDA.TXT file (Figure 1-46).

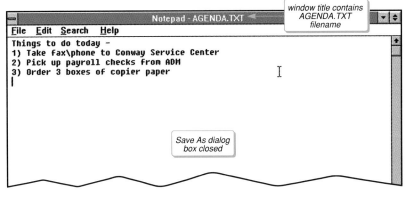

FIGURE 1-46

Correcting Errors Encountered While Saving a Document File

Before you can save a document file on a diskette, you must insert a formatted diskette into the diskette drive. **Formatting** is the process of preparing a diskette for use on a computer by establishing the sectors and cylinders on a disk, analyzing the diskette for defective cylinders, and establishing the root directory. The technique for formatting a diskette is shown in Project 2. If you try to save a file on a diskette and forget to insert a diskette, forget to close the diskette drive door after inserting a diskette, insert an unformatted diskette, or insert a damaged diskette, Windows opens the Save As dialog box in Figure 1-47.

The dialog box contains the messages telling you the condition found and the Retry (Retry) and Cancel buttons. To save a file on the diskette in drive A after receiving this message, insert a formatted diskette into the diskette drive, point to the Retry button, and click the left mouse button.

In addition, you cannot save a document file on a write-protected diskette. A **write-protected diskette** prevents accidentally erasing data stored on the diskette by not letting the disk drive write new data or erase existing data on the diskette. If you try to save a file on a write-protected diskette, Windows opens the Save As dialog box shown in Figure 1-48.

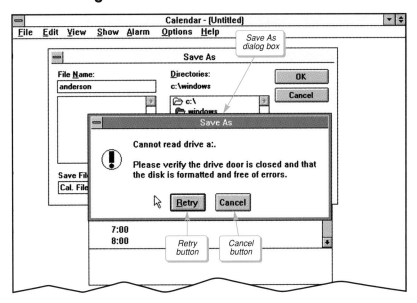

FIGURE 1-47

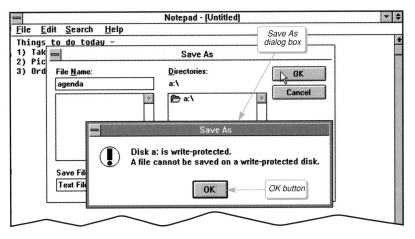

FIGURE 1-48

The Save As dialog box in Figure 1-48 on the previous page contains the messages, Disk a: is write-protected., and, A file cannot be saved on a write-protected disk., and the OK button. To save a file on diskette after inserting a write-protected diskette into drive A, remove the diskette from the diskette drive, remove the write-protection from the diskette, insert the diskette into the diskette drive, point to the OK button, and click the left mouse button.

Quitting an Application

When you have finished saving the AGENDA.TXT file on disk, you can quit the Notepad application as shown in Figure 1-34 through Figure 1-37 on pages WIN21 and WIN22. The steps are summarized below.

TO QUIT AN APPLICATION

Step 1: Point to File on the Notepad menu bar.
Step 2: Select File by clicking the left mouse button, and then point to the Exit command.
Step 3: Choose the Exit command by clicking the left mouse button.

If you have made changes to the document since saving it on the diskette, Notepad will ask if you want to save the changes. If so, choose the Yes button in the dialog box; otherwise, choose the No button.

▶ OPENING A DOCUMENT FILE

C hanges are frequently made to a document saved on disk. To make these changes, you must first open the document file by retrieving the file from disk using the Open command. After modifying the document, you save the modified document file on disk using the Save command. Using the Notepad application, you will learn to (1) open a document file and (2) save an edited document file on diskette. In the process, you will add the following line to the AGENDA.TXT file: 4) Buy copier toner.

Starting the Notepad Application and Maximizing the Notepad Window

To start the Notepad application and maximize the Notepad window, perform the following step.

TO START AN APPLICATION AND MAXIMIZE ITS WINDOW ▼

STEP 1 ▶

Double-click the Notepad icon in the Accessories group window. When the Notepad window opens, click the Maximize button.

Double-clicking the Notepad icon opens the Notepad window. Clicking the Maximize button maximizes the Notepad window (Figure 1-49).

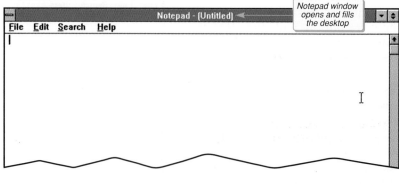

FIGURE 1-49

Opening a Document File

Before you can modify the AGENDA.TXT document, you must open the file from the diskette on which it was stored. To do so, ensure the diskette containing the file is inserted into drive A, then perform the following steps.

TO OPEN A DOCUMENT FILE ▼

STEP 1 ►

Select File on the menu bar, and then point to the Open command.

Windows opens the File menu and the mouse pointer points to the Open command (Figure 1-50).

STEP 2 ►

Choose the Open command from the File menu by clicking the left mouse button, and then point to the Drives drop-down list box arrow.

The Open dialog box opens (Figure 1-51). The File Name text box contains the *.txt entry and the File Name list box is empty because no files with the .TXT extension appear in the current directory. The current path is c:\windows. The Directories list box contains the directory structure of the current subdirectory (WINDOWS). The selected drive in the Drives drop-down list box is c:. The mouse pointer points to the Drives drop-down list box arrow.

STEP 3 ►

Choose the Drives drop-down list box arrow by clicking the left mouse button, and then point to the drive a: icon.

Windows displays the Drives drop-down list (Figure 1-52). The drive a: icon and drive c: icon appear in the drop-down list. The current selection is c:. The mouse pointer points to the drive a: icon.

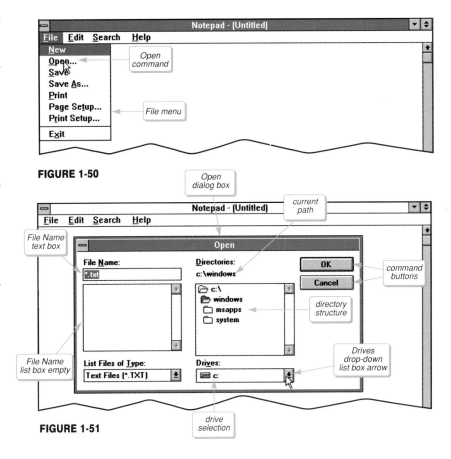

FIGURE 1-50

FIGURE 1-51

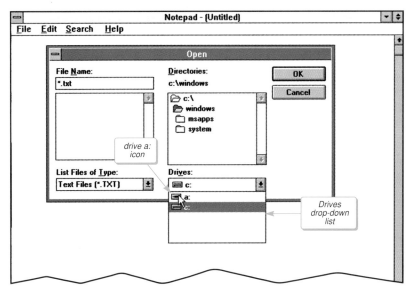

FIGURE 1-52

STEP 4 ▶

Select the drive a: icon by clicking the left mouse button, and then point to the agenda.txt entry in the File Name list box.

The light on drive A turns on, and Windows checks for a diskette in drive A. If there is no diskette in drive A, a dialog box opens to indicate this fact. The current selection in the Drives drop-down list box is highlighted (Figure 1-53). The File Name list box contains the filename agenda.txt, the current path is a:\, and the Directories list box contains the directory structure of drive A. The mouse pointer points to the agenda.txt entry.

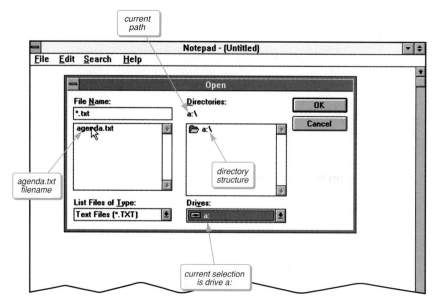

FIGURE 1-53

STEP 5 ▶

Select the agenda.txt file by clicking the left mouse button, and then point to the OK button.

Notepad highlights the agenda.txt entry in the File Name text box, and the agenda.txt filename appears in the File Name text box (Figure 1-54). The mouse pointer points to the OK button.

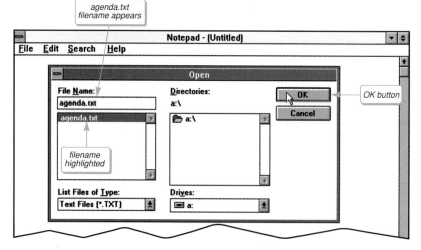

FIGURE 1-54

STEP 6 ▶

Choose the OK button from the Open dialog box by clicking the left mouse button.

Windows retrieves the agenda.txt file from the diskette in drive A and opens the AGENDA.TXT document in the Notepad window (Figure 1-55).

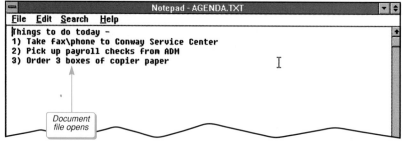

FIGURE 1-55

Editing the Document File

You edit the AGENDA.TXT document file by entering the fourth line of text.

TO EDIT THE DOCUMENT ▼

STEP 1 ▶

Press the DOWN ARROW key four
times to position the insertion
point, and then type the new line,
4) Buy Copier toner.

The new line appears in the Note-pad document (Figure 1-56).

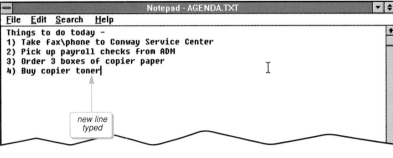

FIGURE 1-56

Saving the Modified Document File

After modifying the AGENDA.TXT document, you should save the modified
document on disk using the same AGENDA.TXT filename. To save a modified
file on disk, choose the Save command. The Save command differs from the
Save As command in that you choose the Save command to save changes to an
existing file while you choose the Save As command to name and save a new file
or to save an existing file under a new name.

TO SAVE A MODIFIED DOCUMENT FILE ▼

STEP 1 ▶

Select File on the Notepad menu
bar, and then point to the Save
command.

*Windows opens the File menu
and the mouse pointer points to
the Save command (Figure 1-57).*

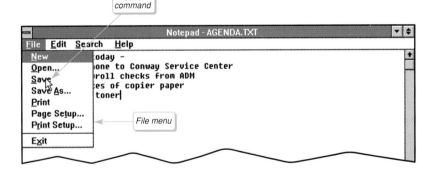

FIGURE 1-57

STEP 2 ▶

Choose the Save command from
the File menu by clicking the left
mouse button.

*Windows closes the File menu,
displays the hourglass icon
momentarily, and saves the
AGENDA.TXT document on the
diskette in drive A (Figure 1-58).*

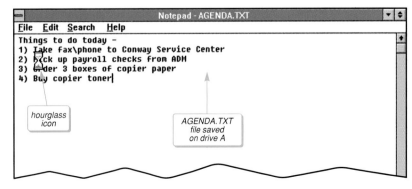

FIGURE 1-58

STEP 3 ▶

Remove the diskette from Drive A (Figure 1-59).

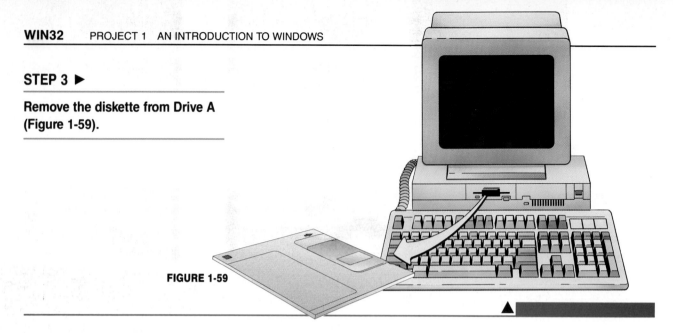

FIGURE 1-59

When you have finished saving the modified AGENDA.TXT file, quit the Notepad application by performing the following steps.

TO QUIT NOTEPAD

Step 1: Select File on the Notepad menu bar.
Step 2: Choose the Exit command.

▶ USING WINDOWS HELP

If you need help while using an application, you can use Windows online Help. **Online Help** is available for all applications except Clock. To illustrate Windows online Help, you will start the Paintbrush application and obtain help about the commands on the Edit menu. **Paintbrush** is a drawing program that allows you to create, edit, and print full-color illustrations.

TO START AN APPLICATION

STEP 1 ▶

Double-click the Paintbrush icon (🖌) in the Accessories group window in Program Manager, and then click the Maximize button on the Paintbrush — [Untitled] window.

Windows opens and maximizes the Paintbrush window (Figure 1-60).

FIGURE 1-60

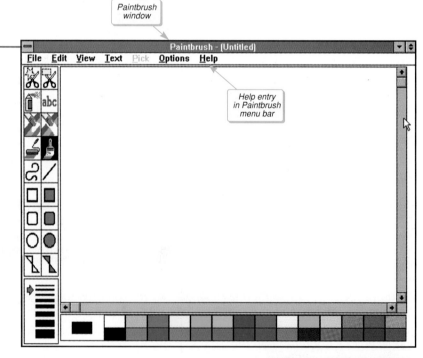

TO OBTAIN HELP ▼

STEP 1 ▶

Select Help on the Paintbrush menu bar, and then point to the Contents command.

Windows opens the Help menu (Figure 1-61). The Help menu contains four commands. The mouse pointer points to the Contents command.

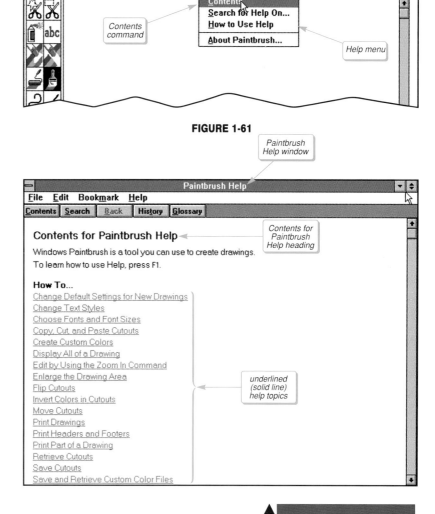

FIGURE 1-61

STEP 2 ▶

Choose the Contents command from the Help menu by clicking the left mouse button. Then click the Maximize button on the Paintbrush Help window.

Windows opens the Paintbrush Help window (Figure 1-62), and when you click the Maximize button, it maximizes the window.

FIGURE 1-62

The Contents for Paintbrush Help screen appears in the window. This screen contains information about the Paintbrush application, how to learn to use online Help (press F1), and an alphabetical list of all help topics for the Paintbrush application. Each **help topic** is underlined with a solid line. The solid line indicates additional information relating to the topic is available. Underlined help topics are called jumps. A **jump** provides a link to viewing information about another help topic or more information about the current topic. A jump may be either text or graphics.

Choosing a Help Topic

To choose an underlined help topic, scroll the help topics to make the help topic you want visible, then point to the help topic and click the left mouse button. When you place the mouse pointer on a help topic, the mouse pointer changes to a hand (🖑). To obtain help about the Edit menu, perform the steps on the next page.

TO CHOOSE A HELP TOPIC ▼

STEP 1 ►

Point to the down scroll arrow (Figure 1-63).

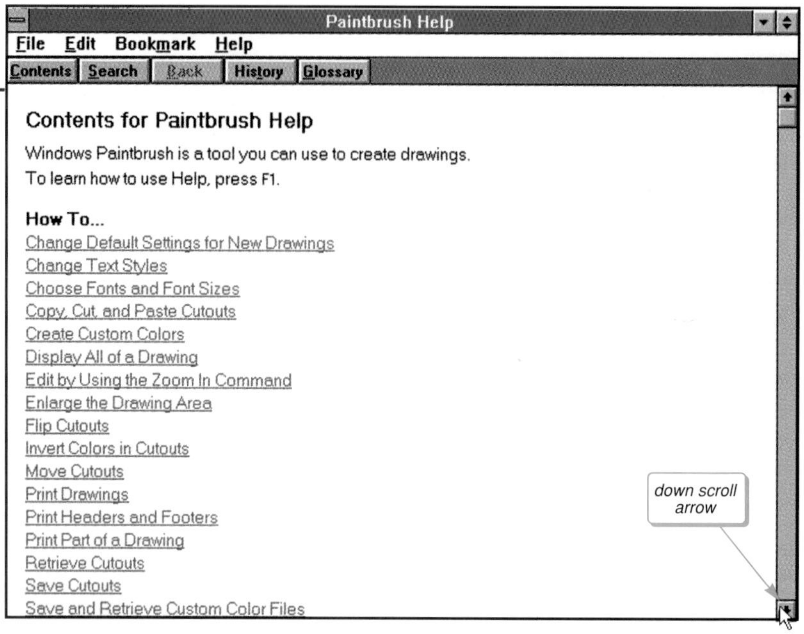

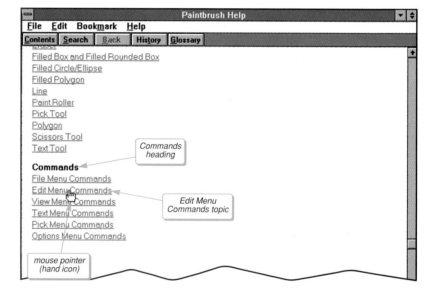

FIGURE 1-63

STEP 2 ►

Hold down the left mouse button (scroll) until the Edit Menu Commands help topic is visible, and then point to the Edit Menu Commands topic.

The Commands heading and the Edit Menu Commands topic are visible (Figure 1-64). The mouse pointer changes to a hand icon and points to the Edit Menu Commands topic.

FIGURE 1-64

STEP 3 ►

Choose the Edit Menu Commands topic by clicking the left mouse button.

The Edit Menu Commands screen contains information about each of the commands in the Edit menu (Figure 1-65). Two terms (scroll bar and cutout) are underlined with a dotted line. Terms underlined with a dotted line have an associated glossary definition. To display a term's glossary definition, point to the term and click the left mouse button.

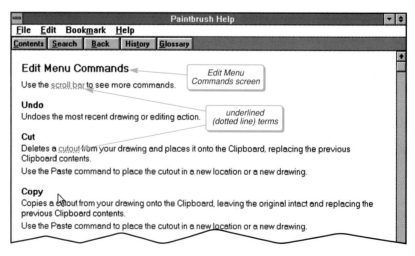

FIGURE 1-65

TO DISPLAY A DEFINITION ▼

STEP 1 ▶

Point to the term, scroll bar.

The mouse pointer changes to a hand and points to the term, scroll bar (Figure 1-66).

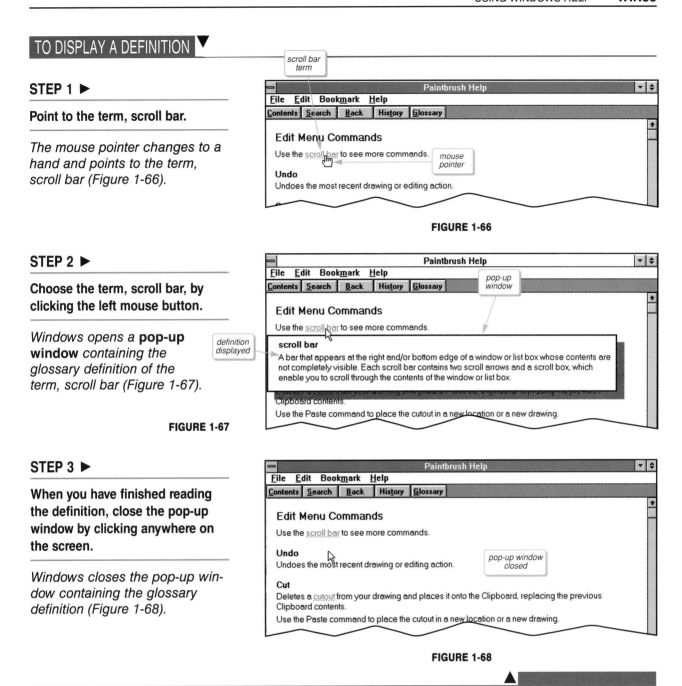

FIGURE 1-66

STEP 2 ▶

Choose the term, scroll bar, by clicking the left mouse button.

Windows opens a **pop-up window** *containing the glossary definition of the term, scroll bar (Figure 1-67).*

FIGURE 1-67

STEP 3 ▶

When you have finished reading the definition, close the pop-up window by clicking anywhere on the screen.

Windows closes the pop-up window containing the glossary definition (Figure 1-68).

FIGURE 1-68

Exiting the Online Help and Paintbrush Applications

After obtaining help about the Edit Menu commands, quit Help by choosing the Exit command from the Help File menu. Then, quit Paintbrush by choosing the Exit command from the Paintbrush File menu. The steps are summarized below.

TO QUIT PAINTBRUSH HELP

Step 1: Select File on the Paintbrush Help menu bar.
Step 2: Choose the Exit command.

TO QUIT PAINTBRUSH

Step 1: Select File on the Paintbrush menu bar.
Step 2: Choose the Exit command.

▶ QUITTING WINDOWS

Y ou always want to return the desktop to its original state before beginning your next session with Windows. Therefore, before exiting Windows, you must verify that any changes made to the desktop are not saved when you quit windows.

Verify Changes to the Desktop Will Not be Saved

Because you want to return the desktop to its state before you started Windows, no changes should be saved. The Save Settings on Exit command on the Program Manager Options menu controls whether changes to the desktop are saved or are not saved when you quit Windows. A check mark (✓) preceding the Save Settings on Exit command indicates the command is active and all changes to the layout of the desktop will be saved when you quit Windows. If the command is preceded by a check mark, choose the Save Settings from Exit command by clicking the left mouse button to remove the check mark, so the changes will not be saved. Perform the following steps to verify that changes are not saved to the desktop.

TO VERIFY CHANGES ARE NOT SAVED TO THE DESKTOP ▼

STEP 1 ▶

Select Options on the Program Manager menu bar, and then point to the Save Settings on Exit command.

The Options menu opens (Figure 1-69). A check mark (✓) precedes the Save Settings on Exit command.

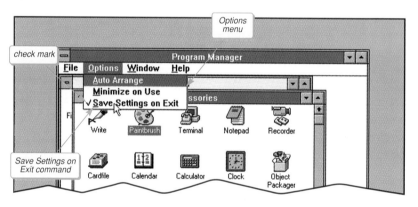

FIGURE 1-69

STEP 2 ▶

To remove the check mark, choose the Save Settings on Exit command from the Options menu by clicking the left mouse button.

Windows closes the Options menu (Figure 1-70). Although not visible in Figure 1-70, the check mark preceding the Save Settings from Exit command has been removed. This means any changes made to the desktop will not be saved when you exit Windows.

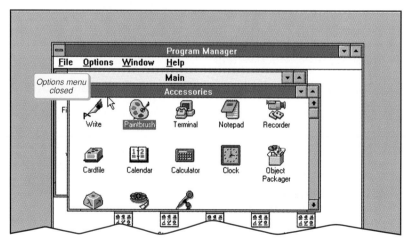

FIGURE 1-70

Quitting Windows Without Saving Changes

After verifying the Save Settings on Exit command is not active, quit Windows by choosing the Exit Windows command from the File menu, as shown below.

TO QUIT WINDOWS ▼

STEP 1 ►

Select File on the Program Manager menu bar, and then point to the Exit Windows command.

Windows opens the File menu and the mouse pointer points to the Exit Windows command (Figure 1-71).

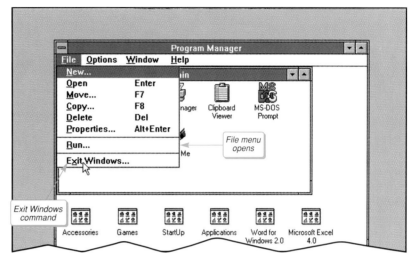

FIGURE 1-71

STEP 2 ►

Choose the Exit Windows command from the File menu by clicking the left mouse button and point to the OK button.

The Exit Windows dialog box opens and contains the message, This will end your Windows session., and the OK and Cancel buttons (Figure 1-72). Choosing the OK button exits Windows. Choosing the Cancel button cancels the exit from Windows and returns you to the Program Manager window. The mouse pointer points to the OK button.

STEP 3 ►

Choose the OK button by clicking the left mouse button.

When you quit Windows, all windows are removed from the desktop and control is returned to the DOS operating system.

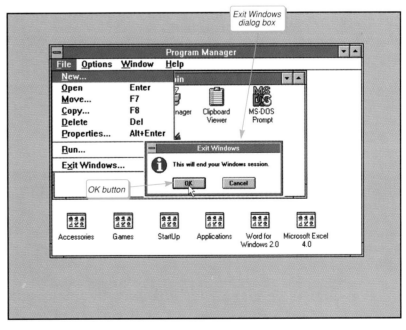

FIGURE 1-72

▶ PROJECT SUMMARY

In this project you learned about user interfaces and the Microsoft Windows graphical user interface. You started and exited Windows and learned the parts of a window. You started Notepad, entered and printed a note, edited the note, opened and saved files, and exited the applications. You opened group windows, maximized application windows, and scrolled the windows. You used the mouse to select a menu, choose a command from a menu, and respond to dialog boxes. You used Windows online Help to obtain help about the Paintbrush application.

▶ KEY TERMS

active icon (*WIN18*)
active window (*WIN15*)
application (*WIN3*)
application software (*WIN3*)
application window (*WIN5*)
check box (*WIN13*)
choosing (*WIN11*)
choosing a command (*WIN11*)
choosing a help topic (*WIN33*)
clicking (*WIN7*)
command (*WIN10*)
command button (*WIN13*)
Control menu (*WIN16*)
creating a document (*WIN19*)
current selection (*WIN13*)
desktop (*WIN4*)
dialog box (*WIN12*)
directory (*WIN23*)
directory path (*WIN24*)
directory structure (*WIN24*)
displaying a definition (*WIN35*)
document (*WIN14*)
document file (*WIN23*)
double-clicking (*WIN8*)
dragging (*WIN9*)
drop-down list box (*WIN13*)
ellipsis (*WIN11*)
edit a document file (*WIN31*)
error correction (*WIN16,*
   WIN18, WIN27)
extension (*WIN23*)
file and disk concepts
   (*WIN22–WIN24*)

filename (*WIN23*)
formatting (*WIN27*)
graphical user interface (GUI)
   (*WIN3*)
group icons (*WIN5*)
group window (*WIN5*)
GUI (*WIN3*)
help topic (*WIN33*)
hourglass icon (*WIN4*)
icons (*WIN5*)
insertion point (*WIN17*)
jump (*WIN33*)
keyboard (*WIN9*)
keyboard shortcuts (*WIN10*)
Maximize button (*WIN18*)
maximizing a window (*WIN18*)
menu (*WIN10*)
menu bar (*WIN10*)
Microsoft Windows (*WIN2*)
mouse (*WIN5*)
mouse operations (*WIN6–WIN9*)
mouse pointer (*WIN6*)
naming a file (*WIN23*)
Notepad (*WIN14*)
online Help (*WIN32*)
opening a document file
   (*WIN28*)
opening a window (*WIN14*)
option button (*WIN12*)
Paintbrush (*WIN32*)
pointing (*WIN6*)
pop-up window (*WIN35*)

printing a document (*WIN20*)
Program Manager (*WIN5*)
program-item icons (*WIN5*)
quitting an application (*WIN21,*
   WIN28)
quitting Windows (*WIN36*)
Restore button (*WIN18*)
root directory (*WIN23*)
saving a document (*WIN24*)
saving a modified document file
   (*WIN31*)
scroll arrows (*WIN16*)
scroll bar (*WIN16*)
scroll box (*WIN16*)
selected button (*WIN12*)
selecting (*WIN11*)
selecting a menu (*WIN11*)
starting an application (*WIN16*)
starting Microsoft Windows
   (*WIN4*)
subdirectory (*WIN23*)
text box (*WIN13*)
title bar (*WIN4*)
user friendly (*WIN3*)
user interface (*WIN3*)
using Windows help (*WIN32*)
window (*WIN4*)
window border (*WIN4*)
window title (*WIN4*)
Windows (*WIN2*)
write-protected diskette
   (*WIN27*)

In Microsoft Windows you can accomplish a task in a number of ways. The following table provides a quick reference to each task presented in this project with it available options. The commands listed in the Menu column can be executed using either the keyboard or mouse.

Task	Mouse	Menu	Keyboard Shortcuts
Choose a Command from a menu	Click command name, or drag highlight to command name and release mouse button		Press underlined character; or press arrow keys to select command, and press ENTER
Choose a Help Topic	Click Help topic		Press TAB, ENTER
Display a Definition	Click definition		Press TAB, ENTER
Enlarge an Application Window	Click Maximize button	From Control menu, choose Maximize	
Obtain Online Help		From Help menu, choose Contents	Press F1
Open a Document		From File menu, choose Open	
Open a Group Window	Double-click group icon	From Window menu, choose group window name	Press CTRL + F6 (or CTRL + TAB) to select group icon, and press ENTER
Print a File		From File menu, choose Print	
Quit an Application	Double-click control menu box, click OK button	From File menu, choose Exit	
Quit Windows	Double-click Control menu box, click OK button	From File menu, choose Exit Windows, choose OK button	
Remove a Definition	Click open space on desktop		Press ENTER
Save a Document on Disk		From File menu, choose Save As	
Save an Edited Document on Disk		From File menu, choose Save	
Save Changes when Quitting Windows		From Options menu, choose Save Settings on Exit if no check mark precedes command	
Save No Changes when Quitting Windows		From Options menu, choose Save Settings on Exit if check mark precedes command	
Scroll a Window	Click up or down arrow, drag scroll box, click scroll bar		Press UP or DOWN ARROW
Select a Menu	Click menu name on menu bar		Press ALT + underlined character (or F10 + underlined character)
Start an Application	Double-click program-item icon	From File menu, choose Open	Press arrow keys to select program-item icon, and press ENTER

STUDENT ASSIGNMENT 1
True/False

Instructions: Circle T if the statement is true or F if the statement is false.

T F   1. A user interface is a combination of computer hardware and computer software.
T F   2. Microsoft Windows is a graphical user interface.
T F   3. The Program Manager window is a group window.
T F   4. The desktop is the screen background on which windows are displayed.
T F   5. A menu is a small picture that can represent an application or a group of applications.
T F   6. Clicking means quickly pressing and releasing a mouse button twice without moving the mouse.
T F   7. CTRL + SHIFT + LEFT ARROW is an example of a keyboard shortcut.
T F   8. You can carry out an action in an application by choosing a command from a menu.
T F   9. Selecting means marking an item.
T F   10. Windows opens a dialog box to supply information, allow you to enter information, or select among several options.
T F   11. A program-item icon represents a group of applications.
T F   12. You open a group window by pointing to its icon and double-clicking the left mouse button.
T F   13. A scroll bar allows you to view areas of a window that are not currently visible.
T F   14. Notepad and Paintbrush are applications.
T F   15. Choosing the Restore button maximizes a window to its maximize size.
T F   16. APPLICATION.TXT is a valid name for a document file.
T F   17. The directory structure is the relationship between the root directory and any subdirectories.
T F   18. You save a new document on disk by choosing the Save As command from the File menu.
T F   19. You open a document by choosing the Retrieve command from the File menu.
T F   20. Help is available while using Windows only in the *User's Guide* that accompanies the Windows software.

STUDENT ASSIGNMENT 2
Multiple Choice

Instructions: Circle the correct response.

1. Through a user interface, the user is able to _____.
   a. control the computer
   b. request information from the computer
   c. respond to messages displayed by the computer
   d. all of the above
2. _____ is quickly pressing and releasing a mouse button twice without moving the mouse.
   a. Double-clicking
   b. Clicking
   c. Dragging
   d. Pointing

3. To view the commands in a menu, you _____ the menu name.
   a. choose
   b. maximize
   c. close
   d. select
4. A _____ is a window that displays to supply information, allow you to enter information, or choose among several options.
   a. group window
   b. dialog box
   c. application window
   d. drop-down list box
5. A _____ is a rectangular area in which Windows displays text or you enter text.
   a. dialog box
   b. text box
   c. drop-down list box
   d. list box
6. The title bar of one group window that is a different color or intensity than the title bars of the other group windows indicates a(n) _____ window.
   a. inactive
   b. application
   c. group
   d. active
7. To view an area of a window that is not currently visible in a window, use the _____.
   a. title bar
   b. scroll bar
   c. menu bar
   d. Restore button
8. The _____ menu in the Notepad application contains the Save, Open, and Print commands.
   a. Window
   b. Options
   c. Help
   d. File
9. Before exiting Windows, you should check the _____ command to verify that no changes to the desktop will be saved.
   a. Open
   b. Exit Windows
   c. Save Settings on Exit
   d. Save Changes
10. Online Help is available for all applications except _____.
    a. Program Manager
    b. Calendar
    c. Clock
    d. File Manager

STUDENT ASSIGNMENT 3
Identifying Items in the Program Manager Window

Instructions: On the desktop in Figure SA1-3, arrows point to several items in the Program Manager window. Identify the items in the space provided.

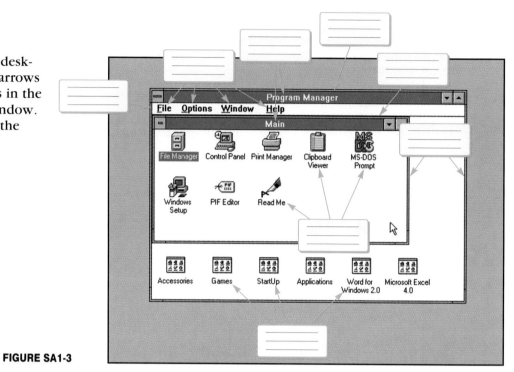

FIGURE SA1-3

STUDENT ASSIGNMENT 4
Starting an Application

Instructions: Using the desktop shown in Figure SA1-4, list the steps in the space provided to open the Accessories window and start the Notepad application.

Step 1: _____

_____

_____

Step 2: _____

_____

_____

Step 3: _____

_____

_____

Step 4: _____

_____

_____

FIGURE SA1-4

COMPUTER LABORATORY EXERCISE 1
Improving Your Mouse Skills

Instructions: Use a computer to perform the following tasks.

1. Start Microsoft Windows.
2. Double-click the Games group icon (⊞) to open the Games window if necessary.
3. Double-click the Solitaire program-item icon (🂠).
4. Click the Maximize button to maximize the Solitaire window.
5. From the Help menu in the Solitaire window (Figure CLE1-1), choose the Contents command. One-by-one click on the help topics in green. Double-click on the Control-menu box in the title bar of the Solitaire Help window to close it.
6. Play the game of Solitaire.
7. To quit Solitaire choose the Exit command from the Game menu.

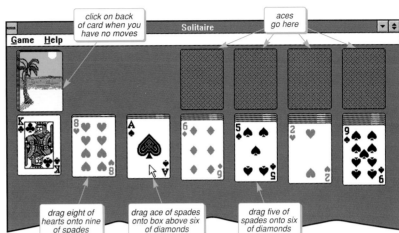

FIGURE CLE1-1

COMPUTER LABORATORY EXERCISE 2
Windows Tutorial

Instructions: Use a computer to perform the following tasks.

1. Start Microsoft Windows.
2. From the Help menu in the Program Manager window, choose the Windows Tutorial command.
3. Type the letter M. Follow the instructions (Figure CLE1-2) to step through the mouse practice lesson. Press the ESC key to exit the tutorial.
4. From the Help menu in the Program Manager window, choose the Windows Tutorial command.

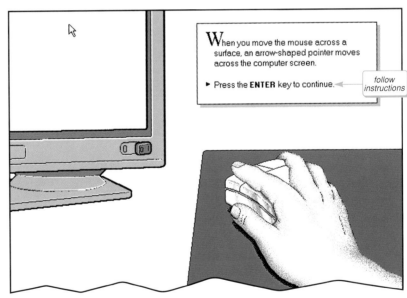

FIGURE CLE1-2

5. Type the letter W. Click the Instructions button (Instructions) and read the information. When you are finished, choose the Return to the Tutorial button (Return to the Tutorial). Next choose the Contents button (Contents) in the lower right corner of the screen.
6. Choose the second item (Starting an Application) from the Contents list. The Windows tutorial will step you through the remaining lessons. Respond as needed to the questions and instructions. Press the ESC key to exit the tutorial.

COMPUTER LABORATORY EXERCISE 3
Creating, Saving, and Printing Documents

Instructions: Use a computer to perform the
following tasks.

1. Start Microsoft Windows if necessary.
2. Double-click the Accessories icon to open
    the Accessories window.
3. Double-click the Notepad icon to start the
    Notepad application.
4. Click the Maximize button to maximize the
    Notepad window.
5. Enter the note shown at the right at the
    insertion point on the screen.
6. Insert the Student Diskette that accompa-
    nies this book into drive A.
7. Select the File menu on the Notepad menu
    bar.
8. Choose the Save As command.
9. Enter grocery in the File Name text box.
10. Change the current selection in the Drives drop-down list box to a:.
11. Click the OK button to save the document on drive A.
12. Select the File menu on the Notepad menu bar.
13. Choose the Print command to print the document on the printer (Figure CLE1-3).
14. Remove the Student Diskette from drive A.
15. Select the File menu on the Notepad menu bar.
16. Choose the Exit command to quit Notepad.

Grocery List —
1/2 Gallon of Low Fat Milk
1 Dozen Medium Size Eggs
1 Loaf of Wheat Bread

```
                          GROCERY.TXT


        Grocery List -
        1/2 Gallon of Low Fat Milk
        1 Dozen Medium Size Eggs
        1 Loaf of Wheat Bread
```

FIGURE CLE1-3

COMPUTER LABORATORY EXERCISE 4
Opening, Editing, and Saving Documents

Instructions: Use a computer to perform the following tasks. If you have questions on how to procede,
use the Calendar Help menu.

1. Start Microsoft Windows if necessary.
2. Double-click the Accessories icon to open the Accessories window.
3. Double-click the Calendar icon (🔢) to start the Calendar application.
4. Click the Maximize button to maximize the Calendar window.
5. Insert the Student Diskette that accompanies this book into drive A.
6. Select the File menu on the Calendar menu bar.

7. Choose the Open command.
8. Change the current selection in the Drives drop-down list box to a:.
9. Select the thompson.cal filename in the File Name list box. The THOMPSON.CAL file contains the daily appointments for Mr. Thompson.
10. Click the OK button in the Open dialog box to open the THOMPSON.CAL document. The document on your screen is shown in Figure CLE1-4a.
11. Click the Left or Right Scroll arrow repeatedly to locate the appointments for Thursday, September 29, 1994.
12. Make the changes shown below to the document.

TIME	CHANGE
11:00 AM	Stay at Auto Show one more hour
2:00 PM	Change the Designer's Meeting from 2:00 PM to 3:00 PM
4:00 PM	Remove the Quality Control Meeting

13. Select the File menu on the Calendar menu bar.
14. Choose the Save As command to save the document file on drive A. Use the filename PETER.CAL.
15. Select the File menu on the Calendar menu bar.
16. Choose the Print command.
17. Choose the OK button to print the document on the printer (Figure CLE1-4b).
18. Remove the Student Diskette from drive A.
19. Select the File menu on the Calendar menu bar.
20. Choose the Exit command to quit Calendar.

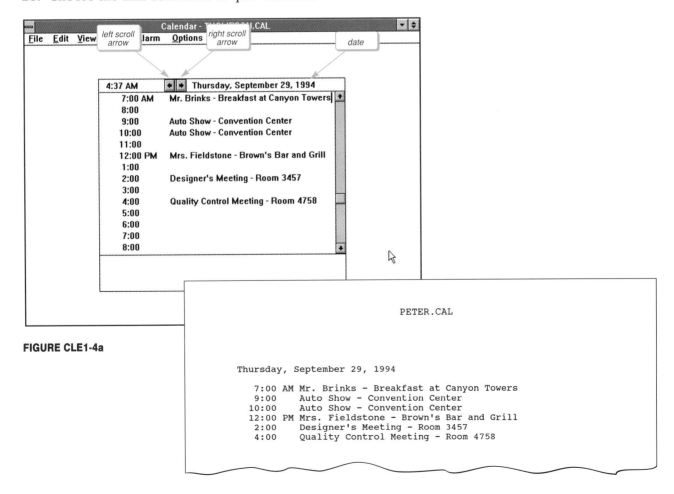

FIGURE CLE1-4a

FIGURE CLE1-4b

COMPUTER LABORATORY EXERCISE 5
Using Online Help

Instructions: Use a computer to perform the following tasks.

1. Start Microsoft Windows if necessary.
2. Double-click the Accessories icon to open the Accessories window.
3. Double-click the Cardfile icon ( ) to start the Cardfile application.
4. Select the Help menu.
5. Choose the Contents command.
6. Click the Maximize button to maximize the Cardfile Help window.
7. Choose the Add More Cards help topic.
8. Select the File menu on the Cardfile Help menu bar.
9. Choose the Print Topic command to print the Adding More Cards help topic on the printer (Figure CLE1-5a).
10. Display the definition of the term, index line.
11. Remove the index line definition from the desktop.
12. Choose the Contents button.
13. Choose the Delete Cards help topic.
14. Choose the Selecting Cards help topic at the bottom of the Deleting Cards screen.

Adding More Cards

Cardfile adds new cards in the correct alphabetic order and scrolls to display the new card at the front.

To add a new card to a file
1 From the Card menu, choose Add.
2 Type the text you want to appear on the index line.
3 Choose the OK button.
4 In the information area, type text.

FIGURE CLE1-5a

15. Select the File menu on the Cardfile Help menu bar.
16. Choose the Print Topic command to print the Selecting Cards help topic (Figure CLE 1-5b).
17. Select the File menu on the Cardfile Help menu bar.
18. Choose the Exit command to quit Cardfile Help.
19. Select the File menu on the Cardfile window menu bar.
20. Choose the Exit command to quit Cardfile.

Selecting Cards

To select a card in Card view
▶ Click the card's index line if it is visible.
   Or click the arrows in the status bar until the index line is visible, and then click it.
   If you are using the keyboard, press and hold down CTRL+SHIFT and type the first letter of the index line.

To select a card by using the Go To command
1 From the Search menu, choose Go To.
2 Type text from the card's index line.
3 Choose the OK button.

To select a card in List view
▶ Click the card's index line.
   Or use the arrow keys to move to the card's index line.

See Also
Moving Through a Card File

FIGURE CLE1-5b

$\mathcal{M}$ICROSOFT $\mathcal{W}$INDOWS 3.1

P R O J E C T   T W O

▼

DISK AND FILE MANAGEMENT

OBJECTIVES You will have mastered the material in this project when you can:

▸ Identify the elements of the directory tree window
▸ Understand the concepts of diskette size and capacity
▸ Format and copy a diskette
▸ Select and copy one file or a group of files
▸ Change the current drive
▸ Rename or delete a file

▸ Create a backup diskette
▸ Search for help topics using Windows online Help
▸ Switch between applications
▸ Activate, resize, and close a group window
▸ Arrange the icons in a group window
▸ Minimize an application window to an icon

▸ INTRODUCTION

F **ile Manager** is an application included with Windows that allows you to organize and work with your hard disk and diskettes and the files on those disks. In this project, you will use File Manager to (1) format a diskette; (2) copy files between the hard disk and a diskette; (3) copy a diskette; (4) rename a file on diskette; and (5) delete a file from diskette.

Formatting a diskette and copying files to a diskette are common operations illustrated in this project that you should understand how to perform. While performing the Computer Laboratory Exercises and the Computer Laboratory Assignments at the end of each application project, you will save documents on a diskette that accompanies this textbook. To prevent the accidental loss of stored documents on a diskette, it is important to periodically make a copy of the entire diskette. A copy of a diskette is called a **backup diskette**. In this project, you will learn how to create a backup diskette to protect against the accidental loss of documents on a diskette.

You will also use Windows online Help in this project. In Project 1, you obtained help by choosing a topic from a list of help topics. In this project, you will use the Search feature to search for help topics.

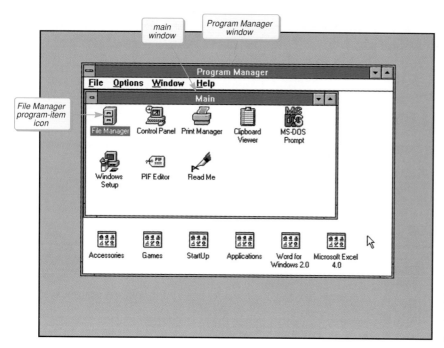

FIGURE 2-1

▶ STARTING WINDOWS

As explained in Project 1, when you turn on the computer, an introductory screen consisting of the Windows logo, Windows name, version number, and copyright notices displays momentarily. Next, a blank screen containing an hourglass icon displays. Finally, the Program Manager and Main windows open on the desktop (Figure 2-1). The File Manager program-item icon displays in the Main window. If your desktop does not look similar to the desktop in Figure 2-1, your instructor will inform you of the modifications necessary to change your desktop.

Starting File Manager and Maximizing the File Manager Window

To start File Manager, double-click the File Manager icon (📖) in the Main window. To maximize the File Manager window, choose the Maximize button on the File Manager window by pointing to the Maximize button and clicking the left mouse button.

TO START AN APPLICATION AND MAXIMIZE ITS WINDOW ▼

STEP 1 ▶

Double-click the File Manager icon in the Main window (see Figure 2-1), then click the Maximize button on the File Manager title bar.

Windows opens and maximizes the File Manager window (Figure 2-2).

FIGURE 2-2

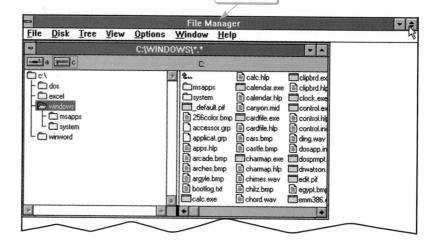

▶ FILE MANAGER

When you start File Manager, Windows opens the File Manager window (Figure 2-3). The menu bar contains the File, Disk, Tree, View, Options, Window, and Help menus. These menus contain the commands to organize and work with the disks and the files on those disks.

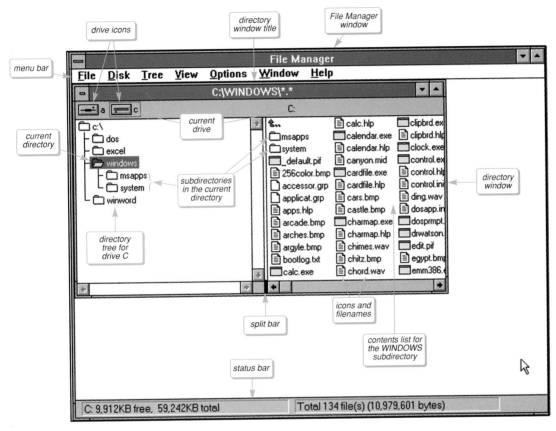

FIGURE 2-3

Below the menu bar is a **directory window** titled C:\WINDOWS*.*. The window title consists of a directory path (C:\WINDOWS), backslash (\), and filename (*.*). The directory path is the path of the current directory on drive C (WINDOWS subdirectory). The backslash separates the path and filename. The filename (*.*) references a group of files whose filename and extension can be any valid filename and extension.

Below the title bar is a horizontal bar that contains two **drive icons**. The drive icons represent the disk drives attached to the computer. The first drive icon (▬ **a:**) represents drive A (diskette drive) and the second drive icon (▤ **c:**) represents drive C (hard drive). Depending upon the number of disk drives attached to your computer, there may be more than two drive icons in the horizontal bar. A rectangular box surrounding the drive C icon indicates drive C is the **current drive**. The entry to the right of the icons (C:) also indicates drive C is the current drive.

The directory window is divided into two equal-sized areas. Each area is separated by a split bar. The **directory tree** in the area on the left contains the directory structure. The **directory tree** in the **directory structure** shows the relationship between the root directory and any subdirectories on the current drive (drive C). You can drag the **split bar** to the left or right to change the size of the two areas.

In the left area, a file folder icon represents each directory or subdirectory in the directory structure (see Figure 2-3). The shaded open file folder (📂) and subdirectory name for the current directory (WINDOWS subdirectory) are highlighted. The unopened file folder icons (📁) for the two subdirectories in the WINDOWS subdirectory (MSAPPS and SYSTEM) are indented below the icon for the WINDOWS subdirectory.

The area on the right contains the contents list. The **contents list** is a list of the files in the current directory (WINDOWS subdirectory). Each entry in the contents list consists of an icon and name. The shaded file folder icons for the two subdirectories in the current directory (MSAPPS and SYSTEM) display at the top of the first column in the list.

The status bar at the bottom of the File Manager window indicates the amount of unused disk space on the current drive (9,912KB free), amount of total disk space on the current drive (59,242KB total), number of files in the current directory (134 files), and the amount of disk space the files occupy (10,979,601 bytes).

▶ FORMATTING A DISKETTE

Before saving a document file on a diskette or copying a file onto a diskette, you must format the diskette. **Formatting** prepares a diskette for use on a computer by establishing the sectors and cylinders on the diskette, analyzing the diskette for defective cylinders, and establishing the root directory. To avoid errors while formatting a diskette, you should understand the concepts of diskette size and capacity that are explained in the following section.

Diskette Size and Capacity

How a diskette is formatted is determined by the size of the diskette, capacity of the diskette as established by the diskette manufacturer, and capabilities of the disk drive you use to format the diskette. **Diskette size** is the physical size of the diskette. Common diskette sizes are 5 1/4-inch and 3 1/2-inch.

Diskette capacity is the amount of space on the disk, measured in kilobytes (K) or megabytes (MB), available to store data. A diskette's capacity is established by the diskette manufacturer. Common diskette capacities are 360K and 1.2MB for a 5 1/4-inch diskette and 720K and 1.44MB for a 3 1/2-inch diskette.

A diskette drive's capability is established by the diskette drive manufacturer. There are 3 1/2-inch diskette drives that are capable of formatting a diskette with a capacity of 720K or 1.44MB and there are 5 1/4-inch diskette drives capable of formatting a diskette with a capacity of 360K or 1.2MB.

Before formatting a diskette, you must consider two things. First, the diskette drive you use to format a diskette must be capable of formatting the size of diskette you want to format. You can use a 3 1/2-inch diskette drive to format a 3 1/2-inch diskette, but you cannot use a 3 1/2-inch diskette drive to format a

5 1/4-inch diskette. Similarly, you can use a 5 1/4-inch diskette drive to format a 5 1/4-inch diskette, but you cannot use a 5 1/4-inch diskette drive to format a 3 1/2-inch diskette.

Second, the diskette drive you use to format a diskette must be capable of formatting the capacity of the diskette you want to format. A 5 1/4-inch diskette drive capable of formatting 1.2MB diskettes can be used to either format a 360K or 1.2MB diskette. However, because of the differences in the diskette manufacturing process, you cannot use a diskette drive capable of formatting 360K diskettes to format a 1.2MB diskette. A 3 1/2-inch diskette drive capable of formatting 1.44MB diskettes can be used to format either a 720K or 1.44MB diskette. Since the 1.44 MB diskette is manufactured with two square holes in the plastic cover and the 720K diskette is manufactured with only one square hole, you cannot use a diskette drive capable of formatting 720K diskette to format a 1.44MB diskette.

The computer you use to complete this project should have a 3 1/2-inch diskette drive capable of formatting a diskette with 1.44MB of disk storage. Trying to format a 3 1/2-inch diskette with any other diskette drive may result in an error. Typical errors encountered because of incorrect diskette capacity and diskette drive capabilities are explained later in this project. For more information about the diskette drive you will use to complete the projects in this textbook, contact your instructor.

Formatting a Diskette

To store a file on a diskette, the diskette must already be formatted. If the diskette is not formatted, you must format the diskette using File Manager. When formatting a diskette, use either an unformatted diskette or a diskette containing files you no longer need. Do not format the Student Diskette that accompanies this book.

To format a diskette using File Manager, you insert the diskette into the diskette drive, and then choose the **Format Disk command** from the Disk menu. Perform the following steps to format a diskette.

TO FORMAT A DISKETTE ▼

STEP 1

Insert an unformatted diskette or a formatted diskette containing files you no longer need into drive A.

STEP 2 ▶

Select the Disk menu, and then point to the Format Disk command.

Windows opens the Disk menu (Figure 2-4). The mouse pointer points to the Format Disk command.

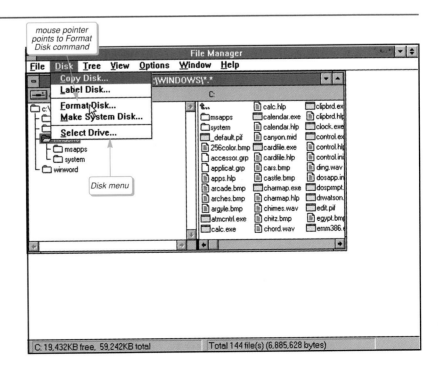

FIGURE 2-4

STEP 3 ▶

Choose the Format Disk command from the Disk menu, and then point to the OK button.

Windows opens the Format Disk dialog box (Figure 2-5). The current selections in the Disk In and Capacity boxes are Drive A: and 1.44 MB, respectively. With these selections, the diskette in drive A will be formatted with a capacity of 1.44MB. The Options list box is not required to format a diskette in this project. The mouse pointer points to the OK button.

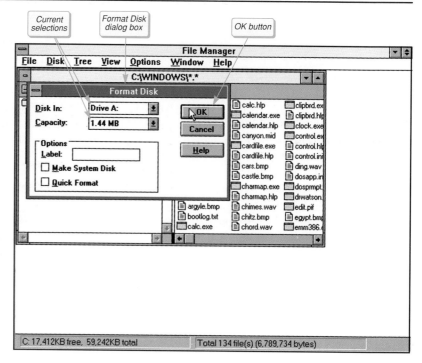

FIGURE 2-5

STEP 4 ▶

Choose the OK button by clicking the left mouse button, and then point to the Yes button.

Windows opens the Confirm Format Disk dialog box (Figure 2-6). This dialog box reminds you that if you continue, Windows will erase all data on the diskette in drive A. The mouse pointer points to the Yes button.

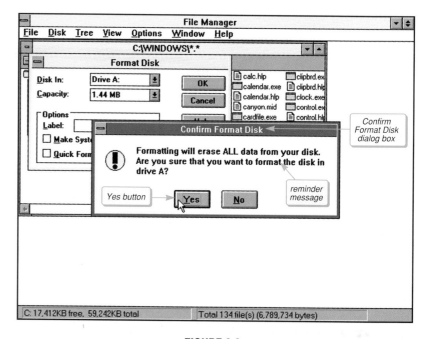

FIGURE 2-6

STEP 5 ▶

Choose the Yes button by clicking the left mouse button.

Windows opens the Formatting Disk dialog box (Figure 2-7). As the formatting process progresses, a value from 1 to 100 indicates what percent of the formatting process is complete. Toward the end of the formatting process, the creating root directory message replaces the 1% completed message to indicate Windows is creating the root directory on the diskette. The formatting process takes approximately two minutes.

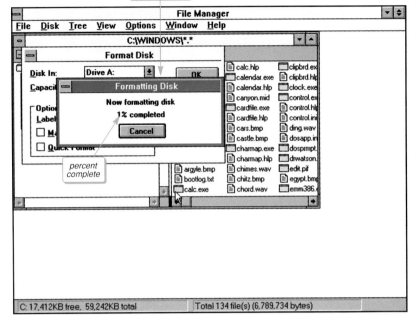

FIGURE 2-7

When the formatting process is complete, Windows opens the Format Complete dialog box (Figure 2-8). The dialog box contains the total disk space (1,457,664 bytes) and available disk space (1,457,664 bytes) of the newly formatted diskette. The values for the total disk space and available disk space in the Format Complete dialog box may be different for your computer.

STEP 6 ▶

Choose the No button by pointing to the No button, and then clicking the left mouse button.

Windows closes the Format Disk and Format Complete dialog boxes.

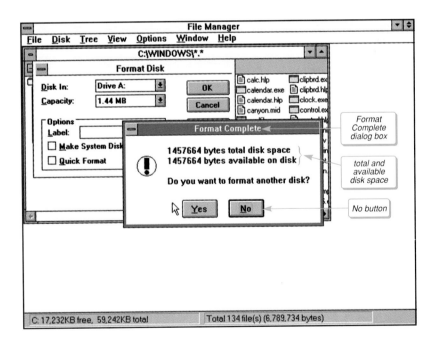

FIGURE 2-8

Correcting Errors Encountered While Formatting a Diskette

When you try to format a diskette but forget to insert a diskette into the diskette drive or the diskette you inserted is write-protected, damaged, or does not have the correct capacity for the diskette drive, Windows opens the Format Disk Error dialog box shown in Figure 2-9. The dialog box contains an error message (Cannot format disk.), a suggested action (Make sure the disk is in the drive and not write-protected, damaged, or of wrong density rating.), and the OK button. To format a diskette after forgetting to insert the diskette into the diskette drive, insert the diskette into the diskette drive, choose the OK button, and format the diskette.

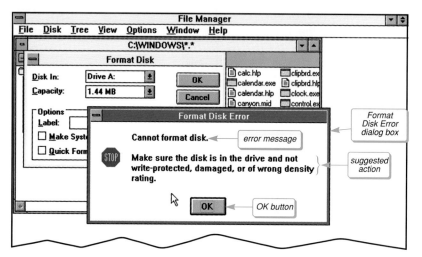

FIGURE 2-9

If the same dialog box opens after inserting a diskette into drive A, remove the diskette and determine if the diskette is write-protected, not the correct capacity for the diskette drive, or damaged. If the diskette is write-protected, remove the write-protection from the diskette, choose the OK button and format the diskette. If the diskette is not write-protected, check the diskette to determine if the diskette is the same capacity as the diskette drive. If it is not, insert a diskette with the correct capacity into the diskette drive, choose the OK button and format the diskette. If the diskette is not write-protected and the correct capacity, throw the damaged diskette away and insert another diskette into drive A, choose the OK button, and format the new diskette.

▶ COPYING FILES TO A DISKETTE

After formatting a diskette, you can save files on the diskette or copy files to the diskette from the hard drive or another diskette. You can easily copy a single file or group of files from one directory to another directory using File Manager. When copying files, the drive and directory containing the files to be copied are called the **source drive** and **source directory**, respectively. The drive and directory to which the files are copied are called the **destination drive** and **destination directory**, respectively.

To copy a file, select the filename in the contents list and drag the high-lighted filename to the destination drive icon or destination directory icon. Groups of files are copied in a similar fashion. You select the filenames in the contents list and drag the highlighted group of filenames to the destination drive or destination directory icon. In this project, you will copy a group of files consisting of the ARCADE.BMP, CARS.BMP, and EGYPT.BMP files from the WINDOWS subdirectory of drive C to the root directory of the diskette that you formatted earlier in this project. Before copying the files, maximize the directory window to make it easier to view the contents of the window.

Maximizing the Directory Window

To enlarge the C:\WINDOWS*.* window, click the Maximize button on the right side of the directory window title bar. When you maximize a directory window, the window fills the File Manager window.

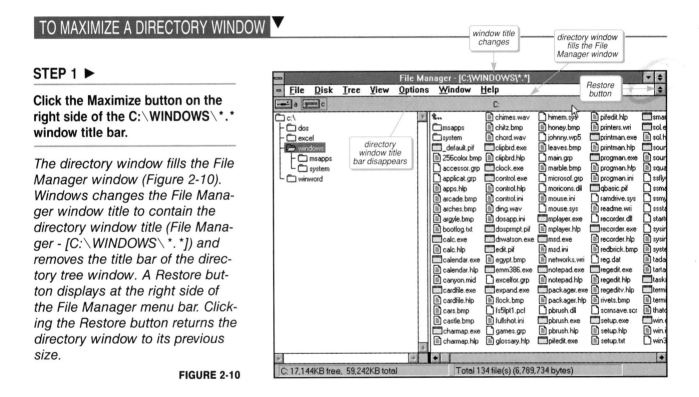

TO MAXIMIZE A DIRECTORY WINDOW ▼

STEP 1 ▶

Click the Maximize button on the right side of the C:\WINDOWS*.* window title bar.

The directory window fills the File Manager window (Figure 2-10). Windows changes the File Manager window title to contain the directory window title (File Manager - [C:\WINDOWS*.]) and removes the title bar of the directory tree window. A Restore button displays at the right side of the File Manager menu bar. Clicking the Restore button returns the directory window to its previous size.*

FIGURE 2-10

Selecting a Group of Files

Before copying a group of files, you must select (highlight) each file in the contents list. You select the first file in a group of files by pointing to its icon or filename and clicking the left mouse button. You select the remaining files in the group by pointing to each file icon or filename, holding down the CTRL key, clicking the left mouse button, and releasing the CTRL key. The steps on the following pages show how to select the group of files consisting of the ARCADE.BMP, CARS.BMP, and EGYPT.BMP files.

TO SELECT A GROUP OF FILES ▼

STEP 1 ►

Point to the ARCADE.BMP filename in the contents list (Figure
2-11).

FIGURE 2-11

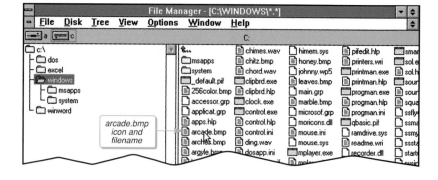

STEP 2 ►

Select the ARCADE.BMP file by
clicking the left mouse button, and
then point to the CARS.BMP
filename.

*When you select the first file, the
highlight on the current directory
(WINDOWS) in the directory tree
changes to a rectangular box
(Figure 2-12). The ARCADE.BMP
entry is highlighted, and the
mouse pointer points to the
CARS.BMP filename.*

FIGURE 2-12

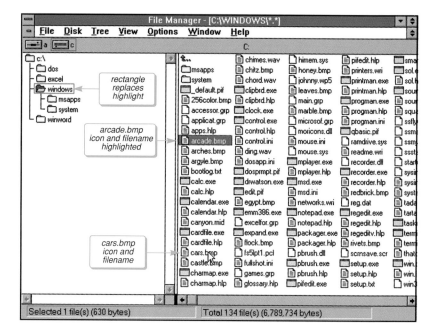

STEP 3 ►

Hold down the CTRL key, click the
left mouse button, release the CTRL
key, and then point to the
EGYPT.BMP filename.

*Two files, ARCADE.BMP and
CARS.BMP are highlighted
(Figure 2-13). The mouse pointer
points to the EGYPT.BMP
filename.*

FIGURE 2-13

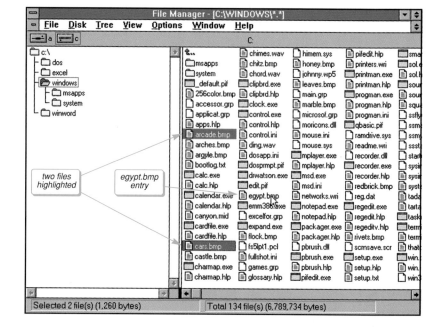

STEP 4 ▶

Hold down the CTRL key, click the left mouse button, and then release the CTRL key.

The group of files consisting of the ARCADE.BMP, CARS.BMP, and EGYPT.BMP files is highlighted (Figure 2-14).

FIGURE 2-14

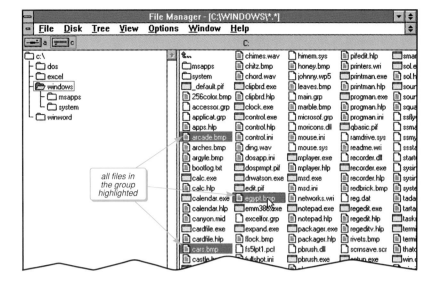

The ARCADE.BMP, CARS,BMP, and EGYPT.BMP files in Figure 2-14 are not located next to each other (sequentially) in the contents list. To select this group of files you selected the first file by pointing to its filename and clicking the left mouse button. Then, you selected each of the other files by pointing to their filenames, holding down the CTRL key, and clicking the left mouse button. If a group of files is located sequentially in the contents list, you select the group by pointing to the first filename in the list and clicking the left mouse button, and then hold down the SHIFT key, point to the last filename in the group and click the left mouse button.

Copying a Group of Files

After selecting each file in the group, insert the formatted diskette into drive A, and then copy the files to drive A by pointing to any highlighted filename and dragging the filename to the drive A icon.

TO COPY A GROUP OF FILES ▼

STEP 1

Verify that the formatted diskette is in drive A.

STEP 2 ▶

Point to the highlighted ARCADE.BMP entry (Figure 2-15).

FIGURE 2-15

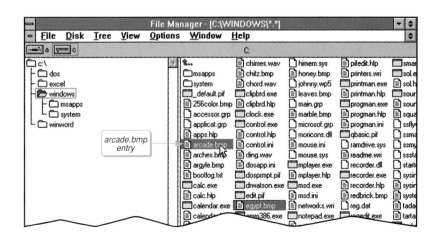

STEP 3 ▶

Drag the ARCADE.BMP filename over to the drive A icon.

As you drag the entry, the mouse pointer changes to an outline of a group of documents (   ) (Figure 2-16). The outline contains a plus sign to indicate the group of files is being copied, not moved.

FIGURE 2-16

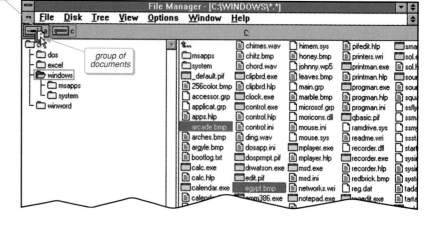

STEP 4 ▶

Release the mouse button, and then point to the Yes button.

Windows opens the Confirm Mouse Operation dialog box (Figure 2-17). The dialog box opens to confirm that you want to copy the files to the root directory of drive A (A:\). The highlight over the CARS.BMP entry is replaced with a dashed rectangular box. The mouse pointer points to the Yes button.

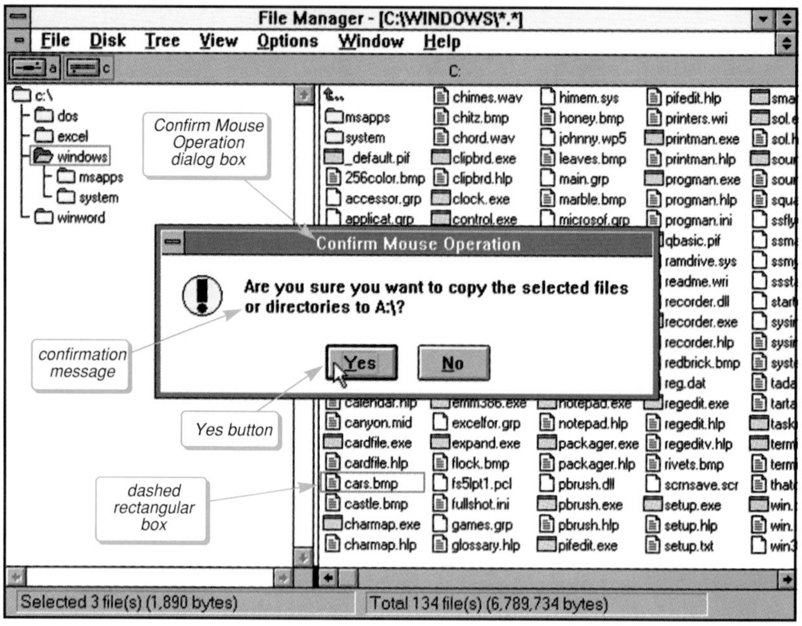

FIGURE 2-17

STEP 5 ▶

Choose the Yes button by clicking the left mouse button.

Windows opens the Copying dialog box, and the dialog box remains on the screen while Windows copies each file to the diskette in drive A (Figure 2-18). The dialog box in Figure 2-18 indicates the EGYPT.BMP file is currently being copied.

FIGURE 2-18

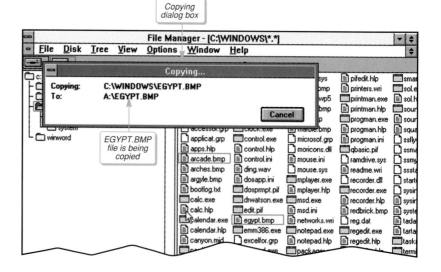

Correcting Errors Encountered While Copying Files

When you try to copy a file to an unformatted diskette, Windows opens the Error Copying File dialog box illustrated in Figure 2-19. The dialog box contains an error message (The disk in drive A is not formatted.), a question (Do you want to format it now?), and the Yes and No buttons. To continue the copy operation, format the diskette by choosing the Yes button. To cancel the copy operation, choose the No button.

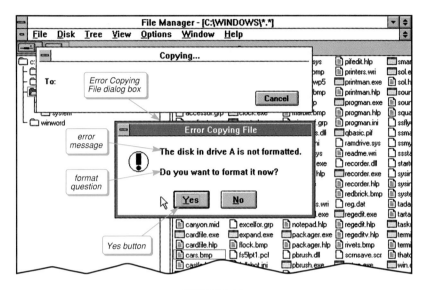

FIGURE 2-19

When you try to copy a file to a diskette but forget to insert a diskette into the diskette drive, Windows opens the Error Copying File dialog box shown in Figure 2-20. The dialog box contains an error message (There is no disk in drive A.), a suggested action (Insert a disk, and then try again.), and the Retry and Cancel buttons. To continue the copy operation, insert a diskette into drive A, and then choose the Retry button.

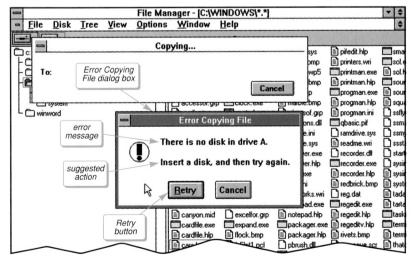

FIGURE 2-20

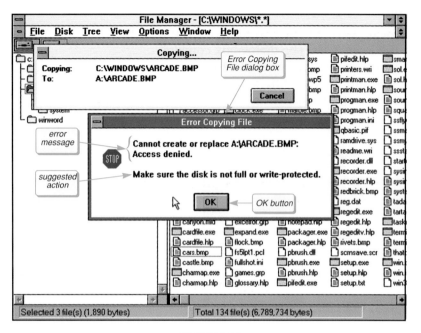

FIGURE 2-21

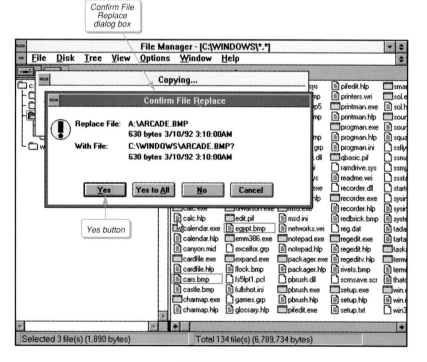

FIGURE 2-22

If you try to copy a file to a diskette that does not have enough room for the file, or you have inserted a write-protected diskette into the diskette drive, Windows opens the Error Copying File dialog box in Figure 2-21. The dialog box contains an error message (Cannot create or replace A:\ARCADE.BMP: Access denied.), a suggested action (Make sure the disk is not full or write-protected.), and the OK button. To continue with the copy operation, first remove the diskette from the diskette drive. Next, determine if the diskette is write-protected. If it is, remove the write-protection from the diskette, insert the diskette into the diskette drive, and then choose the OK button. If you determine the diskette is not write-protected, insert a diskette that is not full into the diskette drive, and then choose the OK button.

Replacing a File on Disk

If you try to copy a file to a diskette that already contains a file with the same filename and extension, Windows opens the Confirm File Replace dialog box (Figure 2-22). The Confirm File Replace dialog box contains information about the file being replaced (A:\ARCADE.BMP), the file being copied (C:\WINDOWS\ARCADE.BMP), and the Yes, Yes to All, No, and Cancel buttons. If you want to replace the file, on the diskette with the file being copied, choose the Yes button. If you do not want to replace the file choose the No button. If you want to cancel the copy operation, choose the Cancel button.

Changing the Current Drive

After copying a group of files, you should verify the files were copied onto the correct drive and into the correct directory. To view the files on drive A, change the current drive to drive A by pointing to the drive A icon and clicking the left mouse button.

TO CHANGE THE CURRENT DRIVE ▼

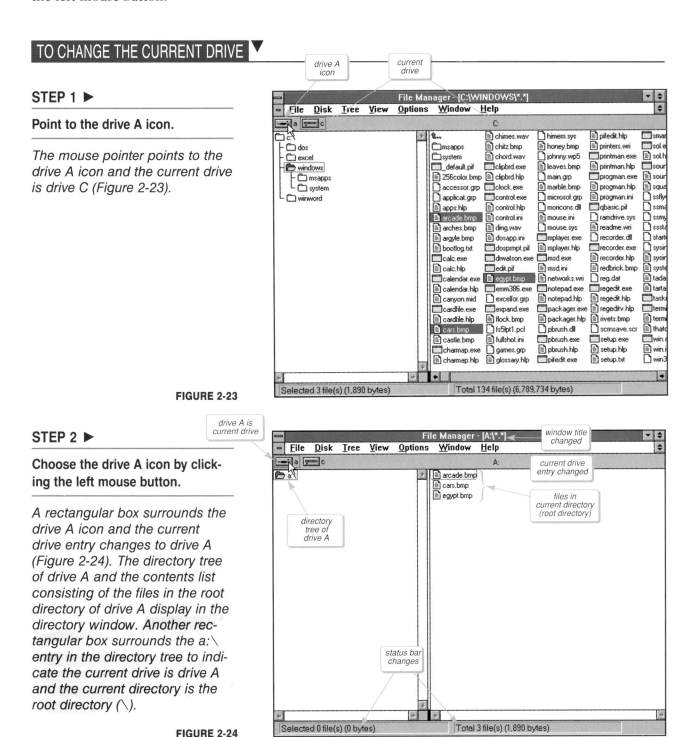

STEP 1 ►

Point to the drive A icon.

The mouse pointer points to the drive A icon and the current drive is drive C (Figure 2-23).

FIGURE 2-23

STEP 2 ►

Choose the drive A icon by clicking the left mouse button.

A rectangular box surrounds the drive A icon and the current drive entry changes to drive A (Figure 2-24). The directory tree of drive A and the contents list consisting of the files in the root directory of drive A display in the directory window. Another rectangular box surrounds the a:\ entry in the directory tree to indicate the current drive is drive A and the current directory is the root directory (\).

FIGURE 2-24

Correcting Errors Encountered While Changing the Current Drive

When you try to change the current drive before inserting a diskette into the diskette drive, Windows opens the Error Selecting Drive dialog box illustrated in Figure 2-25. The dialog box contains an error message (There is no disk in drive A.), a suggested action (Insert a disk, and then try again.), and the Retry and Cancel buttons. To change the current drive after forgetting to insert a diskette into drive A, insert a diskette into drive A, and choose the Retry button.

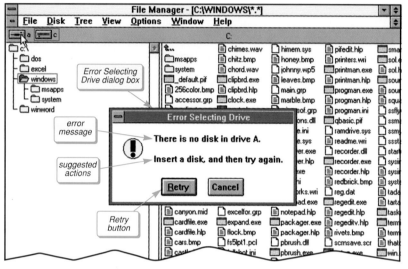

FIGURE 2-25

When you try to change the current drive and there is an unformatted diskette in the diskette drive, Windows opens the Error Selecting Drive dialog box shown in Figure 2-26. The dialog box contains an error message (The disk in drive A is not formatted.), a suggested action (Do you want to format it now?), and the Yes and No buttons. To change the current drive after inserting an unformatted diskette into drive A, choose the Yes button to format the diskette and change the current drive. Choose the No button to cancel the change.

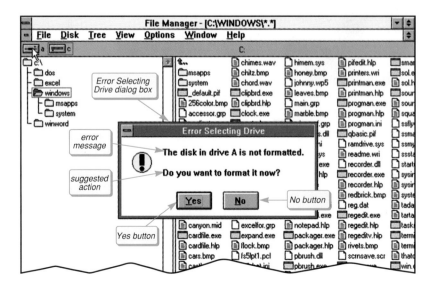

FIGURE 2-26

▶ RENAMING A FILE

S ometimes you may want to rename a file by changing its name or file-name extension. You change the name or extension of a file by selecting the filename in the contents list, choosing the **Rename command** from the File menu, entering the new filename, and choosing the OK button. In this project, you will change the name of the CARS.BMP file on the diskette in drive A to AUTOS.BMP.

TO RENAME A FILE ▼

STEP 1 ▶

Select the CARS.BMP entry by clicking the CARS.BMP filename in the contents list.

The CARS.BMP entry is high-lighted (Figure 2-27).

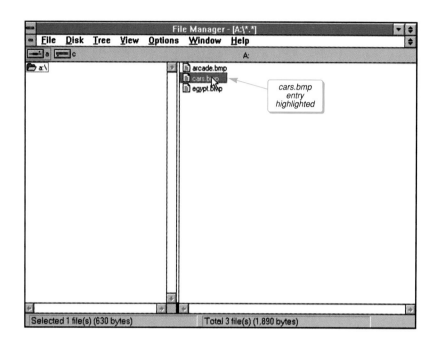

FIGURE 2-27

STEP 2 ▶

Select the File menu, and then point to the Rename command.

Windows opens the File menu (Figure 2-28). The mouse pointer points to the Rename command.

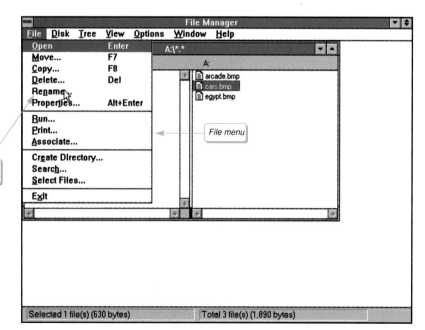

FIGURE 2-28

STEP 3 ▶

Choose the Rename command from the File menu by clicking the left mouse button.

Windows opens the Rename dialog box (Figure 2-29). The dialog box contains the Current Directory : A:\ message, the From and To text boxes, and the OK, Cancel, and Help buttons. The From text box contains the CARS.BMP filename and To text box contains an insertion point.

FIGURE 2-29

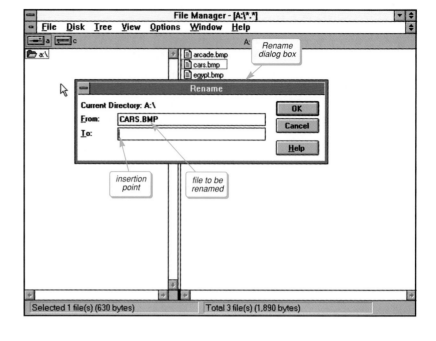

STEP 4 ▶

Type `autos.bmp` **in the To text box, and then point to the OK button.**

The To text box contains the AUTOS.BMP filename and the mouse points to the OK button (Figure 2-30).

FIGURE 2-30

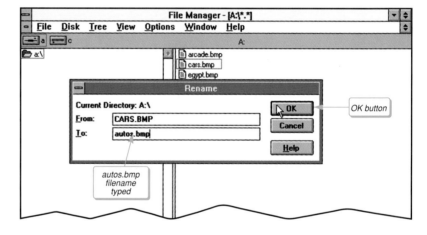

STEP 5 ▶

Choose the OK button by clicking the left mouse button.

The filename in the cars.bmp entry changes to autos.bmp (Figure 2-31).

FIGURE 2-31

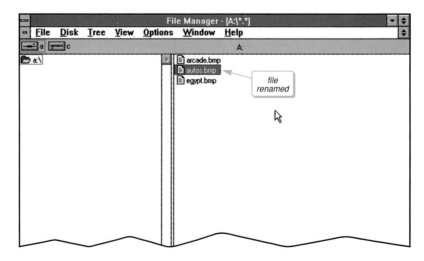

▶ DELETING A FILE

When you no longer need a file, you can delete it by selecting the file-name in the contents list, choosing the **Delete command** from the File menu, choosing the OK button, and then choosing the Yes button. In this project, you will delete the EGYPT.BMP file from the diskette in drive A.

TO DELETE A FILE ▼

STEP 1 ▶

Select the EGYPT.BMP entry.

The EGYPT.BMP entry is high-lighted (Figure 2-32).

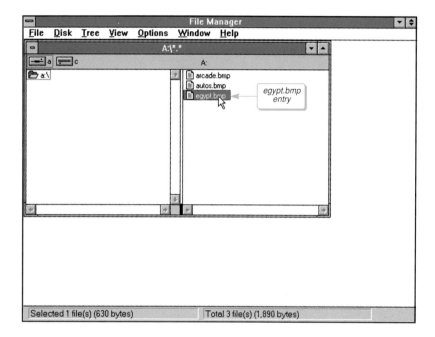

FIGURE 2-32

STEP 2 ▶

Select the File menu from the menu bar, and then point to the Delete command.

Windows opens the File menu (Figure 2-33). The mouse pointer points to the Delete command.

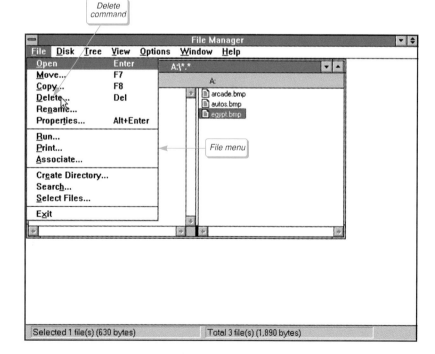

FIGURE 2-33

STEP 3 ▶

Choose the Delete command from the File menu by clicking the left mouse button, and then point to the OK button.

Windows opens the Delete dialog box (Figure 2-34). The dialog box contains the Current Directory: A:\ message, Delete text box, and the OK, Cancel, and Help buttons. The Delete text box contains the name of the file to be deleted (EGYPT.BMP), and the mouse pointer points to the OK button.

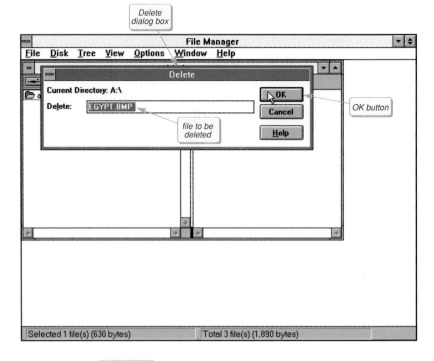

FIGURE 2-34

STEP 4 ▶

Choose the OK button by clicking the left mouse button, and then point to the Yes button.

Windows opens the Confirm File Delete dialog box (Figure 2-35). The dialog box contains the Delete File message and the path and filename of the file to delete (A:\EGYPT.BMP). The mouse pointer points to the Yes button.

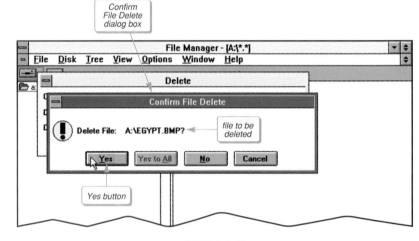

FIGURE 2-35

STEP 5 ▶

Choose the Yes button by clicking the left mouse button.

Windows deletes the EGYPT.BMP file from the diskette on drive A, removes the EGYPT.BMP entry from the contents list, and highlights the AUTOS.BMP file (Figure 2-36).

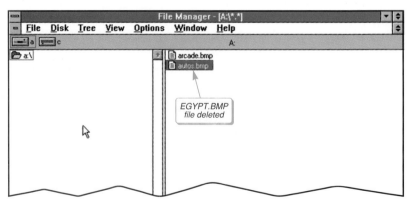

STEP 6

Remove the diskette from drive A.

FIGURE 2-36

▶ CREATING A BACKUP DISKETTE

T o prevent accidental loss of a file on a diskette, you should make a backup copy of the diskette. A copy of a diskette made to prevent accidental loss of data is called a **backup diskette**. Always be sure to make backup diskettes before installing software stored on diskettes onto the hard drive.

The first step in creating a backup diskette is to protect the diskette to be copied, or **source diskette**, from accidental erasure by write-protecting the diskette. After write-protecting the source diskette, choose the **Copy Disk command** from the Disk menu to copy the contents of the source diskette to another diskette, called the **destination diskette**. After copying the source diskette to the destination diskette, remove the write-protection from the source diskette and identify the destination diskette by writing a name on the paper label supplied with the diskette and affixing the label to the diskette.

In this project, you will use File Manager to create a backup diskette for a diskette labeled Business Documents. The Business Documents diskette contains valuable business documents that should be backed up to prevent accidental loss. The source diskette will be the Business Documents diskette and the destination diskette will be a formatted diskette that will later be labeled Business Documents Backup. To create a backup diskette, both the Business Documents diskette and the formatted diskette must be the same size and capacity.

File Manager copies a diskette by asking you to insert the source diskette into drive A, reading data from the source diskette into main memory, asking you to insert the destination disk, and then copying the data from main memory to the destination disk. Depending on the size of main memory on your computer, you may have to insert and remove the source and destination diskettes several times before the copy process is complete. The copy process takes about three minutes to complete.

TO COPY A DISKETTE ▼

STEP 1 ▶

Write-protect the Business Documents diskette by opening the write-protect window (Figure 2-37).

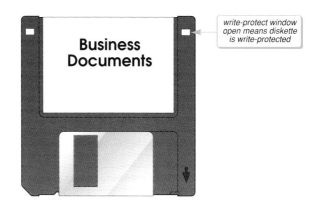

write-protect window
open means diskette
is write-protected

Business
Documents

FIGURE 2-37

STEP 2 ▶

Select the Disk menu from the menu bar, and then point to the Copy Disk command.

Windows opens the Disk menu (Figure 2-38). The mouse pointer points to the Copy Disk command.

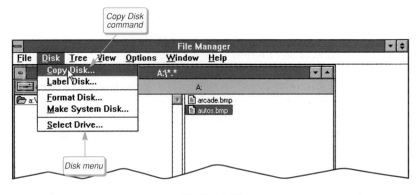

FIGURE 2-38

STEP 3 ▶

Choose the Copy Disk command from the Disk menu by clicking the left mouse button, and then point to the Yes button.

Windows opens the Confirm Copy Disk dialog box (Figure 2-39). The dialog box reminds you that the copy process will erase all data on the destination disk. The mouse pointer points to the Yes button.

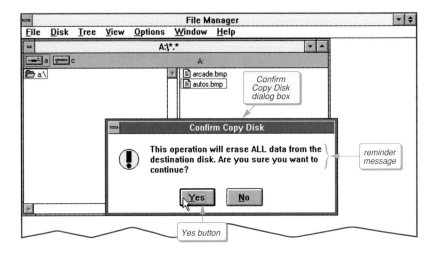

FIGURE 2-39

STEP 4 ▶

Choose the Yes button by clicking the left mouse button, and then point to the OK button.

Windows opens the Copy Disk dialog box (Figure 2-40). The dialog box contains the Insert source disk message and the mouse pointer points to the OK button.

STEP 5 ▶

Insert the source diskette, the Business Documents diskette, into drive A.

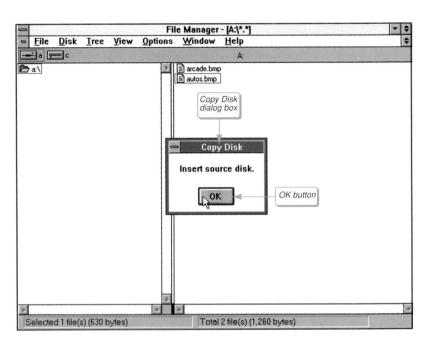

FIGURE 2-40

STEP 6 ▶

Choose the OK button in the Copy Disk dialog box by clicking the left mouse button.

Windows opens the Copying Disk dialog box (Figure 2-41). The dialog box contains the messages, Now Copying disk in Drive A:. and 1% completed. As the copy process progresses, a value from 1 to 100 indicates what percent of the copy process is complete.

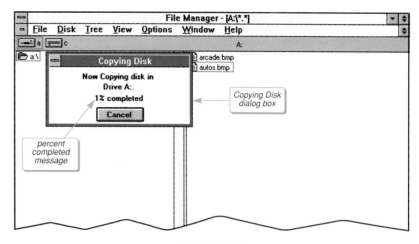

FIGURE 2-41

When as much data from the source diskette as will fit in main memory is copied to main memory, Windows opens the Copy Disk dialog box (Figure 2-42). The dialog box contains the message, Insert destination disk, and the OK button.

STEP 7 ▶

Remove the source diskette (Business Documents diskette) from drive A and insert the destination diskette (Business Documents Backup diskette) into drive A.

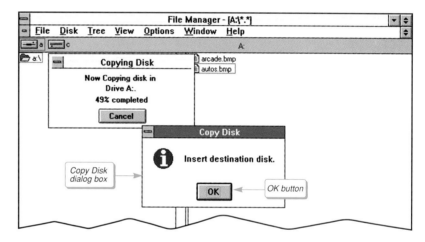

FIGURE 2-42

STEP 8 ▶

Choose the OK button from the Copy Disk dialog box.

Windows opens the Copying Disk dialog box (Figure 2-43). A value from 1 to 100 displays as the data in main memory is copied to the destination disk.

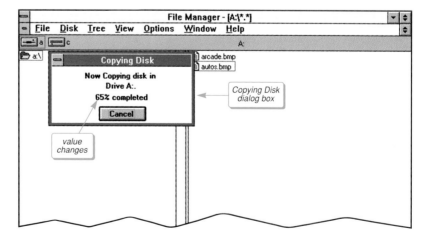

FIGURE 2-43

STEP 9 ▶

Remove the Business Documents Backup diskette from drive A and remove the write-protection from the Business Documents diskette by closing the write-protect window.

The write-protection is removed from the 3 1/2—inch Business Documents diskette (Figure 2-44).

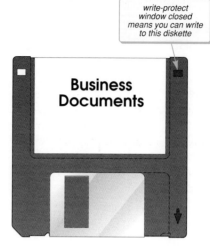

FIGURE 2-44

STEP 10 ▶

Identify the Business Documents Backup diskette by writing the words Business Documents Backup on the paper label supplied with the diskette and then affix the label to the diskette (Figure 2-45).

FIGURE 2-45

Depending on the size of main memory on your computer, you may have to insert and remove the source and destination diskettes several times before the copy process is complete. If prompted by Windows to insert the source diskette, remove the destination diskette (Business Documents Backup diskette) from drive A, insert the source diskette (Business Documents diskette) into drive A, and then choose the OK button. If prompted to insert the destination diskette, remove the source diskette (Business Documents diskette) from drive A, insert the destination diskette (Business Documents Backup diskette) into drive A, and then choose the OK button.

In the future if you change the contents of the Business Documents diskette, choose the Copy Disk command to copy the contents of the Business Documents diskette to the Business Documents Backup diskette. If the Business Documents diskette becomes unusable, you can format a diskette, choose the Copy Disk command to copy the contents of the Business Documents Backup diskette (source diskette) to the formatted diskette (destination diskette), label the formatted diskette, Business Documents, and use the new Business Documents diskette in place of the unusable Business Documents diskette.

Correcting Errors Encountered While Copying A Diskette

When you try to copy a disk and forget to insert the source diskette when prompted, insert an unformatted source diskette, forget to insert the destination diskette when prompted, or insert a write-protected destination diskette, Windows opens the Copy Disk Error dialog box illustrated in Figure 2-46. The dialog box contains the Unable to copy disk error message and OK button. To complete the copy process after forgetting to insert a source diskette or inserting an unformatted source diskette, choose the OK button, insert the formatted source diskette into the diskette drive, and choose the **Disk Copy command** to start over the disk copy process. To complete the copy process after forgetting to insert a destination diskette or inserting a write-protected destination diskette, choose the OK button, insert a nonwrite-protected diskette in the diskette drive, and choose the Disk Copy command to start over the disk copy.

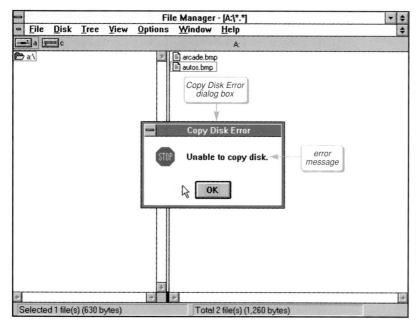

FIGURE 2-46

▶ SEARCHING FOR HELP USING ONLINE HELP

I n Project 1, you obtained help about the Paintbrush application by choosing the Contents command from the Help menu of the Paintbrush window (see pages WIN32 through WIN35). You then chose a topic from a list of help topics on the screen. In addition to choosing a topic from a list of available help topics, you can use the Search feature to search for help topics. In this project, you will use the Search feature to obtain help about copying files and selecting groups of files using the keyboard.

Searching for a Help Topic

In this project, you used a mouse to select and copy a group of files. If you want to obtain information about how to select a group of files using the keyboard instead of the mouse, you can use the Search feature. A search can be performed in one of two ways. The first method allows you to select a search topic from a list of search topics. A list of help topics associated with the search topic displays. You then select a help topic from this list. To begin the search, choose the **Search for Help on command** from the Help menu.

◼ TO SEARCH FOR A HELP TOPIC ▼

STEP 1 ►

Select the Help menu from the File Manager window menu bar, and then point to the Search for Help on command.

Windows opens the Help menu (Figure 2-47). The mouse pointer points to the Search for Help on command.

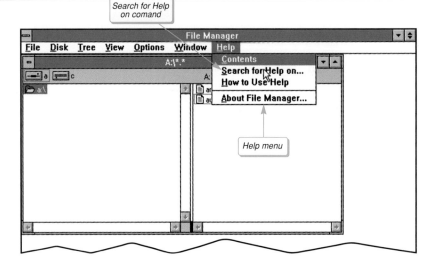

FIGURE 2-47

STEP 2 ►

Choose the Search for Help on command from the Help menu by clicking the left mouse button.

Windows opens the Search dialog box (Figure 2-48). The dialog box consists of two areas separated by a horizontal line. The top area contains the Search For text box, Search For list box, and Cancel and Show Topics buttons. The Search For list box contains an alphabetical list of search topics. A vertical scroll bar indicates there are more search topics than appear in the list box. The Cancel button cancels the Search operation. The Show Topics button is dimmed and cannot be chosen. The bottom area of the dialog box contains the empty Help Topics list box and the dimmed Go To button.

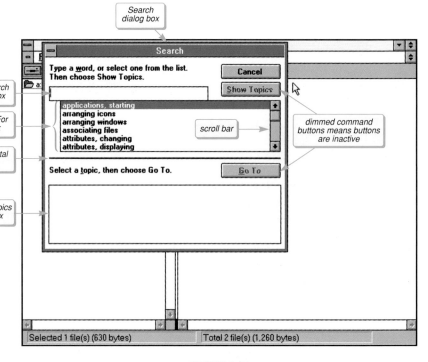

FIGURE 2-48

STEP 3 ▶

Point to the down scroll arrow in the Search For list box (Figure 2-49).

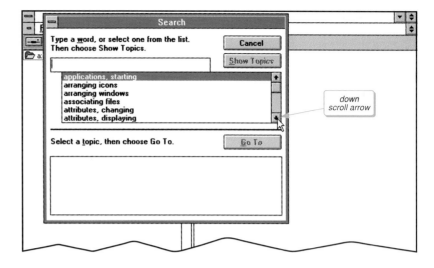

FIGURE 2-49

STEP 4 ▶

Hold down the left mouse button until the selecting files search topic is visible, and then point to the selecting files search topic (Figure 2-50).

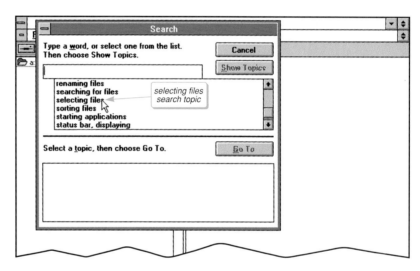

FIGURE 2-50

STEP 5 ▶

Select the selecting files search topic by clicking the left mouse button, and then point to the Show Topics button (Show Topics).

The selecting files search topic is highlighted in the Search For list box and displays in the Search For text box (Figure 2-51). The Show Topics button is no longer dimmed and the mouse pointer points to the Show Topics button.

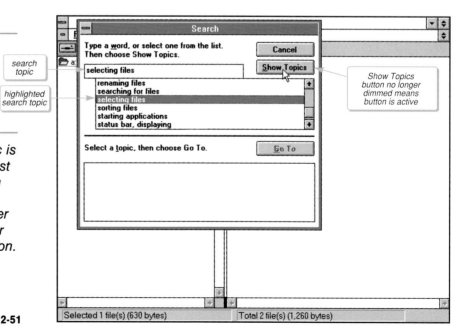

FIGURE 2-51

STEP 6 ▶

Choose the Show Topics button by clicking the left mouse button, and then point to the Using the Keyboard to Select Files help topic.

The Help Topics list box contains four help topics (Figure 2-52). The Go To button (Go To) is no longer dimmed, and the mouse pointer points to the Using the Keyboard to Select Files help topic.

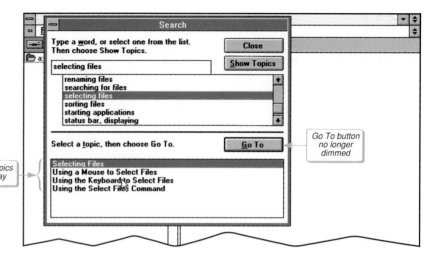

FIGURE 2-52

STEP 7 ▶

Select the Using the Keyboard to Select Files help topic by clicking the left mouse button, and then point to the Go To button.

The Using the Keyboard to Select Files help topic is highlighted in the Help Topics list box and the mouse pointer points to the Go To button (Figure 2-53).

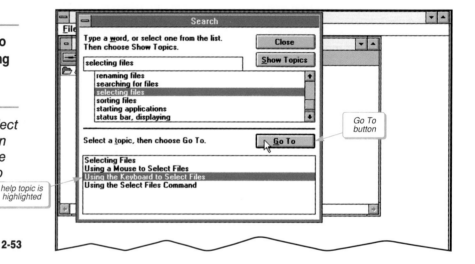

FIGURE 2-53

STEP 8 ▶

Choose the Go To button by clicking the left mouse button.

Windows closes the Search dialog box and opens the File Manager Help window (Figure 2-54). The Using the Keyboard to Select Files screen displays in the window.

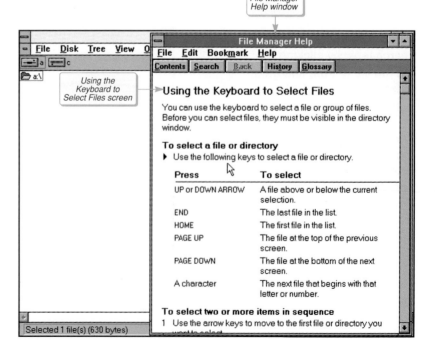

FIGURE 2-54

STEP 9 ▶

Click the Maximize button (⊕) to maximize the File Manager Help window (Figure 2-55).

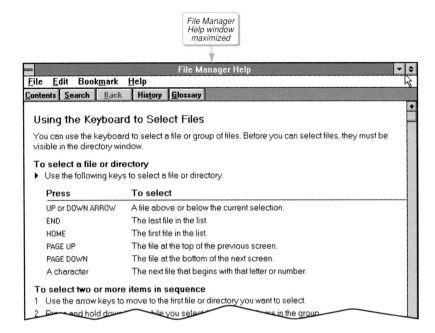

FIGURE 2-55

Searching for Help Using a Word or Phrase

The second method you can use to search for help involves entering a word or phrase to assist the Search feature in finding help related to the word or phrase. In this project, you copied a group of files from the hard disk to a diskette. To obtain additional information about copying files, choose the Search button and type `copy` from the keyboard.

TO SEARCH FOR A HELP TOPIC ▼

STEP 1 ▶

Point to the Search button (Search) (Figure 2-56).

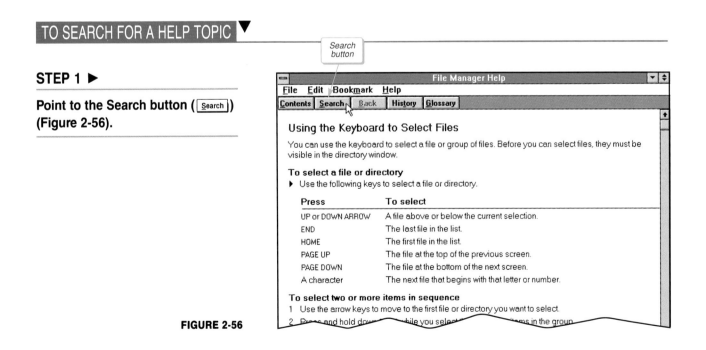

FIGURE 2-56

STEP 2 ▶

Choose the Search button by clicking the left mouse button, and then type `copy`.

Windows opens the Search dialog box (Figure 2-57). As you type the word copy, each letter of the word displays in the Search For text box and the Search For Topics in the Search For Topics list box change. When the entry of the word is complete, the word copy displays in the Search For text box and the Search For topics beginning with the four letters c-o-p-y display first in the Search For list box.

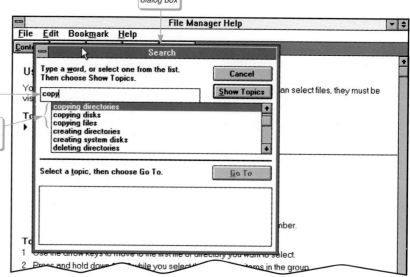

FIGURE 2-57

STEP 3 ▶

Select the copying files search topic by pointing to the topic and clicking the left mouse button, and then point to the Show Topics button.

The copying files search topic is highlighted in the Search For list box and displays in the Search For text box (Figure 2-58).

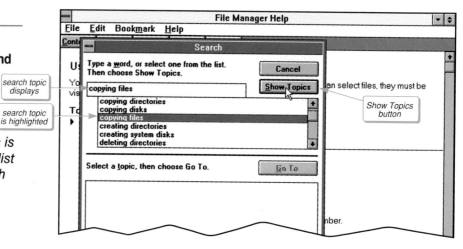

FIGURE 2-58

STEP 4 ▶

Choose the Show Topics button by clicking the left mouse button, and then point to the Go To button.

Only the Copying Files and Directories help topic display in the Help Topic list box (Figure 2-59).

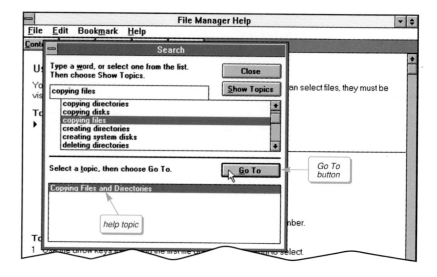

FIGURE 2-59

STEP 5 ▶

Choose the Go To button by clicking the left mouse button.

Windows closes the Search dialog box and displays the Copying Files and Directories help screen (Figure 2-60).

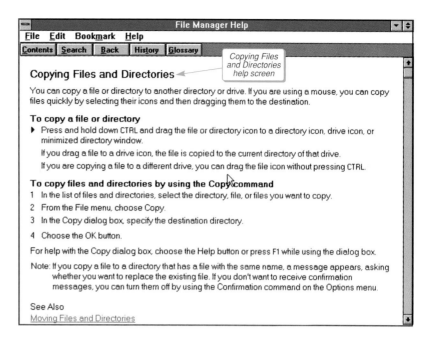

FIGURE 2-60

Quitting File Manager and Online Help

When you finish using File Manager and Windows online Help, you should quit the File Manager Help and File Manager applications. One method of quitting these applications is to first quit the File Manager Help application, and then quit the File Manager application. However, because quitting an application automatically quits the help application associated with that application, you can simply quit the File Manager application to quit both applications. Because the Program Manager and File Manager windows are hidden behind the File Manager Help window (see Figure 2-60), you must move the File Manager window on top of the other windows before quitting File Manager. To do this, you must switch to the File Manager application.

▶ SWITCHING BETWEEN APPLICATIONS

E ach time you start an application and maximize its window, its application window displays on top of the other windows on the desktop. To display a hidden application window, you must switch between applications on the desktop using the ALT and TAB keys. To switch to another application, hold down the ALT key, press the TAB key one or more times, and then release the ALT key. Each time you press the TAB key, a box containing an application icon and application window title opens on the desktop. To display the File Manager window, you will have to press the TAB key only once.

TO SWITCH BETWEEN APPLICATIONS ▼

STEP 1 ▶

Hold down the ALT key, and then press the TAB key.

A box containing the File Manager application icon and window title (File Manager) displays (Figure 2-61).

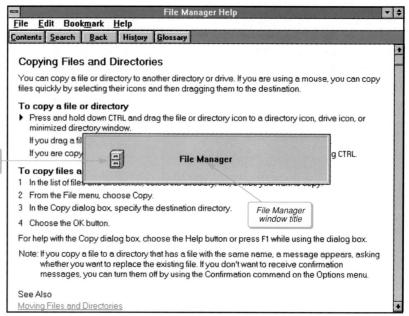

File Manager icon

File Manager window title

FIGURE 2-61

STEP 2 ▶

Release the ALT key.

The File Manager window moves on top of the other windows on the desktop (Figure 2-62).

File Manager window visible

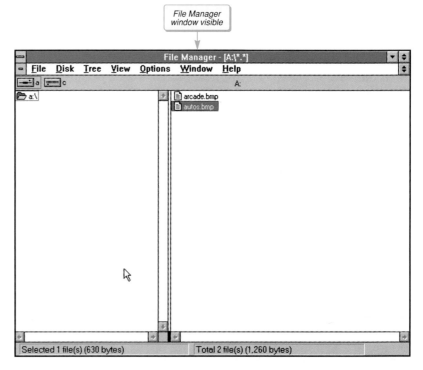

FIGURE 2-62

Verify Changes to the File Manager Window Will Not Be Saved

Because you want to return the File Manager window to its state before you started the application, no changes should be saved. The **Save Settings on Exit command** on the Options menu controls whether changes to the File Manager window are saved or not saved when you quit File Manager. A check mark (✔) preceding the Save Settings on Exit command indicates the command is active and all changes to the layout of the File Manager window will be saved when you quit File Manager. If the command is preceded by a check mark, choose the Save Settings on Exit command by clicking the left mouse button to remove the check mark, so the changes will not be saved. Perform the following steps to verify that changes are not saved to the File Manager window.

TO VERIFY CHANGES WILL NOT BE SAVED ▼

STEP 1 ▶

Select the Options menu from the File Manager menu bar.

The Options menu opens (Figure 2-63). A check mark (✔) precedes the Save Settings on Exit command.

STEP 2 ▶

To remove the check mark, choose the Save Settings on Exit command from the Options menu by pointing to the Save Settings on Exit command and clicking the left mouse button.

Windows closes the Options menu. Although not visible, the check mark preceding the Save Settings on Exit command has been removed. This means any changes made to the desktop will not be saved when you exit File Manager.

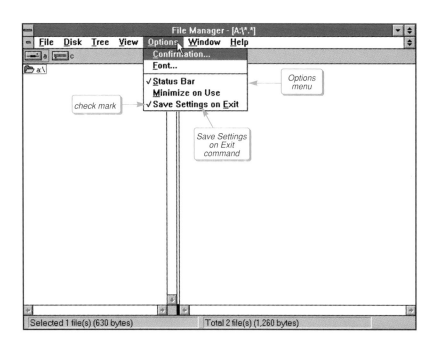

FIGURE 2-63

Quitting File Manager

After verifying no changes to the File Manager window will be saved, the Save Settings on Exit command is not active, so you can quit the File Manager application. In Project 1 you chose the Exit command from the File menu to quit an application. In addition to choosing a command from a menu, you can also quit an application by pointing to the **Control-menu box** in the upper left corner of the application window and double-clicking the left mouse button, as shown in the steps on the next page.

TO QUIT AN APPLICATION ▼

STEP 1 ▶

Point to the Control-menu box in the upper left corner of the File Manager window (Figure 2-64).

STEP 2 ▶

Double-click the left mouse button to exit the File Manager application.

Windows closes the File Manager and File Manager Help windows, causing the Program Manager window to display.

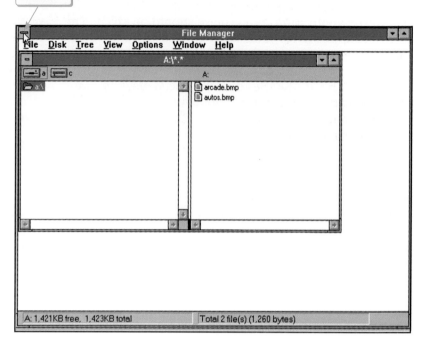

FIGURE 2-64

TO QUIT WINDOWS

Step 1: Select the Options menu from the Program Manager menu bar.
Step 2: If a check mark precedes the Save Settings on Exit command, choose the Save Settings on Exit command.
Step 3: Point to the Control-menu box in the upper left corner of the Program Manager window.
Step 4: Double-click the left mouse button.
Step 5: Choose the OK button to exit Windows.

▶ ADDITIONAL COMMANDS AND CONCEPTS

I n addition to the commands and concepts presented in Project 1 and this project, you should understand how to activate a group window, arrange the program-item icons in a group window, and close a group window. These topics are discussed on the following pages. In addition, methods to resize a window and minimize an application window to an application icon are explained.

Activating a Group Window

Frequently, several group windows are open in the Program Manager window at the same time. In Figure 2-65, two group windows (Main and Accessories) are open. The Accessories window is the active group window, and the inactive Main window is partially hidden behind the Accessories window. To view a group window that is partially hidden, activate the hidden window by selecting the Window menu and then choosing the name of the group window you wish to view.

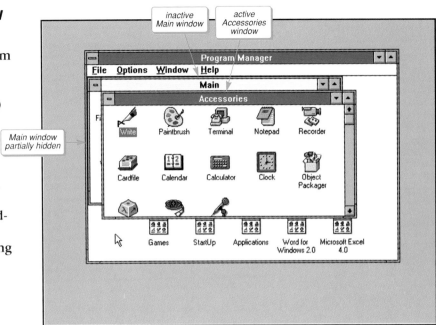

FIGURE 2-65

TO ACTIVATE A GROUP WINDOW ▼

STEP 1 ►

Select the Window menu from the Program Manager menu bar, and then point to the Main group window name.

The Window menu consists of two areas separated by a horizontal line (Figure 2-66). Below the line is a list of the group windows and group icons in the Program Manager window. Each entry in the list is preceded by a value from one to seven. The number of the active window (Accessories) is preceded by a check mark and the mouse pointer points to the Main group window name.

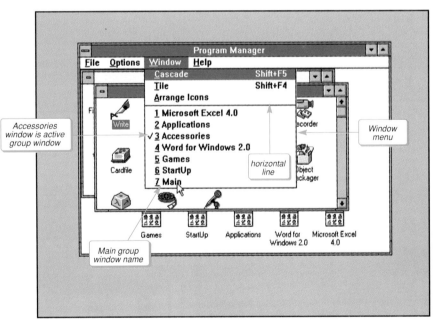

FIGURE 2-66

STEP 2 ▶

Choose the Main group window name by clicking the left mouse button.

The Main window moves on top of the Accessories window (Figure 2-67). The Main window is now the active window.

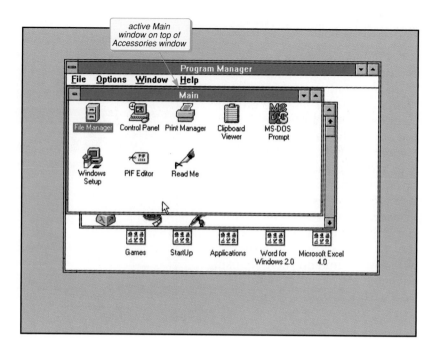

FIGURE 2-67

An alternative method of activating an inactive window is to point to any open area of the window and click the left mouse button. This method cannot be used if the inactive window is completely hidden behind another window.

Closing a Group Window

When several group windows are open in the Program Manager window, you may want to close a group window to reduce the number of open windows. In Figure 2-68, the Main, Accessories, and Games windows are open. To close the Games window, choose the Minimize button on the right side of the Games title bar. Choosing the Minimize button removes the group window from the desktop and displays the Games group icon at the bottom of the Program Manager window.

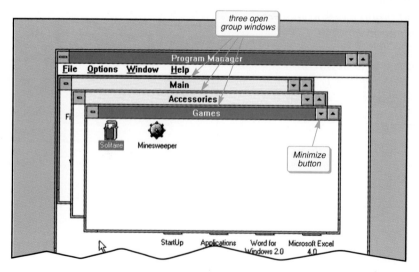

FIGURE 2-68

TO CLOSE A GROUP WINDOW ▼

STEP 1 ▶

Choose the Minimize button (▾) on the Games title bar.

The Games window closes and the Games icon displays at the bottom edge of the Program Manager window (Figure 2-69).

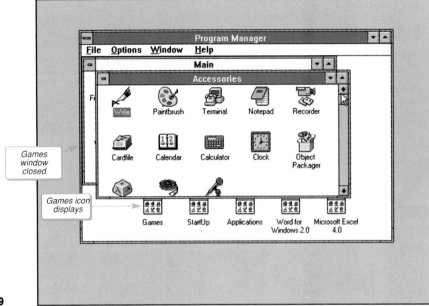

FIGURE 2-69

Resizing a Group Window

When more than six group icons display at the bottom of the Program Manager window, some group icons may not be completely visible. In Figure 2-70, the name of the Microsoft SolutionsSeries icon is partially visible. To make the icon visible, resize the Main window by dragging the bottom window border toward the window title.

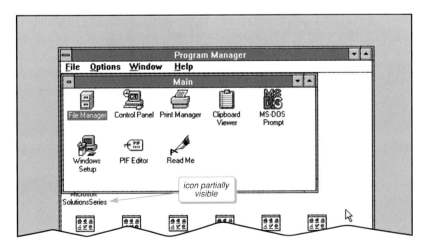

FIGURE 2-70

TO RESIZE A WINDOW ▼

STEP 1 ▶

Point to the bottom border of the Main window.

As the mouse pointer approaches the window border, the mouse pointer changes to a double-headed arrow icon (⇕) (Figure 2-71).

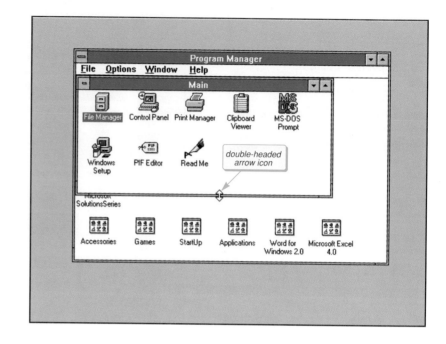

FIGURE 2-71

STEP 2 ▶

Drag the bottom border toward the window title until the Microsoft SolutionsSeries icon is visible.

The Main window changes shape, and the Microsoft Solu- tionsSeries icon is visible (Figure 2-72).

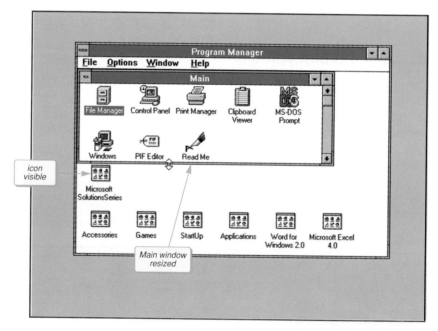

FIGURE 2-72

In addition to dragging a window border to resize a window, you can also drag a window corner to resize the window. By dragging a corner, you can change both the width and length of a window.

Arranging Icons

Occasionally, a program-item icon is either accidentally or intentionally moved within a group window. The result is that the program-item icons are not arranged in an organized fashion in the window. Figure 2-73 shows the eight program-item icons in the Main window. One icon, the File Manager icon, is not aligned with the other icons. As a result, the icons in the Main window appear unorganized. To arrange the icons in the Main window, choose the **Arrange Icons command** from the Window menu.

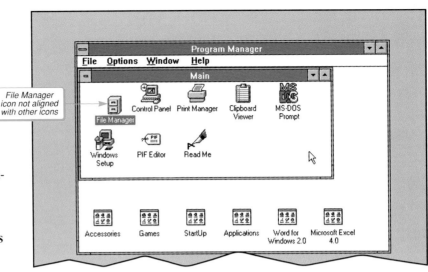

FIGURE 2-73

TO ARRANGE PROGRAM-ITEM ICONS ▼

STEP 1 ►

Select the Window menu from the Program Manager menu bar, and then point to the Arrange Icons command.

Windows opens the Window menu (Figure 2-74). The mouse pointer points to the Arrange Icons command.

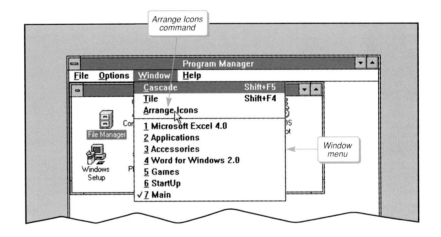

FIGURE 2-74

STEP 2 ►

Choose the Arrange Icons command by clicking the left mouse button.

The icons in the Main window are arranged (Figure 2-75).

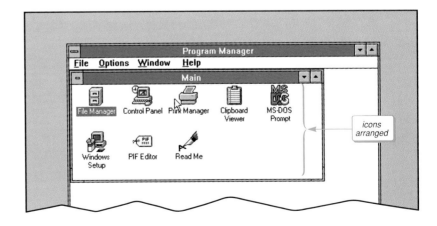

FIGURE 2-75

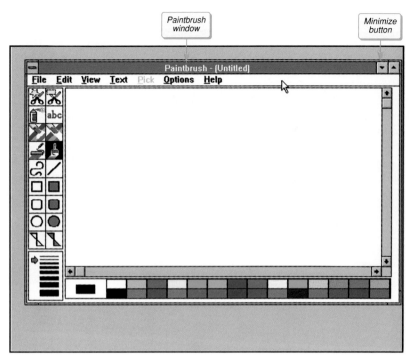

Paintbrush window

Minimize button

FIGURE 2-76

Minimizing an Application Window to an Icon

When you finish work in an application and there is a possibility of using the application again before quitting Windows, you should minimize the application window to an application icon instead of quitting the application. An **application icon** represents an application that was started and then minimized. Minimizing a window to an application icon saves you the time of starting the application and maximizing its window if you decide to use the application again. In addition, you free space on the desktop without quitting the application. The desktop in Figure 2-76 contains the Paintbrush window. To minimize the Paintbrush window to an application icon, click the Minimize button on the right side of the Paintbrush title bar.

TO MINIMIZE AN APPLICATION WINDOW TO AN ICON ▼

STEP 1 ►

Click the Minimize button on the right side of the Paintbrush title bar.

Windows closes the Paintbrush window and displays the Paint-brush application icon at the bottom of the desktop (Figure 2-77).

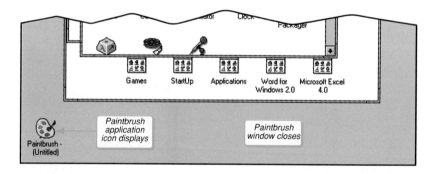

Paintbrush application icon displays

Paintbrush window closes

FIGURE 2-77

After minimizing an application window to an application icon, you can start the application again by double-clicking the application icon.

► PROJECT SUMMARY

In this project, you used File Manager to format and copy a diskette, copy a group of files, and rename and delete a file. You searched for help about File Manager using the Search feature of online Help, and you switched between applications on the desktop. In addition, you activated, resized, and closed a group window, arranged the icons in a group window, and minimized an application window to an application icon.

▶ KEY TERMS

application icon (*WIN86*)
Arrange Icons command
  (*WIN85*)
backup diskette (*WIN47*)
Cascade command (*WIN94*)
contents list (*WIN49*)
Control-menu box (*WIN79*)
Copy Disk command (*WIN67*)
current drive (*WIN48*)
Delete command (*WIN65*)
destination directory (*WIN54*)
destination diskette (*WIN67*)
destination drive (*WIN54*)

directory structure (*WIN49*)
directory tree (*WIN49*)
directory window (*WIN48*)
Disk Copy command (*WIN71*)
Disk menu (*WIN51*)
diskette capacity (*WIN50*)
diskette size (*WIN50*)
drive icon (*WIN48*)
File Manager (*WIN48*)
Format Disk command (*WIN51*)
formatting (*WIN50*)
Help menu (*WIN72*)

Options menu (*WIN79*)
Rename command (*WIN63*)
Save Settings on Exit command
  (*WIN79*)
Search for Help on command
  (*WIN72*)
source directory (*WIN54*)
source diskette (*WIN67*)
source drive (*WIN54*)
split bar (*WIN49*)
Tile command (*WIN94*)
Window menu (*WIN81*)

Q U I C K R E F E R E N C E

In Windows you can accomplish a task in a number of ways. The following table provides a quick reference to each task presented in the project with its available options. The commands listed in the Menu column can be executed using either the keyboard or mouse.

Task	Mouse	Menu	Keyboard Shortcuts
Activate a Group Window	Click group window	From Window menu, choose window title	
Arrange Program-Item Icons in a Group Window		From Window menu, choose Arrange Icons	
Change the Current Drive	Click drive icon		Press TAB to move highlight to drive icon area, press arrow keys to outline drive icon, and press ENTER
Close a Group Window	Click Minimize button or double-click control-menu box	From Control menu, choose Close	Press CTRL + F4
Copy a Diskette		From Disk menu, choose Copy Disk	
Copy a File or Group of Files	Drag highlighted filename(s) to destination drive or directory icon	From File menu, choose Copy	
Delete a File		From File menu, choose Delete	Press DEL
Format a Diskette		From Disk menu, choose Format Disk	

(continued)

QUICK REFERENCE (continued)

Task	Mouse	Menu	Keyboard Shortcuts
Maximize a Directory Window	Click Maximize button	From Control menu, choose Maximize	
Minimize an Application Window	Click Minimize button	From Control menu, choose Minimize	Press ALT, SPACE BAR, N
Rename a File		From File menu, choose Rename	
Resize a Window	Drag window border or corner	From Control menu, choose Size	
Save Changes when Quitting File Manager		From Options menu, choose Save Settings on Exit if no check mark precedes command	
Save No Changes when Quitting Windows		From Options menu, choose Save Settings on Exit if check mark precedes command	
Search for a Help Topic		From Help menu, choose Search for Help on	
Select a File in the Contents List	Click the filename		Press arrow keys to outline filename, press SHIFT + F8
Select a Group of Files in the Contents List	Select first file, hold down CTRL key and select other files		Press arrow keys to outline first file, press SHIFT + F8, press arrow keys to outline each additional filename, and press SPACEBAR
Switch between Applications	Click application window		Hold down ALT, press TAB (or ESC), release ALT

S T U D E N T   A S S I G N M E N T S

STUDENT ASSIGNMENT 1
True/False

Instructions: Circle T if the statement is true or F if the statement if false.

T   F   1. Formatting prepares a diskette for use on a computer.

T   F   2. It is not important to create a backup diskette of the Business Documents diskette.

T   F   3. Program Manager is an application you can use to organize and work with your hard disk and diskettes and the files on those disks.

T   F   4. A directory window title bar usually contains the current directory path.

T   F   5. A directory window consists of a directory tree and contents list.

T   F   6. The directory tree contains a list of the files in the current directory.

T   F   7. The disk capacity of a 3 1/2-inch diskette is typically 360K or 1.2MB.

T   F   8. The source drive is the drive from which files are copied.

T   F   9. You select a single file in the contents list by pointing to the filename and clicking the left mouse button.

T F 10. You select a group of files in the contents list by pointing to each filename and clicking the left mouse button.

T F 11. Windows opens the Error Copying File dialog box if you try to copy a file to an unformatted diskette.

T F 12. You change the filename or extension of a file using the Change command.

T F 13. Windows opens the Confirm File Delete dialog box when you try to delete a file.

T F 14. When creating a backup diskette, the disk to receive the copy is the source disk.

T F 15. The first step in creating a backup diskette is to choose the Copy Disk command from the Disk menu.

T F 16. On some computers, you may have to insert and remove the source and destination diskettes several times to copy a diskette.

T F 17. Both the Search for Help on command and the Search button initiate a search for help.

T F 18. An application icon represents an application that was started and then minimized.

T F 19. You hold down the TAB key, press the ALT key, and then release the TAB key to switch between applications on the desktop.

T F 20. An application icon displays on the desktop when you minimize an application window.

STUDENT ASSIGNMENT 2
Multiple Choice

Instructions: Circle the correct response.

1. The _____ application allows you to format a diskette.
    a. Program Manager
    b. File Manager
    c. online Help
    d. Paintbrush

2. The _____ contains the directory structure of the current drive.
    a. contents list
    b. status bar
    c. split bar
    d. directory tree

3. The _____ key is used when selecting a group of files.
    a. CTRL
    b. ALT
    c. TAB
    d. ESC

4. After selecting a group of files, you _____ the group of files to copy the files to a new drive or directory.
    a. click
    b. double-click
    c. drag
    d. none of the above

5. The commands to rename and delete a file are located on the _____ menu.
    a. Window
    b. Options
    c. Disk
    d. File

6. The first step in creating a backup diskette is to _____.
    a. write-protect the destination diskette
    b. choose the Copy command from the Disk menu
    c. write-protect the source diskette
    d. label the destination diskette

STUDENT ASSIGNMENT 2 (continued)

7. When searching for help, the _____ button displays a list of Help topics.
   a. Go To
   b. Topics
   c. Show Topics
   d. Search
8. You use the _____ and _____ keys to switch between applications on the desktop.
   a. ALT, TAB
   b. SHIFT, ALT
   c. ALT, CTRL
   d. ESC, CTRL
9. When you choose a window title from the Window menu, Windows _____ the associated group window.
   a. opens
   b. closes
   c. enlarges
   d. activates
10. To resize a group window, you can use the _____.
    a. title bar
    b. window border
    c. resize command on the Window menu
    d. arrange Icons command on the Options menu

STUDENT ASSIGNMENT 3
Identifying the Parts of a Directory Window

Instructions: On the desktop in Figure SA2-3, arrows point to several items in the C:\WINDOWS*.* directory window. Identify the items in the space provided.

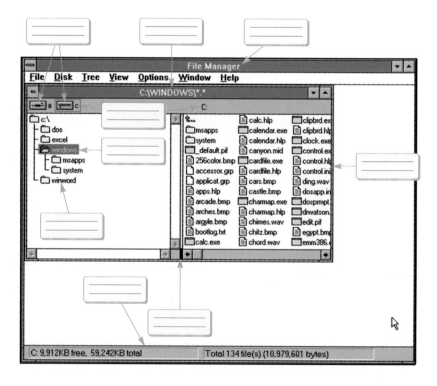

FIGURE SA2-3

STUDENT ASSIGNMENT 4
Selecting a Group of Files

Instructions: Using the desktop in Figure SA2-4, list the steps to select the group of files consisting of the ARCADE.BMP, CARS.BMP, and EGYPT.BMP files in the space provided.

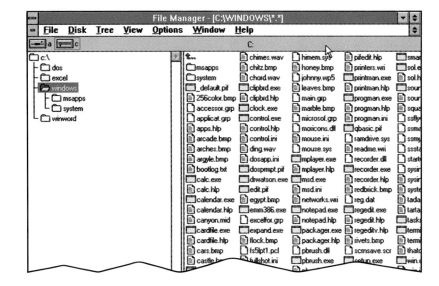

FIGURE SA2-4

Step 1: _____

Step 2: _____

Step 3: _____

Step 4: _____

STUDENT ASSIGNMENT 5
Copying a Group of Files

Instructions: Using the desktop in Figure SA2-5, list the steps to copy the group of files selected in Student Assignment 4 to the root directory of drive A. Write the steps in the space provided.

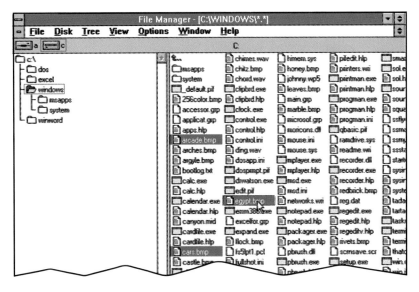

FIGURE SA2-5

Step 1: _____

Step 2: _____

Step 3: _____

Step 4: _____

STUDENT ASSIGNMENT 6
Searching for Help

Instructions: Using the desktop in Figure SA2-6, list the steps to complete the search for the Using the Keyboard to Select Files help topic. The mouse pointer points to the down scroll arrow. Write the steps in the space provided.

FIGURE SA2-6

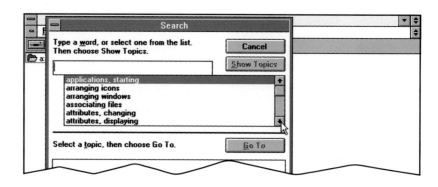

Step 1: _____

Step 2: _____

Step 3: _____

Step 4: _____

Step 5: _____

Step 6: _____

C O M P U T E R   L A B O R A T O R Y   E X E R C I S E S

COMPUTER LABORATORY EXERCISE 1
Selecting and Copying Files

Instructions: Perform the following tasks using a computer.

Part 1:

1. Start Windows.
2. Double-click the File Manager icon to start File Manager.
3. Click the Maximize button on the File Manager window to enlarge the File Manager window.
4. Click the Maximize button on the C:\WINDOWS*.* window to enlarge the C:\WINDOWS*.* window.
5. Select the CHITZ.BMP file.
6. Hold down the CTRL key and click the LEAVES.BMP filename to select the LEAVES.BMP file. The CHITZ.BMP and LEAVES.BMP files should both be highlighted.
7. Insert the Student Diskette into drive A.
8. Drag the group of files to the drive A icon.
9. Choose the Yes button in the Confirm Mouse Operation dialog box.
10. Choose the drive A icon to change the current drive to drive A.
11. Select the CHITZ.BMP file.
12. Choose the Delete command from the File menu.
13. Choose the OK button in the Delete dialog box.
14. Choose the Yes button in the Confirm File Delete dialog box.
15. If the LEAVES.BMP file is not highlighted, select the LEAVES.BMP file.

16. Choose the Rename command from the File menu.
17. Type AUTUMN.BMP in the To text box.
18. Choose the OK button in the Rename dialog box to rename the LEAVES.BMP file.

Part 2:

1. Hold down the ALT key, press the TAB key, and release the ALT key to switch to the Program Manager application.
2. Double-click the Accessories icon to open the Accessories window.
3. Double-click the Paintbrush icon to start Paintbrush.
4. Click the Maximize button on the Paintbrush window to enlarge the Paintbrush window.
5. Choose the Open command from the File menu.
6. Click the Down Arrow button in the Drives drop down list box to display the Drives drop down list.
7. Select the drive A icon.
8. Select the AUTUMN.BMP file in the File Name list box.
9. Choose the OK button to retrieve the AUTUMN.BMP file into Paintbrush.
10. Choose the Print command from the File menu.
11. Click the Draft option button in the Print dialog box.
12. Choose the OK button in the Print dialog box to print the contents of the AUTUMN.BMP file.
13. Remove the Student Diskette from drive A.
14. Choose the Exit command from the File menu to quit Paintbrush.
15. Hold down the ALT key, press the TAB key, and release the ALT key to switch to the File Manager application.
16. Select the Options menu.
17. If a check mark precedes the Save Settings on Exit command, choose the Save Settings on Exit command.
18. Choose the Exit command from the File menu of the File Manager window to quit File Manager.
19. Choose the Exit Windows command from the File menu of the Program Manager window.
20. Click the OK button to quit Windows.

COMPUTER LABORATORY EXERCISE 2
Searching with Online Help

Instructions: Perform the following tasks using a computer.

1. Start Microsoft Windows.
2. Double-click the Accessories icon to open the Accessories window.
3. Double-click the Write icon to start the Write application.
4. Click the Maximize button on the Write window to enlarge the Write window.
5. Choose the Search for Help on command from the Help menu.
6. Scroll the Search For list box to make the cutting text topic visible.
7. Select the cutting text topic.
8. Choose the Show Topics button.
9. Choose the Go To button to display the Copying, Cutting, and Pasting Text topic.
10. Click the Maximize button on the Write Help window to enlarge the window.
11. Choose the Print Topic command from the File menu to print the Copying, Cutting, and Pasting Text topic on the printer.
12. Choose the Search button.
13. Enter the word paste in the Search For list box.
14. Select the Pasting Pictures search topic.
15. Choose the Show Topics button.
16. Choose the Go To button to display the Copying, Cutting, and Pasting Pictures topic.
17. Choose the Print Topic command from the File menu to print the Copying, Cutting, and Pasting Pictures topic on the printer.

COMPUTER LABORATORY EXERCISE 2 (continued)

18. Choose the Exit command from the File menu to quit Write Help.
19. Choose the Exit command from the File menu to quit Write.
20. Select the Options menu.
21. If a check mark precedes the Save Settings on Exit command, choose the Save Settings on Exit command.
22. Choose the Exit Windows command from the File menu.
23. Click the OK button to quit Windows.

COMPUTER LABORATORY EXERCISE 3
Working with Group Windows

Instructions: Perform the following tasks using a computer.

1. Start Windows. The Main window should be open in the Program Manger window.
2. Double-click the Accessories icon to open the Accessories window.
3. Double-click the Games icon to open the Games window.
4. Choose the Accessories window title from the Window menu to activate the Accessories window.
5. Click the Minimize button on the Accessories window to close the Accessories window.
6. Choose the **Tile command** from the Window menu. The Tile command arranges a group of windows so no windows overlap, all windows are visible, and each window occupies an equal portion of the screen.
7. Move and resize the Main and Games windows to resemble the desktop in Figure CLE2-3. To resize a window, drag the window border or corner. To move a group window, drag the window title bar. Choose the Arrange Icons command from the Window menu to arrange the icons in each window.

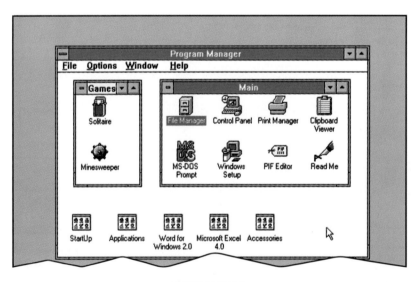

FIGURE CLE2-3

8. Press the PRINTSCREEN key to capture the desktop.
9. Open the Accessories window.
10. Choose the **Cascade command** from the Window menu. The Cascade command arranges a group of windows so the windows overlap and the title bar of each window is visible.
11. Double-click the Paintbrush icon to start Paintbrush.
12. Click the Maximize button on the Paintbrush window to enlarge the Paintbrush window.
13. Choose the Paste command from the Edit menu to place the picture of the desktop in the window.
14. Choose the Print command from the File menu.

15. Click the Draft option button.
16. Choose the OK button in the Print dialog box to print the desktop.
17. Choose the Exit command from the File menu of the Paintbrush window.
18. Choose the No button to not save current changes and quit Paintbrush.
19. Select the Options menu.
20. If a check mark precedes the Save Settings on Exit command, choose the Save Settings on Exit command.
21. Choose the Exit Windows command from the File menu.
22. Click the OK button.

COMPUTER LABORATORY EXERCISE 4
Backing Up Your Student Diskette

Instructions: Perform the following tasks using a computer to back up your Student Diskette.

Part 1:

1. Start Windows.
2. Double-click the File Manager icon to start the File Manager application.
3. Click the Maximize button on the File Manager window to enlarge the File Manager window.
4. Write-protect the Student Diskette.
5. Choose the Copy Disk command from the Disk menu.
6. Choose the Yes button in the Confirm Copy Disk dialog box.
7. Insert the source diskette (Student Diskette) into drive A.
8. Choose the OK button in the Copy Disk dialog box.
9. When prompted, insert the destination diskette (the formatted diskette created in this project) into drive A.
10. Choose the OK button in the Copy Disk dialog box.
11. Insert and remove the source and destination diskette until the copy process is complete.
12. Click the drive A icon to change the current drive to drive A.
13. Press the PRINTSCREEN key to capture the desktop.
14. Select the Options menu on the File Manager menu bar.
15. If a check mark precedes the Save Settings on Exit command, choose the Save Settings on Exit command.
16. Choose the Exit command from the File menu on the File Manager menu bar to quit File Manager.

Part 2:

1. Double-click the Accessories icon to open the Accessories window.
2. Double-click the Paintbrush icon to start Paintbrush.
3. Click the Maximize button to enlarge the Paintbrush window.
4. Choose the Paste command from the Edit menu to place the picture of the desktop in the window.
5. Choose the Print command from the File menu.
6. Click the Draft option button.
7. Choose the OK button in the Print dialog box to print the picture of the desktop on the printer.
8. Choose the Exit command from the File menu.
9. Choose the No button to not save current changes and quit Paintbrush.
10. Select the Options menu.
11. If a check mark precedes the Save Settings on Exit command, choose the Save Settings on Exit command.
12. Choose the Exit Windows command from the File menu of the Program Manager menu bar.
13. Click the OK button to quit Windows.
14. Remove the diskette from drive A.
15. Remove the write-protection from the Student Diskette.

INDEX

Active command, WIN36, WIN79
Active icon, **WIN18**
Active window, **WIN15**–16, WIN81–82
ALT key, switching between applications and, WIN77–78
Application(s), **WIN3**
  inactive, WIN17
  quitting, WIN21–22, WIN28, WIN32, WIN79–80
  starting, WIN16–17
  switching between, WIN77–78
Application icon, **WIN86**
Application software, **WIN3**
Application window
  displaying hidden, WIN77–80
  maximizing, WIN18
Arrange Icons command, **WIN85**
Asterisk (*), group of files and, WIN23
Auxiliary storage device, WIN23

Backslash (\), directory and, WIN24, WIN48
Backup diskette, **WIN47**, **WIN67**–71, WIN95
Bottom window border, WIN83–84
Buttons, WIN12, WIN13

Calendar application, WIN44–45
Cancel command button, WIN21
Cancel copy operation, WIN60
Cardfile application, WIN46
Cascade command, **WIN94**
Check boxes, **WIN13**
Check mark, active command and, WIN36, WIN79
Choosing a command, **WIN11**
Close, WIN16
Closing
  group window, WIN82–83
  pop-up window, WIN35
Command, **WIN10**
  active, WIN36, WIN79
Command buttons, **WIN13**
Confirm Copy Disk dialog box, WIN68
Confirm File Delete dialog box, WIN66
Confirm File Replace dialog box, WIN60
Confirm Format Disk dialog box, WIN52
Confirm Mouse Operation dialog box, WIN58
Contents command, WIN33
Contents list, **WIN49**, WIN61, WIN63
Control menu, **WIN16**
Control-menu box, **WIN79**–80
Copy Disk command, **WIN67**, WIN68, WIN70
Copy Disk dialog box, WIN68–69
Copy Disk Error dialog box, WIN71
Copying Disk dialog box, WIN69
Copying dialog box, WIN58
Copying, WIN54–62, WIN71, WIN92–93
  searching for help about, WIN75–77
CRT screen, WIN3
CTRL key, selecting files and, WIN55–57
Current directory, number of files in, WIN49
Current drive, **WIN48**
  changing, WIN61–62
  disk space on, WIN49
Current path, WIN24
Current selection, **WIN11**

Delete command, **WIN65**–66
Delete dialog box, WIN66
Delete text box, WIN66
Desktop, **WIN4**, WIN18, WIN49
Destination directory, **WIN54**
Destination directory icon, WIN55
Destination diskette, **WIN67**, WIN69, WIN70
Destination drive, **WIN54**
Destination drive icon, WIN55
Dialog boxes, **WIN12**–14
Directory, **WIN23**, WIN54–55
Directory path, **WIN24**, WIN48
Directory structure, **WIN24, WIN49**
Directory tree, **WIN49,** WIN61
Directory window, **WIN48**–49
  maximizing, WIN55
Disk, replacing file on, WIN60

Disk Copy command, **WIN71**
Disk drives, WIN48
Disk management, WIN47–71
Disk menu
  Copy Disk, WIN67, WIN68, WIN70
  Format Disk, WIN51–53
Diskette, WIN23
  protecting, WIN67
  saving document on, WIN24–28
Diskette capacity, **WIN50**–51
Diskette drive, WIN48, WIN50–51
Diskette size, **WIN50**–51
Document(s), **WIN14**
  creating, WIN19, WIN44
  printing, WIN20–21, WIN44
Document file, **WIN23**
Dragging window border to resize window, WIN83–84
Drive, WIN23, WIN48, WIN50–51, WIN54, WIN61–62
Drive icons, **WIN48**
Drives drop-down list box, WIN29
Drop-down list box, **WIN13**–14

Editing document file, WIN31, WIN44–45
Edit menu, help and, WIN32–34
Ellipsis, commands and, **WIN11, WIN12**, WIN25
Error Copying File dialog box, WIN59
Error correction
  changing current drive and, WIN62
  copying files and, WIN59–60, WIN71
  double-clicking group icon and, WIN16
  double-clicking program-item icon and, WIN18
  saving document file and, WIN27–28
Error Selecting Drive dialog box, WIN62
Exit command, WIN21–22, WIN28, WIN37
Exiting
  online help, WIN35
  Windows, WIN36–37
Extension, file, **WIN23**

File(s)
  copying to a diskette, WIN54–62
  in current directory, WIN49
  deleting, WIN65–66
  disk space occupied by, WIN49
  editing, WIN31
  naming, WIN23
  opening, WIN28–32
  renaming, WIN63–64
  replacing on disk, WIN60
  saving, WIN31–32
  selecting group of, WIN55–57, WIN92–93
File management, WIN47–80
  deleting files, WIN65–66
  formatting diskettes, WIN50–54
File Manager, **WIN47**–49
  quitting, WIN77, WIN79–80
  starting, WIN50
File Manager Help applications, quitting, WIN77
File Manager Help window, WIN74–75
File Manager icon, WIN50
File Manager menu bar, WIN48
File Manager window, WIN48, WIN55
  maximizing, WIN50
  saving changes to, WIN79
File menu, WIN11
Filename, **WIN23**, WIN48
  changing, WIN63–64
Filename extension, changing, WIN63
File Name list box, WIN30
File Name text box, WIN25
Format Disk command, **WIN51**–53
Format Disk dialog box, WIN52
Format Disk Error dialog box, WIN54
Formatting a diskette, **WIN27, WIN50**–54
  error correction and, WIN54
Formatting Complete dialog box, WIN53
Formatting Disk dialog box, WIN53

Games, Solitaire, WIN43
Glossary definition, help and, WIN34
Go To button, WIN74
Graphical user interface (GUI), **WIN3**
Group icons, WIN14

error correction while double-clicking, WIN16
Group of files
  copying, WIN57–58, WIN92–93
  selecting, WIN55–57, WIN92–93
Group window(s), WIN81–85, WIN94–95
  activating, WIN81–82
  active window, WIN15–16
  closing, WIN82–83
  hidden, WIN81
  opening, WIN14–15
  resizing, WIN83–84

Hard disk, WIN23
Hard drive, WIN48
Help, online, **WIN32**–35, WIN46, WIN71–77, WIN93–94
  exiting, WIN35, WIN77
  searching with, WIN71–77, WIN93–94
Help menu, WIN33
  Search for Help, WIN72
  Windows Tutorial, WIN43
Help topic, **WIN33**–35
  searching for, WIN47, WIN72–75
Help Topics list box, WIN74

Icon(s)
  active, WIN18
  arranging, WIN85
  Control menu for, WIN16
  drive, **WIN48**
  file folder, WIN24
  minimizing application window to, WIN86
Insertion point, **WIN17,** WIN19

Jump, **WIN33**

Keyboard, WIN3, **WIN9**–10
Keyboard shortcuts, **WIN10,** WIN11

Main memory, copying disks and, WIN69, WIN70
Maximize, WIN16
  application window, WIN18
  directory window, WIN55
  File Manager Help window, WIN75
  File Manager window, WIN55
  Help window, WIN33
  Notepad window, WIN28
Maximize button, **WIN18,** WIN50, WIN55
Menu(s), **WIN10**–11, WIN20–21
Menu bar, **WIN10**
Microsoft Windows, *see* Windows, Microsoft
Minimize, WIN16
  application window to an icon, WIN86
Minimize button, WIN83, WIN86
Mouse, WIN3, **WIN5**–9
  clicking, WIN7
  double-clicking, WIN8
  double-clicking and error correction, WIN16–18
  dragging, WIN9
  pointing with, WIN6
Mouse pointer, **WIN6**
  block arrow, WIN6
  double-headed arrow icon, WIN84
  hand, WIN33
  I-beam, WIN17
Mouse skills exercise, WIN43
Move, WIN16

Naming files, WIN23
Next, WIN16
Notepad application, **WIN14**–22
  quitting, WIN32
  starting, WIN28
Notepad dialog box, WIN21, WIN22
Notepad menu, File, WIN25

Open command, WIN29, WIN44–45
Opening file, WIN28–32
Option(s), turning on or off, WIN13
Option buttons, **WIN12**
Options menu, Save Settings on Exit, WIN36, WIN79, WIN80

Paintbrush application, **WIN32**–34, WIN93, WIN94, WIN95
  quitting, WIN35
Phrase, searching for help using, WIN75–77

Pop-up window, **WIN35**
Print command, WIN20–21
Print dialog box, WIN12–14
Printing, WIN44
  by choosing command from menu, WIN20–21
Program Manager menu, WIN10
Program Manager window, WIN80
  activating group window, WIN81
Program-item icons, WIN14
  double-clicking, WIN16–17
  error correction while double-clicking, WIN18

Quitting,
  without saving changes, WIN37

Rename command, **WIN63**–64
Rename dialog box, WIN64
Resizing group window, WIN83–84
Restore, WIN16
Restore button, **WIN18,** WIN55
Retrieving files, WIN29–30
Retry button, WIN59, WIN62
Root directory, **WIN23,** WIN24, WIN49

Save As command, WIN25
Save As dialog box, WIN25, WIN27–29
Save command, WIN31
Save Settings on Exit command, WIN36, **WIN79,** WIN80
Saving, WIN24–28, WIN44
  modified document file, WIN31–32
Screen, WIN3, WIN4
Scroll arrows, **WIN16**
Scroll bar, **WIN16**
Scroll box, **WIN16**
Search dialog box, WIN72, WIN76
Search feature, help and, WIN47, WIN71–77, WIN93–94
Search for Help on command, **WIN72**
Search topics, WIN72
Selected button, **WIN12**
Selecting a menu, **WIN11**
Selecting files search topic, WIN73
Selection, current, **WIN13**
SHIFT key, selecting group of files and, WIN57
Show Topics button, WIN73–74, WIN76
Size, Control menu and, WIN16
Size, group window, WIN83–84
Software, user interface and, WIN3
Source directory, WIN54
Source diskette, **WIN67,** WIN68–69
Source drive, **WIN54**
Split bar, directory window and, **WIN49**
Status bar, WIN49
Subdirectories, **WIN23,** WIN49

Text box, **WIN13**
Tile command, **WIN94**
Title bar, **WIN4**
  dialog box and, WIN12
Tutorial, WIN43
TXT extension, WIN25–26

User friendly, **WIN3**
User interface, WIN3

Window border, **WIN4**
  dragging to resize window, WIN83–84
Window corner, dragging, WIN84
Window menu, WIN81, WIN85, WIN94
Window title, **WIN4**
Windows, **WIN4**
  activating group, WIN81–82
  dialog box and, WIN12
  directory, WIN48–49
  minimizing to icon, WIN86
Windows, Microsoft, **WIN2,** WIN3
  communicating with, WIN5–14
  mouse operations and, WIN5–9
  quitting, WIN36–37
  starting, WIN4–5, WIN49–50
  tutorial, WIN43
  using, WIN14–22
Word, searching for help using, WIN75–77
Write application, WIN93
Write-protect window, WIN70
Write-protected diskette, **WIN27,** WIN28, WIN54, WIN60, WIN67, WIN70

SPREADSHEETS

USING *Lotus 1-2-3* RELEASE 5 FOR *Windows*

▶ PROJECT ONE

BUILDING A WORKSHEET

Objectives **L2**
Introduction **L2**
What Is Lotus 1-2-3 for Windows? **L3**
Project One **L3**
Starting Lotus 1-2-3 Release 5 for Windows **L4**
The 1-2-3 Window **L6**
Selecting a Cell **L10**
Entering Labels **L11**
Entering Values **L17**
Calculating a Sum **L19**
Copying a Cell to Adjacent Cells **L20**
Saving a Worksheet **L25**
Using Formatting Templates to Format the Worksheet **L27**
Charting a Worksheet **L30**
Printing a Worksheet **L37**
Closing the Worksheet **L39**
Exiting 1-2-3 **L39**
Opening a Worksheet File **L40**
Correcting Errors **L42**
1-2-3 Online Help **L46**
1-2-3 Classic Menu **L48**
Project Summary **L49**
Key Terms and Index **L49**
Quick Reference **L50**
Student Assignments **L51**
Computer Laboratory Exercises **L56**
Computer Laboratory Assignments **L58**

▶ PROJECT TWO

FORMULAS AND WORKSHEET ENHANCEMENT

Objectives **L62**
Introduction **L62**
Project Two **L63**
Starting Lotus 1-2-3 Release 5 for Windows **L65**
Entering Worksheet Titles **L65**
Entering Data **L66**
Saving the Worksheet **L84**
Understanding Fonts and Font Attributes **L84**
Formatting Labels **L85**
Formatting Values **L90**
Changing the Widths of Columns and Heights of Rows **L93**
Adding Color to the Worksheet **L98**
Charting the Worksheet **L102**
Checking Spelling **L108**
Print Preview and Printing the Worksheet Data Separately from the Chart **L112**
Printing the Chart Separately from the Worksheet **L115**
Displaying and Printing the Formulas in the Worksheet **L116**
Project Summary **L117**
Key Terms and Index **L118**
Quick Reference **L118**
Student Assignments **L119**
Computer Laboratory Exercises **L124**
Computer Laboratory Assignments **L127**

▶ PROJECT THREE

WHAT-IF ANALYSIS

Objectives **L134**
Introduction **L134**
Project Three **L134**
Starting Lotus 1-2-3 Release 5 for Windows **L137**
Changing Worksheet Style Defaults **L137**
Creating Text Blocks **L139**
Using Drag and Fill to Enter a Data Sequence in a Range **L142**
Using Drag and Drop to Copy Cells **L145**
Entering the Revenue Values **L148**
Rounding **L149**
Absolute Cell References **L149**
Saving the File **L158**
Formatting Text Blocks **L158**
Formatting the Worksheet **L164**
Multiple Worksheets **L173**
Creating a Stacked Bar Chart **L176**
Enhancing a Stacked Bar Chart **L183**
Checking the Spelling of a Worksheet **L187**
Print Preview and Printing a Worksheet in Landscape **L187**
Changing Values in Cells Referenced in a Formula **L191**
Project Summary **L193**
Key Terms and Index **L194**
Quick Reference **L194**
SmartIcon Reference **L196**
Student Assignments **L196**
Computer Laboratory Exercises **L200**
Computer Laboratory Assignments **L202**

▶ PROJECT FOUR

MULTIPLE WORKSHEETS

Objectives **L209**
Introduction **L209**
Project Four **L209**
Starting Lotus 1-2-3 Release 5 for Windows **L212**
Creating Multiple Worksheets **L212**
Creating a Consolidated Worksheet **L218**
Formatting Multiple Worksheets **L226**
Saving the File **L237**
Creating a Pie Chart **L237**
Printing Multiple Worksheets **L246**
Project Summary **L254**
Key Terms and Index **L254**
Quick Reference **L254**
Student Assignments **L255**
Computer Laboratory Exercises **L260**
Computer Laboratory Assignments **L261**

▶ PROJECT FIVE

CHARTS AND MAPS

Objectives **L269**
Introduction **L269**
Types of Charts **L269**
Creating a Chart **L271**
Line Charts **L272**
Mixed Charts **L284**
High-Low-Close-Open Charts **L295**

Chart Summary **L299**
Maps **L299**
Project Summary **L305**
Key Terms and Index **L306**
Quick Reference **L306**
Student Assignments **L308**
Computer Laboratory Exercises **L312**
Computer Laboratory Assignments **L313**

▶ PROJECT SIX

DATA ANALYSIS

Objectives **L318**
Introduction **L318**
Project Six **L319**
Creating the Seminar Variables Section **L321**
Creating the Management Seminars Section **L324**
Formatting the Worksheet **L334**
Saving the File **L336**
Using Backsolver to Analyze Worksheet Data **L336**
Using a 1-Variable What-If Table to Analyze Worksheet Data **L338**
Creating a Macro to Automate Data Entry **L346**
Working with a Macro Button **L352**
Running a Macro with a Button **L355**
Documenting the Macro **L358**
Creating a Macro to Print the Worksheet **L358**
Formatting the Macros Worksheet **L363**
Using Version Manager to Analyze Data **L363**
Protecting Data **L370**
Project Summary **L374**
Key Terms and Index **L374**
Quick Reference **L375**
Student Assignments **L375**
Computer Laboratory Exercises **L380**
Computer Laboratory Assignments **L383**

▶ PROJECT SEVEN

WORKING WITH DATABASE TABLES

Objectives **L391**
Introduction **L391**
Project Seven **L391**
Starting Lotus 1-2-3 Release 5 for Windows **L393**
Creating a Database Table **L393**
Formatting the Database Table **L395**
Saving the File **L397**
Sorting a Database Table **L397**
Finding Records Using Criteria **L402**
Query Tables **L410**
Creating a Crosstab Table to Summarize Database Table Information **L421**
Project Summary **L427**
Key Terms and Index **L427**
Quick Reference **L427**
Student Assignments **L428**
Computer Laboratory Exercises **L432**
Computer Laboratory Assignments **L434**

INDEX L442

Lotus 1-2-3 RELEASE 5 FOR Windows

P R O J E C T O N E

▼

BUILDING A WORKSHEET

OBJECTIVES You will have mastered the material in this project when you can:

- ▶ Start 1-2-3 for Windows
- ▶ Describe the worksheet
- ▶ Select a cell or range of cells
- ▶ Enter labels and values
- ▶ Use the SmartSum icon to sum a range of cells in a row or in a column
- ▶ Copy a cell to a range of adjacent cells
- ▶ Use the Gallery command on the Style menu to format a range

- ▶ Chart a worksheet
- ▶ Save a worksheet
- ▶ Print a worksheet
- ▶ Close a worksheet
- ▶ Exit 1-2-3 for Windows
- ▶ Open a worksheet
- ▶ Correct errors on a worksheet
- ▶ Use 1-2-3's online Help
- ▶ Use 1-2-3's Tutorial

▶ INTRODUCTION

L otus 1-2-3 Release 5 for Windows allows you to enter data in a worksheet, perform calculations on that data, ask what-if questions regarding the data in the worksheet, make decisions based on the results found in the worksheet, chart data in a worksheet, and develop presentation-quality reports.

As a result of the capabilities of Lotus 1-2-3 Release 5 for Windows, you can accomplish such tasks as sales forecasting and inventory control, investment planning and financial reporting, or marketing analysis and product development. In addition, you can present the data as a worksheet or as a chart in printed reports.

1-2-3 also allows you to change data and automatically recalculate your worksheets. You can create sets of different data for a given application to show the effects of certain changes in the data. For example, you can develop an optimistic set of data for projected sales and a pessimistic set of data for projected sales to show the effect each set would have on the projected profit for a company.

▶ What Is Lotus 1-2-3 for Windows?

Lotus 1-2-3 for Windows is an electronic spreadsheet that allows you to enter data, perform calculations, make decisions, organize data, chart data, and develop professional reports. An electronic spreadsheet, or worksheet, is an automated version of the accountant's ledger consisting of rows and columns of data. 1-2-3 offers the following features for your use:

- ▶ **Worksheets**   Worksheets allow you to enter, calculate, manipulate, and analyze data such as numbers and text.
- ▶ **Charts**   Charts pictorially represent data found in a worksheet. 1-2-3 can create two- or three-dimensional line, bar, pie, and other types of charts.
- ▶ **Databases**   Databases allow you to manage data. Using 1-2-3, you can store and retrieve data, sort data, find and extract specific data, and substitute new data for old.

▶ Project One

To illustrate the features of 1-2-3, this book presents a series of projects that use 1-2-3 to solve typical business problems. Project 1 uses 1-2-3 to produce the worksheet data and three-dimensional (3D) bar chart shown in Figure 1-1.

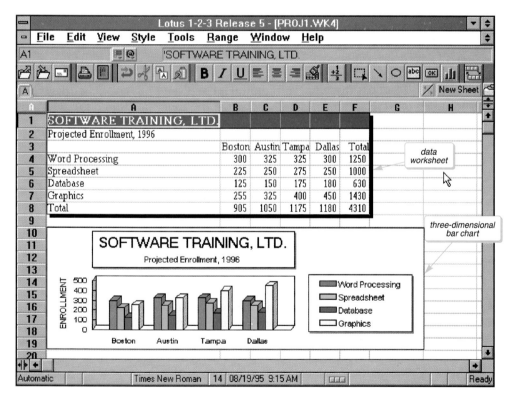

FIGURE 1-1

The worksheet contains SOFTWARE TRAINING, LTD.'s projected enrollment in software training classes for Boston, Austin, Tampa, and Dallas in 1996. The training classes fall into four categories: Word Processing, Spreadsheet, Database, and Graphics. 1-2-3 calculates the total projected enrollment for each city, the total projected enrollment for each training class; and, for all classes in all cities, the total projected enrollment for the entire year.

The 3D bar chart in Figure 1-1 on the previous page graphically displays the projected enrollment for the four categories of classes by city. 1-2-3 creates the chart based on the data in the worksheet.

Worksheet Preparation Steps

The following worksheet preparation steps provide an overview of how the worksheet and chart illustrated in Figure 1-1 on the previous page will be built in this project.

1. Start Lotus 1-2-3 Release 5 for Windows.
2. Enter the worksheet titles (SOFTWARE TRAINING, LTD. and Projected Enrollment, 1996), the column titles (Boston, Austin, Tampa, Dallas, and Total), and the row titles (Word Processing, Spreadsheet, Database, Graphics, and Total).
3. Enter the projected class enrollments (Word Processing, Spreadsheet, Database, and Graphics) for Boston, Austin, Tampa, and Dallas.
4. Enter the formulas to calculate the total projected enrollment for each city, the total projected enrollment for each category of class, and the total projected enrollment for the year.
5. Use a format template to format the worksheet titles (change the color of row 1, change the color of the title, change the font, adjust the height of row 1, and adjust the width of column A) and the body of the worksheet (add an outline and drop shadow, change the font, and adjust the width of the columns).
6. Create the 3D bar chart based on data in the worksheet.
7. Save the worksheet and chart on disk.
8. Print the worksheet.
9. Close the worksheet and exit 1-2-3 for Windows.

The following pages contain a detailed explanation of each of these steps.

▶ STARTING LOTUS 1-2-3 RELEASE 5 FOR WINDOWS

T o start Lotus 1-2-3 Release 5 for Windows, Windows must be running, Program Manager must display on the screen, and the Lotus Applications group window must be open. Perform the following steps to start Lotus 1-2-3 Release 5 for Windows.

TO START LOTUS 1-2-3 RELEASE 5 FOR WINDOWS ▼

STEP 1 ►

Use the mouse to point to the Lotus 1-2-3 Release 5 program-item icon ( ) in the Lotus Applications group window (Figure 1-2).

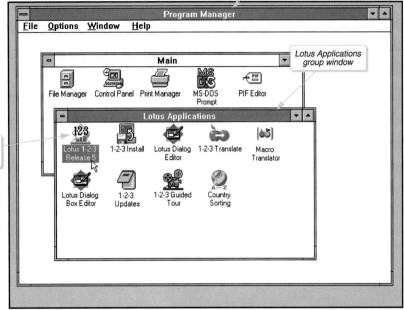

FIGURE 1-2

STEP 2 ►

Double-click the left mouse button. When the Welcome to 1-2-3 dialog box displays on the screen, point to the OK button in the Welcome to 1-2-3 dialog box.

1-2-3 displays the 1-2-3 program title screen briefly and then opens the 1-2-3 window containing a blank 1-2-3 worksheet with the title, Untitled, in the title bar (Figure 1-3). 1-2-3 displays the Welcome to 1-2-3 dialog box. The Create a new worksheet option button contains a solid black circle indicating it is selected. Be aware that the Welcome to 1-2-3 dialog box does not always appear. It will be bypassed if you have previously chosen the Don't show this screen again check box. The mouse pointer points to the OK button.

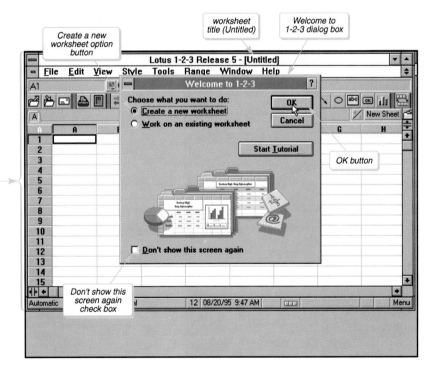

FIGURE 1-3

STEP 3 ▶

Choose the OK button in the Welcome to 1-2-3 dialog box. When the New File dialog box displays on the screen, point to the OK button in the New File dialog box.

1-2-3 displays the New File dialog box (Figure 1-4). The Create a plain worksheet check box contains an X indicating it is selected. The mouse pointer points to the OK button in the New File dialog box.

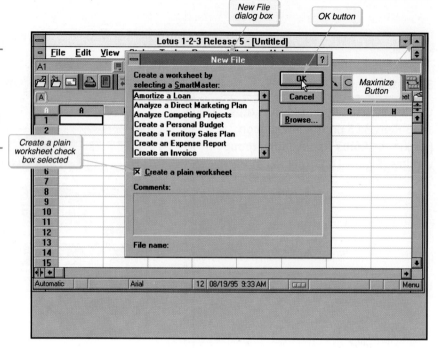

FIGURE 1-4

STEP 4 ▶

Choose the OK button in the New File dialog box. When the New File dialog box is removed from the screen, maximize the 1-2-3 window by pointing to the Maximize button (▲) in the upper right corner of the window and clicking the left mouse button.

1-2-3 removes the New File dialog box from the screen and maximizes the 1-2-3 window (Figure 1-5).

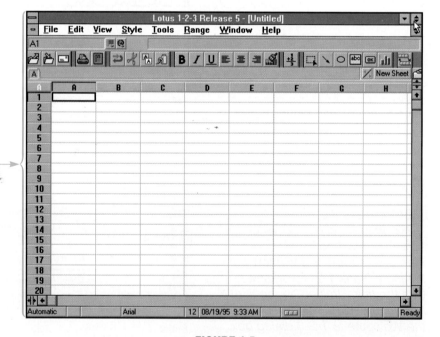

FIGURE 1-5

▶ THE 1-2-3 WINDOW

The 1-2-3 window (Figure 1-6) is divided into three areas: the control panel, the work area, and the status bar. The **control panel** consists of the top three lines of the 1-2-3 window. The **work area** is the area between the control panel and the status bar. The **status bar** displays at the bottom of the 1-2-3 window. Together, these parts enable you to create and display worksheets and charts.

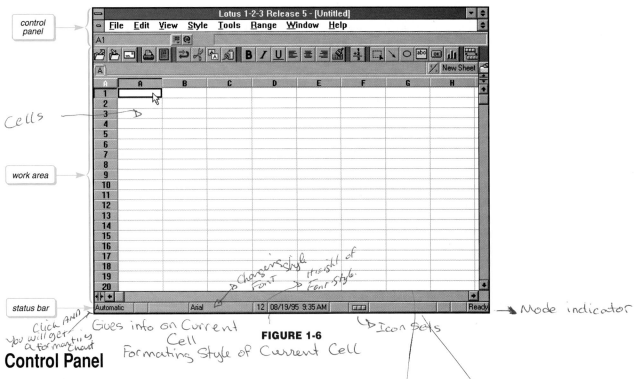

FIGURE 1-6

Handwritten annotations:
Cells
Click AND you will get a formatting chart
Gives info on Current Cell
Formating Style of Current Cell
Changes Style of Font I
It is ight of Font Style.
Icon Sets
Mode indicator

Control Panel

The control panel (Figure 1-7) displays information about 1-2-3 and the active window. It contains the title bar, the main menu, and the edit line.

TITLE BAR   The title bar contains the Control menu box, the application name (Lotus 1-2-3 Release 5), the file name (Untitled), the Minimize button, and the Restore button. 1-2-3 also uses the title bar to display specific information, as you will be shown throughout the projects.

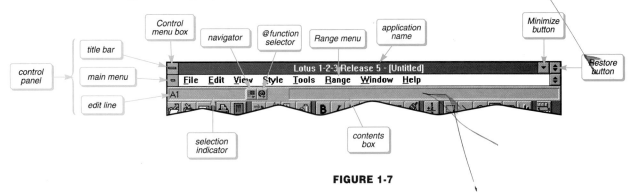

FIGURE 1-7

MAIN MENU   The **main menu** displays the 1-2-3 menu names. Each menu name represents a menu of commands you can choose to retrieve, save, print, and manipulate data in the worksheet. To display a menu, such as the File menu or the Edit menu, select the menu name by pointing to the menu name on the menu bar and clicking the left mouse button.

One name on the main menu changes depending on the type of work you are doing. If you are working with a chart rather than a worksheet, the **Chart menu** name replaces the **Range menu** name.

EDIT LINE The **edit line** is used to display and edit data. The edit line consists of the selection indicator, navigator, @function selector, and contents box. The **selection indicator** displays the location of the current selection in a worksheet. The **contents box** displays the entry you are typing. The purpose of the navigator and the @function selector will be explained when they are used in subsequent projects.

Work Area

The work area contains the set of SmartIcons and the 1-2-3 worksheet.

SMARTICONS **SmartIcons** allow you to perform frequently used commands more quickly than you can when using the main menu. For example, to print a worksheet you can click the Print icon on the set of SmartIcons rather than choose the Print command from the File menu.

Each **icon** contains a picture that helps you remember its function. You click the icon to cause the command to execute. In addition, when you point the mouse pointer to any icon on the set of SmartIcons, a description appears in a text bubble below the icon. Figure 1-8 illustrates the default set of SmartIcons that displays when you start 1-2-3 and names the function of each icon. 1-2-3 automatically displays different SmartIcon sets depending on the task you are performing. For example, when you are working on a chart, 1-2-3 displays charting SmartIcons.

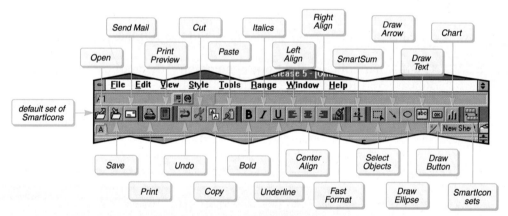

FIGURE 1-8

The use of each of the SmartIcons will be explained in detail as it is used in the projects.

THE 1-2-3 WORKSHEET The **1-2-3 worksheet** is an electronic spreadsheet that is organized into a rectangular grid of columns (vertical) and rows (horizontal) (Figure 1-9). A **column letter**, which is a letter of the alphabet above the grid, identifies each **column**. A **row number**, which is a number down the left side of the grid, identifies each **row**. Eight complete columns (lettered A through H) and twenty complete rows (numbered 1 through 20) appear on the screen when the worksheet is maximized.

A single work-sheet contains 256 columns, labeled A through Z, AA through AZ, BA through BZ, and so on to IV, and 8,192 rows, numbered 1 through 8192. The columns and rows not visible on the screen can be displayed by scrolling.

Initially, 1-2-3 displays only one worksheet on the screen. You can insert additional worksheets and create a multi-sheet file that has up to 256 worksheets. Each worksheet is identified by a letter from A to IV. The worksheet letter appears in the top left corner of the worksheet above the row numbers and in the **worksheet tab**, located above the worksheet letter.

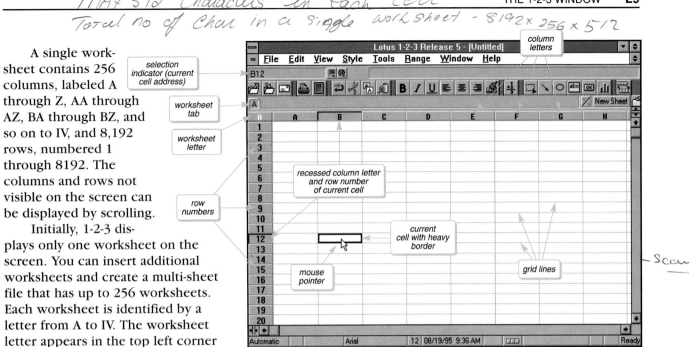

FIGURE 1-9

Scan

Scan

Horizontal Scroll you can see all the Columns.

The intersection of each column and each row is a cell. A **cell** is the basic unit of a worksheet into which you enter data. Each cell has a unique address, which is the column letter of the intersection followed by the row number of the intersection. For example, in Figure 1-9, the address of the cell with the heavy border is B12 because it is located at the intersection of column B and row 12. If there is more than one worksheet, 1-2-3 adds a letter to identify the worksheet. This letter is separated from the cell address by a colon (for example A:B12).

The **current cell** on a worksheet is the cell into which you can enter data. 1-2-3 identifies the current cell in three ways. First, 1-2-3 places the **cell pointer** (a heavy border) around the current cell. Second, 1-2-3 displays the cell address of the current cell in the selection indicator. Third, the column letter and the row number of the current cell are recessed in the worksheet border. In Figure 1-9, the current cell is B12.

The horizontal and vertical lines on the worksheet itself are called **grid lines**. They are intended to make it easier to see and identify each cell on the worksheet.

The **mouse pointer** is a symbol used to point to areas of the screen and indicate which area of the screen will be affected when you click a mouse button. The pointer is often shaped like an arrow, but it can change shape depending on the task you are performing and its location on the screen. In Figure 1-9, the mouse pointer has the shape of a block arrow (⇖). The other **mouse pointer shapes** will be described when they appear on the screen in this and subsequent projects.

Only a small fraction of the worksheet displays on the screen at one time (Figure 1-10 on the next page). Scroll bars, scroll arrows, and scroll boxes you can use to move the window around the worksheet are located below and to the right of the worksheet window.

Press Home Key To got to A1. wherever you Are.

or

Press F5 + key in the location you want to go to

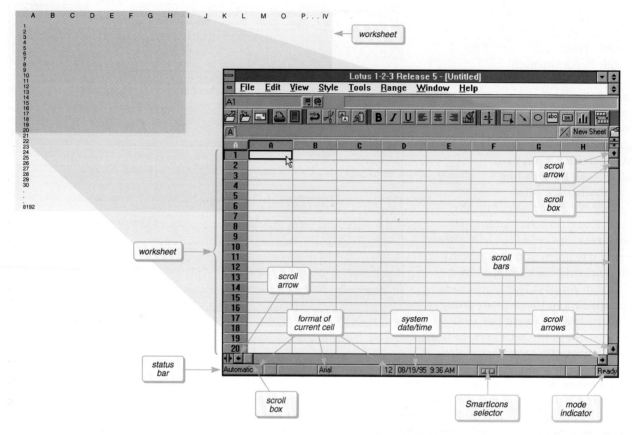

FIGURE 1-10

STATUS BAR The **status bar** displays at the bottom of the 1-2-3 window. The status bar contains a collection of selection buttons that display information about the 1-2-3 worksheet, and menus that allow you to make adjustments to the worksheet. The left half of the status bar in Figure 1-10 displays information about the current cell. The system date and time display toward the middle of the status bar. Clicking the SmartIcons selector ( ) to the right of the date and time will display names of other sets of SmartIcons.

The indicator at the far right is the mode indicator. **Mode indicators**, such as Ready and Wait, specify the current mode of 1-2-3. When the mode is Ready, as shown in Figure 1-10, 1-2-3 is ready to accept the next command or data entry. When the mode indicator is Wait, 1-2-3 is in the process of completing a command, such as saving a file.

▶ SELECTING A CELL

To enter data into the current cell, you must first **select** the current cell into which the data will be entered. The easiest method to select the current cell is to move the mouse pointer to the desired cell and click the left mouse button.

An alternative method is to use the arrow keys located just to the right of the alphabetic keys on the keyboard. After you press an arrow key, the adjacent cell in the direction of the arrow on the key becomes the current cell.

As noted previously, you know a cell is the current cell when the cell pointer surrounds the cell and the cell address displays in the selection indicator in the edit line.

▶ ENTERING LABELS

1 -2-3 for Windows recognizes two types of entries into a cell: labels and values. Any text entry containing a letter is considered a **label** by 1-2-3. A **value** represents numeric data. Labels are used for titles such as worksheet titles, column titles, and row titles. Labels can also contain numbers or a combination of numbers and letters.

In Project 1, the worksheet titles, SOFTWARE TRAINING, LTD. and Projected Enrollment, 1996, identify the worksheet (Figure 1-11). The column titles are the names of the four cities on the worksheet (Boston, Austin, Tampa, Dallas) and Total. The row titles are Word Processing, Spreadsheet, Database, Graphics, and Total and identify each row in the worksheet.

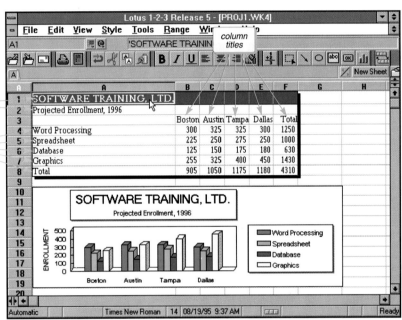

FIGURE 1-11

Entering the Worksheet Titles

The following example explains the steps to enter the worksheet titles into cell A1 and cell A2 of the worksheet.

TO ENTER THE WORKSHEET TITLES ▼

STEP 1 ▶

Select cell A1 by pointing to cell A1 and clicking the left mouse button.

1-2-3 places the cell pointer around cell A1 and displays the cell address A1 in the selection indicator (Figure 1-12). Cell A1 is the current cell.

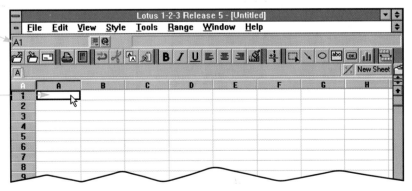

FIGURE 1-12

STEP 2 ►

Press the CAPS LOCK key, type the label, SOFTWARE TRAINING, LTD. and press the CAPS LOCK key again.

*When you type the first character, the cell pointer disappears, the mode indicator in the status bar changes from Ready to Label, and 1-2-3 displays two buttons in the edit line: the **Cancel button** (⊠) and the **Confirm button** (☑) (Figure 1-13). As you type characters, each character displays in the cell followed immediately by a blinking vertical bar (|) called the **insertion point**. The insertion point indicates where the next character typed will display. 1-2-3 also displays the data in the con-*
tents box as it is typed. Notice also that the mouse pointer changes from a block arrow to an I-beam (I). Whenever the mouse pointer is located in the current cell when you enter data, it will change to an I-beam. If you make a typing mistake, press the BACKSPACE key until the error is erased, and then retype the text.

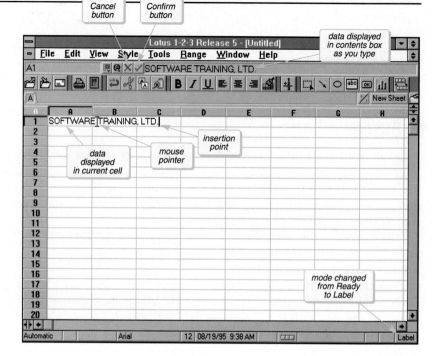

FIGURE 1-13

STEP 3 ►

After you type the label, point to the Confirm button.

The mouse pointer points to the Confirm button in the edit line (Figure 1-14).

labels can have
3 prefixs
1 - Single quote for
left alignment
(set as default)
^ - Center alignment
" - Right alignment

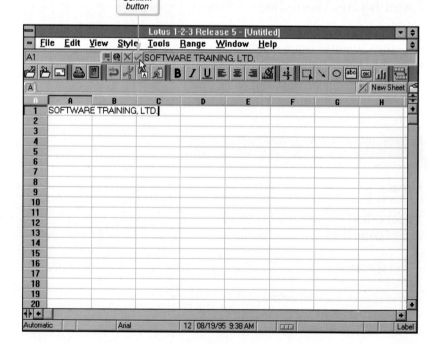

FIGURE 1-14

STEP 4 ▶

Click the Confirm button to confirm the entry.

1-2-3 confirms the entry of the label in cell A1 (Figure 1-15). The mode indicator changes to Ready and both the Cancel button and the Confirm button disappear from the edit line. The cell pointer displays around the current cell, A1. Notice the label overflows into column B and column C.

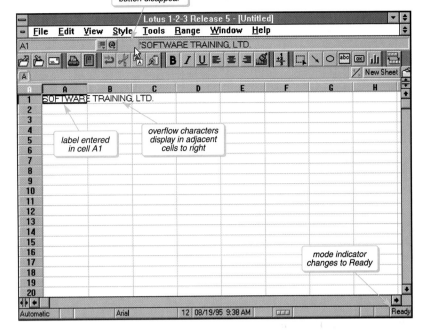

FIGURE 1-15

STEP 5 ▶

Press the DOWN ARROW key.

Cell A2 becomes the current cell (Figure 1-16). Notice that the row number and column letter of the current cell are recessed.

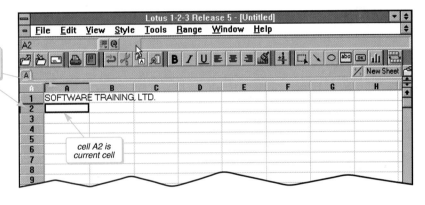

FIGURE 1-16

STEP 6 ▶

Type the label, `Projected Enrollment, 1996`**, and click the Confirm button in the edit line to confirm the entry.**

1-2-3 confirms the entry of the label in cell A2 (Figure 1-17). The label overflows into column B and column C.

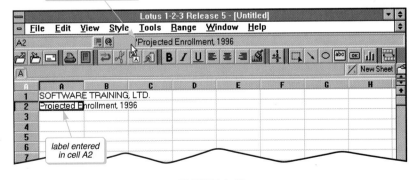

FIGURE 1-17

In the example above, rather than using the mouse and Confirm button to confirm the entry, you can press the ENTER key after typing the label. Pressing the ENTER key replaces Step 3 and Step 4.

When you confirm a label entry into a cell, a series of events occur. First, when the label displays in the contents box in the edit line, 1-2-3 displays it preceded by a **label-prefix character**, which identifies the entry as a label and determines how the label is positioned in the cell. Figure 1-17 on the previous page shows the worksheet title in cell A2 preceded by a single apostrophe in the edit line. The apostrophe label-prefix character causes 1-2-3 to **left-align** the label in the cell. Therefore, the P in the word Projected begins in the leftmost position of cell A2. When you type a label, 1-2-3 automatically enters a single apostrophe as the label-prefix character.

Second, when the label you enter contains more characters than can be displayed in the width of the cell, 1-2-3 displays the overflow characters in adjacent cells to the right as long as these adjacent cells contain no data. In Figure 1-17, column A has a width of nine, which is the default width of all columns on the 1-2-3 worksheet. The label in cell A1 contains twenty-three characters and the label in cell A2 contains twenty-six characters. Therefore, because the cells in column B and column C contain no data, 1-2-3 displays the overflow characters in columns B and C.

Third, when you confirm an entry into a cell by clicking the Confirm button in the edit line or pressing the ENTER key, the cell in which the data is entered remains the current cell.

Correcting a Mistake While Typing

If you type the wrong letter and notice the error before clicking the Confirm button or pressing the ENTER key, use the **BACKSPACE key** to erase all the characters back to and including the ones that are not correct. The insertion point will indicate where in the label the next character you type will display. Then, retype the remainder of the label entry.

To cancel the entire entry before confirming it, click the Cancel button or press the ESC key.

If you find an error in data you have already entered into a cell, select the cell and retype the entire entry. Later in this project, additional error-correction techniques will be explained.

Entering Column Titles

To enter the **column titles**, select the appropriate cell and then enter the label, as illustrated in the following steps.

TO ENTER COLUMN TITLES

STEP 1 ▶

Select cell B3 by pointing to cell B3 and clicking the left mouse button.

Cell B3 becomes the current cell (Figure 1-18). The cell address in the selection indicator changes from A2 to B3.

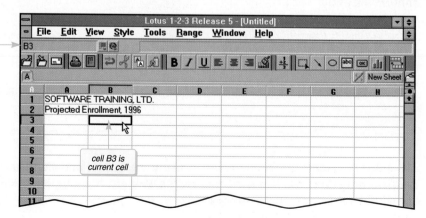

FIGURE 1-18

STEP 2 ▶

Type the column title, Boston.

1-2-3 displays Boston in the contents box in the edit line and in cell B3, which is the current cell (Figure 1-19). Because the mouse pointer is located in the current cell while data is entered, it changes to an I-beam.

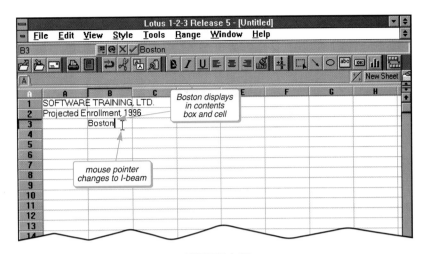

FIGURE 1-19

STEP 3 ▶

Press the RIGHT ARROW key.

1-2-3 makes cell C3 the current cell (Figure 1-20). When you press an arrow key to confirm an entry, 1-2-3 enters the data and then makes the adjacent cell in the direction of the arrow (up, down, left, or right) the current cell.

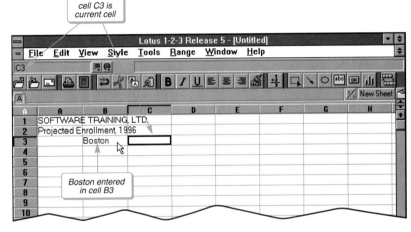

FIGURE 1-20

STEP 4 ▶

Repeat Step 2 and Step 3 for the remaining column titles. That is, enter Austin **in cell C3,** Tampa **in cell D3,** Dallas **in cell E3, and** Total **in cell F3. Confirm the last column title entry in cell F3 by clicking the Confirm button or by pressing the ENTER key.**

The column titles display as shown in Figure 1-21.

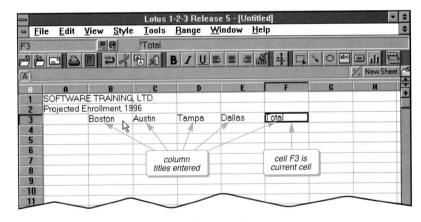

FIGURE 1-21

When confirming an entry in a cell, use the arrow keys if the next entry is in an adjacent cell. If the next entry is not in an adjacent cell, click the Confirm button in the edit line or press the ENTER key, and then use the mouse to select the appropriate cell for the next entry.

Entering Row Titles

The next step in developing the worksheet in Project 1 is to enter the row titles in column A. This process is described in the following steps.

TO ENTER ROW TITLES ▼

STEP 1 ▶

Select cell A4 by pointing to cell A4 and clicking the left mouse button.

Cell A4 is the current cell (Figure 1-22).

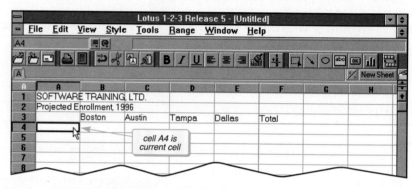

FIGURE 1-22

STEP 2 ▶

Type the row title, Word Processing, **and press the DOWN ARROW key.**

1-2-3 enters the row title, Word Processing, into cell A4 and makes cell A5 the current cell (Figure 1-23). The label overflows from cell A4 into cell B4.

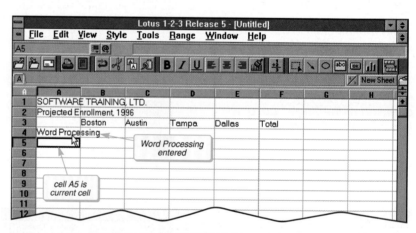

FIGURE 1-23

STEP 3 ▶

Type Spreadsheet **in cell A5, and press the DOWN ARROW key. Continue this sequence by entering** Database **in cell A6,** Graphics **in cell A7, and** Total **in cell A8. Confirm the last row title in cell A8 by clicking the Confirm button or pressing the ENTER key.**

The row titles display as shown in Figure 1-24.

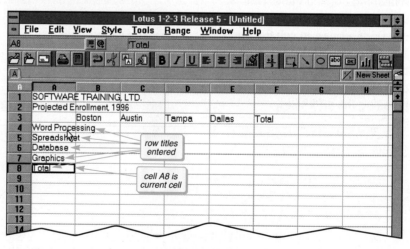

FIGURE 1-24

▶ ENTERING VALUES

A value is the second type of entry you can enter into cells. A **value** represents numeric data and can include the digits zero through nine and any one of the following characters: + – ( ) , / . $ % @ *.

If a cell entry contains any other character from the keyboard, 1-2-3 identifies the entry as a label and treats it accordingly.

In Project 1, the projected enrollment for Boston, Austin, Tampa, and Dallas for each of the categories, Word Processing, Spreadsheet, Database, and Graphics, must be entered in rows 4, 5, 6, and 7. The following steps illustrate how to enter these values one row at a time.

TO ENTER VALUES ▼

STEP 1 ▶

Select cell B4 by pointing to cell B4 and clicking the left mouse button.

1-2-3 makes cell B4 the current cell (Figure 1-25). Notice the overlapping entry from cell A4 still displays in cell B4.

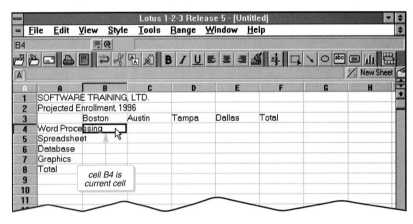

FIGURE 1-25

STEP 2 ▶

Type the number 300.

When you type the first digit, the overlapping portion of the label in cell A4 is replaced with the new value (3). You will change column A to a proper width to display the title, Word Processing, when you format the worksheet after you have entered all the data. The mode indicator changes from Ready to Value and the Confirm and Cancel buttons display in the edit line (Figure 1-26). The value 300 displays in the contents box and in the cell.

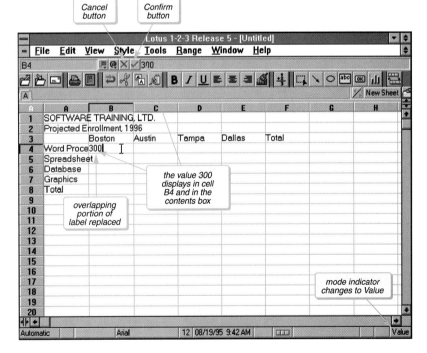

FIGURE 1-26

STEP 3 ▶

Press the RIGHT ARROW key.

1-2-3 confirms the value 300 in cell B4 and makes cell C4 the current cell (Figure 1-27).

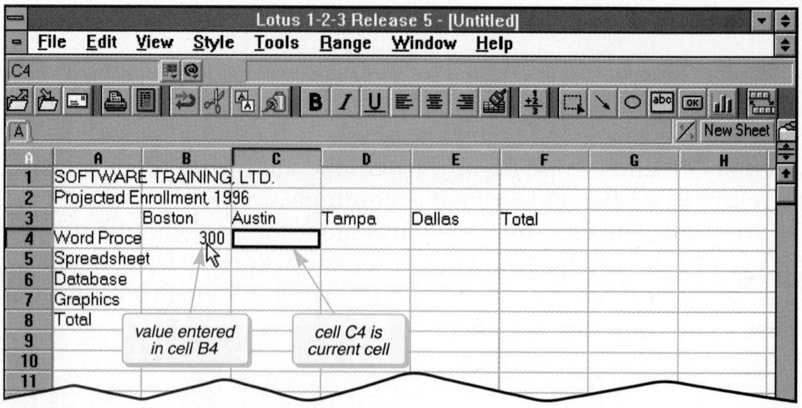

FIGURE 1-27

STEP 4 ▶

Using the same technique as in Step 2 and Step 3, enter 325 into cell C4, enter 325 into cell D4, and enter 300 into cell E4. Press the ENTER key or click the Confirm button to enter the value into cell E4.

Row 4 contains the projected enrollment for Word Processing classes in 1996 (Figure 1-28).

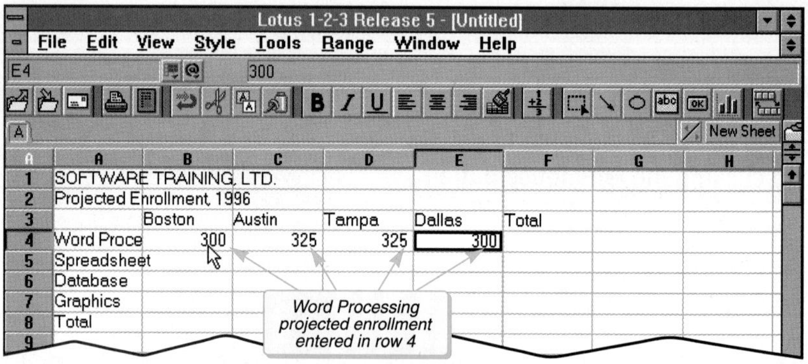

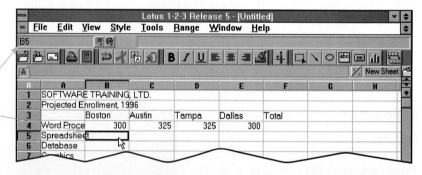

FIGURE 1-28

STEP 5 ▶

Select cell B5 by pointing to cell B5 and clicking the left mouse button.

1-2-3 makes cell B5 the current cell (Figure 1-29).

FIGURE 1-29

STEP 6 ▶

Repeat the procedures used in Step 2 through Step 4 to enter the Spreadsheet, Database, and Graphics projected enrollments for the year. Press the ENTER key or click the Confirm button to enter the value into cell E7.

The Spreadsheet, Database, and Graphics projected enrollments are entered in rows 5, 6, and 7, respectively (Figure 1-30).

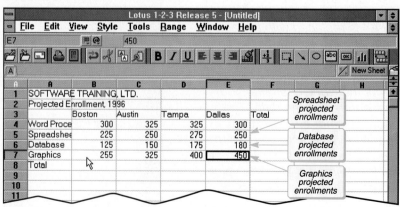

FIGURE 1-30

You have now entered all labels and values required for this worksheet. Notice several important points. First, by default, 1-2-3 enters values **right-aligned** in the cells, which means they occupy the rightmost positions in the cells.

Second, although the long labels, Word Processing and Spreadsheet, in cells A4 and A5 do not display completely in the worksheet, 1-2-3 stores the entire label in each cell. To see the entire label, select the desired cell. The label displays in the contents box in the edit line. As noted previously, when you format the worksheet, column A will be wide enough to display the entire label.

Third, you can use 1-2-3 to calculate the totals in row 8 and column F. The capability of 1-2-3 to perform calculations is one of its major features.

▶ CALCULATING A SUM

The next step in creating the SOFTWARE TRAINING, LTD. worksheet is to calculate the total projected enrollment for Boston. To calculate this value and enter it into cell B8, 1-2-3 must add the numbers in cells B4, B5, B6, and B7. 1-2-3's @functions provide a convenient means to accomplish this task.

An **@function** is a set of predefined instructions that accomplishes a specific task, such as adding a column or a row of numbers. When using 1-2-3, an @function is identified by an @ sign followed by the name of the function. For example, the function that adds a column or a row of numbers is called the @SUM function.

To use the @SUM function, you must first identify the cell in which the sum will be stored after it is calculated. Then, you can use the SmartSum icon ( ) on the set of SmartIcons to enter the function into the cell and actually calculate the sum of the numbers. The following steps illustrate how to use the SmartSum icon to sum the projected enrollments for Boston in cells B4, B5, B6, and B7 and enter the sum in cell B8. If the work area of your screen does not contain the set of SmartIcons as displayed in Figure 1-30 on the previous page, click the SmartIcons selector in the status bar (see Figure 1-10 on page L10), and choose Default Sheet.

TO SUM A COLUMN OF NUMBERS USING THE SMARTSUM ICON ▼

STEP 1 ▶

Select the cell that will contain the sum – cell B8.

Cell B8 is the current cell (Figure 1-31).

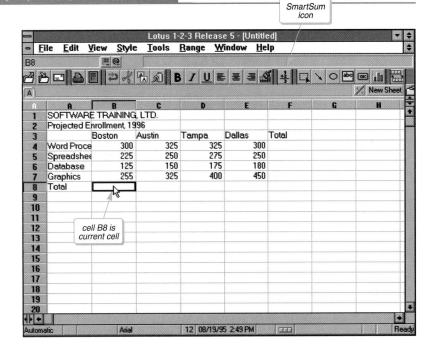

FIGURE 1-31

STEP 2 ▶

Point to and click the SmartSum icon on the set of SmartIcons displayed below the edit line.

1-2-3 displays the sum of the projected enrollments for Boston, (905 = 300 + 225 + 125 + 255), in cell B8 (Figure 1-32). 1-2-3 also displays @SUM(B4..B7) in the contents box in the edit line. The @SUM entry identifies the @SUM function. The B4..B7 entry within parentheses following the function name SUM is 1-2-3's way of identifying cells B4, B5, B6, and B7 as

the cells containing the values to be summed. Although the @SUM function assigned to cell B8 is not displayed in the cell, it remains in the cell and displays in the contents box when cell B8 is selected.

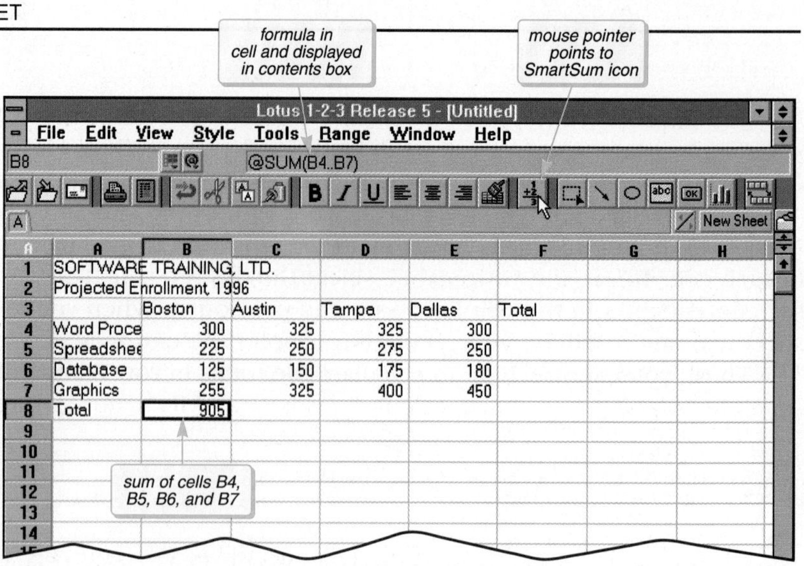

formula in cell and displayed in contents box

mouse pointer points to SmartSum icon

sum of cells B4, B5, B6, and B7

FIGURE 1-32

When you enter the @SUM function using the SmartSum icon, 1-2-3 automatically sums the nearest adjacent group of cells. This group of cells, B4, B5, B6, and B7, is called a range. A **range** is a rectangular group of cells in a worksheet. Ranges can be as small as a single cell and as large as an entire worksheet. A range is represented by the addresses of its top leftmost and bottom rightmost cells, separated by two periods, (for example, B4..B7). Once you define a range, you can work with all the cells in the range rather than one cell at a time.

When using the @SUM function as implemented by the SmartSum icon, 1-2-3 first will attempt to sum a range containing values above the current cell. If no cells directly above the current cell contain values, 1-2-3 will sum values in the adjacent cells to the left of the current cell. If values are found in the row to the left of the current cell as well as in the column above the current cell, you must first select the range to be summed and then click the SmartSum icon on the set of SmartIcons.

▶ COPYING A CELL TO ADJACENT CELLS

I n the SOFTWARE TRAINING, LTD. worksheet, you must also use 1-2-3 to calculate the totals for Austin, Tampa, and Dallas. The total projected enrollment for Austin is the sum of the values in the range C4..C7. Similarly, for Tampa, the range to sum is D4..D7, and for Dallas the range is E4..E7.

To calculate these sums, you can follow the steps shown in Figure 1-31 and Figure 1-32. A more efficient method, however, is to **copy** the @SUM function from cell B8 to the range C8..E8 (cells C8, D8, and E8). The copy cannot be an exact duplicate of the @SUM function in cell B8, though, because one column to the right is being moved for each respective total. Therefore, when you copy cell addresses, 1-2-3 adjusts the address for each new position. As a result, the @SUM function and range in cell C8 will be @SUM(C4..C7), the @SUM function and the range in cell D8 will be @SUM(D4..D7), and the @SUM function and the range in cell E8 will be @SUM(E4..E7). Each adjusted cell reference is called a **relative reference**.

The easiest way to copy the @SUM function from cell B8 to cells C8, D8, and E8 is by using 1-2-3's quick menu. 1-2-3 provides a **quick menu** that contains frequently used commands you can use with the currently selected range. The commands available on the quick menu change depending on the current selection. For example, the list of commands available when a range is selected is different from the list available when a chart is selected. You activate the quick menu by pressing the right mouse button.

To copy the @SUM function from cell B8 to the adjacent cells, C8, D8, and E8, complete the following steps.

TO COPY ONE CELL TO ADJACENT CELLS IN A ROW ▼

STEP 1 ▶

Select the cell to be copied – cell B8.

The cell to be copied, cell B8, is selected (Figure 1-33).

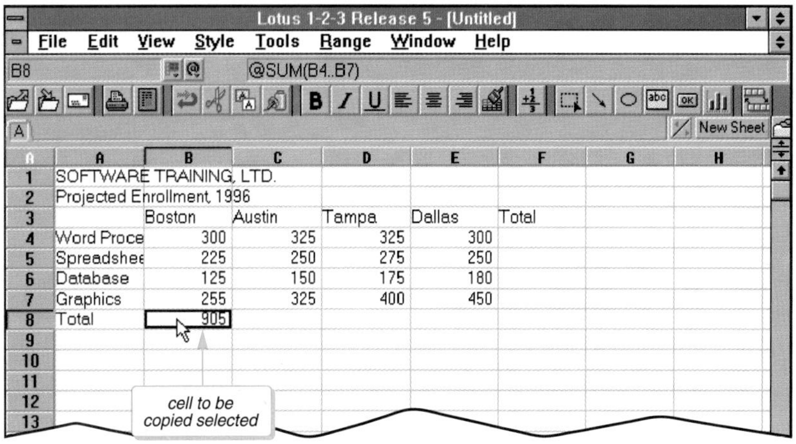

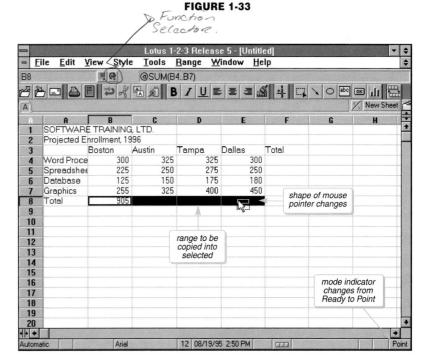

FIGURE 1-33

STEP 2 ▶

Point to cell B8. With the mouse pointer shaped as an arrow, drag the range of cells in to which the @SUM function will be copied (cells C8, D8, and E8).

The mouse pointer changes to an arrow pointing to a picture of a cell ( ) indicating you are selecting a range (Figure 1-34). When you drag the mouse pointer through the cells, 1-2-3 surrounds the first cell by a dark border and the remaining cells in the range have a dark background. The mode indicator changes from Ready to Point.

FIGURE 1-34

STEP 3 ▶

Release the left mouse button. Point to the selected range, click the *right* mouse button, and point to the Copy Right command on the quick menu.

1-2-3 displays the quick menu with the most commonly used commands for the current selection (Figure 1-35). The mouse pointer points to the Copy Right command.

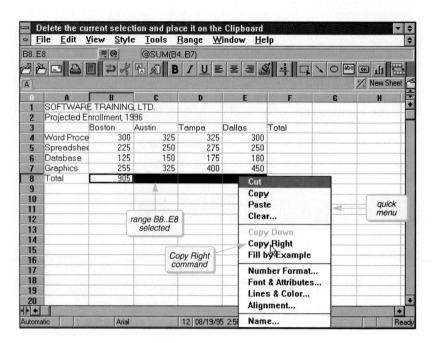

FIGURE 1-35

STEP 4 ▶

Choose the Copy Right command by clicking the left mouse button.

1-2-3 copies the @SUM function in cell B8 to the range C8..E8 (Figure 1-36). In addition, 1-2-3 calculates the sum for cells C4..C7 and enters the result in cell C8, the sum for cells D4..D7 and enters the result in cell D8, and the sum for cells E4..E7 and enters the result in cell E8.

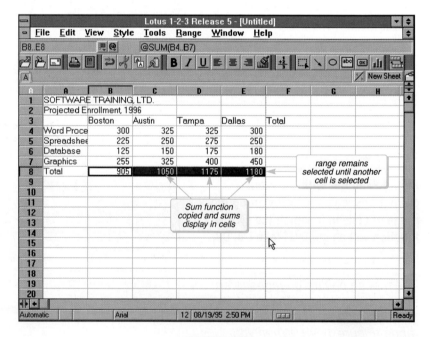

FIGURE 1-36

▲

After 1-2-3 copies the cell contents, the range B8..E8 remains selected. Select any cell to remove the range selection.

The Copy Right command is also found on the Edit menu located on the main menu bar.

Summing a Row Total

The next step in building the SOFTWARE TRAINING, LTD. worksheet is to calculate the total projected enrollment for the Word Processing, Spreadsheet, Database, and Graphics classes, and then to calculate the total projected enrollment for the year. These totals will be entered in column F. The @SUM function is used in the same manner as it was when you calculated the total projected enrollment by cities in row 8. The following steps illustrate this process.

TO SUM A ROW OF VALUES USING THE SMARTSUM ICON ▼

STEP 1 ▶

Select the cell that will contain the total for Word Processing – cell F4 (Figure 1-37).

FIGURE 1-37

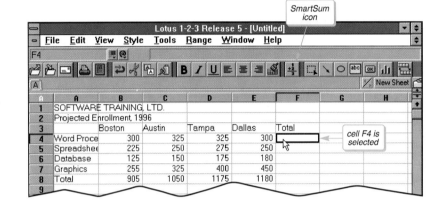

STEP 2 ▶

Click the SmartSum icon on the set of SmartIcons displayed below the edit line.

1-2-3 displays @SUM(B4..E4) in the contents box and the sum of cells B4, C4, D4, and E4 in cell F4 (Figure 1-38). The @SUM entry identifies the @SUM function. The B4..E4 entry within parentheses following the function name, @SUM, is 1-2-3's way of identifying cells B4, C4, D4, and E4 as the cells containing the values to be summed.

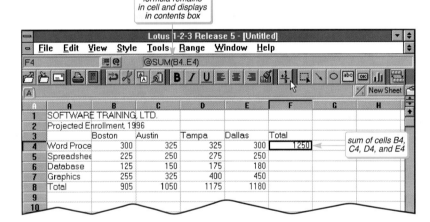

FIGURE 1-38

Copying Adjacent Cells in a Column

The next task is to copy the @SUM function from cell F4 to the range F5..F8 (cells F5, F6, F7, and F8) to obtain the total projected enrollments for the Spreadsheet, Database, and Graphics classes, and the total projected enrollment for the year. Use the **Copy Down command** from the quick menu to accomplish this task as shown in the following steps.

TO COPY ONE CELL TO ADJACENT CELLS IN A COLUMN ▼

STEP 1 ►

Select cell F4 and drag the range F5..F8.

1-2-3 selects the range F4..F8 (Figure 1-39).

FIGURE 1-39

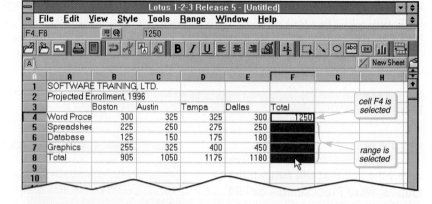

STEP 2 ►

With the mouse pointer in the selected range, click the right mouse button and point to the Copy Down command on the quick menu.

1-2-3 displays the quick menu associated with the selected range (Figure 1-40). The mouse pointer points to the Copy Down command.

FIGURE 1-40

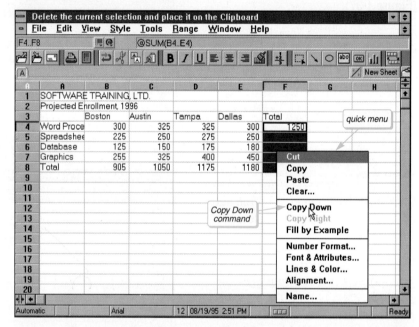

STEP 3 ►

Choose the Copy Down command.

1-2-3 copies the @SUM function to the selected range and displays the calculated results in each of the cells (Figure 1-41). When 1-2-3 copies the function, each range address in the function is adjusted to reflect the proper rows of numbers to sum.

FIGURE 1-41

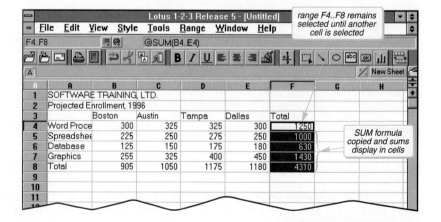

After the copy is complete, the range remains selected. To remove the range selection, select any cell.

The Copy Down command is also found on the Edit menu located on the main menu bar.

▶ SAVING A WORKSHEET

If you accidentally turn off your computer or if the electrical power fails, you will lose all your work on the worksheet unless you have saved it on disk. Therefore, after you have worked on a worksheet for a period of time, or when you complete the worksheet, you should save it on disk. You can save a worksheet on a hard disk or on a diskette. The Project 1 worksheet is to be saved on a diskette located in drive A. Using the following procedure, however, you can save a worksheet on either hard disk or diskette, and on any drive available on your computer.

TO SAVE A WORKSHEET ▼

STEP 1 ▶

Move the cell pointer to cell A1 by pointing to cell A1 and clicking the left mouse button. Point to the Save icon ( ) on the set of SmartIcons and click the left mouse button.

1-2-3 displays the Save As dialog box (Figure 1-42). The default file name file0001.wk4 is selected in the File name text box. The mode indicator changes from Ready to Menu indicating a dialog box is active.

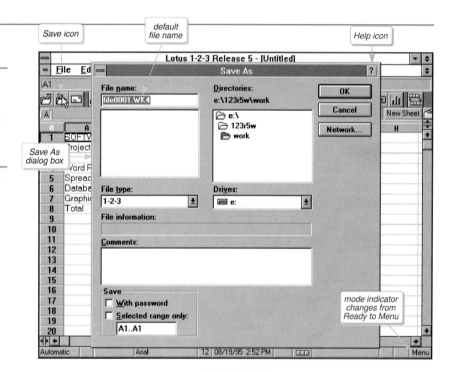

FIGURE 1-42

STEP 2 ▶

Type the file name, `proj1`, in the File name text box.

The file name you type appears in the File name text box (Figure 1-43). This is the name 1-2-3 will use to store the worksheet file.

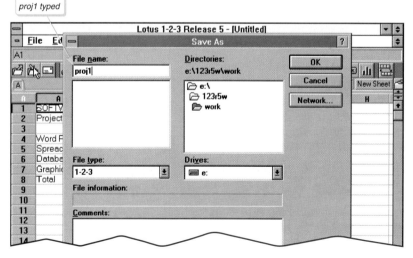

FIGURE 1-43

STEP 3 ▶

Click the Drives drop-down list box arrow and point to a:.

A list of the available drives on your computer displays (Figure 1-44).

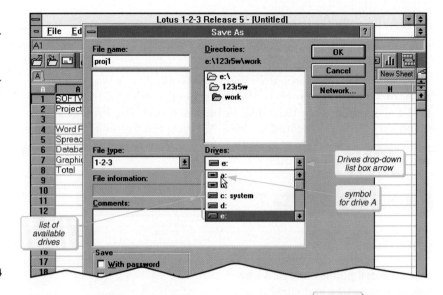

FIGURE 1-44

STEP 4 ▶

Select drive a: by pointing to a: in the drop-down list box and clicking the left mouse button. Point to the OK button in the Save As dialog box.

Drive A becomes the selected drive (Figure 1-45). If you wish, you may enter comments about the file in the Comments text box as shown. The mouse pointer points to the OK button.

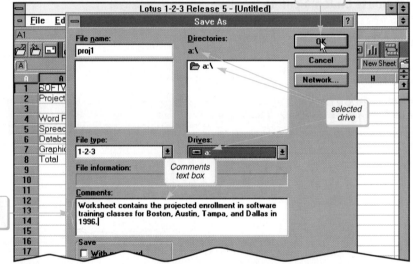

FIGURE 1-45

STEP 5 ▶

Choose the OK button in the Save As dialog box.

*1-2-3 saves the file on the diskette located in drive A using the PROJ1.WK4 file name and places the file name in the title bar (Figure 1-46). 1-2-3 automatically places the file extension **.WK4** following the file name of worksheet files. Although the worksheet is saved on disk, it also remains in main memory and displays on the screen.*

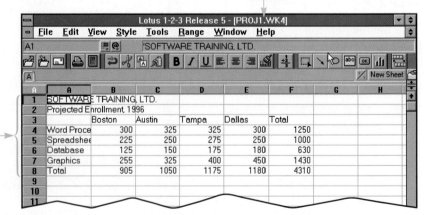

FIGURE 1-46

After saving the worksheet for the first time, continue to save the worksheet often to avoid loss of data if there is a power failure. When saving the worksheet again using the same file name, use the Save icon on the set of SmartIcons below the edit line or the **Save command** from the File menu. If you use the Save icon, 1-2-3 saves the worksheet without displaying a dialog box and without changing the file name. If you want to save the worksheet under a different name, use the **Save As command** from the File menu.

To obtain help about the use of the Save As dialog box in Figure 1-42 on page L25, you can click the Help icon in the top right corner of the dialog box. All 1-2-3 dialog boxes contain the Help icon.

▶ USING FORMATTING TEMPLATES TO FORMAT THE WORKSHEET

Y ou have now entered all the labels, values, and functions for the worksheet. The next step is to format the worksheet. **Formatting a worksheet** emphasizes certain entries and makes the worksheet easier to read and understand.

Figure 1-47a shows the worksheet before formatting. Figure 1-47b shows the worksheet after formatting. As you can see from the two figures, adding color, an outline and drop-shadow, and adjusting column widths and row heights makes the worksheet easier to read and look more professional.

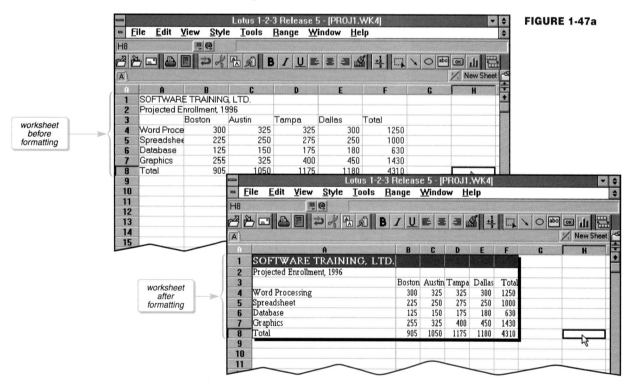

FIGURE 1-47a

worksheet before formatting

worksheet after formatting

FIGURE 1-47b

1-2-3 contains a number of customized format styles called **templates** that allow you to quickly format the worksheet. The templates can be used to give your worksheet a professional appearance. To format the worksheet using a template, first select the range to format. Then from the **Style menu** on the main menu bar, choose the **Gallery command**.

Complete the steps on the next page to automatically format the Project 1 worksheet using a template called Simple3.

TO USE FORMATTING TEMPLATES ▼

STEP 1 ►

Select cell A1, the upper left corner cell of the rectangular range to format (Figure 1-48).

Cell A1 is selected.

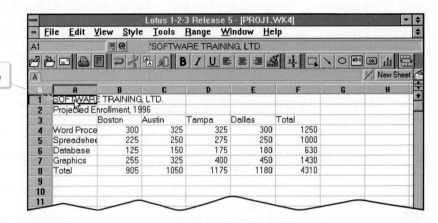

FIGURE 1-48

STEP 2 ►

Drag the mouse pointer to cell F8, the lower right corner cell of the range to format, and release the left mouse button.

The range to format is selected (Figure 1-49).

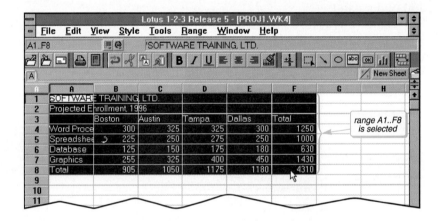

FIGURE 1-49

STEP 3 ►

Select the Style menu by clicking the Style menu name on the menu bar and point to the Gallery command.

1-2-3 displays the Style menu (Figure 1-50). The mouse pointer points to the Gallery command. The mode indicator changes from Ready to Menu indicating a menu is selected.

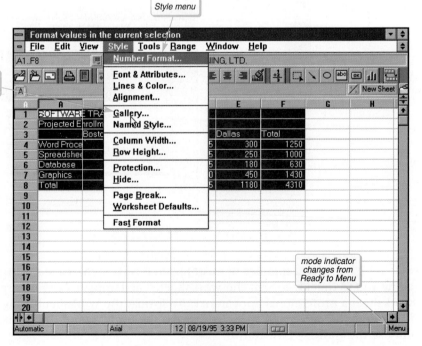

FIGURE 1-50

STEP 4 ▶

Choose the Gallery command from the Style menu.

1-2-3 displays the Gallery dialog box (Figure 1-51). On the left is the Template list box listing template names. These names identify each of the predefined formatting template styles available in 1-2-3. In Figure 1-51, the Template name, Chisel1, is highlighted. In the Sample area of the dialog box is an example of the format that corresponds to the highlighted template name, Chisel1. Each of the template names corresponds to a different format. Below the sample format is the Range text box that displays the selected range to be formatted.

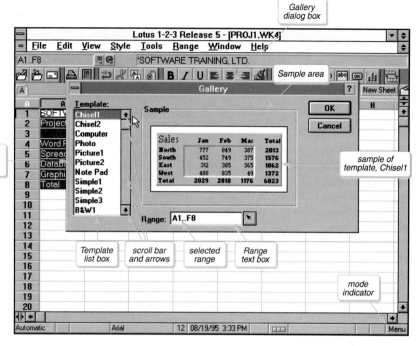

FIGURE 1-51

STEP 5 ▶

Point to the template name, Simple3, in the Template list box and click the left mouse button.

The template name, Simple3, is selected. The Sample area shows an example of the Simple3 template format (Figure 1-52).

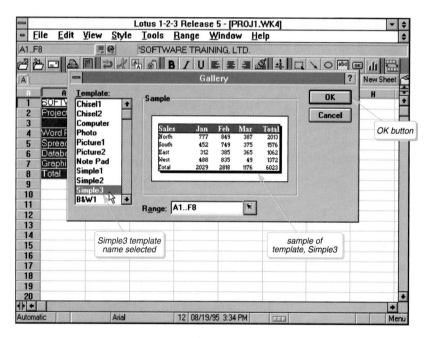

FIGURE 1-52

STEP 6 ▶

Choose the OK button in the Gallery dialog box. Select any cell in the worksheet outside the range A1..F8.

1-2-3 displays the worksheet with the range A1..F8 using the customized template, Simple3 (Figure 1-53). Notice the characteristics associated with the Simple3 template include adding the color blue to the first row and increasing the row height. The title text color is white. The column widths are adjusted so the data fits properly in the columns. An outline and drop shadow are added to the worksheet.

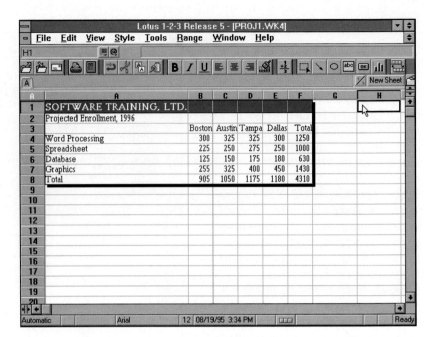

FIGURE 1-53

1-2-3 provides fourteen style templates to customize your data quickly. Each style template has different characteristics. Customizing a worksheet with the style templates will not always give correct results if the worksheet title and subtitle are included in the range to format. Should this occur, do not include the titles in the range to format.

The worksheet is now complete. All the data is entered and the formatting is done. The next step is to chart the projected enrollment for the four cities.

As noted previously, saving the worksheet often is a good practice to prevent lost data if something unexpected happens. Click the Save icon on the set of SmartIcons to save the formatted worksheet.

▶ CHARTING A WORKSHEET

Charts can help you compare values, understand relationships among values, and identify trends when comparing values.

A **chart** is a graphical representation of the data in the worksheet. A **bar chart** is useful when comparing two or more values. A bar chart shows values as vertical rectangular bars. A 3D bar chart displays each individual bar in a three-dimensional perspective. The 3D bar chart drawn by 1-2-3 in this project is based on the data in the SOFTWARE TRAINING, LTD. worksheet (see Figure 1-54).

The chart contains the title from the worksheet. Each vertical colored bar represents one of the classes shown in the rows. Thus, for Boston, the red column represents the projected enrollment for Word Processing (300), the green column represents the projected enrollment for Spreadsheet (225), the blue column represents the projected enrollment for Database (125), and the yellow column represents the projected enrollment for Graphics (255). For Austin, Tampa, and Dallas, the same color columns represent the comparable projected enrollments. This representation of color for values in the worksheet is called the **chart legend**. The totals are not included because they do not present meaningful comparisons on a bar chart.

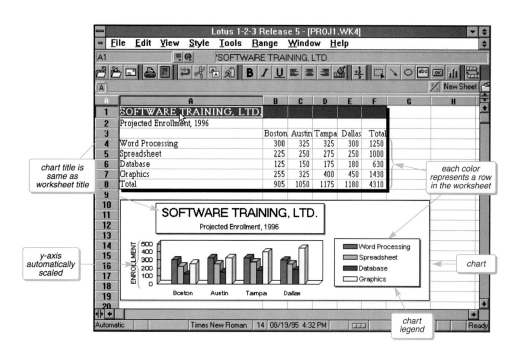

FIGURE 1-54

1-2-3 automatically scaled the enrollment values along the vertical **y axis** of the chart on the basis of the minimum and maximum values in projected enrollments. The value 500 is greater than any value in the worksheet, so it is the maximum value 1-2-3 included in the chart.

To create a chart like the one shown in Figure 1-54, including the titles, legend, and chart formatting, you must select the range to chart, click the Chart icon, and select the area on the worksheet where you want the chart drawn.

In Figure 1-54, the chart is located immediately below the worksheet. You determine the location of the chart on the worksheet and also its size by dragging the mouse pointer from the upper left corner of the chart location to the lower right corner of the chart location after you have clicked the Chart icon.

Follow the detailed steps below and on the following two pages to draw a 3D bar chart that compares the projected enrollment for the four cities.

TO CREATE A 3D BAR CHART ▼

STEP 1 ▶

Select the cells to be charted — range A1..E7 — by dragging from cell A1 to cell E7. Point to the Chart icon (▥).

The cells selected include the worksheet titles, the column titles, the row titles, and the projected enrollments for Boston, Austin, Tampa, and Dallas (Figure 1-55). The total row and total column are not selected.

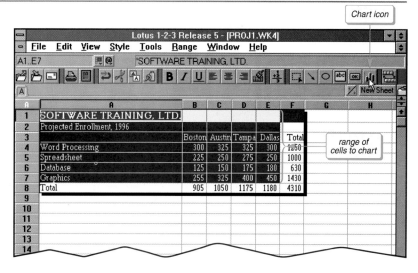

FIGURE 1-55

STEP 2 ▶

Click the Chart icon on the set of SmartIcons and move the mouse pointer onto the worksheet.

The mouse pointer changes to a crosshair with a picture of a bar chart ( ) (Figure 1-56). A message displays in the title bar giving you instructions to complete the task.

FIGURE 1-56

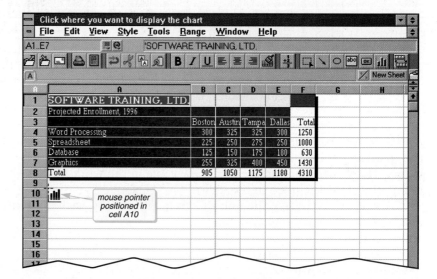

STEP 3 ▶

Move the mouse pointer to the upper left corner of the chart location (cell A10) immediately below the worksheet (Figure 1-57).

FIGURE 1-57

STEP 4 ▶

Drag the mouse pointer to the lower right corner of cell G19, which is the lower right corner of the chart location.

The mouse pointer is positioned at the lower right corner of cell G19, and the proposed chart location is surrounded by a dotted rectangle (Figure 1-58).

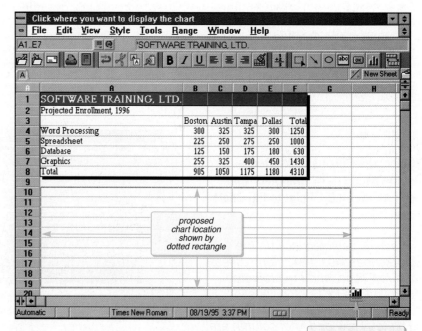

FIGURE 1-58

STEP 5 ▶

Release the left mouse button.

*1-2-3 creates and displays the default two-dimensional bar chart comparing the projected enrollments for the four cities (Figure 1-59). The column titles that were selected in row 3 display as x-axis labels. The row titles that were selected in column A display as the chart legend. The default axes titles, X-Axis and Y-Axis, identify each axis. The small selection squares, or **handles**, on the border of the chart indicate the chart is selected. The default name of the chart, CHART1, displays in the selection indicator indicating the chart is selected. A new menu name, Chart, replaces the Range menu name on the main menu and a new set of charting icons displays on the set of SmartIcons. Both the new menu name and the charting icons appear on the screen only if the chart is selected.*

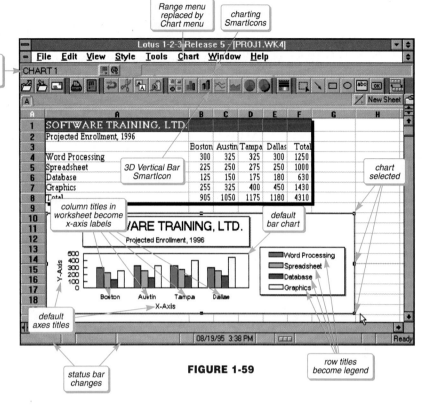

FIGURE 1-59

STEP 6 ▶

Point to the 3D Vertical Bar icon ( ) on the set of SmartIcons and click the left mouse button.

1-2-3 displays the 3D bar chart (Figure 1-60). The chart remains selected as indicated by the handles. To deselect the chart, select any cell outside the chart.

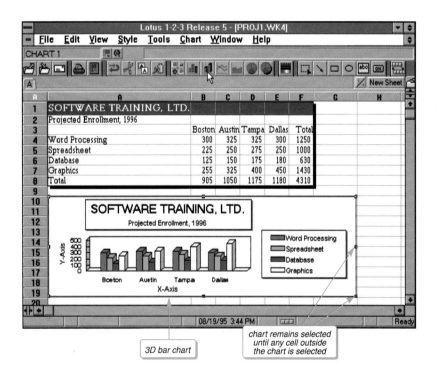

FIGURE 1-60

The 3D vertical bar chart in Figure 1-60 compares the projected enrollment for each training class for each city. When selecting the range to chart, if a label is anywhere in the first row of the selected range, it becomes the chart title. If a label is anywhere in the second row of the selected range, it becomes the chart subtitle. If the selected range includes column and row headings, 1-2-3 uses the labels to create the axes labels and legend. The **chart legend** identifies each bar column in the chart.

While the chart is selected, you can move the chart to any location on the worksheet. To move the chart, position the mouse pointer inside the chart on a white area and drag the chart to the desired location. You can also resize the chart by dragging the handles.

When you create a chart, 1-2-3 provides default axes titles, X-Axis and Y-Axis, identifying the data charted on each axis (Figure 1-60). You can change the axes titles to more accurately describe the data charted along each axis. To complete the chart for Project 1, the x-axis title is deleted from the chart and the y-axis title is changed to Enrollment. To change the axes titles perform the following steps.

TO CHANGE THE AXES TITLES ▼

STEP 1 ►

Point to the X-Axis title in the 3D vertical bar chart.

The mouse pointer changes to an arrowhead with a capital A ( ) (Figure 1-61).

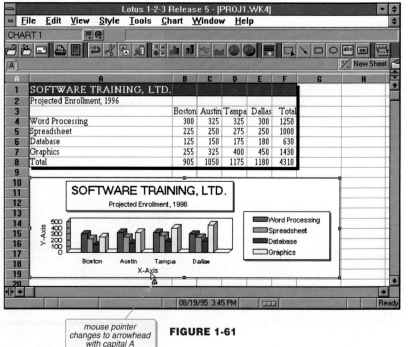

mouse pointer changes to arrowhead with capital A

FIGURE 1-61

STEP 2 ▶

Click the right mouse button. Point to the Clear command on the quick menu.

Handles indicate the X-Axis title is selected (Figure 1-62). 1-2-3 displays the quick menu containing commands you can use on the X-Axis title (Figure 1-62).

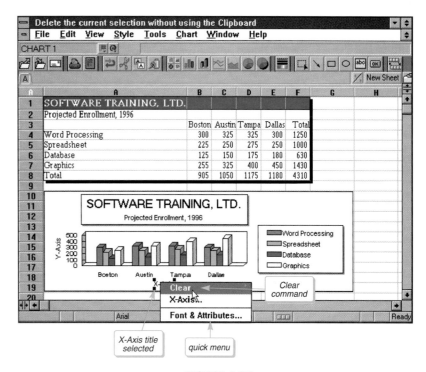

FIGURE 1-62

STEP 3 ▶

Choose the Clear command from the quick menu by clicking the left mouse button.

1-2-3 removes the X-Axis title from the chart (Figure 1-63). In addition, the chart is resized to fill the allocated space. Notice the enrollment numbers on the y-axis are less crowded in Figure 1-63 than in Figure 1-62.

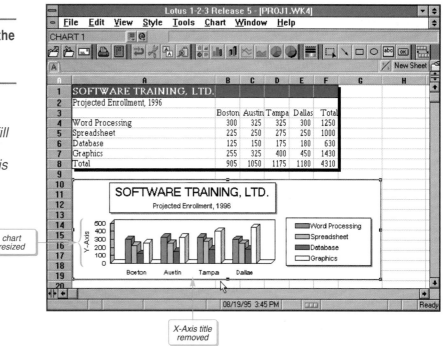

FIGURE 1-63

STEP 4 ▶

Point to the Y-Axis title, click the right mouse button, and point to the Y-Axis command.

1-2-3 selects the Y-Axis title and displays the quick menu (Figure 1-64). The mouse pointer points to the Y-Axis command.

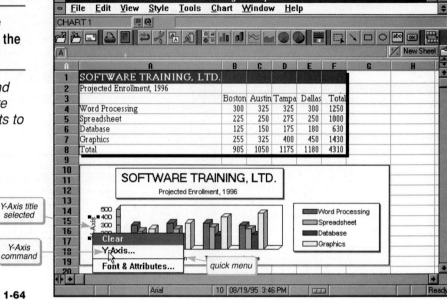

FIGURE 1-64

STEP 5 ▶

Choose the Y-Axis command from the quick menu.

1-2-3 displays the Y-Axis dialog box (Figure 1-65). The default Y-Axis title is highlighted in the Axis title text box. The mode indicator changes from Ready to Edit, indicating text is being edited.

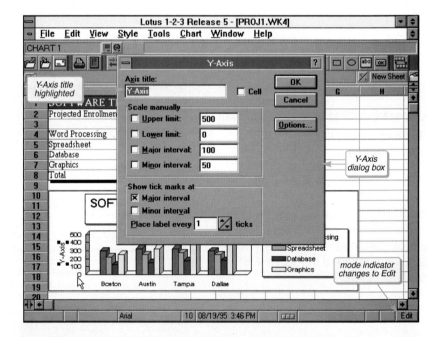

FIGURE 1-65

STEP 6 ▶

Type ENROLLMENT **in the Axis title text box and point to the OK button in the Y-Axis dialog box.**

ENROLLMENT replaces the Y-Axis title (Figure 1-66).

FIGURE 1-66

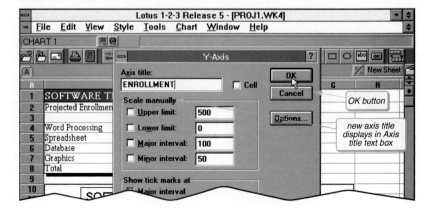

STEP 7 ▶

Choose the OK button in the Y-Axis dialog box. Select any cell in the worksheet outside the chart.

The 3D bar chart displays with the new y-axis title (Figure 1-67). Notice the Range menu name replaces the Chart menu name and the Default set of SmartIcons displays below the Edit line.

new y-axis title

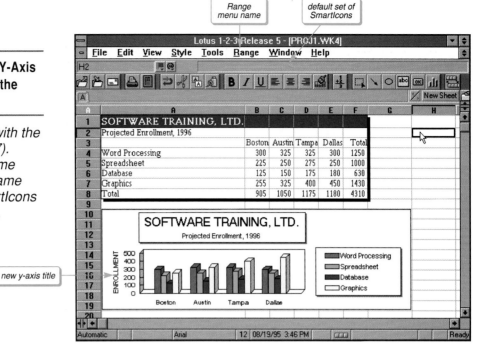

FIGURE 1-67

The worksheet and chart are now complete. To save the latest changes to the worksheet, including the chart, click the Save icon on the set of SmartIcons. After 1-2-3 saves the latest changes to the worksheet, the worksheet remains on the screen.

▶ PRINTING A WORKSHEET

 fter you save the worksheet, the next step is often to print the worksheet and its associated chart. To print a worksheet and chart, you can use the **Print icon** on the set of SmartIcons, as illustrated in the following steps.

TO PRINT A WORKSHEET AND CHART ▼

STEP 1 ▶

Point to the Print icon (🖨) on the set of SmartIcons (Figure 1-68).

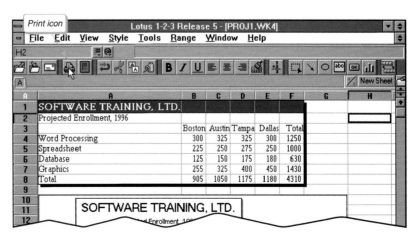

FIGURE 1-68

STEP 2 ►

Click the Print icon on the set of SmartIcons. Point to the OK button in the Print dialog box.

1-2-3 displays the Print dialog box (Figure 1-69). The Current worksheet option button in the Print area is selected. This option prints both the worksheet and chart. The default for the dialog box is that one copy of the document is to print and all pages in the document are to print.

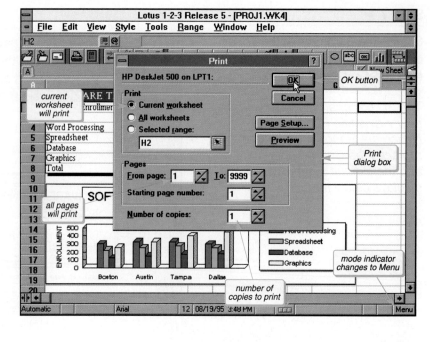

FIGURE 1-69

STEP 3 ►

Choose the OK button in the Print dialog box.

1-2-3 momentarily displays the Printing dialog box (Figure 1-70) that allows you to cancel the print job at any time while the system is internally creating the worksheet image and sending it to the printer. Then the document is printed on the printer (Figure 1-71).

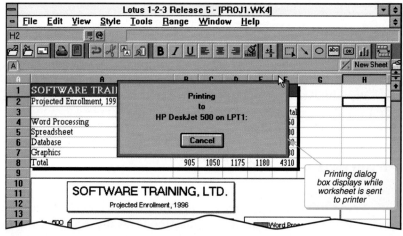

FIGURE 1-70

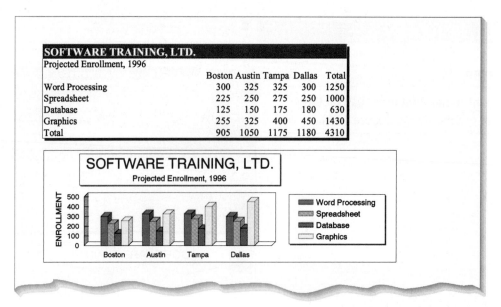

FIGURE 1-71

▶ CLOSING THE WORKSHEET

O nce the worksheet and chart are completed, saved, and printed, you can **close the worksheet** and work on another worksheet or another 1-2-3 project. When you close the worksheet, it is removed from memory. To close the worksheet, use the following steps.

TO CLOSE A WORKSHEET ▼

STEP 1 ▶

Select the File menu and point to the Close command (Figure 1-72).

STEP 2 ▶

Choose the Close command from the File menu.

1-2-3 closes the worksheet and returns you to a new blank worksheet from which you can create another worksheet.

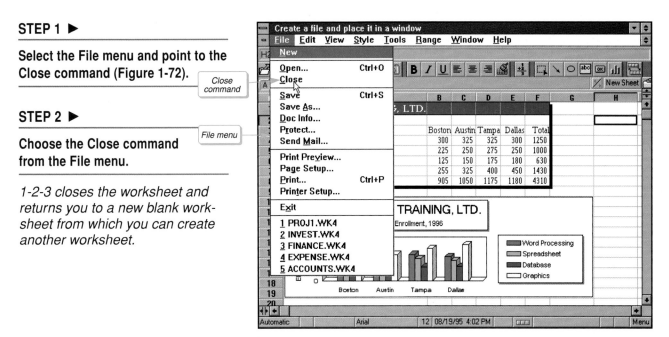

FIGURE 1-72

If you have made changes to the worksheet without saving it after making those changes, 1-2-3 will present a Close dialog box asking if you want to save the file with the changes when you choose the Close command. If you want to save the file, click the Yes button (Yes) in the Close dialog box; otherwise, click the No button (No).

▶ EXITING 1-2-3

fter you have completed all your tasks, you will normally want to **exit 1-2-3** and return to Windows Program Manager. To exit 1-2-3, perform the steps on the next page.

TO EXIT 1-2-3 ▼

STEP 1 ▶

Select the File menu and point to the Exit command (Figure 1-73).

STEP 2 ▶

Choose the Exit command from the File menu.

1-2-3 returns control to Windows Program Manager from which you can select other programs or terminate your computer activity.

FIGURE 1-73

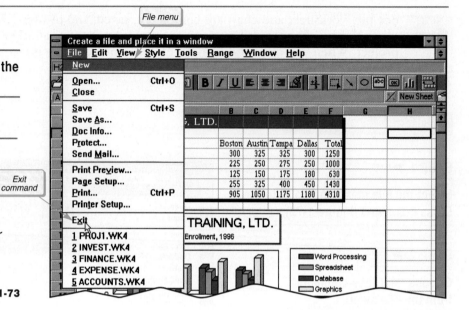

▶ OPENING A WORKSHEET FILE

O nce you have created, saved, and printed a worksheet and exited 1-2-3, you may need to retrieve the worksheet again to make changes to it or otherwise process it. When you do, start 1-2-3 again. Then open the worksheet to be revised.

Opening a worksheet file makes the worksheet available for use or modification. A variety of methods exist for opening a worksheet. One method of opening a worksheet stored on a diskette in drive A is explained in the following steps.

TO OPEN A WORKSHEET FILE ▼

STEP 1 ▶

Start 1-2-3 as explained on page L5. When the Welcome to 1-2-3 dialog box displays, point to the Work on an existing worksheet option button and click the left mouse button. Point to the OK button (Figure 1-74).

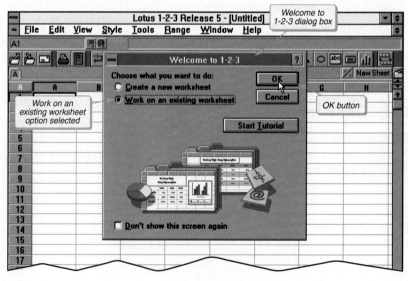

FIGURE 1-74

STEP 2 ▶

Choose the OK button in the Welcome to 1-2-3 dialog box.

1-2-3 displays the Open File dialog box (Figure 1-75).

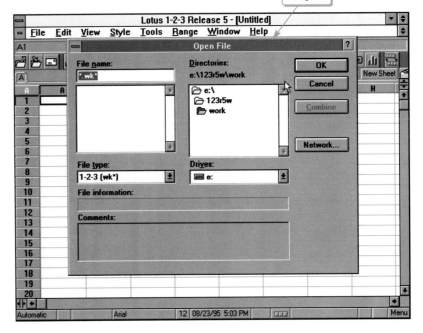

FIGURE 1-75

STEP 3 ▶

Click the Drives drop-down list box arrow and select drive a:. Then select proj1.wk4 by pointing to proj1.wk4 in the File name list box and clicking the left mouse button. Point to the OK button in the Open File dialog box.

1-2-3 displays the file names on drive a: in the File name list box (Figure 1-76). Selecting proj1.wk4 in the list places the file name, proj1.wk4 in the File name text box. If you entered comments in the Comments text box when the file was saved, they display in the Comments text box. The mouse pointer points to the OK button.

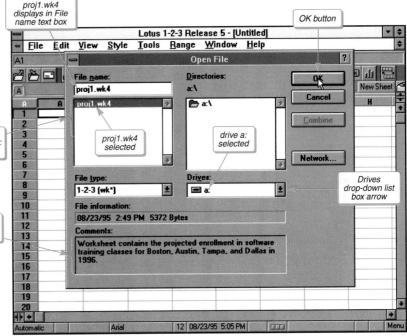

FIGURE 1-76

STEP 4 ▶

Choose the OK button in the Open File dialog box.

1-2-3 displays the worksheet, proj1.wk4, on the screen (Figure 1-77). You can revise or print the worksheet as required.

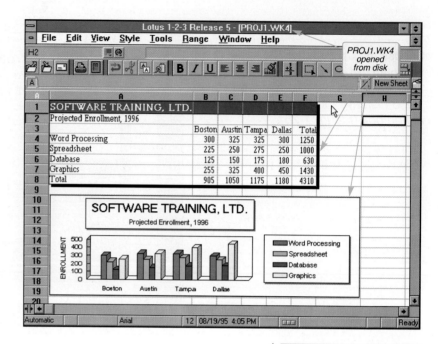

FIGURE 1-77

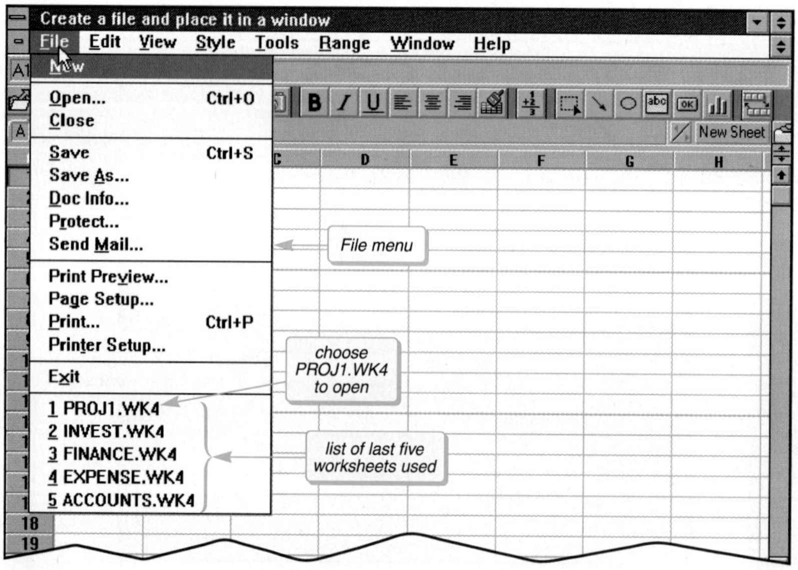

FIGURE 1-78

Another method of opening a file uses the File menu. 1-2-3 saves the names of the last five worksheets on which you have worked and lists their names at the bottom of the File menu (see Figure 1-78). To open one of these worksheets, point to the appropriate file name and click the left mouse button. The worksheet will open and display on the screen.

The set of SmartIcons contains the Open icon ( ) that you can use to display the Open File dialog box. This is useful if you need to open another worksheet while the current worksheet displays.

▶ CORRECTING ERRORS

After completing a worksheet, you may need to modify it to correct a typing error or to change data that was entered correctly the first time but has since changed. You may **edit data** by deleting, inserting, or replacing characters. 1-2-3 provides several methods for editing data in a worksheet. These methods are described in the sections that follow.

Correcting Errors Prior to Confirming a Data Entry into a Cell

If you notice an error in the cell or contents box prior to confirming the entry, do one of the following:

1. Use the BACKSPACE key to erase back to the error, and then type the correct characters; or
2. If the error is too severe, click the Cancel button in the contents box or press the ESC key to erase the entire entry in the cell. Then, reenter the data from the beginning.

Editing Data in a Cell

If you find an error in the worksheet after entering the data, select the cell with the error. 1-2-3 provides two methods to correct the error:

1. If the entry is short, retype it and click the Confirm button or press the ENTER key. The new entry will replace the old entry.
2. If the entry in the cell is long and the errors are minor, **Edit mode** is a better choice. Use Edit mode as described below:
   a. Double-click the cell containing the error. 1-2-3 switches to Edit mode, and the insertion point appears in the cell. The cell contents also display in the contents box in the edit line.
   b. Make your changes, as specified in the next two steps.
      (1) To insert a character in the cell, place the insertion point to the left of the location where you want to insert the character. Type the character. 1-2-3 inserts the character at the location of the insertion point and moves all characters one position to the right.
      (2) To delete a character in the cell, place the insertion point to the left of the character you want to delete and press the DEL key, or place the insertion point to the right of the character you want to delete and press the BACKSPACE key. To delete multiple characters, repeat the process.

While the insertion point is located in the cell, you might have occasion to move it to various points in the cell. Table 1-1 illustrates the means for moving the insertion point in the cell.

▶ **TABLE 1-1**

TASK	MOUSE	KEYBOARD
Move the Insertion Point to the Beginning of the Data	Position mouse pointer and click to left of first character	Press HOME
Move the Insertion Point to the End of the Data	Position mouse pointer and click to right of last character	Press END
Move the Insertion Point One Character to the Left of the Current Location	Click one character to left	Press LEFT ARROW
Move the Insertion Point One Character to the Right of the Current Location	Click one character to right	Press RIGHT ARROW
Move the Insertion Point Anywhere in the Cell	Click cell at appropriate position	Press LEFT ARROW or RIGHT ARROW
Highlight One or More Characters	Drag mouse pointer over data	Press SHIFT+LEFT ARROW or SHIFT+RIGHT ARROW
Delete Highlighted Characters		Press DEL

When you are finished editing data in a cell, click the Confirm button or press the ENTER key.

It is not uncommon to make keyboard and grammatical errors. Understanding how to use Edit mode will allow you to correct mistakes easily.

Undoing Most Recent Actions

1-2-3 provides an **Undo icon** on the set of SmartIcons that you can use to cancel your most recent command or action. For example, if you accidentally delete data, point to the Undo icon (🔁) (see Figure 1-79) and click the left mouse button. 1-2-3 restores the cell contents to what they were prior to the deletion. The Undo option is effective only if you choose it immediately after making a change and before taking any other action.

Some commands and actions cannot be canceled by using the Undo option. You cannot undo the effects of Print commands or File commands. You also cannot use Undo to reverse a previous use of Undo.

The Undo command is also found on the Edit menu located on the main menu bar.

Clearing a Cell or Range of Cells

If you enter data into the wrong cell or range of cells, you can correct the error by **deleting the data**, or **clearing the data**. To delete data in a cell, never select the cell and press the SPACEBAR to enter a blank character. A blank character is text and is different from an empty cell, even though the cell may appear empty.

1-2-3 provides three methods to clear the contents of a cell or a range of cells:

TO CLEAR CELL CONTENTS — DEL KEY

Step 1: Select the cell or range of cells.
Step 2: Press the DEL key.

TO CLEAR CELL CONTENTS — EDIT MENU AND CLEAR COMMAND

Step 1: Select the cell or range of cells.
Step 2: From the Edit menu, choose the Clear command.
Step 3: When 1-2-3 displays the Clear dialog box (see Figure 1-79), select the desired option. To completely clear the cell, select the Both option button.
Step 4: Choose the OK button in the Clear dialog box.

TO CLEAR CELL CONTENTS — CUT ICON

Step 1: Select the cell or range of cells.
Step 2: Click the **Cut icon** (✂) on the set of SmartIcons.

Each of these three methods has differences you should understand. In the first method, when you press the DEL key, the data in the cell or range of cells is cleared but any style features remain. Thus, even after you clear the cells using this method, styles such as color and drop-shadows remain. To also clear the styles, you must use one of the other two methods.

When you use the Edit menu and Clear command, you can clear the data in a cell or a range, clear the style in a cell or a range, or both. When you choose the Clear command from the Edit menu, 1-2-3 displays the Clear dialog box (Figure 1-79). Select the option in the Clear dialog box that specifies what you want to delete. For example, you may want to delete the cell's style format but retain the cell contents to reapply a different style format. In the Clear dialog box, selecting the Styles only option removes all styles from the cell but retains the cell contents.

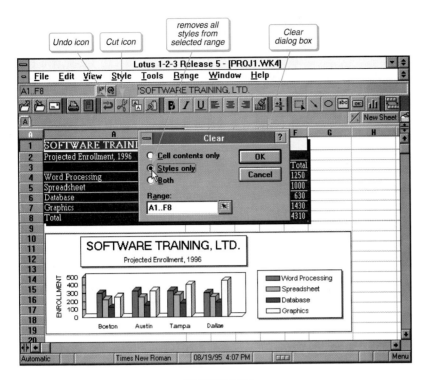

FIGURE 1-79

When you use the Cut icon, 1-2-3 clears both the data and the styles for the cell without displaying a dialog box. Actually, the data and the associated styles are placed on the Windows Clipboard for potential pasting elsewhere, but if you never paste the data into the same or another 1-2-3 worksheet, in effect the data and styles have been entirely cleared from the worksheet.

Clearing the Entire Worksheet

Sometimes so many errors are made in a worksheet that it is easier to start over. To clear an entire worksheet, perform the following steps.

TO CLEAR THE ENTIRE WORKSHEET

Step 1:   Select the entire worksheet by clicking the worksheet letter that is just above row heading 1 and immediately to the left of column heading A.

Step 2:   Follow any of the three methods specified on the previous page to clear the cell contents.

TO DELETE A CHART

Step 1:   Select the chart by clicking anywhere within the chart boundaries.

Step 2:   Choose the Clear command from the Edit menu, or press the DEL key, or click the Cut icon.

When deleting a chart using any of the previous methods, no dialog box displays before the action is carried out.

An alternative to the steps to clear an entire worksheet and chart is to choose the Close command from the File menu and choose No in the Close dialog box. 1-2-3 closes the worksheet and returns you to a blank worksheet from which you can create a new worksheet.

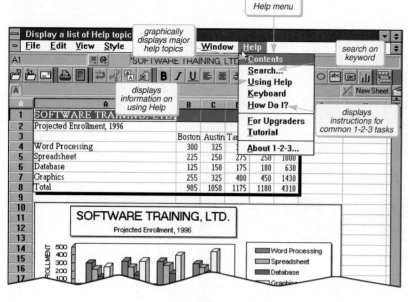

FIGURE 1-80

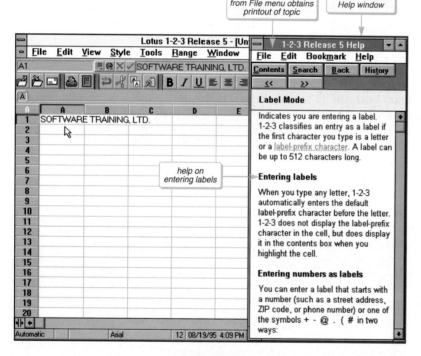

FIGURE 1-81

▶ 1-2-3 ONLINE HELP

A t any time while you are using 1-2-3, you can select the Help menu (Figure 1-80) to gain access to **online Help**. The 1-2-3 Help menu provides commands for navigating around the Help system. The **Contents command** graphically displays twelve major help topics. The **Search command** displays a Search dialog box where you can enter a keyword for which you are searching. Choose the **Using Help command** to learn how to use 1-2-3 online Help. The **How Do I? command** presents instructions for common 1-2-3 tasks such as how to use SmartIcons, how to enter data in a worksheet, and how to chart data.

Pressing the F1 function key allows you to obtain context-sensitive help on various topics. **Context-sensitive** help means that 1-2-3 will display immediate information on the activity you are performing when you press the F1 function key. For example, if you are entering a label into a cell as illustrated in Figure 1-81 and you want an explanation and advice on what to do next, press the F1 function key. The 1-2-3 Release 5 Help window containing help about Label Mode displays, as shown in Figure 1-81. You can continue displaying the Help window while you work in 1-2-3 by choosing the **Always on Top command** from the Help menu in the Help window.

You can print the help topic information in the Help window by choosing the **Print Topic command** from the File menu in the Help window. You can also print entire sections of Help consisting of related help topics. For example, you can print all related help topics describing how to create a chart. To print a section of Help, choose the Contents command from the Help menu and click the icon for **Printing Sections of Help**.

You close a Help window by choosing the **Exit command** from the File menu in the Help window or by pressing the ESC key on the keyboard.

As pointed out previously, all 1-2-3 dialog boxes contain the Help icon (?) in the top right corner of the dialog box. To obtain help about the use of the dialog box, click the Help icon. The Help window opens and displays information about the dialog box.

1-2-3's online Help has features that make it powerful and easy to use. The best way to familiarize yourself with online Help is to use it.

1-2-3 Tutorial

To improve your 1-2-3 skills, you can step through the 1-2-3 **Tutorial**. Before you begin the Tutorial, point to the Save icon on the set of SmartIcons and click the left mouse button to save the worksheet with the latest changes. To start the 1-2-3 Tutorial, use the following steps.

TO START THE 1-2-3 TUTORIAL ▼

STEP 1: ▶

Select the Help menu and point to the Tutorial command.

1-2-3 displays the Help menu and the mouse pointer points to the Tutorial command (Figure 1-82).

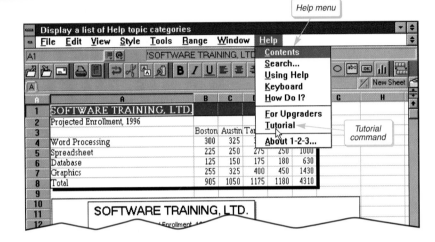

FIGURE 1-82

STEP 2: ▶

Choose the Tutorial command from the Help menu.

1-2-3 displays the 1-2-3 Tutorial window and the Lotus 1-2-3 Release 5 Tutorial main menu (Figure 1-83).

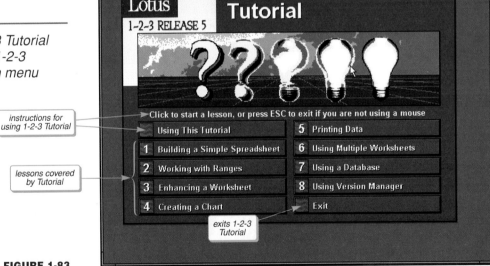

FIGURE 1-83

You can select one of the eight lessons from the Lotus 1-2-3 Release 5 Tutorial menu by pointing to the lesson number and clicking the left mouse button (Figure 1-83).

The lesson titled, Using This Tutorial, gives instructions for using the Tutorial. Each lesson takes five to ten minutes to complete. Choose Exit from the Lotus 1-2-3 Release 5 Tutorial menu to exit the 1-2-3 Tutorial.

▶ 1-2-3 CLASSIC MENU

I n addition to the main menu, 1-2-3 also offers the 1-2-3 Classic menu. The **1-2-3 Classic menu** was used in previous non-Windows versions of 1-2-3. When 1-2-3 for Windows is in Ready mode, pressing the SLASH (/) key or the COLON (:) key on the keyboard opens the 1-2-3 Classic window (Figure 1-84 and Figure 1-85). A different set of commands displays depending on which key was pressed. To close a Classic menu without completing a command, press the ESC key.

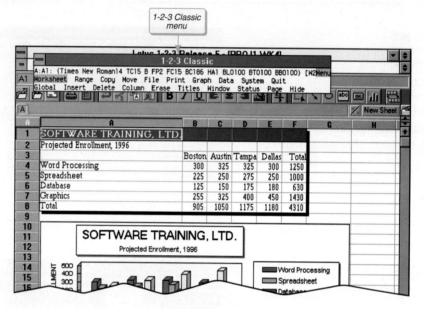

FIGURE 1-84

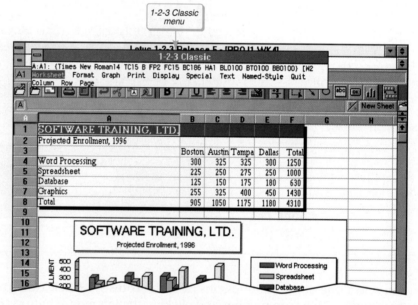

FIGURE 1-85

Discussions in this book focus on the 1-2-3 for Windows menus. It is strongly suggested that the 1-2-3 Classic menu not be used for any 1-2-3 operations.

▶ PROJECT SUMMARY

Project 1 introduced you to starting 1-2-3 Release 5 for Windows and entering labels and values into a worksheet. You learned how to select a range and how to use the SmartSum icon to sum values in a column or row. In the project, you also learned how to copy a cell to adjacent cells.

Once the worksheet was built, you learned how to format a worksheet with the Gallery command on the Style menu. Using the Chart icon you added a chart to the worksheet.

After the worksheet was built, you saved it on disk, printed it, and closed the file. Finally, you learned how to edit data in cells and previewed the use of 1-2-3 online Help.

▶ KEY TERMS AND INDEX

.WK4 *(L26)*
@function *(L19)*
1-2-3 Classic menu *(L48)*
1-2-3 worksheet *(L8)*
address *(L8)*
Always on Top command *(L46)*
BACKSPACE key *(L14)*
bar chart *(L30)*
Cancel button *(L12)*
cell *(L8)*
cell pointer *(L9)*
chart *(L3, L30)*
chart legend *(L30, L34)*
Chart menu *(L7, L33)*
clear a cell *(L44)*
Clear command *(L35)*
clearing the data *(L44)*
Close command *(L39)*
close worksheet *(L39)*
column *(L8)*
column letter *(L8)*
column titles *(L14)*
Confirm button *(L12)*
contents box *(L8)*
Contents command *(L46)*
context-sensitive *(L46)*
control panel *(L6)*
copy *(L20)*
Copy Down command *(L23)*
Copy Right command *(L22)*
current cell *(L9)*

Cut icon *(L44)*
database *(L3)*
deleting the data *(L44)*
DEL key *(L44)*
edit data *(L42)*
edit line *(L8)*
Edit mode *(L43)*
ENTER key *(L13)*
exit 1-2-3 *(L39)*
Exit command *(L46)*
File menu *(L39)*
formatting a worksheet *(L27)*
Gallery command *(L27)*
grid lines *(L9)*
handles *(L33)*
Help icon *(L26, L46)*
Help menu *(L46)*
How Do I? command *(L46)*
icon *(L7)*
insertion point *(L12)*
label *(L11)*
label-prefix character *(L14)*
left-align *(L14)*
legend *(L34)*
main menu *(L7)*
mode indicators *(L10)*
mouse pointer *(L9)*
mouse pointer shapes *(L9)*
online Help *(L46)*
opening a worksheet file *(L40)*
Print icon *(L37)*

Print Topic command *(L46)*
Printing Sections of Help icon
    (L46)
quick menu *(L21)*
range *(L20)*
Range menu *(L7)*
relative reference *(L20)*
right-align *(L19)*
row *(L8)*
row number *(L8)*
Save As command *(L27)*
Save command *(L27)*
Search command *(L46)*
select a cell *(L10)*
selection indicator *(L8)*
SmartIcons *(L8)*
status bar *(L6, L10)*
Style menu *(L27)*
template *(L27)*
Tutorial *(L47)*
Tutorial command *(L47)*
Undo icon *(L44)*
Using Help command *(L46)*
value *(L11, L17)*
work area *(L6)*
worksheet *(L3)*
worksheet tab *(L9)*
x-axis *(L33)*
y-axis *(L31)*
Y-Axis command *(L36)*

In Lotus 1-2-3 for Windows, you can accomplish a task in a number of ways. The following table presents a quick reference to each task presented in this project with its available options. The commands listed in the Menu column can be executed using either the keyboard or mouse.

Task	Mouse	Menu	Keyboard Shortcuts
Cancel an Entry in the Edit Line	Click Cancel button in edit line		Press ESC
Cancel a Range Selection	Click anywhere in worksheet		Press ESC
Chart a Worksheet	Click Chart icon	From Tools menu, choose Chart	
Clear a Selected Cell or Range	Click Cut icon	From Edit menu or quick menu, choose Clear	Press DEL
Clear a Worksheet	Click Cut icon	From Edit menu or quick menu, choose Clear	Press DEL
Close a Worksheet		From File menu, choose Close	Press CTRL+F4
Confirm an Entry in a Cell	Click Confirm button in edit line or click any cell		Press ENTER or press arrow key
Copy Data or Formula Down		From Edit menu or quick menu, choose Copy Down	
Copy Data or Formula Right		From Edit menu or quick menu, choose Copy Right	
Edit Data in a Cell	Double-click cell or click in edit line		Press F2
Exit 1-2-3	Double-click Control menu box	From File menu, choose Exit	Press ALT+F4
Help	Click Help icon in dialog box	Select Help menu	Press F1
Open a Worksheet File	Click Open icon	From File menu, choose Open	Press CTRL+O
Print a Worksheet	Click Print icon	From File menu, choose Print	Press CTRL+P
Save a Worksheet	Click Save icon	From File menu, choose Save As or Save	Press CTRL+S
Select a Cell	Click cell	From Edit menu, choose Go To	Press arrow key
Select an Entire Worksheet	Click worksheet letter to left of column A and above row 1		
Select a Range	Drag mouse		Press SHIFT+ARROW
Start 1-2-3	Double-click 1-2-3 Release 5 program-item icon	From Program Manager File menu, choose Run and enter 1-2-3.EXE	
Sum a Column or Row	Click SmartSum icon		
Undo Last Action	Click Undo icon	From Edit menu, choose Undo	Press CTRL+Z

STUDENT ASSIGNMENT 1
True/False

Instructions: Circle T if the statement is true or F if the statement is false.

T F   1. To start Lotus 1-2-3 for Windows, double-click the Lotus 1-2-3 Release 5 for Windows program-item icon in the Lotus Applications group window.

T F   2. A single 1-2-3 worksheet can contain up to 256 columns and 8,192 rows.

T F   3. Columns are identified by numbers and rows are identified by letters of the alphabet.

T F   4. The intersection of each column and each row is defined as a grid line.

T F   5. The current cell is the cell into which you can enter data.

T F   6. To confirm an entry and keep the same current cell, press an arrow key.

T F   7. When you enter a label, the label is placed right-aligned in the current cell.

T F   8. The label-prefix character determines how a label is positioned in the cell.

T F   9. To cancel an entire entry before confirming it, press the BACKSPACE key.

T F 10. When you press an arrow key to confirm an entry, 1-2-3 confirms the entry of the data and then makes the adjacent cell in the direction of the arrow the current cell.

T F 11. A value is entered into a cell left-justified.

T F 12. A range is represented by the addresses of its top leftmost and bottom rightmost cells, separated by two periods.

T F 13. When you copy cell addresses in a formula, 1-2-3 automatically adjusts the addresses for each new position of the formula.

T F 14. A quick menu contains frequently used commands you can use with a currently selected range.

T F 15. You can activate the quick menu by pressing the left mouse button.

T F 16. To copy a formula from one cell to adjacent cells in a column, select the cell containing the formula, drag the range into which the formula will be copied, and choose the Copy Right command from the quick menu.

T F 17. 1-2-3 provides fourteen style templates to format a worksheet quickly.

T F 18. When you chart data on a worksheet, only values can be included in the range which is charted.

T F 19. To exit 1-2-3 and return to Windows Program Manager, choose the Close command from the File menu.

T F 20. Pressing the DEL key when a chart is selected removes the chart from the worksheet.

STUDENT ASSIGNMENT 2
Multiple Choice

Instructions: Circle the correct response.

1. A _____ is a rectangular group of cells in a worksheet.
   a. range
   b. block
   c. grid line
   d. window

(continued)

STUDENT ASSIGNMENT 2 (continued)

2. To enter a label into a cell, the cell must be _____.
   a. the current cell
   b. blank
   c. defined as a label
   d. filled
3. Mode indicators display in the _____ bar.
   a. menu
   b. title
   c. status
   d. control
4. Which character below is not considered a value by 1-2-3?
   a.)
   b. $
   c. \
   d. @
5. When you enter a label into the current cell, the label is _____.
   a. aligned to the right
   b. aligned to the left
   c. centered
   d. aligned across columns
6. To remove the selection from a range of cells, _____.
   a. click any cell in the worksheet
   b. press the DEL key
   c. click the Cut icon on the set of SmartIcons
   d. print the worksheet
7. Which of the following is a valid @Sum function?
   a. SUM(A1..A5)
   b. @SUM(B10..C20)
   c. @SUM(F1,F5)
   d. @SUM(B5:B12)
8. You cannot undo the effects of _____ commands.
   a. Print
   b. Clear
   c. File
   d. both a and c
9. When a range is selected and you press the DEL key, 1-2-3 _____.
   a. clears all data
   b. clears all styles
   c. clears both data and styles
   d. displays a dialog box asking you what features to clear
10. To clear both cell contents and styles from a selected cell, _____.
   a. press the DEL key
   b. from the Edit menu, choose the ERASE command
   c. click the Cut icon on the set of SmartIcons
   d. press the SPACEBAR

STUDENT ASSIGNMENT 3
Understanding the 1-2-3 Worksheet

Instructions: In Figure SA1-3, arrows point to the major components of a 1-2-3 worksheet. Identify the various parts of the worksheet in the spaces provided.

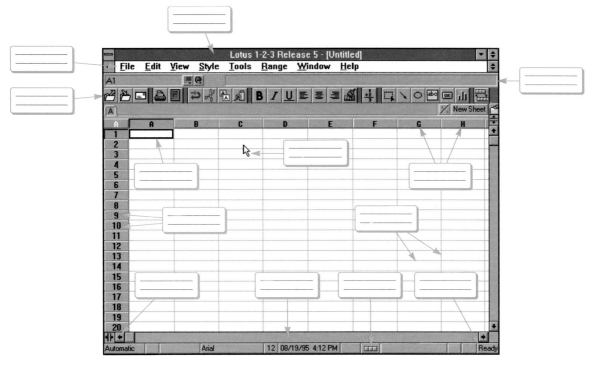

FIGURE SA1-3

STUDENT ASSIGNMENT 4
Understanding SmartIcons

Instructions: In the worksheet in Figure SA1-4, arrows point to several of the icons on the default set of SmartIcons. In the spaces provided, identify each icon.

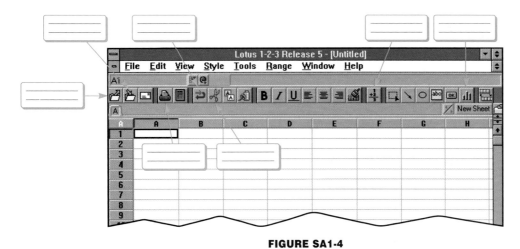

FIGURE SA1-4

STUDENT ASSIGNMENT 5
Understanding the Edit Line on the Worksheet

Instructions: Answer the following questions concerning the contents of the edit line in Figure SA1-5.

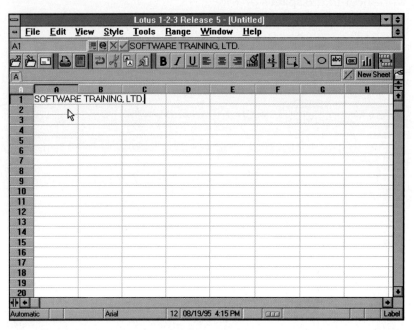

FIGURE SA1-5

1. What does the A1 signify in the selection indicator in the edit line?

_____

_____

2. What is the purpose of the button that contains the letter X in the edit line?

_____

_____

3. What is the purpose of the button that contains the check mark in the edit line?

_____

_____

4. How would you complete the entry into cell A1 of the label, SOFTWARE TRAINING, LTD., that displays in the contents box without using the mouse and maintain cell A1 as the current cell?

_____

_____

5. What is the term for the vertical line that follows the label, SOFTWARE TRAINING, LTD., in cell A1 and what does it indicate?

_____

_____

STUDENT ASSIGNMENT 6
Summing Values

Instructions: The worksheet in Figure SA1-6 contains data but no totals. In the spaces provided below the worksheet, list the steps to accomplish the required tasks.

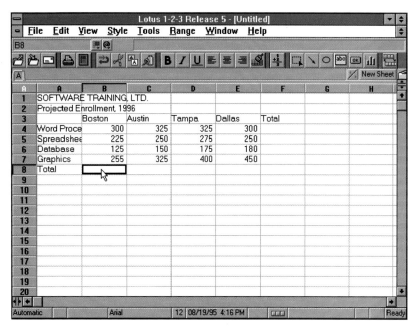

FIGURE SA1-6

Task 1: Sum the values in the Boston column, and place the result in cell B8.

Steps: _____

_____

Task 2: Sum the values in the Austin, Tampa, and Dallas columns, and place the results in cells C8, D8, and E8, respectively.

Steps: _____

_____

Task 3: Sum the values in the Word Processing row, and place the result in cell F4.

Steps: _____

_____

Task 4: Sum the values in the Spreadsheet, Database, Graphics, and Total rows, and place the results in cells F5, F6, F7, and F8, respectively.

Steps: _____

_____

COMPUTER LABORATORY EXERCISE 1
Using the Help Menu

Instructions: Perform the following tasks using a computer.

1. Start Lotus 1-2-3 for Windows.
2. Select the Help menu.
3. Choose the Contents command from the Help menu. Maximize the Help window if necessary.
4. When the 1-2-3 Release 5 Help Contents topic displays, click the 1-2-3 Window icon (▣).
5. When the 1-2-3 Window pop-up box displays, use the mouse pointer to point to Parts of the 1-2-3 Window topic and click the left mouse button.
6. Read the Parts of the 1-2-3 Window topic. Use the scroll arrow in the lower right corner of the Help window to scroll through and read all of the topic.
7. Ready the printer, select the File menu from the main menu bar in the Help window, and choose the Print Topic command to print a hard copy of the help topic, Parts of the 1-2-3 Window.
8. Click the Contents button in the upper left corner of the Help window to return to the original Help screen.
9. Use the technique described in steps 3 and 4 to display help on any other topic listed.
10. Close the Help window by choosing the Exit command from the File menu in the Help window.
11. Select the Help menu in the 1-2-3 window and choose the Tutorial command.
12. Select and read these lessons: Using This Tutorial and Building a Simple Spreadsheet.

COMPUTER LABORATORY EXERCISE 2
Using the Gallery Command from the Style Menu and Sizing a Chart

Instructions: Start 1-2-3. Open the CLE1-2.WK4 file from the Lotus4 subdirectory on the Student Diskette that accompanies this book. The worksheet CLE1-2.WK4 is shown in Figure CLE1-2. The worksheet resembles the SOFTWARE TRAINING, LTD. worksheet created in Project 1.

Perform the following tasks:

1. Select the range A1..F8.
2. From the Style menu, choose the Gallery command. Review the fourteen styles in the Template list box by selecting each one using the mouse and viewing the example in the Sample area.
3. Select the Simple2 template and choose the OK button in the Gallery dialog box.
4. Select the chart by clicking anywhere within the chart frame.

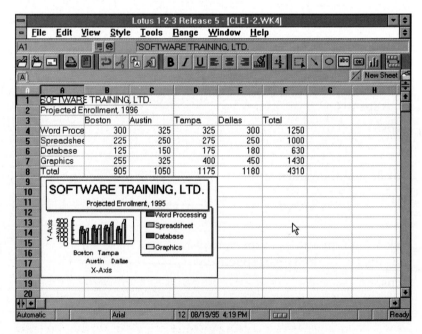

FIGURE CLE1-2

L56

5. Drag the chart handles until the chart is the approximate size of the chart shown in Figure 1-59 on page L33.

6. Click the Print icon to print the worksheet with the Simple2 template. When the Print dialog box displays, choose the Current worksheet option in the Print area. Choose the OK button in the Print dialog box.

7. Close the CLE1-2.WK4 worksheet. Choose the No button in the Close dialog box.

COMPUTER LABORATORY EXERCISE 3
Changing Data in a Worksheet

Instructions: Start 1-2-3. Open the CLE1-3.WK4 file from the Lotus4 subdirectory on the Student Diskette that accompanies this book. The worksheet CLE1-3.WK4 is shown in Figure CLE1-3. Use the data in the table below the worksheet to make the changes specified in the table.

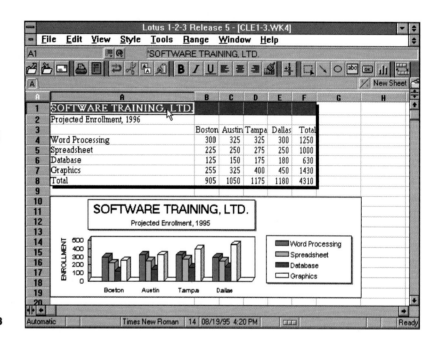

FIGURE CLE1-3

CELL	CURRENT CELL CONTENTS	CHANGE CELL CONTENTS TO
A1	SOFTWARE TRAINING, LTD.	TRAINING, LTD.
D3	Tampa	Miami
D4	325	400
D5	275	450
D6	175	475
D7	400	100

Perform the following tasks:

1. Make the changes to the worksheet described in the table. As you edit the title of the worksheet, watch the worksheet and chart change to display the new title. As you edit the values in the cells, watch the total projected enrollments change (cells D8, F4, F5, F6, F7, and F8). Each of the values in these six cells is based on the @SUM function. When you enter a new value, 1-2-3 automatically recalculates the @SUM functions. The chart also changes as each cell is edited. After you have made the changes listed in the table, the total projected enrollment for Miami in cell D8 should equal 1425, and the total projected enrollment for the year in cell F8 should equal 4560.

2. Print the revised worksheet.

3. Close the CLE1-3.WK4 worksheet. Choose the No button in the Close dialog box.

COMPUTER LABORATORY ASSIGNMENT 1
Creating a Current Employees Worksheet

Purpose: To provide experience in creating a worksheet that requires entering labels and values, calculating sums, applying a style template to the worksheet, creating a chart, saving a worksheet, and printing a worksheet.

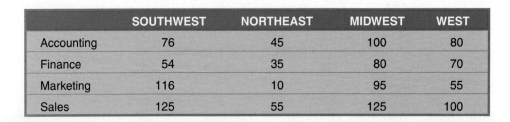

	SOUTHWEST	NORTHEAST	MIDWEST	WEST
Accounting	76	45	100	80
Finance	54	35	80	70
Marketing	116	10	95	55
Sales	125	55	125	100

Problem: Create a worksheet listing the total current employees of TOOL PRODUCTS, INC. by department and by region. The current employees are shown in the table above the worksheet. The worksheet is shown in Figure CLA1-1.

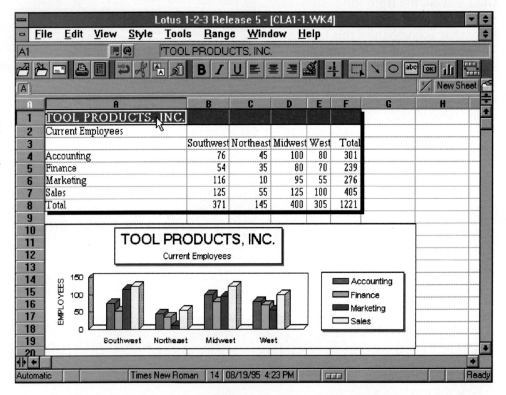

FIGURE CLA1-1

Instructions:

1. Create the worksheet using the data from the table.
2. Calculate the total employees for Southwest, Northeast, Midwest, and West on the worksheet.
3. Calculate the total employees for Accounting, Finance, Marketing, and Sales on the worksheet.
4. Calculate the total employees currently working for TOOL PRODUCTS, INC. on the worksheet.
5. Apply the style template, Simple3, as shown in the worksheet in Figure CLA1-1.
6. Create the 3D bar chart as shown in Figure CLA1-1 from the worksheet data.
7. Save the worksheet you create on a diskette. Use a file name consisting of the initials of your first and last names followed by the assignment number. Example: KS1-1
8. Print the worksheet with the chart you have created.
9. Follow directions from your instructor for turning in this assignment.

L58

COMPUTER LABORATORY ASSIGNMENT 2
Creating a Vacation Packages Sold Worksheet

Purpose: To provide experience in creating a worksheet that requires entering labels and values, calculating sums, applying a style template to the worksheet, creating a chart, saving a worksheet, and printing a worksheet.

	HAWAII	CARIBBEAN	ALASKA	EUROPE
August 05	435	368	248	435
August 12	378	395	197	425
August 19	458	259	165	465
August 26	289	172	241	475

Problem: Create a worksheet for VACATION TRAVELER totaling the vacation packages sold during the month of August. The worksheet contains the total weekly vacation packages sold to Hawaii, the Caribbean, Alaska, and Europe. The weekly packages sold are shown in the table above the worksheet. The worksheet is shown in Figure CLA1-2.

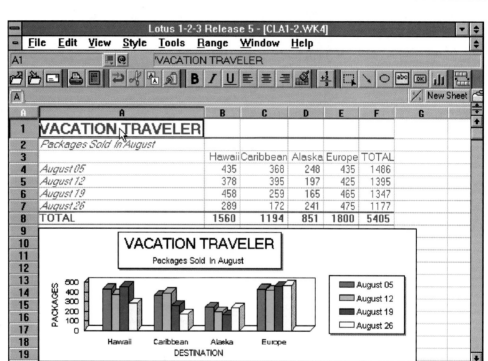

FIGURE CLA1-2

Instructions:

1. Create the worksheet shown in Figure CLA1-2 using the data in the table.
2. On the worksheet, calculate the total vacation packages sold to Hawaii, the Caribbean, Alaska, and Europe.
3. Calculate the total vacation packages sold for August 5, August 12, August 19, and August 26 on the worksheet.
4. Calculate the total vacation packages sold for the entire month of August on the worksheet.
5. Apply the style template, Simple1, shown in Figure CLA1-2.
6. Create the 3D bar chart as shown in Figure CLA1-2.
7. Save the worksheet and chart you create on a diskette. Use a file name consisting of the initials of your first and last names followed by the assignment number. Example: KS1-2.
8. Print the worksheet and chart you created.
9. Follow directions from your instructor for turning in this assignment.

COMPUTER LABORATORY ASSIGNMENT 3
Creating a Diving Rental Worksheet

Purpose: To provide experience in creating a worksheet that requires entering labels and values, calculating sums, applying a style template to the worksheet, creating a chart, saving a worksheet, and printing a worksheet.

	APRIL	MAY	JUNE
Wet Suits	150	295	320
Tanks	100	75	85
Regulators	165	165	245

Problem: Create a worksheet for OCEAN DIVING RENTALS totaling the rentals for Wet Suits, Tanks, and Regulators for the months of April, May, and June. The rentals for these months are shown in the table above the worksheet. The worksheet is shown in Figure CLA1-3.

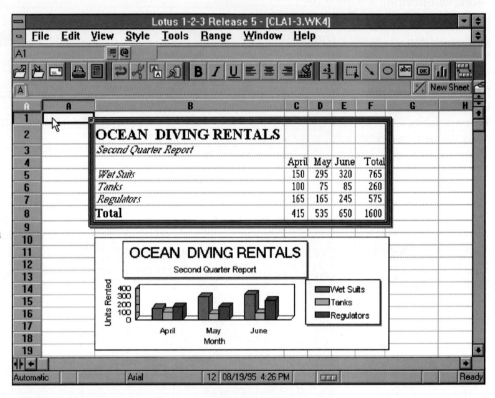

FIGURE CLA1-3

Instructions:

1. Create a worksheet in the format shown using the data from the table. Begin the worksheet title, OCEAN DIVING RENTALS, in cell B2 as shown in Figure CLA1-3.
2. Calculate totals for April, May, and June rentals on the worksheet.
3. Calculate totals for Wet Suits, Tanks, and Regulators rentals on the worksheet.
4. Calculate total rentals for the entire second quarter.
5. Apply the style template shown in Figure CLA1-3 to the worksheet.
6. Create the 3D bar chart shown in Figure CLA1-3.
7. Save the worksheet you create on a diskette. Use a file name consisting of the initials of your first and last names followed by the assignment number. Example: KS1-3.
8. Print the worksheet and chart you have created.
9. Make the following changes to the diving rentals: April, Wet Suits — 300, May, Regulators — 200, June, Tanks — 200. The new totals should be: April — 565 , May — 570 , June — 765.
10. Save the modified worksheet on a diskette. Use a file name consisting of the initials of your first and last names followed by the assignment number and the letter A. Example: KS1-3A.
11. Print the modified worksheet and chart.
12. Follow directions from your instructor for turning in this assignment.

COMPUTER LABORATORY ASSIGNMENT 4
Creating a Video Inventory Worksheet

Purpose: To provide experience in planning and creating a worksheet using the skills learned in Project 1.

Problem: The owners of the local video store where you are employed have asked you to prepare a worksheet containing the inventory of all the videos in each of their four stores. Each video falls into one of four categories: Drama, Comedy, Action, and Children.

Instructions:

1. Design and create a worksheet that contains an inventory listing of all videos in each of the four stores.
2. Calculate the total videos for each store on the worksheet.
3. Calculate the total videos for each category on the worksheet.
4. Calculate the total videos for all four stores on the worksheet.
5. Determine the most appropriate style template to apply to the worksheet.
6. Create a 3D bar chart from the data in the worksheet.
7. Save the worksheet you create on a diskette. Use a file name consisting of the initials of your first and last names followed by the assignment number. Example: KS1-4.
8. Print the worksheet and chart you have created.
9. Follow directions from your instructor for turning in this assignment.

▼

FORMULAS AND WORKSHEET ENHANCEMENT

OBJECTIVES You will have mastered the material in this project when you can:

- ▸ Use arithmetic operators in formulas
- ▸ Use Point mode to enter formulas
- ▸ Use the @function selector
- ▸ Use the @MAX and @MIN functions
- ▸ Use the status bar to increase the size of the font in a cell
- ▸ Bold characters
- ▸ Italicize characters
- ▸ Align labels across columns
- ▸ Align labels vertically in a cell
- ▸ Align labels horizontally in a cell
- ▸ Wrap labels to enter multiple lines in a cell
- ▸ Format values in the currency format
- ▸ Format values in the comma format

- ▸ Format values in the percent format
- ▸ Change the width of a column
- ▸ Change the width of nonadjacent columns
- ▸ Change the height of a row
- ▸ Change the background color of a worksheet
- ▸ Change text color
- ▸ Create a three-dimensional (3D) pie chart
- ▸ Add a title to a chart
- ▸ Format chart titles
- ▸ Use the spell checker
- ▸ Preview a worksheet
- ▸ Print worksheet data separately from a chart

▶ INTRODUCTION

I n Project 1, you learned that a worksheet is useful for presenting data, performing calculations, and charting data. In addition to the @SUM function for adding values, 1-2-3 can perform calculations using specific formulas you enter.

To graphically present data contained in the worksheet, you can produce many types of charts in addition to the three-dimensional bar chart seen in Project 1.

You can also enhance the appearance of your worksheet and make your presentation more effective by formatting values with dollar signs and commas, changing labels to a bold or italic format, changing text and worksheet background colors, and changing the widths of columns and heights of rows.

PROJECT TWO

To illustrate these capabilities, Project 2 explains the steps to produce the worksheet and chart shown in Figure 2-1. The worksheet contains the portfolio analysis of an investment in precious gems. The name of the gem, the purchase date, the number of gems purchased, and the purchase price per gem occupy the first four columns. In the fifth column, titled Initial Value, 1-2-3 calculates the amount of the initial value using a formula that multiplies the

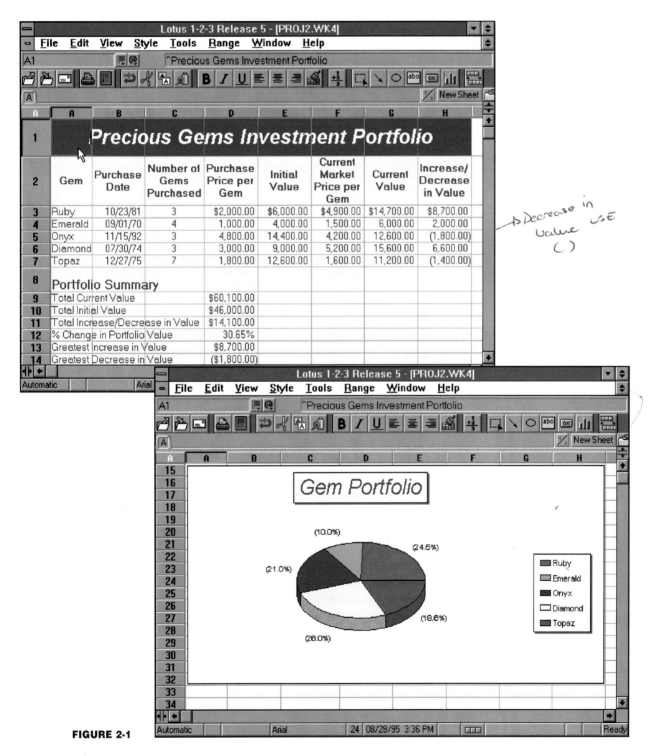

FIGURE 2-1

number of gems purchased (column C) times the purchase price per gem (column D). For example, three rubies were purchased at a price of $2,000.00 per ruby. The initial value of the investment in rubies (3 times $2,000.00) is $6,000.00.

Column F of the worksheet shown in Figure 2-1 on the previous page contains the current market price per gem. The current market price of a ruby is $4,900.00. 1-2-3 calculates the current value (column G) using a formula that multiplies the number of gems purchased (column C) times the current market price per gem (column F). The current value of the rubies is $14,700.00 (3 times $4,900.00).

When an investor purchases and holds gems over a period of time, the current market price per gem can increase or decrease from the initial purchase price per gem. If the current market price per gem is greater than the initial purchase price per gem, the value of the investment in the gem increases. If the current market price per gem goes down and is less than the purchase price per gem, the value of the investment decreases. 1-2-3 calculates the increase or decrease in value of the investment in column H using the formula, current value (column G) minus initial value (column E). From the worksheet illustrated in Figure 2-1, you can see the investment in rubies shows an increase in value ($14,700.00 – $6,000.00 equals $8,700.00).

The bottom of the worksheet displays the portfolio summary of the investment portfolio. The total current value ($60,100.00) is the sum of the values in column G. The total initial value ($46,000) is the sum of the values in column E. Total increase or decrease in value ($14,100) is calculated by the formula, total current value minus total initial value. The % change in portfolio value (30.65%) is equal to total increase or decrease in value ($14,100.00) divided by the total initial value ($46,000.00). The portfolio summary also includes the greatest increase in value for one set of gems ($8,700.00) and the greatest decrease in value for one set of gems ($1,800.00) in the investment portfolio.

Finally, the worksheet contains a chart called a three-dimensional pie chart based on the current value of the gems in the investment portfolio. A **pie chart** is used to show how 100% of an amount is divided. Each slice, or wedge, of the pie represents a contribution to the whole. The pie chart in Figure 2-1 on the previous page shows the percentage of the portfolio each set of gems represents.

Worksheet Preparation Steps

The following list is an overview of the procedure to prepare the worksheet and chart shown in Figure 2-1.

1. Start Lotus 1-2-3 Release 5 for Windows.
2. Enter the worksheet title (Precious Gems Investment Portfolio) and the column titles (Gem, Purchase Date, Number of Gems Purchased, Purchase Price per Gem, Initial Value, Current Market Price per Gem, Current Value, and Increase/Decrease in Value).
3. Enter the gem name, purchase date, number of gems purchased, and the purchase price per gem for the first gem in the investment portfolio.
4. Enter the formula to calculate the initial value (number of gems purchased times purchase price per gem).
5. Enter the current market price per gem.
6. Enter the formula to calculate the current value (number of gems purchased times current market price per gem).
7. Enter the formula to calculate the increase/decrease in value (current value minus initial value).
8. Enter the data for the remaining gems in the portfolio.
9. Copy the formulas for initial value, current value, and increase/decrease in value for each gem.
10. Enter the titles for the portfolio summary.

11. Enter the formulas to calculate total current value, total initial value, total increase/decrease in value, % change in portfolio value, greatest increase in value, and greatest decrease in value for the portfolio.
12. Save the worksheet.
13. Format the worksheet.
14. Create the pie chart.
15. Print the worksheet data and print the chart.

The following sections contain a detailed explanation of each of these steps.

► STARTING LOTUS 1-2-3 RELEASE 5 FOR WINDOWS

o start Lotus 1-2-3 Release 5 for Windows, follow the steps you used in Project 1. These steps are summarized below.

TO START LOTUS 1-2-3 RELEASE 5 FOR WINDOWS

Step 1: From Program Manager, open the Lotus Applications group window.
Step 2: Double-click the Lotus 1-2-3 Release 5 program-item icon.

► ENTERING WORKSHEET TITLES

he worksheet title shown in Figure 2-1 on page L63 is centered over columns A through H in row 1. Because the centered label must first be entered into the leftmost column of the area over which it is centered, you must enter it into cell A1. The column headings in row 2 begin in cell A2 and extend through cell H2. To enter the titles on the worksheet, first select the cells in which the titles belong and then type the titles, as illustrated in the following steps.

STEP 1 ►

Select cell A1 by pointing to cell A1 and clicking the left mouse button. Type the worksheet title, `Precious Gems Investment Portfolio`, and press the DOWN ARROW key.

1-2-3 enters the worksheet title into cell A1 and the cell pointer moves to cell A2 (Figure 2-2). Notice that the title entered in cell A1 overflows into cell B1 and cell C1 because these two cells are empty.

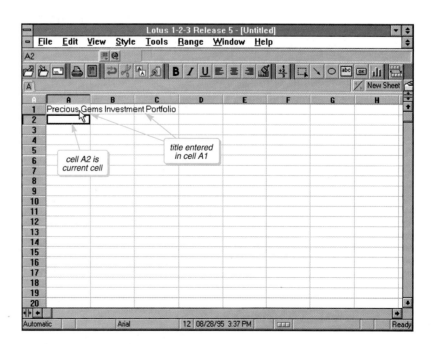

FIGURE 2-2

STEP 2 ▶

In cells A2 through H2, type the column titles, Gem, Purchase Date, Number of Gems Purchased, Purchase Price per Gem, Initial Value, Current Market Price per Gem, Current Value, **and** Increase/ Decrease in Value.

The column titles display as shown in row 2 (Figure 2-3). Notice the blank space before the D in Decrease in cell H2. This space is necessary for the label to display properly when the cell is formatted. Although the titles do not entirely display in Figure 2-3, this will be corrected when you format the worksheet.

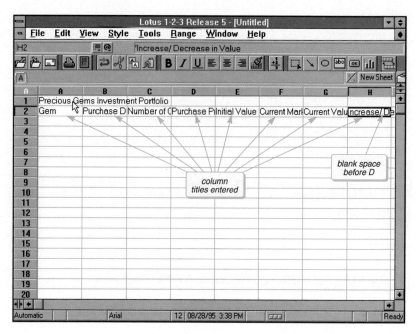

FIGURE 2-3

▶ ENTERING DATA

After entering the worksheet title and column titles, the next step is to enter the data in the worksheet. The data consists of labels (gem name), values (purchase date, number of gems purchased, and so on), and formulas that calculate initial value, current value, and increase/decrease in value.

To enter the gem name, purchase date, number of gems purchased, and purchase price per gem, perform the following steps.

TO ENTER LABELS, DATES, AND VALUES ▼

STEP 1 ▶

Select the cell to contain the gem name – cell A3 – and type the gem name, Ruby. **Press the** RIGHT ARROW **key and type the purchase date,** 10/23/81, **in cell B3. Confirm the entry in cell B3 by clicking the Confirm button or pressing the** ENTER **key.**

1-2-3 displays the date you type in the contents box and in the cell (Figure 2-4). The date format, 12/31/93, displays in the format selector in the status bar. Notice the date is entered right-aligned in the cell.

FIGURE 2-4

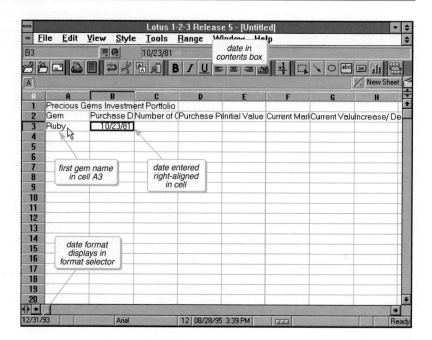

STEP 2 ▶

Press the RIGHT ARROW **key and enter the number of gems purchased** (3) **in cell C3. Then press the** RIGHT ARROW **key and enter the purchase price per gem** (2000) **in cell D3. Press the** RIGHT ARROW **key. Do not type a dollar sign for the purchase price per gem.**

The values you enter are stored in the cells (Figure 2-5).

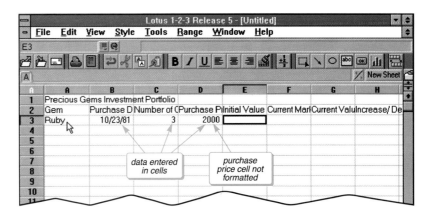

FIGURE 2-5

When you enter a value in a cell, 1-2-3 examines the entry and selects an appropriate format. This is called **automatic format** and is the worksheet default setting that 1-2-3 uses when you create a new worksheet. In Figure 2-4, you entered a value in a date format, 10/23/81. 1-2-3 recognizes the entry as a date and stores it right-aligned in the cell.

1-2-3 can recognize a date in a number of different **date formats**. Table 2-1 contains the different formats in which a date can be entered and automatically formatted to the appropriate date format.

▶ **TABLE 2-1**

DATE ENTERED	FORMAT NAME	DATE FORMAT
09-Jun-95	Day-Month-Year	31-Dec-93
01-Jan	Day-Month	31-Dec
Apr-97	Month-Year	Dec-93
12/16/85	Long International	12/31/93

In Step 1 on page L66, when you entered the date in cell B3, 1-2-3 recognized the entry as a date in the Long International Date format and applied the Long International Date format (12/31/93) to the cell. This is the format displayed in the format selector in the status bar. The **format selector** displays the format of the current cell (Figure 2-4)

When entering the dollar amounts, you do not type a dollar sign and comma. You will format the numbers in the worksheet with dollar signs and commas in a later step.

Entering Formulas

The initial value, current value, and increase/decrease in value fields in the worksheet are calculated based on formulas. To continue creating the worksheet, you must enter the formulas in their respective cells.

In 1-2-3, a **formula** is an equation that calculates a new value using existing values in cells within the worksheet. For example, the initial value is calculated from the values in the number of gems purchased column and the purchase price per gem column (initial value equals number of gems purchased times purchase price per gem). The result of the calculation is displayed in the worksheet cell where the formula is entered.

The first element entered in a formula alerts 1-2-3 that you are entering a formula, not a label. A formula can begin with a number or a special character (+,-,=,(,@,.,$, or #). If a formula begins with a cell address, the cell address must be preceded by a character that defines the cell as a value, such as a plus sign (+). The first character can be followed by the combination of cell references, numbers, operators, and @functions necessary to calculate the required value.

In a formula, a cell reference identifies a cell that contains data to be used in the formula. For example, when you place the formula +C3*D3 in cell E3, 1-2-3 will multiply the value in cell C3 by the value in cell D3 and place the product in cell E3. The asterisk (*) in the formula is the multiplication operator. An **operator** is a mathematical symbol that tells 1-2-3 what type of operation to perform. 1-2-3 recognizes five possible operators in a formula. These operators are summarized in Table 2-2.

Formulas can contain more than two cell references or numeric values and can also contain **multiple operators**. For example, the formula, +C2*(D3-E3)/A5, is a valid formula. To determine the results of this formula, 1-2-3 performs the operations left to right within the formula according to their order of precedence. The **order of precedence** in 1-2-3 corresponds to standard algebraic rules. First, any operation contained within parentheses is performed. Therefore, in the sample formula, the first operation is to subtract the value in cell E3 from the value in cell D3.

Then, exponentiation is performed, followed by any multiplication or division operations. Finally, addition and subtraction are performed. If two or more operators within the formula have the same order of precedence, 1-2-3 performs the operations from left to right. Thus, in the sample formula, 1-2-3 would multiply the result of the subtraction of values in cells D3 and E3 by the value in cell C2 and then divide the result by the value in cell A5.

▶ **TABLE 2-2**

OPERATOR	FUNCTION
+	Addition
−	Subtraction
*	Multiplication
/	Division
^	Exponentiation

When writing formulas, you must take care to ensure the proper calculations are performed. One method to ensure the correct sequence is to use **parentheses**. For example, if a formula in cell C4 is supposed to calculate the average of values in cells A1, B3, and C3, the formula +A1+B3+C3/3 will not obtain the proper result because 1-2-3 will first divide the value in cell C3 by 3 and then add the values in cells A1, B3, and the result of the division.

The correct way to write the formula is (A1+B3+C3)/3. In this formula, 1-2-3 will first add the values in cells A1, B3, and C3. Then, it will divide the answer by 3, resulting in the average of the three numbers.

The examples in Table 2-3 further illustrate the manner in which 1-2-3 evaluates formulas.

▶ **TABLE 2-3**

CELL	FORMULA	RESULT
C5 = 12	+C5+C6/C7	14
C6 = 6	(C5+C6)/C7	6
C7 = 3		
A1 = 12	+A1+A2*A3−A4/A5	95
A2 = 6	+A1+A2*(A3−A4)/A5	48
A3 = 14	(A1+A2*(A3−A4))/A5	42
A4 = 2		
A5 = 2		
A1 = 2	+D5^A1+D6	110
D5 = 10	(D5^A1)+D6	110
D6 = 10		

Whenever you enter a formula, review the formula carefully to ensure the correct calculation will occur.

In Project 2, the initial value is calculated by multiplying the number of gems purchased times the purchase price per gem. From the worksheet shown in Figure 2-5 on page L67, notice that for rubies, the number of gems purchased is contained in cell C3 and the purchase price per gem is located in cell D3. Therefore, the formula to calculate the initial value for rubies is +C3*D3.

The following steps illustrate entering the formula that calculates the initial value.

TO ENTER A FORMULA ▼

STEP 1 ▶

Ensure cell E3 (the cell that will contain the formula) is selected, and type a plus sign (+).

1-2-3 displays the plus sign in the contents box and in cell E3 (Figure 2-6). The plus sign tells 1-2-3 you are entering a formula. In addition, the Cancel and Confirm buttons appear in the edit line and the mode indicator changes from Ready to Value.

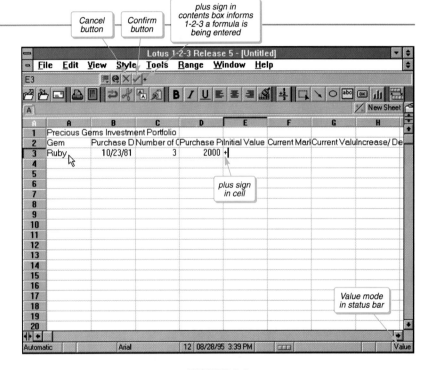

FIGURE 2-6

STEP 2 ▶

Select the first cell in the formula – cell C3 – by pointing to the cell and clicking the left mouse button.

When you select the cell, the mouse pointer changes to an arrow pointing to a cell, indicating a range is selected (Figure 2-7). 1-2-3 enters the cell reference (C3) in the formula in both the cell and the contents box and highlights the cell reference in the cell. The mode indicator changes from Value to Point, indicating you are pointing to a cell to be included in a formula.

FIGURE 2-7

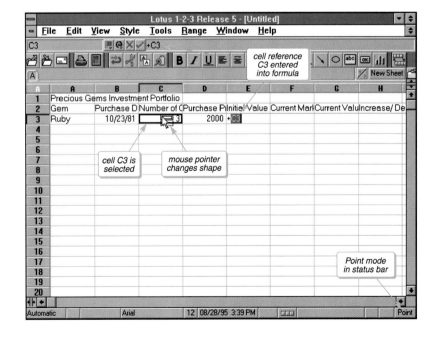

STEP 3 ▶

Type the multiplication operator (*).

1-2-3 displays the multiplication operator in both the contents box and the cell where you are entering the formula (Figure 2-8). In addition, 1-2-3 removes the temporary highlight from cell C3. The mode indicator changes from Point to Value.

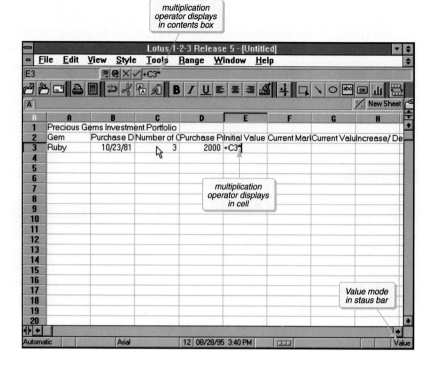

FIGURE 2-8

STEP 4 ▶

Select the second cell in the formula – cell D3 – by clicking the cell.

1-2-3 places the cell reference (D3) in the formula in both the cell and the contents box (Figure 2-9). The mode indicator changes from Value to Point and the mouse pointer changes to an arrow pointing to a cell.

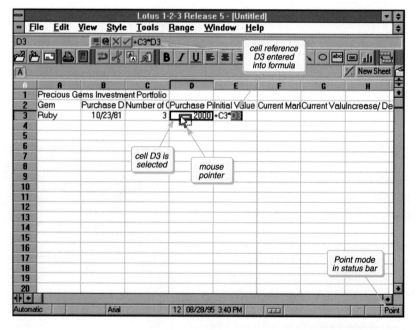

FIGURE 2-9

STEP 5 ▶

Confirm the entry by clicking the
Confirm button or pressing the
ENTER key.

*1-2-3 displays the value calculated
by the formula (6000) in cell E3
and the formula itself in the contents box (Figure 2-10).*

FIGURE 2-10

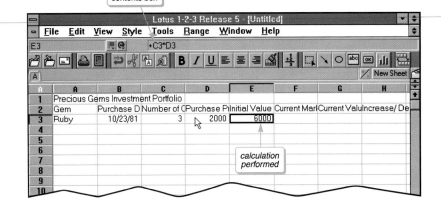

In the previous steps, you selected the cells used in the formula by using the
mouse to select the cells. You can also type the cell reference when you enter a
formula. For example, to enter the formula in cell E3 as shown in the illustration
above, you can type +C3*D3 and then press the RIGHT ARROW key, click the Confirm button, or press the ENTER key. This method, however, is prone to error
because you may type the incorrect cell reference. It is recommended, therefore,
that you use the mouse and **Point mode** for identifying the cell references to
enter into a formula.

To continue the row for the investment in rubies, you must enter the current
market price per gem into cell F3 and then enter the formula to calculate the current value in cell G3. To calculate the current value for rubies, the number of gems
purchased in cell C3 is multiplied by the current market price per gem in cell F3.
Therefore, the formula is +C3*F3. The steps to enter the current market price per
gem and the formula for the current value follow.

TO ENTER A VALUE AND A FORMULA ▼

STEP 1 ▶

Select cell F3, type the current
market value for a Ruby (4900),
press the RIGHT ARROW key, and type
a plus sign (+).

*1-2-3 displays 4900 (the current
market price per gem) in cell F3.
Cell G3 is selected, and a plus
sign displays in both the contents
box and cell G3 (Figure 2-11). The
mode indicator in the status bar
changes from Ready to Value.*

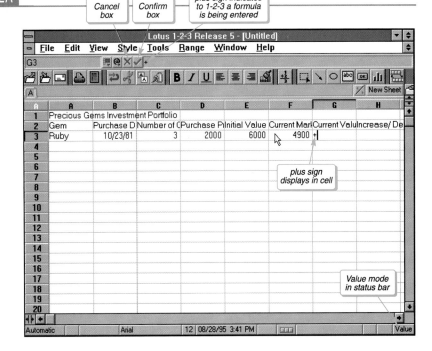

FIGURE 2-11

STEP 2 ▶

Select the first cell in the formula – cell C3 – by clicking the cell.

1-2-3 highlights cell C3 and places the cell reference in the formula (Figure 2-12). The mode indicator in the status bar changes from Value to Point.

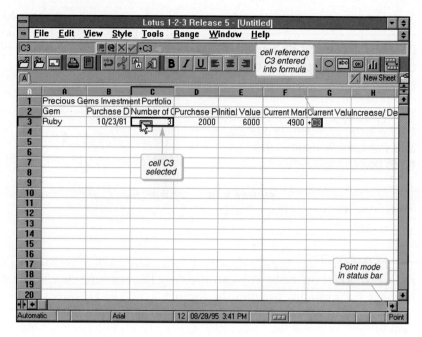

FIGURE 2-12

STEP 3 ▶

Type the multiplication operator (*) and select the second cell in the formula – cell F3.

1-2-3 places the multiplication operator in the formula, highlights cell F3, and places the cell reference in the formula (Figure 2-13).

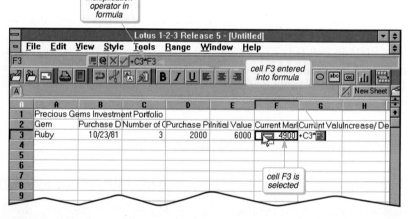

FIGURE 2-13

STEP 4 ▶

Confirm the entry by clicking the Confirm button or pressing the ENTER key.

1-2-3 enters the formula into cell G3, calculates the result, and displays the result (14700) in cell G3 (Figure 2-14). The formula displays in the contents box.

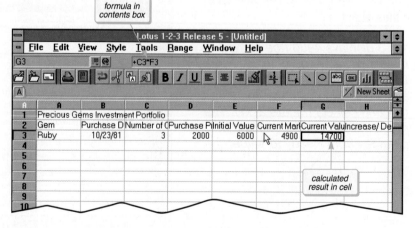

FIGURE 2-14

The last formula you must enter in the row for rubies calculates the increase or decrease in the value of the investment by subtracting the initial value (cell E3) from the current value (cell G3). The formula for this calculation is +G3-E3. To enter this formula into cell H3, perform the following steps.

TO ENTER A FORMULA ▼

STEP 1 ▶

Select cell H3, type a plus sign (+), select cell G3, type a minus sign (-), and select cell E3.

The formula appears in the contents box and in cell H3 (Figure 2-15).

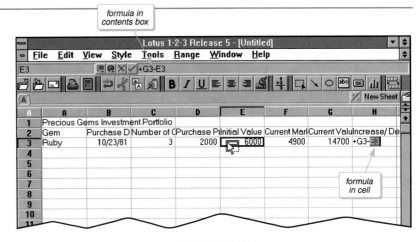

FIGURE 2-15

STEP 2 ▶

Click the Confirm button or press the ENTER key.

1-2-3 enters the formula into cell H3, calculates the result, and displays the result in cell H3 (Figure 2-16).

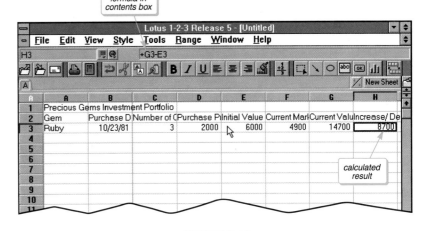

FIGURE 2-16

Entering the Worksheet Data

After you have entered the row for the investment in rubies in the worksheet, you must enter the data for the investment in emeralds into row 4 of the worksheet. Use the same method for entering this row of data as you used for row 3, except in this row, enter no formulas; enter merely the gem, purchase date, number of gems purchased, purchase price per gem, and current market price per gem. Complete the steps on the next page to enter the data for the investment in emeralds.

TO ENTER THE DATA FOR THE INVESTMENT IN EMERALDS

Step 1: Select cell A4 and type the gem (Emerald).
Step 2: Press the RIGHT ARROW key and type the purchase date (09/01/70) in cell B4.
Step 3: Press the RIGHT ARROW key and type the number of gems purchased (4) in cell C4.
Step 4: Press the RIGHT ARROW key, type the purchase price per gem (1000) in cell D4, and click the Confirm button or press the ENTER key.
Step 5: Select cell F4, type the current market price per gem (1500) and click the Confirm button or press the ENTER key.

The data for the investment in emeralds in row 4 displays as shown in Figure 2-17. The formulas are not entered.

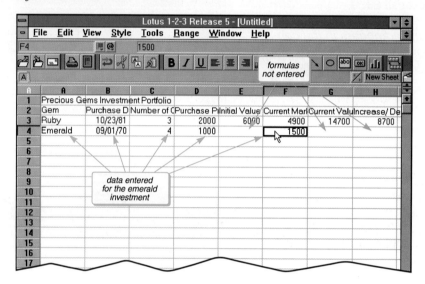

FIGURE 2-17

Notice in Figure 2-17 the data has been entered but no formulas have been entered into row 4. You will copy the formulas from row 3 after all the other data in the worksheet is entered. It is more efficient to copy them all at one time rather than row by row.

The next step is to enter the data for the remaining gems in the portfolio; that is, enter the gem, the purchase date, the number of gems purchased, the purchase price per gem, and the current market price per gem for the remaining gems, onyx, diamond, and topaz in the worksheet. Follow these steps to enter the data for the investment in onyx, diamond and topaz.

TO ENTER THE DATA FOR THE INVESTMENT IN ONYX, DIAMOND, AND TOPAZ

Step 1: Select cell A5 and enter Onyx. Then, enter 11/15/92 in cell B5, 3 in cell C5, 4800 in cell D5, and 4200 in cell F5.
Step 2: Select cell A6 and enter Diamond. Then, enter 07/30/74 in cell B6, 3 in cell C6, 3000 in cell D6, and 5200 in cell F6.
Step 3: Select cell A7 and enter Topaz. Then, enter 12/27/75 in cell B7, 7 in cell C7, 1800 in cell D7, and 1600 in cell F7.

The data for the investment in onyx, diamond, and topaz in rows 5, 6, and 7 displays as shown in Figure 2-18. The formulas are not entered.

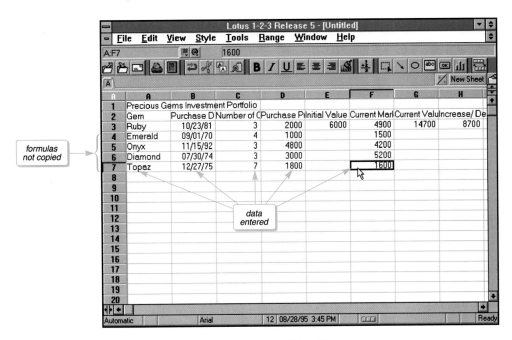

formulas
not copied

data
entered

FIGURE 2-18

In Project 1, you learned that a range is a rectangular group of cells in a work-sheet, for example, A1..A10. When more than one range is to be treated together, but the ranges are not all in one place, you can select a collection of ranges. A **collection of ranges** is two or more ranges selected at the same time, so the next action affects all the ranges in the collection at once. The ranges in a collection can touch or not touch, or overlap. To select a collection of ranges, first select the first range, then press and hold down the CTRL key as you select the other ranges.

In Project 2, once the data is in the worksheet, you must copy the formulas. That is, the initial value formula in cell E3 is copied to cells E4..E7, the current value formula in cell G3 is copied to cells G4..G7, and the increase/decrease in value formula in cell H3 is copied to cells H4..H7. To copy the cells in multiple columns at one time using a collection of ranges, complete the following steps.

TO COPY CELLS IN MULTIPLE COLUMNS

STEP 1 ▶

Select the first cell containing the formula to copy – cell E3 – and the range where you want to copy the formula – E4..E7. Then, point to the cell containing the second formula to copy – cell G3.

1-2-3 highlights the first range to copy into. The mouse pointer points to cell G3 (Figure 2-19).

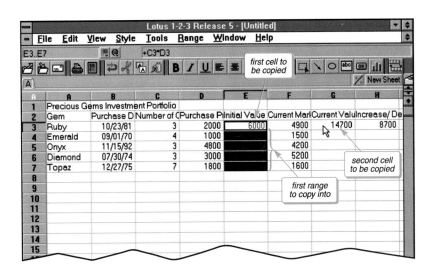

first cell to
be copied

second cell
to be copied

first range
to copy into

FIGURE 2-19

STEP 2 ▶

Hold down the CTRL key and select the range G3..H7. Then release the CTRL key and the mouse button.

1-2-3 highlights the range G3..H7 (Figure 2-20). Notice that two ranges are selected: E3..E7 and G3..H7.

FIGURE 2-20

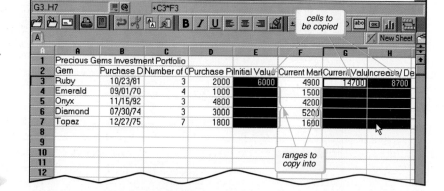

STEP 3 ▶

With the mouse pointer anywhere within the selected ranges, click the right mouse button, and point to the Copy Down command on the quick menu.

1-2-3 displays the quick menu when you press the right mouse button. The mouse pointer points to the Copy Down command (Figure 2-21).

FIGURE 2-21

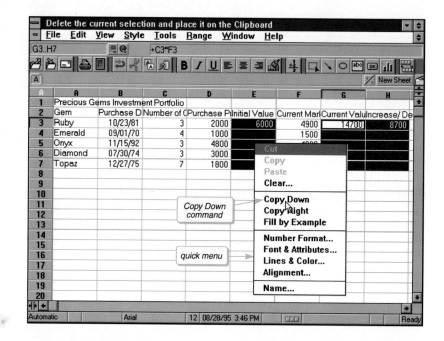

STEP 4 ▶

Choose the Copy Down command from the quick menu.

1-2-3 copies the formulas in each of the cells, E3, G3, and H3, down their respective columns (Figure 2-22). Thus, cell E4 contains the formula +C4*D4, cell G4 contains the formula +C4*F4, cell H4 contains the formula +G4–E4, and so on. The cell references within the cells are modified to reference the proper rows. Notice that 1-2-3 displays negative values in column H (Increase/Decrease in Value) with minus signs.

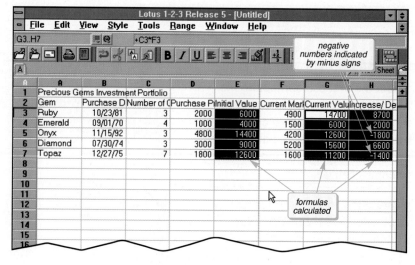

FIGURE 2-22

The Copy Down command is also found on the Edit menu on the main menu bar.

Notice when you copy the cells, 1-2-3 performs the arithmetic in the formulas as part of the copying process and then displays the results in the cells.

To remove a range from a collection, hold down the CTRL key and click the range you want to remove.

Entering Portfolio Summary Data

The next step is to enter the portfolio summary data. This data includes the total current value, total initial value, total increase/decrease in value, % change in portfolio value, greatest increase in value, and greatest decrease in value.

To calculate the total current value, you can use the @SUM function to sum the values in the range G3..G7. Similarly, you can use the @SUM function to sum the values in the range E3..E7 to obtain the total initial value. The total increase/decrease in value is determined by the formula, total current value minus total initial value (+D9−D10). Finally, determine the % change in portfolio value by dividing the total increase or decrease in value by the total initial value (+D11/D10).

In Project 1, you used the SmartSum icon on the set of SmartIcons to enter the @SUM function to sum a range of values. When you enter the @SUM function using the SmartSum icon, 1-2-3 automatically enters the @SUM function and sums the nearest adjacent group of cells. In Project 2, the group of cells to sum for the total current value (G3..G7) is not the nearest adjacent group of cells. Therefore, to calculate the total current value, you should use the **@function selector (@)** in the edit line to enter the @SUM function. 1-2-3 will enter the @function, @SUM(*list*), in the worksheet. **List** refers to an individual cell, or a range of cells that is required by the @SUM function. Similarly, you can use the @function selector in the edit line to enter the @SUM function to sum the values in the range G3..G7 to obtain the total initial value.

Perform the steps on the next several pages to enter the portfolio summary row titles and the accompanying formulas.

▼ TO ENTER ROW TITLES AND FORMULAS

STEP 1 ▶

Select cell A8 and enter `Portfolio Summary`. **Then, enter** `Total Current Value` **in cell A9,** `Total Initial Value` **in cell A10,** `Total Increase/ Decrease in Value` **in cell A11,** `% Change in Portfolio Value` **in cell A12,** `Greatest Increase in Value` **in cell A13, and** `Greatest Decrease in Value` **in cell A14 (Figure 2-23).**

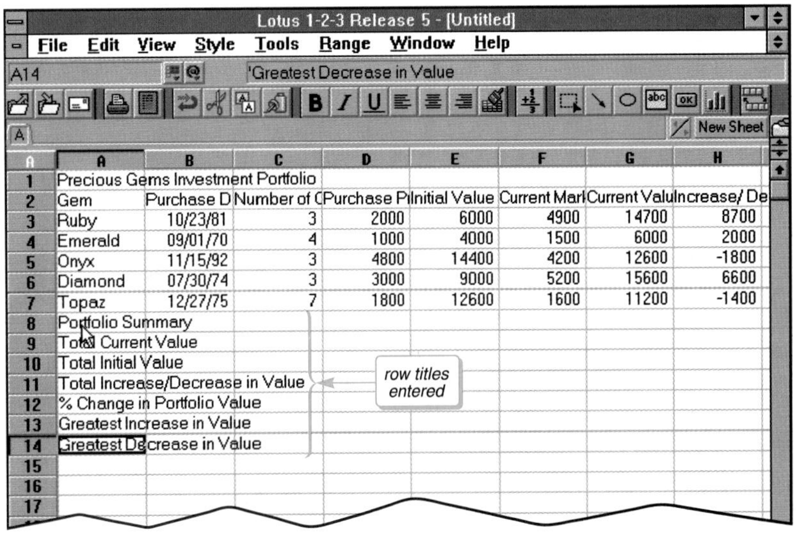

FIGURE 2-23

STEP 2 ▶

Select cell D9 where the total current value will appear and click the @function selector in the edit line. When the @Function menu displays, point to the SUM function name.

*Cell D9 is selected and 1-2-3 displays the @Function menu containing commonly used @functions (Figure 2-24). The mouse pointer points to the SUM function name on the @Function menu. Notice the description of the **List All command** displays in the title bar above the main menu bar because the List All command is highlighted in the @Function menu.*

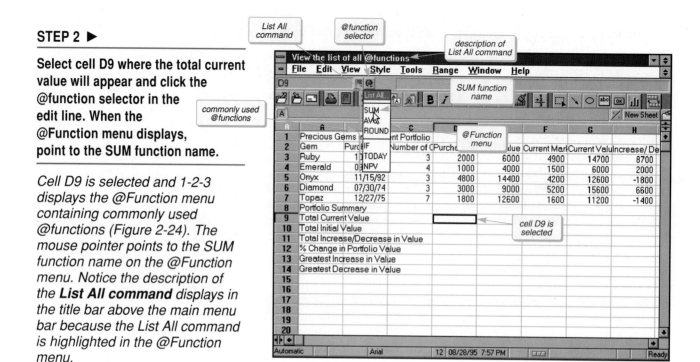

FIGURE 2-24

STEP 3 ▶

Choose the @SUM function from the @Function menu by clicking the left mouse button.

1-2-3 displays the @SUM function in the contents box and in cell D9 and highlights the word, list, for the range to be summed (Figure 2-25). The mode indicator displays Edit, indicating an entry is being edited.

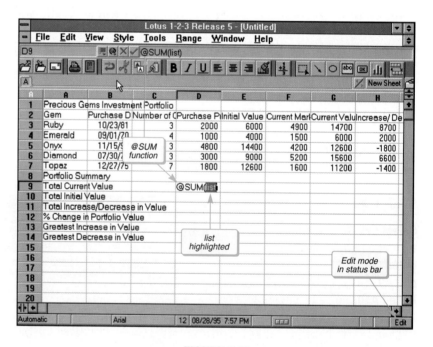

FIGURE 2-25

STEP 4 ▶

Point to cell G3 and drag cells G3 through G7 to select the range that will replace *list* in the @SUM function.

1-2-3 highlights the range G3..G7 and enters the range reference in the @SUM function (Figure 2-26). The mode indicator displays Point, indicating you are selecting a range.

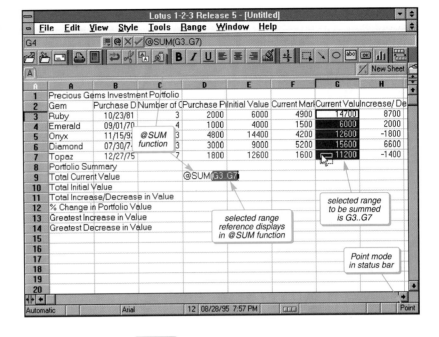

FIGURE 2-26

STEP 5 ▶

Click the Confirm button or press the ENTER key.

1-2-3 enters the @SUM function into cell D9, calculates the sum of cells G3..G7, and displays the sum in cell D9 (Figure 2-27). The @SUM function itself displays in the contents box.

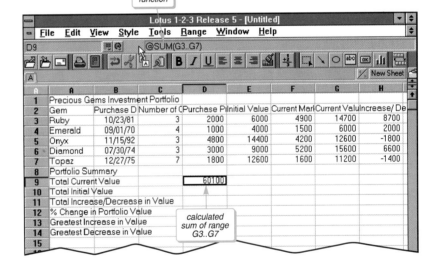

FIGURE 2-27

STEP 6 ▶

Select cell D10 where the total initial value will appear and click the @function selector to display the @Function menu. When the @Function menu displays, choose the SUM function name.

Cell D10 is selected. 1-2-3 displays the @SUM function in the contents box and in the cell and highlights the word, list, for the range to be summed (Figure 2-28).

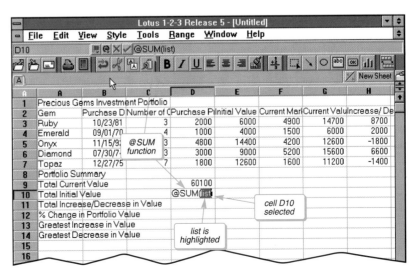

FIGURE 2-28

STEP 7 ▶

Point to cell E3 and drag cells E3 through E7 to select the range that will replace *list* in the @SUM function. Then, click the Confirm button or press the ENTER key.

1-2-3 enters the @SUM function into cell D10, calculates the sum of range E3..E7, and displays the sum in cell D10 (Figure 2-29).

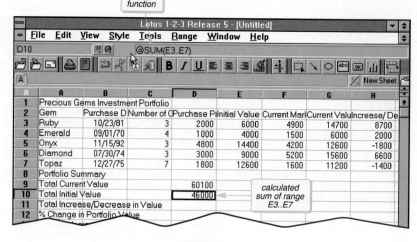

FIGURE 2-29

STEP 8 ▶

Enter the formula for total increase/decrease in value by first selecting cell D11, and then typing a plus sign (+). Select cell D9, type the subtraction operator (-), select cell D10, and click the Confirm button or press the ENTER key.

1-2-3 enters the formula to calculate total increase/decrease in value and displays the result in cell D11 (Figure 2-30).

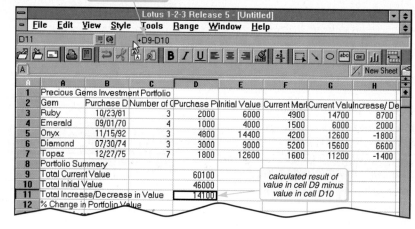

FIGURE 2-30

STEP 9 ▶

Enter the formula for % change in value by first selecting cell D12, and then typing a plus sign (+). Select cell D11, type the division operator (/), select cell D10, and click the Confirm button or press the ENTER key.

1-2-3 enters the formula to calculate % change in value and displays the result in cell D12 (Figure 2-31).

FIGURE 2-31

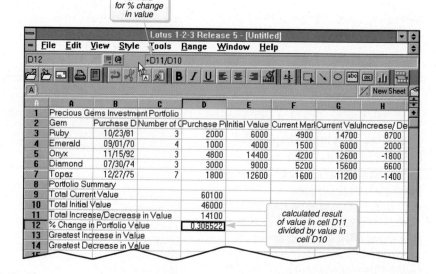

The final requirement for entering data in the worksheet is to calculate the greatest increase in value and the greatest decrease in value shown in column H of the investment portfolio worksheet. This is accomplished by using the @MAX and @MIN functions. The **@MAX function** is used to display the largest value in a range, and the **@MIN function** is used to display the smallest value in a range.

To enter a function into a worksheet cell, you can type the entire function from the keyboard and press the ENTER key or you can choose the function from the **@Function List** using the @function selector. Choosing from the @Function List is the easier, more reliable method because 1-2-3 automatically enters the @function in the correct format. To enter the @MAX and @MIN functions using the @Function List, perform the following steps.

TO ENTER THE @MAX AND @MIN FUNCTIONS FROM THE @FUNCTION LIST ▼

STEP 1 ▶

Select cell D13 where the greatest increase in value will display and click the @function selector in the edit line. When the @Function menu displays, point to the List All command.

Cell D13 is selected and 1-2-3 displays the @Function menu containing commonly used functions (Figure 2-32). The mouse pointer points to the List All command in the @Function menu.

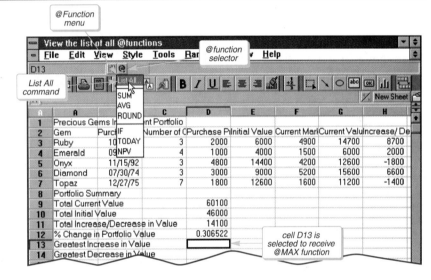

FIGURE 2-32

STEP 2 ▶

Choose the List All command from the @Function menu.

1-2-3 displays the @Function List dialog box (Figure 2-33). The All @functions option in the Category drop-down box lists all @functions alphabetically in the @Functions list box. To see more @functions than are displayed in the @Functions list box, use the scroll arrows to the right of the list. The help box below the @Functions list box displays the correct syntax and a description of the selected @function in the @Functions list box. The mode indicator changes from Ready to Menu, indicating 1-2-3 is displaying a dialog box.

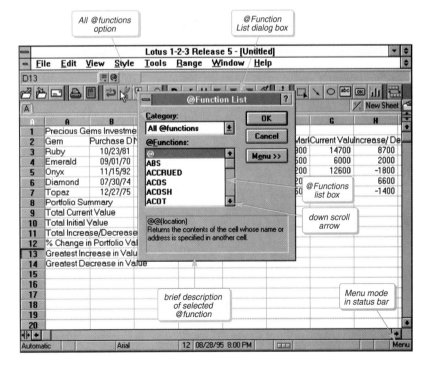

FIGURE 2-33

STEP 3 ▶

Scroll down in the @Functions list box until the MAX function name appears, select the MAX function name by pointing to the function name and clicking the left mouse button, then point to the OK button.

The MAX function name in the @Functions list box is selected (Figure 2-34). The @MAX function name showing the correct syntax and a description of the @MAX function displays in the help box below the @Functions list box. Instead of scrolling to display the function name in the @Functions list, you can type the first letter of the function name when the @Functions list box displays. 1-2-3 highlights the first function name that starts with the character you typed. The mouse pointer points to the OK button.

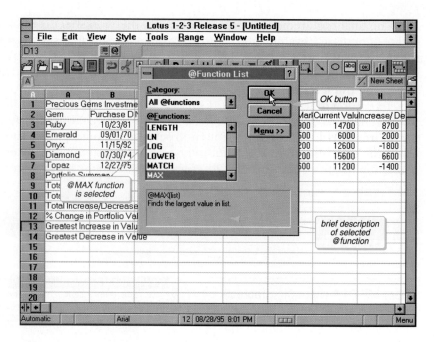

FIGURE 2-34

STEP 4 ▶

Choose the OK button in the @Function List dialog box.

1-2-3 displays the @MAX function in both the contents box and cell D13 (Figure 2-35). In the cell, list is highlighted, which means you can enter the range.

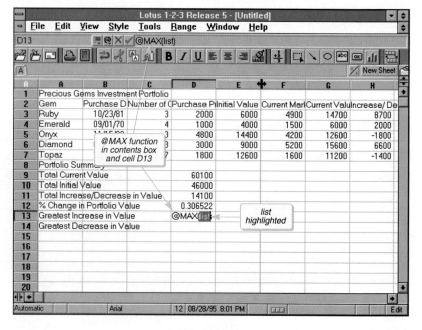

FIGURE 2-35

STEP 5 ▶

Point to cell H3, press the left mouse button, drag down to cell H7 and release the left mouse button.

The selected range (H3..H7) displays in the @MAX function in the cell and in the contents box (Figure 2-36).

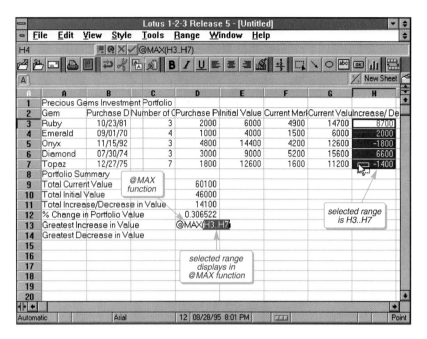

FIGURE 2-36

STEP 6 ▶

Click the Confirm button or press the ENTER key.

1-2-3 enters the @MAX function in cell D13 and determines the largest value in the range specified in the @MAX function (Figure 2-37). The value 8700 displays in cell D13 because it is the largest value in the range H3..H7.

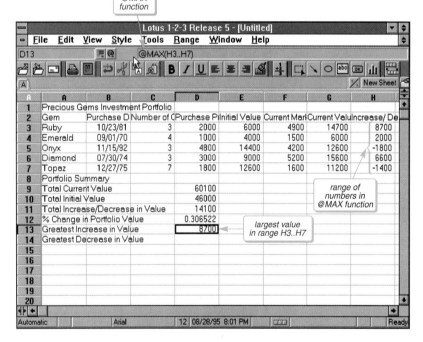

FIGURE 2-37

STEP 7 ▶

Select cell D14, select the @function selector, and choose the List All command. Scroll down in the @Functions list box, select the MIN function name, and choose the OK button in the @Function List dialog box. Then, select the range H3..H7 and click the Confirm button or press the ENTER key.

1-2-3 enters the @MIN function in cell D14 and determines the smallest value in the range specified in the @MIN function (Figure 2-38). The value –1800 displays in cell D14 because it is the smallest value in the range H3..H7.

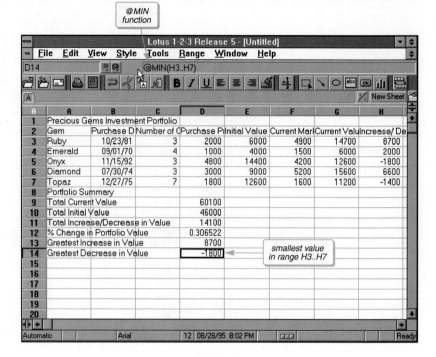

FIGURE 2-38

The worksheet data is now complete. All the data and formulas are contained within the worksheet.

▶ SAVING THE WORKSHEET

 Now that the worksheet data is entered, you should save the worksheet on disk. To save the worksheet on a diskette in drive A using the file name PROJ2, perform the following steps.

TO SAVE THE WORKSHEET

Step 1: From the File menu, choose the Save As command.
Step 2: When the Save As dialog box displays, type proj2.
Step 3: Select drive a: from the Drives drop-down list box.
Step 4: Choose the OK button in the Save As dialog box.

▶ UNDERSTANDING FONTS AND FONT ATTRIBUTES

Fonts and font attributes determine the design and appearance of characters on the screen and in print. A **font** is a typeface that defines the appearance and shape of letters, numbers, and special characters. Each font is identified by a name and a point size. Some of the commonly used font names are Arial and Times New Roman. The font **point size** is gauged by a measurement system called points. A single point is approximately 1/72 of an inch. Thus, a font with point size twelve is about 1/6 of an inch in height.

Font attributes indicate how the characters display. Widely used font attributes include bold, italics, and underlining.

When 1-2-3 begins, the default font for the entire worksheet is Arial with a point size of 12, no bold, no underline, and no italics. With 1-2-3, you can change the font, point size, and font attributes for a single cell, a range of cells, or for an entire worksheet.

▶ FORMATTING LABELS

A lthough you have completed the worksheet by entering all the data, formulas, and functions, the labels and values need to be formatted to improve the appearance and readability of the worksheet.

In Project 1, you used the Gallery command from the Style menu to quickly apply a built-in style to format the worksheet. You may not always find an acceptable style template to use, however. This section and the section that follows describe how to format the worksheet without using the Gallery command.

Formatting the Worksheet Title

In the worksheet shown in Figure 2-1 on page L63, the worksheet title in cell A1 is centered across columns A through H, and displays in bold and italics with a larger point size than the rest of the labels and values. In addition, the title displays with white characters and a blue background. The following steps specify the action to take to format the text and center it across columns. The steps to change color are given later in the project.

TO CENTER, BOLD, ITALICIZE, AND ENLARGE THE WORKSHEET TITLE ▼

STEP 1 ▶

Select the worksheet title in cell A1. Click the Bold icon (**B**) on the set of SmartIcons. Click the Italics icon (*I*) on the set of SmartIcons. Then, click the point-size selector in the status bar and point to the number 24 in the pop-up list box of point sizes.

The format of the characters in cell A1 changes to bold and italic (Figure 2-39). 1-2-3 displays a pop-up list of point sizes. The selected point size is 12 and the mouse pointer points to 24 on the list.

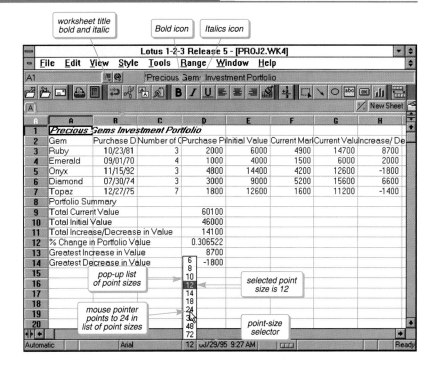

FIGURE 2-39

STEP 2 ▶

Choose point size 24.

1-2-3 displays the worksheet title in the default font, Arial, 24 point, and enlarges the row height for row 1 to fit the new font size (Figure 2-40).

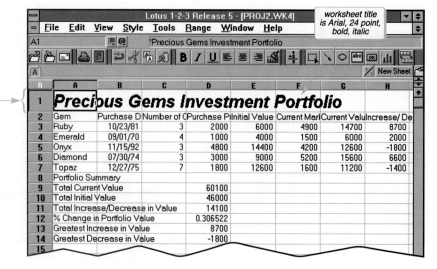

FIGURE 2-40

STEP 3 ▶

Drag the range A1..H1. Then, with the mouse pointer within the selected range, click the right mouse button, and point to the Alignment command.

1-2-3 highlights the range across which the worksheet title will be centered and displays the quick menu (Figure 2-41). The mouse pointer points to the Alignment command.

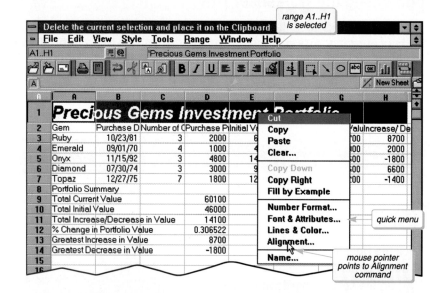

FIGURE 2-41

STEP 4 ▶

Choose the Alignment command from the quick menu.

1-2-3 displays the Alignment dialog box (Figure 2-42). The Horizontal area contains five options to align data horizontally in a cell or range of cells. The Across columns check box aligns data across selected columns. The Vertical area contains three options to align data vertically in a cell. The Range text box indicates the range selected on the worksheet.

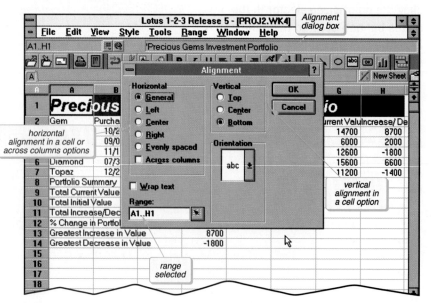

FIGURE 2-42

STEP 5 ▶

Select the Across columns check box and the Center option button in the Horizontal area. Then, select the Center option button in the Vertical area and point to the OK button in the Alignment dialog box.

Selecting the Center option button and the Across columns check box in the Horizontal area indicates the title should be centered horizontally across the selected columns (Figure 2-43). The selection of the Center option button in the Vertical area indicates that the title is to be centered vertically in the cells. The mouse pointer points to the OK button.

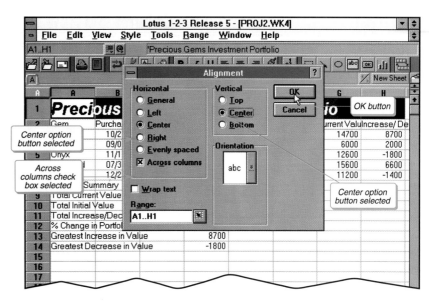

FIGURE 2-43

STEP 6 ▶

Choose the OK button. Select any cell.

1-2-3 centers the worksheet title horizontally across the range A1..H1 and vertically within row 1 (Figure 2-44).

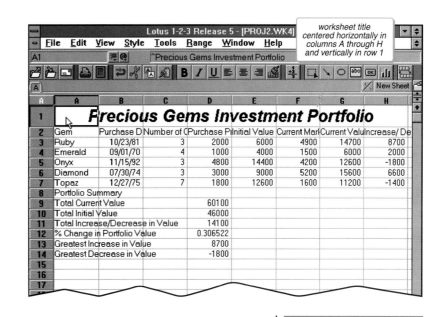

FIGURE 2-44

Be sure the cells to the right of the data you want to align are blank when aligning data horizontally across columns. For example, to center the label in cell A1 (Figure 2-43) across columns A through H, columns B, C, D, E, F, G, and H must be blank in row 1.

The Alignment command is also found on the **Style menu** on the main menu bar.

Recall from Project 1 that if for some reason you want to remove all styles in the selected cell, choose the Clear command from the Edit menu or the quick menu and select the Styles only option. To remove the bold or italic attribute from a selected cell, click that particular icon on the set of SmartIcons.

Formatting the Column and Row Titles

The column titles in row 2 display in bold (see Figure 2-1 on page L63) and are center-aligned both horizontally and vertically in the cell. In addition, the column titles display within each cell on multiple lines. Displaying labels on multiple lines within a cell is called **wrap text**. The row title in row 8 displays in bold and 14 point. The steps on the next two pages show you how to center, wrap, and bold text for the column and row titles.

TO CENTER, WRAP, AND BOLD TEXT IN A CELL ▼

STEP 1 ▶

Select the range to format – A2..H2 – by dragging. With the mouse pointer within the selected range, click the right mouse button, and point to the Alignment command.

The range A2..H2 is selected and 1-2-3 displays the quick menu that contains commands for the selected range (Figure 2-45). The mouse pointer points to the Alignment command in the quick menu.

FIGURE 2-45

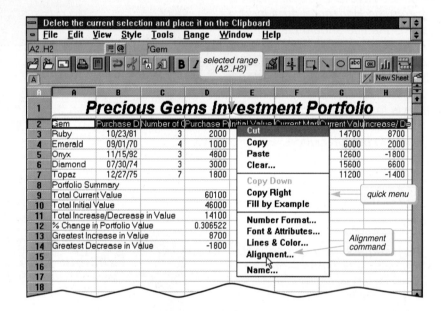

STEP 2 ▶

Choose the Alignment command from the quick menu. When the Alignment dialog box displays, select the Center option button in the Horizontal area. Select the Center option button in the Vertical area. Then, select the Wrap text check box and point to the OK button.

When you choose the Alignment command, 1-2-3 displays the Alignment dialog box (Figure 2-46). Selecting the Center option buttons in the Horizontal and Vertical areas mean the column titles will be centered horizontally and vertically in their respective cells. The Wrap text selection means

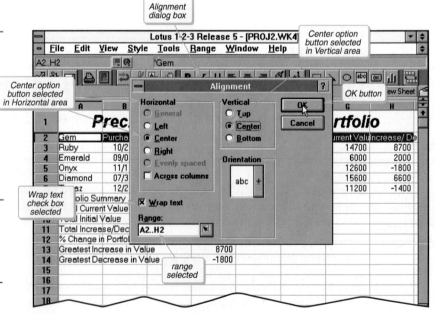

FIGURE 2-46

1-2-3 will wrap text at the right edge of the column and carry it to the next line in the cell. The mouse pointer points to the OK button.

STEP 3 ▶

Choose the OK button in the Alignment dialog box.

1-2-3 centers the text horizontally and vertically in each cell (Figure 2-47). The column titles wrap on multiple lines within each cell and 1-2-3 automatically increases the row height to fit the largest entry.

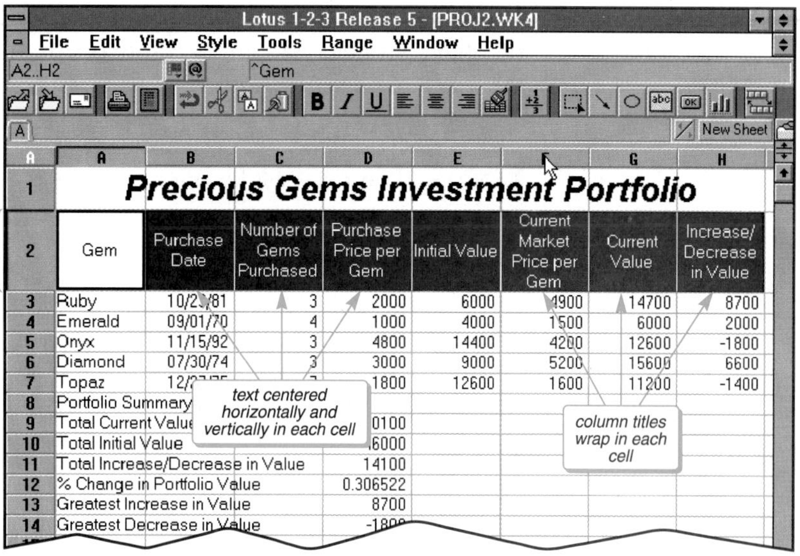

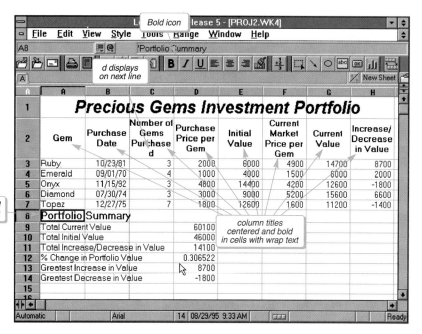

FIGURE 2-47

STEP 4 ▶

With the range A2..H2 selected, hold down the CTRL key and select cell A8. Release the CTRL key. Click the Bold icon on the set of SmartIcons. Point to cell A8 and click the left mouse button to remove the range A2..H2 from the collection. Then, point to the point-size selector in the status bar and click the left mouse button. When the pop-up list box displays, choose point size 14 in the pop-up list box of point sizes.

The column titles and the label in cell A8 display in bold (Figure 2-48). When you click cell A8, 1-2-3 removes the range A2..H2 from the collection. Cell A8 becomes the current cell. The row title in row 8 displays in bold for-mat and 14 point size. Notice the d in Purchased in cell C2 now dis-plays on the next line. The width of column C will be adjusted later.

FIGURE 2-48

When you have a long label in a cell and you do not want it to overflow into the adjacent cells, use the Wrap text option to display the text line by line within the cell.

▶ FORMATTING VALUES

To change how values display in a worksheet you can change the format of the value. Formats determine how values look on the screen and in print, but they do not affect the way 1-2-3 stores these values or uses them in calculations. In the worksheet in Project 2, the values are displayed in three different formats – currency format, comma format, and percent format (see Figure 2-1 on page L63 to review the formatting).

Currency Format

The values in columns D, E, F, G, and H of row 3, and the values in rows 9, 10, 11, 13, and 14 display in currency format. **Currency format** displays values with a currency symbol, thousands separator, and decimal positions ($10,000.00). 1-2-3 supports 45 different types of currency symbols such as the British pound and the Japanese yen. Project 2 illustrates the U.S. dollar currency format. To format values in a currency format, perform the following steps.

TO FORMAT IN THE CURRENCY FORMAT ▼

STEP 1 ▶

Select the first range of cells to be formatted – D3..H3, hold down the CTRL key, select the remaining ranges – D9..D11 and D13..D14, and release the CTRL key.
Then, click the format selector (Automatic) in the status bar and point to US Dollar in the pop-up list of format styles.

The noncontiguous ranges to receive the format are selected and 1-2-3 displays the pop-up list of format styles (Figure 2-49). The mouse pointer points to the US Dollar format.

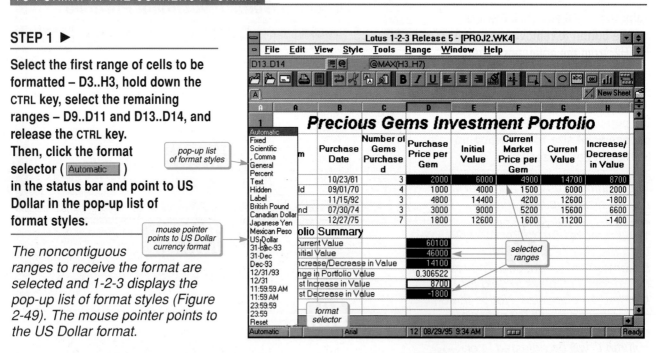

FIGURE 2-49

STEP 2 ▶

Choose US Dollar from the pop-up list of format styles.

1-2-3 formats the selected ranges with the currency format consisting of a dollar sign, two digits to the right of the decimal point, and a comma separating every three digits to the left of the decimal point (Figure 2-50). Negative values display within parentheses. The format selector displays the format applied to the selected range (US Dollar). The decimal selector (2) displays the number of decimal places for the currency format (2).

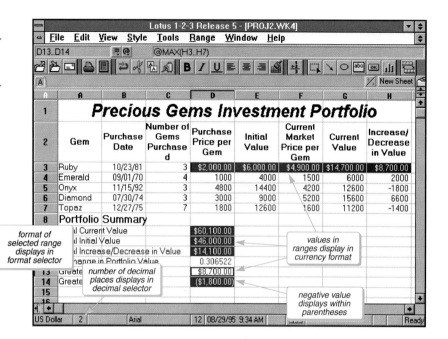

FIGURE 2-50

When applying the currency format to a range of cells, the default number of decimal places is two positions to the right of the decimal. The currency format is also found under the Number Format command on the Style menu on the main menu bar.

Comma Format

To format the values in columns D, E, F, G, and H of rows 4, 5, 6, and 7 with the **comma format**, which is identical to the currency format except no dollar sign is placed in the cell, perform the following steps.

TO FORMAT IN THE COMMA FORMAT ▼

STEP 1 ▶

Select the range of cells to format – cells D4..H7. Then, click the format selector in the status bar and point to ,Comma in the pop-up list of format styles.

1-2-3 highlights the range to receive the format and displays the pop-up list of format styles (Figure 2-51). The mouse pointer points to the ,Comma format.

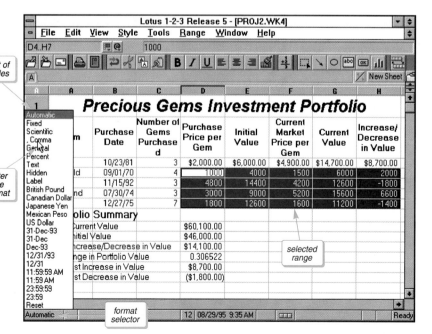

FIGURE 2-51

STEP 2 ▶

Choose ,Comma from the pop-up list of format styles.

1-2-3 formats the selected range with the comma format (Figure 2-52). The ,Comma format displays numeric values with two digits to the right of the decimal point and a comma between every third digit to the left of the decimal point. 1-2-3 displays negative values in column H within parentheses instead of the minus signs used before applying the ,Comma format.

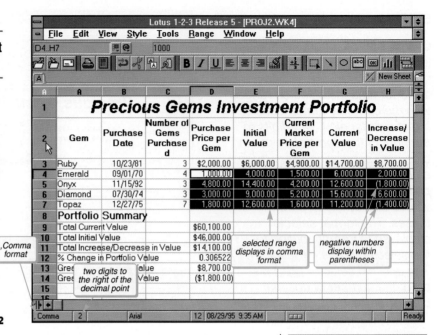

FIGURE 2-52

You can remove the highlight from the cells in Figure 2-52 by clicking any cell in the worksheet.

The comma format is also found under the Number Format command on the Style menu on the main menu bar.

Percent Format

The third format displayed in Project 2 (Figure 2-1 on Page L63) is the percent format in cell D12. The value in cell D12 is displayed with a percent sign and two decimal places (30.65%). This format is referred to as the **percent format**. To format values in a percent format, perform the following step.

TO FORMAT IN THE PERCENT FORMAT ▼

STEP 1 ▶

Select the cell to format – cell D12. Click the format selector in the status bar. Then, choose the Percent format from the pop-up list of format styles.

1-2-3 formats the selected range with the percent format (Figure 2-53). The percent format displays the value rounded with two digits to the right of the decimal point.

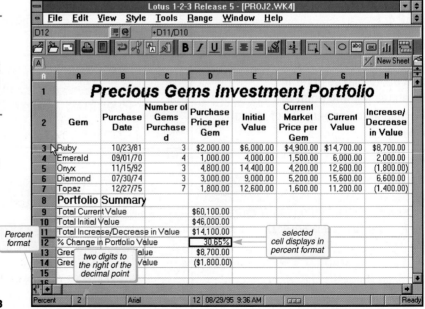

FIGURE 2-53

The percent format is also found under the Number Format command on the Style menu on the main menu bar.

To reset a formatted cell or range of cells to the default format for the worksheet, select the cell or range of cells, click the format selector in the status bar, and choose Reset from the pop-up list of format styles.

Centering Values

The number of gems purchased values displayed in the range C3..C7 should be center-aligned horizontally in the cell. To horizontally center values in a cell, complete the following step.

TO CENTER VALUES HORIZONTALLY IN A CELL ▼

STEP 1 ▶

Select the range of cells to center, C3..C7. Then, click the Center icon (▤) on the set of SmartIcons.

1-2-3 centers the number of gems purchased value in the range C3..C7 (Figure 2-54).

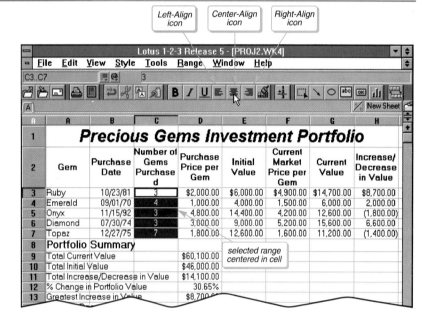

FIGURE 2-54

The set of SmartIcons includes three alignment icons — Left-Align (▤), Center-Align (▤), and Right-Align (▤). The pictures on the icons indicate which way the icons align data horizontally in a cell. The **Left-Align icon** aligns the cell contents to the left in each cell of the selected range. The **Center-Align icon** centers the cell contents within each cell of the selected range. The **Right-Align icon** aligns the cell contents to the right in each cell of the selected range.

▶ CHANGING THE WIDTHS OF COLUMNS AND HEIGHTS OF ROWS

When 1-2-3 begins and a blank worksheet displays on the screen, all the columns have a default width of 9 characters and a height of 14 points. At any time, you can change the width of the columns or height of the rows to make the worksheet easier to read or to ensure that the entries will display properly in the cells to which they are assigned.

Changing the Widths of Columns

1-2-3 provides two ways to increase or decrease the width of the columns in a worksheet. First, you can change the width of a single column or multiple columns by using the mouse and dragging a column border. Second, you can change the width of a column by using the **Column Width command**. This project demonstrates both methods.

In the worksheet for Project 2, column A is decreased to a width of 7 characters using the mouse and dragging the column border. Then, column C is increased to a width of 10 characters using the Column Width command so the d in Purchased displays properly.

Perform the following steps to change the column width by dragging the column border.

TO CHANGE A COLUMN WIDTH BY DRAGGING ▼

STEP 1 ▶

Move the mouse pointer to the right border of the column whose width you want to change (column A).

The mouse pointer changes to a black, two-headed horizontal arrow (✛) (Figure 2-55). This mouse pointer shape indicates you can drag the column border left or right.

FIGURE 2-55

STEP 2 ▶

Drag the column border to the left until the width displayed in the selection indicator is 7Characters.

As you drag, the proposed column border represented by a black line moves to the left and 1-2-3 displays the new column width in the selection indicator (Figure 2-56).

FIGURE 2-56

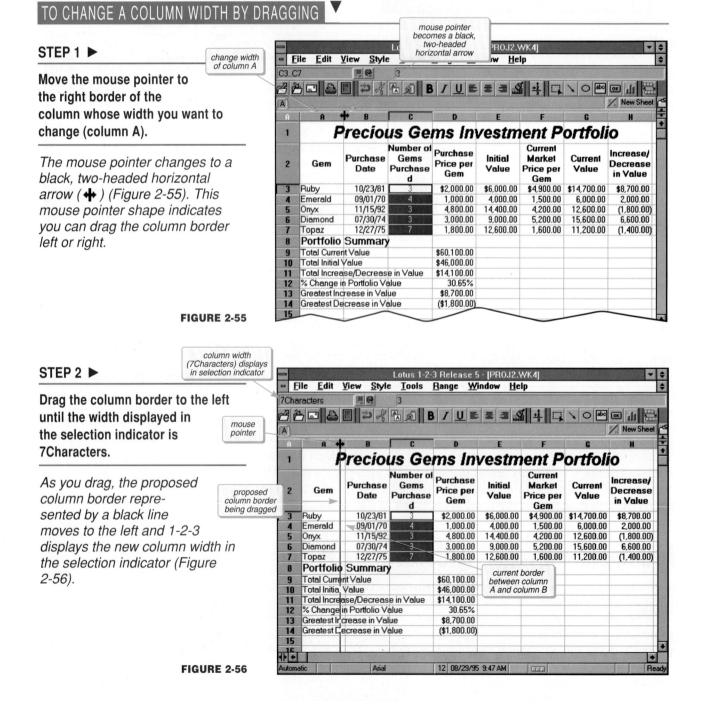

STEP 3 ▶

Release the left mouse button.

The worksheet displays with the width of 7 characters for column A (Figure 2-57).

column A
width now 7
characters

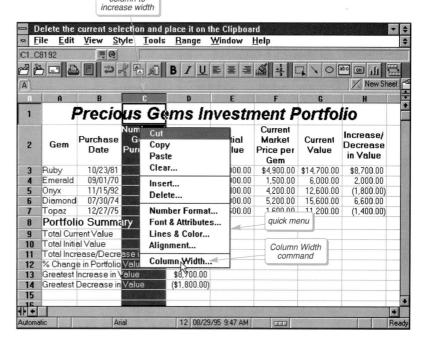

FIGURE 2-57

Notice in Figure 2-57 the word Gem is recentered in the new width of 7 characters. The term 7Characters is used as a width measurement but, because of proportional spacing, does not necessarily mean 7 characters will fit in the column. For example, 5 capital Ms and 18 capital Is, both in Arial 12 point, will fit in one cell formatted to a width of 7 characters.

To change the column width of column C using the Column Width command, perform the following steps.

TO CHANGE A COLUMN WIDTH USING THE COLUMN WIDTH COMMAND ▼

STEP 1 ▶

Move the mouse pointer to column heading C and click the left mouse button. Point to the selected column and click the right mouse button. When the quick menu displays, point to the Column Width command.

Column C is selected and the quick menu displays with the commonly used commands for the selected range (Figure 2-58). The mouse pointer points to the Column Width command.

FIGURE 2-58

STEP 2 ▶

Choose the Column Width command. When the Column Width dialog box displays, click the Set width to characters text box up arrow once to display the number 10. Point to the OK button in the Column Width dialog box.

When 1-2-3 displays the Column Width dialog box, the Set width to characters option button is selected and the default column width 9 displays in the characters text box. Clicking the up arrow once displays the number 10 in the characters text box. The range selected displays in the Column(s) text box (Figure 2-59). The mouse pointer points to the OK button.

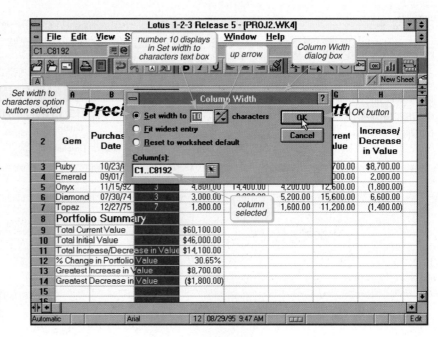

FIGURE 2-59

STEP 3 ▶

Choose the OK button in the Column Width dialog box. Point to the date-time/height-width indicator in the status bar and click the left mouse button.

1-2-3 increases the width of columns C to 10 characters (Figure 2-60). Notice the d in Purchased displays properly in the cell. The height and width of cell C1 displays in the date-time/height-width indicator in the status bar.

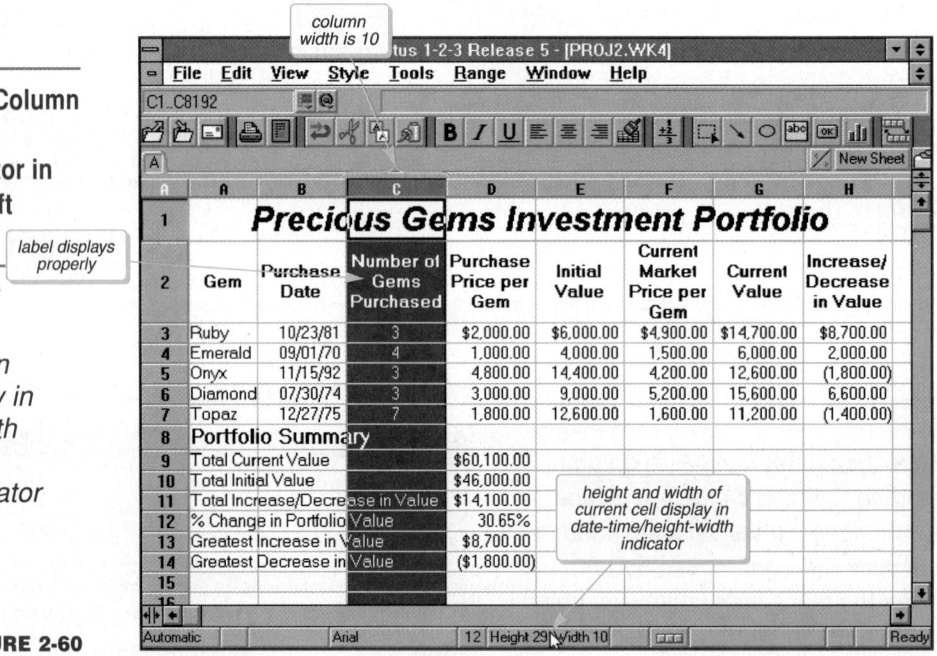

FIGURE 2-60

Select any cell to remove the range selection.

1-2-3 displays the column width of the current cell in the date-time/height-width indicator in the status bar. If the indicator displays the date and time, click it to display the column width and row height of the selected cell. If several columns are selected that contain different measurements, the indicator will be blank.

The Column Width dialog box in Figure 2-59 displays additional options for changing the widths of columns. The Fit widest entry option adjusts the column to the width of the widest entry in the selected range. The Reset to worksheet default option resets the column to the default width of the worksheet.

The column width can vary between zero and 240 characters. When you decrease the column width to zero, the column is hidden. **Hiding columns** is a technique you can use to hide sensitive data on a worksheet that you do not want other people to see. You cannot move the cell pointer to a hidden column or enter data in a hidden column. When you print a worksheet, hidden columns do not print.

To display a hidden column, first select the columns surrounding the column you want to display (for example, to display hidden column C, select one cell in columns B and D). Then, choose the Hide command from the Style menu, and click the Show button in the Hide dialog box.

Changing the Heights of Rows

When you change the font size of a cell entry, such as the Precious Gems Investment Portfolio title in cell A1, 1-2-3 automatically adjusts the **row height** to match the height of the data in the row. You can also manually adjust the height of a row to add space that improves the appearance of the worksheet.

The row height is measured in point size. The default row height is 14 points. The following steps show how to use the mouse to increase the height of row 1 and row 8 so there is extra space between the worksheet title in row 1 and the column titles in row 2, and extra space between the data in row 7 and the summary row title in row 8.

TO INCREASE THE ROW HEIGHT BY DRAGGING THE ROW BORDER ▼

STEP 1 ▶

Move the mouse pointer to the border line between row heading 1 and row heading 2.

The mouse pointer changes to a black, two-headed vertical arrow (✚)(Figure 2-61). This mouse pointer indicates you can drag the row border up or down.

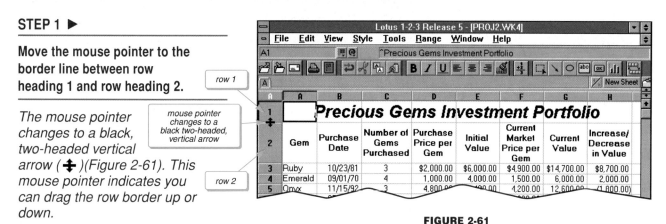

FIGURE 2-61

STEP 2 ▶

Drag the row border down until the height displayed in the selection indicator is 42Points.

As you drag, the proposed row border represented by a solid black horizontal line moves with the mouse pointer (Figure 2-62). The row height (42Points) displays in the selection indicator.

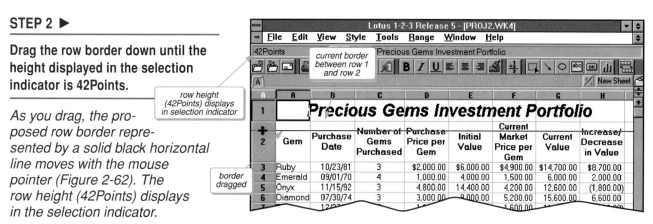

FIGURE 2-62

STEP 3 ▶

Release the left mouse button.

The worksheet displays with the new height of 42 points for row 1 (Figure 2-63). 1-2-3 vertically recenters the text so it remains centered in the new row height. The date-time/ height-width indicator in the status bar displays the height of row 1 (42) and the width for column A (7).

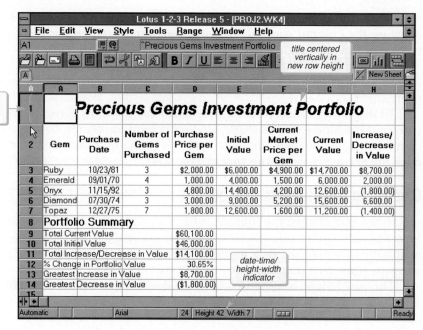

FIGURE 2-63

STEP 4 ▶

Repeat the procedures used in Step 1 through Step 3 to increase the height of row 8 to 28 points.

1-2-3 changes the row height of row 8 to 28 points (Figure 2-64).

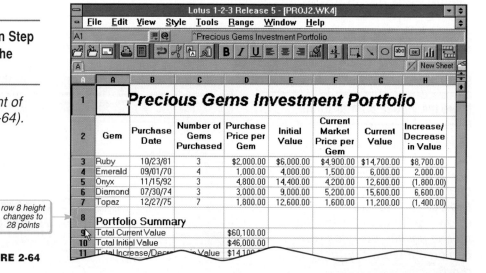

FIGURE 2-64

Changing the height of row 1 to 42 points and row 8 to 28 points spaces the report nicely and gives it a good appearance. Different values could have been chosen for the rows.

The row height can vary between 1 and 255 points. You cannot hide a row. If the date-time/height-width indicator in the status bar shows the date and time information, clicking the date-time/height-width indicator displays information about the column width or row height of the current cell.

▶ ADDING COLOR TO THE WORKSHEET

A dding color to a range emphasizes the range on the screen and draws attention to the data. Using color in a worksheet also allows you to group similar data visually. 1-2-3 provides a color scheme of 256 different colors you can use to change cell backgrounds, text, and lines in a worksheet. In Figure 2-1 on page L63, the worksheet title and row are colored to highlight them and set the title apart from the worksheet entries. The background and data in the worksheet are colored to emphasize the data in the worksheet.

Changing the Color of the Worksheet Title

The worksheet title, Precious Gems Investment Portfolio, in Figure 2-1 on page L63, is assigned to cell A1, is centered over columns A through H, and displays in white with a background color of blue. Complete the following steps to change the color of the font and background in the worksheet title.

TO COLOR THE WORKSHEET TITLE ▼

STEP 1 ▶

Select the range to color – A1..H1. With the mouse pointer in the selected range, click the right mouse button, and choose the Lines & Color command from the quick menu. When the Lines & Color dialog box displays, point to the Background color drop-down box arrow in the Interior area.

1-2-3 displays the Lines & Color dialog box (Figure 2-65). The mouse pointer points to the Background color drop-down box arrow. The selected range displays in the Range text box.

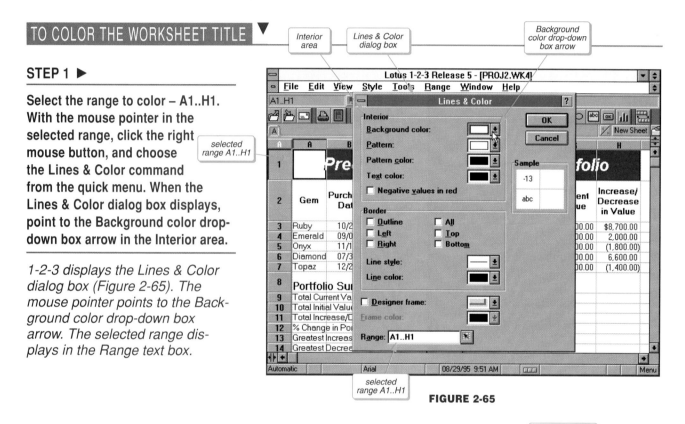

FIGURE 2-65

STEP 2 ▶

Click the Background color drop-down box arrow in the Interior area and point to the fifth color from the left in the top row of the Background color drop-down box (blue).

1-2-3 displays the Background color drop-down box (Figure 2-66). The current color (Color: 15) has a flashing outline around it. The mouse pointer points to the desired blue color.

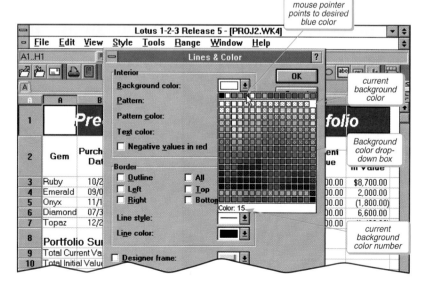

FIGURE 2-66

STEP 3 ▶

Choose the background color by clicking the left mouse button. Click the Text color drop-down box arrow in the Interior area and point to the second color from the left in the top row of the Text color drop-down box (white).

The background color you selected (blue) displays in the Background color drop-down box (Figure 2-67). 1-2-3 displays the Text color drop-down box. The current color (Color: 255) has a flashing outline around it. The mouse pointer points to the desired white color.

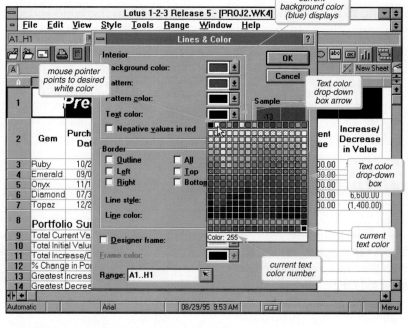

FIGURE 2-67

STEP 4 ▶

Choose the text color (white) by clicking the left mouse button and point to the OK button in the Lines & Color dialog box.

The Sample area shows how the selections you make in the dialog box will appear in the worksheet (Figure 2-68). The mouse pointer points to the OK button in the Lines & Color dialog box.

FIGURE 2-68

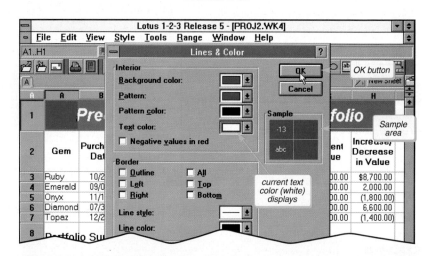

STEP 5 ▶

Choose the OK button in the Lines & Color dialog box. Select any cell in the worksheet.

1-2-3 displays row 1 with a blue background and the worksheet title text in white (Figure 2-69).

FIGURE 2-69

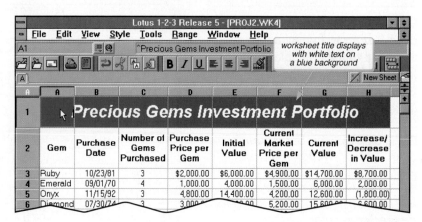

The Lines & Color command is also found on the Style menu on the main menu bar.

Changing the Color of the Worksheet

The worksheet labels and values display in blue with a background color of yellow (see Figure 2-1 on page L63). The steps to change the color of the text and background of the worksheet are the same as the previous set of steps except for the range and color selections. The following steps illustrate changing the color for the worksheet background and text.

TO COLOR THE WORKSHEET ▼

STEP 1 ▶

Select the range to color – A2..H14. With the mouse pointer in the selected range, click the right mouse button, and choose the Lines & Color command from the quick menu. When the Lines & Color dialog box displays, click the Background color drop-down box arrow in the Interior area and point to the fourth color from the left in the second row of the Background color drop-down box (yellow).

1-2-3 displays the Lines & Color dialog box (Figure 2-70). The mouse pointer points to the desired yellow color in the Background color drop-down box.

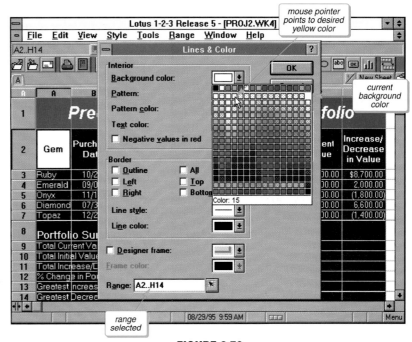

FIGURE 2-70

STEP 2 ▶

Choose the background color by clicking the left mouse button. Click the Text color drop-down box arrow in the Interior area and select the fifth color from the left in the top row of the Text color drop-down box (blue). Point to the OK button in the Lines & Color dialog box.

The yellow background color you selected displays in the Background color drop-down box in the Interior area (Figure 2-71). The text color you selected displays in the Text color drop-down box. The selected range displays in the Range text box. The mouse pointer points to the OK button in the Lines & Color dialog box.

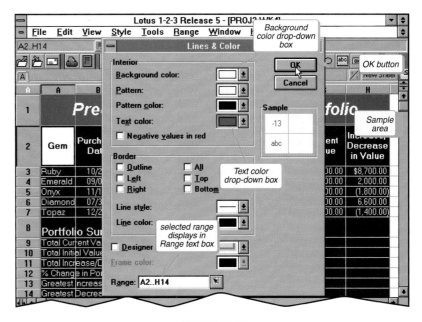

FIGURE 2-71

STEP 3 ▶

Choose the OK button in the Lines & Color dialog box. Select any cell in the worksheet.

1-2-3 displays the background of the worksheet in the selected yellow color and the labels and values in the selected blue color (Figure 2-72).

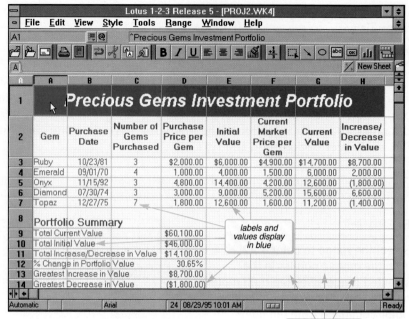

FIGURE 2-72

The worksheet is now complete. All the data and formulas are entered and the formatting is done. The next step is to chart the current value for the gems in the investment portfolio.

As noted previously, saving the worksheet often prevents lost data if something unexpected happens. Click the Save icon on the set of SmartIcons to save the worksheet.

▶ CHARTING THE WORKSHEET

One of the more widely used charts is the pie chart. A **pie chart** is commonly used to show percentages of a whole. A pie chart is circular in form and is divided into wedges called **slices**. Each slice in the pie chart shows how individual values compare to one another and to the total. A pie chart can display only one range of numeric data.

In Project 1, you created a three-dimensional bar chart from data in adjacent columns. In this project, you will prepare a three-dimensional pie chart based on the current values in column G (Figure 2-73) and the gem names in column A.

Notice that the pie chart shows what proportion of the entire investment portfolio each gem's current value represents. For example, in Figure 2-73, the yellow slice representing diamonds occupies 26% of the investment portfolio and the red slice representing rubies occupies 24.5% of the investment portfolio.

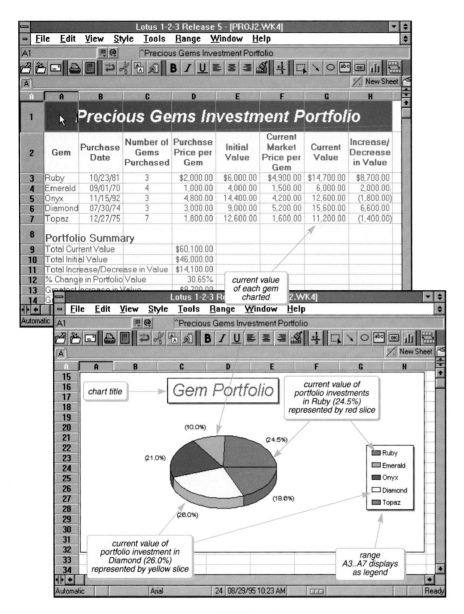

FIGURE 2-73

The title, Gem Portfolio, displays centered above the pie chart. The legend in the chart tells you what each slice of the pie represents. In Figure 2-73, the legend displays to the right of the pie chart by default.

The pie chart in Figure 2-73 uses only two columns of data, an X range and an A range. The **X range**, A3..A7, represents the labels that display in the legend. The **A range**, G3..G7, is used to create the slices in the pie. Because five types of gems appear in the portfolio, the pie chart has five slices.

The procedure to create a pie chart is: (1) select the range of data in the worksheet to chart; (2) indicate where you want to place the chart in the worksheet; (3) obtain the default bar chart; (4) change the chart to a three-dimensional pie chart; (5) add a chart title; and (6) format the chart. The steps required in this process are shown on the next two pages.

TO CREATE A THREE-DIMENSIONAL PIE CHART ▼

STEP 1 ▶

Select the first range in the collection – cells A3..A7, hold down the CTRL key, and select the second range in the collection – cells G3..G7. Release the CTRL key and point to the Chart icon on the set of SmartIcons.

1-2-3 highlights the two noncontiguous ranges (Figure 2-74). Holding down the CTRL key allows you to select many noncontiguous ranges at the same time. The mouse pointer points to the Chart icon on the set of SmartIcons.

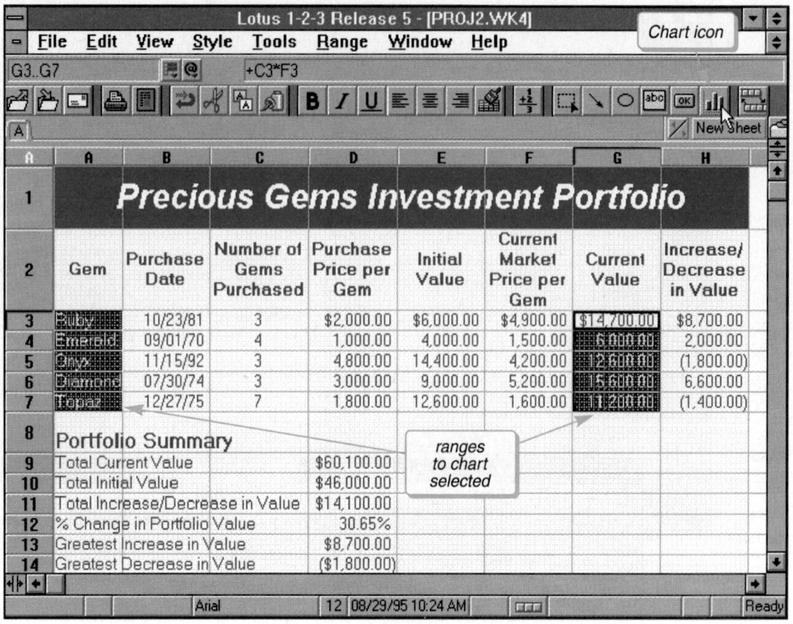

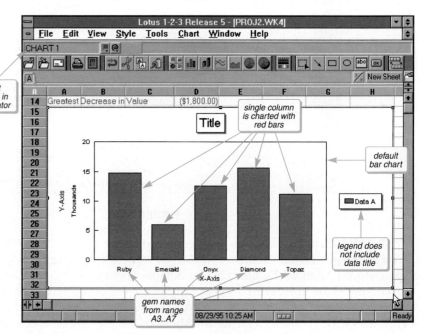

FIGURE 2-74

STEP 2 ▶

Click the Chart icon on the set of SmartIcons. Scroll down until row 14 is the topmost row in the window, and move the mouse pointer to the top left corner of cell A15. Drag to the lower right corner of cell H32. Release the left mouse button.

When you move the mouse pointer onto the worksheet, the shape changes to a crosshair with a picture of a bar chart. 1-2-3 displays the default bar chart in cells A15..H32 (Figure 2-75). The default chart name, CHART 1 displays in the selection indicator. When a single row or column of numbers is selected, such as the range G3..G7 for current value, 1-2-3 displays the bars in a single color (red) because only one value (Current Value) is charted. The gem names from the range A3..A7 in the worksheet display as the x-axis labels. The legend identifies the data charted as Data A.

FIGURE 2-75

STEP 3 ▶

Click the 3D Pie icon on the set of SmartIcons.

1-2-3 displays the 3D pie chart (Figure 2-76). Each slice displays the percentage of the whole pie that the slice occupies. For example, the red slice representing the current value invested in rubies occupies 24.5% of the whole and the green slice of the pie representing the current value invested in emeralds occupies 10% of the whole. The gem names from the range A3..A7 in the worksheet display as the chart legend located to the right of the pie chart. The default chart title displays centered above the pie chart.

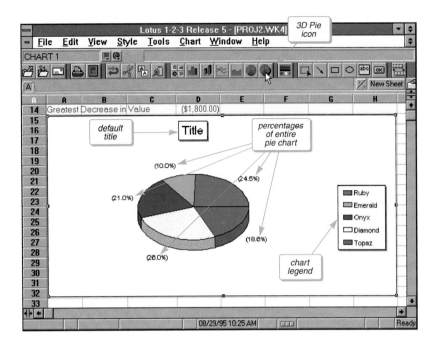

FIGURE 2-76

Adding Titles to a Chart

The next step in preparing the chart is to enter the title, Gem Portfolio. The steps to accomplish this follow.

TO ADD A TITLE TO A CHART ▼

STEP 1 ▶

Position the mouse pointer over the title frame on the chart, click the right mouse button to display the quick menu, and point to the Headings command.

1-2-3 selects the title frame by placing handles on the four corners and displays the quick menu (Figure 2-77).

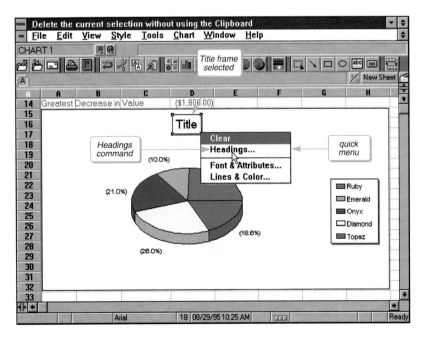

FIGURE 2-77

STEP 2 ▶

Choose the Headings command to display the Headings dialog box. When the Headings dialog box displays, type the chart title, Gem Portfolio, in the Line 1 text box in the Title area. Point to the OK button in the Headings dialog box.

When 1-2-3 displays the Headings dialog box, the Line 1 text box is automatically selected. The title you typed displays in the Line 1 text box (Figure 2-78).The mouse pointer points to the OK button.

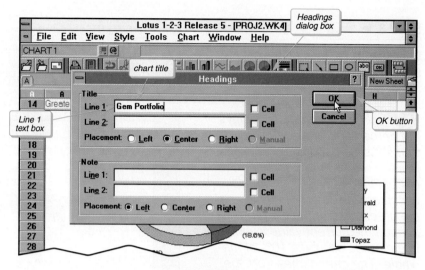

FIGURE 2-78

STEP 3 ▶

Choose the OK button in the Headings dialog box.

1-2-3 replaces the default title with the chart title you typed and centers it above the pie chart (Figure 2-79).

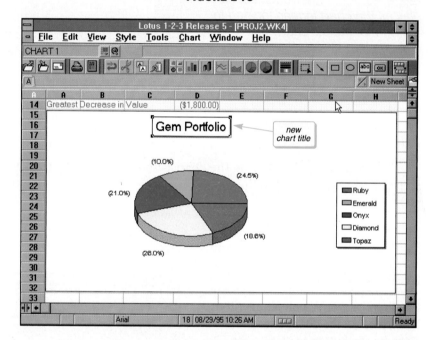

FIGURE 2-79

The Headings command is also found on the **Chart menu** on the main menu bar.

Formatting the Chart Titles

After placing the title on the chart, you can format the title. In Project 2, the font size of the title is increased, italicized, and displayed in the color blue. The following steps accomplish these tasks.

TO FORMAT CHART TITLES ▼

STEP 1 ▶

Point to the chart title frame and click the right mouse button. Then, point to the Font & Attributes command on the quick menu (Figure 2-80).

FIGURE 2-80

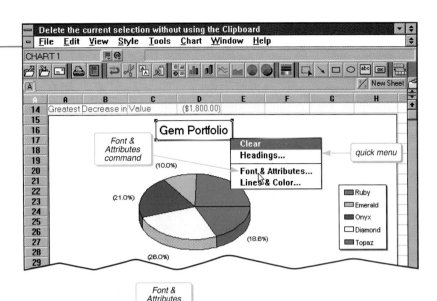

STEP 2 ▶

Choose the Font & Attributes command to display the Font & Attributes dialog box. Select 24 in the Size box and the Italics check box in the Attributes area. Then, click the Color drop-down box arrow. When the Color drop-down box displays, point to the fifth color from the left in the top row of the Color drop-down box (blue).

1-2-3 displays the Font & Attributes dialog box (Figure 2-81). Point size 24 is selected. The Italics check box is selected in the Attributes area. The mouse pointer points to the desired blue color in the Color drop-down box.

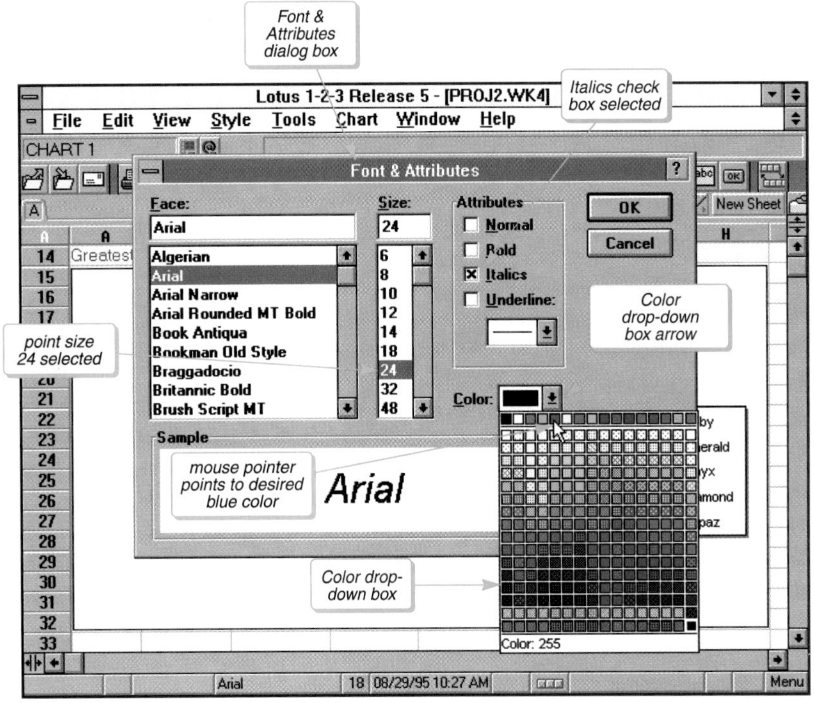

FIGURE 2-81

STEP 3 ▶

Choose blue in the Color drop-down box by clicking the left mouse button. Then, point to the OK button in the Font & Attributes dialog box.

The sample characters in the Sample area show how the selected font, attributes, and color will display in the worksheet (Figure 2-82).

FIGURE 2-82

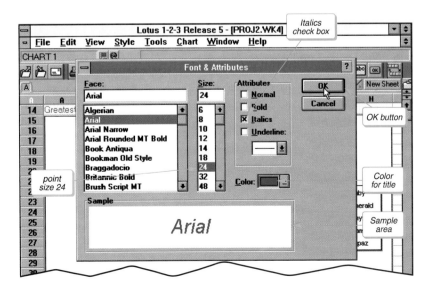

STEP 4 ▶

Choose the OK button in the Font & Attributes dialog box.

1-2-3 applies the format changes and displays the chart title with the selections you made (Figure 2-83).

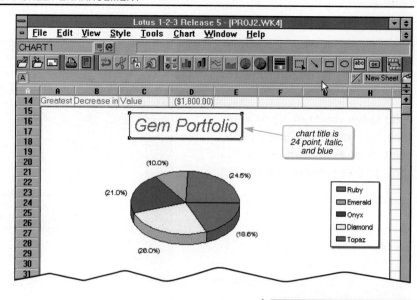

FIGURE 2-83

The Font & Attributes command is also found on the Style menu on the main menu bar.

▶ CHECKING SPELLING

After creating a worksheet, you should check the worksheet for spelling errors. 1-2-3 provides you with the capability to check the spelling of all words in a worksheet through the use of its spell checker.

The spell checker checks for spelling errors against its **language dictionary**. If you have any specialized terms that are not in the language dictionary, you can add them to a **user dictionary** through the Spell Check dialog box. When the 1-2-3 spell checker finds a word in the worksheet that is not in the dictionaries, 1-2-3 displays the unknown word in the Spell Check dialog box and provides a list of alternative words to use.

To activate the spell checker, choose the **Spell Check command** from the **Tools menu**. To illustrate 1-2-3's reaction to a misspelled word, in the following example, the label in cell E2 is spelled Intial Value. Perform the following steps to spell check the worksheet.

TO SPELL CHECK A WORKSHEET ▼

STEP 1 ▶

Select cell A1. Select the Tools menu and point to the Spell Check command.

1-2-3 displays the Tools menu and the mouse pointer points to the Spell Check command (Figure 2-84). Notice the intentionally misspelled word, Intial, in cell E2.

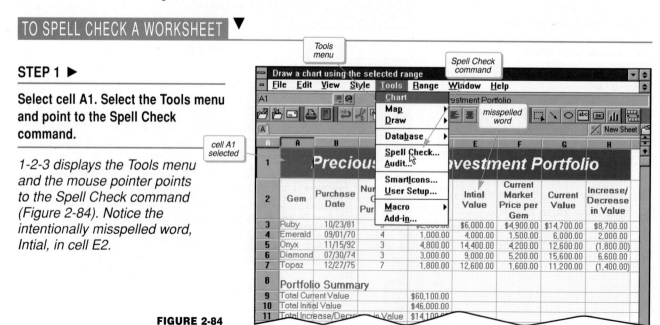

FIGURE 2-84

STEP 2 ▶

Choose the Spell Check command from the Tools menu. Then, point to the OK button in the Spell Check dialog box.

1-2-3 displays the Spell Check dialog box (Figure 2-85). The Check area contains three option buttons, which determine the area of the worksheet to be spell checked. The Entire file option checks the spelling in the worksheet and the chart. The Current worksheet option checks the spelling in the worksheet but not the chart. The Range option checks the spelling in all cells in a selected range. The Entire file option button is selected. The mouse pointer points to the OK button in the Spell Check dialog box.

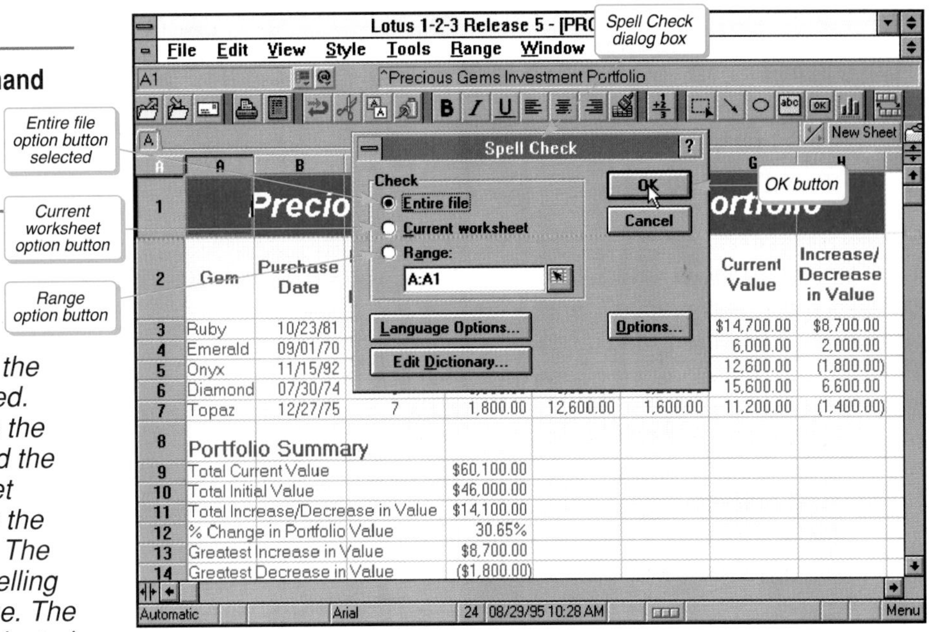

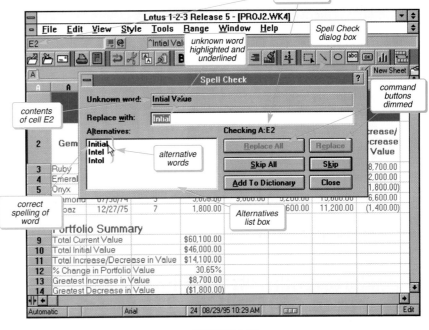

FIGURE 2-85

STEP 3 ▶

Choose the OK button in the Spell Check dialog box. When 1-2-3 displays the Spell Check dialog box containing Intial Value, in the Unknown word text box, point to the correct spelling, Initial, in the Alternatives text box.

1-2-3 scans the worksheet until it finds a word that is not in the language dictionary. 1-2-3 moves the cell pointer to cell E2 in the worksheet, the cell containing the misspelled word, and displays the Spell Check dialog box (Figure 2-86). The Unknown word text box displays the contents of cell E2 in the worksheet and underlines the unknown word, Intial. 1-2-3 high- lights the unknown word in the

FIGURE 2-86

Replace with text box and displays alternative spellings for the word Intial in the Alternatives list box. The Replace All button and the Replace button are dimmed indicating they cannot be chosen. The mouse pointer points to the alternative word, Initial. Notice the cell address containing the unknown word displays in the Spell Check dialog box and the selection indicator in the worksheet.

STEP 4 ▶

Select Initial in the Alternatives list box by clicking the left mouse button. Point to the Replace button (Replace) in the Spell Check dialog box.

1-2-3 highlights Initial in the Alternatives list box and places the word in the Replace with text box (Figure 2-87). Notice the Replace All button and the Replace button are no longer dim and can be chosen. The mouse pointer points to the Replace button in the Spell Check dialog box.

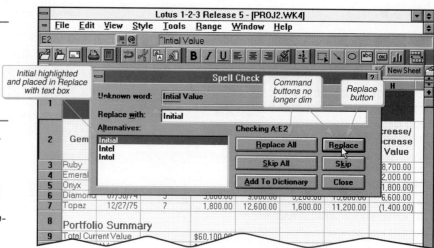

FIGURE 2-87

STEP 5 ▶

To accept the alternative word, choose the Replace button in the Spell Check dialog box.

1-2-3 replaces the word Intial with the word Initial in cell E2 in the worksheet and immediately continues checking the spelling of the worksheet. Because Increase/Decrease is not in the language dictionary, 1-2-3 moves the mouse pointer to cell A11 the active cell (Figure 2-88). No alternative words are listed.

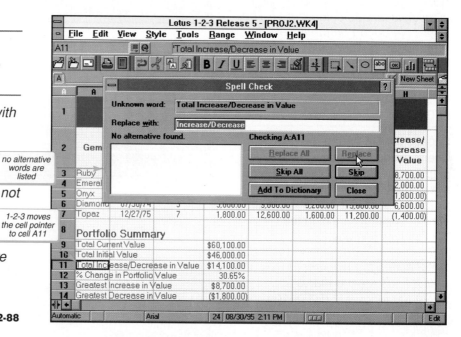

FIGURE 2-88

STEP 6 ▶

Because Increase/Decrease is not misspelled, point to the Skip button (Skip) in the Spell Check dialog box.

The mouse pointer points to the Skip button in the Spell Check dialog box (Figure 2-89).

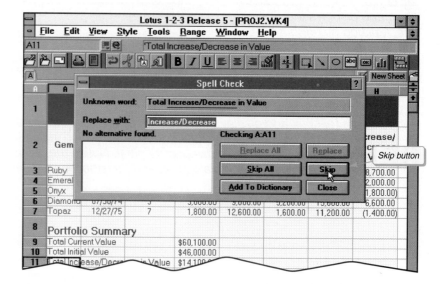

FIGURE 2-89

STEP 7 ▶

Choose the Skip button in the Spell Check dialog box. When 1-2-3 displays the word, X-Axis, in the Unknown word text box, point to the Skip button.

1-2-3 skips Total Increase/ Decrease in Value and continues to search for words not in the language dictionary. Next, 1-2-3 displays X-Axis in the Unknown word text box (Figure 2-90). The word X-Axis is the default title for the x-axis of the chart and is not in the language dictionary. Whenever you spell check a chart, 1-2-3 will stop at the term, X-Axis. Notice 1-2-3 displays Checking CHART 1 when an unknown word is found in the chart and moves the cell pointer to cell A14. The mouse pointer points to the Skip button in the Spell Check dialog box.

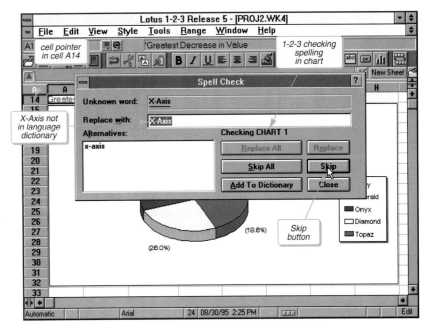

FIGURE 2-90

STEP 8 ▶

Choose the Skip button in the Spell Check dialog box. When 1-2-3 displays the word, Y-Axis, choose the Skip button to continue. When 1-2-3 displays the Spell Check dialog box indicating the spell check is complete, choose the OK button.

1-2-3 skips X-Axis and continues to search for unknown words in the chart. Next, 1-2-3 displays Y-Axis in the Unknown word text box. The word, Y-Axis, is the default title for the y-axis of the chart and is not in the language dictionary. Whenever you spell check a chart, 1-2-3 will stop at the term, Y-Axis. After checking the worksheet, 1-2-3 displays the message Spell check complete! indicating the spell check is finished. Choosing the OK button in this Spell Check dialog box removes the dialog box from the screen.

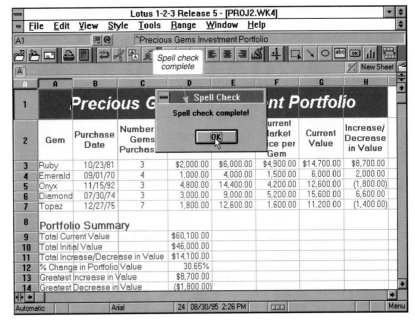

FIGURE 2-91

When 1-2-3 finds an unknown word, and no words display in the Alternatives list box or if none of the words listed is correct, type the correct word in the Replace with text box and choose the Replace button to continue. You can also correct a word that is placed in the Replace text box by adding or deleting one or more characters.

The Replace All button (Replace All) in the Spell Check dialog box (see Figure 2-87 on page L110) replaces all occurrences of the alternative word. The Skip All (Skip All) button in the Spell Check dialog box (Figure 2-87) skips all occurrences of an unknown word. To add an unknown word to the user dictionary, choose the Add To Dictionary button (Add To Dictionary) in the Spell Check dialog box.

The spell checker also looks for repeated words, such as the the, in a worksheet. You can press either the DEL key and then choose the Replace button to delete the repeated word, or choose the Skip button to ignore the repeated words.

To stop the spell checker before it completes the spell check, you can choose the Close button (Close) in the Spell Check dialog box (Figure 2-90 on the previous page). 1-2-3 stops checking the spelling and saves all corrections you have made up to that point.

▶ PRINT PREVIEW AND PRINTING THE WORKSHEET DATA SEPARATELY FROM THE CHART

P rinting worksheet data separately from the chart is useful when both the data and chart do not fit all on one printed page or if you want to display just the chart on an overhead transparency in order to graphically display the data from the worksheet.

Previewing the worksheet before printing it allows you to see the exact layout of the printed report prior to the actual printing. If the report displays properly, you can print it after previewing the report. Otherwise, you can return to the worksheet and make the necessary changes before printing. Previewing a worksheet can save time and paper. Complete the steps below and on the following two pages to preview and print the worksheet data.

TO PREVIEW THE WORKSHEET AND PRINT THE WORKSHEET DATA ONLY ▼

STEP 1 ▶

Point to the Print Preview icon (▤) on the set of SmartIcons and click the left mouse button. When the Print Preview dialog box displays on the screen, ensure the Current worksheet option button in the Preview area is selected. Then, point to the Page Setup button (Page Setup...) in the Print Preview dialog box.

1-2-3 displays the Print Preview dialog box (Figure 2-92). The current worksheet option button is selected in the Preview area. The mouse pointer points to the Page Setup button in the Print Preview dialog box.

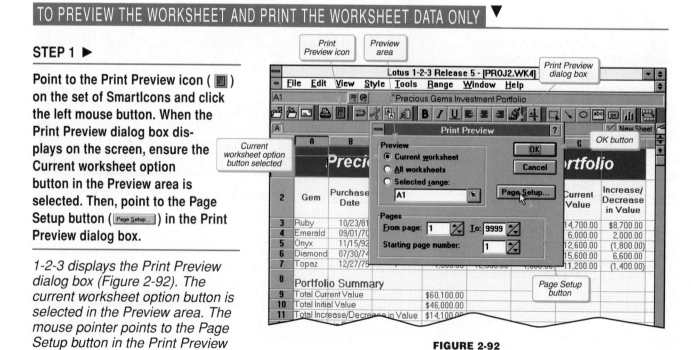

FIGURE 2-92

STEP 2 ▶

Choose the Page Setup button in the Print Preview dialog box. When the Page Setup dialog box displays on the screen, remove the X from the Drawn objects check box in the Show area by pointing to the check box and clicking the left mouse button. Point to the OK button in the Page Setup dialog box.

1-2-3 displays the Page Setup dialog box (Figure 2-93). Removing the X from the Drawn objects check box prevents the chart from printing. The mouse pointer points to the OK button in the Page Setup dialog box.

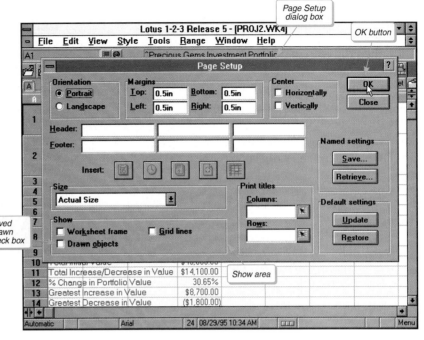

FIGURE 2-93

STEP 3 ▶

Choose the OK button in the Page Setup dialog box. When the Print Preview dialog box displays on the screen again, choose the OK button. 1-2-3 displays the Print Preview window. Point to the Print icon (🖨) in the Print Preview window.

1-2-3 displays the report as it will appear on the printed page in the Print Preview window (Figure 2-94). 1-2-3 displays the preview page in black and white if your printer does not print in color. Notice the chart does not display below the worksheet data in the Print Preview window.

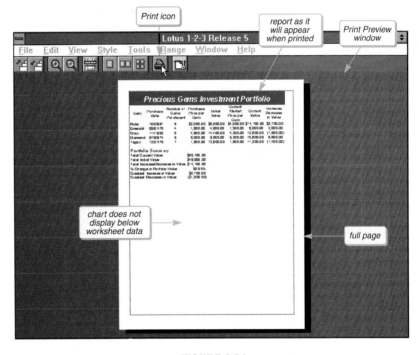

FIGURE 2-94

STEP 4 ▶

Click the Print icon in the Print Preview window. When 1-2-3 displays the Print dialog box on the screen, verify the Current worksheet option button is selected in the Print area. Point to the OK button in the Print dialog box.

1-2-3 displays the Print dialog box on the screen (Figure 2-95). The Current worksheet option button is selected in the Print area. The mouse pointer points to the OK button in the Print dialog box.

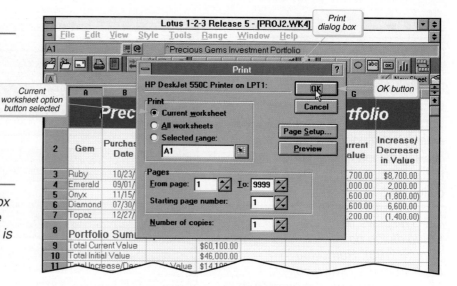

FIGURE 2-95

STEP 5 ▶

Choose the OK button in the Print dialog box.

A brief message appears on the screen describing the status of the printing operation and the report is printed without the chart (Figure 2-96).

FIGURE 2-96

Precious Gems Investment Portfolio

Gem	Purchase Date	Number of Gems Purchased	Purchase Price per Gem	Initial Value	Current Market Price per Gem	Current Value	Increase/ Decrease in Value
Ruby	10/23/81	3	$2,000.00	$6,000.00	$4,900.00	$14,700.00	$8,700.00
Emerald	09/01/70	4	1,000.00	4,000.00	1,500.00	6,000.00	2,000.00
Onyx	11/15/92	3	4,800.00	14,400.00	4,200.00	12,600.00	(1,800.00)
Diamond	07/30/74	3	3,000.00	9,000.00	5,200.00	15,600.00	6,600.00
Topaz	12/27/75	7	1,800.00	12,600.00	1,600.00	11,200.00	(1,400.00)

Portfolio Summary

Total Current Value	$60,100.00
Total Initial Value	$46,000.00
Total Increase/Decrease in Value	$14,100.00
% Change in Portfolio Value	30.65%
Greatest Increase in Value	$8,700.00
Greatest Decrease in Value	($1,800.00)

Notice that removing the X from the Drawn objects check box in the Page Setup dialog box removes the chart from the Print Preview window and prevents the chart from printing with the worksheet data. The chart continues to display in the worksheet in the 1-2-3 window, however.

To print the chart with the worksheet data, choose the Page Setup command from the File menu and select the Drawn objects check box in the Show area (see Figure 2-93 on the previous page).

1-2-3 displays several icons at the top of the Print Preview window (see Figure 2-94 on the previous page). The first two icons on the left allow you to page back and forth in a multiple-page report. The report that 1-2-3 displays is reduced in size. Click the Zoom Out (🔍) icon or Zoom In (🔍) icon to reduce or magnify the page. While you are zoomed in, use the arrow keys to view different areas of the page.

Clicking the Page Setup icon (▦) in the Print Preview window (Figure 2-94 on the previous page) displays the Page Setup dialog box so you can change the way the printed output appears. Use the Close icon (▣) (Figure 2-94) to close the Print Preview window and return to the worksheet without printing the report.

The **Print Preview command** and **Page Setup command** are also found on the File menu on the main menu bar.

▶ PRINTING THE CHART SEPARATELY FROM THE WORKSHEET

To print the chart separately from the worksheet, you can first select the chart and then click the Print icon on the set of SmartIcons. Print the chart separately from the worksheet data by performing the following steps.

TO PRINT A CHART SEPARATELY FROM THE WORKSHEET DATA ▼

STEP 1 ▶

Use the down scroll arrow to display the chart on the screen. Select the chart by pointing anywhere inside the chart and clicking the left mouse button. Click the Print icon on the set of SmartIcons. When the Print dialog box displays, point to the OK button.

The chart displays on the screen (Figure 2-97). The handles on the chart indicate the chart is selected. The Selected chart option button in the Print area is automatically selected. 1-2-3 enters the default chart name, CHART 1, into the Selected chart box. The mouse pointer points to the OK button.

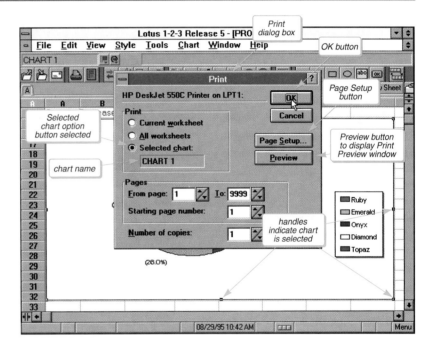

FIGURE 2-97

STEP 2 ▶

Choose the OK button in the Print dialog box.

1-2-3 prints the chart centered on the page (Figure 2-98).

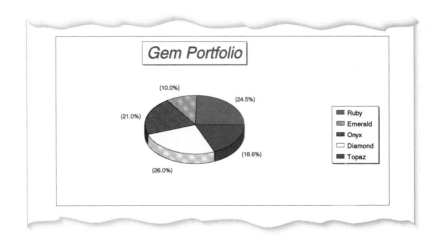

FIGURE 2-98

To preview the chart before printing, click the Print Preview icon on the set of SmartIcons or choose the Preview button (Preview) in the Print dialog box (see Figure 2-97 on the previous page). Notice in Figure 2-97 you can also display the Page Setup dialog box from the Print dialog box.

▶ DISPLAYING AND PRINTING THE FORMULAS IN THE WORKSHEET

T he printed report in Figure 2-96 on page L114 prints the results of the formulas. You can format the worksheet to print the actual formulas. Printing the actual formulas is useful for debugging a worksheet because the formulas and functions display and print instead of the numeric values. **Debugging** is the process of finding and correcting errors in the worksheet.

You can use the Text format to display numeric formulas instead of their results. When you change from values to formulas, 1-2-3 displays the formulas left-aligned in the cell. If a formula is too long to fit in the column width, the formula is truncated unless the cell to the right is blank. If the cell to the right is blank, the formulas spill over and display in full.

In Project 2, the ranges to format in the Text format are E3..E7, G3..H7, and D9..D14. To display and print the formulas in the worksheet, perform the following steps.

TO DISPLAY AND PRINT THE FORMULAS IN THE WORKSHEET ▼

STEP 1 ▶

Select the first range of cells you want to format – E3..E7, hold down the CTRL key, select the second range – G3..H7, and select the third range – D9..D14. Release the CTRL key. Then, click the format selector in the status bar and choose Text from the pop-up list of format styles. Select any cell.

1-2-3 formats the selected ranges with the Text format (Figure 2-99). The formulas display as they were entered, left-aligned in each cell. Notice the formulas in cells D9, D10, D13, and D14 spill over into column E.

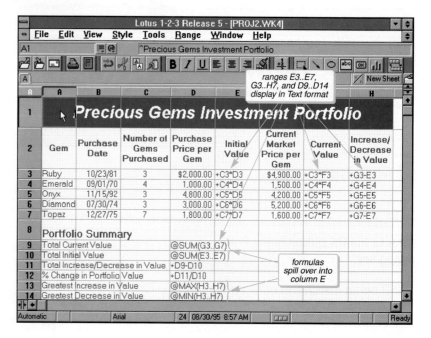

FIGURE 2-99

STEP 2 ▶

Click the Print icon on the set of SmartIcons. When the Print dialog box displays on the screen, verify the Current worksheet option button in the Print area is selected. Choose the OK button in the Print dialog box.

1-2-3 prints the formulas in the worksheet (Figure 2-100).

Precious Gems Investment Portfolio

Gem	Purchase Date	Number of Gems Purchased	Purchase Price per Gem	Initial Value	Current Market Price per Gem	Current Value	Increase/ Decrease in Value
Ruby	10/23/81	3	$2,000.00	+C3*D3	$4,900.00	+C3*F3	+G3-E3
Emerald	09/01/70	4	1,000.00	+C4*D4	1,500.00	+C4*F4	+G4-E4
Onyx	11/15/92	3	4,800.00	+C5*D5	4,200.00	+C5*F5	+G5-E5
Diamond	07/30/74	3	3,000.00	+C6*D6	5,200.00	+C6*F6	+G6-E6
Topaz	12/27/75	7	1,800.00	+C7*D7	1,600.00	+C7*F7	+G7-E7

Portfolio Summary
Total Current Value	@SUM(G3..G7)
Total Initial Value	@SUM(E3..E7)
Total Increase/Decrease in Value	+D9-D10
% Change in Portfolio Value	+D11/D10
Greatest Increase in Value	@MAX(H3..H7)
Greatest Decrease in Value	@MIN(H3..H7)

FIGURE 2-100

To reset the formulas to values, select the ranges E3..E7, G3..H7, and D9..D14, click the format selector in the status bar, and choose Reset. The cells in the ranges are reset to the Automatic format, which is the format in which you entered the data.

If you want the cells in the ranges to display using the format they had prior to changing to the Text format, you must either reformat the cells or, prior to changing to the Text format, save the worksheet and then use the saved worksheet.

After printing the formulas in the worksheet, you can close the worksheet and work on another 1-2-3 project. To close the worksheet, choose the Close command from the File menu. To quit 1-2-3, choose the Exit command from the File menu.

▶ PROJECT SUMMARY

Project 2 presented steps and techniques to show you how to enter formulas, format numbers, calculate the maximum and minimum values in a range, change column widths and row heights, and add color to a worksheet. You created a pie chart from data in the worksheet and entered and formatted the chart title. To check the spelling of a worksheet, you used the Spell Check command. You learned how to use Print Preview to view a worksheet before printing and you printed the worksheet and chart on separate pages.

▶ KEY TERMS AND INDEX

@Function List *(L81)*
@Function menu *(L78)*
@function selector *(L77)*
@MAX function *(L81)*
@MIN function *(L81)*
Alignment command *(L86)*
A range *(L103)*
automatic format *(L67)*
Center icon *(L93)*
Chart menu *(L106)*
collection of ranges *(L75)*
Column Width command *(L94)*
comma format *(L91)*
currency format *(L90)*
date formats *(L67)*
debugging *(L116)*
font *(L84)*

font attributes *(L84)*
Font & Attributes command *(L107)*
format selector *(L67)*
formula *(L67)*
Headings command *(L105)*
hiding columns *(L97)*
language dictionary *(L108)*
Left icon *(L93)*
Lines & Color command *(L101)*
list *(L77)*
List All command *(L78)*
multiple operators *(L68)*
operator *(L68)*
order of precedence *(L68)*
Page Setup command *(L115)*
parentheses *(L68)*

percent format *(L92)*
pie chart *(L64)*, *(L102)*
Point mode *(L71)*
point size *(L84)*
Print Preview command *(L115)*
Right icon *(L93)*
row height *(L97)*
slice *(L102)*
Spell Check command *(L108)*
Style menu *(L87)*
SUM function *(L62)*, *(L77)*
Text format *(L116)*
Tools menu *(L108)*
user dictionary *(L108)*
wrap text *(L88)*
X range *(L103)*

QUICK REFERENCE

In Lotus 1-2-3 Release 5 for Windows, you can accomplish a task in a number of ways. The following table presents a quick reference to each task presented in this project with its available options. The commands listed in the Menu column can be executed using either the keyboard or mouse.

Task	Mouse	Menu	Keyboard Shortcuts
Add Chart Title		From Chart menu or quick menu, choose Headings	
Bold	Click Bold icon	From Style menu or quick menu, choose Font & Attributes	Press CTRL+B
Center Data Horizontally in a Cell	Click Center icon	From Style menu or quick menu, choose Alignment	Press CTRL+E
Center Data Vertically in a Cell		From Style menu or quick menu, choose Alignment	
Change Color		From Style menu or quick menu, choose Lines & Color	
Change Column Width	Drag column border to desired width	From Style menu or quick menu, choose Column Width	
Change Font Size		From Style menu or quick menu, choose Font & Attributes	
Change Row Height	Drag row border to desired height	From Style menu or quick menu, choose Row Height	
Check Spelling		From Tools menu, choose Spell Check	

Task	Mouse	Menu	Keyboard Shortcuts
Create 3D Pie Chart	Click 3D Pie icon	From Chart menu or quick menu, choose Type	
Format in Comma Format	Click format selector in status bar	From Style menu, chose Number Format	
Format in Currency Format	Click format selector in status bar	From Style menu, choose Number Format	
Format in Percent Format	Click format selector in status bar	From Style menu, choose Number Format	
Format in Text Format	Click format selector in status bar	From Style menu, choose Number Format	
Italicize	Click Italics icon	From Style menu or quick menu, choose Font & Attributes	Press CTRL+I
Left-Align Data in a Cell	Click Left icon	From Style menu or quick menu, choose Alignment	Press CTRL+L
Print Preview	Click Print Preview icon	From File menu, choose Print Preview	
Print Worksheet without Chart		From File menu, Choose Page Setup	
Right-Align Data in a Cell	Click Right icon	From Style menu, choose Alignment	Press CTRL+R

STUDENT ASSIGNMENTS

STUDENT ASSIGNMENT 1
True/False

Instructions: Circle T if the statement is true or F if the statement is false.

T F 1. 1-2-3 considers a date entry to be an alphabetic field and stores the entry left-aligned in a cell.
T F 2. In 1-2-3, a formula is an equation that calculates a new value from existing values in cells within the worksheet.
T F 3. When entering the formula, B2-B3, in a cell, B2 must be preceded by a plus sign to define the entry as a formula.
T F 4. The five operators for formulas are +, -, *, \, and %.
T F 5. If cell A1 contains the value 6, cell B1 contains the value 10, and cell C1 contains the value 12, then the formula +A1+B1+C1/2 produces the answer value 14.
T F 6. In the formula +A1+A2*A3–A4/A5, the addition operation (+) is the first operation performed.
T F 7. Two or more ranges selected at the same time are called a collection.
T F 8. You can use the @MAX function to find the largest value in a range.
T F 9. A font size of 24 points is approximately one inch in height.
T F 10. Displaying labels on multiple lines within a single cell is called cell wrap.
T F 11. 1-2-3 allows centering data horizontally and vertically in a cell.
T F 12. Changing the format of a value affects the way 1-2-3 displays the value on the screen.
T F 13. The comma format is identical to the currency format except no comma displays with the currency format.

STUDENT ASSIGNMENT 1 (continued)

T F 14. To increase or decrease the height of a row, use the mouse to point to the row heading number and drag it up or down.

T F 15. To change from a bar chart to a three-dimensional pie chart, you can click the 3D Pie Chart SmartIcon on the set of charting SmartIcons.

T F 16. A pie chart is commonly used to show percentages of a whole.

T F 17. Only one range of values can be displayed in a pie chart.

T F 18. You cannot use the spelling checker to check the spelling in a chart.

T F 19. Previewing a worksheet allows you to see the exact layout of your printed report prior to printing the report.

T F 20. To return to the worksheet from the Print Preview window, choose the Close icon from the top of the Print Preview window.

STUDENT ASSIGNMENT 2
Multiple Choice

Instructions: Circle the correct response.

1. An equation that calculates a new value from existing values in cells within the worksheet is a(n)

   _____.
   a. cell reference
   b. order of precedence
   c. formula
   d. operator

2. For use in a formula, _____ is not a valid operator.
   a. %
   b. *
   c. –
   d. ^

3. Which of the following is a valid formula?
   a. C10*(F5-G9)/A1
   b. =C10*(F5-G9))/+A1
   c. +C10*(F5-G9)/A1
   d. @C10*((F5-G9)/A1

4. 1-2-3 evaluates operators in formulas in the following order: Evaluates any operation within parentheses first, then _____.
   a. exponentiation, followed by any multiplication or division operations, and finally, addition or subtraction
   b. addition and subtraction, followed by any multiplication or division operations
   c. addition and subtraction, followed by any division and multiplication, and finally exponentiation
   d. multiplication or division, followed by any addition and subtraction

5. If cell C4 contains 50, cell D6 contains 10, and cell F12 contains 25, the formula (F12+C4)/D6 yields _____.
   a. 7.5
   b. 30
   c. 75
   d. 25

6. To select a collection of ranges, select the first range in the collection, hold down the _____ key, and select the remaining ranges in the collection.
    a. SHIFT
    b. ENTER
    c. CTRL
    d. ALT
7. When 1-2-3 formats values with the ,Comma format, any negative values display with _____.
    a. minus signs
    b. dollar signs
    c. parentheses
    d. both b and c
8. To change the background color of a worksheet, choose the _____ command from the quick menu.
    a. Font & Attributes
    b. Lines & Color
    c. Number Format
    d. Alignment
9. A pie chart is used to show _____.
    a. comparisons of data
    b. percentages of a whole
    c. trends over time
    d. relationships between two sets of data
10. To format a worksheet to print the actual formulas, choose the _____ format.
    a. Fixed
    b. Text
    c. Label
    d. General

STUDENT ASSIGNMENT 3
Writing Formulas

Instructions: In the spaces provided, write the formulas to accomplish the calculations specified.

1. Add the values in cells D20 and D25 and divide the result by the value in cell E30.

    _____

2. Multiply the value in cell S4 by the quotient of cell A1 divided by cell C1.

    _____

3. Multiple the value in cell A1 by the greatest value in the range A13..H20.

    _____

4. Subtract the value in cell F25 from the value in cell F24 and divide the result by the value in cell A10.

    _____

5. Divide the smallest value in the range A1..A14 by 2 times the product of cells D1 and D2.

    _____

STUDENT ASSIGNMENT 4
Evaluating Formulas

Instructions: Using the values shown in the worksheet in Figure SA2-4, evaluate the formulas in the problems below Figure SA2-4.

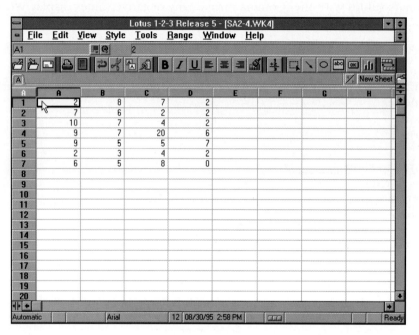

FIGURE SA2-4

1. +A3+B1+C5 _____

2. @SUM(A1..A7)–@SUM(B1..B7) _____

3. +A7^D6/B6 _____

4. @MAX(A1..D7)–@MIN(A1..D7) _____

5. (C4-C7)/A1*A2 _____

STUDENT ASSIGNMENT 5
Correcting a Worksheet

Instructions: The worksheet in Figure SA2-5 contains four errors. Identify the errors and describe the method to correct each error in the spaces provided below Figure SA2-5.

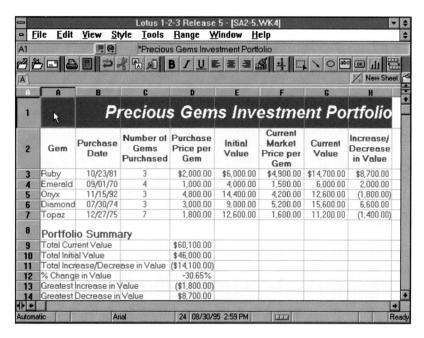

FIGURE SA2-5

Error 1: _____

Correction: _____

Error 2: _____

Correction: _____

Error 3: _____

Correction: _____

Error 4: _____

Correction: _____

STUDENT ASSIGNMENT 6
Understanding Dialog Boxes

Instructions: Write the command that causes the dialog box to display and allow you to make the indicated changes.

CHANGES   **COMMAND**

1. Center labels and values in a cell and across columns.   _____

2. Change the background color of a cell.   _____

3. Change the title of a chart.   _____

4. Wrap text for a range of cells.   _____

5. Add color to and change the attributes of fonts.   _____

6. Check the spelling in a worksheet.   _____

7. Change the width of columns.   _____

8. Enter the name of the worksheet you are saving.   _____

C O M P U T E R   L A B O R A T O R Y   E X E R C I S E S

COMPUTER LABORATORY EXERCISE 1
Using the Help Menu

Instructions: Perform the following tasks using a computer.

1. Start Lotus 1-2-3 Release 5 for Windows.
2. Select the Help menu.
3. Choose the Search command.
4. Type Number Formats in the Search text box.
5. Click the Show Topics button.
6. Use the scroll arrows in the Search dialog box to display the Style Number Format topic.
7. Select Style Number Format and click the Go To button.
8. Read the Style Number Format topic and answer the following questions:
   a. What is the name of the default format for a worksheet?

   _____

   b. List the formats that allow you to specify decimal places in the format.

   _____

   c. Point to Currency. What shape does the mouse pointer become?

   _____

   d. Click Currency. How many decimal places will the Currency format allow? Click the left mouse button again.

   _____

   e. Which format displays formulas as entered rather than the calculated values?

   _____

9. Choose the Exit command from the File menu.

COMPUTER LABORATORY EXERCISE 2
Formatting the Worksheet

Instructions: Start Lotus 1-2-3 Release 5 for Windows. Open the CLE2-2.WK4 file from the Lotus4 sub-directory on the Student Diskette that accompanies this book. The worksheet, shown in Figure CLE2-2, contains labels and values, but none of the worksheet is formatted. Format the worksheet as follows.

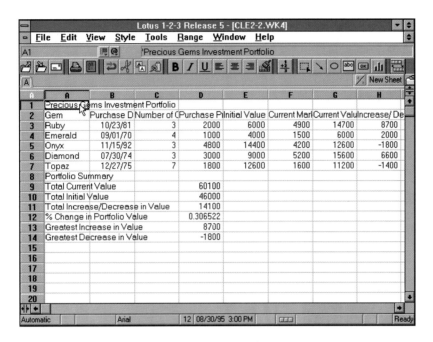

FIGURE CLE2-2

1. Display the worksheet title, column titles, and the label in cell A8 in bold.
2. Increase the worksheet title to 32 point size and center it horizontally and vertically across the range A1..H1.
3. Center all column titles horizontally and vertically in each cell and display them on multiple lines within each cell. Center the cell contents in the range C3..C7.
4. Change the height of row 8 to 28 points.
5. Display the range D3..H3 in the currency format with two decimal places. Display the range D4..H7 in the comma format with two decimal places. Display all dollar amounts in rows 9 through 13 with dollar signs, commas, and two decimal places. Display the % change in portfolio value in the percent format with two decimal places.
6. Change the column width of column A to 7 characters and column C to 10 characters.
7. Change the background color of the range A1..H1 to blue. Change the text color in cell A1 to yellow.
8. Change the background color of the range A2..H14 to yellow. Change the cell contents of the range A2..H14 to blue.
9. Print the formatted worksheet.

COMPUTER LABORATORY EXERCISE 3
Displaying Formulas

Instructions: Start Lotus 1-2-3 Release 5 for Windows. Open the CLE2-3.WK4 file from the Lotus4 subdirectory the Student Diskette that accompanies this book. The worksheet you will see on your screen is shown in Figure CLE2-3a.

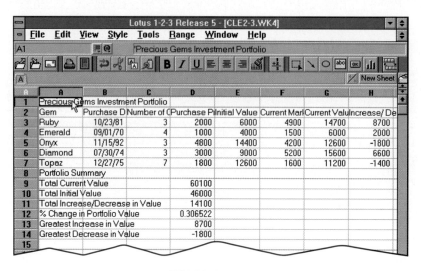

FIGURE CLE2-3a

1. Select the collection E3..H7; D9..D14. Click the format selector in the status bar and choose Text. The screen will change. The formulas display in the cells.
2. Change the column widths to the following: A = 8; B = 8; C = 8; D = 9; E = 6; F = 7; G = 6; H = 8. Your worksheet should now look like the worksheet in Figure CLE2-3b.

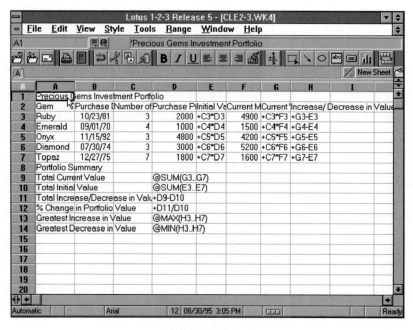

FIGURE CLE2-3b

3. Print the worksheet with all the formulas displayed.

COMPUTER LABORATORY ASSIGNMENT 1
Creating an Oil Production Report

Purpose: To provide experience creating a worksheet that requires entering formulas, using the @SUM and @MAX functions, formatting labels and values, adding color to a worksheet, creating a three-dimensional pie chart with a formatted title, previewing the worksheet, and printing the report.

Problem: Create an Oil Production report for the Chief Executive Officer of an oil exploration and production company. The data for the worksheet is shown in the following table.

DATE	DRILLING LOCATION	BARRELS OF OIL PRODUCED	PRICE PER BARREL
02/25/95	Oklahoma	524	14
02/28/95	Texas	612	15
03/02/95	Louisiana	349	13
03/05/95	California	959	15
03/15/95	Alaska	995	15
04/01/95	Montana	320	13

The worksheet is shown in Figure CLA2-1a.

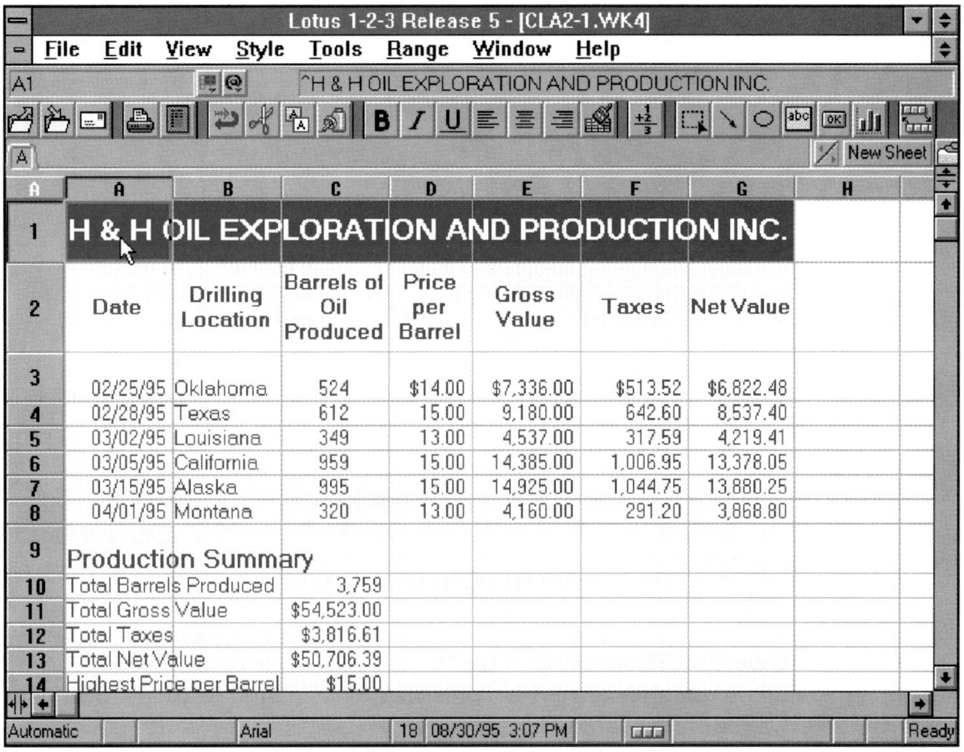

FIGURE CLA2-1a

(continued)

COMPUTER LABORATORY ASSIGNMENT 1 (continued)

Instructions:

1. Create a worksheet in the format shown in Figure CLA2-1a on the previous page using the text and numbers from the table.
2. On the worksheet, calculate the gross value by multiplying the barrels of oil produced by the price per barrel.
3. On the worksheet, calculate taxes by multiplying the gross value by 7%.
4. On the worksheet, calculate the net value by subtracting taxes from gross value.
5. Calculate the production summary totals by summing the values in each of the respective columns.
6. Determine the highest price per barrel in row 14.
7. Format the worksheet as shown. The title displays with 18 point font size and is centered horizontally and vertically across the range A1..G1. The row heights are: 1 = 35; 2 = 50; 3 = 28; 9 = 28. Column D width is 7.
8. The background color for range A1..G1 is blue and the text color is white. The background color for the range A2..G14 is yellow and the text color is blue.
9. Create the three-dimensional pie chart shown in Figure CLA2-1b from the net value on the worksheet. Enter and format the title as shown.

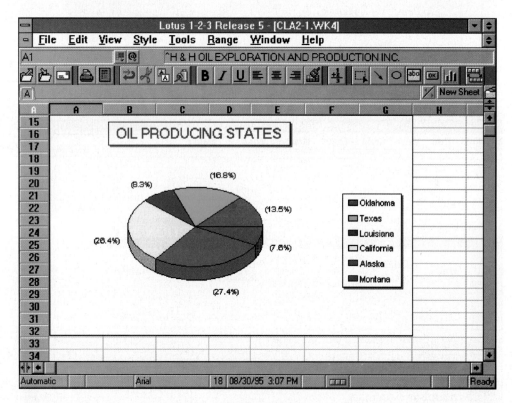

FIGURE CLA2-1b

10. Check the spelling of the worksheet.
11. Save the worksheet you create on a diskette. Use a file name consisting of the initials of your first and last names followed by the assignment number. Example: KS2-1.
12. Print the worksheet data and chart separately.
13. Print the formulas in the worksheet.
14. Follow directions from your instructor for turning in this assignment.

COMPUTER LABORATORY ASSIGNMENT 2
Creating a Monthly Sales Report

Purpose: To provide experience creating a worksheet that requires entering formulas, using the @SUM and @MAX functions, formatting labels and values, adding color to a worksheet, creating a three-dimensional pie chart, checking the spelling of the worksheet, and printing the worksheet data and chart separately.

Problem: Create a Monthly Sales Report using the data in the following table.

PLANT	FLATS SOLD	FLAT PRICE	SALES RETURNS
Azalea	135	12.50	62.50
Hibiscus	240	9.75	78.00
Star Jasmine	111	11.75	105.75
Nandina	236	7.50	75.00
Agapanthus	85	15.20	60.80
Impatiens	185	11.34	56.70

The worksheet is shown in Figure CLA2-2a.

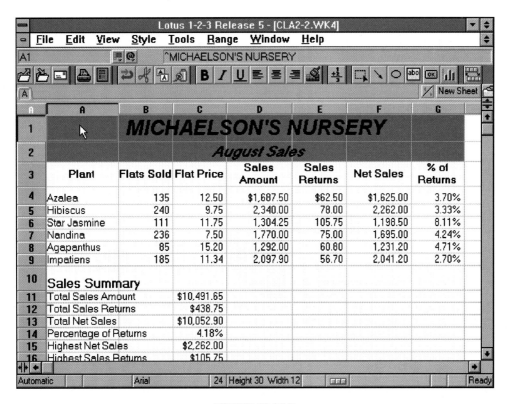

FIGURE CLA2-2a

(continued)

COMPUTER LABORATORY ASSIGNMENT 2 (continued)

Instructions:

1. Create a worksheet in the format shown in Figure CLA2-2a on the previous page using the text and numbers from the table.
2. On the worksheet, calculate the Sales Amount by multiplying the Flats Sold by the Flat Price.
3. On the worksheet, calculate Net Sales by subtracting the Sales Returns from the Sales Amount.
4. Calculate the % of Returns by dividing the Sales Returns by the Sales Amount.
5. Calculate the Total Sales Amount and Total Sales Returns by summing the values in each of the respective columns.
6. Calculate the Total Net Sales by subtracting the Total Sales Returns from the Total Sales Amount.
7. Calculate the Percentage of Returns in row 14 by dividing the Total Sales Returns by the Total Sales Amount.
8. Determine the Highest Net Sales in row 15. Determine the Highest Sales Returns in row 16.
9. Format the worksheet as shown. The title, MICHAELSON'S NURSERY, displays in 24 point and is centered across the range A1..G1. The title, August Sales, displays in 18 point and is centered across the range A2..G2. The row heights are: 1 = 30; 2 = 22; 3 = 28; 4 = 20; 10 = 28. The column widths are: A = 12; D = 11, F = 11. Background color for the titles in row 1 and row 2 is located in the top row, third from the right (color 118) in the Background color drop-down box in the Lines & Colors dialog box. The background color for the range A3..G16 is yellow.
10. Create the three-dimensional pie chart shown in Figure CLA2-2b from the Net Sales on the worksheet. Enter the title as shown. The title displays in 24 point font size and bold.

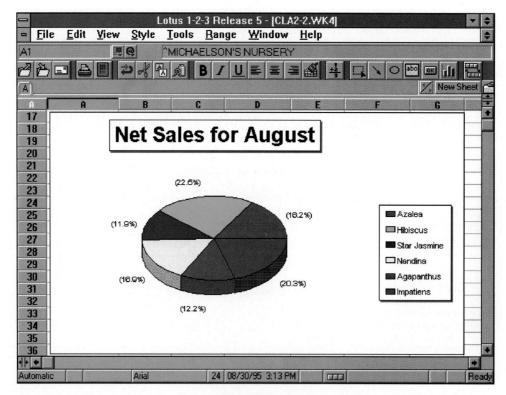

FIGURE CLA2-2b

11. Check the spelling of the worksheet.
12. Save the worksheet you create on a diskette. Use a file name consisting of the initials of your first and last names followed by the assignment number. Example: KS2-2.
13. Print the worksheet data separately from the chart you have created.
14. Print the formulas in the worksheet.
15. Follow directions from your instructor for turning in this assignment.

COMPUTER LABORATORY ASSIGNMENT 3
Creating an Accounts Receivable Report

Purpose: To provide experience creating a worksheet that requires entering formulas, using the @SUM, @MAX, and @MIN functions, formatting labels and values, adding color to a worksheet, creating a three-dimensional pie chart, checking the spelling of the worksheet, and printing the worksheet data and chart separately.

Problem: Create an Accounts Receivable Report using the data in the following table.

ACCOUNT NUMBER	CUSTOMER NAME	BEGINNING BALANCE	PURCHASES	PAYMENTS	RETURNS
902	Brison	629.17	24.18	600.00	0.00
710	Connolly	420.71	129.00	250.00	43.50
765	Arvin	912.00	0.00	500.00	126.25
468	Slack	17.90	251.05	17.90	0.00
195	Dolby	788.00	135.00	650.00	79.00
172	Tech Corp	112.60	21.80	75.00	0.00

The worksheet is shown in Figure CLA2-3a.

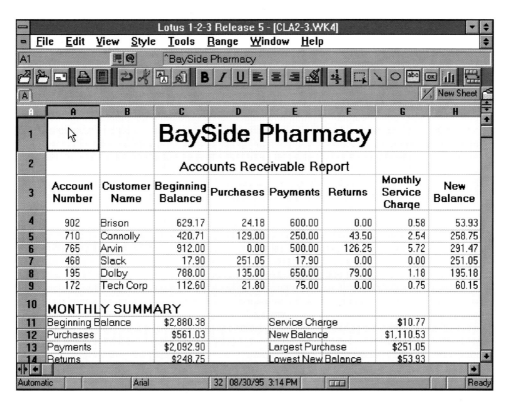

FIGURE CLA2-3a

(continued)

COMPUTER LABORATORY ASSIGNMENT 3 (continued)

Instructions:

1. Create a worksheet in the format shown in Figure CLA2-3a on the previous page using the text and numbers from the table.
2. On the worksheet, calculate the Monthly Service Charge by multiplying 2% times (Beginning Balance − Payments − Returns).
3. On the worksheet, calculate the New Balance by adding Beginning Balance plus Purchases minus Payments minus Returns plus Monthly Service Charge.
4. Calculate the totals by summing the values in each of the respective columns.
5. Determine the Largest Purchase in row 13. Determine the Lowest New Balance in row 14.
6. Format the worksheet as shown. The title, BaySide Pharmacy, displays in 32 point and is centered across the range A1..H1. The title, Accounts Receivable Report, displays in 14 point and is centered across the range A2..H2. The row heights are: 1 = 40; 2 = 26; 3 = 40; 4 = 22; and 10 = 28. Column width for D is 10 characters. All labels in rows 1, 2, 3, and 10 are bold.
7. Create the three-dimensional pie chart in Figure CLA2-3b from the New Balance on the worksheet. Enter the titles as shown. The first chart title, Accounts Receivable Report, displays in 24 point and bold. The second chart title, BaySide Pharmacy, displays in 18 point and italics.
8. Check the spelling of the worksheet.
9. Save the worksheet you create on a diskette. Use a file name consisting of the initials of your first and last names followed by the assignment number. Example: KS2-3.
10. Print the worksheet data separately from the chart you have created.
11. Print the formulas in the worksheet.
12. Follow directions from your instructor for turning in this assignment.

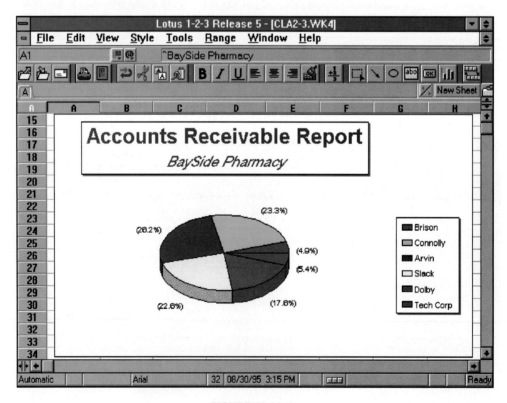

FIGURE CLA2-3b

COMPUTER LABORATORY ASSIGNMENT 4
Creating a Monthly Payroll Report

Purpose: To provide experience creating a worksheet that requires entering formulas, using the @SUM, @MAX, and @MIN functions, formatting labels and values, adding color to a worksheet, creating a three-dimensional pie chart, checking the spelling of the worksheet, and printing the worksheet data and chart separately.

Problem: You have started your own business and need to prepare a monthly payroll worksheet for your employees. You have gathered the following information:

EMPLOYEE	HOURLY PAY RATE	HOURS WORKED	DEPENDENT
Parsons	9.75	40	1
Frier	8.50	25	3
Hamilton	11.00	35	4
Nemoy	8.25	40	2
Alverez	9.25	38	2

Instructions:

1. Design and create a worksheet that includes the four fields listed in the table. In addition, you must calculate Gross Pay, Federal Tax, State Tax, and Net Pay. Use the following information for creating the formulas:
   a. Gross Pay = Hourly Pay Rate * Hours Worked
   b. Federal Tax = 28% * (Gross Pay - (Dependents * 40.00)
   c. State Tax = 10% * (Gross Pay - (Dependents * 40.00))
   d. Net Pay = Gross Pay - (Federal Tax + State Tax)
2. Calculate the totals for Gross Pay, Federal Tax, State Tax, and Net Pay.
3. Determine the highest and lowest net pay paid to your employee.
4. Format the worksheet appropriately.
5. Create a three-dimensional pie chart based on Net Pay. Include an appropriate chart title.
6. Check the spelling of the worksheet.
7. Save the worksheet you create on a diskette. Use a file name consisting of the initials of your first name and last name followed by the assignment number. Example KS2-4.
8. Print the worksheet data separately from the chart
9. Print the formulas in the worksheet.
10. Follow directions from your instructor for turning in this assignment.

▼

WHAT-IF ANALYSIS

OBJECTIVES You will have mastered the material in this project when you can:

- ▸ Change the default style settings for a worksheet
- ▸ Create a sequence
- ▸ Use drag and drop to copy a range
- ▸ Use the @ROUND function
- ▸ Enter a formula containing absolute cell references
- ▸ Add a text block to a worksheet
- ▸ Use the Zoom Out and Custom commands to change the display size of cells

- ▸ Add borders to cells
- ▸ Use the New Sheet button to insert a second worksheet into the current worksheet file
- ▸ Add a name to a worksheet tab
- ▸ Create a 3D stacked bar chart
- ▸ Display a table of values below a chart
- ▸ Print in landscape page orientation
- ▸ View different parts of a worksheet through window panes
- ▸ Use 1-2-3 to answer what-if questions

▶ INTRODUCTION

In Project 1 and Project 2, you learned that a worksheet is useful for performing calculations and presenting data both on a worksheet and in a chart. You can also use worksheets to solve business, financial, and accounting problems that would otherwise be difficult to solve.

In particular, 1-2-3 worksheets provide a means for asking **what-if questions** and obtaining almost immediate answers. For example, a business person might ask, *What if we decreased our projected expenses by 1% — how would the decrease affect our net income?* 1-2-3 can easily answer this question. This capability of quickly analyzing the effect of changing values in a worksheet is important when making business decisions.

▶ PROJECT THREE

The worksheet to be developed in Project 3 is shown in Figure 3-1. The worksheet contains the monthly projected revenue, returns, expenses, and net income for a six-month period for Medical Research, Inc. The worksheet also includes, in column I, the six-month projected total for all revenues, returns, expenses, and net income.

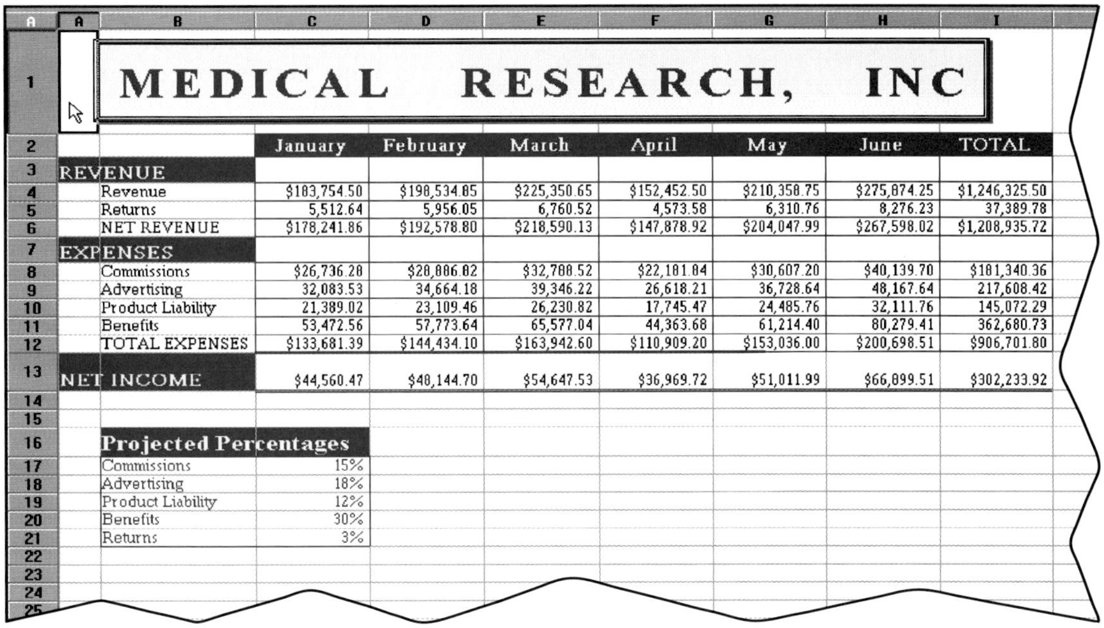

MEDICAL RESEARCH, INC

		January	February	March	April	May	June	TOTAL
REVENUE								
	Revenue	$183,754.50	$198,534.85	$225,350.65	$152,452.50	$210,358.75	$275,874.25	$1,246,325.50
	Returns	5,512.64	5,956.05	6,760.52	4,573.58	6,310.76	8,276.23	37,389.78
	NET REVENUE	$178,241.86	$192,578.80	$218,590.13	$147,878.92	$204,047.99	$267,598.02	$1,208,935.72
EXPENSES								
	Commissions	$26,736.28	$28,886.82	$32,788.52	$22,181.84	$30,607.20	$40,139.70	$181,340.36
	Advertising	32,083.53	34,664.18	39,346.22	26,618.21	36,728.64	48,167.64	217,608.42
	Product Liability	21,389.02	23,109.46	26,230.82	17,745.47	24,485.76	32,111.76	145,072.29
	Benefits	53,472.56	57,773.64	65,577.04	44,363.68	61,214.40	80,279.41	362,680.73
	TOTAL EXPENSES	$133,681.39	$144,434.10	$163,942.60	$110,909.20	$153,036.00	$200,698.51	$906,701.80
NET INCOME		$44,560.47	$48,144.70	$54,647.53	$36,969.72	$51,011.99	$66,899.51	$302,233.92

Projected Percentages	
Commissions	15%
Advertising	18%
Product Liability	12%
Benefits	30%
Returns	3%

FIGURE 3-1

The title for the worksheet, MEDICAL RESEARCH, INC, is entered in a text block over the range B1..I1. A **text block** is a drawn object into which you can type text not confined to cells. You can size the text block and place it anywhere on the worksheet.

The returns for each month as shown in row 5 are determined by multiplying the revenue in row 4 times the returns percentage in cell C21. The returns percentage shown in Figure 3-1 is 3%. Therefore, for January, the returns are 5,512.64 ($183,754.50 * 3%).

The net revenue for each month as shown in row 6 is determined by subtracting the returns in row 5 from the revenue in row 4 for each month. In Figure 3-1, the net revenue for January is $178,241.86 ($183,754.50 - 5,512.64).

Each of the monthly projected expenses in the range C8..H11 — commissions, advertising, product liability, and benefits — is determined by multiplying the net revenue in row 6 by the appropriate expense percentage in the projected percentages section for each month. As an example, the projected expenses for January are as follows:

1. Commissions are $26,736.28 ($178,241.86 * 15%).
2. Advertising is 32,083.53 ($178,241.86 * 18%).
3. Product Liability is 21,389.02 ($178,241.86 * 12%).
4. Benefits are 53,472.56 ($178,241.86 * 30%).

The total expenses for each month in row 12 of Figure 3-1 are the sum of the monthly projected expenses in rows 8 through 11.

The net income for each month in row 13 is calculated by subtracting the monthly total expenses in row 12 from the corresponding monthly net revenue in row 6. Finally, the six-month totals in column I are determined by summing the monthly values in each row.

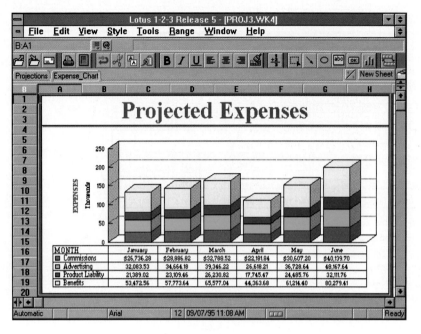

FIGURE 3-2

Recall from Project 1 that you can have more than one worksheet in a file. In this project, you will add a second worksheet to the file and create a 3D stacked bar chart on this second worksheet. The 3D stacked bar chart in Figure 3-2 graphically illustrates the projected expenses for the six-month period. Each expense for the month is a different color, and they are stacked one on top of the other so the stack represents the total expenses for a given month. Below each vertical stack are the values that each expense represents.

Because the monthly returns in row 5 and the monthly expenses in rows 8 through 11 (see Figure 3-1 on the previous page) are dependent on the projected percentages, when you change a percentage, 1-2-3 will recalculate the values. Therefore, you can see the impact of changing these projected percentages on the net income in row 13.

Worksheet Preparation Steps

The following worksheet preparation steps provide an overview of how the worksheet in Figure 3-1 and the chart in Figure 3-2 will be built in this project.

1. Start Lotus 1-2-3 Release 5 for Windows.
2. Change the worksheet default style settings for fonts and column widths.
3. Create a text block and enter MEDICAL RESEARCH INC, the worksheet title.
4. Enter the column titles (January, February, March, April, May, June, and TOTAL).
5. Enter the row titles (REVENUE, Revenue, Returns, NET REVENUE, EXPENSES, Commissions, Advertising, Product Liability, Benefits, TOTAL EXPENSES, NET INCOME, and Projected Percentages).
6. Copy the projected expense labels to the projected percentages section.
7. Enter the projected percentages shown in Figure 3-1.
8. Enter the projected revenue.
9. Enter the formulas to calculate returns, net revenue, commissions, advertising, product liability, benefits, total expenses, net income, and total.
10. Format the text block (increase the font size and resize the text block).
11. Format the column and row titles (bold the text and increase the font size, change the background color, and change the text color).
12. Format the values on the worksheet.
13. Add borders to the worksheet.
14. Format the projected percentages section (increase the font size, change the background color, and change the text color).
15. Insert a second worksheet.
16. Name the worksheets.
17. Create the 3D stacked bar chart based on data in the worksheet.
18. Save the worksheet and chart on disk.
19. Print the worksheet and chart.

▶ STARTING LOTUS 1-2-3 RELEASE 5 FOR WINDOWS

o start Lotus 1-2-3 Release 5 for Windows, follow the steps you used in previous projects. These steps are reviewed below.

TO START LOTUS 1-2-3 RELEASE 5 FOR WINDOWS

Step 1: From Program Manager, open the Lotus Applications group window.
Step 2: Double-click the Lotus 1-2-3 Release 5 program-item icon.

▶ CHANGING WORKSHEET STYLE DEFAULTS

ach time you start 1-2-3, the worksheet has certain default style settings and characteristics already set. For example, the columns are 9 characters wide, labels are entered left-aligned in a cell, and the font is Arial 12 point. These settings are known as **worksheet style defaults** and affect the entire worksheet. In Project 3, the font of the worksheet is changed from the default Arial to Times New Roman. The column width of all columns is increased from a width of 9 to a width of 11. To change the worksheet style defaults, perform the steps below and on the next two pages.

TO CHANGE WORKSHEET STYLE DEFAULTS ▼

STEP 1 ▶

Select the Style menu, and point to the Worksheet Defaults command.

1-2-3 displays the Style menu, and the mouse pointer points to the Worksheet Defaults command (Figure 3-3). Notice the default font for the worksheet, Arial 12 point, displays in the status bar. The column widths are set to 9 characters.

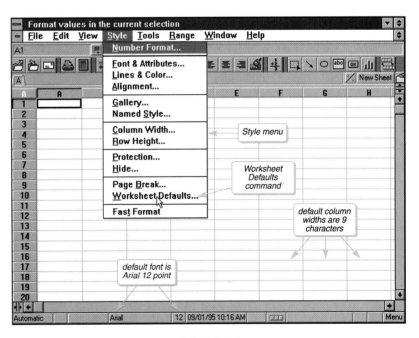

FIGURE 3-3

STEP 2 ▶

Choose the Worksheet Defaults command from the Style menu.

1-2-3 displays the Worksheet Defaults dialog box (Figure 3-4). The default font, Arial 12 point, is selected in the Font area. The Other area displays the default column width (9) and alignment of data (Left). The Number format area displays the default format for values (Automatic). The default text color (black) and the cell background color (white) display in the Colors area.

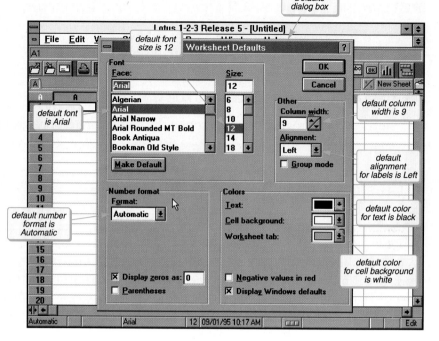

FIGURE 3-4

STEP 3 ▶

Point to the down scroll arrow in the Face list box and scroll until Times New Roman is visible. Select Times New Roman in the Face list box. In the Other area, click the up arrow in the Column width text box twice to display 11. Then, point to the OK button in the Worksheet Defaults dialog box.

Times New Roman is selected in the Face list box and displays in the Face text box. The Column width textbox displays 11 and the mouse pointer points to the OK button in the Worksheet Defaults dialog box (Figure 3-5).

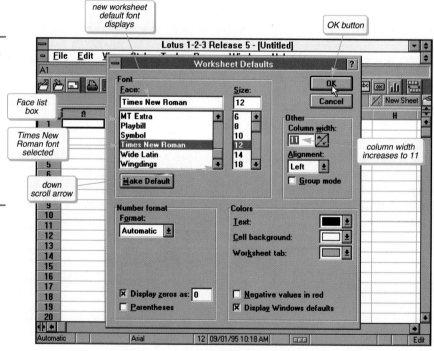

FIGURE 3-5

STEP 4 ▶

Choose the OK button in the Worksheet Defaults dialog box.

1-2-3 displays a blank worksheet with the new worksheet defaults (Figure 3-6). Times New Roman displays in the font selector in the status bar. All columns on the worksheet now have a width of 11. Notice the difference in the column widths of 9 in Figure 3-3 on page L137, and 11 in Figure 3-6. Only six complete columns now display in Figure 3-6.

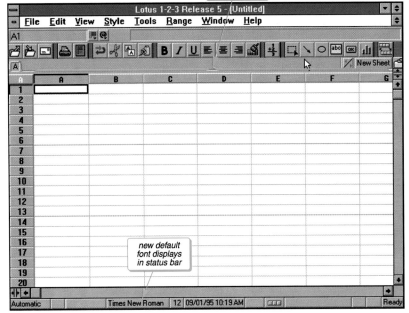

FIGURE 3-6

These worksheet default settings for the font type of Times New Roman and the column width of 11 apply to the current worksheet only.

▶ CREATING TEXT BLOCKS

1-2-3 includes a set of basic drawing tools for creating and working with drawn objects to enhance worksheets and charts. **Drawn objects** are graphic objects you can draw on a 1-2-3 worksheet or chart. In Project 3, you draw a text block and enter the worksheet title in the block. You will increase the height of row 1 to allow sufficient room for the text block. The procedure for creating a text block is described in the steps on the next two pages.

TO CREATE A TEXT BLOCK ▼

STEP 1 ▶

Move the mouse pointer to the border line between row heading 1 and row heading 2. Drag the row border down until the height displayed in the selection indicator is 30Points. Release the left mouse button. Point to the Draw Text icon (▣) on the set of SmartIcons.

The worksheet displays with the new height of 30 points for row 1 (Figure 3-7). The mouse pointer points to the Draw Text icon.

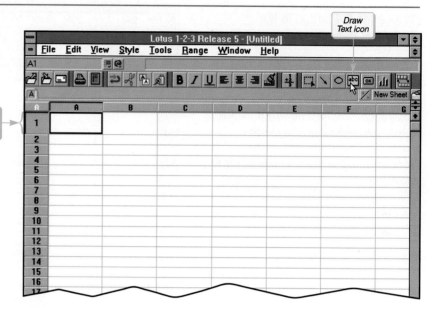

FIGURE 3-7

STEP 2 ▶

Click the left mouse button. Then, move the mouse pointer to the upper left corner of cell A1.

1-2-3 displays an instruction in the title bar prompting you to click and drag to draw a text block (Figure 3-8). The mouse pointer changes to a cross hair indicating you can position a drawn object.

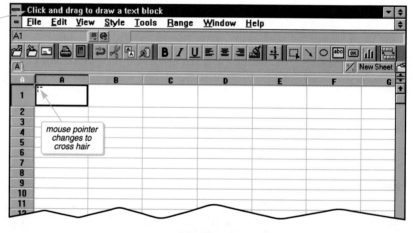

FIGURE 3-8

STEP 3 ▶

Drag the mouse pointer to the lower right corner of cell C1.

The mouse pointer is positioned at the lower right corner of cell C1, and the proposed text block location is surrounded by a dotted rectangle (Figure 3-9).

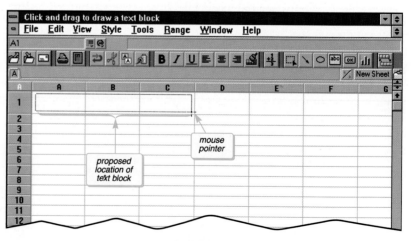

FIGURE 3-9

STEP 4 ▶

Release the left mouse button.

A new set of drawing SmartIcons displays below the edit line (Figure 3-10). 1-2-3 displays the text block, which has a white background. Notice the text block sits in front of the worksheet cells. The name of the text block, Text 1, displays in the selection indicator. The blinking insertion point displays in the top left corner of the text block.

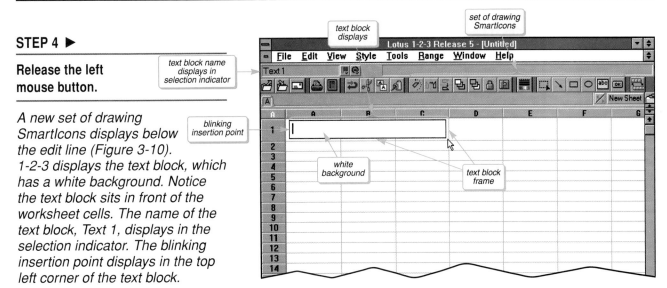

FIGURE 3-10

STEP 5 ▶

Type the worksheet title, MEDICAL RESEARCH, INC and then, click any cell outside the text block.

1-2-3 displays the worksheet title in the text block (Figure 3-11). Notice 1-2-3 enters the text left-aligned.

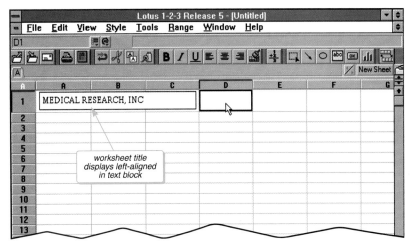

FIGURE 3-11

If you make an error while typing in the text block and notice the error prior to selecting any cell outside the text block, highlight the error and type the correct entry.

Once text is entered in a text block, you can edit the text by positioning the mouse pointer inside the text block and double-clicking the left mouse button. The insertion point appears at the beginning of the text. Use the mouse or arrow keys to position the insertion point, and make your corrections. After all corrections are made to the text, click any cell outside the text block.

To delete a text block, select the text block by clicking the left mouse button anywhere inside the text block and press the DEL key.

The **Draw Text command** is also found on the Tools menu on the main menu bar.

▶ USING DRAG-AND-FILL TO ENTER A DATA SEQUENCE IN A RANGE

1 -2-3 can automatically enter data in a range if the range is to have a certain sequence to it. In Figure 3-1 on page L135, the months January through June display in row 1. Using **drag-and-fill,** you can automatically enter the month names in the row. To create this sequence, first select the cell or range that includes the data you want to use as the starting sequence. Then, position the mouse pointer on the border of the selection at the lower right corner and drag to select the range you want to fill. Perform the following steps to enter the month name January in cell C2, create the sequence, February, March, April, May, and June, in the range D2..H2, and enter the column title TOTAL in cell I2.

TO ENTER A DATA SEQUENCE IN A RANGE USING DRAG-AND-FILL ▼

STEP 1 ▶

Select cell C2. Enter the column title, January. Click the Center icon on the set of SmartIcons. Position the mouse pointer on the lower right corner border of cell C2.

January displays centered in cell C2 (Figure 3-12). The mouse pointer changes to an arrow with double horizontal and vertical traingles.

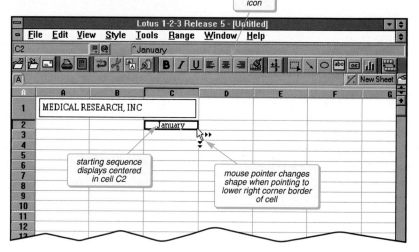

FIGURE 3-12

STEP 2 ▶

Hold down the left mouse button and drag the range you want to fill – cells D2..H2.

The mouse pointer changes to an arrow pointing to a cell as you drag the range D2..H2 (Figure 3-13). Cells C2, D2, and E2 do not display on the screen even though they are selected.

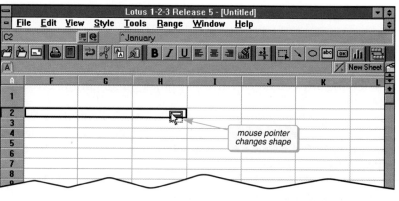

FIGURE 3-13

STEP 3 ▶

Release the left mouse button.

*1-2-3 places the month name
sequence, February through June,
in the range D2..H2 and centers
each label (Figure 3-14). The
month of June displays in cell H2
even though it does not display on
the screen.*

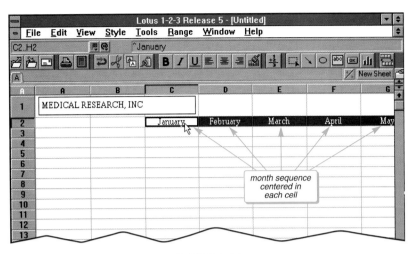

FIGURE 3-14

STEP 4 ▶

**Point to the right scroll arrow at the
bottom of the screen and click until
cell I2 is visible. Select cell I2 and
enter the column title, TOTAL. With
cell I2 selected, click the Center-
Align icon on the set of SmartIcons.**

*1-2-3 displays the column title,
TOTAL, centered in cell I2 (Figure
3-15).*

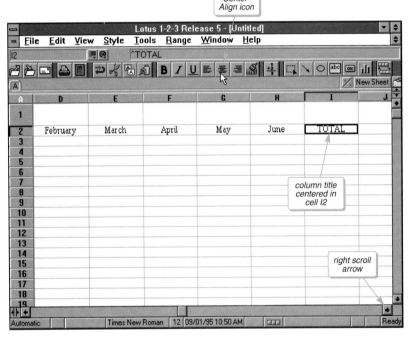

FIGRUE 3-15

In addition to creating a sequence, 1-2-3 also copies the format of cell C2 (centered) to the range D2..H2.

You can create different types of sequences using drag-and-fill. Table 3-1 on the next page illustrates several examples.

▸ **TABLE 3-1**

EXAMPLE	DATA ALREADY IN THE RANGE	NEXT THREE VALUES OF SEQUENCE
1	A	B, C, D
2	Monday	Tuesday, Wednesday, Thursday
3	Product 1	Product 2, Product 3, Product 4
4	100	101, 102, 103
5	Qtr3	Qtr4, Qtr1, Qtr2
6	100, 200	300, 400, 500
7	5, 10	15, 20, 25
8	January, March	May, July, September
9	Monday, Qtr 1	Tuesday, Wednesday, Thursday
10	Accounting	Accounting, Accounting, Accounting

Notice in Examples 6 through 8 in Table 3-1 that you are required to enter the first data in the sequence in one cell and the second data in the sequence in an adjacent cell. If you create a sequence that increments each entry by a value other than 1, 1-2-3 uses the first two cells to establish the proper sequence. If a relationship cannot be determined between the data in the first two cells, (Example 9), 1-2-3 uses only the data in the first cell to create the sequence. If no sequence can be determined, 1-2-3 fills the range with the contents of the first cell (Example 10).

You can also fill a range by using the Fill by Example command. The **Fill by Example command** is found on the Range menu on the main menu bar.

Entering the Row Titles

The next step in preparing the Medical Research, Inc worksheet is to enter the row titles in column A and column B. Perform the following step to enter the row titles in the two columns.

TO ENTER ROW TITLES IN TWO COLUMNS ▼

STEP 1 ▶

Use the left scroll arrow to view column A. Select cell A3. Enter REVENUE **in cell A3. Enter** Revenue **in cell B4,** Returns **in cell B5, and** NET REVENUE **in cell B6. Enter** EXPENSES **in cell A7. Enter** Commissions **in cell B8,** Advertising **in cell B9,** Product Liability **in cell B10,** Benefits **in cell B11, and** TOTAL EXPENSES **in cell B12. Enter** NET INCOME **in cell A13.**

1-2-3 displays the row titles in column A and column B (Figure 3-16).

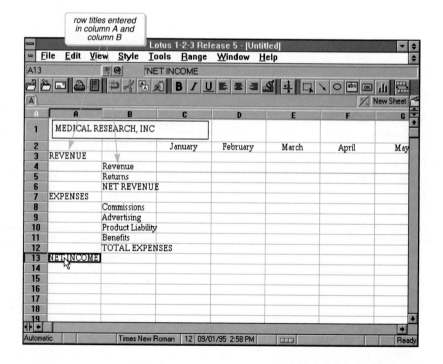

FIGURE 3-16

▶ USING DRAG-AND-DROP TO COPY CELLS

After you have entered data once, you can copy it to other locations on the worksheet. The row titles in the projected percentages table in Figure 3-1 on page L135 in the range B17..B20 are the same as the row titles in the range B8..B11 in Figure 3-16. Therefore, the range B8..B11 can be copied to the range B17..B20. In the first two projects, the Copy Right and Copy Down commands worked well for copying a range of cells to an adjacent area, but you cannot use these commands to copy a range of cells to a nonadjacent area.

The easiest method of copying a cell or range of cells to a nonadjacent area is to use the **drag-and-drop** feature. Drag-and-drop copies selected cells by using the mouse pointer to grab the selection, drag the selection to another area of the worksheet, and drop the selected cells. Perform the following steps to copy the row titles in the range B8..B11 to the range B17..B20.

TO COPY CELLS BY USING DRAG-AND-DROP ▼

STEP 1 ▶

Select the range B8..B11. Move the mouse pointer to the border of the selected range so the mouse pointer changes to a hand ( ).

The range to copy is selected (Figure 3-17). The mouse pointer changes to a hand. This mouse pointer shape indicates 1-2-3 is ready to perform drag-and-drop.

FIGURE 3-17

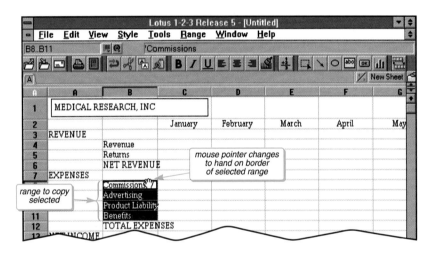

STEP 2 ▶

Press and hold down the CTRL key and then press and hold down the left mouse button.

The mouse pointer changes to a fist with a plus sign ( ) holding the border of the selected range (Figure 3-18). The selected range appears with a dashed outline.

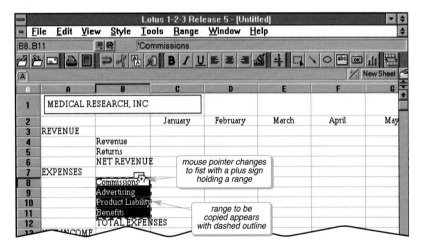

FIGURE 3-18

STEP 3 ▶

Drag the dashed outline to the range B17...B20.

As you drag, the selected range appears as a dashed outline. The dashed outline is positioned over the range B17..B20 (Figure 3-19). Notice the range B8..B11 remains selected.

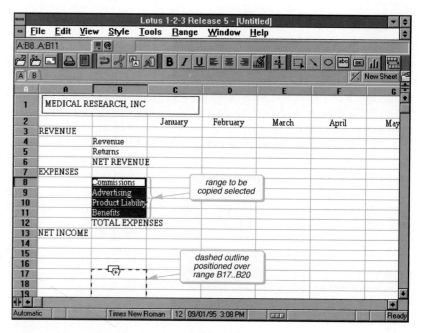

FIGURE 3-19

STEP 4 ▶

Release the left mouse button and the CTRL key. Use the down scroll arrow to view cell B20.

1-2-3 places a copy of the data in the range B17..B20 and leaves the original data intact (Figure 3-20). The selection is removed from the original data.

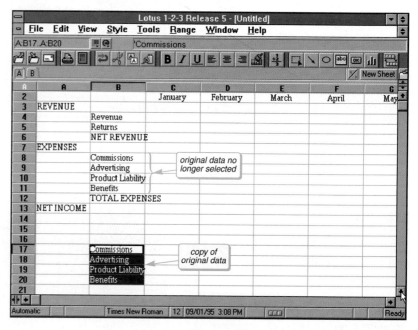

FIGURE 3-20

▲

In the previous example, the drag-and-drop feature was used to copy a range of cells from one area of a worksheet to another area of a worksheet. If you want to move a range of cells, perform the steps on the next page instead of copying a range of cells.

TO MOVE CELLS BY USING DRAG-AND-DROP

Step 1: Select the range to be moved.

Step 2: Position the mouse pointer on the border of the selection until the mouse pointer changes into a hand.

Step 3: Click the left mouse button and drag the selection to the desired location. Then release the left mouse button.

The data is removed from its original location and appears only in its new location. This is basically the same procedure that is used to copy data except the CTRL key is not used to move data.

Completing the Entries in the Projected Percentages Section

The projected percentages section in the range B17..B21 includes a title in cell B16, the row titles just copied, the row title, Returns, in cell B21, and the percent values for all the expenses. Follow these steps to complete the entries in the projected percentages section.

TO ENTER PERCENTAGES AND COMPLETE THE PROJECTED PERCENTAGES SECTION ▼

STEP 1 ▶

Select cell B16. Enter Projected Percentages. **Select cell B21. Enter** Returns.

1-2-3 displays the row titles (Figure 3-21).

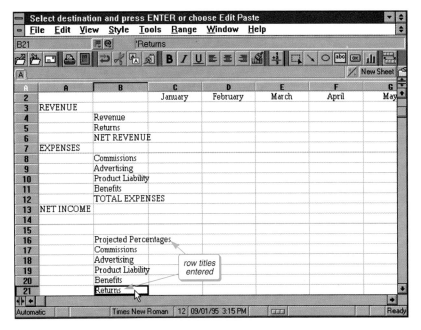

FIGURE 3-21

STEP 2 ▶

Enter the percent values 15% in cell C17, 18% in cell C18, 12% in cell C19, 30% in cell C20, and 3% in cell C21.

1-2-3 displays the projected percentages (Figure 3-22).

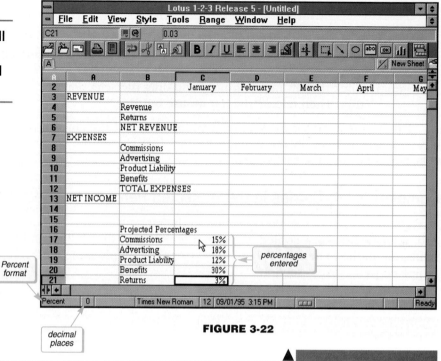

FIGURE 3-22

Recall from Project 2 that Automatic format determines the format of a value by how it looks as you enter it. Entering the percent values in the projected percentages section with a percent sign (%) causes 1-2-3 to recognize the entry as a percent and assign the Percent format to the cells (Figure 3-22).

▶ ENTERING THE REVENUE VALUES

T he next task in preparing the worksheet for Project 3 is to enter the revenue values in the range C4..H4. To enter the revenue values on the worksheet, complete the following steps (see Figure 3-23).

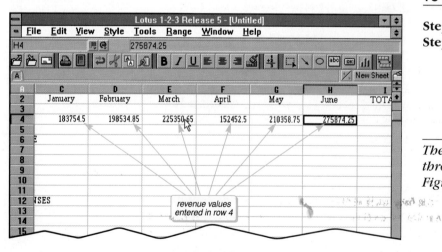

FIGURE 3-23

TO ENTER THE REVENUE VALUES

Step 1: Select cell C4.

Step 2: Enter 183754.5. Enter 198534.85 in cell D4, 225350.65 in cell E4, 152452.5 in cell F4, 210358.75 in cell G4, and 275874.25 in cell H4.

The revenue values for January through June display as shown in Figure 3-23.

▶ ROUNDING

Whenever you multiply numbers containing decimals by a decimal, the possibility exists that the answer will contain more than two digits to the right of the decimal point. This causes problems in applications representing dollars and cents. For example, to calculate the returns for January, the value 183754.50 is multiplied by .03 (3%), resulting in the answer 5512.635. When 5512.635 is formatted to two decimal places, 1-2-3 rounds the displayed value in the cell. Therefore, in the example, the answer to the calculation 183754.50 * .03 will display as 5512.64.

While this action takes care of the display issue, it does not completely solve the problem because even though the numbers are formatted correctly, the rounded values displayed in the cell are not the values 1-2-3 uses in calculations. Thus, even though the value 5512.64 displays in the cell, the value 5512.635 will be used in calculations, resulting in answers on the worksheet that do not correspond to the values displayed in the cells. For example, continuing with the above example, subtracting 5512.635 from 183754.50 results in the answer 178241.865. After applying the comma format with two decimal places, 178,241.87 (183754.50 – 5512.64) displays as the answer. Clearly the subtraction displays the incorrect result. Such a calculation is illustrated in Table 3-2.

▶ **TABLE 3-2**

ACTUAL VALUES USED IN CALCULATIONS	VALUES DISPLAYED WITH COMMA FORMAT, TWO DECIMAL PLACES
183754.50	183,754.50
-5512.635	-5,512.64
178241.865	178,241.87

To prevent these errors, you must use the **@ROUND function** to round values used in calculations so the numbers used in calculations are the same as the numbers in the display. The @ROUND function allows you to round any numeric value to the number of digits to the right or left of the decimal point that you specify. For the calculations in Project 3, the values should have two digits to the right of the decimal point.

The format of the @ROUND function is @ROUND(x,n), where x is the value to round and n is a value specifying the number of positions to the right or left of the decimal point. If the value of n is positive, 1-2-3 rounds the value x to the number of decimal places to the right of the decimal point. If n is negative, 1-2-3 rounds the value x to the number of decimal places to the left of the decimal point. If n is zero, x is rounded to the nearest integer.

All values in Project 3 should contain two decimal places so n should be 2.

▶ ABSOLUTE CELL REFERENCES

The next step in building the worksheet for Project 3 is to place the proper formula in cell C5 to calculate the projected returns for January. The returns value is calculated by multiplying the projected revenue for January (cell C4) by the percent projected for returns (cell C21). Thus, the formula to determine the projected returns for January with the @ROUND function is @ROUND(C4*C21,2).

Before entering the calculation to determine the returns for January, however, you need to become familiar with absolute cell references. Cell references used in a formula are one of two types — a relative cell reference or an absolute cell reference. When you use a **relative cell reference**, the cell reference in the formula will change when you copy the formula from one cell to the next. Relative cell reference is the type used in Project 1 and Project 2.

The projected returns percentage (cell C21) in the formula +C4*C21, however, always remains the same. That is, the formula to calculate the returns for January is C4*C21, the formula for February is D4*C21, and the formula for March is E4*C21. Notice that cell C21 is always used because it contains the percent for the returns value. When a cell's reference does not change as the formula is copied from one cell to the next, the cell reference is called an **absolute cell reference**.

When you enter cell references into a formula, 1-2-3 assumes they are relative cell references. To specify that a cell reference is an absolute cell reference, you must enter the cell number in the absolute cell reference format, which is a dollar sign preceding each part of the address you want to remain absolutely the same. You can add a dollar sign to the worksheet letter, to the column letter, and to the row number. Thus, in the formula, the absolute cell reference for cell C21 is C21.

The steps on this and the next two pages illustrate entering the formula that contains the @ROUND function to calculate the returns for the month of January. The formula uses both relative and absolute cell references.

TO ENTER A FORMULA CONTAINING RELATIVE AND ABSOLUTE CELL REFERENCES ▼

STEP 1 ▶

Click the left scroll arrow twice to view column A. Select cell C5. Click the @function selector in the edit line and point to ROUND on the @Function menu.

Cell C5 is selected and 1-2-3 displays the @Function menu listing commonly used functions (Figure 3-24). The mouse pointer points to ROUND on the @Function menu.

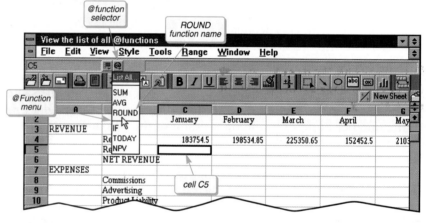

FIGURE 3-24

STEP 2 ▶

Choose the ROUND function from the @function menu.

1-2-3 displays the @ROUND function in the contents box in the edit line and the cell and highlights x, the first required entry in the function (Figure 3-25).

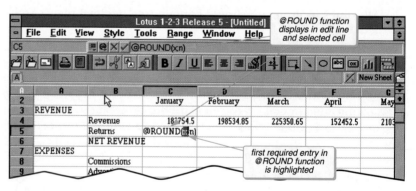

FIGURE 3-25

STEP 3 ▶

Select the first cell to enter into the function – cell C4 – by clicking the cell. Then, type the multiplication operator (*) and select the second cell in the function – cell C21.

1-2-3 displays the @ROUND function and the formula in the contents box in the edit line and the cell (Figure 3-26).

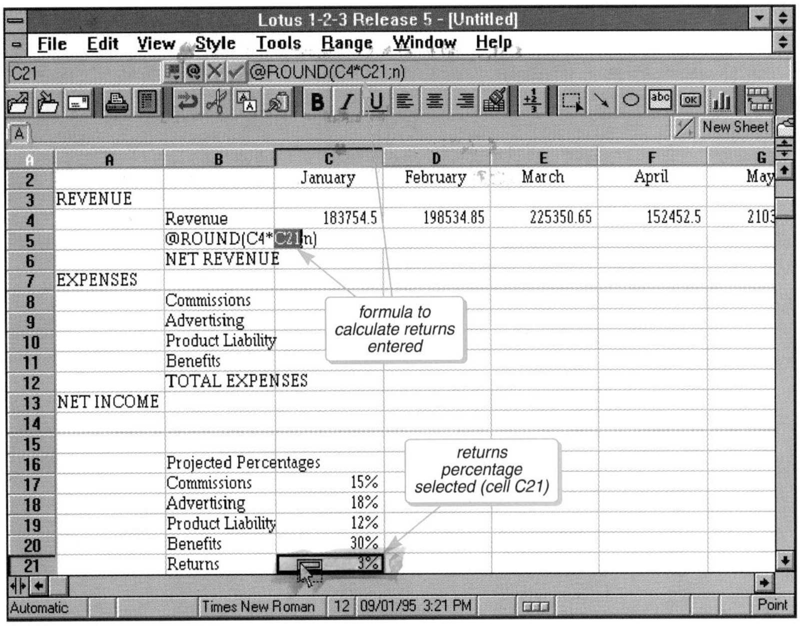

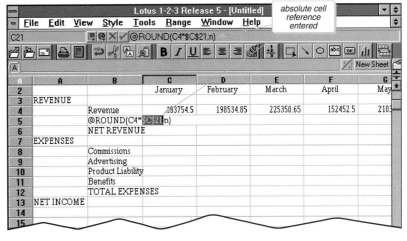

FIGURE 3-26

STEP 4 ▶

Press the F4 function key to change the C21 cell reference to an absolute cell reference.

1-2-3 places a dollar sign in front of the column letter and in front of the row number of the selected cell (Figure 3-27). The dollar signs tell 1-2-3 that cell C21 is an absolute cell reference and should not be changed when the formula is copied.

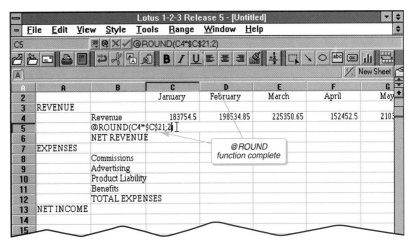

FIGURE 3-27

STEP 5 ▶

Highlight *n* in the @ROUND function by pointing to the *n* and double-clicking the left mouse button. Then, type 2.

The complete @ROUND function displays in the contents box in the edit line and the cell (Figure 3-28). The 2 in the @ROUND function tells 1-2-3 to round the result of the calculation (C4*C21) to two places to the right of the decimal point.

FIGURE 3-28

STEP 6 ▶

Click the Confirm button or press the ENTER key.

1-2-3 confirms the formula into the cell and performs the calculation (Figure 3-29). The result of the calculation displays in the cell and the @ROUND function with the formula displays in the contents box in the edit line.

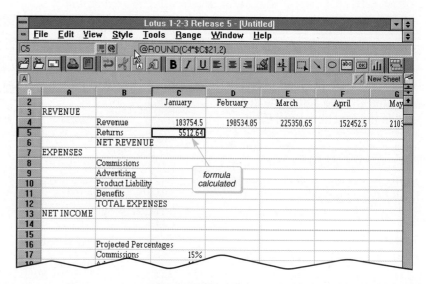

FIGURE 3-29

The next step in building the Project 3 worksheet is to copy the formula in cell C5 containing the @ROUND function to the range D5..H5. When you copy the formula, the reference to cell C4 will change to D4, E4, etc., while the reference to cell C21 will remain the same. To copy a formula with both relative and absolute cell references, complete the following steps.

TO COPY A FORMULA WITH RELATIVE AND ABSOLUTE CELL REFERENCES ▼

STEP 1 ▶

Select the cell containing the formula to copy – cell C5 – and the range where the formula is to be copied – cells D5..H5. Then point to the selected range and click the right mouse button. When the quick menu displays, point to the Copy Right command.

The cell containing the formula to copy (C5) and the range where it is to be copied (D5..H5) are selected (Figure 3-30). 1-2-3 displays the quick menu, and the mouse pointer points to the Copy Right command.

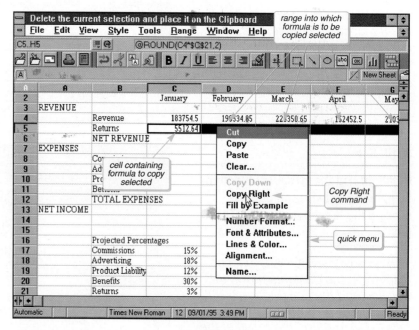

FIGURE 3-30

STEP 2 ▶

Choose the Copy Right command from the quick menu.

1-2-3 copies the formula from cell C5 to the range D5..H5 (Figure 3-31). 1-2-3 performs the calculations, which include rounding the result when required.

FIGURE 3-31

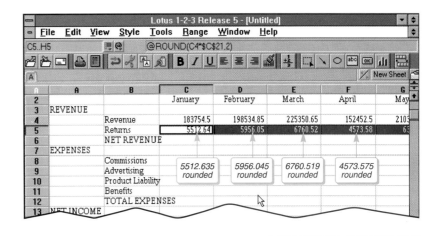

Entering and Copying a Formula

After you enter the returns formula into the Project 3 worksheet, the next step is to enter the net revenue formula into cell C6 and copy the formula to the range D6..H6. The net revenue is calculated by subtracting the returns from revenue. The returns value for January is contained in cell C5 while revenue is in cell C4. Therefore, the formula to calculate the net revenue for January is +C4-C5. The formulas for each of the ensuing months require both cell C4 and C5 to be changed when it is copied. Thus, this formula has no requirement for an absolute cell reference. To enter the formula in the range C6..H6 (see Figure 3-32), perform the following steps.

TO ENTER AND COPY A FORMULA

Step 1: Select cell C6, type a plus sign (+), select cell C4 to place it in the formula, type the subtraction operator (–), select cell C5 to place it in the formula, and click the Confirm button or press the ENTER key.

Step 2: Select the cell containing the formula – cell C6 – and the range where the formula is to be copied – D6..H6.

Step 3: Click the selected range with the right mouse button.

Step 4: Choose the Copy Right command.

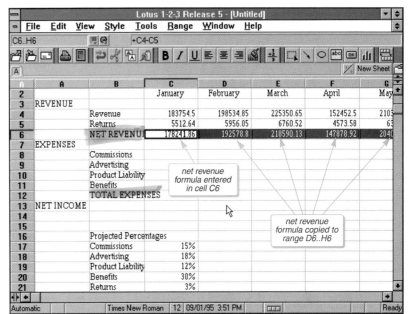

FIGURE 3-32

The worksheet after you have completed these steps is shown in Figure 3-32.

Entering Additional Functions and Formulas

The next step in this project is to determine the four monthly projected expenses for the month of January (see Figure 3-1 on page L135). Each of the projected expenses for January is equal to the January net revenue in cell C6 times the corresponding projected percentage in the range C17..C20. Therefore, the formula to calculate the commissions expense for January is +C6*C17. Because the commissions percentage is contained in a single cell and should be used to calculate the expense for each of the months, cell C17 will be an absolute cell reference in the formula.

Perform the following steps to place the formulas that calculate the projected expenses for January into the spreadsheet.

TO ENTER FORMULAS ▼

STEP 1 ▶

Select cell C8. Click the @function selector in the edit line and choose ROUND from the @Function menu.

1-2-3 displays the @ROUND function in the contents box in the edit line and the cell and highlights x in the function (Figure 3-33).

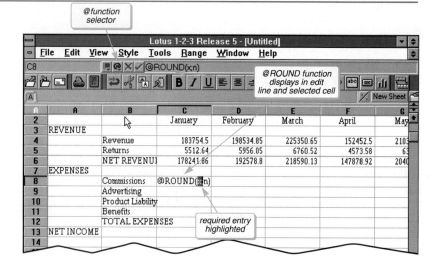

FIGURE 3-33

STEP 2 ▶

Select cell C6. Type the multiplication operator (*), select cell C17, and press the F4 function key. Then, highlight *n* in the @ROUND function by pointing to the *n* and double-clicking the left mouse button. Type 2 and click the Confirm button or press the ENTER key.

1-2-3 confirms the entry into the cell and performs the calculation (Figure 3-34). The result of the calculation is rounded to two places to the right of the decimal point. The result of the calculation displays in the cell, and the @ROUND function and the formula display in the contents box in the edit line.

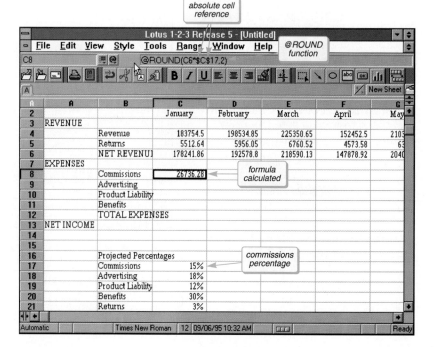

FIGURE 3-34

STEP 3 ▶

Select cell C9. Click the @function selector in the edit line and choose ROUND from the @Function menu. Select cell C6 and type the multiplication operator (*). Select cell C18 and press the F4 function key. Then, double-click *n* in the @ROUND function, type 2 and click the Confirm button or press the ENTER key.

1-2-3 confirms the entry into the cell and performs the calculation (Figure 3-35). The result of the calculation is rounded to two places to the right of the decimal point. The result of the calculation displays in the cell, and the @ROUND function and the formula display in the contents box in the edit line.

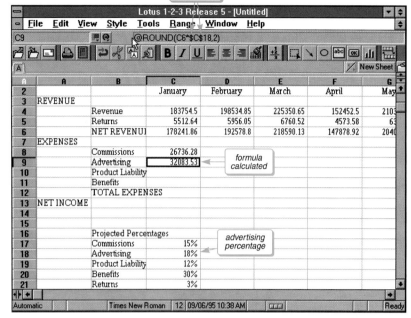

FIGURE 3-35

STEP 4 ▶

Select cell C10. Click the @function selector in the edit line and choose ROUND from the @Function menu. Select cell C6 and type the multiplication operator. Select cell C19 and press the F4 function key. Then, double-click *n* in the @ROUND function, type 2 and click the Confirm button or press the ENTER key.

1-2-3 confirms the entry into the cell and performs the calculation (Figure 3-36). The result of the calculation is rounded to two places to the right of the decimal point. The result of the calculation displays in the cell, and the @ROUND function and the formula display in the contents box in the edit line.

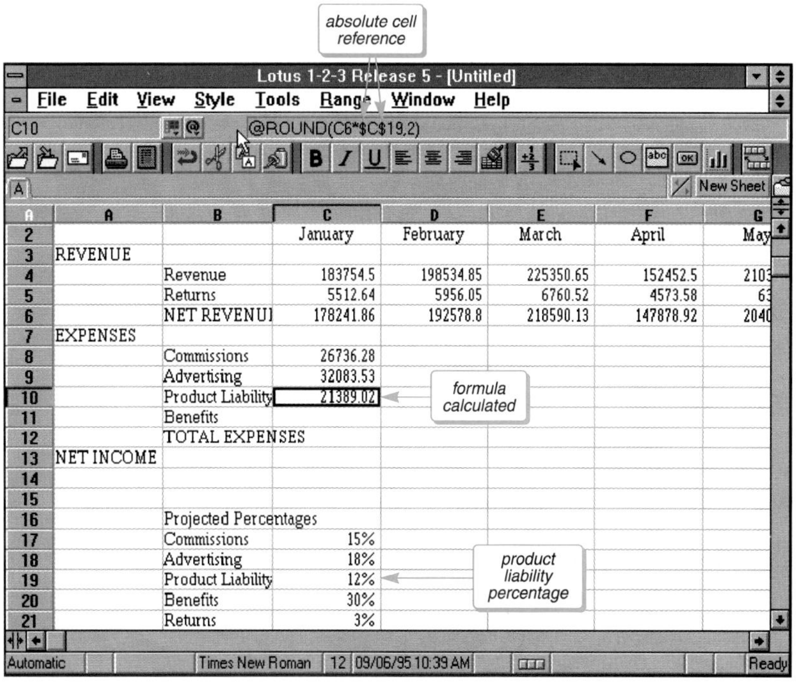

FIGURE 3-36

STEP 5 ▶

Select cell C11. Click the @function
selector in the edit line and choose
the ROUND function. Select cell C6
and type the multiplication operator.
Select cell C20 and press the F4
function key. Then, double-click *n* in
the @ROUND function, type 2 and
click the Confirm button or press the
ENTER key.

*The projected expenses for
January display as shown in
Figure 3-37.*

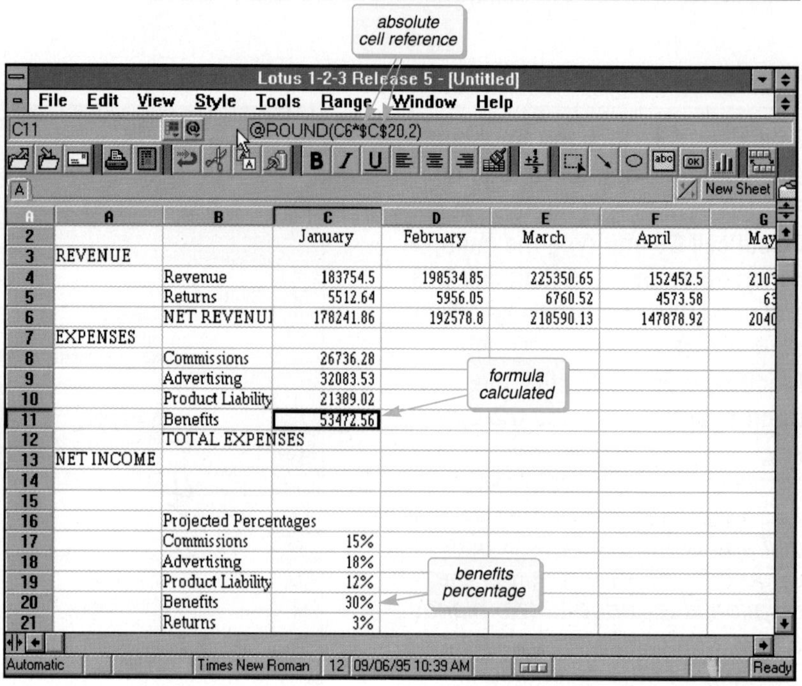

FIGURE 3-37

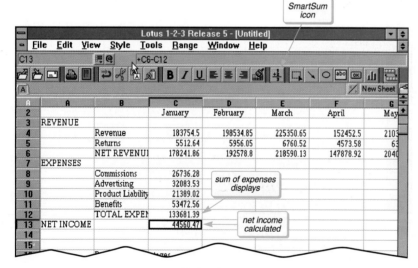

FIGURE 3-38

To calculate the total expenses in cell C12 for January use the SmartSum icon
to enter the @SUM function to add the values in the range C8..C11. You obtain the
net income in cell C13 for January by subtracting total expenses (C12) from net
revenue (C6). The formulas for total expenses and net income require the cells to
be changed when copied. Thus, these formulas have no requirement for an
absolute cell reference. To enter the formulas, perform the following steps (see
Figure 3-38).

TO ENTER FORMULAS

Step 1: Select cell C12. Click the
SmartSum icon on the set of
SmartIcons to enter the
@SUM function.

Step 2: Select cell C13 and type +.
Select cell C6 and type – .
Then select cell C12 and
click the Confirm button or
press the ENTER key.

*The worksheet after completing
these steps is shown in Figure 3-38.*

The formulas to calculate the four projected expenses for January, the total expenses for January, and the net income for January are entered on the worksheet. The next step is to copy the formulas in the range C8..C13 to the cells in the range D8..H13 so 1-2-3 will calculate these formulas for the months of February through June. Copy the formula using the following step (see Figure 3-39).

TO COPY FORMULAS ▼

STEP 1 ►

Select the range containing the formulas to copy – C8..C13 – and the range where the formulas are to be copied – D8..H13. Click the selected range with the right mouse button to display the quick menu. Choose the Copy Right command. Select any cell.

1-2-3 copies the formulas from the range C8..C13 to the range D8..H13, calculates the copied formulas, and rounds the results when required (Figure 3-39).

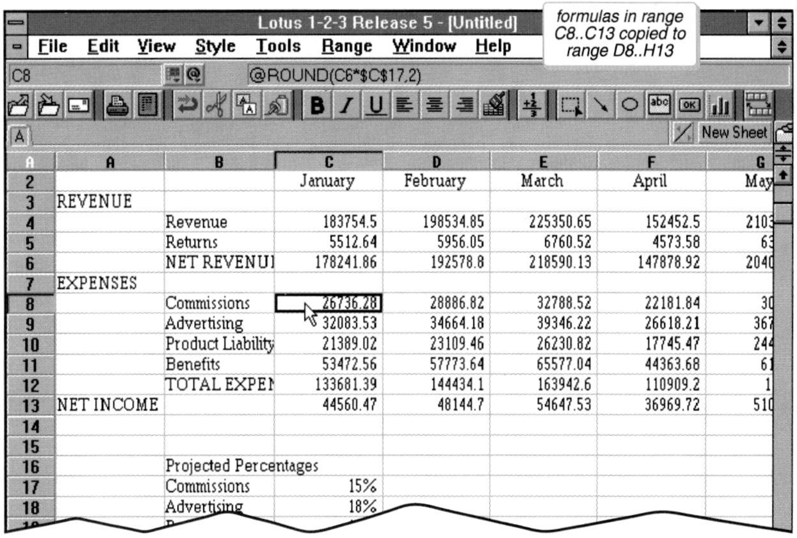

FIGURE 3-39

Completing the Entries

The final step in completing the entries in the worksheet is to determine the row totals in column I. Perform the following steps to obtain the required totals in column I using the SmartSum icon on the set of SmartIcons (see Figure 3-40 on the next page).

TO SUM THE ROW TOTALS

Step 1: Click the right scroll arrow to display column I. Select the range I4..I6, press and hold down the CTRL key, and select the range I8:I13. Release the CTRL key.

Step 2: Click the SmartSum icon on the set of SmartIcons. Select any cell.

1-2-3 places the @SUM function in each cell of the selected ranges and calculates the sum of values across each row of the worksheet. The row totals display in column I as shown in Figure 3-40 on the next page.

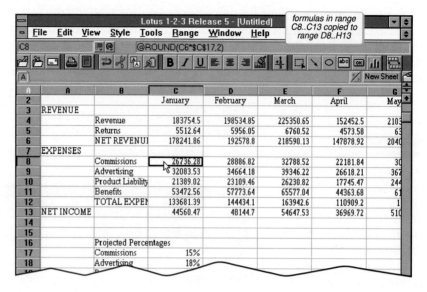

FIGURE 3-40

SAVING THE FILE

Now that the worksheet data is entered, you should save it on disk. To save the worksheet on drive A using the file name PROJ3, complete the following steps.

TO SAVE THE FILE

Step 1: Select cell A1. Click the Save icon on the set of SmartIcons.

Step 2: When the Save As dialog box displays, type `proj3` in the File name text box.

Step 3: Select drive a: from the Drives drop-down list box.

Step 4: Choose the OK button in the Save As dialog box.

1-2-3 saves the worksheet with the file name, proj3, on the diskette in drive A.

FORMATTING TEXT BLOCKS

Text that is entered into a text block can be formatted in the same way text is formatted in a worksheet. Unlike the text in a worksheet, however, the whole text block must be treated as a single unit. For example, you cannot apply different fonts and colors to different parts of the text in the text block.

To format the text block, you must first select the text block. Then, choose the desired command.

Changing the Font Size and Attributes in a Text Block

In Project 3, the title in the text block displays in blue, Times New Roman 32 point, and bold. To change the font size and attributes of the text block, perform the following steps.

TO CHANGE THE FONT SIZE AND ATTRIBUTES OF A TEXT BLOCK ▼

STEP 1 ▶

Position the mouse pointer inside the text block, click the right mouse button, and point to the Font & Attributes command.

Handles appear on the border of the text block indicating the object is selected. 1-2-3 displays the quick menu and the mouse pointer points to the Font & Attributes command (Figure 3-41). Notice the name of the text block, Text 1, displays in the selection indicator.

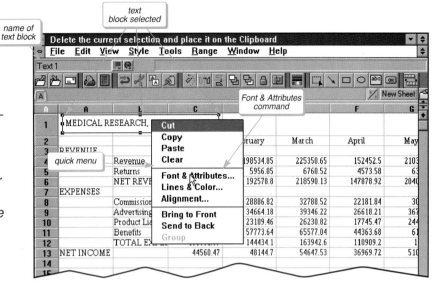

FIGURE 3-41

STEP 2 ▶

Choose the Font & Attributes command from the quick menu to display the Font & Attributes dialog box. Select 32 in the Size list box and click the Bold check box in the Attributes area. Then, point to the OK button.

1-2-3 displays the Font & Attributes dialog box (Figure 3-42). The default Times New Roman font is selected. The Size text box contains 32 and the Bold check box is selected. The mouse pointer points to the OK button.

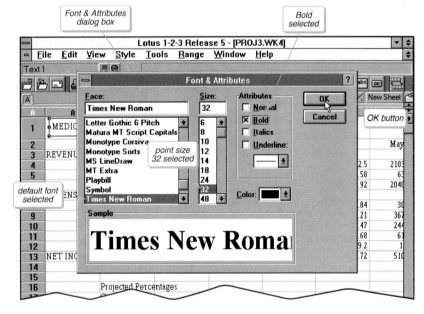

FIGURE 3-42

STEP 3 ▶

Choose the OK button in the Font & Attributes dialog box. Select any cell.

1-2-3 displays the text block with the text in 32 point and bold (Figure 3-43).

FIGURE 3-43

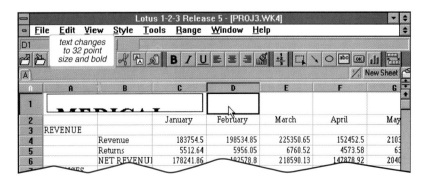

Notice in Figure 3-43 on the previous page after the font size is increased to 32 point, the text block is not large enough to display the entire text, and most of the text has scrolled out of sight. The text block must be resized to properly display the worksheet title.

Resizing Text Blocks

In Figure 3-1 on page L135, the text block displays centered above the worksheet across columns B through I. The height of row 1 must be increased to properly display the text block. The task of resizing the text block is made easier by decreasing the display size of the worksheet cells so the entire worksheet can be viewed on the screen. You will use the **Zoom Out command** on the View menu when you decrease the size of the worksheet cells. To decrease the display size of cells and resize the text block, perform the following steps.

TO DECREASE THE DISPLAY SIZE OF CELLS AND RESIZE THE TEXT BLOCK ▼

STEP 1 ▶

Drag the row border of row 1 down to 80 points. Select the View menu by pointing to the View menu and clicking the left mouse button. Point to the Zoom Out command.

1-2-3 increases the height of row 1 to 80 points and displays the View menu (Figure 3-44). The mouse pointer points to the Zoom Out command.

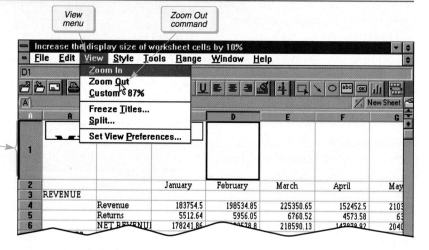

FIGURE 3-44

STEP 2 ▶

Choose the Zoom Out command from the View menu.

1-2-3 reduces the display of the worksheet cells by 10%. Notice columns A through G and most of column H now display on the screen. Rows 1 through 18 also display on the screen (Figure 3-45).

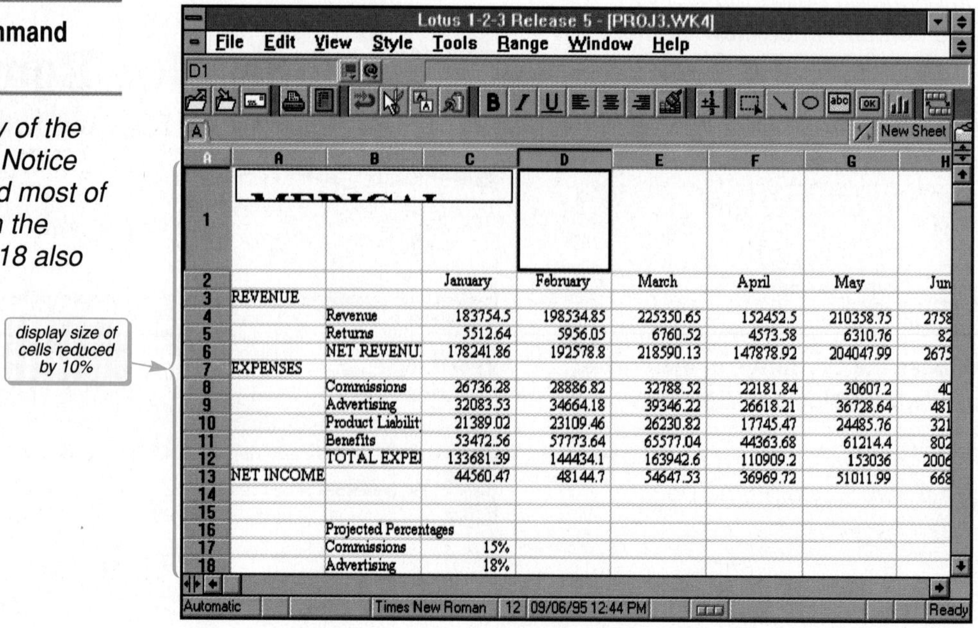

FIGURE 3-45

STEP 3 ►

Choose the Zoom Out command from the View menu to decrease the display size of the cells. Then, select the text block by clicking anywhere within the block. Position the mouse pointer over the right midpoint handle on the frame of the text block.

1-2-3 decreases the display size of the worksheet cells by 10%. The handles on the frame of the text block indicate the chart is selected (Figure 3-46). The mouse pointer changes to a four-headed arrow (⊕) indicating the text block can be sized.

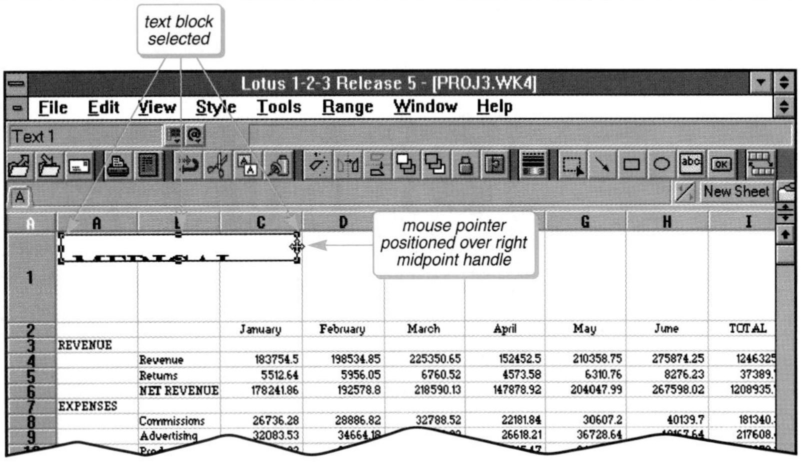

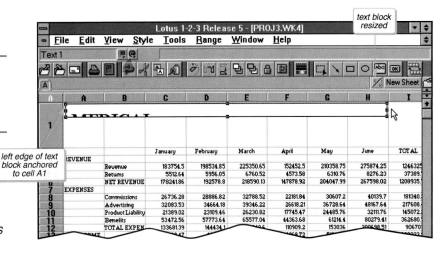

FIGURE 3-46

STEP 4 ►

Drag the right midpoint handle on the text block to increase the width to column H. Then, release the left mouse button.

The text block displays across columns A through H (Figure 3-47). Notice as you drag the right side of the text block, the left edge of the text block remains anchored as the text block width is increased.

FIGURE 3-47

STEP 5 ►

Position the mouse pointer over the bottom midpoint handle on the frame of the text block. Drag the bottom midpoint handle down until the text block height is approximately one inch. Release the left mouse button.

The text block height is increased and the entire worksheet title displays in the text block (Figure 3-48). Notice as you drag the bottom of the text block, the top edge of the text block remains anchored as its height is increased.

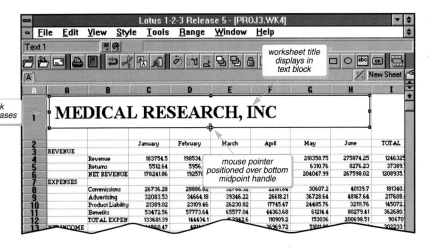

FIGURE 3-48

You can also drag a corner handle to adjust both the height and width of a text block.

Aligning Text in a Text Block

The alignment of text in a text block can also be adjusted. By default, 1-2-3 aligns the text horizontally to the left. Text cannot be aligned vertically in a text block. In Project 3, the text in the text block is evenly spaced within the text block. Perform the following steps to align the text in the text block.

TO ALIGN TEXT IN A TEXT BLOCK ▼

STEP 1 ▶

Position the mouse pointer anywhere inside the text block and click the right mouse button. Choose the Alignment command from the quick menu. When the Alignment dialog box displays, select the Evenly spaced option button in the Align all text area and point to the OK button.

The Alignment dialog box displays (Figure 3-49). The Evenly spaced option button is selected. The mouse pointer points to the OK button.

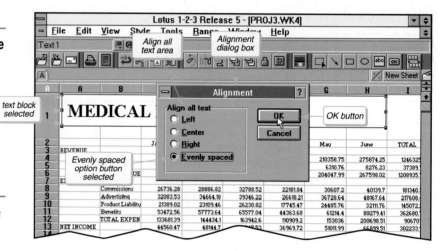

FIGURE 3-49

STEP 2 ▶

Choose the OK button.

1-2-3 displays the text block (Figure 3-50). The text is evenly spaced within the text block.

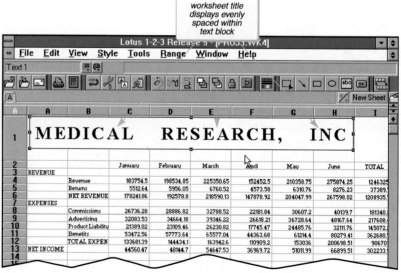

FIGURE 3-50

Moving the Text Block

The last step in formatting the text block is to move the text block to the right so it is centered over the columns of the worksheet. To move the text block, you must first select the text block, then position the mouse pointer inside the text block and drag the text block to the desired location. To move the text block, perform the following steps.

TO MOVE A TEXT BLOCK ▼

STEP 1 ▶

Select the text block by positioning the mouse pointer inside the text block and clicking the left mouse button. With the mouse pointer inside the text block, drag the text block to the right until it is centered.

Selection handles display on the text block (Figure 3-51). When you drag the text block, the mouse pointer changes to a fist holding a range, and a dashed outline appears as the text block is moved to the new location. Notice the text block remains in the original location.

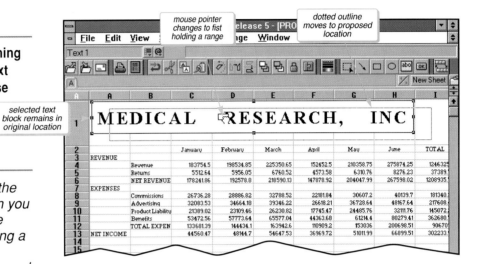

FIGURE 3-51

STEP 2 ▶

Release the mouse button.

The text block displays in the new location (Figure 3-52).

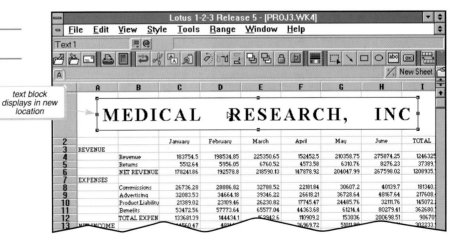

FIGURE 3-52

You can cancel the move by pressing the ESC key before you release the mouse button.

FORMATTING THE WORKSHEET

Formatting the worksheet in Project 3 includes adding a pattern and designer frame to the text block, changing the text color in the text block, changing the appearance of the row and column titles in the worksheet, placing the values in the proper format, changing the column width and row height, adding borders to the cells of the worksheet, and formatting the projected percentages section of the worksheet. When formatting is complete, the worksheet will appear as shown in Figure 3-53.

	A	B	C	D	E	F	G	H	I
1	MEDICAL RESEARCH, INC								
2			January	February	March	April	May	June	TOTAL
3	REVENUE								
4		Revenue	$183,754.50	$198,534.85	$225,350.65	$152,452.50	$210,358.75	$275,874.25	$1,246,325.50
5		Returns	5,512.64	5,956.05	6,760.52	4,573.58	6,310.76	8,276.23	37,389.78
6		NET REVENUE	$178,241.86	$192,578.80	$218,590.13	$147,878.92	$204,047.99	$267,598.02	$1,208,935.72
7	EXPENSES								
8		Commissions	$26,736.28	$28,886.82	$32,788.52	$22,181.84	$30,607.20	$40,139.70	$181,340.36
9		Advertising	32,083.53	34,664.18	39,346.22	26,618.21	36,728.64	48,167.64	217,608.42
10		Product Liability	21,389.02	23,109.46	26,230.82	17,745.47	24,485.76	32,111.76	145,072.29
11		Benefits	53,472.56	57,773.64	65,577.04	44,363.68	61,214.40	80,279.41	362,680.73
12		TOTAL EXPENSES	$133,681.39	$144,434.10	$163,942.60	$110,909.20	$153,036.00	$200,698.51	$906,701.80
13	NET INCOME		$44,560.47	$48,144.70	$54,647.53	$36,969.72	$51,011.99	$66,899.51	$302,233.92
14									
15									
16		Projected Percentages							
17		Commissions	15%						
18		Advertising	18%						
19		Product Liability	12%						
20		Benefits	30%						
21		Returns	3%						
22									

FIGURE 3-53

Adding a Pattern and Designer Frame to a Text Block

You can add a pattern to the interior of the text block. A **pattern** includes designs made up of lines or shapes. You can choose from 64 different patterns. Project 3 uses a gradient fill pattern. A **gradient fill pattern** gradually changes from the color used for the background to the color used for the pattern. For example, in Project 3, the background of the text block is white and the pattern color is yellow. Thus, the gradient pattern chosen gradually changes from white to yellow starting from the bottom of the text block.

A designer frame can also be added to the edges of the text block. A **designer frame** is one of 16 predesigned frames you can use to further enhance the edges of the text block. Project 3 adds one of the designer frames to the text block and changes the color of the frame to blue.

Now that the text block is properly positioned on the worksheet, return the worksheet display to the default setting by choosing the Custom command on the View menu.

To add a pattern and a designer frame to the text block, perform the following steps.

TO RETURN THE WORKSHEET CELLS TO THE DEFAULT DISPLAY AND ADD A PATTERN AND DESIGNER FRAME TO THE TEXT BLOCK ▼

STEP 1 ►

Select the View menu. Point to the Custom – 87% command.

1-2-3 displays the View menu (Figure 3-54). The mouse pointer points to the Custom – 87% command.

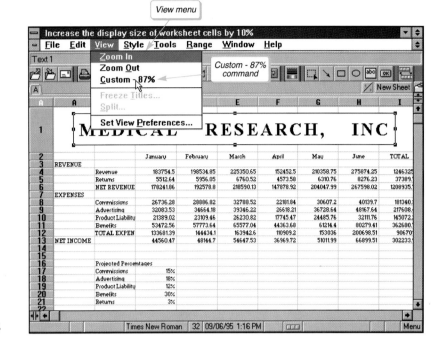

FIGURE 3-54

STEP 2 ►

Choose the Custom – 87% command from the View menu. Position the mouse pointer anywhere inside the text block and click the right mouse button. Choose the Lines & Color command from the quick menu. When the Lines & Color dialog box displays, click the Pattern color drop-down box arrow, and point to the yellow color in the top row of the Pattern color drop-down box.

1-2-3 returns the worksheet cells to the default display size. The Lines & Color dialog box displays (Figure 3-55). The mouse pointer points to the desired yellow color in the Pattern color drop-down box.

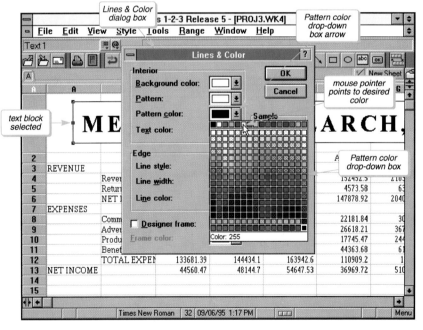

FIGURE 3-55

STEP 3 ▶

Select the yellow color in the top row of the Pattern color drop-down box. Click the Pattern drop-down box arrow and point to the last pattern in the Pattern drop-down box.

1-2-3 displays the Pattern drop-down box and the mouse pointer points to the desired pattern (Figure 3-56). The current pattern for the text block is blinking. The four gradient fill patterns are located in the bottom row of the Pattern drop-down box.

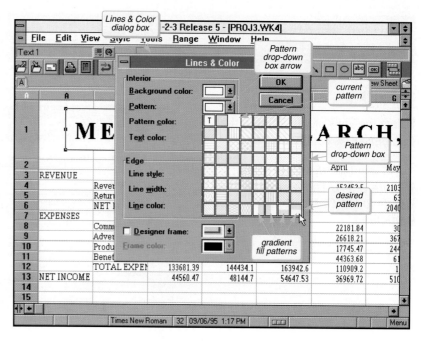

FIGURE 3-56

STEP 4 ▶

Select the last pattern in the Pattern drop-down box. Click the Text color drop-down box arrow, and select the first blue color in the top row of the Text color drop-down box. Click the Designer frame check box. Click the Designer frame drop-down box arrow, and point to the last designer frame in the third row of the Designer frame drop-down box.

The gradient fill pattern you selected displays in the Pattern drop-down box. The text color you selected displays in the Text color drop-down box. When you select the Designer frame check box, an X appears in the box (Figure 3-57). This selection tells 1-2-3 to place a designer frame around the edge of the selected object. 1-2-3 displays the Designer frame drop-down box and the mouse pointer points to the desired designer frame.

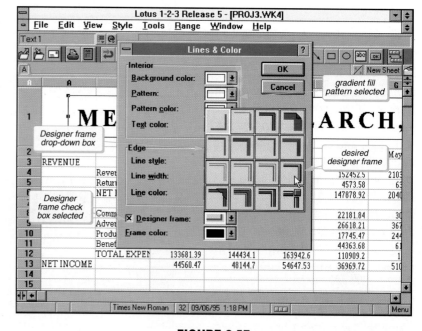

FIGURE 3-57

STEP 5 ►

Select the last designer frame in the third row. Then, click the Frame color drop-down box arrow, select the first blue color in the top row, and point to the OK button in the Lines & Color dialog box.

The Frame color box displays the color blue (Figure 3-58). The Sample area displays the gradient fill pattern, the yellow pattern, blue text, and the blue designer frame. The mouse pointer points to the OK button.

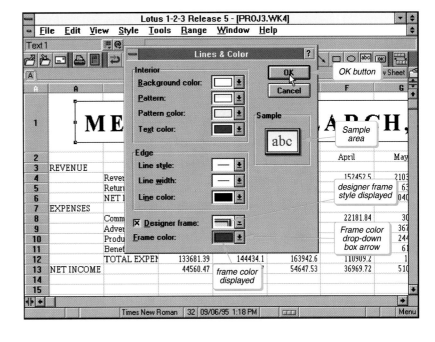

FIGURE 3-58

STEP 6 ►

Choose the OK button in the Lines & Color dialog box.

1-2-3 displays the text block with a blue designer frame around the edge (Figure 3-59). The gradient fill pattern displays in the text block. The text displays in blue.

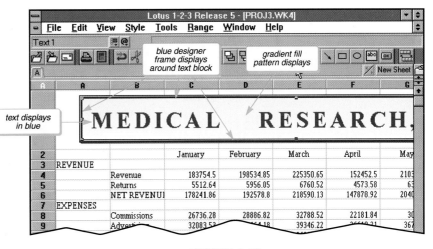

FIGURE 3-59

Formatting the Column and Row Titles

The column and row titles display in 14 point size and bold. The text color is yellow and the background of each cell displays in blue (see Figure 3-53 on page L164). To accomplish this formatting, complete the following steps.

TO FORMAT TITLES

Step 1: Select the collection of ranges: C2..I2; A3..B3; A7..B7; and A13..B13.

Step 2: Point to the selected collection and click the right mouse button. Choose the Font & Attributes command from the quick menu. When the Font & Attributes dialog box displays, select 14 in the Size list box and Bold in the Attributes area. Click the Color drop-down box arrow and select yellow in the top row of the Color drop-down box. Choose the OK button in the Fonts & Attributes dialog box.

Step 3: Point to the selected collection and click the right mouse button. Choose the Lines & Color command from the quick menu. When the Lines & Color dialog box displays, select the first blue color in the top row of the Background color drop-down box. Choose the OK button in the Lines & Color dialog box.

Formatting Values in the Worksheet

The values in the worksheet, even though they are generated by formulas, can still be formatted. The following formatting, as shown in Figure 3-53 on page L164, is required:

1. The revenue for each month and the total use the US dollar format with two digits to the right of the decimal point.
2. The returns for each month and the total use the comma format with two digits to the right of the decimal point.
3. The net revenues for each month and the total use the US dollar format with two digits to the right of the decimal point.
4. The commissions for each month and the total use the US dollar format with two digits to the right of the decimal point.
5. The advertising, product liability, and benefits for each month and their respective totals use the comma format with two digits to the right of the decimal point.
6. The total expenses and net income for each month and their respective totals use the US dollar format with two digits to the right of the decimal point.

To accomplish this formatting, complete the following steps.

TO FORMAT VALUES

Step 1: Select the collection of ranges: C4..I4; C6..I6; C8..I8; and C12..I13. Click the format selector in the status bar and choose US Dollar from the list of format styles.
Step 2: Select the collection C5..I5 and C9..I11. Click the format selector in the status bar and choose ,Comma from the list of format styles.

Adding Borders to Cells

The range C2..I12 contains a blue line around all edges of each cell in the range. The range C13..I13 contains a double line below each cell in the range. To place a line, or **border**, around all edges of a cell or each cell in the range, first select the cell or range where the border is to be displayed. Then use the Lines & Color command from the quick menu, as shown in the following steps.

TO ADD A BORDER TO A RANGE OF CELLS ▼

STEP 1 ▶

Select the range of cells – C2..I12, point to the selected range and click the right mouse button to display the quick menu. Choose the Lines & Color command from the quick menu. When the Lines & Color dialog box displays, point to the All check box in the Border area.

1-2-3 displays the Lines & Color dialog box. The Border area contains six check boxes — Outline, All, Left, Top, Right, and Bottom (Figure 3-60). Outline draws a line around the outside edge of the selected range. Left, Right, Top, or Bottom draw a line along the specified edge of each cell in the selected range. All draws a line around all edges of each cell in the range. The mouse pointer points to the All check box.

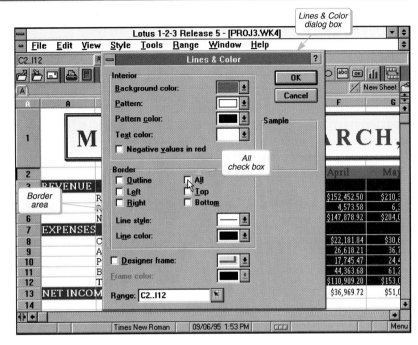

FIGURE 3-60

STEP 2 ▶

Select the All check box by clicking the left mouse button. Then, click the Line color drop-down box arrow, and point to the blue color in the Line color drop-down box.

When you select the All check box, an X appears in all the check boxes in the Border area indicating a line is to be placed around all the edges of the selected range (Figure 3-61). A sample line displays in a box next to each border selection. The mouse pointer points to the blue color in the Line color drop-down box.

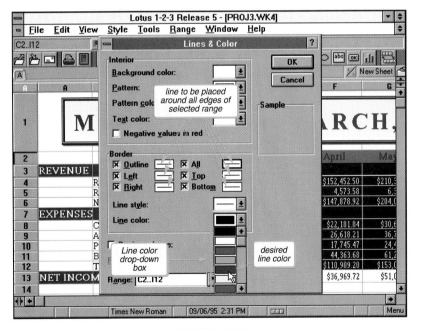

FIGURE 3-61

STEP 3 ▶

Select the blue color in the Line color drop-down box, and point to the OK button in the Lines & Color dialog box.

The Line color box displays the color blue (Figure 3-62). The sample lines next to the border selections also display in the blue color. The mouse pointer points to the OK button in the Lines & Color dialog box.

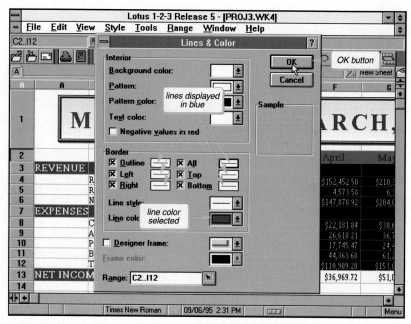

FIGURE 3-62

STEP 4 ▶

Choose the OK button in the Lines & Color dialog box. Select any cell to remove the highlight.

The worksheet redisplays with the range containing a blue border around all the edges of the cells (Figure 3-63).

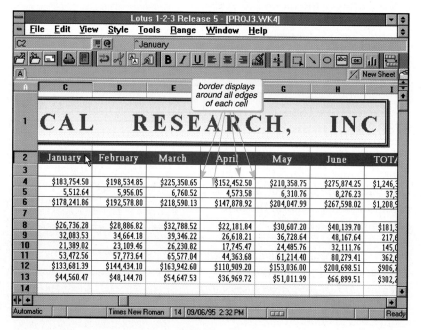

FIGURE 3-63

STEP 5 ▶

Select the range C13..I13. Point to the selected range and click the right mouse button to display the quick menu. Choose the Lines & Color command from the quick menu. When the Lines & Color dialog box displays, select the Bottom check box in the Border area. Then, click the Line style drop-down box arrow, and point to the double line.

The range C13..I13 is selected, and the Lines & Color dialog box displays. The Bottom check box is selected, and the mouse pointer points to the double line in the Line style drop-down box (Figure 3-64). Selecting the Bottom option instructs 1-2-3 to draw a line at the bottom of each cell in the selected range.

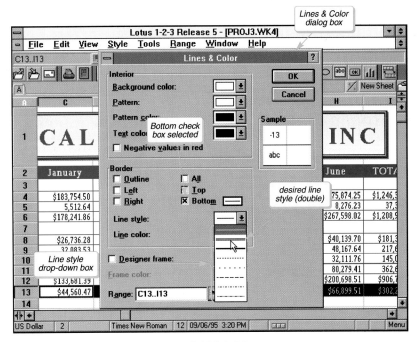

FIGURE 3-64

STEP 6 ▶

Select the double line in the Line style drop-down box. Select the blue color in the Line color drop-down box, and point to the OK button in the Lines & Color dialog box.

The Line style box displays the double line and the Line color box displays the blue color (Figure 3-65). The sample line next to the Bottom border selection also displays in the blue color. The Sample area displays a double line at the bottom. The mouse pointer points to the OK button in the Lines & Color dialog box.

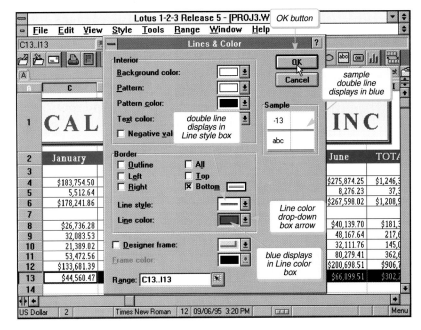

FIGURE 3-65

STEP 7 ▶

Choose the OK button in the Lines & Color dialog box. Select any cell.

The range C13..I13 displays with a blue double line at the bottom of each cell (Figure 3-66).

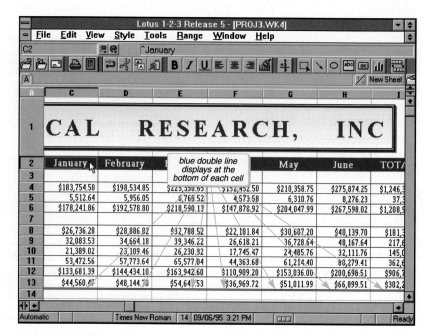

FIGURE 3-66

Changing the Widths of Columns and Heights of Rows

The default width of all columns of the worksheet was increased to 11 characters before creating Project 3. You can override these default settings at any time. The following changes are required:

1. The width of column A is decreased to 4 characters.
2. The width of column B is increased to 15 characters.
3. The heights of row 3 and row 7 are increased to 20 point size.
4. The height of row 13 is increased to 30 point size.

To accomplish these changes (see Figure 3-53 on page L164), complete the following steps.

TO CHANGE COLUMNS WIDTHS AND ROWS HEIGHTS

Step 1: Use the left scroll arrow to display column A. Drag the column border between column A and column B to the left until column A is a width of 4 characters.

Step 2: Drag the column border between column B and column C to the right until column B is a width of 15 characters.

Step 3: Move the mouse pointer to the border line between row headings 3 and 4 and drag the row border down until the height is equal to 20 points.

Step 4: Move the mouse pointer to the border line between row headings 7 and 8 and drag the row border down until the height is equal to 20 points.

Step 5: Use the down scroll arrow to display row 14. Move the mouse pointer to the border line between row headings 13 and 14 and drag the row border down until the height is equal to 30 points.

Formatting the Projected Percentages Section

The last task in formatting the worksheet in Project 3 is to format the projected percentages section. The following formatting, as shown in Figure 3-53 on page L164, is required:

1. The table title in cell B16 displays in 18 point type, bold, and yellow.
2. The range B16..C16 displays with a blue background.
3. The text displays in blue.
4. An outline border surrounds range B17..C21.

To format the projected percentages section of the worksheet, perform the following steps.

TO FORMAT THE PROJECTED PERCENTAGES SECTION

Step 1: Point to cell B16 and click the right mouse button. Choose the Font & Attributes command from the quick menu. When the Font & Attributes dialog box displays, select 18 in the Size list box, Bold in the Attributes area, and the yellow color in the top row of the Color drop-down box. Choose the OK button in the Font & Attributes dialog box.

Step 2: Select the range B16..C16. Point to the selected range and click the right mouse button. Choose the Lines & Color command from the quick menu. When the Lines & Color dialog box displays, select the first blue color in the top row of the Background color drop-down box. Choose the OK button in the Lines & Color dialog box.

Step 3: Select the range B17..C21. Point to the selected range and click the right mouse button. Choose the Lines & Color command from the quick menu. When the Lines & Color dialog box displays, select the first blue color in the top row of the Text color drop-down box. Select the Outline check box in the Border area. Then, select the first blue color in the Line color drop-down box. Choose the OK button in the Lines & Color dialog box. Select cell A1.

The formatting of the worksheet is now complete. To save the changes you have made, click the Save icon on the set of SmartIcons.

▶ MULTIPLE WORKSHEETS

In Project 1 and Project 2, you used only one worksheet to enter data and create a chart based on that data. 1-2-3 also has the capability to create multiple worksheets in each file to give you flexibility in organizing data effectively. Each worksheet is smaller and easier to understand and use than one large worksheet.

Inserting a Worksheet

1-2-3 allows you to insert up to 255 additional worksheets in a file. Each worksheet in the file is identified by letters of the alphabet, from A, B, and C for the first three worksheets, to IV for worksheet 256.

In Project 3, a second worksheet is inserted after worksheet A. You will create a 3D stacked bar chart from data in worksheet A and add the bar chart to worksheet B.

To insert one worksheet, perform the following steps.

TO INSERT ONE WORKSHEET ▼

STEP 1 ►

Point to the New Sheet button ( ) in the top right corner of the 1-2-3 window above column heading G.

The mouse pointer points to the New Sheet button above column heading G on the worksheet (Figure 3-67).

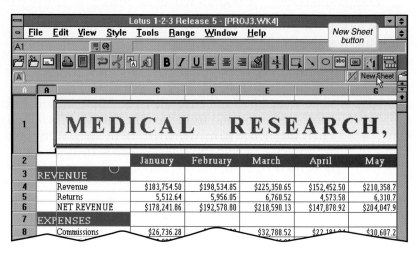

FIGURE 3-67

STEP 2 ►

Click the New Sheet button.

1-2-3 adds a second worksheet to the file and identifies the new worksheet by the letter B in the recessed worksheet tab next to the tab labeled A located at the far left above the column headings (Figure 3-68). Notice the tab for worksheet A is no longer recessed, indicating worksheet A is not the current worksheet. The cell pointer is positioned in cell A1 of worksheet B. The selection indicator displays the current address, B:A1.

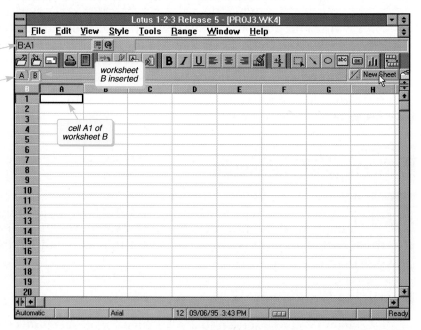

FIGURE 3-68

Notice several important details in worksheet B. First, 1-2-3 inserts the second sheet, worksheet B, after worksheet A. Worksheet B becomes the **current worksheet,** the worksheet in which you can enter data. The first worksheet A is now behind the new worksheet B.

Second, the selection indicator displays the worksheet letter as part of the cell reference. The complete cell address now consists of three elements: the worksheet letter, followed by a colon (B:), the column letter (A), and the row number (1).

Third, 1-2-3 inserts the new worksheet B with the original worksheet style defaults, that is, Arial 12 point as the font and the column width as 9 characters. The changes made to the worksheet A default style settings have no effect on the new worksheet.

To delete a worksheet, point to the worksheet letter just to the left of column A, click the right mouse button, and choose the Delete command from the quick menu. When you delete worksheets, 1-2-3 automatically changes the letters of the remaining worksheets.

Naming Worksheets

You can name a worksheet tab with a more meaningful name to represent the data contained in the worksheet. Perform the following steps to rename worksheet A, Projections, and worksheet B, Expense_Chart.

TO NAME A WORKSHEET ▼

STEP 1 ▶

Double-click the tab for worksheet B. Type `Expense_Chart` **and press the ENTER key.**

When you double-click the worksheet tab, 1-2-3 expands the worksheet tab and a blinking cursor displays. 1-2-3 enters the worksheet name, Expense_Chart, in the worksheet tab (Figure 3-69).

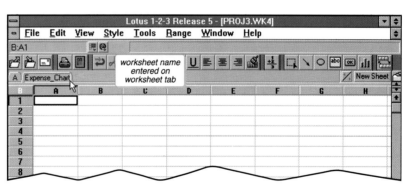

FIGURE 3-69

STEP 2 ▶

Double-click the tab for worksheet A. Type `Projections` **and press the ENTER key.**

When you double-click the tab of worksheet A, 1-2-3 makes worksheet A the current worksheet, and places worksheet B after worksheet A (Figure 3-70). 1-2-3 enters the worksheet name, Projections, in the worksheet tab.

FIGURE 3-70

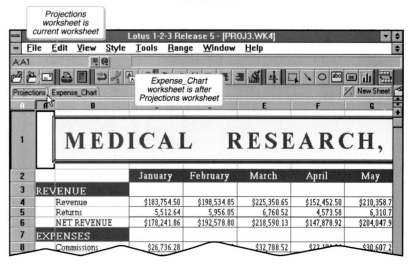

When naming a worksheet tab, there are several guidelines you should follow. First, worksheet names can be from one to fifteen characters in length. Second, avoid using worksheet names that are similar to worksheet letters or cell addresses; for example, do not name a worksheet Q1 or BB. Third, you can't enter duplicate worksheet names in a file. Each worksheet name in a file must be unique. If you try to enter a worksheet name that contains illegal characters, 1-2-3 beeps and displays a message. The following characters cannot be used in worksheet names: blank spaces, !, ;, +, -, *, /, &, >, <, @, #, { or . (period).

To delete a worksheet name, double-click the worksheet tab, press the DEL key and then press the ENTER key.

▶ CREATING A STACKED BAR CHART

A **stacked bar chart** illustrates the relationship between two or more values and their totals by drawing stacked bars vertically across a chart. The stacked bar chart shown in Figure 3-71 shows the total expenses for each month, as well as the expense amount for each type of expense. The red bars represent the projected commissions expense for each month. For example, in January, the commissions expense is approximately $25,000. The green bars represent the projected advertising expense for each month. The red bars and the green bars together represent the combined total of the projected commissions expenses and the projected advertising expenses for each month. For January, the combined total for both projected expenses is a little more than $50,000. Similarly, the blue bars on the chart illustrated in Figure 3-71 show the projected product liability expense for each month. The yellow bars represent the projected benefits expense for each month. From this chart, it is easy to see that the greatest projected expense for the six-month period is for benefits.

A table of values displays below the chart. The x-axis labels display in the top row of the table, and the x-axis title and **legend** text display in the far left column of the table. To display a table of values below a chart, select the Include table of values check box in the Types dialog box. Including a table of values below a chart is a good way to present charts when it is difficult to read the actual numbers from the scale.

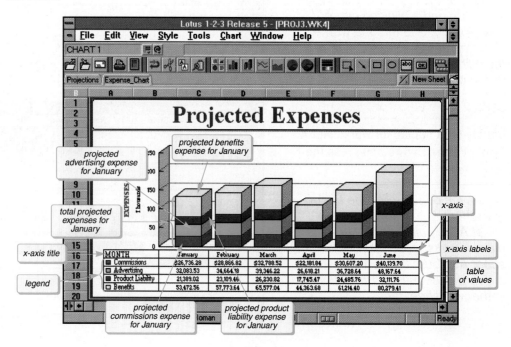

FIGURE 3-71

To create the stacked bar chart and display a table of values, perform the steps below and on the next two pages.

TO CREATE A STACKED BAR CHART AND DISPLAY A TABLE OF VALUES ▼

STEP 1 ▶

Select the range on the worksheet to chart – B8..H11, and point to the Chart icon on the set of SmartIcons.

The row titles and cells containing the projected expenses for January through June are selected (Figure 3-72). Notice the range address in the selection indicator includes the worksheet letter A. The mouse pointer points to the Chart icon on the set of SmartIcons.

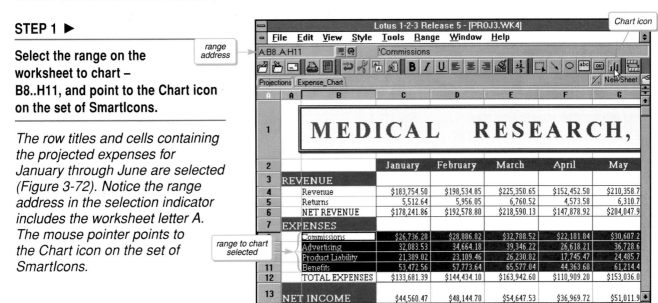

FIGURE 3-72

STEP 2 ▶

Click the Chart icon on the set of SmartIcons. Then, click the Expense_Chart worksheet tab and move the mouse pointer into the work area.

1-2-3 displays the Expense_Chart worksheet and makes cell A1 the current cell. The mouse pointer changes to a crosshair with a picture of a bar chart (Figure 3-73).

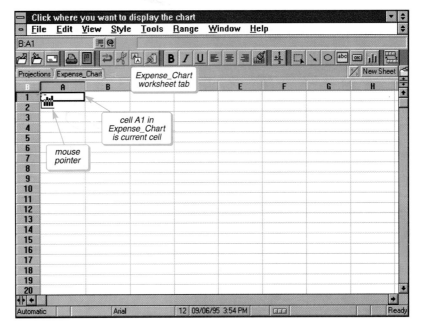

FIGURE 3-73

STEP 3 ►

Click and drag the range A1..H20 in the Expense_Chart worksheet. Then, release the left mouse button.

1-2-3 displays the default bar chart it always displays when a chart is first created (Figure 3-74). The charting set of SmartIcons displays below the edit line. The default title, Title, displays centered above the chart. The row titles that were selected in column B appear as the chart legend, located to the right of the chart. The x- and y-axis default labels display as X-Axis and Y-Axis.

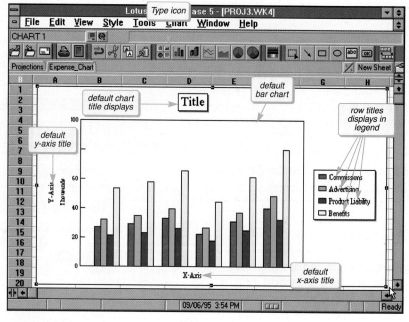

FIGURE 3-74

STEP 4 ►

Click the Type icon ( ) on the set of charting SmartIcons. When the Type dialog box displays, point to the 3D Bar option button in the Types area.

1-2-3 displays the Type dialog box (Figure 3-75). In the Types area, Bar option is selected button indicating the default chart. To the right of the Types area three style buttons display, each represents a style of bar chart.

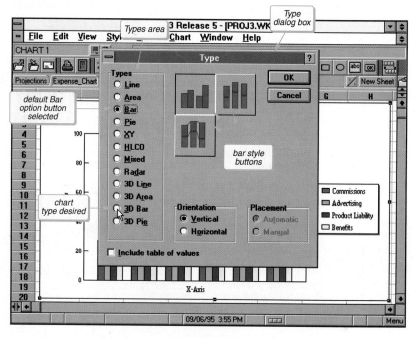

FIGURE 3-75

STEP 5 ▶

Select the 3D Bar option button in
the Types area. Click the 3D Stacked
bar chart style button. Then select
the Include table of values check box
at the bottom of the Type dialog box.
Point to the OK button.

*The 3D Bar option button is
selected (Figure 3-76). The three
style buttons for 3D bar charts display to the right of the Types area.
The first style places the three-
dimensional bars side by side. In
the second style, the three-
dimensional bars are placed in
rows one behind the other. The
third style stacks the three-
dimensional bars. The X in the
Include table of values check box
informs 1-2-3 to include a table of
values below the chart. The mouse
pointer points to the OK button in
the Type dialog box.*

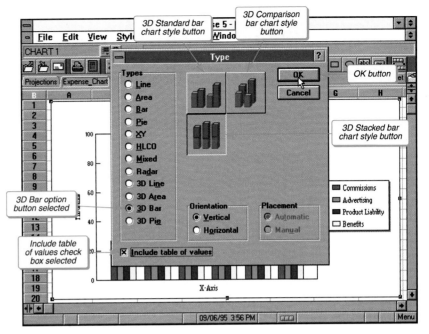

FIGURE 3-76

STEP 6 ▶

Choose the OK button.

*1-2-3 displays the 3D Stacked bar
chart (Figure 3-77). The chart
name, CHART 1, displays in the
selection indicator. Each vertical
bar represents the total projected
expenses for the month. Each seg-
ment in each bar represents the
total projected expense for that
category. A table of values diplays
below the chart. The default
x-axis title displays in the left
column. The legend text
displays below the x-axis title
in the left column. The x-axis
labels do not display in the top row
of the table because the labels
were not selected in the range to
chart.*

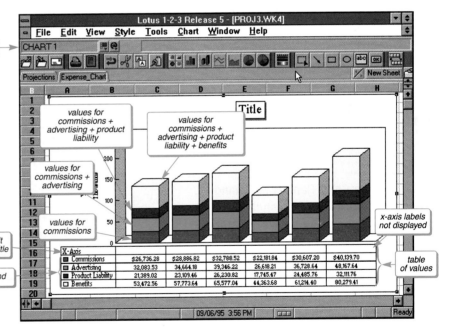

FIGURE 3-76

Adding X-Axis Labels

X-axis labels are words that identify information along the horizontal (X) axis. In Figure 3-71 on page L176, the months, (January, February, March, April, May, and June) are the x-axis labels. These labels are found in the range C7..H7 in the Projections worksheet. Perform the following steps to add x-axis labels to the 3D stacked bar chart.

TO ADD X-AXIS LABELS ▼

STEP 1 ▶

Select the chart. Click the right mouse button to display the quick menu. When the quick menu displays, point to the Chart Ranges command.

The quick menu displays, and the mouse pointer points to the Chart Ranges command (Figure 3-78).

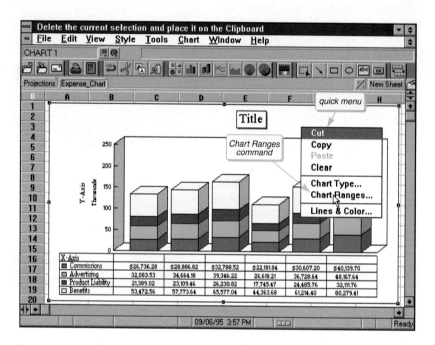

FIGURE 3-78

STEP 2 ▶

Choose the Chart Ranges command from the quick menu. When the Ranges dialog box displays, point to the range selector (▣) located to the right of the Range text box.

1-2-3 displays the Ranges dialog box (Figure 3-79). X-Axis labels is selected in the Series list box. The mouse pointer points to the range selector located to the right of the Range text box at the bottom of the dialog box.

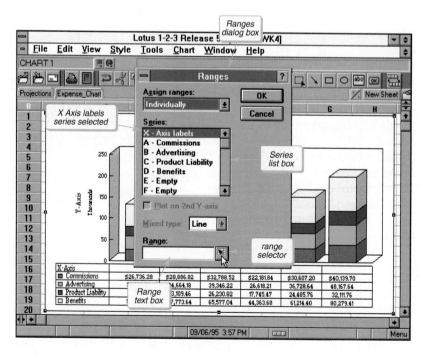

FIGURE 3-79

STEP 3 ▶

Click the range selector. Then, click the Projections worksheet tab. Select the range C2..H2 and release the left mouse button. Point to the OK button in the Ranges dialog box.

After you click the range selector, 1-2-3 removes the Ranges dialog box temporarily so you can select the range. The Ranges dialog box reappears when you release the left mouse button (Figure 3-80). The address of the selected range displays in the Range text box. The mouse pointer points to the OK button. Notice the address reference in the Range text box displays the worksheet name, Projections.

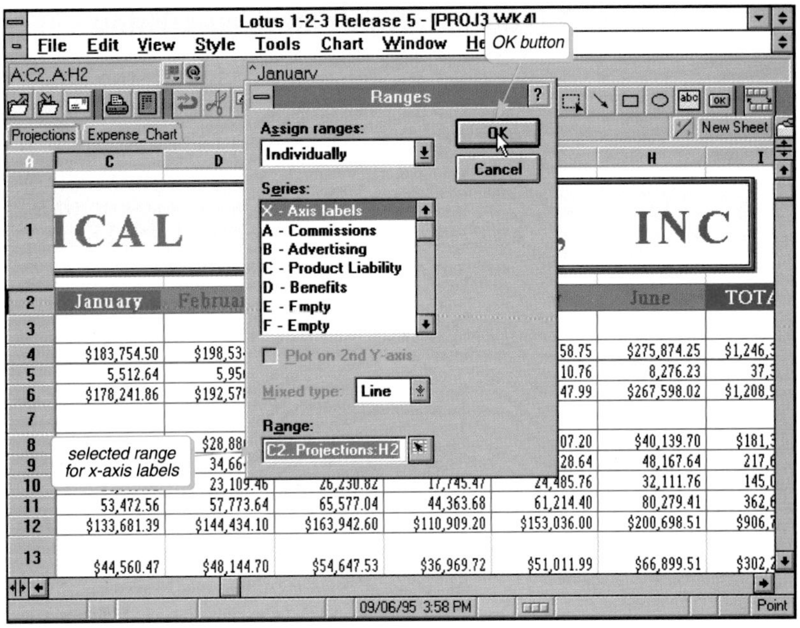

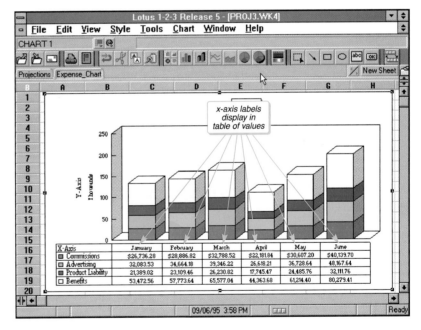

FIGURE 3-80

STEP 4 ▶

Choose the OK button.

1-2-3 displays the 3D stacked bar chart with the x-axis labels, January, February, March, April, May, and June, at the bottom of the chart in the table of values (Figure 3-81).

FIGURE 3-81

You can delete x-axis labels on a chart by highlighting the Range text box entry in the Ranges dialog box (see Figure 3-80), pressing the DEL key, and then choosing the OK button in the Ranges dialog box.

When you create a chart, if the x-axis labels are adjacent to the values in the worksheet to be charted and the x-axis labels are selected, 1-2-3 will automatically display the labels on the chart.

The Ranges command is also found on the Chart menu on the main menu bar.

Adding Chart and Axes Titles

When you create a chart, if the range you select in the worksheet includes the title in the first row, 1-2-3 automatically uses the text to create the chart title. Thus, if Projected Expenses had been in the first row of the selected range to chart, the title would have appeared automatically in the chart.

In the 3D stacked bar chart, the title is Projected Expenses. The x-axis title is MONTH and the y-axis title is EXPENSES. The x-axis title displays in the top left column of the table of values.

The following steps add a chart title, x-axis title, and a y-axis title to the 3D stacked bar chart (see Figure 3-82).

TO ADD CHART AND AXES TITLES TO A 3D STACKED BAR CHART

Step 1: Point to the default chart title in the Expense_Chart worksheet and click the right mouse button. Choose the Headings command. When the Headings dialog box displays, type Projected Expenses in the Line 1 text box in the Title area. Choose the OK button.

Step 2: Point to the x-axis and click the right mouse button. Choose the **X-Axis command**. When the X-Axis dialog box displays, type MONTH in the Axis title text box. Choose the OK button in the X-Axis dialog box.

Step 3: Point to the y-axis default title, Y-Axis, on the chart and click the right mouse button. Choose the **Y-Axis command**. When the Y-Axis dialog box displays, type EXPENSES in the Axis title text box. Choose the OK button in the Y-Axis dialog box.

1-2-3 displays the chart with the chart title, x-axis title, and y-axis title (Figure 3-82).

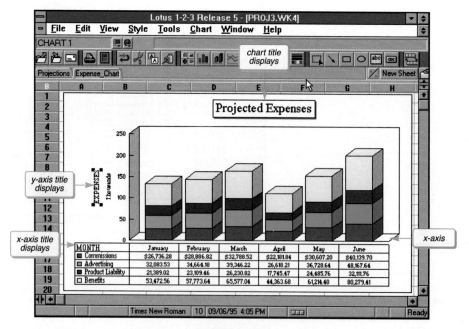

FIGURE 3-82

▶ ENHANCING A STACKED BAR CHART

his section of Project 3 explains the steps required to enhance the stacked bar chart shown in Figure 3-71 on page L176. You can enhance the 3D stacked bar chart to present the data in the clearest, most professional way. Using the following steps and techniques, you will resize the frame surrounding the chart title, add grid lines to the chart, change the font size, color, and style of the text, and add a designer frame to the chart.

Resizing the Chart Title Frame

To change the size of the chart title frame, you must first select the frame edge. Then, drag a selection handle until the chart title frame is the desired size. The following steps explain how to resize the chart title frame.

TO RESIZE THE CHART TITLE FRAME ▼

STEP 1 ▶

Point to the chart title frame and click the left mouse button. When the selection handles appear on the four corners, position the mouse pointer on the bottom left selection handle.

Selection handles appear on the four corners of the chart title frame indicating the edges are selected (Figure 3-83). The mouse pointer changes to a four-headed arrow indicating the frame can be sized.

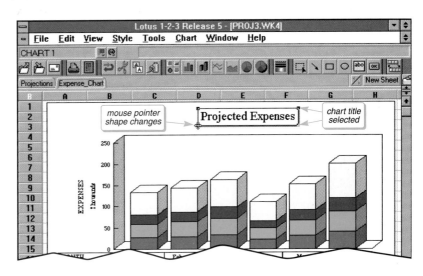

FIGURE 3-83

STEP 2 ▶

Drag the bottom left selection handle of the chart title frame to the left until the frame is the same width as the chart frame. Release the left mouse button.

As you drag the selection handle, both sides of the frame expand keeping the chart title centered within the frame (Figure 3-84). The chart title frame displays with the same width as the chart. The title, Projected Expenses, is centered in the frame.

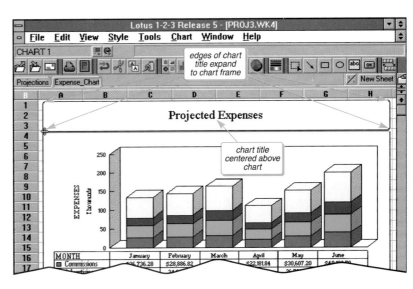

FIGURE 3-84

Adding Grid Lines to the Chart

To further enhance the 3D stacked bar chart, you can add grid lines extending from the y-axis. These vertical axis grid lines display horizontally on the chart and make the chart easier to read and interpret. To accomplish this, perform the following steps.

TO ADD Y-AXIS GRID LINES ▼

STEP 1 ▶

Select the chart plot. Click the right mouse button to display the quick menu. Point to the Grids command.

*Selection handles on the **chart plot** indicate the chart is selected (Figure 3-85). 1-2-3 displays the quick menu. The mouse pointer points to the Grids command.*

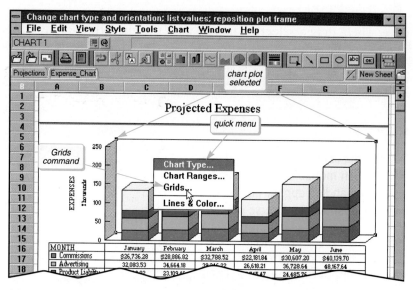

FIGURE 3-85

STEP 2 ▶

Choose the Grids command from the quick menu. When the Grids dialog box displays, click the Y-axis drop-down box arrow. Select Major interval from the Y-axis drop-down box. Then, point to the OK button in the Grids dialog box.

1-2-3 displays the Grids dialog box (Figure 3-86). The Y-axis drop-down box displays the Major interval setting. The Major interval setting adds horizontal grid lines that originate from each number on the y-axis scale. The mouse pointer points to the OK button.

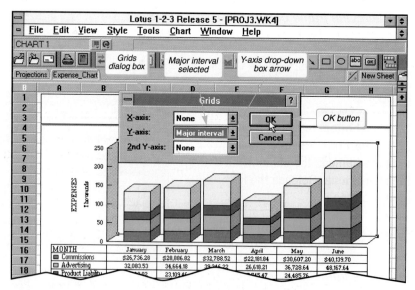

FIGURE 3-86

STEP 3 ▶

Choose the OK button in the Grids dialog box.

The 3D stacked bar chart displays with y-axis grid lines (Figure 3-87). Notice the horizontal grid lines originate from each number on the y-axis scale.

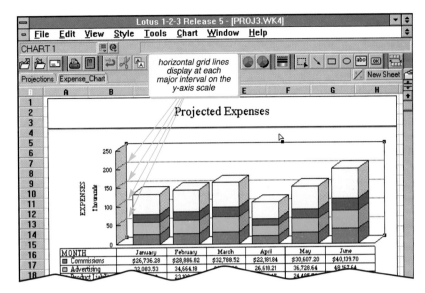

FIGURE 3-87

To remove the y-axis grid lines from the chart, display the Grids dialog box and choose None in the Y-axis drop-down box.

The Grids command is also found on the Chart menu on the main menu bar.

Changing Font Size, Font Color, and Font Style

To change the font size, font color, and font style of text on a chart, first select the text, then choose the Font & Attributes command from the quick menu and make the appropriate selections. In this project, the chart title displays in Times New Roman 32 point, bold, and the color blue. The y-axis title displays in Times New Roman, 12 point bold, and the color blue.

To change the font size, font color, and font style (see Figure 3-88 on the next page), perform the following steps.

TO CHANGE THE FONT SIZE, FONT COLOR, AND FONT STYLE

Step 1: Point to the chart title, Projected Expenses, and click the right mouse button. Choose the Font & Attributes command. When the Font & Attributes dialog box displays, select 32 in the Size list box and Bold in the Attributes area. Click the Color drop-down box arrow and choose the first blue color in the top row of the Color drop-down box. Choose the OK button in the Font & Attributes dialog box.

Step 2: Point to the y-axis title, EXPENSES, and click the right mouse button. Choose the Font & Attributes command. When the Font & Attributes dialog box displays, select Bold in the Attributes area. Click the Color drop-down box arrow, and choose the first blue color in the top row of the Color drop-down box. Choose the OK button in the Font & Attributes dialog box.

1-2-3 displays the 3D stacked bar chart with the appropriate changes as shown in Figure 3-88 on the next page.

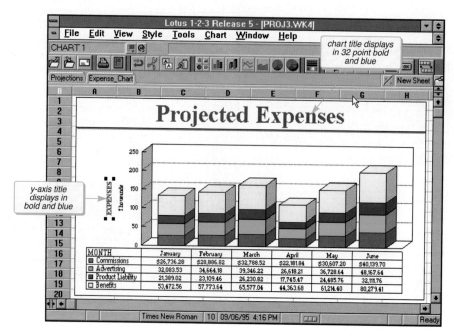

FIGURE 3-88

Adding a Designer Frame to the Chart

To further enhance the chart, you can add a designer frame. The following steps explain how to add a designer frame to a chart (see Figure 3-89).

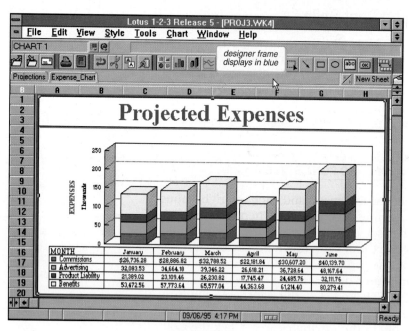

FIGURE 3-89

TO ADD A DESIGNER FRAME TO A CHART

Step 1: Point to the chart frame and click the right mouse button. Choose the Lines & Color command. When the Lines & Color dialog box displays, click the Designer frame drop-down box arrow and select the second designer frame from the right in the bottom row.

Step 2: Click the Frame color drop-down box arrow and select the first blue color in the top row of the Color drop-down box. Choose the OK button in the Lines & Color dialog box.

(1-2-3 displays the chart with the designer frame added (Figure 3-89).

▶ CHECKING THE SPELLING OF A WORKSHEET

After you have completed the worksheet and charted the data, spell check the file as specified in Project 2 on page L108. Click the Projections worksheet tab and select cell A1. Use the **Spell Check command** on the Tools menu to begin checking the spelling. 1-2-3 checks the Projections worksheet and Expense_Chart worksheet for spelling errors. Make any necessary corrections.

As noted previously, saving the worksheet often prevents lost data if something unexpected happens. Click the Save icon on the set of SmartIcons to save the worksheet.

▶ PRINT PREVIEW AND PRINTING A WORKSHEET IN LANDSCAPE

When a worksheet contains more than eight columns or when you increase the width of the columns, the worksheet often will not fit across a piece of paper that is 8.5 inches wide and 11 inches long. In Project 3, because nine columns are to print, use print preview to determine if the Projections worksheet will fit across the page.

To use Print Preview, perform the following steps.

TO USE PRINT PREVIEW ▼

STEP 1 ▶

Select cell A1 of the Projections worksheet. Click the Print Preview icon on the set of SmartIcons. When the Print Preview dialog box displays, select the Current worksheet option button in the Preview area if necessary. Then, point to the OK button in the Print Preview dialog box.

The Current worksheet option in the Print Preview dialog box previews the worksheet that contains the cell pointer (Figure 3-90). The mouse pointer points to the OK button in the Print Preview dialog box.

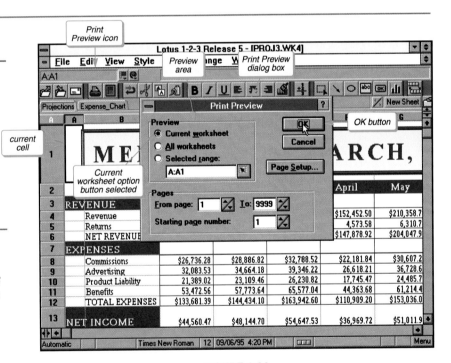

FIGURE 3-90

STEP 2 ▶

Choose the OK button in the Print Preview dialog box. When the Print Preview window displays on the screen, click the Zoom In icon once.

1-2-3 displays a full page of the current worksheet and the report as it will appear on the page. When you magnify the display, the bottom portion of the worksheet does not show on the screen (Figure 3-91). The displayed report does not contain the June column and the TOTAL column, which means these columns will not appear on the printed report.

STEP 3

To return to the worksheet from the Print Preview window, click the Close icon in the Print Preview window.

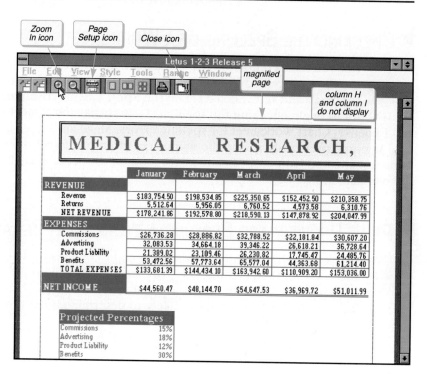

FIGURE 3-91

Printing Landscape Reports

If you print the Projections worksheet on a page with a width of 8.5 inches and a length of 11 inches, 1-2-3 will print column A through column G on the first page of the report and column H and column I on the second page of the report. This is not normally a satisfactory technique.

One option is to print the worksheet across the length of the paper instead of the width of the paper; that is, in effect turn the page ninety degrees so the paper is 11 inches wide and 8.5 inches in height. When you print a report in this manner, you are using the **landscape page orientation** as opposed to the **portrait page orientation** you use when the printed page is 8.5 inches wide by 11 inches long.

To print in the landscape mode using 1-2-3, you must use the Page Setup command to change the page orientation from portrait to landscape. To accomplish this, perform the steps on the next two pages.

TO PRINT A LANDSCAPE REPORT ▼

STEP 1 ▶

Point to the Print icon on the set of SmartIcons and click the left mouse button. When the Print dialog box displays, ensure the Current worksheet option button is selected in the Print area, and point to the Page Setup button.

1-2-3 displays the Print dialog box (Figure 3-92). The Current worksheet option button in the Print area is selected. The mouse pointer points to the Page Setup button. The Page Setup button allows you to change the page orientation.

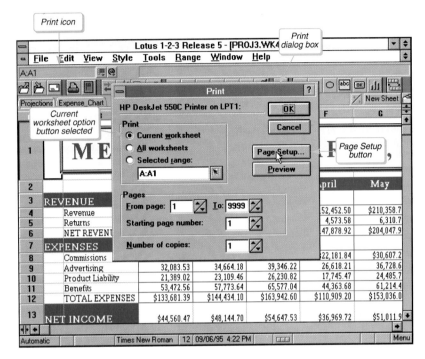

FIGURE 3-92

STEP 2 ▶

Choose the Page Setup button in the Print dialog box. When the Page Setup dialog box displays, select the Landscape option button in the Orientation area. Point to the OK button.

1-2-3 displays the Page Setup dialog box (Figure 3-93). In the Orientation area, you can select either Portrait or Landscape. When you select Landscape or Portrait, 1-2-3 fills the option button of the selection.

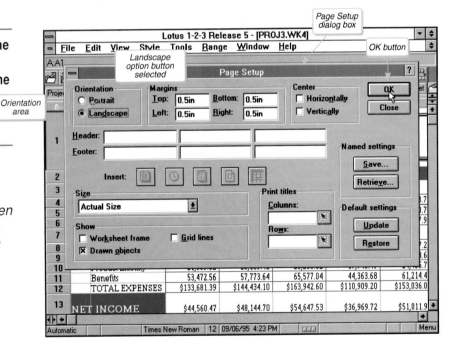

FIGURE 3-93

STEP 3 ▶

Choose the OK button in the Page
Setup dialog box. When the Print
dialog box redisplays, choose the
OK button in the Print dialog box.

*1-2-3 again displays the Print dia-
log box. 1-2-3 prints the Projections worksheet (Figure 3-94).
Notice that the entire worksheet
prints on a single page.*

MEDICAL RESEARCH, INC

	January	February	March	April	May	June	TOTAL
REVENUE							
Revenue	$183,754.50	$198,534.85	$225,350.65	$152,452.50	$210,358.75	$275,874.25	$1,246,325.50
Returns	5,512.64	5,956.05	6,760.52	4,573.58	6,310.76	8,276.23	37,389.78
NET REVENUE	$178,241.86	$192,578.80	$218,590.13	$147,878.92	$204,047.99	$267,598.02	$1,208,935.72
EXPENSES							
Commissions	$26,736.28	$28,886.82	$32,788.52	$22,181.84	$30,607.20	$40,139.70	$181,340.36
Advertising	32,083.53	34,664.18	39,346.22	26,618.21	36,728.64	48,167.64	217,608.42
Product Liability	21,389.02	23,109.46	26,230.82	17,745.47	24,485.76	32,111.76	145,072.29
Benefits	53,472.56	57,773.64	65,577.04	44,363.68	61,214.40	80,279.41	362,680.73
TOTAL EXPENSES	$133,681.39	$144,434.10	$163,942.60	$110,909.20	$153,036.00	$200,698.51	$906,701.80
NET INCOME	$44,560.47	$48,144.70	$54,647.53	$36,969.72	$51,011.99	$66,899.51	$302,233.92

Projected Percentages

Commissions	15%
Advertising	18%
Product Liability	12%
Benefits	30%
Returns	3%

FIGURE 3-94

Once you have printed a worksheet in landscape orientation, landscape orientation remains the selection in the Page Setup dialog box. Therefore, if you are
going to print other reports in 1-2-3, be aware that the reports will print in landscape orientation until you change back to portrait.

You can also display the Page Setup dialog box from the Print Preview window (see Figure 3-91 on page L188) by clicking the Page Setup icon. The Page
Setup command is also found on the File menu on the main menu bar.

Printing a Chart

By using the following steps, you can print the chart.

TO PRINT A CHART

Step 1: Click the Expense_Chart worksheet tab.

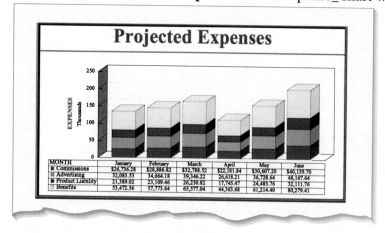

FIGURE 3-95

Step 2: Click the Print icon on the set
of SmartIcons. When the Print
dialog box displays, select the
Current worksheet option in
the Print area. Then, choose the
Page Setup button.

Step 3: Select Portrait in the Orientation area.

Step 4: Click the OK button in the Page
Setup dialog box.

Step 5: Click the OK button in the Print
dialog box.

*1-2-3 prints the chart in portrait
orientation (Figure 3-95).*

▶ CHANGING VALUES IN CELLS REFERENCED IN A FORMULA

The 1-2-3 automatic recalculation feature is a powerful tool used to analyze worksheet data. Using 1-2-3 to examine the impact of changing values in cells that are referenced by a formula in another cell is called **what-if analysis**.

In Project 3, the monthly expenses in the range C8..H11 (see Figure 3-1 on page L135) of the Projections worksheet are dependent on the projected percentages in the range C17..C20. Thus, if you change any of the projected percentages, 1-2-3 immediately recalculates the monthly expenses in rows 8 through 11, the monthly total expenses in row 12 and the monthly net incomes in row 13. As a result, these new values cause 1-2-3 to recalculate a new, six-month net income in cell I13.

The what-if question posed at the beginning of Project 3, *What if the projected percentages decrease by 1% each — how would the decrease affect the net income?*, can now be answered. To answer the question, you need to change only the four percent values in the worksheet. 1-2-3 immediately answers the questions regarding the six-month net income in cell I13 by instantly recalculating these figures.

Splitting the Window into Panes

To ensure that the projected percentages section (range B16..C21) and the net income in cell I13 show on the screen at the same time, you must first display the window so both ranges (B16..C21 and I13) are visible on the screen.

In 1-2-3, you can split the worksheet window into two window panes and view two different parts of a large worksheet at the same time. A **pane** is a part of the window through which you can view a portion of the worksheet. Using the following steps, split the worksheet window into two vertical panes and perform a what-if analysis on the data in the worksheet.

TO SPLIT THE WORKSHEET WINDOW AND ANALYZE DATA BY CHANGING VALUES ▼

STEP 1 ▶

Click the Projections worksheet tab. Select cell A2. Position the mouse pointer on the vertical splitter (⊞) to the left of the left scroll arrow at the bottom of the screen.

The Projections worksheet displays (Figure 3-96). The mouse pointer, when positioned on the vertical splitter, changes shape to a black two-headed horizontal arrow. The pointer indicates you can split the screen into two panes.

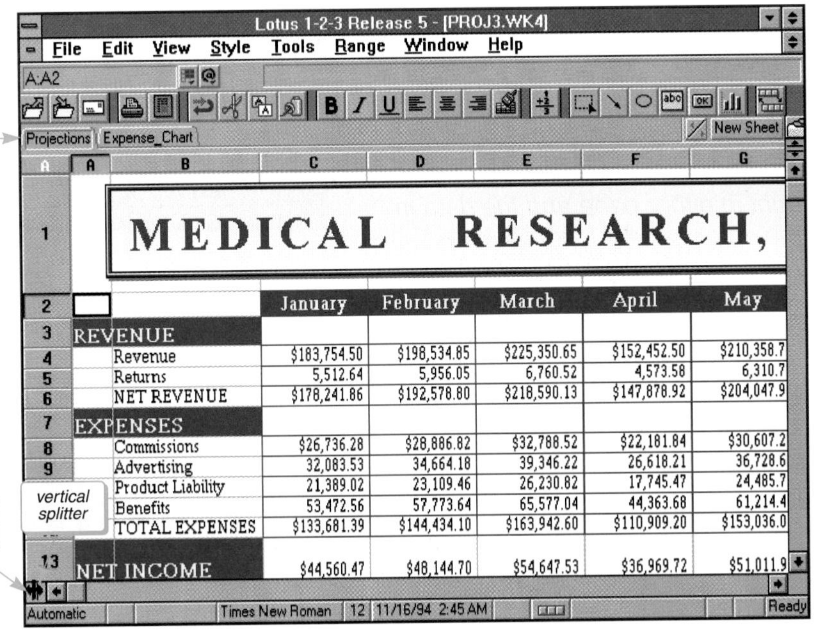

FIGURE 3-96

STEP 2 ►

Drag the mouse pointer and the vertical split bar to the right until the bar rests on the border between column D and column E.

As you drag the mouse pointer positioned on the vertical splitter, a split bar accompanies the pointer (Figure 3-97). The split bar indicates where the window will be separated into panes. The split bar is located on the border between column D and column E. This location informs 1-2-3 to display column E in the right pane and display column D in the left pane.

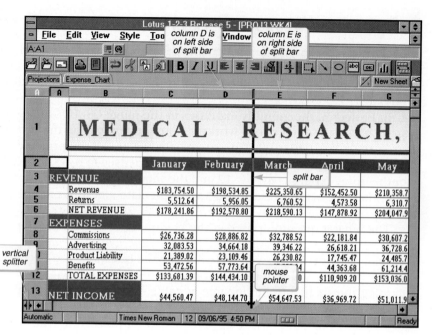

FIGURE 3-97

STEP 3 ►

Release the left mouse button and move the mouse pointer off the vertical split bar. Use the vertical scroll arrow to display the projected percentages in the left pane. Use the right scroll arrow in the right pane to display the totals in column I.

1-2-3 divides the window into side-by-side panes (Figure 3-98). As you scroll to display the projected percentages, notice that both panes move together. Each pane has its own horizontal scroll bar, scroll box, and scroll arrows. This means you can scroll data left or right in either pane and the data in the other pane will not move. Notice only one vertical scroll bar displays for controlling the vertical movement of both panes. The projected percentages section of the worksheet displays in the left pane and the total net income displays in the right pane.

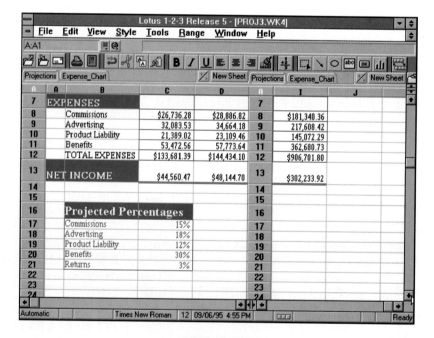

FIGURE 3-98

STEP 4 ▶

Enter 14% in cell C17, 17% in cell C18, 11% in cell C19, and 29% in cell C20.

1-2-3 recalculates all the formulas in the worksheet, including the total expenses in cell I12 and total net income in cell I13 (Figure 3-99).

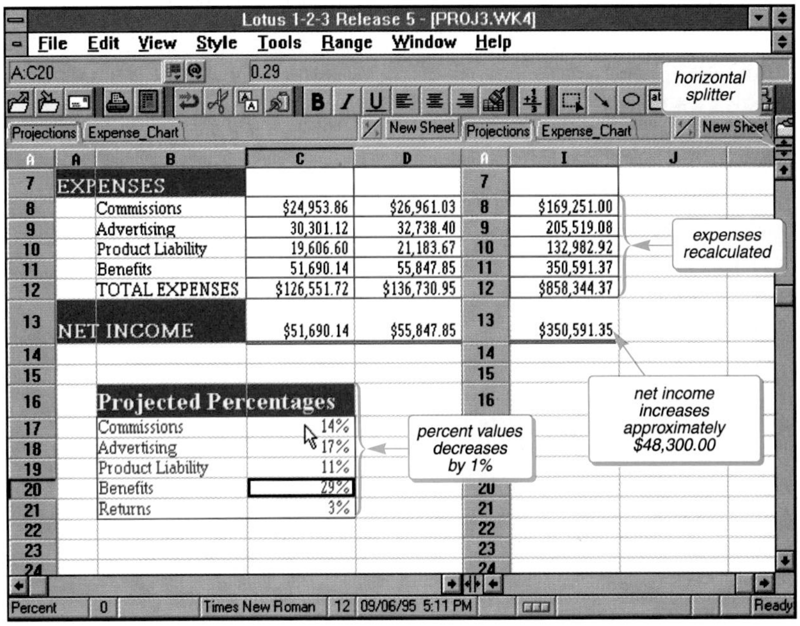

FIGURE 3-99

Notice that when you enter the new values, 1-2-3 recalculates the worksheet. The recalculated values express the results that would be obtained if all the expenses were decreased by 1%.

Compare the total expenses and net incomes in Figure 3-98 on the previous page and Figure 3-99. By reducing the projected commissions, advertising, product liability, and benefits percentages by 1% each, the total expenses in cell I12 decreases from $906,701.80 to $858,344.37, and the net income in cell I13 increases from $302,233.92 (Figure 3-98) to $350,591.35 (Figure 3-99). The 1% reduction in projected expenses translates into a net income gain of $48,357.43.

You can divide the worksheet window into an upper and lower pane by pointing to the **horizontal splitter** (⬍) and dragging the horizontal split bar down to the desired location. This configuration is useful when a worksheet consists of many rows, and you want to view rows at the beginning of the worksheet and other rows in the middle or end of the worksheet. When you split the window into upper and lower panes, each pane has a separate vertical scroll bar.

To return to a single window, place the mouse pointer on the split bar, and drag the split bar back to the vertical or horizontal splitter.

▶ PROJECT SUMMARY

Project 3 introduced you to using 1-2-3 to answer what-if questions. You saw the difference between relative cell references and absolute cell references, how to enter both into a formula, and how to copy both to adjacent cells. The project presented steps showing you how to round values calculated by formulas. In addition, you learned to draw in and format a text block on a worksheet.

Using 1-2-3's charting capabilities, you learned to create a 3D stacked bar chart from data in the worksheet and display the chart in a second worksheet.

▶ KEY TERMS AND INDEX

@ROUND function *(L149)*
absolute cell reference *(L150)*
border *(L168)*
chart plot *(L184)*
Chart Ranges command *(L180)*
copy data to a nonadjacent area *(L145)*
current worksheet *(L175)*
designer frame *(L164)*
drag-and-drop *(L145)*
drag-and-fill *(L142)*
Draw Text command *(L141)*

drawn objects *(L139)*
Fill by Example command *(L144)*
gradient fill pattern *(L164)*
Grids command *(L184)*
horizontal splitter *(L193)*
landscape page orientation *(L188)*
legend *(L176)*
move data *(L147)*
pane *(L191)*
pattern (L164)

portrait page orientation *(L188)*
relative cell reference *(L149)*
Spell Check command *(L187)*
stacked bar chart *(L176)*
text block *(L135, L139)*
vertical splitter *(L191)*
what-if analysis *(L191)*
what-if questions *(L134)*
worksheet style defaults *(L137)*
X-Axis command *(L182)*
Y-Axis command *(L182)*

QUICK REFERENCE

In Lotus 1-2-3 for Windows, you can accomplish a task in a number of ways. The following table presents a quick reference to each task presented in this project with its available options. The commands listed in the Menu column can be executed using either the keyboard or mouse.

Task	Mouse	Menu	Keyboard Shortcuts
Add a Border to a Cell or Range of Cells		From Style menu or quick menu, choose Lines & Color	
Add a Table of Values Below a Chart		From Chart menu, choose Type	
Add Grid Lines to a Chart		From Chart menu or quick menu, choose Grids	
Add X-Axis Labels to a Chart		From Chart menu or quick menu, choose Ranges	
Change the Chart Type	Click Type icon on charting set of SmartIcons	From Chart menu, choose Type	
Change the Default Settings for a Worksheet		From Style menu, choose Worksheet Defaults	
Copy Cells to a Nonadjacent Area	Position mouse pointer on border of selected range, press and hold down CTRL key, and click and drag to new area	From Edit menu or quick menu, choose Copy; from Edit menu or quick menu, choose Paste	Press CTRL+C; press CTRL+V
Create a Sequence	Position mouse pointer on bottom right border of selected range and drag	From Range menu, choose Fill by Example	

Task	Mouse	Menu	Keyboard Shortcuts
Decrease the Worksheet Display		From View menu, choose Zoom Out	
Delete a Worksheet		From Edit menu or quick menu, choose Delete	Press CTRL+MINUS (gray key on numeric keypad)
Draw a Text Block	Click Draw Text icon on Default Sheet of SmartIcons	From Tools menu, choose Draw; choose Text	
Insert a Worksheet	Click New Sheet button	From Edit menu, choose Insert	Press CTRL+PLUS (gray key on numeric keypad)
Make a Selected Cell an Absolute Cell Reference			Press F4
Move Cells to a Nonadjacent Area	Position mouse pointer on border of selected range, click and drag to new area	From Edit menu or quick menu, choose Cut; from Edit menu or quick menu, choose Paste	Press CTRL+X; press CTRL+V
Move the Cell Pointer to the Next Worksheet	Click desired worksheet tab		Press CTRL+PAGE UP
Move the Cell Pointer to the Previous Worksheet	Click desired worksheet tab		Press CTRL+PAGE DOWN
Print in Landscape Orientation		From File menu, choose Page Setup	
Print in Portrait Orientation		From File menu, choose Page Setup	
Remove Window Panes	Drag split bar	From View menu, choose Clear Split	
Return the Worksheet to Its Default Display	Click Custom icon on set of SmartIcons	From View menu, choose Custom - 87%	
Select a Chart Element	Click chart element		
Split the Worksheet into Two Horizontal Panes	Drag horizontal split bar	From View menu, choose Split	
Split the Worksheet into Two Vertical	Drag vertical split bar	From View menu, choose Split	

The icons on the most often used SmartIcon sets are summarized below. Because you can add, delete, and relocate icons on the sets, the number and location of the icons that display on your sets may be different from those shown below.

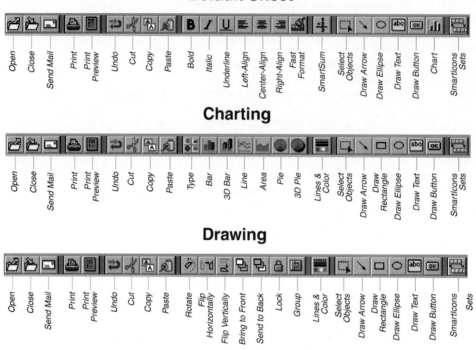

STUDENT ASSIGNMENTS

STUDENT ASSIGNMENT 1
True/False

Instructions: Circle T if the statement if true or F if the statement is false.

T   F   1. If you enter WEEK 1 in cell A1, WEEK 3 in cell A2 and use drag-and-fill to enter a data sequence in the range A1..A4, 1-2-3 assigns cell A4 the value WEEK 4.

T   F   2. To copy a cell or range of cells to a nonadjacent area, use the Copy Right or Copy Down command on the Edit menu.

T   F   3. The format of the @ROUND function is @ROUND(x,n) where x is a value specifying the number of positions to the right or left of the decimal point and n is the value to round.

T F   4. @ROUND(2.67,1) returns the value 2.7 in a cell.
T F   5. An absolute cell reference means a cell's reference will change when a formula containing the cell reference is copied from one cell to another.
T F   6. When you enter cell references into a formula, 1-2-3 assumes they are relative cell references.
T F   7. You can use the F2 function key to change a cell address to an absolute cell reference.
T F   8. To reduce the worksheet display so the entire worksheet can be viewed on the screen, use the Zoom In icon.
T F   9. Drawn objects are graphic objects you can draw on a 1-2-3 worksheet or chart.
T F   10. Once text is entered into a text block, it can be edited at any time by double-clicking anywhere inside the text block.
T F   11. You cannot apply different fonts to text in a text block.
T F   12. By default, 1-2-3 center-aligns text in a text block.
T F   13. To place a border around all edges of a cell, first select the cell where the border will appear, then use the Lines & Color command from the Style menu or the quick menu.
T F   14. You can have as many as 256 worksheets in a single file.
T F   15. A stacked bar chart shows the relationship between two or more values and their totals.
T F   16. The only way to display x-axis labels on a chart is to include the x-axis labels when selecting the range to chart.
T F   17. Use the Headings command from the quick menu or the Chart menu to add or change a chart title.
T F   18. To add a table of values below a chart, place an X in the Include table of values check box located in the Legend dialog box.
T F   19. Once you have printed a worksheet in the landscape orientation, reports will appear in the landscape orientation until you change the setting to portrait orientation.
T F   20. When performing what-if analysis, you normally change the value in one or more cells to answer the questions.

STUDENT ASSIGNMENT 2
Multiple Choice

Instructions: Circle the correct response.

1. To change the settings for an entire worksheet, use the _____ command from the Style menu.
    a. Font & Attributes   c. Worksheet Defaults
    b. Lines & Color   d. Alignment
2. If you enter MONDAY in cell B4 and drag the range B4..E4, cell E4 will contain _____.
    a. Monday   c. THURSDAY
    b. Thursday   d. MONDAY
3. To ensure that whole numbers are used in calculations when the result of a calculation could result in decimals, use the _____.
    a. Comma format in the status bar
    b. @ROUND function in the calculations
    c. Currency format in the status bar
    d. @SUM function in the calculations
4. Cell G11 displays the value 124 in the cell due to the Comma format with zero decimals applied to the original entry of 123.736. The product of G11*10 equals _____.
    a. 1240   c. 1240.74
    b. 1237.40   d. 1237.36
5. When entering a formula, pressing the F4 function key will _____.
    a. change the selected cell to a relative cell reference
    b. confirm the formula into the cell
    c. change the selected cell to an absolute cell reference
    d. delete the formula

STUDENT ASSIGNMENT 2 (continued)

6. To add a double line below each cell in a range, first select the cells in the range, then use the _____ command.
   a. Lines & Color
   b. Border
   c. Font & Attributes
   d. Double Underline

7. Press the _____ function key to change a cell reference to an absolute cell reference.
   a. F1
   b. F2
   c. F3
   d. F4

8. To change the default bar chart to a 3D stacked bar chart, select the chart, then choose the _____ command from the Chart menu or quick menu.
   a. 3D Stacked Bar
   b. 3D Bar
   c. Type
   d. Chart

9. You can add and delete grid lines from a 3D stacked bar chart by choosing the _____ command from the quick menu or the Chart menu.
   a. Set View Preferences
   b. Grids
   c. Lines & Color
   d. Y-Axis

10. When using a worksheet to answer what-if questions, it is possible to vary _____ of the four variables used in the worksheet.
    a. one
    b. two
    c. three
    d. four

STUDENT ASSIGNMENT 3
Drag-and-Fill

Instructions: In the spaces provided, describe the steps required to perform the following tasks.

Task 1: Use drag-and-fill to enter a data sequence in the range A1..G1 with the days of the week. Begin the sequence with Monday. Display the days right-aligned in each cell.

Steps: _____

_____

Task 2: Use drag-and-fill to enter a data sequence in the range F3..F23 with numbers incrementing by 2,000. Begin the sequence with the number 6,000. Display the numbers in the Comma format with zero decimals.

Steps: _____

_____

Task 3: Use drag-and-fill to enter a data sequence in the range D1..D100 with the months of the year. The sequence should be every other month. Begin the sequence with JANUARY. Display the months center-aligned in each cell.

Steps: _____

_____

Task 4: Use drag-and-fill to enter a data sequence in the range C1..C13 with the date of each Monday in the first three months of 1996. The date of the first Monday is 01/02/96. Display each date bold and left-aligned in each cell.

Steps: _____

_____

STUDENT ASSIGNMENT 4
Understanding Dialog Boxes

Instructions: Identify the command that causes the dialog box to display and allow you to make the indicated changes.

CHANGES	COMMAND
1. Change the worksheet font to Times New Roman and increase all column widths to 12.	_____
2. Add a gradient fill pattern to a text block.	_____
3. Add a designer frame to a chart frame.	_____
4. Add a border to a range.	_____
5. Change the alignment of text in a text block.	_____
6. Add grid lines to a chart.	_____
7. Add a table of values to a chart.	_____
8. Change the chart type.	_____
9. Add x-axis labels.	_____
10. Change to landscape orientation for printing reports.	_____

STUDENT ASSIGNMENT 5
Absolute Cell References

Instructions: The worksheet shown in Figure SA3-5 contains a mistake that results in erroneous data. Identify the error and explain how it can be corrected.

Error: _____

_____

_____

Correction: _____

_____

_____

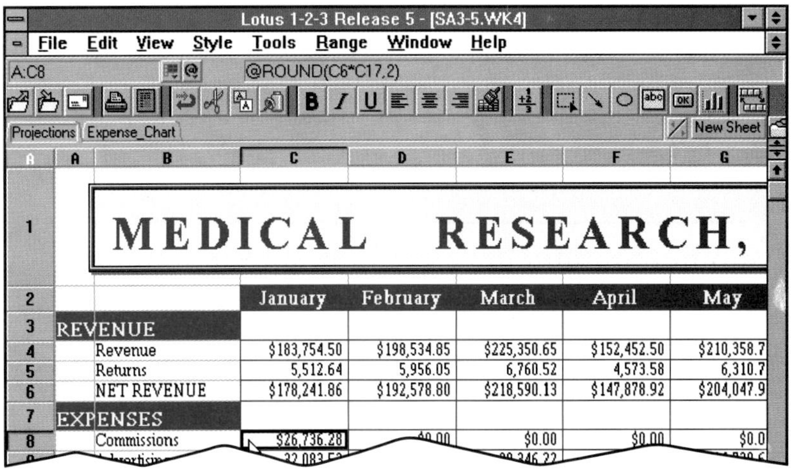

FIGURE SA 3-5

STUDENT ASSIGNMENT 6
Creating and Formatting a Text Block

Instructions: The worksheet shown in Figure SA3-6 on the next page displays a text block. In the spaces provided, describe the steps required to create and format the text block as shown.

(continued)

STUDENT ASSIGNMENT 6 (continued)

Steps to create and format the text block:

_____

_____

_____

_____

_____

_____

_____

FIGURE SA3-6

C O M P U T E R   L A B O R A T O R Y   E X E R C I S E S

COMPUTER LABORATORY EXERCISE 1
Using the Help Menu

Instructions: Perform the following tasks using a personal computer.

1. Start Lotus 1-2-3 Release 5 for Windows.
2. Select the Help menu.
3. Choose Contents from the Help menu.
4. Click the Basics icon from the 1-2-3 Release 5 Help Contents topic.
5. Choose Creating Drawn Objects from the Basics topic.
6. Read the Creating Drawn Objects information, print the topic, and answer the following questions:
   a. When can drawn objects be useful in a 1-2-3 worksheet?

   _____

   _____

   b. Identify and name the two examples of drawn objects that display in the Creating Drawn Objects topic.

   _____

   c. List four things you can do to a drawn object.

   _____

   d. When a drawn object is placed in front of data in a cell, what happens to the data in the cell?

   _____

7. In the Text blocks paragraph, position the mouse pointer over the Tools Draw Text. What shape does the pointer become?

   _____

8. Click the left mouse button. Read the Tools Draw Text information and print the topic.
   a. What is the procedure to create a text block in the default size?

   _____

b. How do you edit a text block?

_____

c. What command would you use to apply color to a text block?

_____

9. To exit from the Help window, choose the Exit command from the File menu.

COMPUTER LABORATORY EXERCISE 2
Entering Formulas

Instructions: Start Lotus 1-2-3 Release 5 for Windows. Open the CLE3-2.WK4 file from the Lotus4 subdirectory on the Student Diskette that accompanies this book. Using the worksheet on your screen and illustrated in Figure CLE3-2, enter the formulas to calculate the expenses, total expenses and net income for the six months. When you have completed this task, format the values in the worksheet, then print the worksheet.

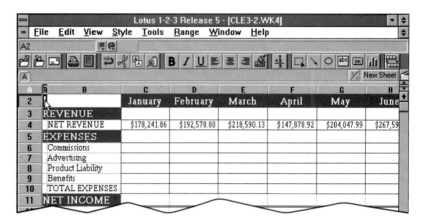

FIGURE CLE3-2

COMPUTER LABORATORY EXERCISE 3
Displaying and Printing a 3D Stacked Bar Chart

Instructions: Start Lotus 1-2-3 Release 5 for Windows. Open the CLE3-3.WK4 file from the Lotus4 subdirectory on the Student Diskette that accompanies this book. Display the range B22..G41. Select the chart and then perform the following tasks:

1. Change the chart to a 3D stacked bar chart.
2. Include a table of values below the chart.
3. Add appropriate titles and axis titles.
4. Add vertical (y) axis grid lines.
5. Print the chart. The chart should look like Figure CLE3-3.
6. Exit 1-2-3.
7. Follow directions from your instructor for turning in this assignment.

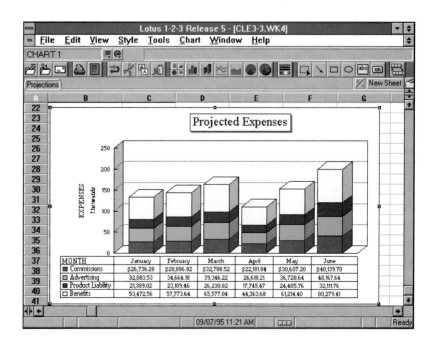

FIGURE CLE3-3

COMPUTER LABORATORY ASSIGNMENT 1
Creating a Current and Projected Salaries Report

Purpose: To provide experience in using Lotus 1-2-3 Release 5 for Windows to create a worksheet that requires entering labels, values, formulas, calculating sums, saving and printing the worksheet, and providing answers to what-if questions.

Problem: Create a worksheet that calculates the current and projected salaries based on a percentage allocated to each department. The current salary proposed for full-time employees and part-time employees is shown in the table.

The worksheet is shown in Figure CLA3-1.

EMPLOYEE	CURRENT SALARY
Full-Time Employees	$1,250,000
Part-Time Employees	$750,000

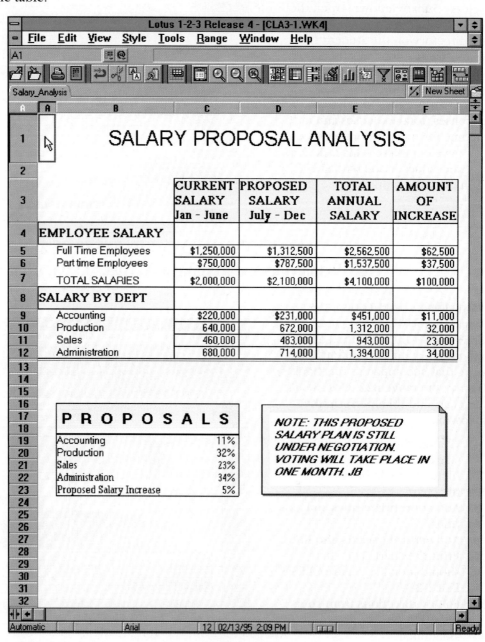

FIGURE CLE3-1

Instructions:

1. Change the font of the worksheet to Times New Roman. Create a worksheet in the format shown in Figure CLA3-1 using the numbers from the table.
2. Create a text block for the Proposals title. Enter the labels and values in the Proposals section of the worksheet. Format the Proposals section as shown in Figure CLA3-1.
3. Perform rounding on all calculations as required. When rounding, round the values to whole numbers.
4. On the worksheet, calculate the proposed salary for July - Dec for full-time employees by multiplying the current salary for Jan - June by the salary increase percentage found in the Proposals section of the worksheet.
5. On the worksheet, calculate the total annual salary for full-time employees by adding the current salary Jan - June to the proposed salary July - Dec.
6. On the worksheet, calculate the amount of increase for full-time employees by subtracting the current salary Jan - June from the proposed salary July - Dec.
7. Copy the formulas assigned to the full-time employees in the range D5..F5 to the part-time employees in row 6.
8. Calculate the total salaries by summing the values for full-time employees and part-time employees for the current salary Jan - June, the proposed salary July - Dec, the total annual salary, and the amount of increase.
9. Calculate the current salary Jan - June for accounting, production, sales, and administration by multiplying the total salaries for Jan - June by the accounting, production, sales, and administration percentages, respectively, found in the Proposals section of the worksheet.
10. Format the worksheet as shown. The column width for column A is 3, for column B is 20, for column C is 11, for column D is 13, for column E is 13, for column F is 11. The row height for row 1 is 55, for row 3 is 50, for row 4 is 25, for row 7 is 20, and for row 8 is 25.
11. Create the text block to the right of the Proposals section that contains NOTE: THIS PROPOSED SALARY PLAN IS STILL UNDER NEGOTIATION. VOTING WILL TAKE PLACE IN ONE MONTH. JB. Format the text block as shown.
12. Save the worksheet you create on a diskette. Use a file name consisting of the initials of your first and last names followed by the assignment number. Example: KS3-1.
13. Print the worksheet you have created on a single page. Check whether the worksheet will fit on a single page by using Print Preview. If it will not fit, then change the Page Setup to print in landscape orientation.
14. If the salary increase is 10%, what will be the total amount of increase for full-time employees?

_____

15. Enter the following percentages for each of the departments in the Proposals section of the worksheet and answer the following questions (assume salary increase is 10%).
    Accounting: 15%   Sales: 20%
    Production: 35%   Administration: 30%
    a. What will be the proposed salary for Accounting?

_____

    b. What will be the proposed salary for Production?

_____

    c. What will be the proposed salary for Sales?

_____

    d. What will be the proposed salary for Administration?

_____

16. Follow directions from your instructor for turning in this assignment.

COMPUTER LABORATORY ASSIGNMENT 2
Creating a Six-Month Budget Report and 3D Stacked Bar Chart

Purpose:　To provide experience in using Lotus 1-2-3 Release 5 for Windows to create a worksheet that requires entering labels, values, formulas, and functions, calculating sums, saving and printing the worksheet, charting data from the worksheet, and providing answers to what-if questions.

Problem:　Create a six-month budget report where the expenses are calculated as percentages of the total income. Create a 3D stacked bar chart from the expense data in the worksheet. The income is shown in the table below.

INCOME	JULY	AUGUST	SEPTEMBER	OCTOBER	NOVEMBER	DECEMBER
Service Fees	19378.85	17435.50	12075.50	10850.50	11850.25	15795.50
Consultations	4844.71	4358.88	3018.88	2712.63	2962.56	3948.88

The worksheet is shown in Figure CLA3-2a.

FIGURE CLA3-2a

Instructions:

1. Change the font of the worksheet to Times New Roman. Set the column width default to 11. Create a worksheet in the format shown in Figure CLA3-2a using the numbers from the table.
2. Create and format the text block as shown.
3. On the worksheet, calculate the total for each item of income (Service Fees and Consultations) by adding the income for July, August, September, October, November, and December.
4. Calculate the total income by adding the service fees and consultations values for July, August, September, October, November, December, and the TOTAL column.
5. Calculate the expenses for advertising, salaries, supplies, truck, and other by multiplying the total income for each month by the advertising, salaries, supplies, truck, and other percentages, respectively, found in the Budgeted Percentages section of the worksheet. Perform rounding as required.

6. Calculate the total expenses for each month and the total for all expenses by adding the advertising, salaries, supplies, truck, and other expenses for each month and for the TOTAL column.

7. Calculate the net income by subtracting the total expenses for each month and for the TOTAL column from the total income for each month and for the TOTAL column.

8. Format the worksheet as shown. The column width for column A is 3 and for column B is 15. The row height for row 2 is 17, for row 3 is 20, for row 7 is 20, for row 14 is 30, and for row 17 is 22.

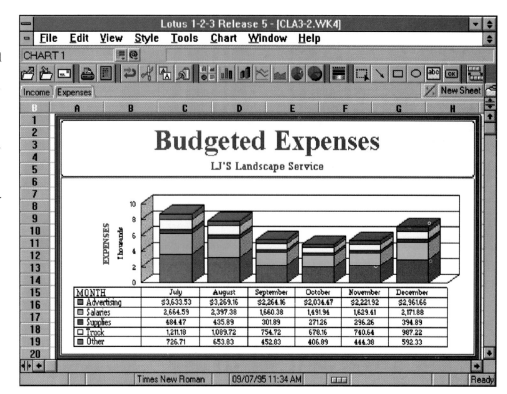

FIGURE CLA3-2b

9. Save the worksheet you create on a diskette. Use a file name consisting of the initials of your first and last names followed by the assignment number. Example: KS3-2.

10. Print the worksheet you have created on a single page. Check whether the worksheet will fit on a single page by using Print Preview. If it will not fit, then change the Page Setup to print in landscape orientation.

11. Insert a new sheet and create the 3D stacked bar chart in Figure CLA3-2b from the expenses contained on the worksheet. Include a table of values below the chart.

12. Format the 3D stacked bar chart as shown in Figure CLA3-2b. The chart title, Budgeted Expenses, is Times New Roman, 32 point bold. The chart title, LJ's Landscape Service, is Times New Roman, 12 point bold.

13. Save the worksheet and new chart using the same file name as in step 9.

14. Print the chart in portrait orientation.

15. Enter the following percentages on the worksheet for each of the budgeted expenses and answer the following questions:

    Advertising: 13%   Supplies: 5%   Other: 2%
    Salaries: 10%   Truck: 4%

a. What is the total net income for the six-month period as shown in the worksheet?

b. What is the advertising expense for December? _____

16. Enter the following percentages on the worksheet for each of the budgeted expenses and answer the following questions:

    Advertising: 35%   Supplies: 15%   Other: 12%
    Salaries: 25%   Truck: 14%

a. What are the total expenses for the six-month period? _____

b. What is the net income for the six-month period as shown in the worksheet?

17. Follow directions from your instructor for turning in this assignment.

COMPUTER LABORATORY ASSIGNMENT 3
Creating an International Manufacturing
Projections Report and 3D Stacked Bar Chart

Purpose: To provide experience in using Lotus 1-2-3 Release 5 for Windows to create a worksheet that requires entering labels, values, formulas, and functions, calculating sums, saving and printing the worksheet, charting data from the worksheet, and providing answers to what-if questions.

Problem: Create an International Manufacturing Projections Report where the sales growth, returns, and expenses are calculated from values in an Assumptions Table. Create a 3D stacked bar chart from the expense data in the worksheet. The worksheet is shown in Figure CLA3-3a.

	A	B	C	D	E	F	G
1		*INTERNATIONAL MANUFACTURING*					
2			QUARTER 1	QUARTER 2	QUARTER 3	QUARTER 4	YEAR TO DATE
3		*REVENUE*					
4		Sales	$250,000	$312,500	$390,625	$488,281	$1,441,406
5		Returns	7,500	9,375	11,719	14,648	43,242
6		NET SALES	$242,500	$303,125	$378,906	$473,633	$1,398,164
7		*EXPENSES*					
8		COGS	$84,875	$106,094	$132,617	$165,772	$489,358
9		Advertising	24,250	30,313	37,891	47,363	139,817
10		Salary	25,750	25,750	25,750	25,750	103,000
11		Rent	15,560	15,560	15,560	15,560	62,240
12		Total Operating Expenses	$150,435	$177,717	$211,818	$254,445	$794,415
13		*OPERATING INCOME*	$92,065	$125,408	$167,088	$219,188	$603,749
14							
15							
16		**ASSUMPTIONS TABLE**					
17		First Quarter Sales	$250,000				
18		Sales Growth	25%				
19		Returns	3%				
20		COGS	35%				
21		Advertising	10%				
22		Salary	$25,750				
23		Rent	$15,560				
24							

FIGURE CLA3-3a

Instructions:

1. Change the default font of the worksheet to Times New Roman. Set the column width default to 14. Create a worksheet in the format shown in Figure CLA3-3a.
2. Create and format the International Manufacturing text block as shown. The row height for row 1 is 80.
3. Create a text block for the Assumptions Table title. Enter the labels and values in the Assumptions Table. Format the Assumptions Table as shown in Figure CLA3-3a.
4. Perform rounding on all calculations as required. When rounding, round the values to whole numbers.

5. On the worksheet, calculate quarter 1 sales by entering the address of the first quarter sales from the Assumptions Table (C17) in cell C4.
6. On the worksheet, calculate quarter 2 sales by multiplying quarter 1 sales times the sales growth percentage found in the Assumptions Table of the worksheet.
7. Calculate returns by multiplying the sales for each quarter by the returns percentage, found in the Assumptions Table of the worksheet.
8. Calculate net sales by subtracting returns from sales for each quarter.
9. Calculate the year-to-date value for sales, returns, and net sales by adding the respective rows for quarter 1, quarter 2, quarter 3, and quarter 4.
10. Calculate the expenses for the COGS and advertising by multiplying the net sales for each quarter by the cost of goods sold and advertising percentages, respectively, found in the Assumptions Table of the worksheet. Calculate the expenses for salary and rent by entering the absolute address of the salary and rent values, respectively, found in the Assumptions Table of the worksheet.
11. Calculate the total operating expenses for each quarter and the year to date for all expenses by adding the COGS, advertising, salary, and rent expenses for each quarter and for the YEAR TO DATE column.
12. Calculate the operating income by subtracting the total operating expenses for each quarter and for the YEAR TO DATE column from the net sales for each quarter and for the YEAR TO DATE column.
13. Format the worksheet as shown. The column width for column A is 3, for column B is 20. The row height for row 2 is 33, for row 3 is 25, for row 7 is 25 and for row 13 is 25.
14. Save the worksheet you create on a diskette. Use a file name consisting of the initials of your first and last names followed by the assignment number. Example: KS3-3.
15. Print the worksheet you have created on a single page. Check whether the worksheet will fit on a single page by using Print Preview. If it will not fit, then change the Page Setup to print in landscape orientation.
16. Insert a new sheet and create the 3D stacked bar chart in Figure CLA3-3b from the expenses contained on the worksheet. Include a table of values below the chart.
17. Format the 3D stacked bar chart as shown in Figure CLA3-3b. The chart title, PROJECTIONS, is Times New Roman, 32 point bold.
18. Save the worksheet and new chart using the same file name as in step 14.
19. Print the chart in portrait orientation.
20. Answer the following questions based on the worksheet.
a. If sales growth is 10%, how is the year-to-date operating income affected?

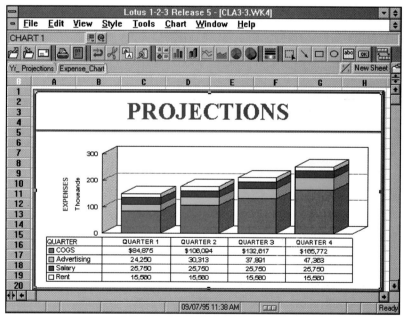

FIGURE CLA3-3b

b. Assume sales growth at 25%. What is the effect on the year-to-date operating income if the returns decrease to 2%?

c. Assume returns at 3%. What is the effect on the year-to-date operating income if the salary doubles?

21. Follow directions from your instructor for turning in this assignment.

COMPUTER LABORATORY ASSIGNMENT 4
Creating a Current Employment and Projected
Employment by Industry Report and 3D Stacked Bar Chart

Purpose: To provide experience in using Lotus 1-2-3 Release 5 for Windows to create a worksheet that requires entering labels, values, formulas, and functions, calculating sums, saving and printing the worksheet, charting data from the worksheet, and providing answers to what-if questions.

Problem: Develop a worksheet that calculates the projected employment for each of the next five years. The Current Employment and Projected Increase by Industry are specified in the table below.

INDUSTRY	CURRENT EMPLOYMENT 1995	PROJECTED INCREASE 1996-2000
Agriculture	255,770	0.10
Manufacturing	445,870	0.05
Medical	425,650	0.20
Real Estate	235,980	0.15
Technical	545,550	0.25

Instructions:

1. Design and create a worksheet that shows the current employment for 1996 and projected employment for each industry for each of the next five years (1997 - 2001).
2. Format the worksheet appropriately.
3. Create a 3D stacked bar chart from the industries' current employment and projected employment contained on the worksheet.
4. Format the chart appropriately.
5. Save the worksheet and chart you create on disk. Use a file name consisting of the initials of your first and last names followed by the assignment number. Example: KS3-4.
6. Print the worksheet and chart you have created. Follow directions from your instructor for turning in this assignment.

1996 - 1997

Round
/nt

B

$\mathcal{L}$OTUS 1-2-3 RELEASE 5 FOR $\mathcal{W}$INDOWS

P R O J E C T   F O U R

MULTIPLE WORKSHEETS

OBJECTIVES   You will have mastered the material in this project when you can:

- Copy data between multiple worksheets
- Use Group mode to format multiple worksheets
- Use the Insert command to insert a new worksheet before the current worksheet
- Create formulas that refer to cells in multiple worksheets
- Add a footnote to a chart
- Display data labels on a pie chart
- Explode a 3D pie slice
- Add an arrow to a chart
- Insert page breaks in multiple worksheets

▶ INTRODUCTION

Project 3 introduced the concept of multiple worksheets by adding a chart to the second worksheet. Rather than having one large worksheet, you can divide a worksheet into smaller segments and place the segments in different worksheets in the same file.

You can also use multiple worksheets to consolidate information. For example, if you were tracking company sales for each month of the year, you could use multiple worksheets that contained worksheets for each month. Then, you could add all the total sales for each month and place the answer in a summary worksheet. Thus, the one file would contain thirteen worksheets; one for each month of the year and one for the summary worksheet.

▶ PROJECT FOUR

The four worksheets that are to be created in Project 4 are illustrated in Figure 4-1 on the next page. The file contains four worksheets: the Imperial Lighting Balance Sheet, the Universal Electronics Balance Sheet, the Imperial Lighting and Universal Electronics Consolidated Balance Sheet, and the Total Assets 3D pie chart.

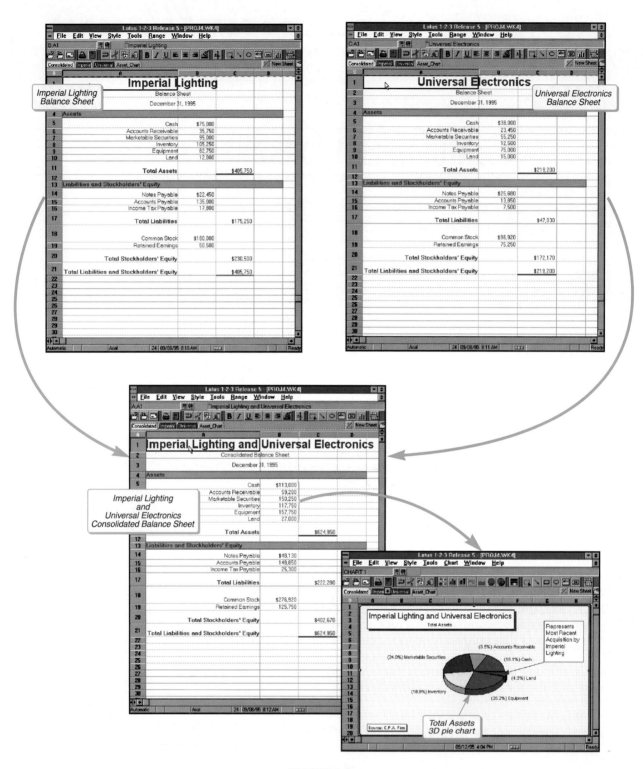

FIGURE 4-1

For Project 4, you will first create the Imperial Lighting balance sheet and the Universal Electronics balance sheet. Each balance sheet illustrates the financial status of the respective company as of the end of the year. You will then create a summary, or consolidated, balance sheet showing the combined financial status of the two corporations. Once the consolidated balance sheet is created, you will chart the total assets from the consolidated balance sheet.

A **balance sheet** is a financial report showing the status of a corporation's assets, liabilities, and owner's equity on a given date. An **asset** is any property owned by a corporation. For example, in Figure 4-1 on the previous page, the balance sheet for Imperial Lighting lists the following assets: Cash ($75,000), Accounts Receivable ($35,750), Marketable Securities ($95,000), Inventory ($105,250), Equipment ($82,750) and Land ($12,000).

A **liability** is an amount owed by a corporation to its creditors. The balance sheet for Imperial Lighting lists the following liabilities: Notes Payable ($22,450), Accounts Payable ($135,000), and Income Tax Payable ($17,800).

Stockholders' equity represents the ownership interest of the stockholders in the corporation. On the balance sheet for the Imperial Lighting, the stockholders' equity section consists of the Common Stock ($180,000) sold by the corporation, and the Retained Earnings ($50,500), which is income retained by the corporation.

Once the balance sheets for both Imperial Lighting and Universal Electronics are completed, you will create a summary, or consolidated, balance sheet for the two companies. A **consolidated balance sheet** is a balance sheet that brings together all assets, liabilities, and stockholders' equity of two or more corporations. You create the consolidated balance sheet by entering and copying formulas that sum the data from the other two worksheets. For example, the cash value in cell B5 of the Consolidated worksheet is the sum of cell B5 of the Imperial worksheet and cell B5 of the Universal worksheet.

Finally, you will create a three-dimensional pie chart illustrating the total assets from the Consolidated worksheet. The pie chart in Figure 4-1 displays the total assets from the Consolidated worksheet for the Imperial Lighting and Universal Electronics corporations.

Each slice of the pie represents an asset and is identified by the corresponding name of the asset and the percentage each asset represents of the total assets. From the chart you can tell that the asset, Equipment, consumes the largest portion of the total assets. One of the slices, Land, is exploded, or slightly separated from the chart. A text block displays on the chart with an arrow pointing to the exploded pie slice. Recall from Project 3 that a **text block** is a drawn object that contains text.

Worksheet Preparation Steps

To prepare the worksheets and pie chart in Figure 4-1, the following worksheet preparation steps are provided as an overview.

1. Start Lotus 1-2-3 Release 5 for Windows.
2. Enter the labels and values for the Imperial balance sheet.
3. Copy the labels and values from the Imperial balance sheet to the Universal balance sheet.
4. Enter the values for the Universal balance sheet.
5. Copy the labels from the Universal balance sheet to the consolidated balance sheet.
6. Enter formulas on the Consolidated worksheet to sum the values from the Imperial worksheet and the Universal worksheet.
7. Format the multiple worksheets (increase the font size of the title, align the labels, format the values, add double-underlining, change column widths and row heights, and apply color and borders).
8. Create the 3D pie chart.
9. Print the multiple worksheets.

The following pages contain a detailed explanation of each of these steps.

▶ STARTING LOTUS 1-2-3 RELEASE 5 FOR WINDOWS

o start Lotus 1-2-3 Release 5 for Windows, follow the steps you used in previous projects. These steps are reviewed below.

TO START LOTUS 1-2-3 RELEASE 5 FOR WINDOWS

Step 1: From Program Manager, open the Lotus Applications group window.
Step 2: Double-click the Lotus 1-2-3 Release 5 program-item icon.

▶ CREATING MULTIPLE WORKSHEETS

he first step in creating the multiple worksheets in Project 4 is to enter the worksheet titles and row titles for the Imperial Lighting balance sheet.

TO ENTER THE WORKSHEET TITLES AND ROW TITLES

Step 1: Select cell A1. Enter `Imperial Lighting`. Enter `Balance Sheet` in cell A2 and `December 31, 1995` in cell A3. Enter `Assets` in cell A4, `Cash` in cell A5, `Accounts Receivable` in cell A6, `Marketable Securities` in cell A7, `Inventory` in cell A8, `Equipment` in cell A9, `Land` in cell A10, and `Total Assets` in cell A11.
Step 2: Select cell A13. Enter `Liabilities and Stockholders' Equity`. Enter `Notes Payable` in cell A14. Enter `Accounts Payable` in cell A15, `Income Tax Payable` in cell A16, and `Total Liabilities` in cell A17.

Step 3: Enter `Common Stock` in cell A18, `Retained Earnings` in cell A19, `Total Stockholders' Equity` in cell A20, and `Total Liabilities and Stockholders' Equity` in cell A21. Press the HOME key.

The worksheet titles and row titles display as shown in Figure 4-2.

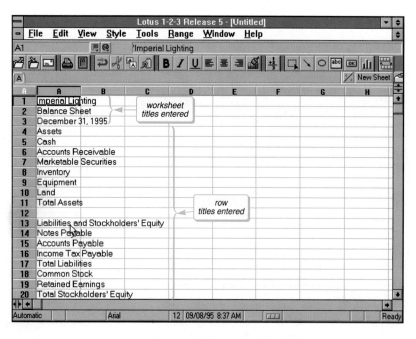

FIGURE 4-2

The next step is to enter the values for the Imperial Lighting balance sheet. To display the labels, the width of column A is increased to 16 characters.

TO ENTER VALUES

Step 1: Drag the column border between column A and column B to the right until column A is a width of 16 characters. Select cell B5. Enter 75000. Enter 35750 in cell B6, 95000 in cell B7, 105250 in cell B8, 82750 in cell B9, and 12000 in cell B10.

Step 2: Select cell B14. Enter 22450. Enter 135000 in cell B15 and 17800 in cell B16.

Step 3: Select cell B18. Enter 180000. Enter 50500 in cell B19.

The worksheet values display as shown in Figure 4-3.

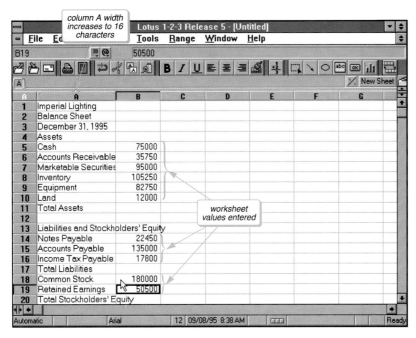

FIGURE 4-3

The last step in creating the Imperial Lighting balance sheet is to enter the totals. Total assets in cell C11 is calculated by entering the @SUM function to sum the range B5..B10. Total Liabilities in cell C17 is calculated by entering the @SUM function to sum the liabilities in the range B14..B16. Calculate Total Stockholders' Equity in cell C20 by summing the range B18..B19. Total Liabilities and Stockholders' Equity in cell C21 is the sum of cell C17 and cell C20.

TO CALCULATE TOTALS

Step 1: Select cell C11. Click the @function selector in the edit line. When the @Function menu displays, choose SUM. Select the range to be summed, B5..B10, and click the Confirm button or press the ENTER key to complete the @SUM function.

Step 2: Select cell C17. Click the @function selector in the edit line. When the @Function menu displays, choose SUM. Select the range to be summed, B14..B16, and click the Confirm button or press the ENTER key.

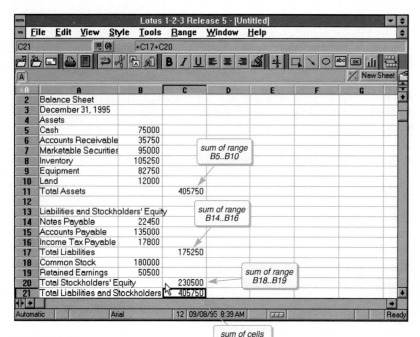

FIGURE 4-4

3D Formula

Step 3: Select cell C20. Click the @function selector in the edit line. When the @Function menu displays on screen, choose SUM. Select the range to be summed, B18..B19, and click the Confirm button or press the ENTER key.

Step 4: Use the down scroll arrow to view cell C21. Select cell C21. Type a plus sign (+). Select cell C17, type a plus sign (+), select cell C20, and click the Confirm button or press the ENTER key to complete the formula.

The completed worksheet displays as shown in Figure 4-4.

Copying Data Between Worksheets Using Drag-and-Drop

Now that you have created the Imperial balance sheet, you can start to build the Universal worksheet with a copy of the Imperial balance sheet. Recall from Project 3 that you can copy data to a nonadjacent area in a worksheet by using the drag-and-drop feature. You can also use drag-and-drop to copy data between worksheets. Perform the following steps to copy the contents of worksheet A to a new worksheet B inserted after worksheet A.

TO COPY DATA BETWEEN WORKSHEETS USING DRAG-AND-DROP ▼

STEP 1 ▶

Use the up scroll arrow to view cell A1. Select the range A1..C21. Move the mouse pointer to the upper right border of the selected range so the mouse pointer changes to a hand. Press and hold down the CTRL key.

The range to copy is selected (Figure 4-5). When you move the mouse pointer to the border of the selected range and press and hold down the CTRL key, the mouse pointer changes to a hand with a plus sign. This mouse pointer shape indicates 1-2-3 is ready to perform drag-and-drop.

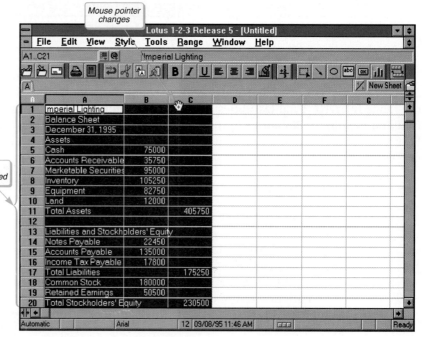

FIGURE 4-5

STEP 2 ▶

While holding down the CTRL key, press and hold down the left mouse button. When the mouse pointer changes to a fist with a plus sign holding a range, drag the fist to the New Sheet button..

When the mouse pointer is positioned on a New Sheet button, 1-2-3 inserts a second worksheet to the file and places the cell pointer in cell A1 of worksheet B (Figure 4-6).

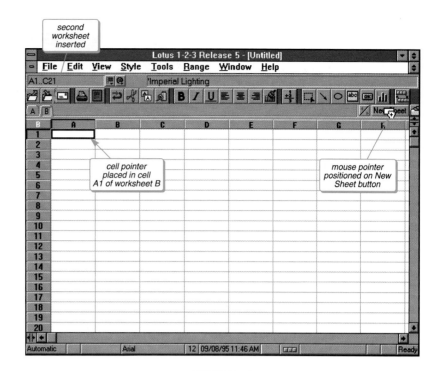

FIGURE 4-6

STEP 3 ▶

Move the mouse pointer onto the worksheet. When a dashed outline displays, drag the dashed outline to the range A1..C21 of worksheet B.

As you drag, the selected range displays a dashed outline. The dashed outline is positioned over the range A1..C21 in worksheet B (Figure 4-7).

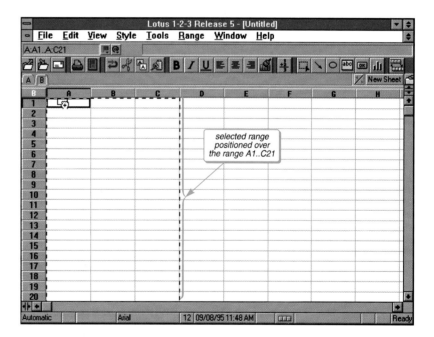

FIGURE 4-7

STEP 4 ▶

Release the left mouse button. Then, release the CTRL key. Select cell A1 to remove the highlight.

1-2-3 places a copy of the data from worksheet A in the range A1..C21 in worksheet B (Figure 4-8).

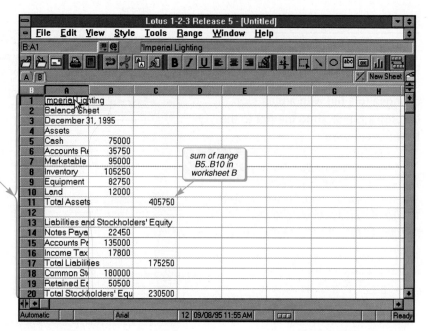

FIGURE 4-8

Notice in Figure 4-6 on the previous page that it was not necessary to click the New Sheet button to insert a new worksheet. When using the drag-and-drop feature to copy data between worksheets, merely positioning the mouse pointer over the New Sheet button inserts a new sheet.

Notice several important points when copying data. First, when 1-2-3 copies formulas containing addresses between worksheets, the addresses automatically adjust to the new location in the worksheets. For example, in Figure 4-8, the total assets in cell C11 is the sum of the range B5..B10 in worksheet B.

Second, in Figure 4-8, 1-2-3 did not copy the column width of the selected range in worksheet A. The width of column A in worksheet B is the default width of 9 characters.

Third, if you drag-and-drop over existing data, 1-2-3 displays a dialog box warning that you are dragging a range to a location that already contains data. If you complete the operation, 1-2-3 will write over the existing data.

To copy data to another existing worksheet in a file, select the range to copy and position the mouse pointer on the border of the selection. When the mouse pointer changes to a hand, press the CTRL key, drag the fist to the desired worksheet *tab*, and then to the location on the worksheet.

In the previous example, using the drag-and-drop feature copies data from one worksheet to another worksheet. If you want to **move data** to another worksheet, perform the following steps instead of copying the data.

TO MOVE DATA TO A NEW WORKSHEET BY USING DRAG-AND-DROP

Step 1: Select the range to be moved.

Step 2: Position the mouse pointer on the border of the selection until the mouse pointer changes to a hand.

Step 3: Click the left mouse button and drag the fist to the New Sheet button.

Step 4: Drag the dashed outline to the desired location. Then release the left mouse button.

The data is removed from its original location and appears only in its new location. This is basically the same procedure that was used to copy data between worksheets, except the CTRL key is not used to move data between worksheets.

Moving data can affect formulas in different ways. If you move cells containing formulas and the cells the formulas refer to, the formulas are adjusted relative to their new worksheet location. If you move a formula, but not the data it refers to, the references in the formula do not change. For example, if only cell C11 in worksheet A was moved to cell C11 in worksheet B, and not the range C11 refers to, the references in the formula in the new location do not change and remain @SUM(A:B5..A:B11).

Entering the Worksheet Title and Data for the Universal Electronics Balance Sheet

The next step in creating the Universal Electronics balance sheet is to enter the worksheet title and values. To complete the worksheet, enter the worksheet title in cell A1 and enter the correct values. Follow these steps to enter the label and values for the Universal balance sheet.

TO ENTER LABEL AND VALUES

Step 1: Select cell A1 in worksheet B. Type `Universal Electronics.`
Step 2: Drag the column border between column A and column B to the right until column A is a width of 16 characters.
Step 3: Select cell B5. Enter `38000`. Enter `23450` in cell B6, `55250` in cell B7, `12500` in cell B8, `75000` in cell B9, and `15000` in cell B10.
Step 4: Select cell B14. Enter `25680`. Enter `13850` in cell B15 and `7500` in cell B16.
Step 5: Select cell B18. Enter `96920`. Enter `75250` in cell B19.

The completed Universal Electronics balance sheet displays as shown in Figure 4-9.

Notice in Figure 4-9 as you enter the values in the range B5..B10, B14..B16, and B18..B19, 1-2-3 recalculates the sums in cell C11, C17, C20, and C21. When you copied the data from worksheet A to worksheet B, the formulas in cells C11, C17, C20, and C21 were also copied and the cell references changed relative to the new location.

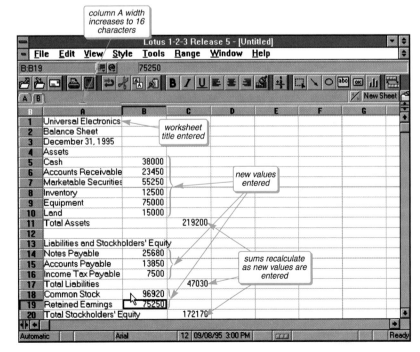

FIGURE 4-9

Naming the Worksheets

Recall from Project 3, you can name a worksheet tab with a more meaningful name to represent the data contained in the worksheet. Perform the following steps to name worksheet A, Imperial, and worksheet B, Universal.

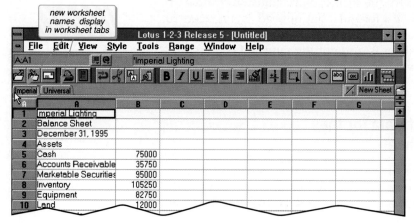

FIGURE 4-10

TO NAME WORKSHEETS

Step 1: Double-click the tab for worksheet B. Type `Universal` and press the ENTER key.

Step 2: Double-click the tab for worksheet A. Type `Imperial` and press the ENTER key.

_____

The worksheet tabs display as shown in Figure 4-10.

▶ CREATING A CONSOLIDATED WORKSHEET

The Consolidated worksheet contains a summary of the Imperial worksheet and the Universal worksheet. For example, in Figure 4-1 on page L210, the Cash entry $113,000 in the Consolidated worksheet represents the sum of cash from the Imperial worksheet ($75,000) and cash from the Universal worksheet ($38,000). The accounts receivable entry in the Consolidated worksheet represents the sum of accounts receivable from the Imperial worksheet (35,750) and accounts receivable from the Universal worksheet (23,450).

The steps to create the Consolidated worksheet are: (1) insert a worksheet before the Imperial worksheet; (2) add the worksheet name, Consolidated, to the new worksheet tab and copy the labels from the Imperial worksheet to the Consolidated worksheet; and (3) enter the formulas to sum the values in the Imperial worksheet and the Universal worksheet. The sections that follow accomplish these tasks.

Inserting a Worksheet Before the Current Worksheet

The next step is to insert a new worksheet before the Imperial worksheet and create the Consolidated balance sheet. You have previously used the New Sheet button below the set of SmartIcons to insert a new worksheet after the current worksheet. To insert a new worksheet before a current worksheet or to insert a specified number of worksheets before or after a current worksheet, you must use **the Insert command** on the Edit menu. Using the Insert command displays a dialog box so you can enter the number of worksheets you want 1-2-3 to insert before or after the current worksheet.

TO INSERT A WORKSHEET BEFORE THE CURRENT WORKSHEET ▼

STEP 1 ►

Ensure the cell pointer is located in cell A1 of the Imperial worksheet. Select the Edit menu by pointing to the Edit menu and clicking the left mouse button. Point to the Insert command.

The cell pointer is located in cell A1 of the Imperial worksheet (Figure 4-11). 1-2-3 displays the Edit menu. The mouse pointer points to the Insert command.

FIGURE 4-11

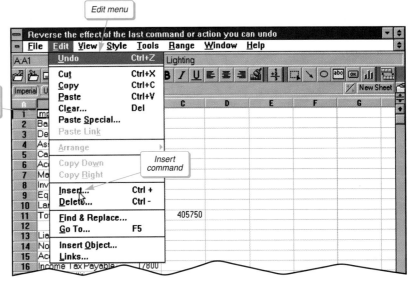

STEP 2 ►

Choose the Insert command from the Edit menu. When the Insert dialog box displays on the screen, point to the Sheet option button.

1-2-3 displays the Insert dialog box (Figure 4-12). The Column option inserts an entire column in a worksheet. The Row option inserts an entire row in a worksheet. The Sheet option inserts an entire worksheet in the file. The Insert selection check box inserts a range of cells in a worksheet.

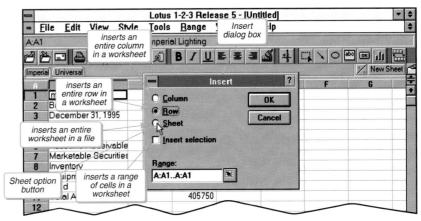

FIGURE 4-12

STEP 3 ►

Click the left mouse button. Select the Before option by pointing to the Before option button and clicking the left mouse button. Point to the OK button in the Insert dialog box.

When you select the Sheet option, the Insert selection check box is replaced with the Before option button, the After option button, and the Quantity text box (Figure 4-13). The Before option inserts the quantity of worksheets specified in

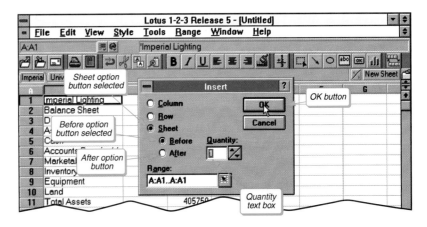

FIGURE 4-13

the Quantity text box before the current worksheet. The After option inserts the quantity of worksheets specified in the Quantity text box after the current worksheet. A maximum of 255 worksheets can be inserted in one file.

STEP 4 ▶

Choose the OK button in the Insert dialog box.

1-2-3 inserts one worksheet before the Imperial worksheet (Figure 4-14). The new worksheet becomes worksheet A. The Imperial worksheet becomes the second worksheet in the file (worksheet B) and the Universal worksheet becomes the third worksheet in the file (worksheet C).

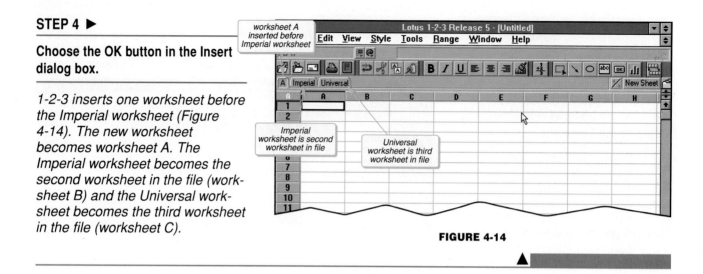

FIGURE 4-14

Copying Data Between Worksheets Using the Copy and Paste Icons

The next step is to name the Consolidated balance sheet worksheet tab and enter the labels. Because the labels in the Consolidated worksheet are exactly the same as the Imperial worksheet, you can copy the labels from the Imperial worksheet to the Consolidated worksheet. The formulas in the Consolidated worksheet, however, are not the same and are not copied.

Another way to copy data is to use the Copy and Paste icons on the set of SmartIcons. The **Copy icon** (⬚) copies the selected cells from the worksheet and copies them onto the Clipboard. The **Clipboard** is a temporary storage area Microsoft Windows uses to store data. Once the selected cells are on the Clipboard, the **Paste icon** (⬚) can be used to paste the Clipboard contents to any area of any worksheet as often as required. The data being copied is called the **source**; the location to which you are copying the data is called the **destination**. Perform the following steps to copy the labels from the Imperial worksheet to worksheet A and name the worksheet tab.

TO COPY DATA BETWEEN WORKSHEETS USING THE COPY AND PASTE ICONS ▼

STEP 1 ▶

Double-click the worksheet tab for worksheet A and type Consolidated. **Click the Imperial worksheet tab. Select the range to copy – A1..A21. Then, point to the Copy icon on the set of SmartIcons.**

1-2-3 enters the new worksheet name in the worksheet tab. 1-2-3 highlights the range to copy (Figure 4-15). The mouse pointer points to the Copy icon on the set of SmartIcons.

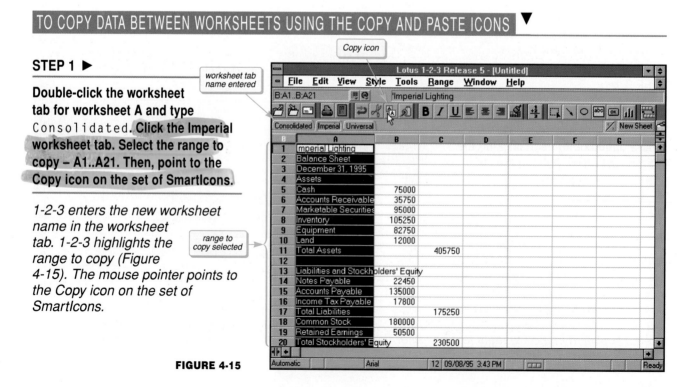

FIGURE 4-15

STEP 2 ▶

Click the Copy icon on the set of SmartIcons. Click the Consolidated worksheet tab. Then, point to the Paste icon on the set of SmartIcons.

1-2-3 copies the selected range to the Clipboard and displays an instruction in the title bar explaining how to paste the data from the Clipboard (Figure 4-16). The cell pointer is located in cell A1 of the Consolidated worksheet. The mouse pointer points to the Paste icon.

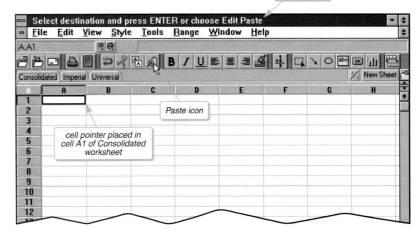

FIGURE 4-16

STEP 3 ▶

Click the Paste icon on the set of SmartIcons. Then, drag the column border between column A and column B to the right until column A is a width of 16 characters. Select cell A1. Type Imperial Lighting and Universal Electronics. **Select cell A2. Type** Consolidated Balance Sheet.

1-2-3 pastes the contents of the Clipboard into the Consolidated worksheet (Figure 4-17). The worksheet title is entered in cell A1 and the worksheet subtitle is entered in cell A2. Column A displays with the width of 16 characters.

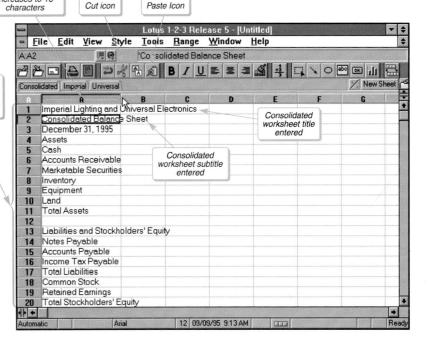

FIGURE 4-17

Consider several important features when using the Copy and Paste icons. First, when using the Paste icon to paste data, you need to select only the top left cell of the destination range. 1-2-3 treats the top left cell as the first cell of the destination range and pastes all the data accordingly.

Second, when using the Paste icon, 1-2-3 writes over any existing data in the destination range without displaying a warning dialog box. If you accidentally paste over existing data, you can undo this activity by clicking the Undo icon on the set of SmartIcons.

Third, you can use the Paste icon to copy data from the Clipboard to as many locations as you want. The copied data remains on the Clipboard until you replace it by using the Copy icon again.

If you want to move data from one worksheet to another, the Cut icon and Paste icon are used. When you **move data**, the source data is removed from its original location and reappears in the destination range. The **Cut icon** ( ) removes the selected cells from the worksheet and copies them onto the Clipboard. Once the selected cells are on the Clipboard, they can be pasted into any worksheet as often as required.

The Copy, Cut, and Paste commands are also found on the Edit menu located on the main menu bar.

Creating Three-Dimensional Formulas

The next step in creating the Consolidated worksheet is to create a formula to sum the values from the Imperial worksheet and the Universal worksheet. You will use the @SUM function to sum the value in cell B5 of the Imperial worksheet and the value in cell B5 of the Universal worksheet and display the result in cell B5 of the Consolidated worksheet.

In previous projects, you worked with ranges in a single worksheet. For example, the range A1..B1 in worksheet A, encompasses cells A1 and B1. The range address does not contain the worksheet letter when there is only one worksheet in a file. To sum the values in two worksheets requires selecting a 3D (three-dimensional) range. A **(3D) three-dimensional range** includes the same cells in two or more contiguous worksheets. The address of a 3D range includes the worksheet letters in the cell addresses. For example, the 3D range A:A1..B:B1 contains cells A1 and B1 in worksheet A and cells A1 and B1 in worksheet B.

To select a 3D range, select the range in the first worksheet of the 3D range, hold down the SHIFT key, and click the worksheet tab of the last worksheet you want to include in the range. Perform the following steps to select a 3D range and enter the @SUM function to sum the values in the Imperial worksheet and the Universal worksheet.

TO CREATE A 3D FORMULA ▼

STEP 1 ▶

Select the cell to contain the @SUM function – B5 in the Consolidated worksheet. Click the @function selector in the edit line. When the @Function menu displays, choose SUM. Click the Imperial worksheet tab and select the first range – cell B5. Press and hold down the SHIFT key and point to the Universal worksheet tab.

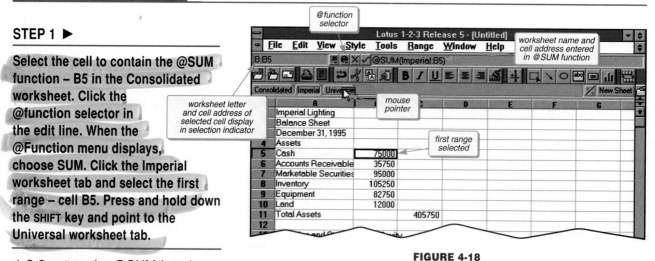

FIGURE 4-18

1-2-3 enters the @SUM function and highlights list in the @SUM function. When you select cell B5, 1-2-3 enters the worksheet name and the cell address of the selected cell in the @SUM function in the contents box (Figure 4-18). 1-2-3 enters the worksheet letter and cell address in the selection indicator in the edit line. The mouse pointer points to the Universal worksheet.

STEP 2 ▶

Click the Universal worksheet tab.

1-2-3 highlights cell B5 in the Universal worksheet and enters the worksheet name and cell address in the @SUM function in the contents box (Figure 4-19).

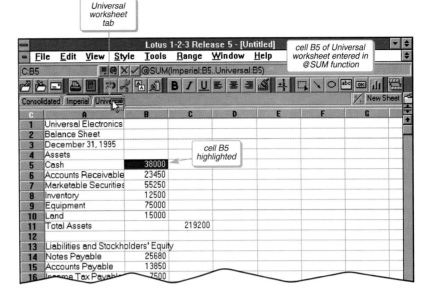

FIGURE 4-19

STEP 3 ▶

Release the SHIFT key and click the Confirm button or press the ENTER key to confirm the entry.

1-2-3 sums the value in cell B5 of the Imperial worksheet and the value in cell B5 of the Universal worksheet and displays the result in cell B5 of the Consolidated worksheet (Figure 4-20). The @SUM function displays in the contents box.

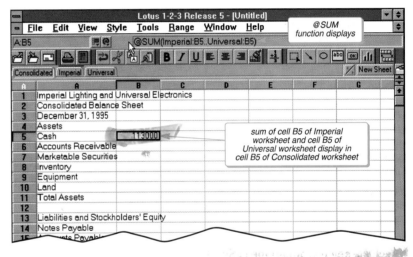

FIGURE 4-20

Once you enter the formula to calculate the sum of the cash assets in the Consolidated worksheet, you can copy the formula to the cells in the range B6..B10 in the Consolidated worksheet so 1-2-3 will calculate the sum of accounts receivable, marketable securities, inventory, equipment, and land for the Imperial Lighting and Universal Electronics worksheets. Then, you can enter the @SUM function in cell C11 to sum the range B5..B10 to calculate the total assets for the Consolidated worksheet. Copy and enter the @SUM function using the following procedure.

TO COPY AND ENTER THE @SUM FUNCTION ▼

STEP 1 ►

Select the cell containing the formula to copy – cell B5 in the Consolidated worksheet and the range where the formula is copied – cells B6..B10. Point to the selected range and click the right mouse button. When the quick menu displays, choose the Copy Down command.

1-2-3 copies the @SUM function from cell B5 to the range B6..B10 in the Consolidated worksheet and calculates the copied @SUM functions (Figure 4-21). Notice the cell references for each row change to reflect the correct row. For example, the formula in cell B6 is @SUM(Imperial:B6..Universal:B6) and the formula in cell B7 is @SUM(Imperial:B7..Universal:B7).

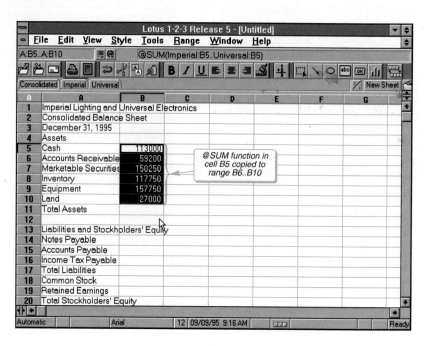

FIGURE 4-21

STEP 2 ►

Select cell C11. Click the @function selector in the edit line. When the @Function menu displays, choose SUM. Select the range B5..B10. Click the Confirm button or press the ENTER key to confirm the entry.

1-2-3 sums the values in the range B6..B10 and enters the result in cell C11 (Figure 4-22). The @SUM function displays in the contents box. Notice when you are entering a formula that sums a range in the current worksheet, 1-2-3 enters the range address only and does not include the worksheet name in the formula in the contents box.

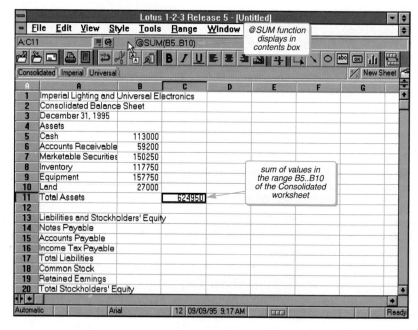

FIGURE 4-22

The next step is to enter the @SUM function in cell B14 of the Consolidated worksheet to sum the notes payable from the Imperial and the Universal worksheets. To enter the @function, complete the following step.

TO ENTER AN @FUNCTION ▼

STEP 1 ►

Select cell B14 in the Consolidated worksheet. Click the @function selector in the edit line and choose SUM from the @Function menu. Click the Imperial worksheet tab, select cell B14, press and hold down the SHIFT key, click the Universal worksheet tab, release the SHIFT key, and click the Confirm button or press the ENTER key.

1-2-3 enters the @SUM function in the contents box and the results of the @SUM function in the cell (Figure 4-23).

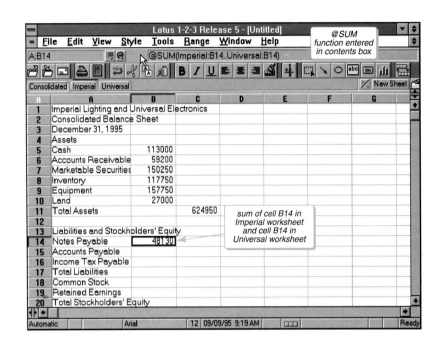

FIGURE 4-23

Next, copy the @SUM function in cell B14 of the Consolidated worksheet to the range B15..B16. Enter the @SUM function in cell C17 to sum the range B14..B16. To complete these tasks, perform the following steps (see Figure 4-24).

TO COPY AN @FUNCTION AND SUM A RANGE

Step 1: Select the range B14..B16 in the Consolidated worksheet. Point to the selected range and click the right mouse button. Choose the Copy Down command.

Step 2: Select cell C17. Click the @function selector in the edit line. When the @Function menu displays, choose SUM. Select the range B14..B16. Click the Confirm button or press the ENTER key to confirm the entry.

The worksheet displays as shown in Figure 4-24.

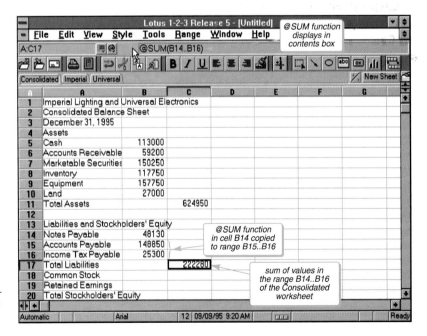

FIGURE 4-24

Completing the Worksheet

The final steps in completing the entries in the worksheet are to sum the common stock and retained earnings values from the Imperial worksheet and the Universal worksheet and display the results in the Consolidated worksheet. Follow these steps to complete the worksheet.

TO COMPLETE THE WORKSHEET

Step 1: Select cell B18 in the Consolidated worksheet. Click the @function selector in the edit line and choose SUM from the @Function menu. Click the Imperial worksheet tab and select cell B18. Press and hold down the SHIFT key, click the Universal worksheet tab, release the SHIFT key, and click the Confirm button or press the ENTER key.

Step 2: Select the range B18..B19 in the Consolidated worksheet. Point to the selected range and click the right mouse button. From the quick menu, choose the Copy Down command.

Step 3: Select cell C20. Click the @function selector in the edit line and choose SUM from @Function menu. Select the range to be summed, B18..B19, and click the Confirm button or press the ENTER key.

Step 4: Use the down scroll arrow to view cell C21. Select cell C21. Type a plus sign (+). Select cell C17, type a plus sign (+), select cell C20, and click the Confirm button or press the ENTER key to complete the formula.

The consolidated totals for common stock, retained earnings, total stockholders' equity, and total liabilities and stockholders' equity display as shown in Figure 4-25.

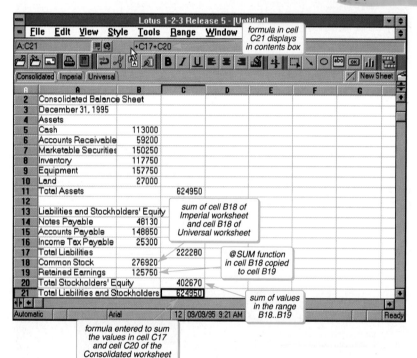

FIGURE 4-25

FORMATTING MULTIPLE WORKSHEETS

The Consolidated worksheet, the Imperial worksheet, and the Universal worksheet display with identical formatting (see Figure 4-1 on page L210). That is, the title in each worksheet displays in Arial 24 point, bold, and centered over the columns; the row headings are aligned to the right; the values are formatted in the U.S. dollar format and the comma format; the column widths and row heights are increased; the text color is blue; and a designer frame has been added.

When the worksheets in a file all have the same layout, you can format all of them at the same time using **Group mode**. With Group mode turned on, any changes made to one worksheet affect all the other worksheets in the file. The sections that follow accomplish these formatting tasks.

Grouping Worksheets

To duplicate the formatting of the Consolidated worksheet in the Imperial worksheet and the Universal worksheet, group the three worksheets by turning on Group mode. While worksheets are grouped, any changes made to the current worksheet are also made automatically on all worksheets in the file. To group multiple worksheets, perform the steps on the next page.

TO GROUP MULTIPLE WORKSHEETS ▼

STEP 1 ▶

Use the up scroll arrow to view cell A1. Select cell A1 in the Consolidated worksheet. Choose the Worksheet Defaults command from the Style menu. When the Worksheet Defaults dialog box displays, select the Group mode check box in the Other area by pointing to the Group mode check box and clicking the left mouse button. Point to the OK button in the Worksheet Defaults dialog box.

The cell pointer is located in cell A1 of the Consolidated worksheet (Figure 4-26). 1-2-3 displays the Worksheet Defaults dialog box. The Group mode check box is selected in the Other area. The mouse pointer points to the OK button.

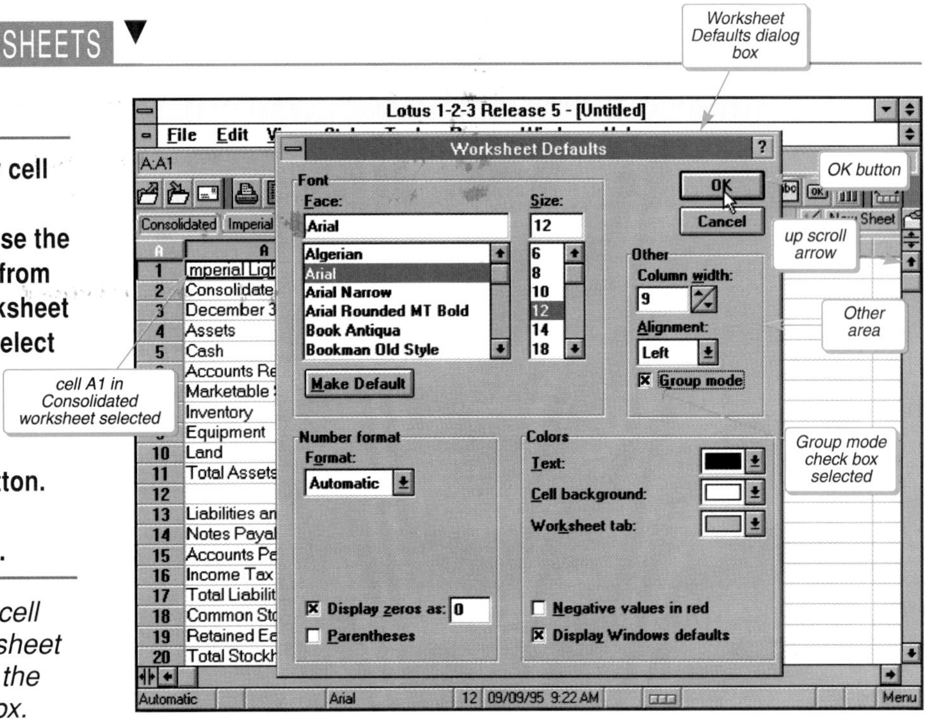

STEP 2 ▶

Choose the OK button in the Worksheet Defaults dialog box.

1-2-3 removes the Worksheet Defaults dialog box from the screen (Figure 4-27). The Group indicator displays in the status bar at the bottom of the screen. The Consolidated worksheet, Imperial worksheet, and Universal worksheet are now grouped. Any changes made to the current worksheet are also made to all worksheets in the file.

FIGURE 4-26

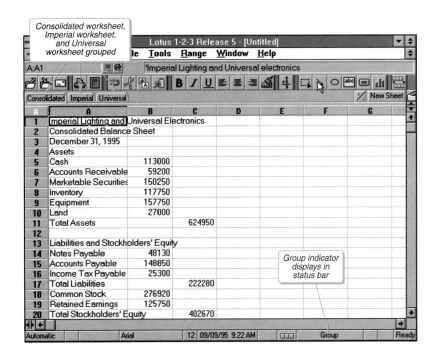

FIGURE 4-27

Use caution when grouping worksheets. When worksheets are grouped, you can lose data if you forget they are grouped. For example, if you delete a row in one worksheet, the row is also deleted in all worksheets in the file.

After applying formats to all the worksheets in a file, you can deselect Group mode to apply different formats to individual worksheets. To ungroup worksheets, choose the Worksheet Defaults command from the Style menu and deselect the Group mode check box. Ungrouping worksheets does not restore the settings applied to a worksheet before grouping them.

Formatting the Worksheet Titles

The worksheet title in row 1 displays in Arial 24 point, bold, and is centered over columns A, B, C, and D. The worksheet titles in row 2 and row 3 are centered over columns A, B, C, and D. Perform the following step to format the titles.

TO FORMAT THE WORKSHEET TITLES

Step 1: Select cell A1. Click the Bold icon on the set of SmartIcons. Click the point-size selector in the status bar and choose 24 from the pop-up list of point sizes. Select the range A1..D3. Point to the selected range and click the right mouse button. Choose the Alignment command from the quick menu. When the Alignment dialog box displays, select the Center option button and the Across columns check box in the Horizontal area. Select the Center option button in the Vertical area. Choose the OK button in the Alignment dialog box. Select any cell.

The worksheet titles display as shown in Figure 4-28.

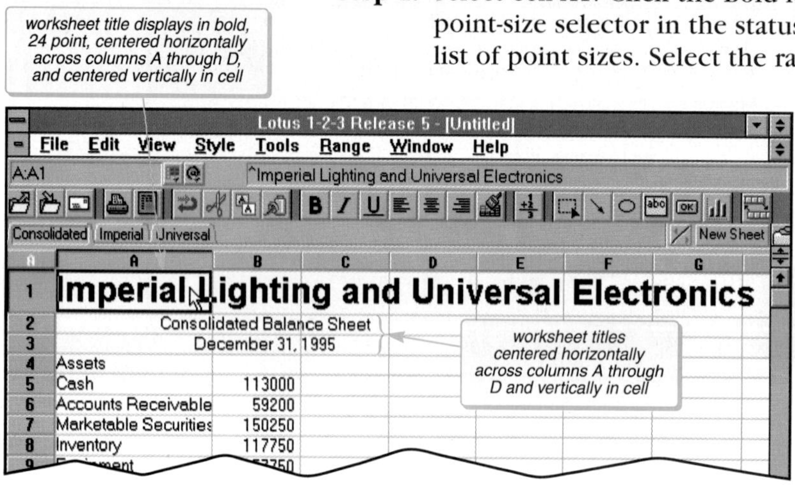

worksheet title displays in bold, 24 point, centered horizontally across columns A through D, and centered vertically in cell

worksheet titles centered horizontally across columns A through D and vertically in cell

FIGURE 4-28

Notice in Figure 4-28, the worksheet title displays across columns A through G even though the title was centered across columns A through D. Increasing the font size to 24 points causes the title to spill over into the adjacent columns. After the column widths are adjusted in a later section, the title will display across columns A through D.

Formatting the Row Titles

Recall from earlier projects that you can use the CTRL key and mouse to make any nonadjacent selection in the worksheet. The row titles in the ranges A5..A11 and A14..A21 are right-aligned in each cell (see Figure 4-29 on the next page). The row titles in cells A4, A11, A13, A17, A20, and A21 are bold. Perform the step on the next page to format the row titles.

TO FORMAT THE ROW TITLES

Step 1: Select the range A5..A11. Hold down the CTRL key and select the range A14..A21. Release the CTRL key. Click the Right icon on the set of SmartIcons. Select cell A4. Hold down the CTRL key and select cell A11, A13, and A17. Use the down scroll arrow to view row 21. Select cells A20 and A21. Release the CTRL key. Click the Bold icon on the set of SmartIcons. Select any cell.

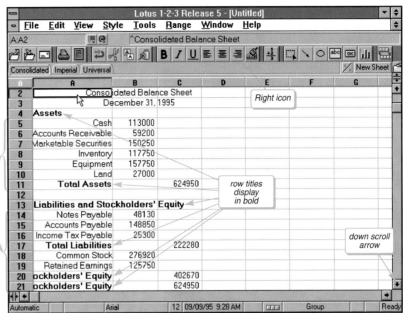

FIGURE 4-29

The worksheet row titles display as shown in Figure 4-29.

Formatting the Values in U.S. Dollar Format and Comma Format

The values in the worksheet display in the U.S. dollar format and comma format with zero decimal places to the right of the decimal point. Cells B5, B14, B18, C11, C17, C20, and C21 are formatted in the U.S. dollar format with zero decimal places. Ranges B6..B10, B15..B16, and cell B19 are formatted in the comma format with zero decimal places. Perform the following steps to format the values in the worksheet in the U.S. dollar and comma formats.

TO FORMAT THE VALUES IN THE U.S. DOLLAR AND COMMA FORMATS

Step 1: Select cell B5. Hold down the CTRL key and select cells C11, B14, C17, B18, C20, and C21. Release the CTRL key. Click the format selector in the status bar and choose US Dollar from the pop-up list. Click the decimal selector in the status bar and choose 0 from the pop-up list.

Step 2: Select the range B6..B10. Hold down the CTRL key and select the range B15..B16 and cell B19. Release the CTRL key. Click the format selector in the status bar and choose the ,Comma format from the pop-up list. Click the decimal selector in the status bar and choose 0 from the pop-up list. Select any cell.

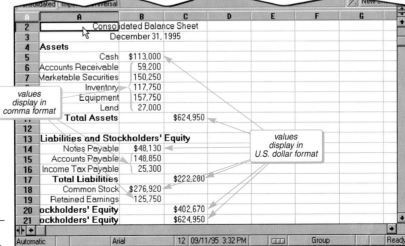

FIGURE 4-30

The values display in U.S. dollar and comma formats as shown in Figure 4-30.

Increasing the Widths of Columns and Heights of Rows

The next step in formatting the worksheets is to increase the widths of columns and the heights of rows. Column A displays with a width of 36 characters and column B and column C display with a width of 12 characters (Figure 4-31).

Rows 3, 11, 17, 20, and 21 have a height of 28 points. Rows 5 and 14 have a height of 22 points. Row 18 displays with a height of 36 points. Perform the following steps to increase column widths and row heights.

TO INCREASE COLUMN WIDTHS AND ROW HEIGHTS

Step 1: Use the up scroll arrow to view cell A2. Point to the right column border of column A. Drag the column border to the right until the width displayed in the selection indicator is 36Characters. Point to the right column border of column B. Drag the column border to the right until the width displayed in the selection indicator is 12Characters. Point to the right column border of column C. Drag the column border to the right until the width displayed in the selection indicator is 12Characters.

Step 2: Point to row heading 3 to the left of column A and click the left mouse button. Hold down the CTRL key and click row headings 11, 17, 20, and 21. Release the CTRL key. Position the mouse pointer on the bottom border between row heading 3 and row heading 4. Drag the border of row heading 3 down until the height for row 3 displays 28Points in the selection indicator. Release the left mouse button.

Step 3: Use the up scroll arrow to view row heading 5. Point to row heading 5 and click the left mouse button. Hold down the CTRL key and click row heading 14. Release the CTRL key. Position the mouse pointer on the bottom border between row heading 5 and row heading 6. Drag the border of row heading 5 down until the height for row 5 displays 22Points in the selection indicator. Release the left mouse button.

Step 4: Use the down scroll arrow to view row 18. Position the mouse pointer on the bottom border between row heading 18 and row heading 19. Drag the border of row heading 18 down until the height for row 18 displays 36Points in the selection indicator. Release the left mouse button. Select any cell.

The worksheet displays as shown in Figure 4-31.

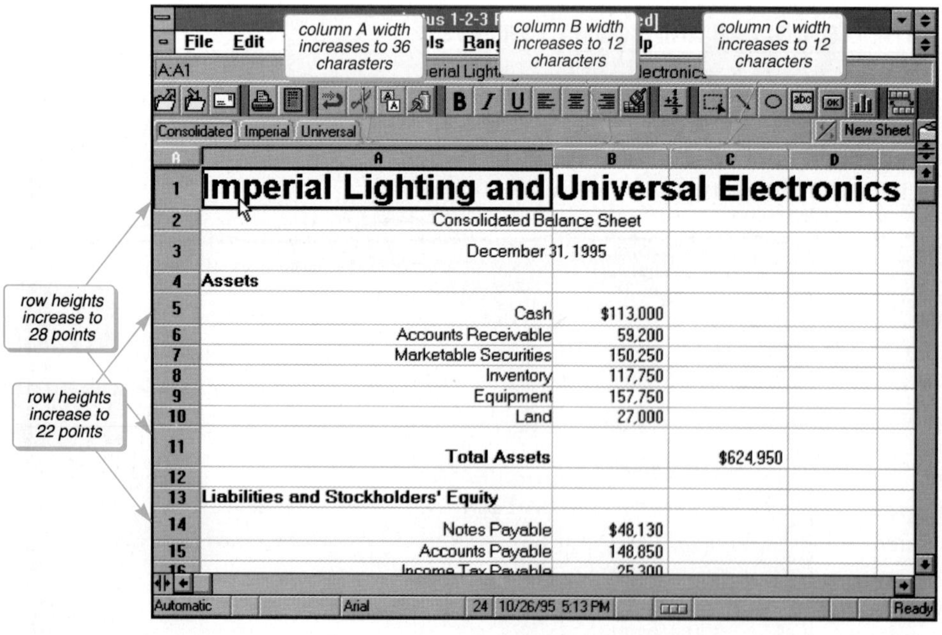

FIGURE 4-31

Adding Color, Underlining, and Designer Frames to the Worksheet

The next task in formatting the worksheets is to add background color, underlining, and designer frames. The font displays in blue, and the background color in row 4 and row 12 is light gray (see Figure 4-32). The ranges A4..D4 and A13..D13 display with a dark gray designer frame. Cells C11 and C21 display with a double underline. To add color, underlining, and designer frames to the worksheet, perform the following steps.

TO ADD COLOR, UNDERLINING, AND DESIGNER FRAMES TO THE WORKSHEET

Step 1: Select the range A1..C21. Point to the selected range and click the right mouse button. Choose the Font & Attributes command from the quick menu. When the Font & Attributes dialog box displays, click the Color drop-down box arrow and select the first blue color down from the top row in the Color drop-down box. Choose the OK button in the Font & Attributes dialog box.

Step 2: Select the range A4..D4. Press and hold the CTRL key and select the range A13..D13. Release the CTRL key. Point to the selected range and click the right mouse button. Choose the Lines & Color command from the quick menu. When the Lines & Color dialog box displays, click the Background color drop-down box arrow in the Interior area and select the light gray color in the top row of the Background color drop-down box. Select the Designer frame check box. Click the Designer frame drop-down box arrow and select the second designer frame from the right in the second row. Then, click the Frame color drop-down box arrow and select the dark gray color in the top row of the Frame color drop-down box. Choose the OK button in the Lines & Color dialog box.

Step 3: Select cell C11. Use the down scroll arrow to view cell C21. Hold down the CTRL key and select cell C21. Release the CTRL key. Point to the selected range and click the right mouse button. Choose the Lines & Color command from the quick menu. When the Lines & Color dialog box displays, select the Bottom check box in the Border area. Click the Line style drop-down box arrow and select the double line from the Line style drop-down list. Click the Line color drop-down box arrow and select blue from the Line color drop-down list. Choose the OK button in the Lines & Color dialog box. Select any cell.

The completed worksheet displays as shown in Figure 4-32.

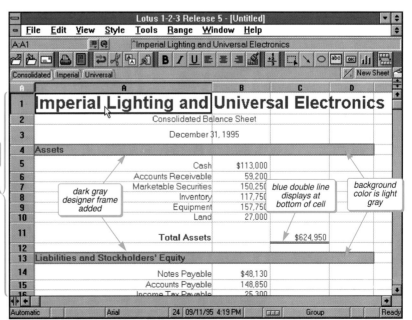

FIGURE 4-32

Changing the Color of the Worksheet Tabs

The final task in formatting the worksheets is to change the color of the worksheet tabs. The Consolidated worksheet tab displays in yellow, the Imperial worksheet tab displays in purple, and the Universal worksheet tab displays in blue (refer to Figure 4-1 on page L210). To change the color of the worksheet tabs, perform the following steps.

TO CHANGE THE COLOR OF THE WORKSHEET TABS ▼

STEP 1 ▶

Point to the Consolidated worksheet tab and click the right mouse button. Choose the Worksheet Defaults command from the quick menu. When the Worksheet Defaults dialog box displays, point to the Worksheet tab drop-down box arrow in the Colors area.

1-2-3 highlights the Consolidated worksheet and displays the Worksheet Defaults dialog box (Figure 4-33). The mouse pointer points to the Worksheet tab drop-down box arrow in the Colors area.

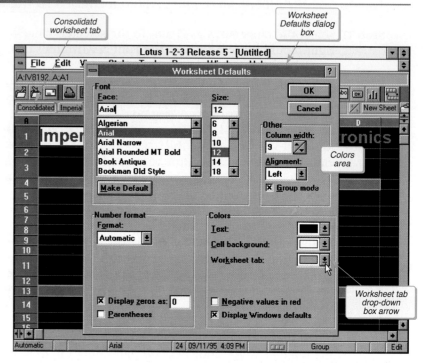

FIGURE 4-33

STEP 2 ▶

Click the Worksheet tab drop-down box arrow and select yellow in the top row of the Worksheet tab drop-down box. Point to the OK button in the Worksheet Defaults dialog box.

The desired yellow color displays in the Worksheet tab drop-down box (Figure 4-34). The mouse pointer points to the OK button.

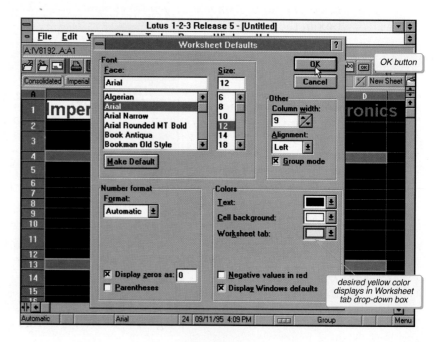

FIGURE 4-34

STEP 3 ▶

Choose the OK button in the Worksheet Defaults dialog box. Select any cell.

1-2-3 closes the Worksheet Defaults dialog box and changes the color of the Consolidated worksheet tab to yellow (Figure 4-35).

FIGURE 4-35

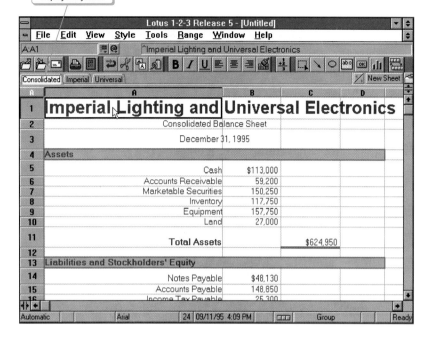

STEP 4 ▶

Repeat Step 1 through Step 3 to change the Imperial worksheet tab color to purple and the Universal worksheet tab color to blue.

The Imperial worksheet tab color displays in purple and the Universal worksheet tab color displays in blue (Figure 4-36).

FIGURE 4-36

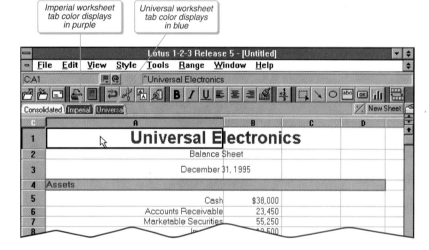

The formatting of the Consolidated worksheet is now complete. Because the Group mode is on, all the formatting changes made to the Consolidated worksheet are also made to the Imperial worksheet and the Universal worksheet. You can view the identical formatting of the Imperial and Universal worksheets by clicking the respective worksheet tab. You can also view the three worksheets on one screen by using the perspective view illustrated in the following section.

Viewing Multiple Worksheets

When a worksheet file contains multiple worksheets, you can display one worksheet at a time on the screen and move between the worksheets by clicking the worksheet tabs. You can also display three worksheets at the same time by splitting the worksheet window into perspective view. **Perspective view** is a layered display of three contiguous worksheets from a file using the **Split command** from the **View menu.** Perform the following steps to view the worksheets in perspective view.

TO VIEW MULTIPLE WORKSHEETS IN PERSPECTIVE VIEW ▼

STEP 1 ▶

Select cell A1 in the Consolidated worksheet. Select the View menu by pointing to the View menu and clicking the left mouse button. Point to the Split command.

1-2-3 displays the View menu (Figure 4-37). The mouse pointer points to the Split command.

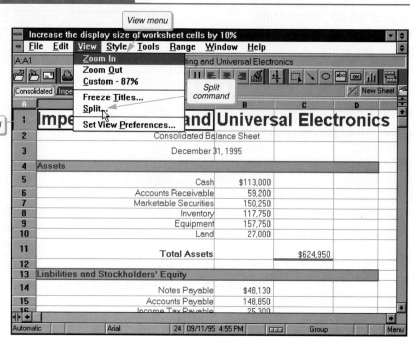

FIGURE 4-37

STEP 2 ▶

Choose the Split command from the View menu. When the Split dialog box displays, select the Perspective option button in the Type area by pointing to the Perspective option and clicking the left mouse button. Ensure the Synchronize scrolling check box contains an X. Then, point to the OK button.

1-2-3 displays the Split dialog box (Figure 4-38). The Perspective option button is selected. An X in the Synchronize scrolling check box causes the worksheets displayed in perspective view to scroll together so the same rows and columns are always visible in all three worksheets. The mouse pointer points to the OK button in the Split dialog box.

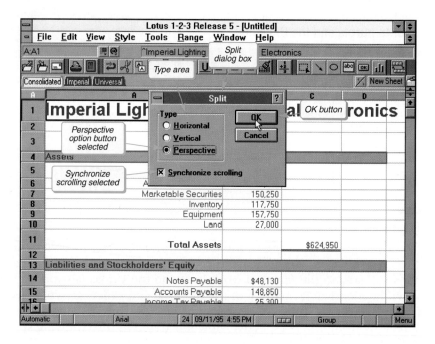

FIGURE 4-38

STEP 3 ▶

Choose the OK button in the Split dialog box.

1-2-3 displays the three work-sheets in perspective view simulta-neously (Figure 4-39). Notice the worksheet tabs do not display in perspective view. Each worksheet is identified by the worksheet letter in the upper left corner of the worksheet. The cell pointer is located in cell A1 of the Consoli-dated worksheet. Only one set of vertical and horizontal scroll bars displays for all three worksheets. When you click the up/down or left/right scroll arrow, all three worksheets scroll together in the direction indicated. Notice the worksheets display with identical formatting.

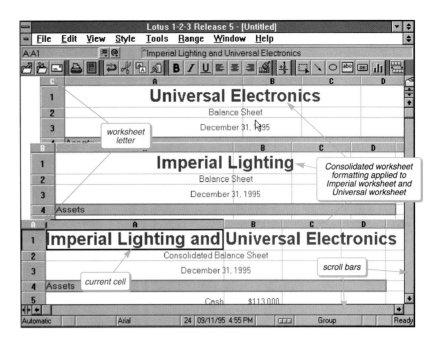

FIGURE 4-39

To move among the worksheets in perspective view, point to the desired cell in the desired worksheet and click the left mouse button. To return to a single worksheet display, choose the **Clear Split command** from the View menu. 1-2-3 will then display only the worksheet in which the cell pointer is positioned.

With all the format settings included in the worksheets, you now can turn off Group mode. Perform the following steps to clear the perspective view and ungroup the worksheets.

TO CLEAR PERSPECTIVE VIEW AND UNGROUP MULTIPLE WORKSHEETS ▼

STEP 1 ▶

Select the View menu and point to the Clear Split command.

1-2-3 displays the View menu, and the mouse pointer points to the Clear Split command (Figure 4-40). The cell pointer is located in cell A1 of the Consolidated worksheet.

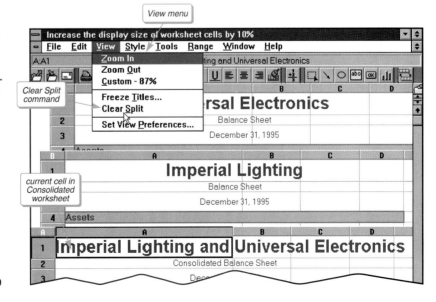

FIGURE 4-40

STEP 2 ▶

Choose the Clear Split command.

1-2-3 restores the worksheet window to display the Consolidated worksheet only (Figure 4-41). The worksheet tabs display above the column letters.

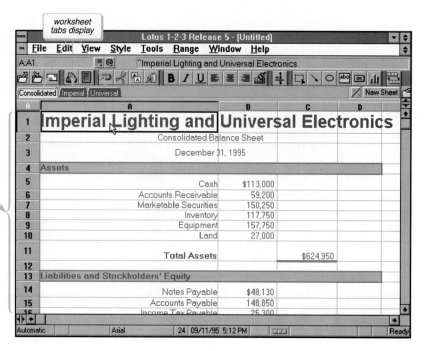

FIGURE 4-41

STEP 3 ▶

Choose the Worksheet Defaults command from the Style menu. When the Worksheet Defaults dialog displays, remove the X from the Group mode check box in the Other area by pointing to the Group mode check box and clicking the left mouse button. Point to the OK button.

The Worksheet Defaults dialog box displays (Figure 4-42). The X is removed from the Group mode check box. The mouse pointer points to the OK button.

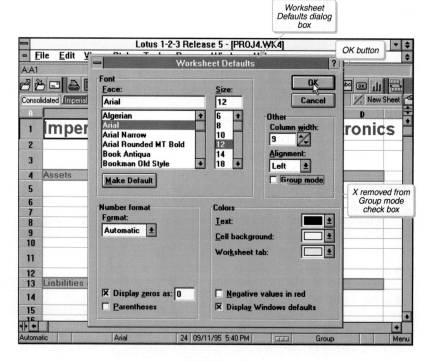

FIGURE 4-42

STEP 4 ▶

Choose the OK button in the
Worksheet Defaults dialog box.

*The Worksheet Defaults dialog box
is removed from the screen (Figure
4-43). The Group indicator no
longer displays in the status bar
and the worksheets are not
grouped. Now, any changes made
to one worksheet will not be made
to the other worksheets in the file.*

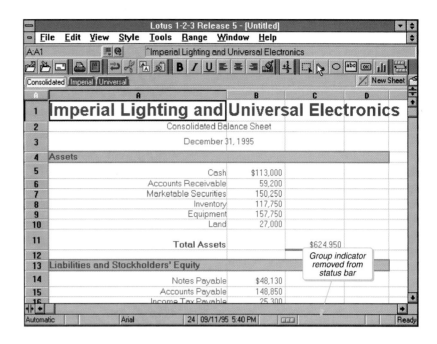

FIGURE 4-43

▶ SAVING THE FILE

ow that the worksheets are completed, you should save them on disk. To save the worksheets on drive A using the file name PROJ4, complete the following steps.

TO SAVE THE FILE

Step 1: Click the Save icon on the set of SmartIcons.
Step 2: When the Save As dialog box displays, type `proj4` in the File name text box.
Step 3: Select a: from the Drives drop-down list box.
Step 4: Choose the OK button in the Save As dialog box.

1-2-3 saves the worksheet as PROJ4.wk4 on the diskette in drive A.

▶ CREATING A PIE CHART

In Project 2, you created a 3D pie chart showing the percentage each gem represented in the investment portfolio. This project reviews the steps required to create a 3D pie chart and also explains how to left-justify a chart title, add a footnote at the bottom of a chart, display labels containing text, explode a slice of the pie chart, and add an arrow to the chart.

The 3D pie chart displayed in Figure 4-44 on the next page charts the assets from the Consolidated worksheet. The chart is divided into slices; the size of each slice represents the percentage that the corresponding asset contributes toward the total. The name of the asset and its percentage are included on the chart. One of the slices, Land, is exploded, or slightly separated, from the chart. This is done to emphasize one slice in the pie chart.

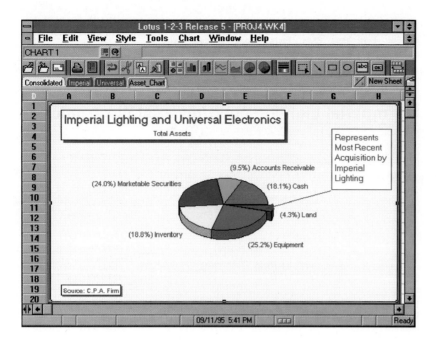

FIGURE 4-44

A text block, which is a drawn object that contains text, is added to the chart with an arrow pointing to the exploded pie slice. The text block for Project 4 is added to the chart to give information about the exploded pie slice.

The range to chart in the Consolidated worksheet is A5..B10 (Figure 4-1 on page L210). The **X data range**, A5..A10, contains the labels that identify the slices of the pie. The **A data range,** B5..B10, contains the values to chart. Only one data range (A) is defined in a pie chart. Perform the following steps to create the chart on a separate worksheet inserted after the Universal worksheet.

TO CREATE A 3D PIE CHART ▼

STEP 1 ▶

Click the Universal worksheet tab by pointing to the worksheet tab and clicking the left mouse button. Click the New Sheet button located below the set of SmartIcons. Double-click the worksheet tab for worksheet D and type `Asset_Chart`. **Press the ENTER key. Click the Consolidated worksheet and select the range to chart, A5..B10. Click the Chart icon** on the set of SmartIcons. Click the Asset_Chart worksheet tab and select the range for the chart, A1..H20. When the default bar chart displays on the screen, point to the 3D Pie icon on the set of SmartIcons.

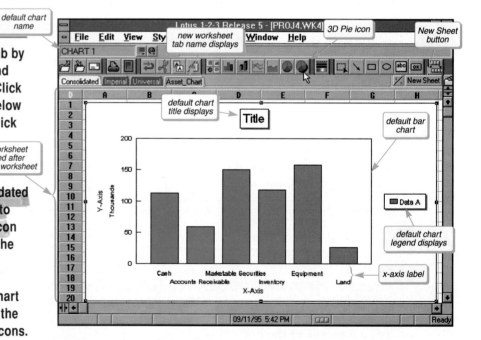

FIGURE 4-45

1-2-3 inserts a blank worksheet after the Universal worksheet. The new worksheet tab name Asset_Chart, displays (Figure 4-45). 1-2-3 displays the default chart (the two-dimensional bar chart). The x-axis labels display below the bar chart because they were selected in the range to chart. The default chart title and default chart legend display on the chart. The mouse pointer points to the 3D Pie icon. The chart name, CHART 1, displays in the selection indicator.

STEP 2 ▶

Click the left mouse button.

1-2-3 displays the 3D pie chart (Figure 4-46). Each slice represents one of the six assets from the Consolidated worksheet. The percentage each slice represents of the total assets displays outside the slices. The default chart title displays centered above the pie chart. The legend displays to the right of the chart because you selected the text in the worksheet.

FIGURE 4-46

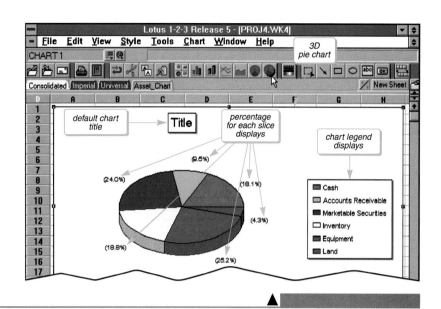

Adding a Title, Subtitle, and Footnote to a Chart

In 1-2-3, you can add a title, subtitle, and footnotes to a chart. By default, 1-2-3 displays the title centered above the chart, and the subtitle is displayed centered below the title. **Footnotes** are explanatory text displayed left-aligned below the chart. 1-2-3 automatically adds a title and subtitle to a chart if you include the labels in the range to be charted. In Project 4, the title and subtitle are aligned to the left. To add the title, subtitle, and footnote to the chart, perform the following steps.

TO ADD A TITLE, SUBTITLE, AND FOOTNOTE TO A CHART ▼

STEP 1 ▶

Point to the default chart title, Title, and click the right mouse button. Choose the Headings command from the quick menu. When the Headings dialog box displays, type Imperial Lighting and Universal Electronics **in the Line 1 text box and** Total Assets **in the Line 2 text box in the Title area. Select the Placement Left option button in the Title area. In the Note area, type** Source: C.P.A. Firm **in the Line 1 text box. Point to the OK button.**

1-2-3 displays the Headings dialog box (Figure 4-47). The Line 1 text box in the Title area contains the last part of the chart title, and the

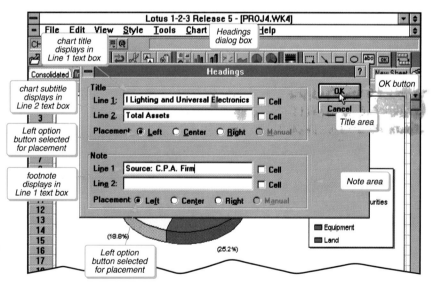

FIGURE 4-47

Line 2 text box contains the chart subtitle. The Line 1 text box is not large enough to contain the whole title, so the title has scrolled off the screen. The Left option causes 1-2-3 to place the headings to the left on the chart. The Line 1 text box in the Note area contains the footnote for the chart. The Left option button is selected for Placement in the Note area. The footnote will be aligned to the left. The mouse pointer points to the OK button.

STEP 2 ▶

Choose the OK button in the
Headings dialog box.

*1-2-3 displays the chart title and
subtitle left-aligned (Figure
4-48). The footnote displays
at the bottom left of the chart.
The size of the pie chart is
reduced slightly to accommodate
the increased size of the title and
subtitle.*

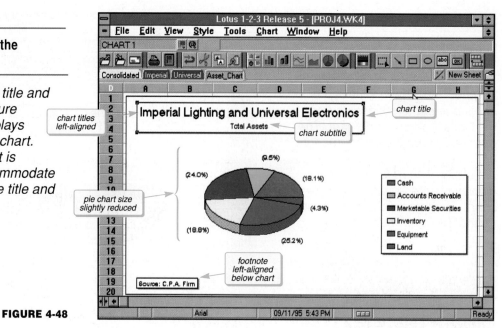

FIGURE 4-48

Titles, subtitles, and footnotes can contain numbers, letters, or special characters. To delete a title, subtitle, or footnote in the Headings dialog box, highlight
the contents of the text box for the title, subtitle, or footnote you want to delete
and press the DEL key. Then, choose the OK button.

Adding Data Labels to a Chart

For each slice of the pie chart, you can show three data labels. By default,
1-2-3 displays the percentage of the whole each slice represents. You can also
show the actual numeric value in each cell you are charting and the slice labels
contained in the X data range. In this project, the slice labels display with the percentages. To add a second data label containing the slice label and increase the
font size to 10, perform the following steps.

TO ADD DATA LABELS ▼

STEP 1 ▶

Point to any percentage on the pie
chart and click the right mouse
button. When the quick menu
displays, point to the Data Labels
command.

*1-2-3 selects the percentages for
each slice and displays the quick
menu (Figure 4-49). The mouse
pointer points to the Data Labels
command.*

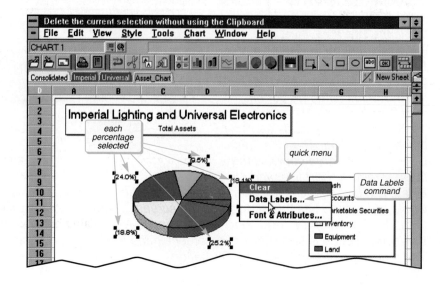

FIGURE 4-49

STEP 2 ▶

Choose the Data Labels command from the quick menu. When the Data Labels dialog box displays, point to the Contents of X data range check box and click the left mouse button. Then, point to the OK button.

1-2-3 displays the Data Labels dialog box (Figure 4-50). In the Show area, the Percentages check box contains an X because 1-2-3 displays the percentage each slice represents by default. The Contents of X data range check box is selected. The X data range contains the labels Cash, Accounts Receivable, Marketable Securities, Inventory, Equipment, and Land. The mouse pointer points to the OK button.

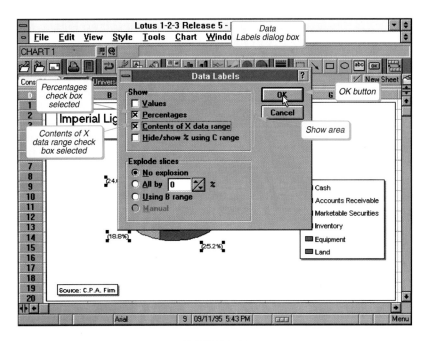

FIGURE 4-50

STEP 3 ▶

Choose the OK button in the Data Labels dialog box. When the Data Labels dialog box is removed from the screen, click the point-size selector in the status bar and select the number 10 in the pop-up list box of point sizes.

1-2-3 displays the pie chart (Figure 4-51). The data labels from the X data range display to the right of the percentages. The percentages and labels display in 10 point font size. Notice the legend does not display when the contents of the X data range display as data labels.

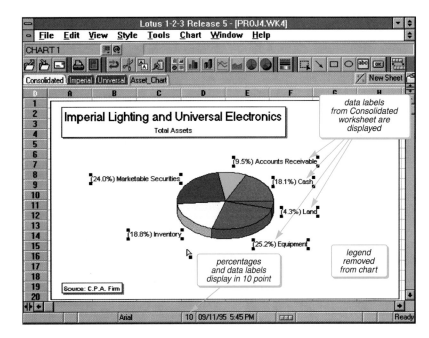

FIGURE 4-51

To remove the selection, click inside the chart where there is no other chart element.

To display the actual values represented by each slice as data labels, select the Values check box in the Show area of the Data Labels dialog box (see Figure 4-50).

To delete data labels you no longer want to display on a pie chart, remove the X from the desired check box in the Data Labels dialog box, and then choose the OK button.

Exploding a Pie Slice

When you want to draw attention to a particular slice in a pie chart, you can explode that slice; that is, separate the slice from the rest of the chart. In this project, the Land slice is exploded. Perform the following steps to explode a slice of the pie chart.

TO EXPLODE A PIE SLICE ▼

STEP 1 ▶

Point to the dark gray Land slice and click the left mouse button.

1-2-3 surrounds the Land slice with handles (Figure 4-52). The mouse pointer changes to an arrowhead and triangle (⬈).

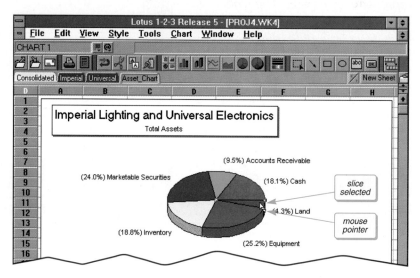

FIGURE 4-52

STEP 2 ▶

Drag the selected pie slice to the desired position and release the left mouse button.

When you drag, the mouse pointer changes to a fist. 1-2-3 redraws the pie chart with the Land slice offset from the rest of the pie chart (Figure 4-53). When you stop dragging, the mouse pointer returns to the arrowhead and triangle shape.

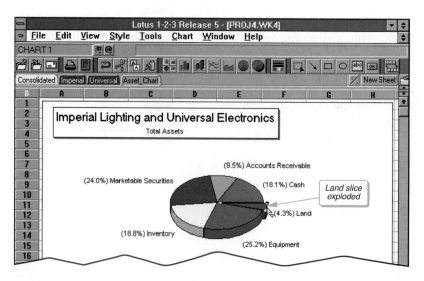

FIGURE 4-53

To remove the selection, click inside the chart where there is no other chart element.

Notice that after you drag a slice away from the main portion of the pie chart, the slices become smaller. If you compare Figure 4-52 to Figure 4-53, you can see that by exploding one slice, the pie chart becomes smaller. If you explode additional slices, the pie chart becomes too small to have an impact on the reader.

To reset the exploded pie slice, select the slice, and drag it toward the center of the pie. You can also choose the Data Labels command from the Chart menu and choose the No explosion option in the Explode slices area in the Data Labels dialog box (see Figure 4-50 on page L241).

Adding a Text Block and an Arrow to a Chart

In Project 3, you created a text block as the worksheet title. In this project, you create a square text block on the pie chart and add an arrow from the text block pointing to the exploded pie slice. To add a square text block, click the Draw Text icon on the set of SmartIcons, press and hold down the SHIFT key, move the mouse pointer to where you want to begin the text block, and drag across the worksheet. When the text block is the size you want, release the SHIFT key and the mouse button. You can then enter text in the text block.

To draw a single straight line with an arrowhead, click the Draw Arrow icon on the set of SmartIcons, move the mouse pointer to where you want to begin drawing the arrow, and drag across the worksheet. When the arrow is the size you want, release the mouse button. The arrowhead appears at the point where you release the mouse button. To draw a square text block, enter the text, and draw an arrow, perform the following steps.

TO CREATE A SQUARE TEXT BLOCK AND AN ARROW ▼

STEP 1 ▶

Point to the Draw Text icon on the set of SmartIcons and click the left mouse button. Then, move the mouse pointer to the upper right area of the chart, press and hold down the SHIFT key, and drag the mouse pointer until the text block is approximately one and one-half inch square on the screen. Release the left mouse button. Release the SHIFT key.

1-2-3 draws the square text block on the chart (Figure 4-54). The drawing set of SmartIcons displays below the edit line. 1-2-3 displays the text block with the insertion point in the top left corner. The default name of the text block, Text 1, displays in the selection indicator.

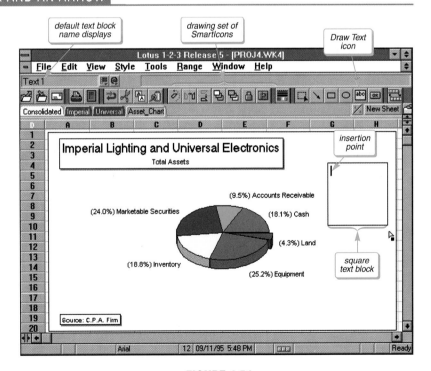

FIGURE 4-54

STEP 2 ▶

Type Represents Most Recent Acquisition by Imperial Lighting. **Then, click anywhere outside the text block. Point to the Draw Arrow icon ( ) on the set of SmartIcons and click the left mouse button. Position the mouse pointer next to the lower left border of the text block.**

As you type the text, 1-2-3 automatically wraps the text to the next line when it reaches the edge of the block. 1-2-3 displays the text inside the text block (Figure 4-55). The mouse pointer changes to a cross hair indicating you can position the arrow. 1-2-3 displays the instruction in drawing the arrow in the title bar of the next step.

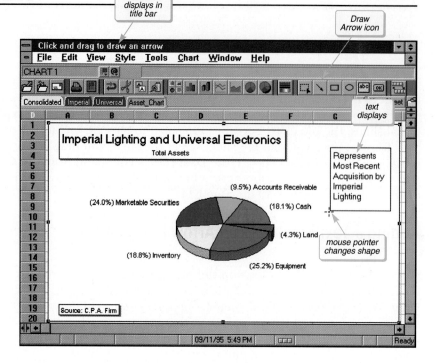

FIGURE 4-55

STEP 3 ▶

Click the left mouse button and drag the line to the center of the exploded pie slice. Release the left mouse button.

As you drag, the proposed line with the arrow appears as a dotted line. An arrowhead appears at the point where you release the mouse button (Figure 4-56). Handles appear on the arrow indicating the arrow is selected. When the mouse pointer is positioned over the selection handle, it changes to a four-headed arrow, indicating the object can be sized. The default name for the arrow, Line 1, displays in the selection indicator.

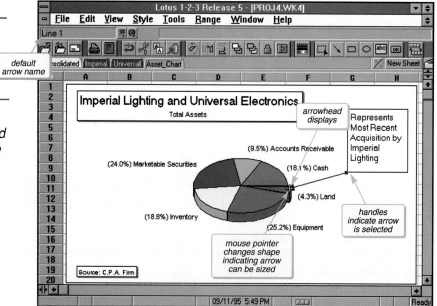

FIGURE 4-56

To move the text block, select the text block, position the mouse pointer over the selected text block, and drag the text block to where you want it to display.

To remove the selection from the arrow, click anywhere on the chart. To change the size of the arrow, first select the arrow by pointing to the arrow and clicking the left mouse button. Then, position the mouse pointer over a selection handle and drag the selection handle until the arrow is the desired size.

To delete the arrow, first select the arrow, then press the DEL key. The Draw Arrow command is also found on the Tools menu on the main menu bar.

Formatting the Pie Chart

To further enhance the appearance of the chart, you can format the chart title, subtitle, data labels, text block and arrow, change the background color and frame to the chart, and change the color of the Asset_Chart worksheet tab. To format the 3D pie chart shown in Figure 4-44 on page L238, perform the following steps.

TO FORMAT THE 3D PIE CHART

Step 1: Select the chart by pointing the mouse pointer inside the chart and clicking the right mouse button. Choose the Lines & Color command from the quick menu. When the Lines & Color dialog box displays, click the Background drop-down box arrow and select the fourth color from the left in the second row from the top (light yellow) in the Background color drop-down box. Click the Designer frame check box. Then, click the Designer frame drop-down box arrow and select the rightmost frame in the third row of the Designer frame drop-down box. Click the Frame color drop-down box arrow and select the first blue color in the top row of the Color drop-down box. Choose the OK button in the Lines & Color dialog box.

Step 2: Point to the chart title frame and click the right mouse button. Choose the Lines & Color command from the quick menu. When the Lines & Color dialog box displays, click the Text color drop-down box arrow and select the first blue color in the top row of the Text color drop-down box. Click the Designer frame drop-down box arrow and select the first frame on the left in the top row of the Designer frame drop-down box. Click the Frame color drop-down box arrow and select the blue color in the top row of the Frame color drop-down box. Choose the OK button in the Lines & Color dialog box.

Step 3: Point to a data label on the chart and click the right mouse button. Choose the Font & Attributes command from the quick menu. When the Font & Attributes dialog box displays, click the Color drop-down box arrow and select the first blue color in the top row of the Color drop-down box. Choose the OK button in the Font & Attributes dialog box.

Step 4: Position the mouse pointer inside the text block and click the left mouse button. Press the CTRL key and click the arrow. Release the CTRL key. Then, point to the arrow and click the right mouse button. Choose the Lines & Color command from the quick menu. When the Lines & Color dialog box displays, click the Text color drop-down box arrow and select the blue color in the top row of the Text color drop-down box. Click the Line color drop-down box arrow in the Edge area and choose the first blue color in the top row of the Line color drop-down box. Choose the OK button in the Lines & Color dialog box.

Step 5: Point to the chart note frame and click the right mouse button. Choose the Lines & Color command from the quick menu. When the Lines & Color dialog box displays, click the Text color drop-down box arrow and select the first blue color in the top row of the Text color drop-down box. Click the Frame color drop-down box arrow and select the blue color in the top row of the Frame color drop-down box. Choose the OK button in the Lines & Color dialog box.

Step 6: Point to the Asset_Chart worksheet tab and click the right mouse button. Choose the Worksheet Defaults command from the quick menu. When the Worksheet Defaults dialog box displays, click the Worksheet tab drop-down box arrow and select cyan (Color: 70) from the top row of the Worksheet tab drop-down box. Choose the OK button in the Lines & Color dialog box.

The formatted 3D pie chart displays as shown in Figure 4-57 on the next page.

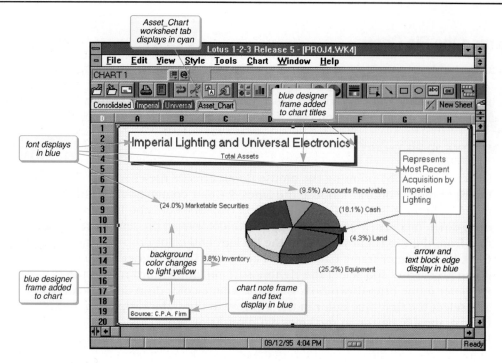

FIGURE 4-57

▶ PRINTING MULTIPLE WORKSHEETS

The four worksheets are now complete. The next step is to print the worksheets. In Project 4 each worksheet is to print on a separate page.

Adding Page Breaks

When you print a file containing multiple worksheets, 1-2-3 does not automatically break pages between the worksheets. To start each worksheet on a new page, you must add a page break at the top of each worksheet after the first worksheet in the file. To add a page break, perform the following steps.

TO ADD A PAGE BREAK ▼

STEP 1 ▶

Click the Imperial worksheet tab and ensure the cell pointer is in cell A1. Select the Style menu and point to the Page Break command.

The cell pointer is in cell A1 of the Imperial worksheet (Figure 4-58). The Style menu displays and the mouse pointer points to the Page Break command.

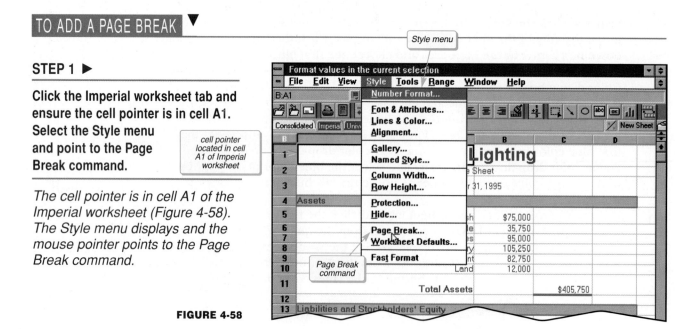

FIGURE 4-58

STEP 2 ▶

Click the left mouse button. When the Page Break dialog box displays, place an X in the Row check box by pointing to the Row check box and clicking the left mouse button. Point to the OK button.

The Page Break dialog box displays (Figure 4-59). Selecting the Row check box will cause 1-2-3 to insert a horizontal page break above the cell pointer.

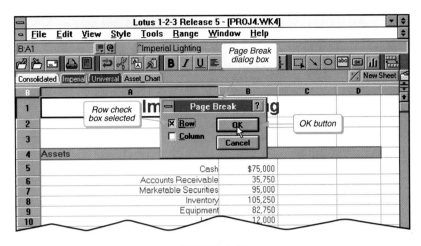

FIGURE 4-59

STEP 3 ▶

Choose the OK button in the Page Break dialog box.

1-2-3 inserts a dashed gray line above row 1 in the Imperial worksheet (Figure 4-60). When the file is printed, row 1 of the Imperial worksheet will print on a new page.

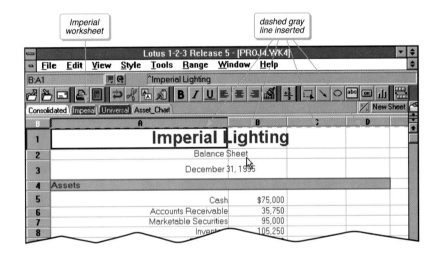

FIGURE 4-60

STEP 4 ▶

Click the Universal worksheet tab. Ensure the cell pointer is located in cell A1. Choose the Page Break command from the Style menu. When the Page Break dialog box displays, place an X in the Row check box by pointing to the Row check box and clicking the left mouse button. Choose the OK button.

1-2-3 inserts a dashed gray line above row 1 in the Universal worksheet (Figure 4-61). When the file is printed, row 1 of the Universal worksheet will print on a new page.

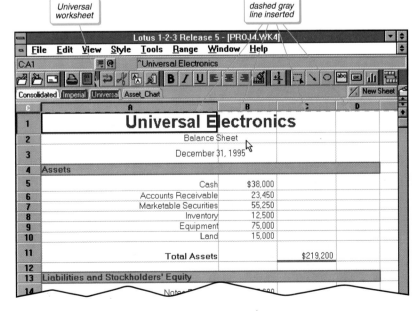

FIGURE 4-61

STEP 5 ►

Click the Asset_Chart worksheet tab. Ensure the cell pointer is located in cell A1. Choose the Page Break command from the Style menu. When the Page Break dialog box displays, select the Row check box. Choose the OK button.

1-2-3 inserts a dashed gray line in row 1 of the Asset_Chart worksheet (Figure 4-62). When the file is printed, row 1 of the Asset_Chart worksheet will print on a new page.

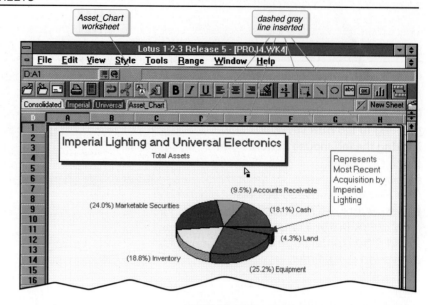

FIGURE 4-62

To remove a page break, select any cell immediately below the row where the page breaks, choose the Page Break command from the Style menu, and deselect the Row check box.

Adding Headers and Footers

A **header** is a single line of text that prints at the top of each page in your report. A **footer** is a single line of text that prints at the bottom of each page. You use headers and footers to print page numbers, the current date or time of printing, the worksheet file name, or other types of information on the pages of a report. Text can be left-aligned, centered, or right-aligned in a header or footer.

In this project, you are to print the word Page and the page number centered at the bottom of each page. To create the footer, use the **Page Setup command** from the File menu to display the Page Setup dialog box. In the center Footer text box, type Page and click the Page Number button below the Footer text box to enter a pound sign (#). The entry, #, is a code instructing 1-2-3 to print the page number. Use the procedures in the following steps to add a footer.

TO ADD A FOOTER ▼

STEP 1 ►

Select the File menu and point to the Page Setup command.

1-2-3 displays the File menu and the mouse pointer points to the Page Setup command (Figure 4-63).

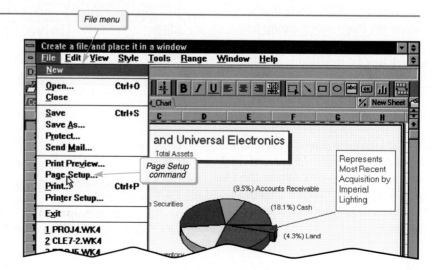

FIGURE 4-63

STEP 2 ▶

Choose the Page Setup command from the File menu. When the Page Setup dialog box displays, position the mouse pointer in the center Footer text box and click the left mouse button. Type `Page` and press the SPACEBAR. Then, point to the Page Number button (▣) below the Footer text boxes.

*1-2-3 displays the Page Setup dialog box (Figure 4-64). When you click the center Footer text box, a blinking insertion point displays in the text box and the row of **Insert buttons** appears raised below the Footer text boxes indicating they can be selected. The text you typed displays in the center Footer text box. The mouse pointer points to the Page Number button.*

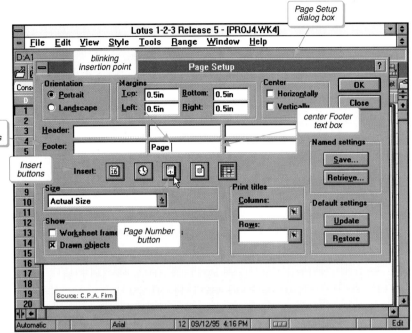

FIGURE 4-64

STEP 3 ▶

Click the Page number button and point to the OK button in the Page Setup dialog box.

1-2-3 inserts the number sign (#) in the center Footer text box (Figure 4-65). This entry will cause 1-2-3 to print the text you typed followed by a page number centered at the bottom of each page. The mouse pointer points to the OK button.

STEP 4

Choose the OK button in the Page Setup dialog box.

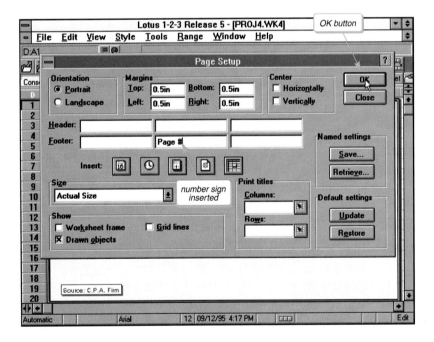

FIGURE 4-65

▲▬▬▬▬▬▬▬▬▬▬

1-2-3 returns to the 1-2-3 window. The footer information entered into the Footer text box does not display on the screen but prints at the bottom of each page when the file is printed. You can use the Print Preview icon on the set of SmartIcons to display the footer to ensure you have entered it correctly.

▸ **TABLE 4-1**

INSERT BUTTON	INFORMATION ENTERED	CODE ENTERED
	date of printing	@ (at sign)
	time of printing	+ (plus sign)
	page number	# (number sign)
	file name	^ (caret)
	contents of a cell	\ (backslash), then type the cell address

The three header and footer text boxes in Figure 4-65 on the previous page are used to control the alignment of the text entered. Enter text in the left text boxes to left-align the text in a header or footer. Text entered in the center text boxes is centered in a header or footer. The right text boxes right-align the text in a header or footer.

1-2-3 provides great flexibility in printing information in a header or footer line. You can enter up to approximately 79 characters of text in each header or footer text box. Table 4-1 shows the Insert buttons you can use in the dialog box and the information and code that is entered in a header or footer.

To remove text entered as a header or footer, choose the Page Setup command from the File menu, highlight the text you want to delete in the Header or Footer text box, press the DEL key, and choose the OK button in the Page Setup dialog box.

Previewing Multiple Worksheets

You have entered the page breaks to print each worksheet on a separate page and entered page numbers on each page. You should preview the worksheets before printing to verify that the footer and page breaks are entered properly. To preview multiple worksheets, perform the following steps.

TO PREVIEW MULTIPLE WORKSHEETS ▼

STEP 1 ▶

Point to the Print Preview icon on the set of SmartIcons and click the left mouse button. When the Print Preview dialog box displays, ensure the All worksheets option button is selected in the Preview area. Then, point to the OK button.

1-2-3 displays the Print Preview dialog box (Figure 4-66). The All worksheets option button is selected. The mouse pointer points to the OK button.

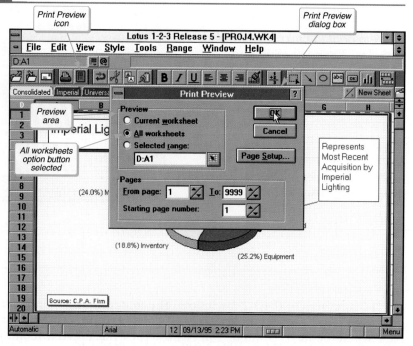

FIGURE 4-66

STEP 2 ▶

Choose the OK button in the Print Preview dialog box. When the Print Preview window displays, point to the Multiple Pages Icon (⊞) in the Print Preview window.

1-2-3 displays the Print Preview window and the first page (Figure 4-67). The mouse pointer points to the Multiple Pages icon. Notice the footer displays centered at the bottom of the page.

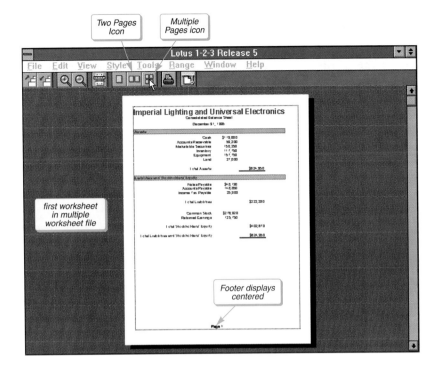

FIGURE 4-67

STEP 3 ▶

Click the left mouse button. Point to the Close icon.

1-2-3 displays the multiple worksheets (Figure 4-68). The mouse pointer points to the Close icon.

STEP 4

Click the Close icon in the Print Preview window.

1-2-3 closes the Print Preview window and returns to the Asset_Chart worksheet.

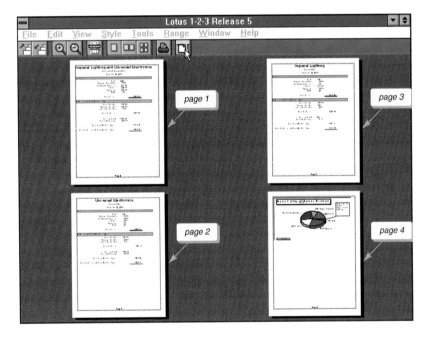

FIGURE 4-68

You can display up to nine worksheets in a file in the Print Preview window. The Two Pages icon (Figure 4-67) displays two worksheets in the Print Preview window.

Printing the Multiple Worksheets

The next step is to print the worksheets. Printing the worksheet is accomplished by performing the steps on the next page.

TO PRINT MULTIPLE WORKSHEETS

Step 1: Click the Print icon on the set of SmartIcons.

Step 2: Select the All worksheets option button in the Print area.

Step 3: Choose the OK button in the Print dialog box.

1-2-3 produces the printouts shown in Figure 4-69 on this and the next page.

Imperial Lighting and Universal Electronics
Consolidated Balance Sheet
December 31, 1995

Assets

Cash	$113,000
Accounts Receivable	59,200
Marketable Securities	150,250
Inventory	117,750
Equipment	157,750
Land	27,000
Total Assets	$624,950

Liabilities and Stockholders' Equity

Notes Payable	$48,130
Accounts Payable	148,850
Income Tax Payable	25,300
Total Liabilities	$222,280
Common Stock	$276,920
Retained Earnings	125,750
Total Stockholders' Equity	$402,670
Total Liabilities and Stockholders' Equity	$624,950

Page 1

Imperial Lighting
Balance Sheet
December 31, 1995

Assets

Cash	$75,000
Accounts Receivable	35,750
Marketable Securities	95,000
Inventory	105,250
Equipment	82,750
Land	12,000
Total Assets	$405,750

Liabilities and Stockholders' Equity

Notes Payable	$22,450
Accounts Payable	135,000
Income Tax Payable	17,800
Total Liabilities	$175,250
Common Stock	$180,000
Retained Earnings	50,500
Total Stockholders' Equity	$230,500
Total Liabilities and Stockholders' Equity	$405,750

Page 2

FIGURE 4-69a

Universal Electronics
Balance Sheet

December 31, 1995

Assets

Cash	$38,000
Accounts Receivable	23,450
Marketable Securities	55,250
Inventory	12,500
Equipment	75,000
Land	15,000
Total Assets	**$219,200**

Liabilities and Stockholders' Equity

Notes Payable	$25,680	
Accounts Payable	13,850	
Income Tax Payable	7,500	
Total Liabilities		**$47,030**
Common Stock	$96,920	
Retained Earnings	75,250	
Total Stockholders' Equity		**$172,170**
Total Liabilities and Stockholders' Equity		**$219,200**

Page 3

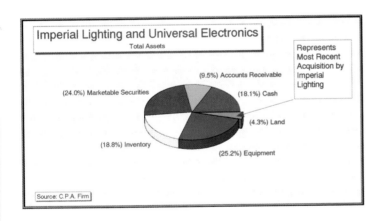

Imperial Lighting and Universal Electronics
Total Assets

(9.5%) Accounts Receivable
(24.0%) Marketable Securities
(18.1%) Cash
(4.3%) Land
(18.8%) Inventory
(25.2%) Equipment

Represents Most Recent Acquisition by Imperial Lighting

Source: C.P.A. Firm

Page 4

FIGURE 4-69b

▶ PROJECT SUMMARY

In Project 4, you learned about multiple worksheets. Using Group mode, you formatted multiple worksheets. With the Copy and Paste commands you copied between worksheets. In addition, you learned how to create 3D formulas and view multiple worksheets in perspective view. Using the techniques and steps presented in the project, you saw how to insert page breaks in multiple worksheets and print each page with a footer. Finally you learned how to add titles, footnotes, data labels, text block, and an arrow to a 3D pie chart.

▶ KEY TERMS AND INDEX

A data range (L238)
asset (L211)
balance sheet (L211)
Clear Split command (L235)
Clipboard (L220)
consolidated balance sheet (L211)
Copy icon (L220)
Cut icon (L222)
Data Labels command (L240)
destination (L220)

footer (L248)
footnote (L239)
Group mode (L226)
header (L248)
Insert buttons (L251)
Insert command (L218)
liability (L211)
move data (L216),(L222)
Page Break command (L246)
Page Setup command (L248)
Paste icon (L220)

perspective view (L233)
source (L220)
Split command (L233)
stockholders' equity (L211)
text block (L211)
3D (three-dimensional) range (L222)
View menu (L233)
Worksheet Defaults command (L232)
X data range (L238)

Q U I C K   R E F E R E N C E

In Lotus 1-2-3 for Windows, you can accomplish a task in a number of ways. The following table presents a quick reference to each task presented in this project with its available options. The commands listed in the Menu column can be executed using either the keyboard or mouse.

Task	Mouse	Menu	Keyboard Shortcuts
Add a Footer		From File menu, choose Page Setup	
Add a Footnote		From Chart menu or quick menu, choose Headings	
Add an Arrow to a Chart	Click Draw Arrow icon on Charting set of SmartIcons	From Tools menu, choose Draw	
Add Data Labels		From Chart menu or quick menu, choose Data Labels	
Clear Perspective View		From View menu, choose Clear Split	
Copy Data Between Worksheets	Click Copy icon on Default Sheet of SmartIcons; Paste icon on Default Sheet of SmartIcons	From Edit menu, or quick menu, choose Copy; from Edit menu or quick menu, choose Paste	Press CTRL+C, CTRL+V

Task	Mouse	Menu	Keyboard Shortcuts
Create a 3D Pie Chart	Click 3D Pie icon on Default Sheet of SmartIcons	From Chart menu, choose Type, or from quick menu, choose Chart Type	
Create a New Chart	Click Chart icon on Default Sheet of SmartIcons	From Tools menu, choose Chart	
Display Multiple Worksheets in Perspective View		From View menu, choose Split	
Explode a Pie Slice	Click desired slice and drag		
Group Worksheets		From Style menu, choose Worksheet Defaults	
Insert a Page Break		From Style menu, choose Page Break	
Insert a Worksheet Before the Current Worksheet		From Edit menu, choose Insert	Press CTRL++
Move Data Between Worksheets	Click Cut icon on Default Sheet of SmartIcons; click Paste icon on Default Sheet of SmartIcons	From Edit menu or quick menu, choose Cut; from Edit menu or quick menu, choose Paste	Press CTRL+X; CTRL+V
Move the Cell Pointer Between Worksheets in	Click desired cell location in worksheet	From Edit menu, choose Go To	Press CTRL+PAGE UP; CTRL+PAGE DOWN
Select a 3D Range	Select range in first worksheet, press and hold down SHIFT key, then click tab of last worksheet to be included in range		

S T U D E N T   A S S I G N M E N T S

STUDENT ASSIGNMENT 1
True/False

Instructions: Circle T if the statement is true or F if the statement is false.

T   F   1. To copy selected data from worksheet A to worksheet B, use the Copy Down command.

T   F   2. Once selected cells are copied to the Clipboard, use the Paste icon to paste the Clipboard contents in the worksheet.

T   F   3. When you use the Paste icon, the Clipboard contents are erased.

(continued)

STUDENT ASSIGNMENT 1 (continued)

T   F   4. When you use the Cut and Paste icons, the source data is removed from its original location and reappears in the destination range.

T   F   5. You can use the New Sheet button below the set of SmartIcons to insert a new worksheet before the current worksheet.

T   F   6. A 3D (three-dimensional) range includes the same cells in two or more contiguous worksheets.

T   F   7. The 3D range, C:C1..D:D1, contains cells C1 in worksheet C and D1 in worksheet D.

T   F   8. To select a 3D range, select the range in the first worksheet of the 3D range, hold down the SHIFT key, and click the worksheet tab of the last worksheet you want to include in the range.

T   F   9. To group multiple worksheets, choose the Worksheet Defaults command from the Style menu and select the Group mode check box in the Worksheet Defaults dialog box.

T   F   10. When Group mode is on, changes made to the current worksheet affect all other worksheets in the file.

T   F   11. Turning off Group mode restores all settings applied to the worksheet before grouping them.

T   F   12. To view three continuous worksheets in perspective view, choose the Split command from the View menu.

T   F   13. You can chart up to 23 data series in a pie chart.

T   F   14. Use the Footnote command from the quick menu to add a footnote to a pie chart.

T   F   15. 1-2-3 automatically adds a title, subtitle, and footnotes to a chart if you include the labels in the range to be charted.

T   F   16. When creating a pie chart, 1-2-3 displays the percentage that each slice represents of the whole as a default.

T   F   17. When you choose to display the contents of the X data range as a data label on a pie chart, the legend will not display.

T   F   18. To separate a slice from a pie chart, first select the slice, then drag the slice to the desired position.

T   F   19. To draw a square text block, hold down the CTRL key as you drag across the worksheet.

T   F   20. 1-2-3 automatically inserts a page break between multiple worksheets.

STUDENT ASSIGNMENT 2
Multiple Choice

Instructions: Circle the correct response.

1. To copy between worksheets, you can use the _____.
   a. Cut and Paste icons
   b. Copy and Paste icons
   c. Copy Down command
   d. Move and Paste icons

2. To move data from worksheet A to worksheet B in the same file, use the _____.
   a. Cut and Paste icons
   b. Copy and Paste icons
   c. Copy Down command
   d. Move and Paste icons

3. To insert a worksheet before the current worksheet in the same file, you can _____.
   a. click the New Sheet button below the set of SmartIcons
   b. choose the Insert command on the Style menu
   c. double-click the New Sheet button below the set of SmartIcons
   d. choose the Insert command on the Edit menu

4. To select a 3D range, select the range in the first worksheet of the 3D range, hold down the _____ key, and click the worksheet tab of the last worksheet you want to include in the range.
   a. INSERT
   b. CTRL
   c. SHIFT
   d. ALT

5. The 3D range A:A1..B:B2 contains cells _____.
   a. A1 and B2 in worksheet A and A1 and B2 in worksheet B
   b. A1 in worksheet A and B2 in worksheet B
   c. A1, A2, B1, and B2 in worksheet A and A1, A2, B1, and B2 in worksheet B
   d. A1 and A2 in worksheet A and B1 and B2 in worksheet B

6. To group worksheets, choose the _____ command and select the Group mode check box.
   a. Worksheet Defaults
   b. Set View Preferences
   c. Users Setup
   d. Lines & Color

7. After selecting a range to chart, clicking the Chart icon on the set of SmartIcons will display a _____.
   a. blank chart
   b. line chart
   c. bar chart
   d. pie chart

8. To add a page break to a worksheet, you can use the Page Break command on the _____ menu.
   a. Style
   b. View
   c. Edit
   d. File

9. To create a footer, use the _____ command from the File menu.
   a. Print
   b. Page Setup
   c. Print Preview
   d. Printer Setup

10. You can use the _____ icon on the set of SmartIcons to display a footer to ensure it is entered correctly.
   a. Print Preview
   b. Print
   c. Copy
   d. Paste

STUDENT ASSIGNMENT 3
Understanding Multiple Worksheets

Instructions: Explain the steps to accomplish the following tasks.

Task 1: Insert one worksheet before worksheet A.

Steps: _____

_____

_____

(continued)

STUDENT ASSIGNMENT 3 (continued)

Task 2: Display three consecutive worksheets in perspective view.

Steps: _____

_____

_____

Task 3: Select the 3D range A:A1..D:D10.

Steps: _____

_____

_____

Task 4: Copy the range A1..B10 in worksheet A to the same range in worksheet B.

Steps: _____

_____

_____

Task 5: Duplicate the settings of worksheet A to worksheets B and C.

Steps: _____

_____

_____

STUDENT ASSIGNMENT 4
Understanding the Insert Buttons in the Page Setup Dialog Box

Instructions: Figure SA4-4 shows the Insert buttons in the Page Setup dialog box used to insert data in a header or footer. In the spaces provided, briefly explain the function of the buttons identified by the arrows.

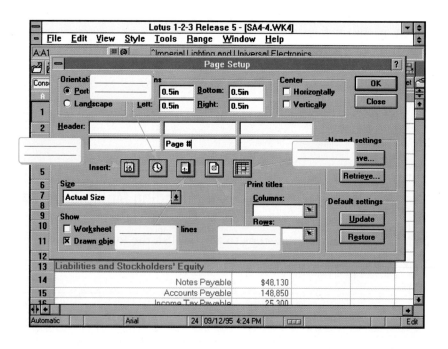

FIGURE SA4-4

STUDENT ASSIGNMENT 5
Adding Page Breaks to Multiple Worksheets

Instructions: In the space provided, explain the steps necessary to add page breaks to allow each worksheet shown in Figure SA4-5 to print on a separate page.

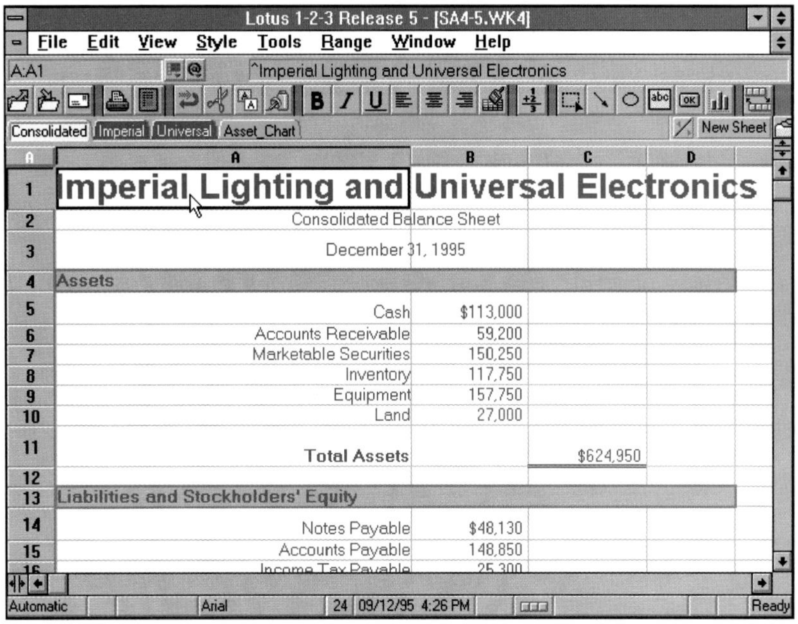

FIGURE SA4-5

Steps: _____

_____

_____

_____

_____

STUDENT ASSIGNMENT 6
Understanding 1-2-3 Dialog Boxes

Instructions: Write the command that causes the dialog box to display and allows you to make the indicated changes.

CHANGES	COMMAND
1. Add a footer to a printed page.	_____
2. Add data labels to a pie chart.	_____
3. Display multiple worksheets in perspective view.	_____
4. Insert a page break.	_____
5. Insert a worksheet before the current worksheet.	_____
6. Add color to a worksheet tab.	_____

COMPUTER LABORATORY EXERCISE 1
Using the Help Menu

Instructions: Perform the following tasks using a personal computer.

1. Start Lotus 1-2-3 Release 5 for Windows.
2. Select the Help menu.
3. Choose Contents from the Help menu and Basics from the 1-2-3 Release 5 Help Contents.
4. Choose Copying, Moving, and Pasting Data from Basics.
5. Read Copying, Moving, and Pasting Data, print the topic, and answer the following questions.
   a. How are the copy and move operations similar?

   _____

   _____

   b. If you accidentally cut the wrong data, what should you do?

   _____

   _____

   c. How do you know you have successfully copied data to the Clipboard?

   _____

   _____

   d. After you finish copying data, what happens to the data on the Clipboard?

   _____

   _____

6. Exit the Help window.

COMPUTER LABORATORY EXERCISE 2
Creating a Consolidated Worksheet

Instructions: Start 1-2-3. Open the CLE4-2.WK4 file from the Lotus4 subdirectory on the Student Diskette that accompanies this book. Using the worksheet on your screen and illustrated in Figure CLE4-2, enter the formulas to create the Consolidated worksheet. This is the same consolidated balance sheet created in Project 4. When you have completed the Consolidated worksheet, format the values in the worksheet, then print the Consolidated worksheet only.

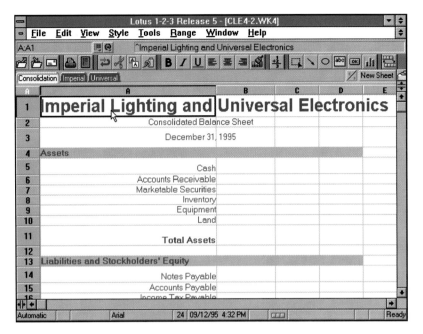

FIGURE CLE4-2

COMPUTER LABORATORY EXERCISE 3
Creating a 3D Pie Chart

Instructions: Start 1-2-3. Open the CLE4-3.WK4 file from the Lotus4 subdirectory on the Student Diskette that accompanies this book. Insert a second worksheet and then perform the following tasks.

1. Select the range A5..B10 in the Imperial worksheet.
2. Create a 3D pie chart on the second worksheet.
3. Add a title, subtitle, and a footnote to the chart.
4. Show the percentages and the contents of the X data range as data labels.
5. Explode the smallest pie slice.
6. Follow directions from your instructor for turning in this exercise.
7. Exit 1-2-3.

COMPUTER LABORATORY ASSIGNMENTS

COMPUTER LABORATORY ASSIGNMENT 1
Creating a Sales Summary Worksheet

Purpose: To provide experience in using Lotus 1-2-3 Release 5 for Windows to create a summary worksheet that requires creating multiple worksheets, entering labels, values, formulas, calculating sums, adding footers, creating a pie chart, and saving and printing the worksheets.

Problem: Create a summary worksheet that combines the sales, returns, and net sales of the Century Plaza store and Monarch Plaza store for the Musician's Warehouse. The sales and returns for the two stores are shown in the table on the next page.

(continued)

COMPUTER LABORATORY ASSIGNMENT 1 (continued)

ITEM	CENTURY PLAZA	MONARCH PLAZA
Sales:		
Cassette Tapes	275,000	343,750
Compact Discs	523,000	653,750
Videos	478,200	597,750
Returns:		
Cassette Tapes	52,300	65,375
Compact Discs	15,530	19,413
Videos	4,750	6,250

The Summary worksheet is shown below in Figure CLA4-1a.

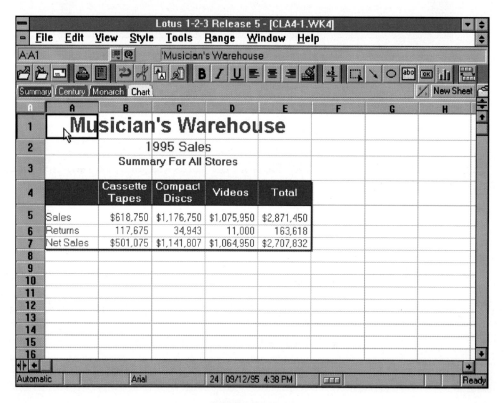

FIGURE CLA4-1a

Instructions:

1. Create a Sales worksheet for the Century Plaza store using the labels and values from the table. Calculate the net sales by subtracting returns from sales for cassette tapes, compact discs, and videos. Calculate the total for sales, returns, and net sales by summing the values in each row.
2. Create a Sales worksheet for the Monarch Plaza store using the labels and values from the table. Calculate the net sales by subtracting returns from sales for cassette tapes, compact discs, and videos. Calculate the total for sales, returns, and net sales by summing the values in each row.
3. Create a Summary worksheet. Calculate the sales for cassette tapes, compact discs, and videos by adding the corresponding sales for the Century Plaza store and the Monarch Plaza store. For example, calculate sales for cassette tapes in the Summary worksheet by adding the Century Plaza store sales for cassette tapes and Monarch Plaza store sales for cassette tapes.

4. Format the worksheets as shown. The row heights are: 1 = 29; 2 = 18; 3 = 28; 4 = 28; and 5 = 22. The title in row 1 is 24 point and the subtitle in row 2 is 14 point. The designer frame is the second designer frame from the left in the top row of the Designer frame drop-down box.
5. Create the 3D pie chart from the Summary worksheet by plotting the total sales and total returns. Display the data labels as shown in Figure CLA4-1b.

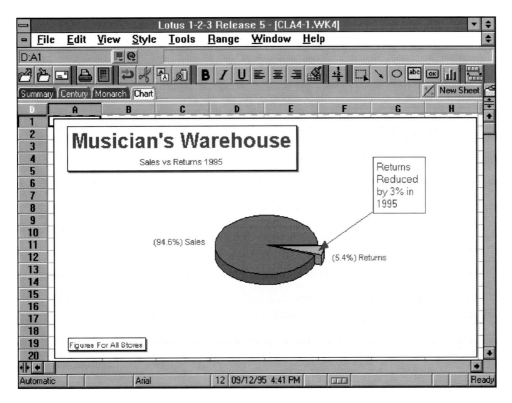

FIGURE CLA4-1b

6. Add the text block and arrow as shown. Explode the Returns pie slice.
7. Save the worksheets and chart using a file name consisting of the initials of your first and last names followed by the assignment number. Example: KS4-1.
8. Print each worksheet and the chart on separate pages. Number the pages in the bottom right corner of each page.
9. Follow directions from your instructor for turning in this assignment.

COMPUTER LABORATORY ASSIGNMENT 2
Creating a Projected Costs Consolidated Worksheet

Purpose: To provide experience in using Lotus 1-2-3 Release 5 for Windows to create a consolidated worksheet that requires creating multiple worksheets, entering labels, values, formulas, calculating sums, adding footers, creating a pie chart, and saving and printing the worksheets.

Problem: Create a consolidated worksheet that combines the projected costs of the West Side Store and East Side Store. The projected costs of West Side and East Side Stores are shown in the table on the next page.

(continued)

COMPUTER LABORATORY ASSIGNMENT 2 (continued)

ITEM	WEST SIDE STORE	EAST SIDE STORE
Direct Costs:		
Direct Labor	37,500	75,000
Materials	76,000	152,000
Overhead Costs:		
Salaries	42,600	65,200
Rent	34,600	40,000
Depreciation	12,000	3,000
Utilities	82,500	16,500
Maintenance	12,000	24,000

The consolidated worksheet is shown below in Figure CLA4-2a.

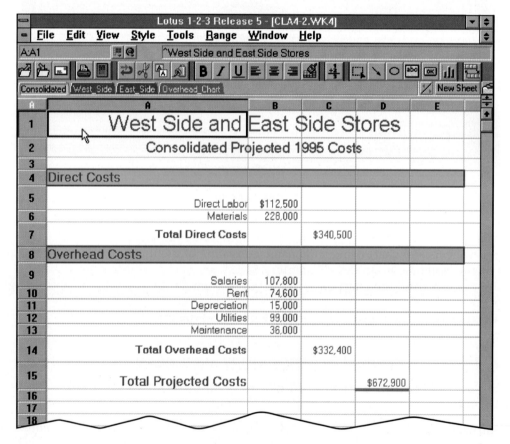

FIGURE CLA4-2a

Instructions:

1. Create a Projected Costs worksheet for the West Side Store using the labels and values from the table. Calculate the total direct costs by adding direct labor and materials. Calculate the total overhead costs by adding salaries, rents, depreciation, utilities, and maintenance. Calculate total projected expenses by adding total direct costs and total overhead costs.

2. Create a Projected Costs worksheet for the East Side Store using the labels and values from the table. Calculate the total direct costs by adding direct labor and materials. Calculate the total overhead costs by adding salaries, rents, depreciation, utilities, and maintenance. Calculate total projected expenses by adding total direct costs and total overhead costs.

3. Create a Consolidated Projected Costs worksheet. Calculate each cost by adding the corresponding cost for the West Side Store and East Side store. For example, calculate direct labor by adding the West Side Store direct labor and East Side Store direct labor.

4. Format the worksheets as shown. Column A is 34 characters wide. The row heights are: 1 = 30; 2 = 22; 4 = 17; 5 = 28; 7 = 28; 8 = 17; 9 = 28; 14 = 28; and 15 = 30. The title in row 1 is 24 point and the subtitle in row 2 is 18 point; the labels in row 4 and 8 are 17 point; and the label in row 15 is 14 point.

5. Create the 3D pie chart from the Consolidated Projected Costs worksheet by plotting the overhead costs (salaries, rent, depreciation, utilities, and maintenance). Display the data labels as shown in Figure CLA4-2b.

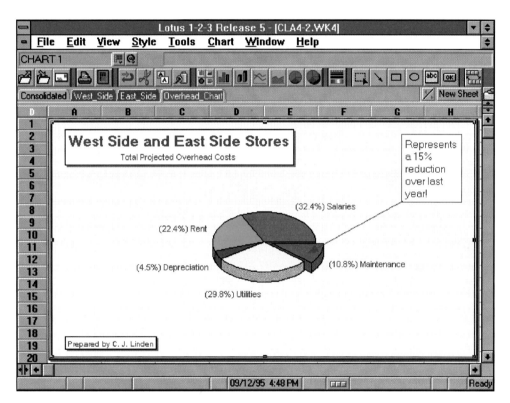

FIGURE CLA4-2b

6. Add the text block and arrow as shown. Explode the Maintenance pie slice.

7. Save the worksheets and chart using a file name consisting of the initials of your first and last names followed by the assignment number. Example: KS4-2.

8. Print each worksheet and the chart on separate pages. Print the current date in the bottom left corner of each page. Number the pages in the bottom right corner of each page.

9. Follow directions from your instructor for turning in this assignment.

COMPUTER LABORATORY ASSIGNMENT 3
Creating a Consolidated Income Statement Worksheet

Purpose: To provide experience in using Lotus 1-2-3 Release 5 for Windows to create a consolidated worksheet that requires creating multiple worksheets, entering labels, values, formulas, calculating sums, adding footers, creating a pie chart, and saving and printing the worksheets.

Problem: Create a consolidated worksheet that combines the income statement of the Brickely Company and the Miller Company. Data for the income statements for both companies is shown in the following table:

ITEM	BRICKELY COMPANY	MILLER COMPANY
Sales	73,600.00	103,040.00
Cost of Goods Sold	42,800.00	59,920.00
Salary	7,000.00	9,800.00
Advertising	5,860.00	8,204.00
Insurance	1,075.00	1,505.00
Store Supplies	750.00	1,025.00

The consolidated worksheet is shown in Figure CLA4-3a.

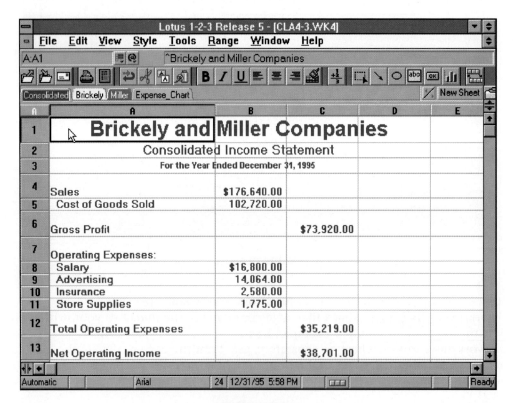

FIGURE CLA4-3a

Instructions:

1. Create an income statement for the Brickely Company using the labels and values from the table. Calculate the gross profit by subtracting the cost of goods sold from sales. Calculate the total operating expenses by adding salary, advertising, insurance, and store supplies. Calculate the net operating expenses by subtracting the total operating expenses from the gross profit.
2. Create an income statement for the Miller Company using the labels and values from the table. Calculate the gross profit by subtracting the cost of goods sold from sales. Calculate the total operating expenses by adding salary, advertising, insurance, and store supplies. Calculate the net operating expenses by subtracting the total operating expenses from the gross profit.
3. Create a consolidated income statement by summing the values from the Brickely Company income statement and the Miller Company income statement. Sum each item by adding the corresponding item for the Brickely Company and the Miller Company. For example, calculate sales on the consolidated income statement by adding the Brickely Company sales and the Miller Company sales.
4. Format the worksheets as shown. Column A is 28 characters wide, and columns B, C, and D are 12 characters wide. The row heights are: 1 = 29; 2 = 17; 3 = 17; 4 = 28; 6 = 29; 7 = 28; 12 = 28; and 13 = 28. The title in row 1 is 24 point; the subtitle in row 2 is 14 point; and the subtitle in row 3 is 10 point.
5. Create the 3D pie chart from the Consolidated worksheet by charting the operating expenses (salary, advertising, insurance, and store supplies.). Display the data labels as shown in Figure CLA4-3b.

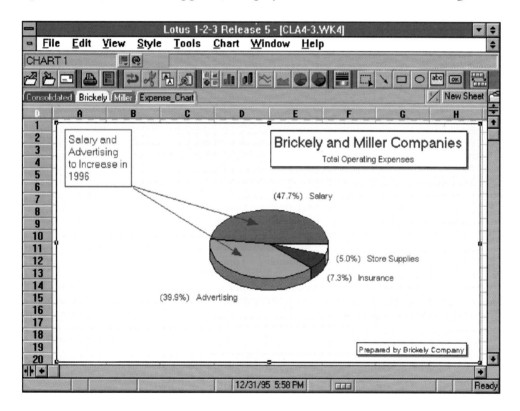

FIGURE CLA4-3b

6. Add the text block and arrows as shown.
7. Save the worksheets and chart using a file name consisting of the initials of your first and last names followed by the assignment number. Example: KS4-3.
8. Print each worksheet and the chart on separate pages. Print the current date in the bottom left corner of each page. Number the pages in the bottom right corner of each page. Print your name in the top right corner of each page.
9. Follow directions from your instructor for turning in this assignment.

COMPUTER LABORATORY ASSIGNMENT 4
Creating a Consolidated Ice Cream Sales Worksheet

Purpose: To provide experience in using Lotus 1-2-3 Release 5 for Windows to create a consolidated worksheet that requires creating multiple worksheets, entering labels, values, formulas, calculating sums, adding footers, creating a pie chart, and saving and printing the worksheets.

Problem: Create a consolidated worksheet that combines the ice cream sales for Rainbow Flavors' two stores for Monday through Friday. The sales data for the two stores is shown in the tables below:

▸ **SOUTH BAY RAINBOW FLAVORS**

FLAVOR	MONDAY	TUESDAY	WEDNESDAY	THURSDAY	FRIDAY
Vanilla	616	675	780	870	800
Chocolate	250	261	237	497	849
Strawberry	400	952	850	447	950
Peanut Butter	850	975	980	950	900
Pralines & Cream	300	553	452	400	350

▸ **EAST HILLS RAINBOW FLAVORS**

FLAVOR	MONDAY	TUESDAY	WEDNESDAY	THURSDAY	FRIDAY
Vanilla	689	756	873	974	896
Chocolate	280	292	265	556	950
Strawberry	448	1000	952	500	1044
Peanut Butter	952	1025	1045	1064	1008
Pralines & Cream	175	275	235	448	392

Instructions:

1. Create a sales worksheet for the South Bay store showing the daily sales for the five flavors of ice cream. Calculate the total gallons sold for each flavor. Calculate the total gallons sold for each day.
2. Create a sales worksheet for the East Hills store showing the daily sales for the five flavors of ice cream. Calculate the total gallons sold for each flavor. Calculate the total gallons sold for each day.
3. Create a consolidated worksheet by summing the values from the South Bay store and the East Hills store. For example, calculate sales for vanilla ice cream on Monday on the consolidated worksheet by adding the South Bay sales for vanilla ice cream on Monday and the East Hills sales for vanilla ice cream on Monday.
4. Calculate the total gallons sold for each flavor on the consolidated worksheet. Calculate the total gallons sold for each day on the consolidated worksheet.
5. Format the worksheet appropriately.
6. Create a 3D pie chart from the consolidated worksheet by plotting the total gallons sold for each flavor. Display appropriate data labels. Explode the flavor that sold the fewest number of gallons.
7. Add a text block and arrow to explain the exploded pie slice.
8. Save the worksheets and chart using a file name consisting of the initials of your first and last names followed by the assignment number. Example: KS4-4.
9. Print each worksheet and the chart on separate pages. Add an appropriate footer to each page.
10. Follow directions from your instructor for turning in this assignment.

▼

CHARTS AND MAPS

OBJECTIVES You will have mastered the material in this project when you can:

▶ Create a line chart
▶ Add x-axis and y-axis grid lines to a chart
▶ Change line type, line color, and symbols on a line chart
▶ Create an HLCO chart
▶ Rotate column headings
▶ Create a mixed chart

▶ Change the second y-axis scale
▶ Add a title to the second y-axis
▶ Add an ellipse to a worksheet
▶ Create a map
▶ Change a map title
▶ Change bin colors on a map

▶ INTRODUCTION

A **chart** is a graphical representation of the data in a worksheet. Charts can help you compare values, understand relationships among values, and see trends when comparing values. In earlier projects, you were introduced to the 3D bar chart, 3D pie chart, and 3D stacked bar chart. Project 5 reviews the techniques used to create these charts and presents additional topics that allow you to produce other types of charts for a variety of applications.

A **map** is a geographical representation of the data in a worksheet. Maps can reveal the significance of data that has a basis in geography. Maps are dynamic; when you change the data on which a map is based, 1-2-3 automatically updates the map to reflect the changes made. Project 5 introduces you to the mapping capability of 1-2-3.

▶ TYPES OF CHARTS

W hen you chart data, it is important to be able to analyze the data in a worksheet and determine the appropriate chart type you should use to best present the data in a meaningful manner. Project 5 explains the use of the line chart, mixed chart, and HLCO chart and how they are created. The following paragraphs explain the use of these chart types.

Line Charts

A **line chart** displays data by drawing lines and placing symbols horizontally across a chart. Line charts are often used for showing trends over a period of time. The line chart in Figure 5-1 shows the Total Exports of Computers, Inc. over a six-month period for three products, Software (computer applications), Desktops

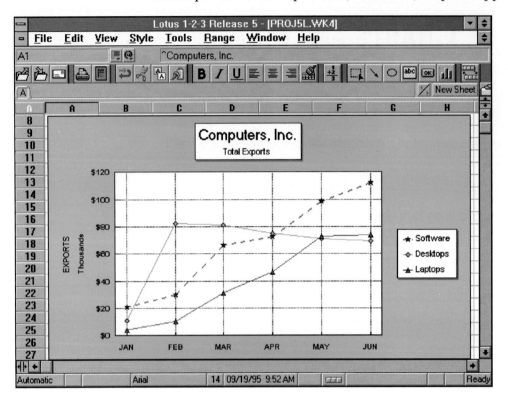

FIGURE 5-1

(desktop computers), and Laptops (laptop computers). From this chart, you can see the exports of Software and Laptops have been increasing since January, but Desktops have been on a decline since February. The small stars, diamonds, and triangles on the chart are called **symbols**. Symbols represent individual values in worksheet cells based on the scale on the left side of the chart.

The line chart in Figure 5-1 does not display precise values in a manner that is easy to see but effectively shows trends over a period of time.

Mixed Charts

A **mixed chart** combines two chart types on the same chart. The chart in Figure 5-2 shows the Total Earnings and Dividends per Share of Chesapeake Air for seven quarters. The total earnings for Chesapeake Air are indicated by the transparent bars outlined in magenta, and the dividends per share are indicated by the blue line.

Notice in Figure 5-2 that the numbers for total earnings on the left are different from the numbers for dividends per share on the right. The numbers on the left represent the total earnings for Chesapeake Air and the bars are scaled to these numbers. The numbers on the right represent the dividends per share for Chesapeake Air and the blue line

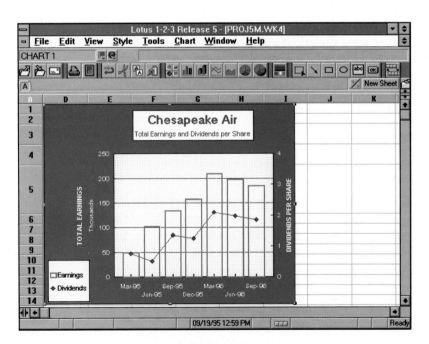

FIGURE 5-2

is scaled to these numbers. This second y-axis is called the **2nd y-axis**. As a result, the blue diamond for Mar-95 represents a value of $0.75; whereas, the bar for Mar-95 represents a value of $50,000.

The mixed chart serves essentially the same function as a bar or line chart. By mixing both lines and bars, a different method of presentation and emphasis is possible.

HLCO Charts

A **HLCO chart,** also known as a stock market chart, tracks data that fluctuates over time, such as charting the highest and lowest price of a stock on a given day. The chart in Figure 5-3 shows the high, low, close, and open price of West Coast Computers stock for a ten-day period in November. Each day is represented by a vertical line where the top of the line is the high value for the day, the bottom is the low value for the day, and the horizontal markers are used for the open and close values. The blue bars on the chart represent the volume of trading transactions for the stock.

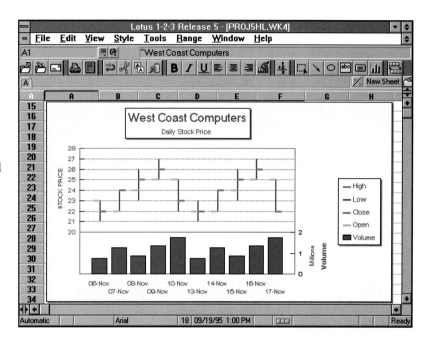

FIGURE 5-3

► CREATING A CHART

To create a chart, select the range in the worksheet you want to chart. Then click the Chart icon on the set of SmartIcons or choose the Chart command from the Tools menu. Drag across the worksheet where you want the chart to display and release the mouse button when the chart is the desired size. 1-2-3 then draws the initial default chart type, a bar chart.

To create a chart other than the bar chart, use the chart icons on the set of charting SmartIcons or choose the Type command from the Chart menu. The Type dialog box displays a list of chart types you can choose. Figure 5-4 illustrates the set of charting SmartIcons. To change the chart type from the set of charting SmartIcons, click the appropriate icon.

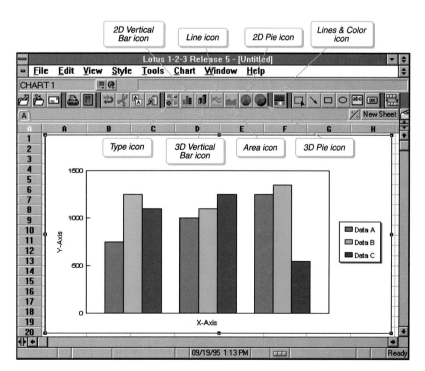

FIGURE 5-4

▶ LINE CHARTS

L ine charts show trends in a set of data over a period of time. In a line chart, 1-2-3 plots each data value as a data point and connects the data points with a line. Each data point is represented with a symbol, such as a triangle, square, or diamond.

Figure 5-5 illustrates a worksheet containing the total exports for three products: Software, Desktops, and Laptops. Also shown is a line chart illustrating the total exports for the months January through June. The symbols appear as stars for Software, diamonds for Desktops, and triangles for Laptops. The magenta line for Software is a dashed line while the green line for Desktops and the blue line for Laptops are solid lines.

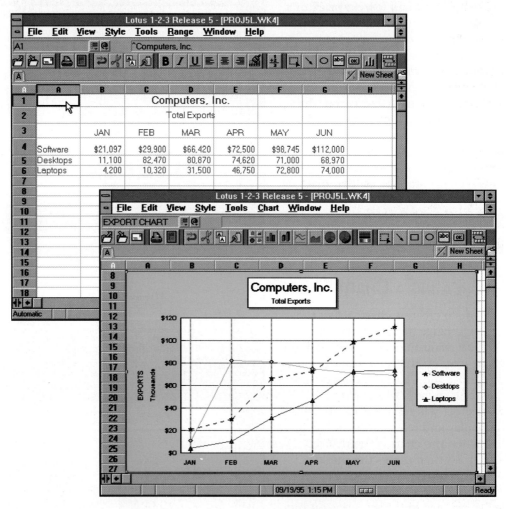

FIGURE 5-5

A line chart is an appropriate choice of charts because it graphically illustrates the export trends of the three products for a six-month period.

Understanding Charting Terms

The following paragraphs review charting terminology. Figure 5-6 illustrates a line chart with various parts of the chart labeled.

All charts except pie charts have a horizontal axis called the **x-axis** and a vertical axis called the **y-axis.** The charted values are identified on the x-axis by **x-axis labels.** In the chart in Figure 5-6, the x-axis labels JAN, FEB, MAR, APR, MAY, and JUN are displayed below the x-axis.

The y-axis provides the measure against which values in the chart are plotted. 1-2-3 automatically divides the y-axis into units based on the lowest and highest values in the worksheet.

1-2-3 plots each row or column of data in the selected range as a **data series**. Each data series (for example, exports for software) has its own color. You can chart up to 23 data series, represented by the letters A through W. The chart in Figure 5-6 contains three data series, Software, Desktops, and Laptops. The first data series, Software, is identified as the A series; the second data series, Desktops, is identified as the B series; and the third data series, Laptops, is identified as the C series.

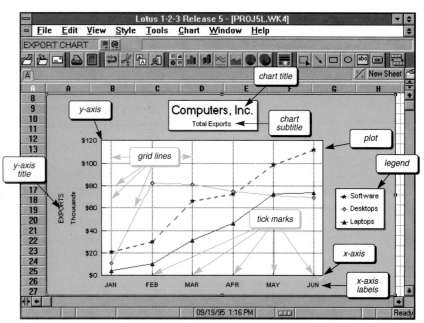

FIGURE 5-6

The main part of the chart is called the **plot**. The plot includes the axes and their labels and titles, and all the data plotted on the axes. 1-2-3 divides the axes with **tick marks** and scales the numbers on the y-axis based on the smallest and largest numbers in the selected range to chart. The plot does not include the titles or legend.

A **legend** in a chart identifies the colors and symbols used in the chart's data series.

Understanding the Rules for Automatic Charting

1-2-3 uses specific rules in creating a chart when you select a range of data to chart and click the Chart icon on the set of SmartIcons or choose the Chart command from the Tools menu. 1-2-3 begins by finding the first cell containing a value that is not a date in the selected range. Then, 1-2-3 counts the number of columns that contain values and the number of rows that contain values.

When there are more columns than rows, or the same number of columns and rows, 1-2-3 plots the data series by rows. The first row in the selected range (after any titles) becomes the x-axis labels, the second row (after any titles) in the selected range becomes the first data series, the third row (after any titles) in the selected range becomes the second data series, and so on. The first column in the selected range becomes the text entries for the legend labels.

When there are more rows than columns, 1-2-3 plots the data series by columns. The first column in the selected range becomes the x-axis labels, the second column becomes the first data series, the third column becomes the second data series, and so on. The first row after the titles becomes the text entries for the legend labels.

1-2-3 does not count blank columns or rows in the selected range.

Creating a Line Chart

In the worksheet, the range of data to chart is A1..G6 (see Figure 5-5 on page 272). The label (Computers, Inc.) in row 1 of the selected range is used for the chart title. The label (Total Exports) in row 2, is used for the chart subtitle. The first cell in the selected range containing a value is cell B4. Starting from cell B4, 1-2-3 counts the number of columns that contain values (6) and the number of rows that contain values (3). Because the selected range to chart contains more columns than rows, 1-2-3 charts the data series by rows. Therefore, the first row after the titles (row 3) is used for the x-axis labels, the second row (row 4) is used for the first data series, the third row (row 5) is used for the second data series, and the fourth row (row 6) is used for the third data series. The first column (column A) in the selected range is used for the text entries of the legend labels. The y-axis title (EXPORTS) is added to the chart.

To create a line chart, perform the following step. It is assumed the worksheet file is open and displayed on the screen.

TO CREATE A LINE CHART ▼

STEP 1 ▶

Select the range to chart – A1..G6 – and click the Chart icon on the set of SmartIcons. Drag the range for the chart, A8..H27. When the default bar chart displays on screen, point to the Line icon (⬚)on the charting set of SmartIcons and click the left mouse button.

1-2-3 displays the default bar chart and then the line chart (Figure 5-7). The Chart menu name displays on the main menu bar. The chart name, CHART 1, displays in the selection indicator. The chart title, Computers, Inc., and chart subtitle, Total Exports, display centered above the line chart because they are located in row one and row two of the selected range. Small symbols identify specific values from the worksheet for each month based on the numbers on the y-axis. The legend displays to the right of the chart. Notice 1-2-3 automatically adds the data series labels to the legend because the labels are located in column A of the selected range. The x-axis labels display below the x-axis because the labels are located in row three of the selected range. The default axes titles, X-Axis and Y-Axis, display on the chart. 1-2-3 always creates default titles for the x-axis and y-axis.

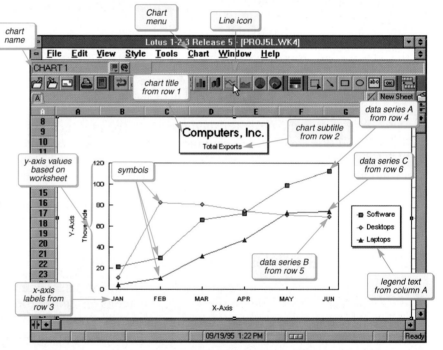

FIGURE 5-7

1-2-3 determines the range of values on the y-axis in Figure 5-7 based on the values in the charted range of the worksheet. The maximum value on the y-axis is 120 (thousand) because the greatest value in the worksheet is 112,000. Notice the interval between the values on the chart is 20 (thousand).

Changing the Line Style, Width, Color, and Symbol

When you create a line chart, 1-2-3 automatically assigns the line style, width, color, and symbol for each line. You can change the line style, line width, line color, and symbol. To make changes to a line, click the appropriate color box in the legend to select the line, then click the right mouse button and choose the Lines & Color command. To change the first data series (Software) to a magenta dashed line with a solid star-shaped symbol, perform the following steps.

TO CHANGE THE LINE STYLE, LINE WIDTH, LINE COLOR, AND SYMBOL ▼

STEP 1 ►

Point to the red box in the legend and click the right mouse button. Choose the Lines & Color command from the quick menu. When the Lines & Color dialog box displays, click the Style drop-down box arrow in the Line area and point to the dashed line (second from the bottom line style) in the Style drop-down box.

Handles appear on the legend box and all the data points in the Software series (Figure 5-8). 1-2-3 displays the Lines & Color dialog box. The mouse pointer points to the desired dashed line in the Style drop-down box.

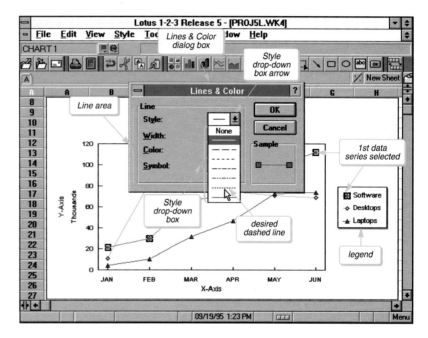

FIGURE 5-8

STEP 2 ►

Select the dashed line style in the Style drop-down box. Click the Width drop-down box arrow and point to the second line width from the top in the Width drop-down box.

The dashed line you chose displays in the Style box (Figure 5-9). The mouse pointer points to the desired line width in the Width drop-down box.

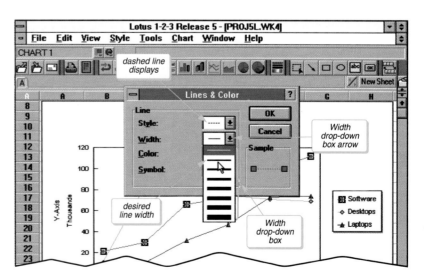

FIGURE 5-9

STEP 3 ▶

Select the line width in the Width drop-down box. Click the Color drop-down box arrow and select the magenta color in the top row of the Color drop-down box. Click the Symbol drop-down box arrow and select the filled star from the Symbol drop-down box. Point to the OK button in the Lines & Color dialog box.

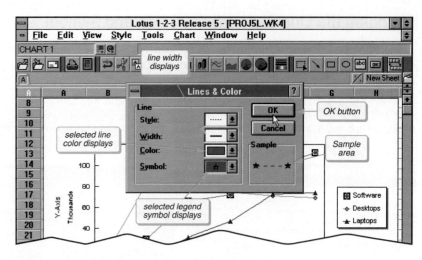

FIGURE 5-10

The line width you selected displays in the Width box (Figure 5-10). The magenta color you selected displays in the Color box. The filled star symbol you selected displays in the Symbol box. The Sample area shows how your selections in the Line area will appear in the worksheet. Notice the Lines & Color dialog box displays fewer options when a legend symbol is selected. You cannot add a designer frame to a legend symbol. The mouse pointer points to the OK button.

STEP 4 ▶

Choose the OK button in the Lines & Color dialog box.

1-2-3 displays the chart (Figure 5-11). The line for Software is now a wider dashed line. The line color is magenta and the symbols on the line are filled stars. Notice the legend symbol for Software now displays the filled star shape with a magenta dashed line.

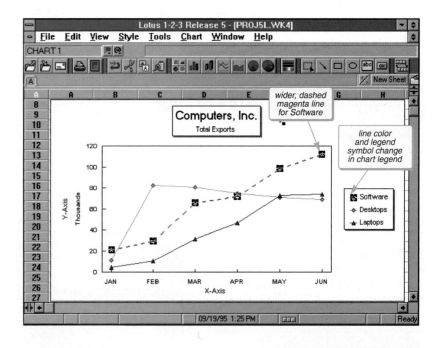

FIGURE 5-11

To remove the selection, click inside the chart where there is no other chart element.

Adding X-Axis and Y-Axis Grid Lines

Grid lines make it easier to interpret the data points in a line chart. The x-axis grid lines (see Figure 5-5 on page L272) extend vertically from the month on the x-axis and are perpendicular to the x-axis. The y-axis grid lines extend horizontally from the values on the y-axis and are perpendicular to the y-axis. To add x-axis and y-axis grid lines to the line chart, perform the following steps.

TO ADD X-AXIS AND Y-AXIS GRID LINES ▼

STEP 1 ▶

Select the chart plot and display the quick menu by pointing inside the plot and clicking the right mouse button. Point to the Grids command.

Selection handles on the chart plot indicate the chart is selected (Figure 5-12). 1-2-3 displays the quick menu. The mouse pointer points to the Grids command.

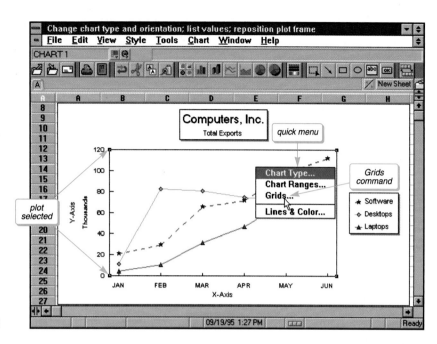

FIGURE 5-12

STEP 2 ▶

Choose the Grids command from the quick menu. When the Grids dialog box displays, click the X-axis drop-down box arrow and select the Major interval setting in the X-axis drop-down box. Click the Y-axis drop-down box arrow and select the Major interval setting in the Y-axis drop-down box. Then, point to the OK button in the Grids dialog box.

1-2-3 displays the Grids dialog box (Figure 5-13). The X-axis and Y-axis boxes display the Major interval setting. The Major interval setting adds grid lines that origi-nate from each month on the x-axis and from each value on the y-axis scale. The mouse pointer points to the OK button.

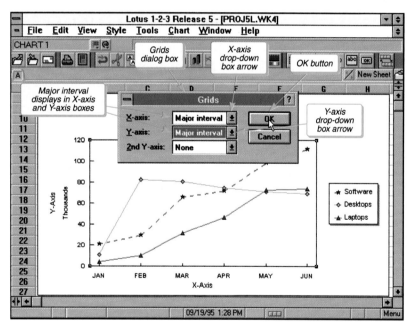

FIGURE 5-13

STEP 3 ▶

Choose the OK button in the Grids dialog box.

1-2-3 displays the line chart (Figure 5-14). The chart displays x-axis and y-axis grid lines. Notice the x-axis grid lines originate from each month on the x-axis. The y-axis grid lines originate from each value on the y-axis scale.

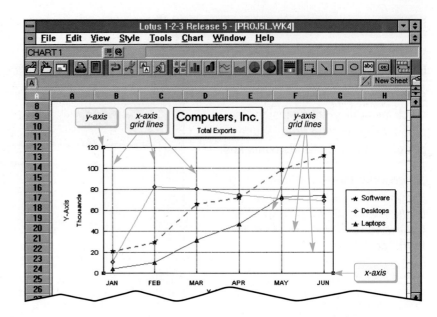

FIGURE 5-14

To remove the grid lines from the chart, select the plot, display the Grids dialog box and select None in the X-axis and Y-axis drop-down boxes.

Changing the Format of Values

By default, 1-2-3 displays the values of the y-axis scale in the General format. **General format** displays values with no commas to the left of the decimal point and no zeros to the right of the decimal point. To change the display of values on the y-axis of the line chart to the US Dollar format with zero decimals, first select the values. Then use the format selector and decimal selector in the status bar to apply the US Dollar format with zero decimals as illustrated in the following steps.

TO CHANGE THE FORMAT OF VALUES ON THE Y-AXIS ▼

STEP 1 ▶

Select the y-axis values by pointing to any value on the y-axis scale and clicking the left mouse button. Click the format selector in the status bar and point to the US Dollar format.

Handles display on all the values on the y-axis indicating they are selected (Figure 5-15). 1-2-3 displays the pop-up list of format styles. General format displays in the format selector and is highlighted in the pop-up list of format styles. The mouse pointer points to the US Dollar format.

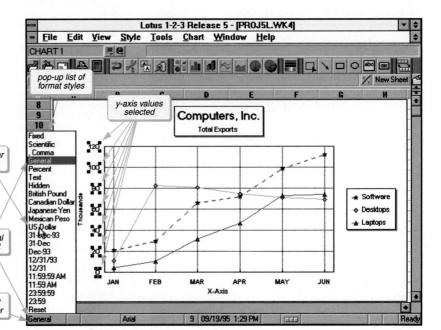

FIGURE 5-15

STEP 2 ▶

Choose the US Dollar format from the pop-up list of format styles. Click the decimal selector in the status bar and point to 0.

The values on the y-axis scale display in the US Dollar format with two decimal places by default (Figure 5-16). 1-2-3 displays the pop-up list of decimal places. The number 2 displays in the decimal selector and is highlighted in the pop-up list of decimal places. The mouse pointer points to 0 (zero).

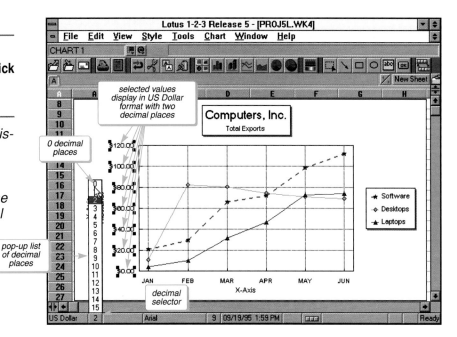

FIGURE 5-16

STEP 3 ▶

Select 0 from the pop-up list of decimal places.

1-2-3 formats the selected values with the US Dollar format consisting of a dollar sign and no decimal places to the right of the decimal point (Figure 5-17). The number format applied to the selected values displays in the status bar.

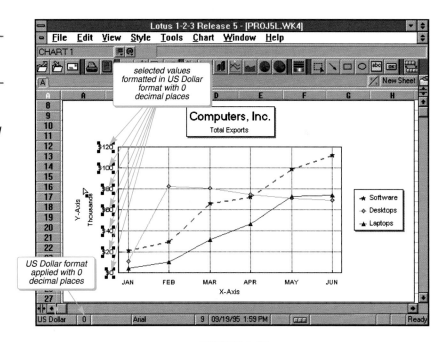

FIGURE 5-17

Changing the Axes Titles and Background Color

To complete the line chart, the x-axis title is deleted from the x-axis, the y-axis title is changed to EXPORTS, and the background color of the chart is changed to cyan. To change the axes titles and background color, perform the following steps (see Figure 5-18 on the next page).

TO CHANGE THE AXES TITLES AND BACKGROUND COLOR

Step 1: Select the x-axis title by pointing to the x-axis title, X-Axis, and clicking the left mouse button. Press the DEL key.

Step 2: Select the y-axis title by pointing to the y-axis title, Y-Axis, and clicking the right mouse button. Choose the Y-Axis command from the quick menu. When the Y-Axis dialog box displays, type EXPORTS in the Axis title text box. Choose the OK button.

Step 3: Select the chart by pointing to the chart frame and clicking the right mouse button. Choose the Lines & Color command from the quick menu. When the Lines & Color dialog box displays, click the Background color drop-down box arrow in the Interior area and select the cyan color (Color: 70) in the top row of the Background color drop-down box. Choose the OK button in the Lines & Color dialog box.

1-2-3 displays the line chart. The axes titles and background color display as shown in Figure 5-18.

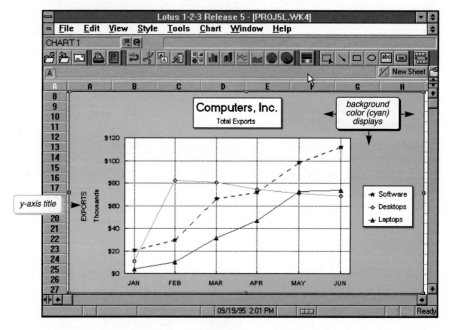

FIGURE 5-18

Renaming a Chart

1-2-3 automatically names charts, starting with CHART 1. You can change the default name to a more descriptive name. To rename the chart, EXPORT CHART, perform the following steps.

TO RENAME A CHART ▼

STEP 1 ▶

Ensure the chart is selected. Select the Chart menu and point to the Name command.

1-2-3 displays the Chart menu and the mouse pointer points to the Name command (Figure 5-19). The default chart name, CHART 1, displays in the selection indicator in the edit line.

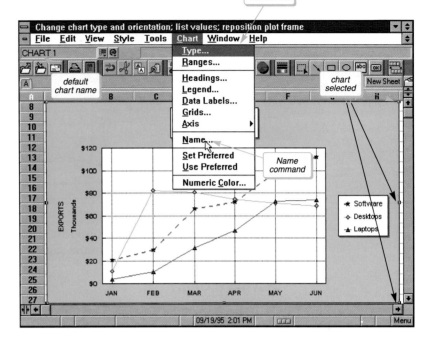

FIGURE 5-19

STEP 2 ▶

Choose the Name command. When the Name dialog box displays, type EXPORT CHART **in the Chart name text box. Then point to the Rename button (Rename).**

1-2-3 displays the Name dialog box (Figure 5-20). The Chart name text box displays the name you typed. The current chart name, CHART 1, is highlighted in the Existing charts list box. This is the chart to be renamed. The mouse pointer points to the Rename button.

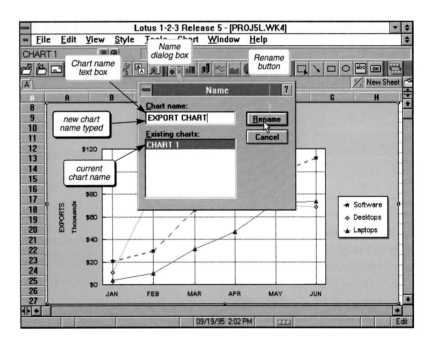

FIGURE 5-20

STEP 3 ▶

Choose the Rename button.

1-2-3 removes the Name dialog box from the screen and changes the name of the chart in the selection indicator to EXPORT CHART (Figure 5-21).

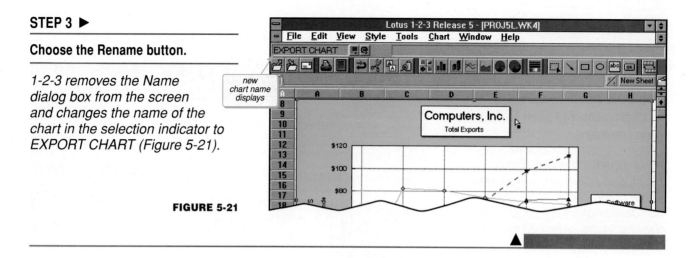

FIGURE 5-21

A chart name can contain up to 15 characters and may include spaces or special characters. You cannot use the same name for more than one chart in a file.

Saving a Chart

The worksheet and chart should now be saved. To save the worksheet and the associated chart, click the Save icon on the set of SmartIcons. You can create and save as many charts in one file as you want.

Printing a Chart

In previous projects, you printed charts in their actual size on the page. You can enlarge a chart to fill the entire page when printed by selecting the **Fill page option** in the Page Setup dialog box. To print the line chart using the Fill page option, perform the following steps.

TO PRINT A CHART USING THE FILL PAGE OPTION ▼

STEP 1 ▶

Ensure the chart is selected. Click the Print icon on the set of SmartIcons. When the Print dialog box displays, click the Page Setup button. When the Page Setup dialog box displays, click the Size drop-down box arrow and point to the Fill page option.

1-2-3 displays the Page Setup dialog box (Figure 5-22). The Fill page option causes 1-2-3 to enlarge the dimensions of the line chart to fill the entire page.

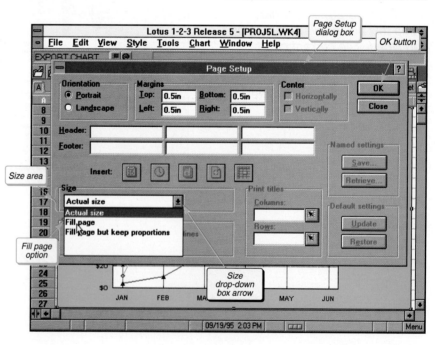

FIGURE 5-22

STEP 2 ►

Select the Fill page option in the Size drop-down list. Choose the OK button in the Page Setup dialog box. When the Print dialog box redisplays, choose the OK button in the Print dialog box.

1-2-3 prints the chart (Figure 5-23). 1-2-3 expands the dimensions of the line chart until it fills the page.

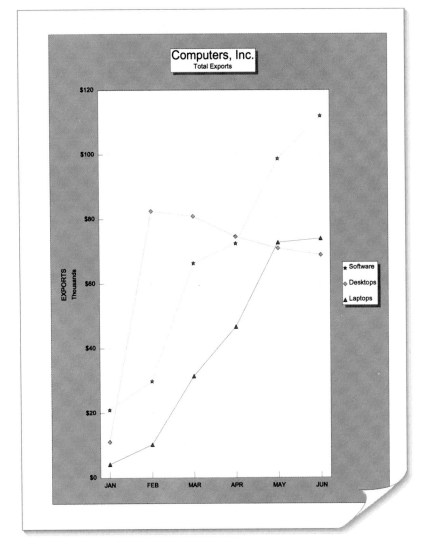

FIGURE 5-23

The **Fill page but keep proportions option** in the Page Setup dialog box in Figure 5-22 centers the chart on the printed page but retains the proportions of the chart.

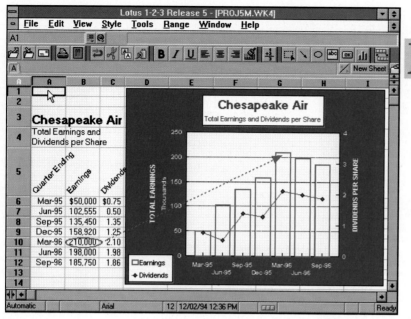

FIGURE 5-24

▶ MIXED CHARTS

Mixed charts allow you to have two different types of charts on a singlechart. Figure 5-24 illustrates a worksheet and a related mixed chart that displays the seven quarter total earnings and dividends per share for Chesapeake Air. The total earnings display as bars on the chart and the dividends per share display as a line with seven data points. Notice that the values on the y-axis are different from the values on the 2nd y-axis. The values on the left correspond to the bars for total earnings and the values on the right correspond to the line for dividends per share.

The column titles on the worksheet (range A5..C5) display on a diagonal. To draw attention to the highest earnings for the quarters, an ellipse is drawn around the highest earnings on the worksheet and an arrow points to the corresponding bar on the chart. The techniques for accomplishing these tasks are explained in this section of Project 5.

Rotating Data in a Cell

To **rotate data** within a cell, you change its orientation in the Alignment dialog box. This option can be useful for labeling columns with narrow widths, as shown in Figure 5-24. The column labels in row 5 use a diagonal orientation of 45 degrees. To change the orientation of data, perform the following steps. It is assumed the worksheet file is open and displayed on the screen.

TO ROTATE DATA IN A CELL ▼

STEP 1 ▶

Select the range A5..C5. Point to the selected range and click the right mouse button. Choose the Alignment command from the quick menu. When the Alignment dialog box displays, point to the Orientation drop-down box arrow.

1-2-3 displays the Alignment dialog box (Figure 5-25). The mouse pointer points to the Orientation drop-down box arrow in the Orientation area.

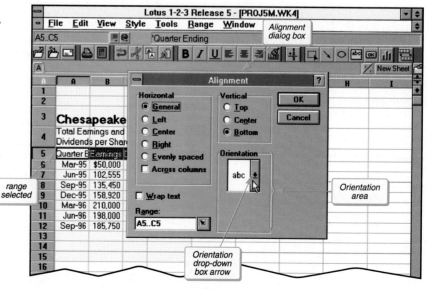

FIGURE 5-25

STEP 2 ▶

Click the Orientation drop-down box arrow. When the Orientation drop-down box displays, use the down scroll arrow to view the angled orientation. Point to the angled orientation.

When you click the Orientation drop-down box arrow, the Orientation drop-down box displays rotation options (Figure 5-26). The mouse pointer points to the desired angled rotation.

FIGURE 5-26

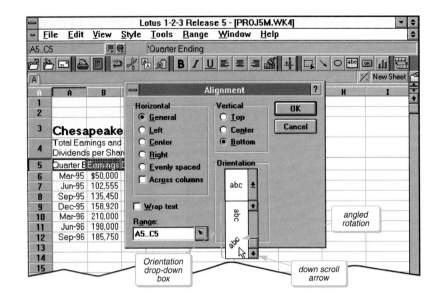

STEP 3 ▶

Select the angled rotation in the Orientation drop-down box. Point to the OK button in the Alignment dialog box.

1-2-3 displays the angled rotation in the Orientation box (Figure 5-27). When you select the angled rotation, 1-2-3 displays the Rotation text box in the Orientation area. The 45 in the Rotation text box indicates the selected data will be rotated 45 degrees. The mouse pointer points to the OK button.

FIGURE 5-27

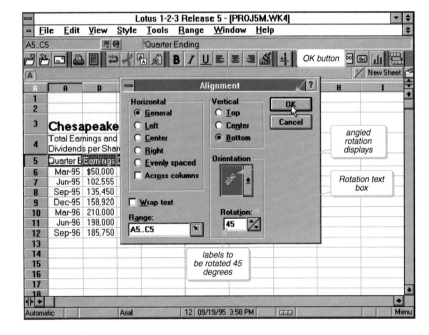

STEP 4 ▶

Choose the OK button in the Alignment dialog box.

1-2-3 rotates the data in each cell 45 degrees (Figure 5-28). Notice the label in cell A5 overlaps cell B5 and displays even though cell B5 contains a label. 1-2-3 increases the height of row 5 to 66 points.

FIGURE 5-28

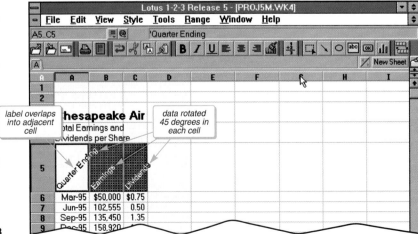

Controlling the exact degree of rotation is achieved by entering the desired rotation degree in the Rotation text box or by clicking the up or down arrows to the right of the Rotation text box (see Figure 5-27 on the previous page) until the desired diagonal degrees display. Data can be rotated from 1 to 90 degrees.

Creating a Mixed Chart

When you create a mixed chart, 1-2-3 plots the first three data series as vertical bars and all other data series as lines by default. Because the mixed chart in Figure 5-24 on page L284 contains only two data ranges, 1-2-3 will display both data ranges as vertical bars by default. You can plot the dividends per share data series as a line on the 2nd y-axis by using the **Ranges command** on the Chart menu. To create the mixed chart for Chesapeake Air and plot the second data range as a line on the 2nd y-axis, perform the following steps.

TO CREATE A MIXED CHART ▼

STEP 1 ▶

Select the range to chart – A3..C12 – and click the Chart icon on the set of SmartIcons. Move the mouse pointer into the worksheet and drag the range D1..I14. Click the Type icon on the set of charting SmartIcons. When the Type dialog box displays on the screen, select Mixed in the Types area by pointing to the Mixed option button and clicking the left mouse button. Then, point to the OK button.

1-2-3 draws the default bar chart and displays the Type dialog box (Figure 5-29). The Mixed option button is selected. The dialog box contains six different style buttons for a mixed chart. The top left style is recessed indicating it is selected. This selection will cause 1-2-3 to display the first three data series as vertical bars and all other data series as lines with symbols. The Vertical option button in the Orientation area displays the x-axis across the bottom of the plot, the y-axis along the left edge of the plot, and the 2nd y-axis along the right edge of the plot. The mouse pointer points to the OK button.

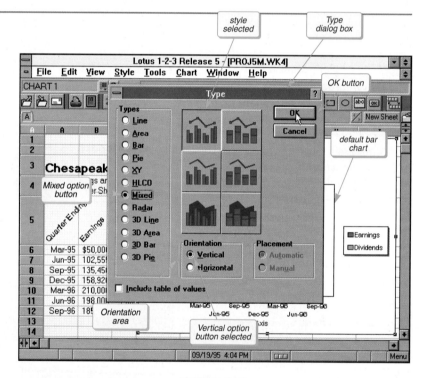

FIGURE 5-29

STEP 2 ▶

Choose the OK button in the Type
dialog box. Select the Chart menu
and point to the Ranges command.

*1-2-3 displays the mixed chart
(Figure 5-30). The values for
total earnings display as two-
dimensional bars. The values for
dividends are plotted as two-
dimensional bars on the y-axis
scale. The values for dividends are
too small to show on the y-axis
scale, however. The Chart menu
displays and the mouse pointer
points to the Ranges command.*

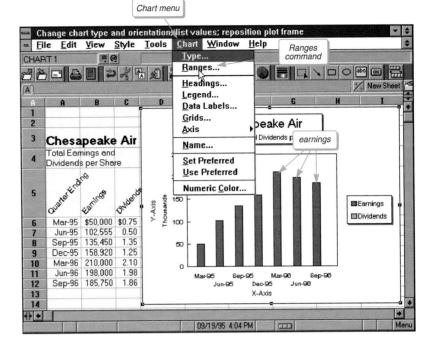

FIGURE 5-30

STEP 3 ▶

Choose the Ranges command.
When the Ranges dialog box
displays, select the B - Dividends
data series in the Series list box by
pointing to B - Dividends and
clicking the left mouse button.
Select the Plot on 2nd Y-axis check
box by pointing to the Plot on 2nd
Y-axis check box and clicking the
left mouse button. Click the Mixed
type drop-down box arrow and
select Line in the Mixed type drop-
down list box. Point to the OK
button.

*1-2-3 displays the Ranges dialog
box (Figure 5-31). The B -
Dividends series is selected. The
Plot on 2nd Y-axis check box is
selected. Line displays in the*
Mixed type box. These selections inform 1-2-3 to plot the values for dividends on the 2nd y-axis as a
line. The range address for the dividends series displays in the Range text box.

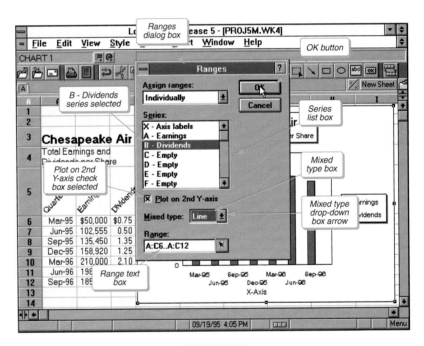

FIGURE 5-31

STEP 4 ▶

Choose the OK button in the Ranges dialog box.

1-2-3 displays the mixed chart (Figure 5-32). The chart contains values on the 2nd y-axis. The A data series values (Earnings) are plotted as two-dimensional bars on the y-axis. The B data series values (Dividends) are plotted as a line with symbols on the 2nd y-axis. Notice 1-2-3 automatically scales the 2nd y-axis based on the highest and lowest values in the Dividend series.

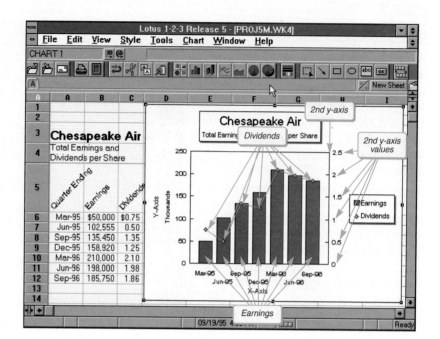

FIGURE 5-32

The style options available for mixed charts in the Type dialog box shown in Figure 5-29 on page L286 include the following: the top left style displays bar and line with symbols; the middle left style displays bar and line with no symbols; and the bottom left style displays bar and area. The top right style displays stacked bar and line with symbols, the middle right style displays stacked bar and line without symbols; and the bottom right style displays stacked bar and area.

Notice in Figure 5-24 on page L284 that, because the range to chart (A3..C12) contained more rows (7) of values than columns (2) of values, 1-2-3 plotted the data by columns. The first column in the range to chart (column A) was used for the x-axis labels. The second column (column B) was used for the first data series (Earnings). The third column (column C) was used for the second data series (Dividends). The first row after the chart titles (row 5) was used for the legend labels.

Changing the Second Y-Axis Scale and Adding a Title

1-2-3 allows you to change the second y-axis scale and add a title to the 2nd y-axis to make the chart easier to read and understand. In this project, the 2nd y-axis is scaled with an upper limit value of 4. To change the 2nd y-axis scale and add a title, perform the steps on the next page.

TO CHANGE THE SECOND Y-AXIS SCALE AND ADD A TITLE ▼

STEP 1 ►

Point to any value on the 2nd y-axis and click the right mouse button. Point to the 2nd Y-Axis command on the quick menu.

The values on the 2nd y-axis are selected (Figure 5-33). 1-2-3 displays the quick menu. The mouse pointer points to the 2nd Y-Axis command.

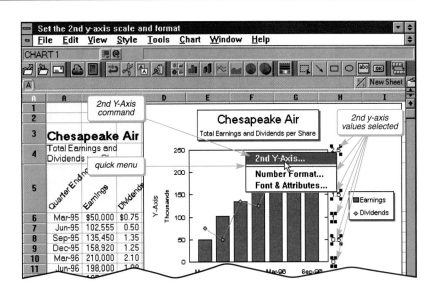

FIGURE 5-33

STEP 2 ►

Choose the 2nd Y-Axis command from the quick menu. When the 2nd Y-Axis dialog box displays, type DIVIDENDS PER SHARE in the Axis title text box. Select the Upper limit check box in the Scale manually area. Type 4 in the Upper limit text box. Then, point to the OK button.

1-2-3 displays the 2nd Y-Axis dialog box (Figure 5-34). The title displays in the Axis title text box. The Upper limit is set to 4.

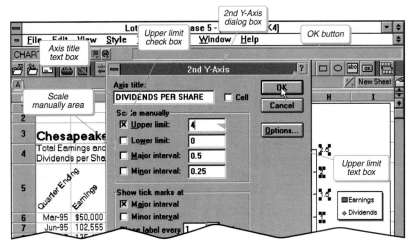

FIGURE 5-34

STEP 3 ►

Choose the OK button in the 2nd Y-Axis dialog box.

1-2-3 displays the mixed chart with the y-axis showing the range 0 – 250 and the 2nd y-axis showing the range 0 – 4 (Figure 5-35). The values on the y-axis represent the Total Earnings, and the values on the 2nd y-axis represent the Dividends per Share.

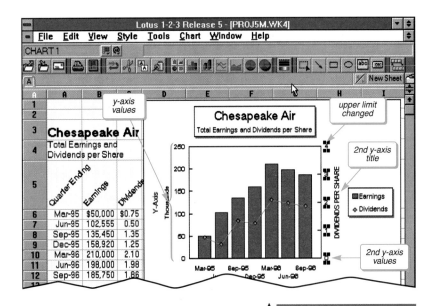

FIGURE 5-35

To return the 2nd y-axis to the default scale, choose the 2nd y-axis command from the quick menu, and deselect all the check boxes in the Scale manually area.

Moving the Chart Legend and Plot

Using the Legend dialog box, you can place the legend to the right or below the plot or you can move the legend anywhere inside the chart frame. The legend in Figure 5-24 on page L284 is located in the lower left corner of the chart frame. To move the legend, first select it; then, position the mouse pointer inside the legend, and drag the legend to the desired location.

When you move the legend to the left side of the chart, the plot does not automatically move over. You must then move the plot to the right. To move the plot, first select it; then, position the mouse pointer inside the plot, and drag the plot to the desired location. You can then resize the plot. To move the chart legend and the chart plot and then resize the chart plot, perform the following steps.

TO MOVE THE CHART LEGEND AND THE CHART PLOT AND RESIZE THE CHART PLOT ▼

STEP 1 ▶

Select the chart legend by pointing inside the legend and clicking the left mouse button. When selection handles appear on the corners of the legend, position the mouse pointer inside the legend and drag to the lower left corner of the chart.

Selection handles appear on the corners of the legend (Figure 5-36). When you drag the legend, the mouse pointer changes to a fist holding a range, and a dotted rectangle appears as the legend as it is moved to the new location. Notice the legend remains in the original location.

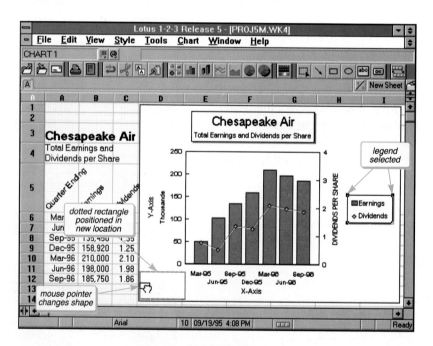

FIGURE 5-36

STEP 2 ▶

Release the left mouse button. Select the chart plot by pointing inside the plot and clicking the left mouse button. When selection handles appear on the corners of the plot, drag the plot to the right approximately one inch.

The chart legend displays in the bottom corner of the chart (Figure 5-37). Selection handles appear on the chart plot indicating the plot is selected. When you drag the plot, the mouse pointer changes to a fist holding a range, and the plot displays as dotted rectangles as it is moved to the right. The smaller dotted rectangle represents the proposed location of the plot frame. The larger dotted rectangle represents the proposed location of the plot frame and the axes.

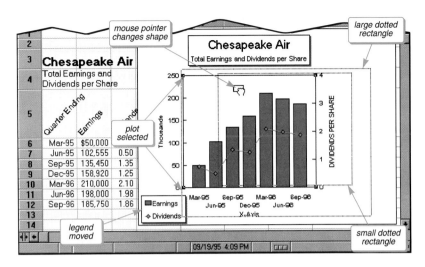

FIGURE 5-37

STEP 3 ▶

Release the left mouse button. Position the mouse pointer over the bottom left selection handle. When the mouse pointer changes to a four-headed arrow, drag the plot to the left approximately one-half inch.

The chart plot displays in the new location (Figure 5-38). The mouse pointer changes to a four-headed arrow. As you drag the chart plot, the left side of the plot expands.

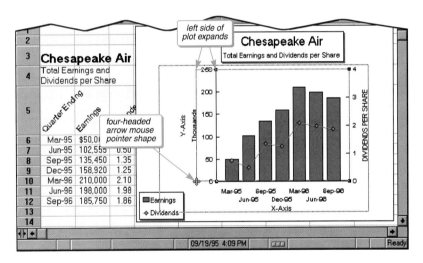

FIGURE 5-38

STEP 4 ▶

Release the left mouse button.

The chart plot is resized (Figure 5-39). The vertical bars are wider and there are more spaces between the labels on the x-axis.

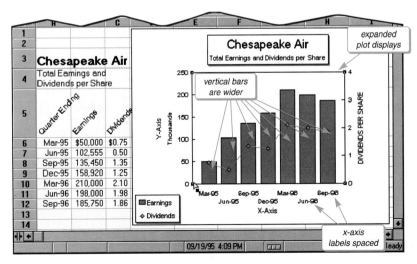

FIGURE 5-39

Drawing an Ellipse and an Arrow

To draw attention to the highest earnings in the mixed chart, an **ellipse** is drawn around the value in cell B10 (see Figure 5-24 on page L284) and an arrow extends from that value in the worksheet to the corresponding bar on the chart. To draw an ellipse, use the **Draw Ellipse icon** ( ) on the charting set of Smart-Icons. To draw an arrow, use the Draw Arrow icon on the charting set of Smart-Icons. To draw an ellipse and an arrow, perform the following steps.

TO DRAW AN ELLIPSE AND AN ARROW ▼

STEP 1 ▶

Point to the Draw Ellipse icon on the set of SmartIcons and click the left mouse button. Position the mouse pointer at the top left corner of cell B10.

The mouse pointer changes to a cross hair indicating you can position the arrow (Figure 5-40). 1-2-3 displays the instruction in the edit line of the next step in drawing an ellipse.

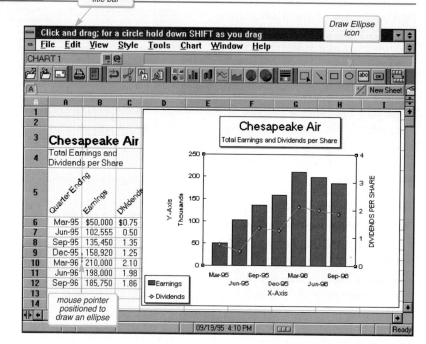

FIGURE 5-40

STEP 2 ▶

Click the left mouse button and drag to the bottom right of cell B10. Release the left mouse button.

As you drag, the proposed ellipse appears as a dotted line. When you release the mouse button, handles appear on the ellipse indicating it is selected (Figure 5-41). When the mouse pointer is positioned over one of the selection handles, the mouse pointer changes to a four-headed arrow, indicating the object can be sized. The default name for the ellipse, Ellipse 1, displays in the selection indicator.

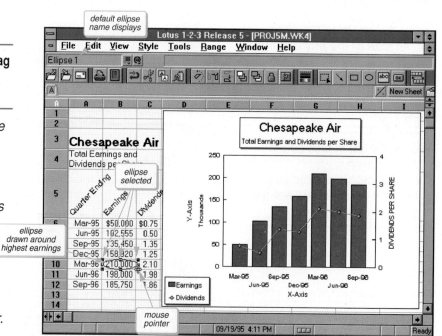

FIGURE 5-41

STEP 3 ▶

Point to the Draw Arrow icon on the set of SmartIcons and click the left mouse button. Position the mouse over the right center selection handle on the ellipse. Drag the line to the top of the bar for Mar-96. Release the left mouse button.

When you click the Draw Arrow icon and move the mouse pointer on the worksheet, the mouse pointer changes to a cross hair indicating you can position the arrow. 1-2-3 displays an instruction in the title bar prompting you to click and drag to draw an arrow. As you drag, the proposed line with the arrow appears as a dotted line. An arrowhead appears at the point where you release the

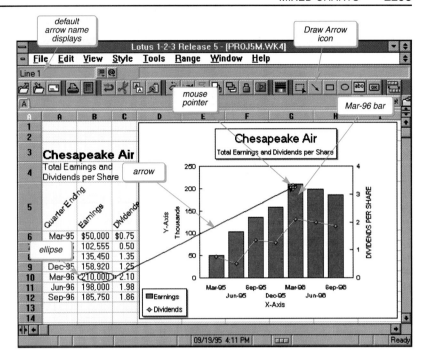

FIGURE 5-42

mouse button (Figure 5-42). Handles appear on the arrow indicating the arrow is selected. When the mouse pointer is positioned over the selection handle, it changes to a four-headed arrow, indicating the object can be sized. The default name for the arrow, Line 1, displays in the selection indicator.

To change the size of an ellipse, first select the ellipse by pointing to the ellipse and clicking the left mouse button. Then, position the mouse pointer over a selection handle and drag the selection handle until the ellipse is the desired size.

To delete the ellipse, first select the ellipse, then press the DEL key. To draw a circle instead of an ellipse, press and hold down the SHIFT key as you drag. The **Draw Ellipse command** is also found on the Tools menu on the main menu bar.

Changing the Pattern and Edge Color of Bars

1-2-3 automatically assigns the color red to the bars in the chart and displays the bars with a solid red pattern. For the Chesapeake Air chart, you are to change the bars to a transparent pattern and change the color on the edge of the bars to magenta.

To change the pattern and edge color of the bars, perform the steps on the next two pages.

TO CHANGE THE PATTERN AND EDGE COLOR OF BARS ▼

STEP 1 ▶

Select the bars and display the quick menu by pointing to the red color in the legend and clicking the right mouse button. Choose the Lines & Color command. When the Lines & Color dialog box displays, click the Pattern drop-down box arrow and point to the T in the Pattern drop-down box.

Handles appear around the bars indicating the bars are selected (Figure 5-43). 1-2-3 displays the Lines & Color dialog box. The mouse pointer points to the desired pattern. When the T pattern is selected, a transparent pattern is assigned to the selected bars.

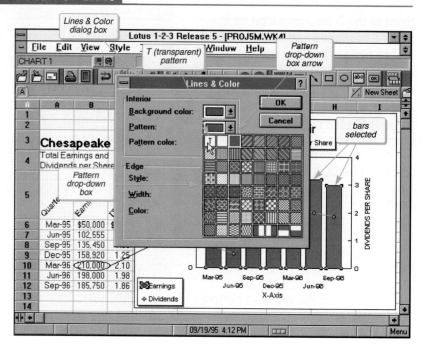

FIGURE 5-43

STEP 2 ▶

Select the T in the Pattern drop-down box. Click the Width drop-down box arrow and select the second width from the top in the Width drop-down box. Click the Color drop-down box arrow and choose the magenta color in the top row of the Color drop-down box. Point to the OK button in the Lines & Color dialog box.

The selected transparent pattern displays in the Pattern box (Figure 5-44). The selected edge width displays in the Width box. The selected edge color displays in the Color box. The Sample area shows how the selections will display. The mouse pointer points to the OK button.

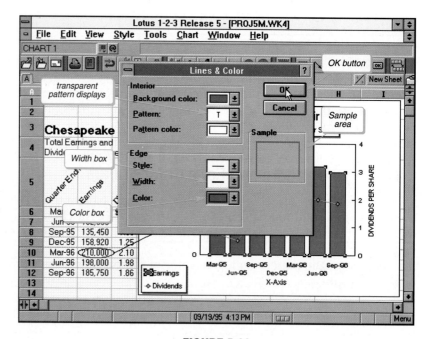

FIGURE 5-44

STEP 3 ▶

Choose the OK button in the Lines & Color dialog box.

1-2-3 displays the bars with a transparent pattern and magenta edges (Figure 5-45). Notice the symbol for earnings in the legend also displays with a transparent pattern and magenta edges.

FIGURE 5-45

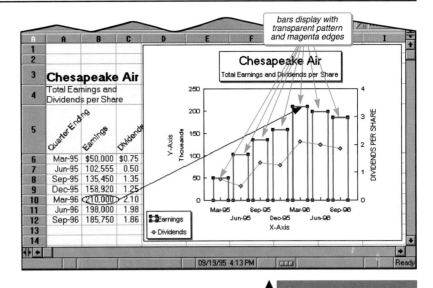

Complete the formatting of the chart by deleting the x-axis default title, changing the y-axis default title, and adding grid lines using the steps and techniques presented for formatting other charts.

▶ HIGH-LOW-CLOSE-OPEN CHARTS

T he High-Low-Close-Open chart (HLCO) is used to chart data that has high and low values over a period of time, such as stock market data and daily air temperatures. The worksheet and related chart in Figure 5-46 illustrate the use of a whisker HLCO chart. A **whisker HLCO** chart illustrates high and low values as a vertical line. Open and close values are shown as markers to the left and right of the vertical line.

The worksheet contains the highest, lowest, opening, and closing price of West Coast Computers stock during a two-week period in November. The set of bars below the HLCO section of the chart represents the daily trading volume for the stock. The chart graphically illustrates this information. In applications of this type, it is frequently necessary to add y-axis grid lines and change the default y-axis scale interval initially displayed by 1-2-3 to obtain a chart that is easier to read and understand.

When you create a HLCO chart, 1-2-3 charts the data ranges as follows: (1) the A and B data series represent the high and low values, respectively; (2) the C and D data series represent the closing and opening values, respectively; and (3) the E data series becomes the bar chart representing the trading volume.

FIGURE 5-46

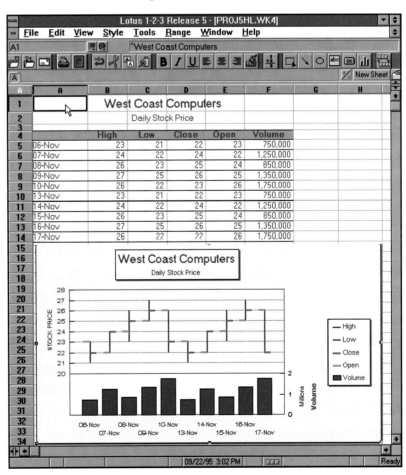

Creating the HLCO Chart

To prepare the chart, add y-axis grid lines, and change the interval for the y-axis scale, perform the following steps. It is assumed the worksheet file is open and displayed on the screen.

TO CREATE A HLCO CHART, ADD Y-AXIS GRID LINES, AND CHANGE THE Y-AXIS SCALE INTERVAL ▼

STEP 1 ▶

Select the range to chart – A1..F14 – on the worksheet (see Figure 5-46 on the previous page), and click the Chart icon on the set of SmartIcons. Move the mouse pointer into the worksheet and drag the range A15..H34. Point to the Type icon on the set of charting SmartIcons.

1-2-3 displays the default bar chart (Figure 5-47). Notice only the values for volume display as vertical bars on the chart. The high, low, close, and open values do not show because these values in the selected range are too small. The mouse pointer points to the Type icon on the set of charting SmartIcons.

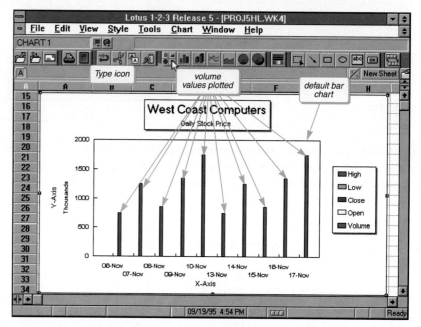

FIGURE 5-47

STEP 2 ▶

Click the Type icon on the set of charting SmartIcons. When the Type dialog box displays, select the HLCO option in the Types area. Then, point to the OK button.

1-2-3 displays the Type dialog box (Figure 5-48). The HLCO option button is selected. This selection will cause 1-2-3 to display an HLCO chart. The Type dialog box contains two different style buttons for an HLCO chart. The left style is recessed indicating it is selected. This selection will cause 1-2-3 to display a set of vertical bars (representing the high and low values for a day) with two markers on each bar (representing the close and open values for a day).The mouse pointer points to the OK button.

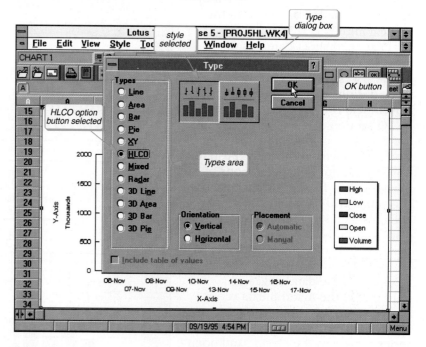

FIGURE 5-48

STEP 3 ▶

Choose the OK button in the Type dialog box.

1-2-3 displays an HLCO chart (Figure 5-49). Each symbol on the chart consists of a vertical bar (red) with two horizontal markers (yellow and blue) on each bar. The top of the red line indicates the stock's highest price for the day. The bottom of the red line indicates the stock's lowest price for the day. The left marker (yellow) indicates the stock's opening price at the start of the day. The right marker (blue) indicates the stock's closing price at the end of the day. The magenta bars below the HLCO chart are plotted on the 2nd y-axis and represent the trading volume for the stock for each day. The default scale of the y-axis is the range 20 to 28 with an interval of 2. The dates from column A display below the x-axis. To improve the readability of the chart, you can add grid lines to the y-axis.

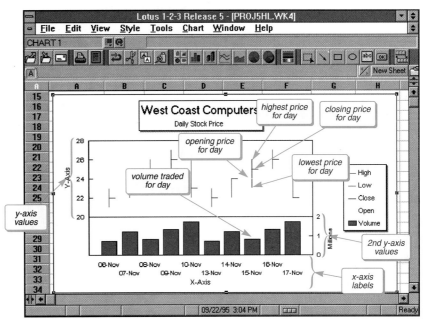

FIGURE 5-49

STEP 4 ▶

Select the chart plot and display the quick menu by pointing inside the plot and clicking the right mouse button. Choose the Grids command from the quick menu. When the Grids dialog box displays, click the Y-axis drop-down box arrow and select Major interval from the Y-Axis drop-down box. Then, choose the OK button in the Grids dialog list.

1-2-3 displays the HLCO (Figure 5-50). The chart displays y-axis grid lines. The y-axis grid lines originate from each value on the y-axis scale. Notice the interval between each value on the y-axis is two. You can change the interval of the y-axis scale to further improve the readability of the chart.

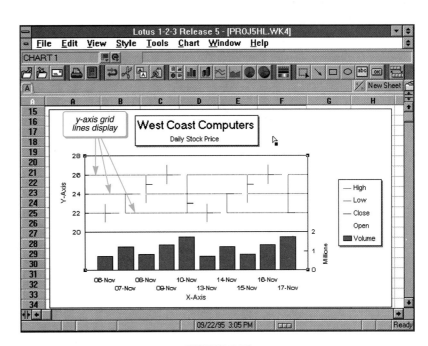

FIGURE 5-50

STEP 5 ▶

Select the y-axis scale and display the quick menu by pointing to any value on the y-axis scale and clicking the right mouse button. Choose the Y-Axis command from the quick menu. When the Y-Axis dialog box displays, select the Major interval check box in the Scale manually area. Type 1 in the Major interval text box in the Scale manually area. Then, point to the OK button in the Y-Axis dialog box.

The y-axis scale is selected (Figure 5-51). 1-2-3 displays the Y-Axis dialog box. The entry in the Major interval text box will increment the values on the y-axis by one.

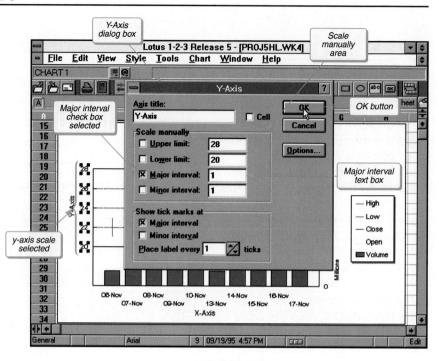

FIGURE 5-51

STEP 6 ▶

Choose the OK button in the Y-Axis dialog box.

1-2-3 displays the HLCO chart with the values on the y-axis incremented by one (Figure 5-52).

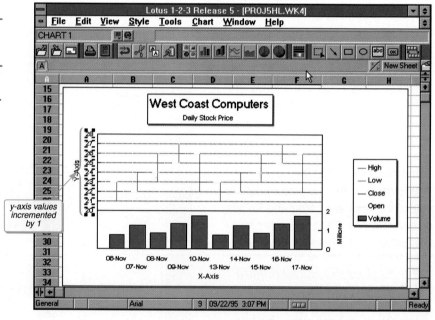

FIGURE 5-52

The second style option available for HLCO charts in the Type dialog box shown in Figure 5-48 on page L296 is called a candlestick HLCO chart. The **candlestick HLCO** chart displays the same information as the whisker HLCO chart but illustrates the close and open values as a widened vertical bar that spans the range between the close and open values.

Complete the formatting of the chart, following the steps previously explained when formatting the other charts.

▶ CHART SUMMARY

I t is important to understand that you can chart worksheet data in a variety of ways using one or more of the charts available with 1-2-3. The chart you use depends on the information you want to convey. Table 5-1 summarizes the charts illustrated in Project 1 through Project 5 and describes when it is best to use a particular chart type.

▶ **TABLE 5-1**

CHART TYPE	TO ILLUSTRATE
Bar	Comparison of two or more values over time
Pie	Parts of the whole
Stacked Bar	The relationship between two or more values and their totals
Line	Data that changes over time
Mixed	Data that changes over time using bars and lines
HLCO	Data that has high and low values over a period of time

▶ MAPS

A worksheet and its related map are illustrated in Figure 5-53. The map displays the annual sales by state for USA Sports, Inc. Column A in the worksheet contains the **map regions**. The map regions for this map are state names to be mapped. Column B contains the sales values for each map region. The map displays to the right of column B on the worksheet. The **map title**, Annual Sales by State, displays above the map. The **map legend** displays in the lower right corner of the map.

When you create a map, 1-2-3 analyzes the values to map and automatically groups the values into categories, called **bins**. 1-2-3 assigns each bin a color, a legend label, and a value that marks the upper limit of the bin. For example, in Figure 5-53, 1-2-3 groups states with sales of zero to $240,000 (Utah, South Dakota, and North Carolina) in the red bin, assigns the legend label as red, and marks $240,000 in the legend as the upper limit of that bin. Continuing with the above example, 1-2-3 groups states with sales of $240,001 to $360,000 (Kansas, Florida, and New York) in the green bin, assigns the legend label as green, and marks $360,000 in the legend as the upper limit of that bin. 1-2-3 uses a maximum of six bins on a map.

FIGURE 5-53

Creating a Map

To create the map shown in Figure 5-53, you must select the range to map, choose the **Map New Map command** from the Tools menu, and select the area where you want the map drawn. Follow the detailed steps below to create a map illustrating the annual sales by states. It is assumed the worksheet file is open and displayed on the screen.

TO CREATE A MAP ▼

STEP 1 ▶

Select cells A3..B18. Select the Tools menu and point to the Map command.

1-2-3 highlights the range to map and displays the Tools menu (Figure 5-54). Notice the column headings in row 2 are not included in the range to map. The mouse pointer points to the Map command. The arrowhead to the right of the Map command indicates a cascading menu is associated with the command. A **cascading menu** *is a supplemental menu with additional menu choices.*

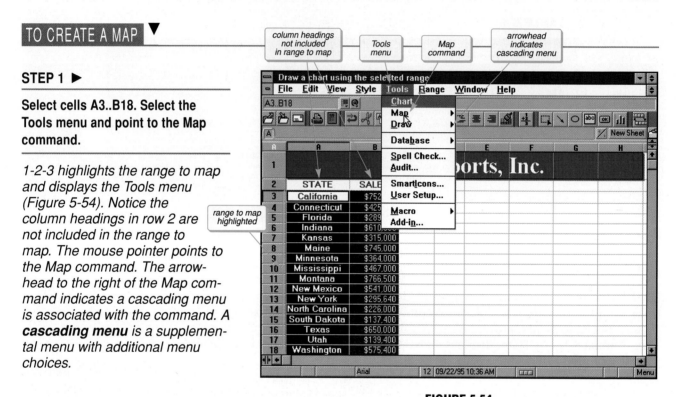

FIGURE 5-54

STEP 2 ▶

Choose the Map command and point to the New Map command on the Map cascading menu.

When you choose the Map command, the Map cascading menu displays because an arrowhead displays to the right of the Map command on the Tools menu (Figure 5-55). The mouse pointer points to the New Map command.

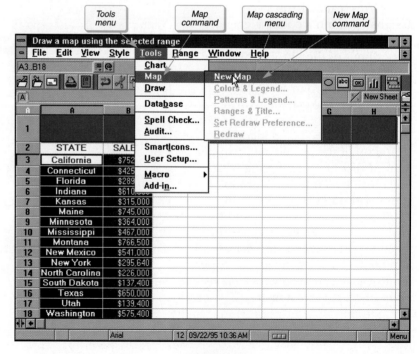

FIGURE 5-55

STEP 3 ▶

Choose the New Map command, move the mouse pointer onto the worksheet, and position the mouse pointer on the center of the bottom border of cell C3.

1-2-3 displays a message in the title bar giving you instructions to complete the task (Figure 5-56). When you move the mouse pointer onto the worksheet, the shape changes to a crosshair with a rotating globe. The mouse pointer is positioned on the center of the bottom border of cell C3.

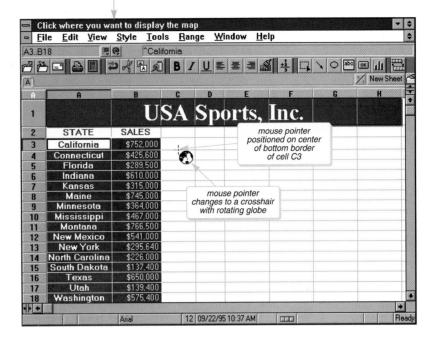

FIGURE 5-56

STEP 4 ▶

Click the left mouse button.

1-2-3 creates and displays a map of the United States (Figure 5-57). The default name of the map, Map 1, displays in the selection indicator and the drawing set of icons displays on the set of SmartIcons. The small selection handles on the border of the map indicate the map is selected. The map legend explains the meaning of the colors on the map. 1-2-3 automatically groups the sales values for the sixteen states into six bins and identifies each bin with a different color in the map legend. The states in the selected range display on the map in the corresponding bin color.

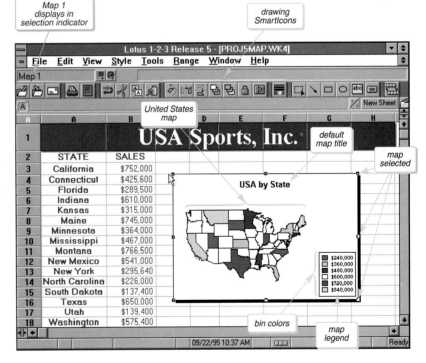

FIGURE 5-57

To deselect the map, select any cell outside the map.

While the map is selected, you can move the map to any location on the worksheet. To move the map, position the mouse pointer inside the map and drag the map to the desired location. You can also resize the map by dragging the handles. Be aware that resizing the map may distort the shape of the states.

Changing the Map Title

The next task in preparing the map is to change the map title. The steps to accomplish this task follow.

TO CHANGE THE MAP TITLE ▼

STEP 1 ▶

Ensure the map is selected. Then, choose the Map command from the Tools menu. Point to the Ranges & Title command on the Map cascading menu.

1-2-3 displays the Tools menu (Figure 5-58). When you choose the Map command, 1-2-3 displays the Map cascading menu. The mouse pointer points to the Ranges & Title command.

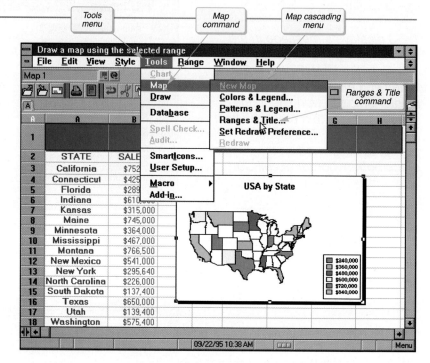

FIGURE 5-58

STEP 2 ▶

Choose the Ranges & Title command. When the Ranges & Title dialog box displays, highlight the default title text in the Title text box. Type Annual Sales by State in the Title text box. Point to the OK button.

1-2-3 displays the Ranges & Title dialog box (Figure 5-59). The title you typed displays in the Title text box. The mouse pointer points to the OK button in the Ranges & Title dialog box.

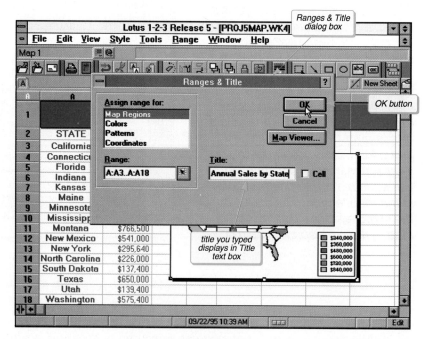

FIGURE 5-59

STEP 3 ▶

Choose the OK button.

1-2-3 replaces the default title with the map title you typed and centers it between the map frame (Figure 5-60).

FIGURE 5-60

Changing Bin Colors

When you create a map, 1-2-3 automatically assigns the bin colors for each data group. You can change the colors for each bin. To make changes to a bin color, select the map by positioning the mouse pointer inside the map and clicking the left mouse button. Then, choose the Map Colors & Legend command from the Tools menu. To change the color of Bin 6 from cyan to purple, perform the following steps.

STEP 1 ▶

Ensure the map is selected. Choose the Map command from the Tools menu. Point to the Colors & Legend command on the Map cascading menu.

1-2-3 displays the Tools menu (Figure 5-61). The mouse pointer points to the Colors & Legend command.

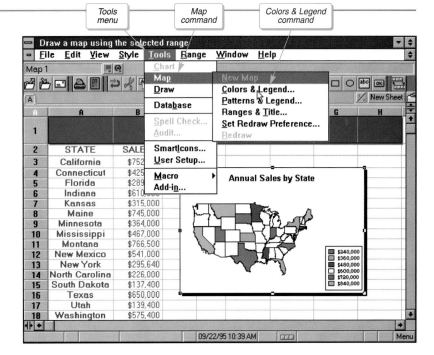

FIGURE 5-61

STEP 2 ▶

Choose the Colors & Legend command. When the Colors & Legend dialog box displays, click the Colors drop-down box arrow and point to Manual in the Colors drop-down list.

1-2-3 displays the Colors & Legend dialog box (Figure 5-62). The Colors drop-down list displays and the mouse pointer points to the Manual option.

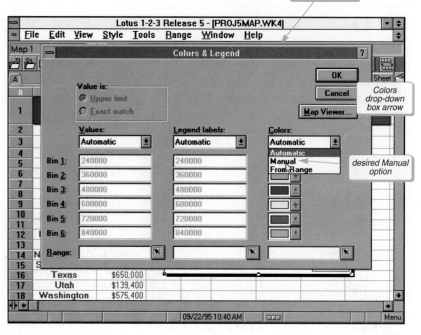

FIGURE 5-62

STEP 3 ▶

Choose Manual from the Colors drop-down list by clicking the left mouse button. Click Bin 6 drop-down box arrow and select purple in the top row of the color palette. Point to the OK button in the Colors & Legend dialog box.

The option you selected displays in the Colors drop-down box (Figure 5-63). When you select the Manual option in the Colors drop-down list, Bin 1 through Bin 6 drop-down box arrows become available so you can specify colors.

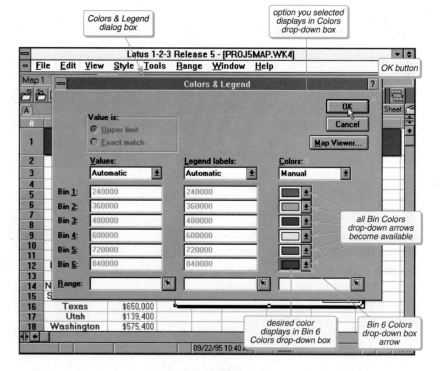

FIGURE 5-63

STEP 4 ▶

Choose the OK button in the Colors & Legend dialog box.

1-2-3 redraws the map and changes the color for those states having sales between $720,001 and $840,000 (California, Montana, and Maine) to purple (Figure 5-64). The legend label for Bin 6 displays in purple in the map legend.

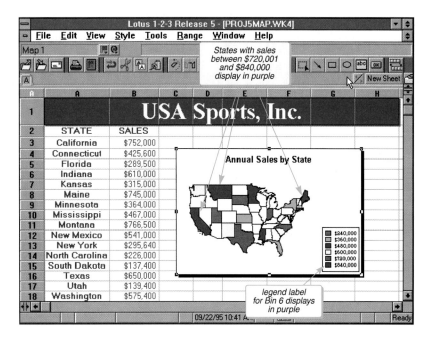

FIGURE 5-64

Complete the formatting of the map by following the steps previously presented to format charts. To print the worksheet and its related map, follow the steps you used when printing charts.

▶ PROJECT SUMMARY

Project 5 illustrated the steps to create line charts, mixed charts, and HLCO charts. You learned the rules 1-2-3 follows when determining how to chart selected data. The project presented techniques to show you how to add grid lines to the x-axis and y-axis, change the color of lines and bars on a chart, plot data on the 2nd y-axis, draw an ellipse and rename charts. Using the procedures explained in this project, you can now create a variety of professional-appearing charts for business or personal use.

Project 5 also introduced you to the mapping capabilities of 1-2-3. You learned how to create a map from worksheet data. The project illustrated the steps to change the title and color of a map.

▶ KEY TERMS AND INDEX

2nd y-axis *(L271)*
2nd Y-Axis command *(L289)*
bins *(L299)*
candlestick HLCO chart *(L298)*
cascading menu *(L300)*
changing bin colors *(L303)*
changing the map title *(L302)*
chart *(L269)*
Colors & Legend command *(L303)*
data series *(L273)*
Draw Elipse command *(L293)*
Draw Ellipse icon *(L292)*
ellipse *(L292)*

Fill page but keep proportions option *(L283)*
Fill page option *(L282)*
General format *(L278)*
HLCO chart *(L271)*
legend *(L273)*
line chart *(L270)*
map *(L269)*
Map command *(L300)*
map legend *(L299)*
Map New Map command *(L300)*
map regions *(L299)*
map title *(L299)*
mixed chart *(L270)*

Name command *(L281)*
New Map command *(L300)*
plot *(L273)*
Ranges command *(L286)*
Ranges & Title command *(L302)*
rotate data *(L284)*
symbols *(L270)*
tick marks *(L273)*
whisker HLCO chart *(L295)*
x-axis *(L273)*
x-axis labels *(L273)*
y-axis *(L273)*

Q U I C K   R E F E R E N C E

In Lotus 1-2-3 for Windows, you can accomplish a task in a number of ways. The following table presents a quick reference to each task presented in this project with its available options. The commands listed in the Menu column can be executed using either the keyboard or mouse.

Task	Mouse	Menu	Keyboard Shortcuts
Add Grid Lines		From Chart menu or quick menu, choose Grids	
Change a Symbol		From Style menu or quick menu, choose Lines & Color	
Change Bin Color on a Map		From Tools menu, choose Map, then choose Colors & Legend	
Change the Line Color		From Style menu or quick menu, choose Lines & Color	
Change the Line Style		From Style menu or quick menu, choose Lines & Color	

Task	Mouse	Menu	Keyboard Shortcuts
Change the Line Width		From Style menu or quick menu, choose Lines & Color	
Change the Map Title		From Tools menu, choose Map, then choose Ranges & Title	
Change the 2nd Y-Axis		From Chart menu, choose Axis; or from quick menu, choose 2nd Y-Axis	
Change the Y-Axis Interval		From Chart menu, choose Axis; or from quick menu, choose Y-Axis	
Create a Line Chart	Click Line icon on Default set of SmartIcons	From Chart menu, choose Type; or from quick menu, choose Chart Type	
Create a Map		From Tools menu, choose Map, then choose New Map	
Create a Mixed Chart		From Chart menu, choose Type; or from quick menu, choose Chart Type	
Create an HLCO Chart		From Chart menu, choose Type; or from quick menu, choose Chart Type	
Draw an Ellipse	Click Draw Ellipse icon on Default set of SmartIcons	From Tools menu, choose Draw	
Move a Map	Position mouse pointer inside map, drag to desired location		
Rename a Chart		From Chart menu, choose Name	
Rotate Data		From Style menu or quick menu, choose Alignment	
Select a Map	Position mouse pointer inside map, click left mouse button		

STUDENT ASSIGNMENT 1
True/False

Instructions: Circle T if the statement is true or F if the statement is false.

T F 1. A chart is a graphical representation of worksheet data.

T F 2. When you change data on which a chart is based, you must rechart the data to reflect the changes made.

T F 3. Line charts are widely used for showing trends over a period of time.

T F 4. A mixed chart combines two chart types on the same chart.

T F 5. Use an HLCO chart to illustrate data that has high and low values over a period of time.

T F 6. All charts have a horizontal axis and a vertical axis.

T F 7. You can chart up to 32 data series on one chart.

T F 8. The plot of a chart includes the chart title and chart subtitle, the axes, the axes labels and titles, and all the data plotted on the axes.

T F 9. If you select more rows of data than columns of data to chart, 1-2-3 plots the data series by rows.

T F 10. When 1-2-3 plots data by rows, the first column in the selected range is used for the text entries for the legend labels.

T F 11. When you create a line chart, 1-2-3 automatically names the chart Line 1.

T F 12. When charting a range of values, 1-2-3 automatically determines the range of values on the y-axis based on the values in the selected range.

T F 13. To change the color of a line on a line chart, select the appropriate color box in the legend, then, choose the Legend command from the quick menu.

T F 14. You can use the Rename command on the Chart menu to give a chart a more meaningful name.

T F 15. To enlarge a chart to fill an entire printed page, choose the Fill page option in the Page Setup dialog box.

T F 16. You can change the rotation of data in a cell by choosing the Orientation command from the Style menu.

T F 17. You can create and save as many charts in one file as you want.

T F 18. To change the 2nd y-axis scale of a chart, first, select the 2nd y-axis; then, choose the Y-Axis command from the quick menu.

T F 19. To draw a circle, click the Draw Ellipse icon on the set of SmartIcons, hold down the SHIFT key, and drag across the worksheet where you want the circle to appear.

T F 20. When you create a map, 1-2-3 analyzes the values to map and automatically groups the values into bins.

STUDENT ASSIGNMENT 2
Multiple Choice

Instructions: Circle the correct response.

1. After selecting a range to chart, clicking the Chart icon on the set of SmartIcons will display a _____ chart.
   a. blank
   b. bar
   c. line
   d. pie

2. The main part of a chart is called the _____.
   a. chart
   b. plot
   c. graph
   d. legend
3. When you create a chart, 1-2-3 automatically names the chart _____.
   a. CHART 1
   b. CHART 1.wk4
   c. CHART 1.cht
   d. BAR 1
4. You can create and save _____ charts in one file.
   a. two (2)
   b. four (4)
   c. ten (10)
   d. any number of
5. When 1-2-3 plots data by columns, the first column is used for the _____.
   a. the first data series
   b. chart title
   c. x-axis labels
   d. legends
6. A line chart can contain up to _____ data series.
   a. 10
   b. 23
   c. 26
   d. 20
7. To change the shape of symbols in a line chart, use the _____.
   a. Legend command from the quick menu
   b. Y-Axis command from the quick menu
   c. Lines & Color command from the quick menu
   d. Type command from the Chart menu
8. To combine lines and bars in a single chart, use a _____ chart.
   a. pie
   b. mixed
   c. stacked bar
   d. bar
9. To change the 2nd y-axis scale on a chart, use the _____.
   a. Y-Axis command from the quick menu
   b. 2nd Y-Axis command from the quick menu
   c. X-Axis command from the quick menu
   d. Ranges command from the quick menu
10. To change the bin color on a map, use the _____.
   a. Legend command from the quick menu
   b. Map command from the Tools menu
   c. Font & Attributes command from the quick menu
   d. Lines & Color command from the Tools menu

STUDENT ASSIGNMENT 3
Understanding Rotating Data

Instructions: In the space provided, explain the steps necessary to rotate the data in the range A5..C5 as shown in Figure SA5-3.

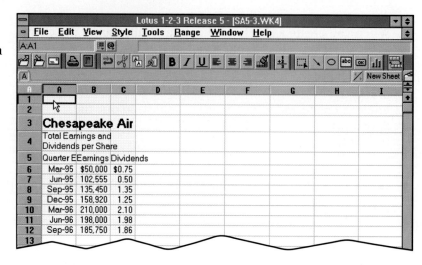

FIGURE SA5-3

Steps: _____

_____

_____

_____

STUDENT ASSIGNMENT 4
Understanding the Charting Set of SmartIcons

Instructions: In the spaces provided in Figure SA5-4, identify each of the icons on the charting set of SmartIcons.

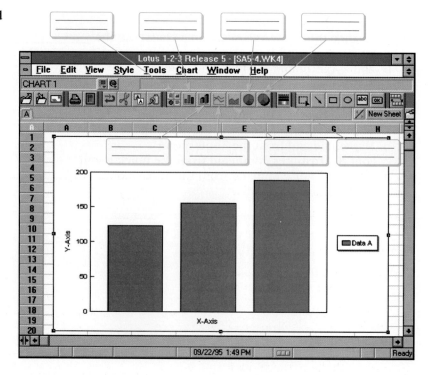

FIGURE SA5-4

STUDENT ASSIGNMENT 5
Understanding the Type Dialog Box

Instructions: In the spaces provided, describe the chart that displays when you select each of the six styles from the Type dialog box shown in Figure SA5-5.

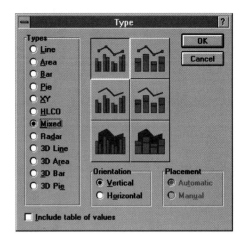

FIGURE SA5-5

Top left style: _____

Middle left style: _____

_____

Bottom left style: _____

Top right style: _____

Middle right style: _____

_____

Bottom right style: _____

STUDENT ASSIGNMENT 6
Understanding 1-2-3 Dialog Boxes

Instructions: Write the command that causes the dialog box to display and allows you to make the indicated changes.

CHANGES	COMMAND
1. Add grid lines to a line chart	
2. Change the symbol on a line chart	
3. Change the y-axis scale	
4. Change the 2nd y-axis scale	
5. Rename a chart	
6. Save a chart	
7. Change the line color on a line chart	
8. Enlarge a chart to fill the entire printed page	
9. Rotate data in a cell	
10. Change the chart type of a chart	
11. Change the title on a map	
12. Change the bin color on a map	

COMPUTER LABORATORY EXERCISE 1
Using the Help Menu

Instructions: Perform the following tasks using a personal computer.

1. Start Lotus 1-2-3 Release 5 for Windows.
2. Select the Help menu.
3. Choose Contents from the Help menu.
4. Click the Commands icon in the 1-2-3 Release 5 Help Contents screen. Choose 1-2-3 Commands from the Commands box.
5. Choose Chart from the Commands topic.
6. Read the Chart Commands topic.
7. In the spaces provided write the name of the command that is associated with each task.

TASK	COMMAND
Set the pattern for a data series	_____
Rename a chart	_____
Change the chart type	_____
Remove grid lines	_____
Reposition the chart note	_____
Delete a data range in a chart	_____
Move the legend in a chart	_____

8. Choose Exit from the Help File menu.

COMPUTER LABORATORY EXERCISE 2
Changing Chart Types and Printing Charts

Instructions: Start 1-2-3. Open the CLE5-2.WK4 file from the Lotus4 subdirectory on the Student Diskette that accompanies this book, and perform the following tasks:

1. Select the chart.
2. Click the 3D Vertical Bar Chart icon on the set of charting SmartIcons.
3. Print the bar chart using the Fill page option in the Page Setup dialog box.
4. Click the 3D Vertical Bar chart icon on the charting set of SmartIcons. Click the Type icon on the charting set of SmartIcons. When the Type dialog box displays, select the Horizontal option button in the Orientation area. Choose the OK button in the Type dialog box.
5. Print the 3D horizontal bar chart using the Fill page but keep proportions option in the Page Setup dialog box.
6. Close the file. Do not save the changes you have made.
7. Follow directions from your instructor for turning in this exercise.
8. Exit 1-2-3.

COMPUTER LABORATORY EXERCISE 3
Adding an Ellipse and Arrow

Instructions: Start 1-2-3. Open the CLE5-3.WK4 file from the Lotus4 subdirectory on the Student Diskette that accompanies this book, and perform the following tasks:

1. Add an ellipse around the value in cell B10.
2. Draw an arrow that extends from the value in cell B10 in the worksheet to the corresponding bar on the chart.
3. Change the color of the ellipse to magenta.
4. Change the color of the arrow to magenta.
5. Print the worksheet and chart.
6. Close the file. Do not save the changes you have made.
7. Follow directions from your instructor for turning in this exercise.
8. Exit 1-2-3.

COMPUTER LABORATORY ASSIGNMENT 1
Creating a Line Chart

Purpose: To provide experience creating a worksheet and related line chart.

Problem: Prepare a worksheet and line chart illustrating the sales by store for Classic Designer. The sales for four quarters are shown in the table below.

STORE	QUARTER 1	QUARTER 2	QUARTER 3	QUARTER 4
Boston	450,000	495,000	562,500	700,000
Dallas	380,000	418,000	475,000	494,000
Atlanta	300,000	275,000	375,000	350,000

The worksheet and chart are shown in Figure CLA5-1.

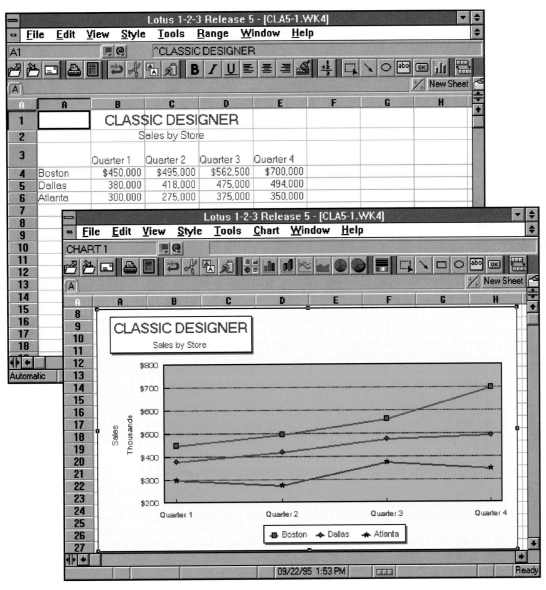

FIGURE CLA5-1

(continued)

COMPUTER LABORATORY ASSIGNMENT 1 (continued)

Instructions:

1. Create and format the worksheet shown in Figure CLA5-1 on the previous page using the numbers from the table.
2. Create a line chart showing the sales for the three stores for four quarters.
3. Change the line color for Boston to magenta.
4. Change the line color for Dallas to dark green.
5. Change the symbol for Atlanta to a star.
6. Display the chart legend below the plot. (To display the chart legend below the plot, select the Below plot option button in the Legend dialog box.)
7. Save the worksheet and chart using a file name consisting of the initials of your first and last names followed by the assignment number. Example: KS5-1.
8. Print the worksheet and chart.
9. Change the line chart to a 3D vertical bar chart.
10. Print the chart.
11. Follow directions from your instructor for turning in this assignment.
12. Exit 1-2-3.

COMPUTER LABORATORY ASSIGNMENT 2
Creating an HLCO Chart

Purpose: To provide experience creating a worksheet and the related HLCO chart.

Problem: Prepare a worksheet and an HLCO chart illustrating the two-week stock activity for Pacific Investors. The high, low, close, and open stock prices and volume are shown in the table below.

DAY	HIGH	LOW	CLOSE	OPEN	VOLUME
Mon	40	32	35	40	1,200,000
Tue	45	35	42	35	750,000
Wed	48	39	47	42	1,375,000
Thurs	50	40	42	47	1,000,000
Fri	42	32	40	42	1,150,000
Mon	40	32	35	40	1,200,000
Tue	45	35	42	35	750,000
Wed	48	39	47	42	1,375,000
Thurs	50	40	42	47	1,000,000
Fri	42	32	40	42	1,150,000

The worksheet and chart are shown in Figure CLA5-2 on the next page.

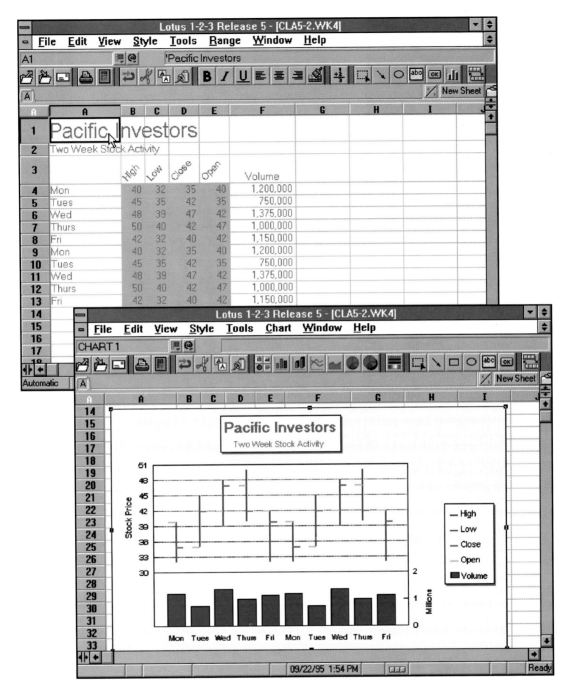

FIGURE CLA5-2

Instructions:

1. Create a worksheet in the format shown in Figure CLA5-2 using the numbers from the table.
2. Rotate the column headings in row 3 forty-five degrees.
3. Create a HLCO chart showing the high, low, close, open, and volume for the Pacific Investor's stock for the two-week period. Notice the y-axis is scaled in intervals of 3.
4. Format the HLCO chart as shown in Figure CLA5-2.
5. Save the worksheet and chart using a file name consisting of the initials of your first and last names followed by the assignment number. Example: KS5-2.
6. Print the worksheet.
7. Print the chart using the Fill page option in the Size area in the Page Setup dialog box.
8. Follow directions from your instructor for turning in this assignment.
9. Exit 1-2-3.

COMPUTER LABORATORY ASSIGNMENT 3
Creating Mixed Charts

Purpose: To provide experience creating a worksheet and related chart.

Problem: Prepare a mixed chart illustrating the sales and profit the Marlow Company for six months of the year based on the following table.

The worksheet and chart are shown in Figure CLA5-3.

	JAN	FEB	MAR	APR	MAY	JUN
Sales	75,000	88,500	104,500	123,000	145,250	171,350
Profit	9,500	7,850	19,540	19,680	32,000	27,400

Instructions:

1. Create a worksheet in the format shown in Figure CLA5-3a using the numbers from the table.
2. Create a mixed chart in the format (shown in Figure CLA 5-3b on the next page) showing the sales and profit for the six months.
3. Plot the profit series on the 2nd y-axis. Manually scale the 2nd y-axis upper limit to 50,000.
4. Format the mixed chart.
5. Save the worksheet and chart using a file name consisting of the initials of your first and last names followed by the assignment number. Example: KS5-3.
6. Print the chart.
7. Follow directions from your instructor for turning in this assignment.
8. Exit 1-2-3.

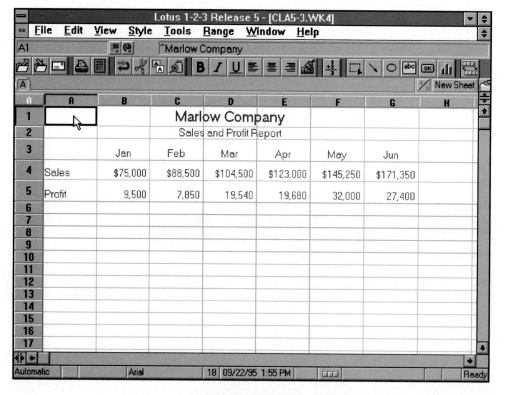

FIGURE CLA5-3a

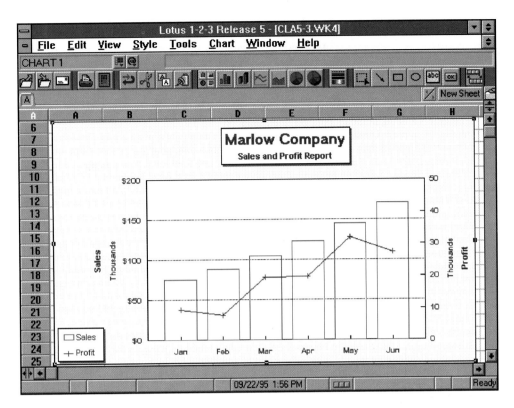

FIGURE CLA5-3b

COMPUTER LABORATORY ASSIGNMENT 4
Creating Charts

Purpose: To provide experience creating a worksheet and appropriate charts.

Problem: Prepare a chart illustrating the sales by type for four quarters based on the following table.

	QUARTER 1	QUARTER 2	QUARTER 3	QUARTER 4
California	561,740	834,650	901,755	899,540
Nevada	300,000	265,400	298,750	358,750
Washington	410,000	563,800	632,400	345,200
Oregon	55,075	85,350	75,460	89,700

Instructions:

1. Analyze the data, and create two different charts that display the data so you can completely analyze the changes in the sales by type over the four quarters.
2. Format the charts.
3. Print the charts.
4. Create a map to illustrate total sales geographically.
5. Print the map.
6. Save the worksheet and charts using a file name consisting of the initials of your first and last names followed by the assignment number. Example: KS5-4.
7. Follow directions from your instructor for turning in this assignment.
8. Exit 1-2-3.

LOTUS 1-2-3 RELEASE 5 FOR WINDOWS

PROJECT SIX

▼

DATA ANALYSIS

You will have mastered the material in this project when you can:

- ▸ Display the system date in a worksheet using the @TODAY function
- ▸ Assign a name to a cell and refer to the cell in a formula by using the assigned name
- ▸ Use Backsolver to determine the input value necessary to achieve a desired goal
- ▸ Build a 1-variable what-if table to analyze data in a worksheet
- ▸ Write a macro to automate data entry into a worksheet

- ▸ Write a macro to print selected ranges in a worksheet
- ▸ Assign a macro to a macro button
- ▸ Run a macro from a macro button
- ▸ Use Version Manager to record and save different versions of data values
- ▸ Protect and unprotect data
- ▸ Seal a file

▶ INTRODUCTION

In the first five projects, you learned how to create worksheets, use formulas, and create charts. This project presents a broader utilization of 1-2-3's powerful capability to analyze data and solve problems in worksheets. For example, what if you know the result you want a formula in a worksheet to return, but you do not know the data required to attain that value? Or what if you wanted to examine a table of profit calculations for a range of sales levels. 1-2-3 has the means of examining data to solve these types of questions.

Project 6 describes three 1-2-3 tools to use in analyzing worksheet data — Backsolver, what-if tables, and Version Manager.

This project also introduces you to the use of macros and cell protection. Using a macro you can reduce a series of actions to the click of a button. Cell protection ensures that you don't accidentally change values that are critical to the worksheet.

▶ PROJECT SIX

P roject 6 is made up of two worksheets: (1) the Analysis worksheet that determines the potential profit for a one-day management training seminar; and (2) the Macros worksheet that contains two macros: one that instructs 1-2-3 to accept new seminar variables from the worksheet user; and one to print a defined range in the worksheet.

The Analysis worksheet in Figure 6-1 includes four distinct sections: (1) a seminar variables section in the range A1..B8; (2) the management seminars section in the range D1..E13; (3) a what-if table in the range A10..B18; and (4) two buttons titled, New Seminar Variables and Print, located below the management seminars section.

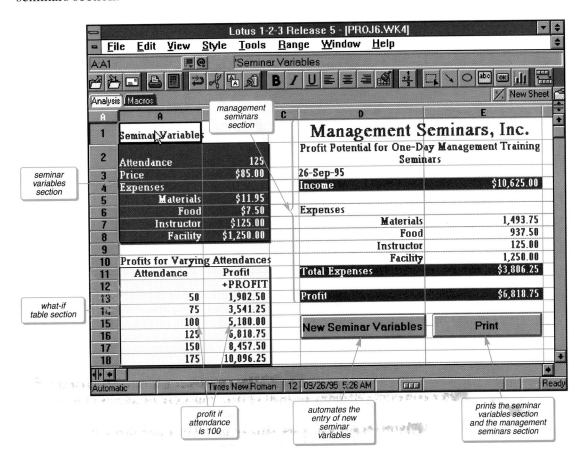

FIGURE 6-1

The seminar variables section of the worksheet in Figure 6-1 contains the variables used in determining the potential profit for the one-day management seminars. The attendance value, 125, is entered in cell B2. The price, $85.00, is entered in cell B3. The projected expenses for the seminar are entered in the range B5..B8: $11.95 for materials in cell B5, $7.50 for food in cell B6, $125.00 for the instructor in cell B7, and $1,250.00 for the facility in cell B8.

The management seminars section of the worksheet in Figure 6-1 on the previous page contains the profit potential for a one-day management training seminar based on the variables entered in the seminar variables section. The income in cell E4 is calculated by multiplying the attendance value in cell B2 by the price in cell B3. Each of the projected expenses in the range E7..E8 — materials and food — is determined by multiplying the appropriate expense value in the seminar variables section by the attendance value in cell B2. These projected expenses for the seminar are as follows:

1. Materials are 1,493.75 ($11.95 * 125)
2. Food is 937.50 ($7.50 * 125)

The instructor and facility expense do not vary as the attendance number changes. Therefore, the instructor and facility expense are the same values as in the seminar variables section.

The value in Total Expenses (cell E11) is $3,806.25 and is calculated by summing the expenses in the range E7..E10. The profit in cell E13, $6,818.75, is calculated by subtracting the total expenses in cell E11 from the income in cell E4.

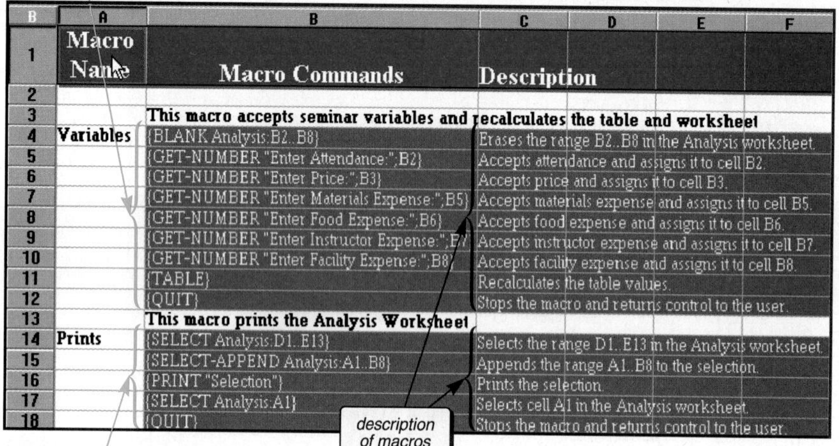

The third section of the worksheet in Figure 6-1 is a what-if table located below the seminar variables section. The what-if table shows the potential profits (range B13..B18) for different attendance values (range A13..A18). The what-if table in Figure 6-1 on the previous page answers six different what-if questions. The questions pertain to the effect the six different attendance values in the range A13..A18 have on the profit. For example, what will be the profit if the attendance value is 100 rather than 125? The answer, $5,180.00, is in cell B15.

macro accepts new seminar variables when you click New Seminar Variables button in Analysis worksheet (Figure 6-1)

	A	B	C	D	E	F
1	**Macro Name**	**Macro Commands**	**Description**			
2						
3		This macro accepts seminar variables and recalculates the table and worksheet				
4	Variables	{BLANK Analysis.B2..B8}	Erases the range B2..B8 in the Analysis worksheet.			
5		{GET-NUMBER "Enter Attendance:",B2}	Accepts attendance and assigns it to cell B2.			
6		{GET-NUMBER "Enter Price:",B3}	Accepts price and assigns it to cell B3.			
7		{GET-NUMBER "Enter Materials Expense:",B5}	Accepts materials expense and assigns it to cell B5.			
8		{GET-NUMBER "Enter Food Expense:",B6}	Accepts food expense and assigns it to cell B6.			
9		{GET-NUMBER "Enter Instructor Expense:",F7}	Accepts instructor expense and assigns it to cell B7.			
10		{GET-NUMBER "Enter Facility Expense:",B8}	Accepts facility expense and assigns it to cell B8.			
11		{TABLE}	Recalculates the table values.			
12		{QUIT}	Stops the macro and returns control to the user.			
13		This macro prints the Analysis Worksheet				
14	Prints	{SELECT Analysis.D1..E13}	Selects the range D1..E13 in the Analysis worksheet.			
15		{SELECT-APPEND Analysis.A1..B8}	Appends the range A1..B8 to the selection.			
16		{PRINT "Selection"}	Prints the selection.			
17		{SELECT Analysis.A1}	Selects cell A1 in the Analysis worksheet.			
18		{QUIT}	Stops the macro and returns control to the user.			

description of macros

FIGURE 6-2

macro prints seminar variables section and management seminars section when you click Print button in Analysis worksheet (Figure 6-1)

The function of the button titled New Seminar Variables in the range D15..D16 (Figure 6-1 on the previous page) is to automate the entry of new seminar variables. The function of the button titled, Print, in the range E15..E16 is to print the seminar variables section and the management seminars section. The buttons play back the macros shown in Figure 6-2.

The Macros worksheet shown in Figure 6-2 contains two macros that are played back when you click the corresponding button on the Analysis worksheet. A **macro command** tells 1-2-3 to carry out an operation, such as select a range or clear the selection. Column A in the Macros worksheet contains the names of the macros, Variables and Prints. Column B contains the macro commands 1-2-3 is to carry out when the macro is played back. Column C includes a description that explains the purpose of the macro command in the same row in column B.

The Variables macro in the range B4..B12 automates entering the seminar variables into cells B2 through B8 on the Analysis worksheet. The Prints macro in the range B14..B18 prints the seminar variables and management seminars section.

Changing the Font of the Worksheet

The first step in Project 6 is to change the font of the worksheet from the default Arial to Times New Roman. The steps to change the font of the worksheet are reviewed below.

TO CHANGE THE FONT OF THE WORKSHEET

Step 1: Choose the Worksheet Defaults command from the Style menu.
Step 2: Select Times New Roman in the Face list box in the Worksheet Defaults dialog box.
Step 3: Choose the OK button in the Worksheet Defaults dialog box.

▶ CREATING THE SEMINAR VARIABLES SECTION

he next step is to enter the title in cell A1, the row titles in the range A2..A8, and the values in the range B2..B8 for the seminar variables section. Perform the following steps to enter the seminar variables section.

TO ENTER THE SEMINAR VARIABLES SECTION

Step 1: Select cell A1. Type `Seminar Variables`. Type `Attendance` in cell A2, `Price` in cell A3, `Expenses` in cell A4, `Materials` in cell A5, `Food` in cell A6, `Instructor` in cell A7, and `Facility` in cell A8.
Step 2: Select cell B2. Type `125`. Type `85` in cell B3. Select cell B5. Type `11.95`. Type `7.5` in cell B6, `125` in cell B7, and `1250` in cell B8. Click the Confirm button or press the ENTER key.

The seminar variables section displays as shown in Figure 6-3.

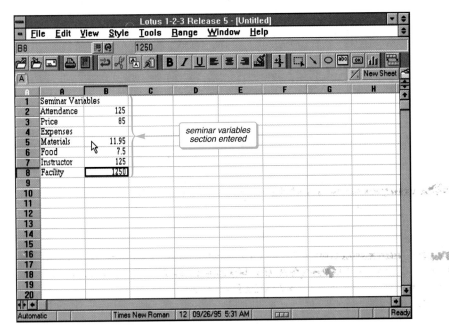

FIGURE 6-3

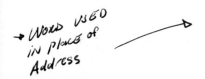

*Word used
in place of
Address*

Naming a Range Using Adjacent Labels

In addition to using a cell reference such as B2 to reference a cell, you can also name a range. A **range name** is a word you use in place of an address. After a range name is assigned to a cell, you can use the range name in formulas. Naming a cell helps make the formula easier to read and understand.

You can name single-cell ranges using labels in adjacent cells. To name the range using the adjacent label, you first select the range that contains the label you want to use to name the range, then choose the **Name command** from the quick menu. For Project 6, each label in the ranges A2..A3 and A5..A8 is assigned to the adjacent cell in column B. To name a range using adjacent labels, complete the following steps.

TO NAME A RANGE USING ADJACENT LABELS ▼

STEP 1 ►

Select the range containing the labels – A2..A3. Point to the selected range and click the right mouse button. When the quick menu displays, point to the Name command.

1-2-3 highlights the range A2..A3 and displays the quick menu (Figure 6-4). The mouse pointer points to the Name command. Cells A2 and A3 contain the labels you want to use as range names.

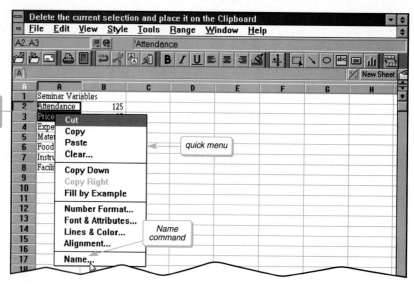

FIGURE 6-4

STEP 2 ►

Choose the Name command. When the Name dialog box displays, be sure To the right displays in the For cells drop-down box. Then, point to the Use Labels button

(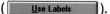).

1-2-3 displays the Name dialog box (Figure 6-5). The mouse pointer points to the Use Labels button. To the right displays in the For cells drop-down box under the Use Labels button. The To the right direction tells 1-2-3 where the cells you want to name are in relation to the labels. The range selected displays in the Range text box.

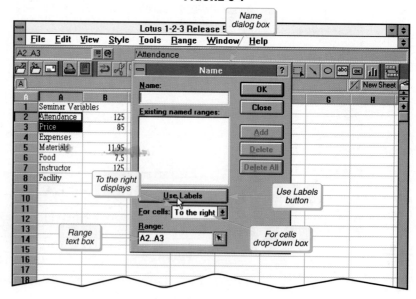

FIGURE 6-5

STEP 3 ▶

Click the Use Labels button in the Name dialog box. Point to the range selector (▣) to the right of the Range text box.

1-2-3 enters the labels from the selected range in the Existing named ranges list box (Figure 6-6). The mouse pointer points to the range selector. Notice 1-2-3 enters all range names as upper-case letters and in alphabetical order.

FIGURE 6-6

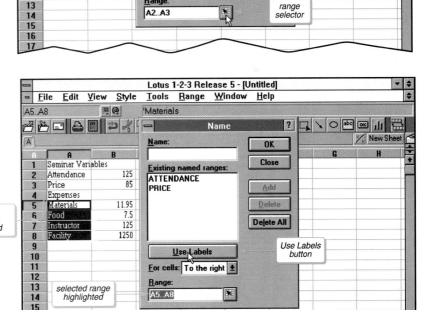

STEP 4 ▶

Click the Range selector. When the Name dialog box disappears, select the range A5..A8. When the Name dialog box reappears, point to the Use Labels button.

When you click the range selector, 1-2-3 removes the Name dialog box so you can select the range. 1-2-3 highlights the range A5..A8 (Figure 6-7). The selected range is highlighted in the Range text box. The mouse pointer points to the Use Labels button.

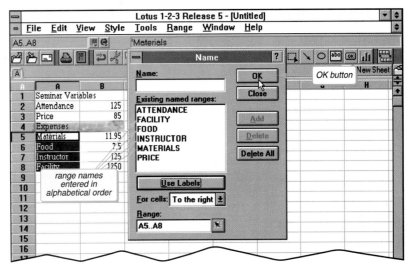

FIGURE 6-7

STEP 5 ▶

Click the Use Labels button in the Name dialog box and point to the OK button.

1-2-3 enters the labels from the selected range in the Existing named ranges list box in alphabetical order (Figure 6-8). The mouse pointer points to the OK button.

STEP 6

Choose the OK button.

FIGURE 6-8

In the steps on the previous pages, each label in the range became the range name of the adjacent cell. For example, cell B2 was given the name ATTENDANCE and cell B3 was given the name PRICE. These range names can be used in formulas within the worksheet.

A range name can include up to 15 characters. If the label you use to name an adjacent cell contains more than 15 characters, 1-2-3 will use only the first 15 characters for the range name. Consider the following guidelines when using labels to name adjacent cells in a worksheet: (1) do not start a label with exclamation point (!) and do not include spaces, commas, semicolons, periods, or the following characters: + - * / & < > @ # or {; (2) do not use a name that is a valid cell address, such as Q2; and (3) use the underscore (_) to replace the spaces between a two-word name; for example, TOTAL_EXPENSES.

The Name command is also found in the Range menu on the main menu bar.

▶ CREATING THE MANAGEMENT SEMINARS SECTION

he next step is to enter the management seminars section titles in cell D1 and cell D2. Perform the following step to enter the titles.

TO ENTER WORKSHEET TITLES

Step 1: Select cell D1. Type `Management Seminars, Inc.`. Type `Profit Potential for One-Day Management Training Seminars` in cell D2. Click the Confirm button or press the ENTER key

The worksheet titles display as shown in Figure 6-9.

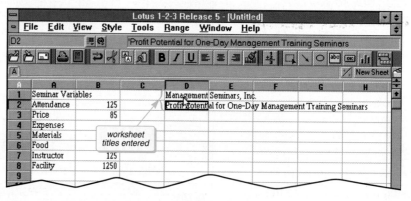

FIGURE 6-9

Displaying the System Date

The next step is to enter the system date in cell D3. You can use the @TODAY function to enter the system date in the worksheet. The **@TODAY function** returns a date number that represents the current date according to the system date in your computer. The **date number** is an integer in the range 1 to 73050 corresponding to the dates January 1, 1900 through December 31, 2099. For example, @TODAY returns the date number 34968 on September 26, 1995. To display the system date in cell D3, perform the steps on the next page.

TO DISPLAY THE SYSTEM DATE ▼

STEP 1 ▶

Select cell D3. Click the @function selector in the edit line and point to the TODAY function name.

Cell D3 is selected and 1-2-3 displays the @Function menu listing commonly used function names (Figure 6-10). The mouse pointer points to the TODAY function name.

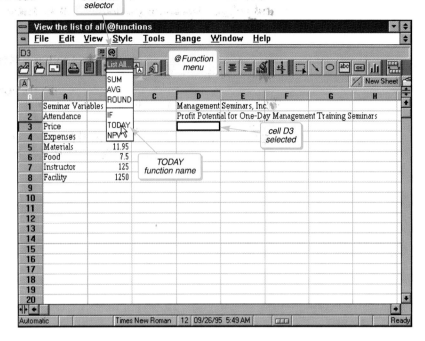

FIGURE 6-10

STEP 2 ▶

Choose TODAY from the @Function menu. Click the Confirm button or press the ENTER key.

1-2-3 displays the @TODAY function in the contents box in the edit line and the date number in the cell (Figure 6-11). The date number 34968 represents the number of days past January 1, 1900.

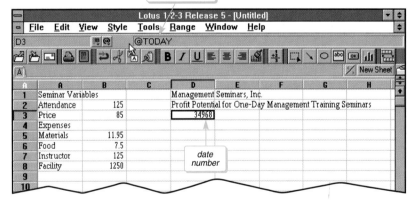

FIGURE 6-11

Notice in Figure 6-11 the date number displays in the cell right-aligned because 1-2-3 treats a date as a value. The date number will be formatted in a later section.

The @TODAY function is one of nineteen date and time functions available in the **Calendar category**. 1-2-3 has a total of 228 @functions divided into ten categories. Table 6-1 on the following page lists the categories and summaries of each category's purpose.

▶ **TABLE 6-1**

CATEGORY OF FUNCTIONS	PURPOSE
Calendar	Calculates values that represent dates and times
Database	Performs statistical calculations and queries in databases
Engineering	Performs advanced mathematical operations and specific engineering calculations
Financial	Performs financial analysis, determines depreciation, and calculates cash flows
Information	Provides information about cells, ranges, and operating system
Logical	Tests whether a condition is true or false
Lookup	Finds and returns the contents of a cell
Mathematical	Performs standard arithmetic operations
Statistical	Performs statistical calculations on data in a worksheet
Text	Performs operations on the text in cells

1-2-3's online Help provides detailed information about each of the @functions. You can also obtain help by typing the @ sign and the function name in a cell, and then pressing F1. 1-2-3 then displays a Help topic with detailed information about the specific @function.

Entering the Row Titles

The next step is to enter the row titles for the management seminars section. Perform the following step to enter the row titles.

TO ENTER ROW TITLES

Step 1: Select cell D4 and type Income. Select cell D6 and type Expenses. Type Materials in cell D7, type Food in cell D8, type Instructor in cell D9, type Facility in cell D10, and type Total Expenses in cell D11. Select cell D13 and type Profit. Click the Confirm button or press the ENTER key.

The row titles display as shown in Figure 6-12.

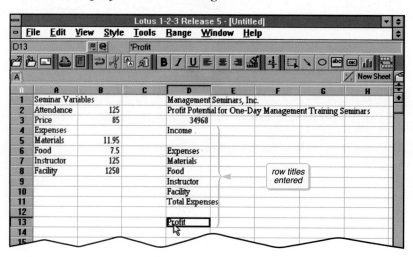

FIGURE 6-12

Using Range Names in Formulas

The next step is to enter the formulas in the management seminars section of the worksheet. When you name a range, you can use the range name in a formula instead of typing the range address or selecting the range. One way to enter a range name into a formula is to type it. However, you can also use the navigator in the edit line to select a named range to insert into a formula.

In the steps on page L323, cell B2 was given the range name, ATTENDANCE, and cell B3, PRICE (Figure 6-6 on page L323). The formula in cell E4 to calculate the income for a one-day seminar is +ATTENDANCE*PRICE. To enter this formula using range names, perform the following steps.

TO USE RANGE NAMES IN A FORMULA ▼

STEP 1 ▶

Select cell E4. Type + to begin the formula in cell E4. Point to the navigator (▦) on the edit line.

Typing a plus sign informs 1-2-3 you are entering a formula. The plus sign, Cancel button, and Confirm button display in the contents box (Figure 6-13). The mouse pointer points to the navigator in the edit line.

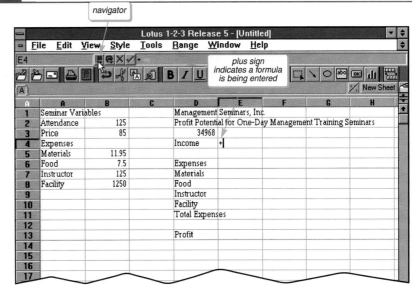

FIGURE 6-13

STEP 2 ▶

Click the navigator and point to ATTENDANCE.

1-2-3 displays the navigator drop-down box listing the named ranges in the current file (Figure 6-14). The mouse pointer points to the desired named range. Notice the named ranges display in uppercase letters and in alphabetical order.

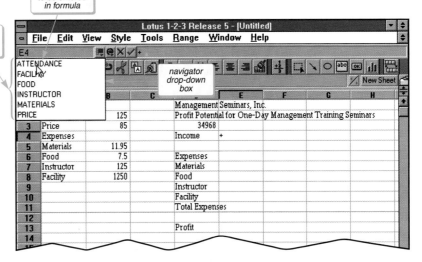

FIGURE 6-14

STEP 3 ▶

Click the left mouse button. Type the multiplication operator (*). Then, click the navigator and point to PRICE.

1-2-3 places the named range ATTENDANCE in the formula displayed in the cell and the contents box instead of the cell reference B2 (Figure 6-15). Whenever you select a cell or range of cells that have been given a range name, 1-2-3 will display the range name instead of the cell reference. The navigator drop-down box displays and the mouse pointer points to PRICE.

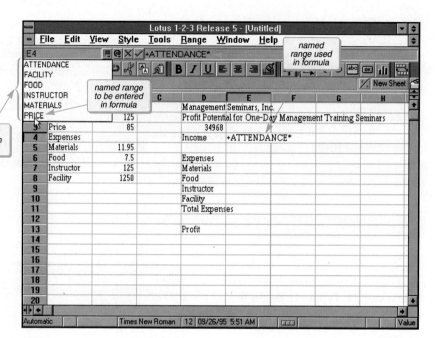

FIGURE 6-15

STEP 4 ▶

Click the left mouse button. Click the Confirm button or press the ENTER key.

1-2-3 enters the formula into cell E4 and calculates the formula (Figure 6-16). The formula in the contents box, +ATTENDANCE* PRICE, is the same as the formula, +B2*B3. Using range names in formulas creates formulas that are easier to read and understand.

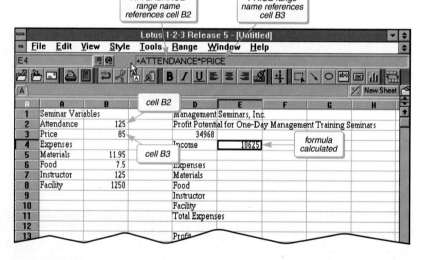

FIGURE 6-16

Because the value in cell E4 will be used to calculate the profit in cell E13 (profit = income – total expenses), you can use the label in cell D4 to assign a name to cell E4. Perform the following steps to name the range using the adjacent label.

TO NAME A RANGE USING ADJACENT LABELS

Step 1: Select cell D4 and click the right mouse button.

Step 2: Choose the Name command from the quick menu. When the Name dialog box displays, ensure that To the right displays in the For cells drop-down box. Click the Use Labels button.

Step 3: Choose the OK button in the Name dialog box.

The next step is to enter the formulas in the range E7..E10 to calculate the expenses for the one-day management seminars. The formula in cell E7 to calculate the materials expense for a one-day seminar is +ATTENDANCE*MATERIALS. The formula in cell E8 to calculate the food expense for a one-day seminar is +ATTENDANCE*FOOD. The instructor and facility expenses do not vary according to the attendance value. Therefore, the formula in cell E9 to calculate the instructor expense is +INSTRUCTOR and the formula in cell E10 to calculate the facility expense is +FACILITY. Perform the following steps to use range names in formulas.

TO USE RANGE NAMES IN FORMULAS ▼

STEP 1 ▶

Select cell E7. Type a plus sign (+), click the navigator, select ATTENDANCE, type the multiplication operator (*), click the navigator and select MATERIALS. Click the Confirm button or press the ENTER key.

*1-2-3 displays the formula in the contents box and enters the results in cell E7 (Figure 6-17). The formula in the contents box, +ATTENDANCE*MATERIALS, is the same as the formula, +B2*B5.*

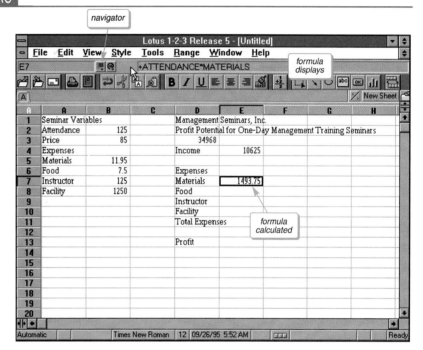

FIGURE 6-17

STEP 2 ▶

Select cell E8. Type a plus sign (+), click the navigator, select ATTENDANCE, type the multiplication operator (*), click the navigator and select FOOD. Click the Confirm button or press the ENTER key.

*1-2-3 displays the formula in the contents box and enters the results in cell E7 (Figure 6-18). The formula in the contents box, +ATTENDANCE*FOOD, is the same as the formula, +B2*B6.*

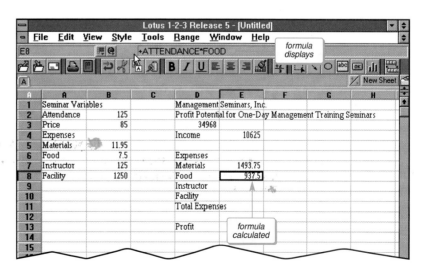

FIGURE 6-18

STEP 3 ▶

Select cell E9. Type a plus sign +, click the navigator and select INSTRUCTOR. Click the Confirm button or press the ENTER key.

The formula in cell E9 contains the plus sign and the range name for cell B7 (Figure 6-19). No other element in the formula is required because only cell B7 is used so, in effect, the contents of cell B7 are copied into cell E9.

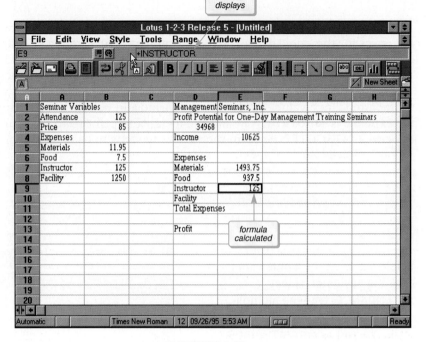

FIGURE 6-19

STEP 4 ▶

Select cell E10. Type a plus sign +, click the navigator and select FACILITY. Click the Confirm button or press the ENTER key.

The formula in cell E10 contains the plus sign and the range name for cell B8 (Figure 6-20). No other element in the formula is required because only cell B8 is used.

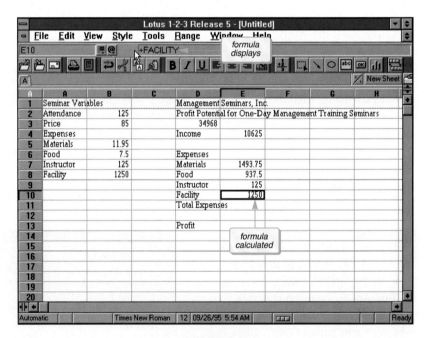

FIGURE 6-20

Range names can also be given to more than one cell. When naming more than one cell, you must type the name in the Name dialog box. To name the range E7..E10 EXPENSES by typing, follow the steps on the next page.

TO NAME A RANGE BY TYPING ▼

STEP 1 ▶

Select the range E7..E10. Point to the selected range and click the right mouse button. Choose the Name command from the quick menu. When the Name dialog box displays, type the range name, EXPENSES, in the Name text box. Point to the ADD button (Add).

1-2-3 displays the Name dialog box (Figure 6-21). As you type the range name, the Add and Delete buttons in the Name dialog box display indicating they can be chosen. The range name you typed displays in the Name text box. The range names defined previously display in the Existing named ranges list box. The mouse pointer points to the Add button.

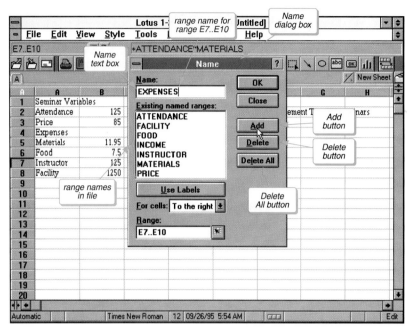

FIGURE 6-21

STEP 2 ▶

Choose the Add button. Point to the OK button.

When you select the Add button, 1-2-3 adds the name to the list of existing named ranges and clears the Name text box (Figure 6-22). The mouse pointer points to the OK button. Notice 1-2-3 dims the Delete button when you select the Add button. The range name you added displays in alphabetical order in the Existing named ranges list box.

STEP 3

Choose the OK button.

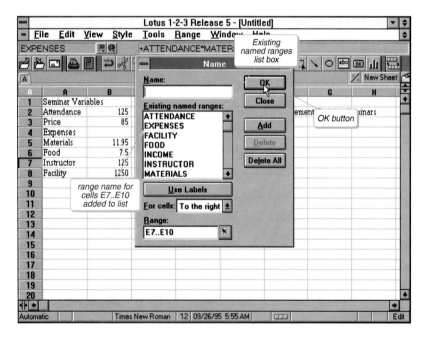

FIGURE 6-22

The Name dialog box (see Figure 6-21 on the previous page) contains two buttons of which you should be aware. First, the Delete button (Delete) is used to delete a range name. To delete a range name, select the name to delete in the Existing named ranges list box, choose the Delete button, and then choose the OK button.

The Delete All button (Delete All) is used to delete all the range names in the file. To delete all the range names in a file, choose the Delete All button, and then choose the OK button.

When you delete a range name, the data in the range is left unchanged. If the range you delete is used in a formula, 1-2-3 replaces the range name with its associated cell address.

Completing the Management Seminars Section

The next step is to calculate the total expenses and name the range. Use the SmartSum icon to enter the @SUM function in cell E11 to sum the range E7..E10. To enter an @function and name the range, perform the following steps.

TO ENTER AN @FUNCTION AND NAME THE RANGE

Step 1: Select cell E11. Click the SmartSum icon on the set of SmartIcons.

Step 2: Point to cell E11 and click the right mouse button. Choose the Name command from the quick menu. Type TOTAL_EXPENSES in the Name text box. Choose the Add button. Choose the OK button in the Name dialog box.

The worksheet displays as shown in Figure 6-23.

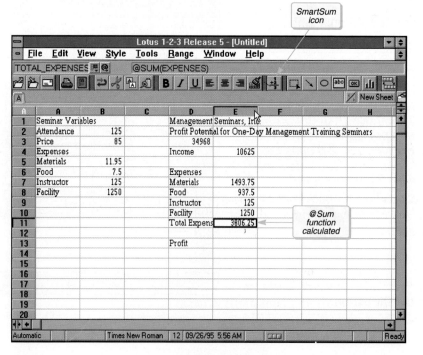

FIGURE 6-23

Notice in Figure 6-23 you typed the range name for cell E11 in the Name text box instead of using the label adjacent to the cell. Recall you cannot use spaces in a range name. Therefore, you were instructed to type the range name, TOTAL_EXPENSES, using an underscore.

The last step in creating the Management Seminars section is to calculate the profit and name the range. The formula to calculate profit is INCOME - TOTAL_EXPENSES. Perform the following steps to use range names in a formula and then name the range.

TO USE RANGE NAMES IN A FORMULA AND THEN NAME THE RANGE

Step 1: Select cell E13. Type a plus sign (+), click the navigator, select INCOME, type the minus sign (-), click the navigator, and select TOTAL_EXPENSES. Click the Confirm button or press the ENTER key.

Step 2: Select cell D13 and click the right mouse button. Choose the Name command from the quick menu. When the Name dialog box displays, ensure that To the right displays in the For cells drop-down box. Then, click the Use Labels button. Choose the OK button in the Name dialog box.

The worksheet displays as shown in Figure 6-24.

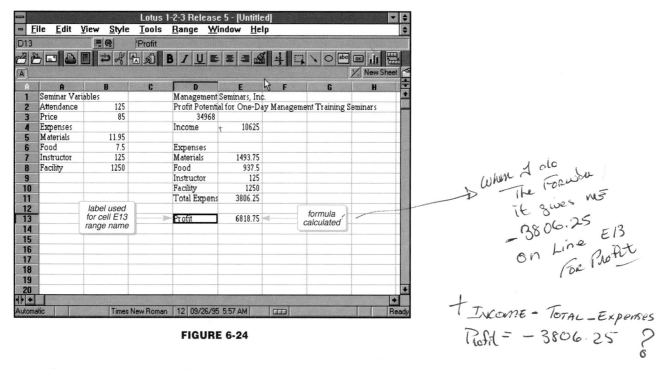

FIGURE 6-24

The use of range names can result in a worksheet that is easier to read and understand when analyzing formulas. Whenever you create a worksheet with multiple formulas, consider using range names.

▶ FORMATTING THE WORKSHEET

F ormatting the worksheet in Project 6 includes changing the color of the text, changing the background color of cells, aligning labels, and placing the values in the proper format. When formatting is complete, the worksheet will appear as shown in Figure 6-25.

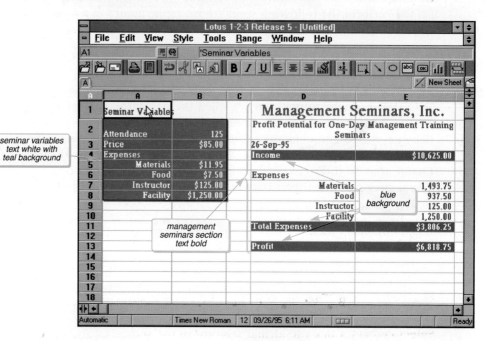

FIGURE 6-25

To accomplish this formatting, complete the following steps.

TO FORMAT THE WORKSHEET

Step 1: Select the collection A1; D1..E13. Point to the selected collection and click the right mouse button. Choose the Font & Attributes command from the quick menu. When the Font & Attributes dialog box displays, select Bold in the Attributes area. Click the Color drop-down box arrow and select the first blue in the top row of the Color drop-down box. Choose the OK button in the Font & Attributes dialog box.

Step 2: Select the range A2..B8. Point to the selected range and click the right mouse button. Choose the Lines & Color command from the quick menu. When the Lines & Color dialog box displays, select teal (Color: 118) in the top row of the Background color drop-down box. Select white in the top row of the Text color drop-down box. Click the Designer frame drop-down box arrow and choose the second designer frame from the left in the top row of the Designer frame drop-down box. Choose the OK button in the Lines & Color dialog box. Click the Bold icon on the set of SmartIcons.

STEP 2 ▶

Choose the Analyze command and point to the Backsolver command on the Analyze cascading menu.

When you choose the Analyze command, the Analyze cascading menu displays because there is an arrowhead to the right of the Analyze command on the Range menu (Figure 6-27). The mouse pointer points to the Backsolver command.

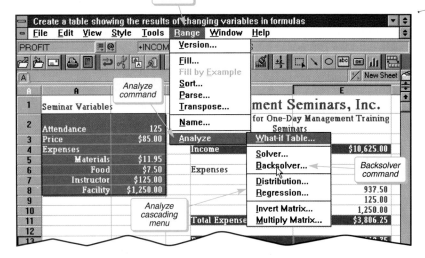

FIGURE 6-27

STEP 3 ▶

Choose the Backsolver command. When the Backsolver dialog box displays, highlight 0 in the Equal to value text box. Type 3500. Then, point to the range selector to the right of the By changing cell(s) text box.

1-2-3 displays the Backsolver dialog box (Figure 6-28). Cell E13 is the Make cell because the profit formula is located in that cell. The Equal to value is 3500 because this is the profit you want from the one-day management seminar. The mouse pointer points to the range selector to the right of the By changing cell(s) text box.

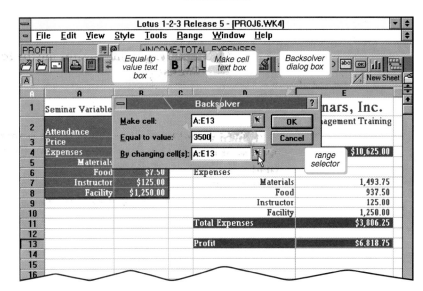

FIGURE 6-28

STEP 4 ▶

Click the range selector. Select cell B2. Point to the OK button in the Backsolver dialog box.

When you click the range selector, 1-2-3 temporarily removes the Backsolver dialog box while you select cell B2. When the Backsolver dialog box reappears, cell B2 displays in the By changing cell(s) text box because 1-2-3 must change the attendance variable to make the formula in cell E13 equal to $3,500 (Figure 6-29). The mouse pointer points to the OK button.

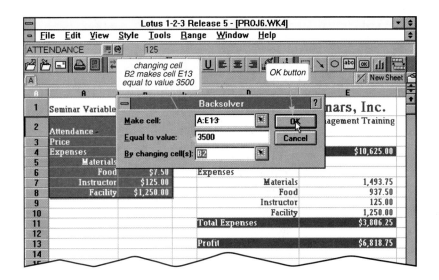

FIGURE 6-29

STEP 5 ►

Choose the OK button.

Backsolver recalculates the work-sheet to meet the specified result of $3,500.00 profit. Backsolver finds the attendance value that results in a profit of $3,500.00 (Figure 6-30).

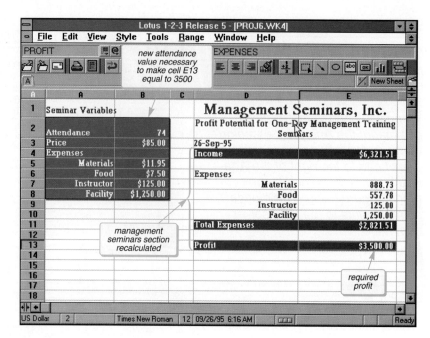

FIGURE 6-30

Using Backsolver, you determined that an attendance level of 74 people is necessary to achieve a profit of $3,500.00.

Notice in this example the cell to vary does not have to be directly referenced. For example, the formula in cell E13 is INCOME – TOTAL_EXPENSES. There is no mention of the attendance value in the formula. However, because income, which is referenced in the formula in cell E13, is based on the attendance value, Backsolver is able to determine the desired profit by varying the attendance value.

When you use Backsolver, 1-2-3 permanently changes the value of By changing cell(s) (see Figure 6-29 on the previous page). If you want to restore the original values, click the Undo icon on the set of SmartIcons immediately after using Backsolver.

▶ USING A 1-VARIABLE WHAT-IF TABLE TO ANALYZE WORKSHEET DATA

The next step is to create a 1-variable what-if table in the range A10..B18 of the worksheet. A **1-variable what-if table** creates a table displaying the results of changing a single variable in a formula. Figure 6-31a illustrates the set up of a 1-variable what-if table. With a 1-variable what-if table, you supply the formula and the different values you want 1-2-3 to subsitute for the variable, and 1-2-3 fills the table with the results of the formula in cell B12. The variable in this what-if table is the attendance value.

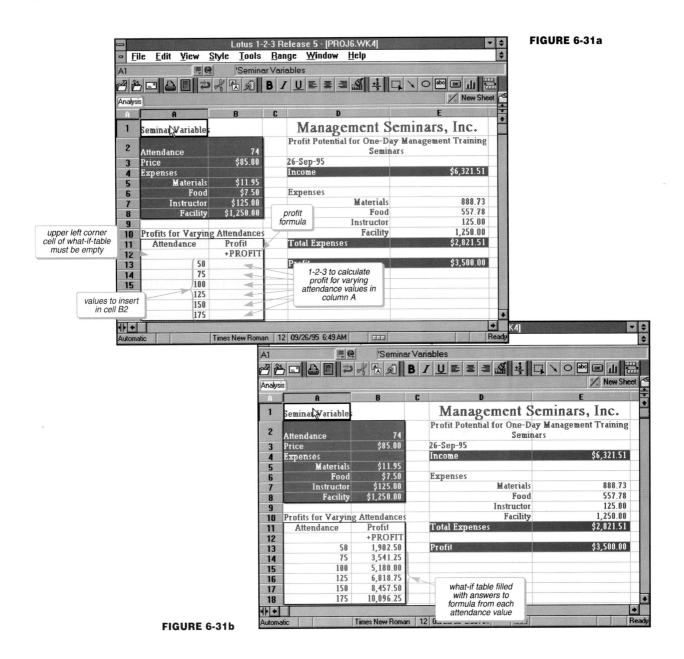

FIGURE 6-31a

FIGURE 6-31b

Figure 6-31b shows the profit with different attendance values. The attendance values used in this project range from 50 to 175 in increments of 25.

The steps to construct the 1-variable what-if table illustrated in Figure 6-31b are as follows: (1) enter the what-if table title and column headings in the range A10..B11; (2) use the Fill by Example command to enter the varying attendance values in column A; (3) enter the formula in cell B12 for which the table is to determine answers; and (4) calculate the 1-variable what-if table. The sections on the next five pages use these steps to construct the 1-variable what-if table shown in Figure 6-31b.

Entering the What-if Table Title and Column Headings

Perform the following steps to enter the what-if table title in cell A10 and the column headings in cells A11 and B11.

TO ENTER THE WHAT-IF TABLE TITLE AND COLUMN TITLES

Step 1: Select cell A10. Type `Profits for Varying Attendances`.
Step 2: Type `Attendance` in cell A11. Type `Profit` in cell B11. Click the Confirm button or press the ENTER key.

The what-if table title and column headings display as shown in Figure 6-32.

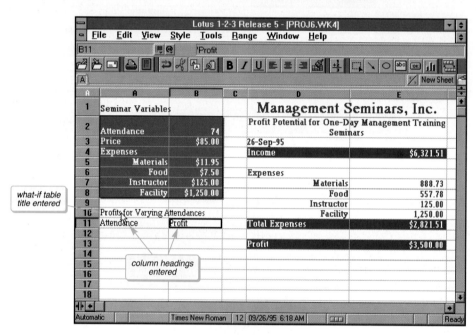

FIGURE 6-32

Using Drag-and-Fill to Create a Data Sequence

The next step in creating the what-if table is to enter the sequence of attendance values in the range A13..A18. Recall from Project 3 that you can use drag-and-fill to enter a data sequence in a range. For this project, the data sequence in the range A13..A18 starts with 50 and increments by 25. When creating a sequence that increments with a value other than 1, you must enter the first two values in the sequence. To create a data sequence, perform the following steps.

TO CREATE A DATA SEQUENCE

Step 1: Select cell A13. Type `50`. Type `75` in cell A14. Click the Confirm button or press the ENTER key.
Step 2: Select the range A13..A14.
Step 3: Position the mouse pointer on the bottom right corner of cell A14. When the mouse pointer changes shape to a block arrow with horizontal and vertical double arrows, drag the range A15..A18.

1-2-3 creates the sequence of values in increments of 25 as shown in Figure 6-33.

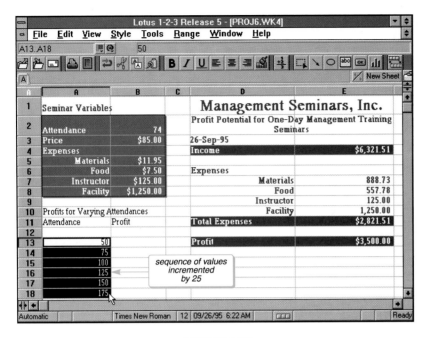

FIGURE 6-33

The attendance values in column A (see Figure 6-31b on page L339) are the input values you want 1-2-3 to use in the formula in cell B12. Notice the top left cell in the table — cell A12 — is blank. The cell immediately above the sequence and to the left of the formula in the table must be empty for a 1-variable what-if table.

Also in this example, it is not required that the cell to vary be directly referenced in the formula in cell B12. For example, the formula in cell B12 (see Figure 6-31b) on page L331, +PROFIT, is the named range for cell E13. The formula in cell E13 is INCOME – TOTAL_EXPENSES. There is no mention of the attendance value in the formula. However, because income, which is referenced in the formula in cell E13, is based on the attendance value, 1-2-3 is able to determine the desired profit by varying the attendance value.

Entering a Formula in a 1-Variable What-if Table

The next step in creating the 1-variable what-if table is to enter the formula in cell B12. The formula you want in the what-if table is the formula that calculates the profit for the management seminars located in cell E13, INCOME – TOTAL_EXPENSES. Recall that earlier in this project cell E13 was assigned the range name, PROFIT. You use the navigator to enter the range name in cell B12. The following steps use the navigator to enter the range name to define the formula in the 1-variable what-if table.

TO ENTER THE FORMULA IN THE 1-VARIABLE WHAT-IF TABLE

Step 1: Select cell B12. Type +.

Step 2: Click the navigator and select PROFIT. Click the Confirm button or press the ENTER key.

1-2-3 displays the profit value in cell B12 as shown in Figure 6-34 on the next page.

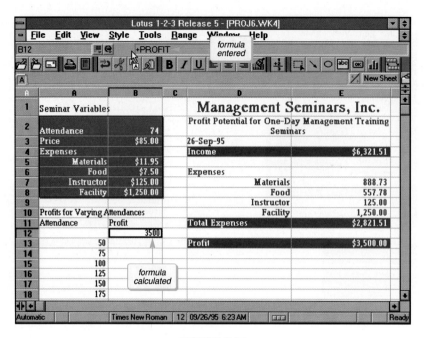

FIGURE 6-34

Calculating the 1-Variable What-if Table

The last step in creating the 1-variable what-if table is to use the Analyze What-if Table command on the Range menu to define the range A12..B18 as the what-if table and identify the attendance value in cell B2 as the input cell, the one you want to vary. To calculate the 1-variable what-if table, perform the following steps.

TO CALCULATE THE 1-VARIABLE WHAT-IF TABLE ▼

STEP 1 ►

Select the range A12..B18. Choose the Analyze command from the Range menu. Point to the What-if Table command.

1-2-3 displays the Range menu (Figure 6-35). When you choose the Analyze command, 1-2-3 displays the Analyze cascading menu because an arrowhead is to the right of the Analyze command. The mouse pointer points to the What-if Table command. Notice the selected range does not include the title in cell A10 or the column headings in row 11. The column headings are not part of the what-if table even though they identify the values in the what-if table. The formula in cell B12 is included in the selected range.

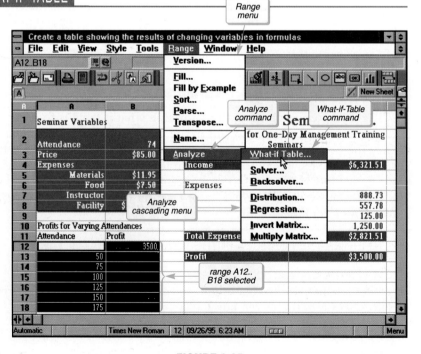

FIGURE 6-35

STEP 2 ▶

Choose the What-if Table command. When the What-if Table dialog box displays, click the Number of variables drop-down box arrow. Then, point to 1 in the Number of variables drop-down box.

1-2-3 displays the What-if Table dialog box (Figure 6-36). The mouse pointer points to the desired number of variables. The selected range displays in the Table range text box.

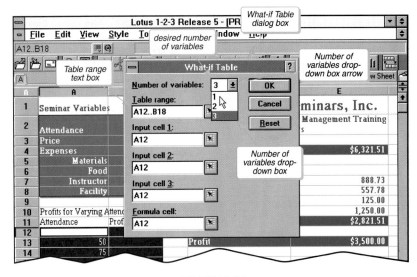

FIGURE 6-36

STEP 3 ▶

Select 1 in the Number of variables drop-down box. Point to the range selector located to the right of the Input cell 1 text box.

The selected number of variables displays in the Number of variables box (Figure 6-37). The mouse pointer points to the range selector.

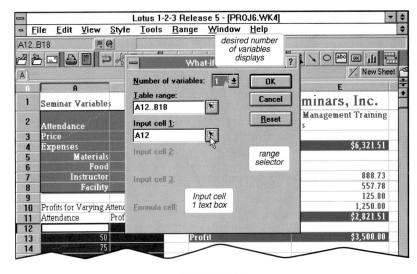

FIGURE 6-37

STEP 4 ▶

Click the range selector. When 1-2-3 removes the What-if Table dialog box, select cell B2. When the What-if Table dialog box displays again, point to the OK button.

1-2-3 displays the cell reference in the Input cell 1 text box (Figure 6-38). The mouse pointer points to the OK button in the What-if Table dialog box.

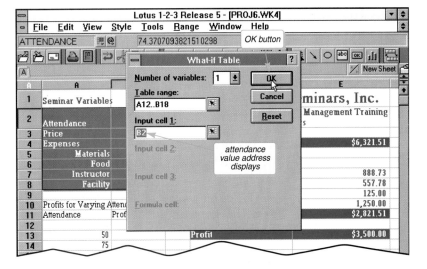

FIGURE 6-38

STEP 5 ▶

Choose the OK button.

1-2-3 substitutes the values in the range A13..A18 in the formula in cell B12 and places the results in the range B13..B18 (Figure 6-39).

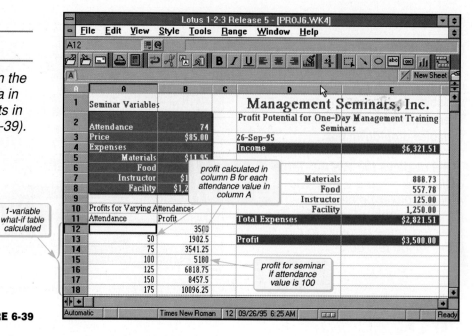

FIGURE 6-39

Notice in Figure 6-39, the profit calculation represents the value that would display in cell E13 if the corresponding attendance value were entered in cell B2. For example, if the attendance value of 100 were entered in cell B2, the profit of $1,830 would display in cell E13. Using the What-if Table command generates six different profit calculations for six different attendance values in a single operation.

When creating a 1-variable what-if table, remember the following important points:

1. You can have as many what-if tables in a worksheet as you want.
2. You delete a what-if table as you do any other item on a worksheet.
3. The top left cell in the what-if table range (cell A12 in Figure 6-39) must be empty.
4. The formula to be evaluated must be entered in the second column of the first row of the table range (cell B12).
5. The input cell you are varying (cell B2 in Figure 6-39) must be located outside the table range (range A12..B18 in Figure 6-39).

Entering New Seminar Variables and Recalculating the What-if Table

With the what-if table section of the worksheet complete, you can enter new seminar variables and generate new profit information. For example, assume attendance for a one-day seminar decreased to 50 and price increased to $95.00. How would these changes impact the profit for the varying attendance rates in the what-if table?

The entries 1-2-3 places in the what-if table are values, not formulas, and are not subject to recalculation when you make changes on the worksheet. Therefore, to cause the what-if table to recalculate new values, you must use the F8 function key. The steps on the next page show how to enter the new price and recalculate the what-if table.

TO ENTER NEW SEMINAR VARIABLES AND RECALCULATE THE TABLE

Step 1: Select cell B2. Type 50.

Step 2: Select cell B3. Enter 95. Click the Confirm button or press the ENTER key.

Step 3: Press F8.

1-2-3 recalculates the what-if table as shown in Figure 6-40.

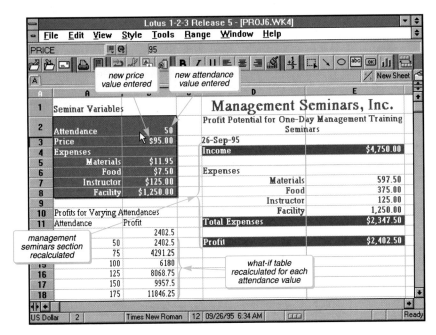

FIGURE 6-40

Formatting the 1-Variable What-if Table and Naming the Worksheet Tab

To format the 1-variable what-if table and name the worksheet tab, perform the following steps.

TO FORMAT THE 1-VARIABLE WHAT-IF TABLE AND NAME THE WORKSHEET TAB

Step 1: Select the range A10..B18. Point to the selected range and click the right mouse button. Choose the Font & Attributes command from the quick menu. When the Font & Attributes dialog box displays, select Bold in the Attributes area. Click the Color drop-down box arrow and select the first blue in the top row of the Color drop-down box. Choose the OK button in the Fonts & Attributes dialog box.

Step 2: Select the range A11..B11. Click the Center icon on the set of Smart-Icons.

Step 3: Select cell B12. Click the format selector on the status bar. Choose the Text format from the pop-up list of formats. Click the Right icon on the set of SmartIcons.

Step 4: Select the range B13..B18. Click the format selector on the status bar. Choose the ,Comma format from the pop-up list of formats.

Step 5: Select the range A11..B18. Point to the selected range and click the right mouse button. Choose the Lines & Color command from the quick menu. When the Lines & Color dialog box displays, click the Background color drop-down box arrow and select the forth color from the left in the second row. Click the Designer frame drop-down box arrow and choose the second designer frame from the left in the top row of the Designer frame drop-down box. Choose the OK button.

Step 6: Double-click the worksheet tab. Type `Analysis`. Press the ENTER key.

Step 7: Point to the worksheet tab and click the right mouse button. Choose the Worksheet Defaults command from the quick menu. When the Worksheet Defaults dialog box displays, click the Worksheet tab drop-down box arrow and select the fourth color from the left in the second row. Choose the OK button.

The worksheet displays as shown in Figure 6-41.

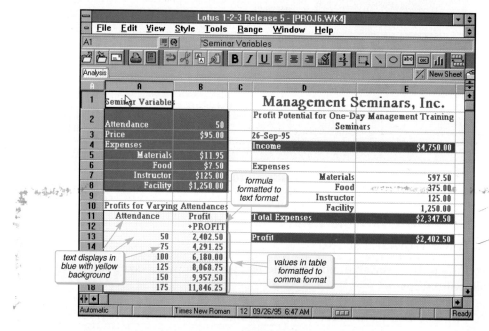

FIGURE 6-41

▶ CREATING A MACRO TO AUTOMATE DATA ENTRY

T o perform 1-2-3 tasks automatically, you can create macros. A **macro** is made up of a series of commands that tell 1-2-3 what to do to complete a task. Macro commands such as the ones in Figure 6-42 are used to automate routine worksheet tasks, such as entering new data into a worksheet and printing a worksheet.

B	A	B	C	D	E	F
1	Macro Name	Macro Commands	Description			
2						
3		This macro accepts seminar variables and recalculates the table and worksheet				
4	Variables	{BLANK Analysis:B2..B8}	Erases the range B2..B8 in the Analysis worksheet.			
5		{GET-NUMBER "Enter Attendance:";B2}	Accepts attendance and assigns it to cell B2.			
6		{GET-NUMBER "Enter Price:";B3}	Accepts price and assigns it to cell B3.			
7		{GET-NUMBER "Enter Materials Expense:";B5}	Accepts materials expense and assigns it to cell B5.			
8		{GET-NUMBER "Enter Food Expense:";B6}	Accepts food expense and assigns it to cell B6.			
9		{GET-NUMBER "Enter Instructor Expense:";B7}	Accepts instructor expense and assigns it to cell B7.			
10		{GET-NUMBER "Enter Facility Expense:";B8}	Accepts facility expense and assigns it to cell B8.			
11		{TABLE}	Recalculates the table values.			
12		{QUIT}	Stops the macro and returns control to the user.			
13		This macro prints the Analysis Worksheet				
14	Prints	{SELECT Analysis:D1..E13}	Selects the range D1..E13 in the Analysis worksheet.			
15		{SELECT-APPEND Analysis:A1..B8}	Appends the range A1..B8 to the selection.			
16		{PRINT "Selection"}	Prints the selection.			
17		{SELECT Analysis:A1}	Selects cell A1 in the Analysis worksheet.			
18		{QUIT}	Stops the macro and returns control to the user.			

FIGURE 6-42

Project 6 illustrates two macros. The instructions that make up the first macro (range B4..B12) automate the data entry in the seminar variables section. When the macro is run, a dialog box prompts the user to enter the required seminar variables in the range B2..B8. The instructions that make up the second macro (range B14..B18) print two nonadjacent ranges of the Analysis worksheet.

Macro Commands

1-2-3 has more than 200 macro commands from which you can choose to create a macro. Many of these commands automate menu choices or dialog box selections. This project uses the seven macro commands listed in Table 6-2.

▶ TABLE 6-2

MACRO COMMAND	DESCRIPTION
{BLANK location}	Erases the contents of location. Location is the address of a cell or range.
{GET-NUMBER prompt:result}	Lets the user enter a number. Prompt is the text that displays at the top of the dialog box, result is the address of a cell where you want 1-2-3 to store what the user entered
{PRINT what}	Prints the current file. What is the text that specifies what to print.
{QUIT}	Ends a macro and returns control to the user.
{SELECT name}	Selects a range. Name is the address of the range.
{SELECT-APPEND name}	Selects a range without deselecting those currently selected. Name is the address of the range.
{TABLE}	Recalculates the tables values.

All macro commands have a structure, or **syntax**. When you create a macro, you must use the correct syntax, or the macro will not run. Following the conventions for spacing and punctuation is vitally important. The illustration below shows the syntax of a macro command.

{Keyword argument1;argument2;...;argumentn}

The macro command must begin and end with braces ({ }). The braces tell 1-2-3 where the macro command begins and ends. The keyword is the first word in a macro command. The **keyword** tells 1-2-3 what action to perform. Some macro commands are a single command enclosed in braces. For example, in Figure 6-42 on the previous page, the macro command to stop the macro is {QUIT}.

Most macro commands require arguments. **Arguments** supply the information 1-2-3 needs to complete the command. For example, in Figure 6-42, BLANK, tells 1-2-3 to erase the contents of a range. The argument, Analysis: B2..B8, tells 1-2-3 what range to erase. A blank space follows the keyword BLANK and the argument. When more than one argument is used with a macro command, separate the arguments with a semicolon. Leave no spaces between arguments.

The macro syntax must be correct for the command to run properly.

Planning a Macro Command

When you run a macro from the worksheet, 1-2-3 executes the macro commands one at a time beginning at the top of the macro and working downward. Thus, when planning a macro, you should remember the order in which you place the commands in the macro determines the sequence of execution.

Once you determine what you want the macro to do, you should write it out on paper. Before entering the macro commands into the computer, step through the instructions and see how the command affects the worksheet.

Entering Macro Commands in the Worksheet

You can enter a macro in any single column of the worksheet. However, it is best to enter a macro in a separate worksheet rather than in a worksheet containing data. For this project, you are to enter the macro commands in a second worksheet inserted after the Analysis worksheet. Perform the following steps to insert a second worksheet, change the font, name the worksheet tab, enter the column headings, and enter macro commands in the worksheet.

TO ENTER MACRO COMMANDS IN THE WORKSHEET ▼

STEP 1 ▶

Click the New Sheet button below the set of SmartIcons. Choose the Worksheet Defaults command from the Style menu and select Times New Roman as the worksheet default font. Double-click the worksheet tab. Type `Macros`. Press the ENTER key. Select cell A1. Type `Macro Name`. Type `Macro Commands` in cell B1. Type `Description` in cell C1. **Select cell B3. Type** `This macro accepts seminar variables and recalculates the table and worksheet`. **Point to the right column border of column B. Drag the column border to the right until the width displayed in the selection indicator is 34Characters.**

1-2-3 inserts the second worksheet after the Analysis worksheet (Figure 6-43). The worksheet name you typed displays in the worksheet tab. The column titles you typed display in the worksheet. Column B displays with a width of 34 characters. The worksheet default font, Times New Roman, displays on the status bar.

STEP 2 ▶

Type `{BLANK Analysis:B2..B8}` **in cell B4. Select cell B5.**

1-2-3 displays the macro command you typed in cell B4 (Figure 6-44). Notice the macro command begins with an open brace ({). The only space in the macro command is after the keyword, BLANK. The macro command ends with a close brace (}). This command instructs 1-2-3 to erase the contents in the range B2..B8 in the Analysis worksheet.

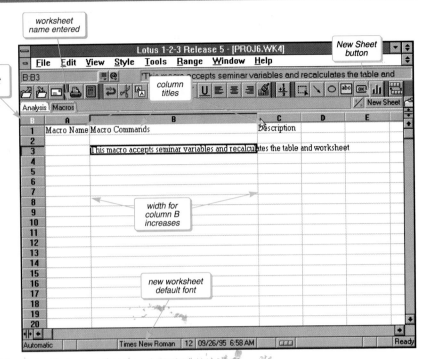

FIGURE 6-43

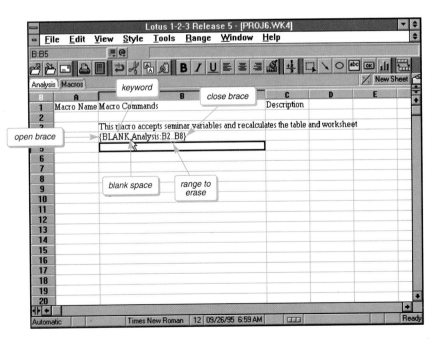

FIGURE 6-44

STEP 3 ▶

Type {GET-NUMBER "Enter Attendance:";B2} **in cell B5. Select cell B6.**

1-2-3 displays the macro command you typed (Figure 6-45). The text entered between the quotation marks has no syntax and can contain spaces and any type of punctuation. The argument separator (;) follows the quotation mark. Notice the only space outside the quotation marks is located after the keyword, GET-NUMBER. This command instructs 1-2-3 to display a dialog box that contains a text box. The text contained within the quotation marks will display in the dialog box. The number entered in the text box by the user will be entered in cell B2 in the worksheet.

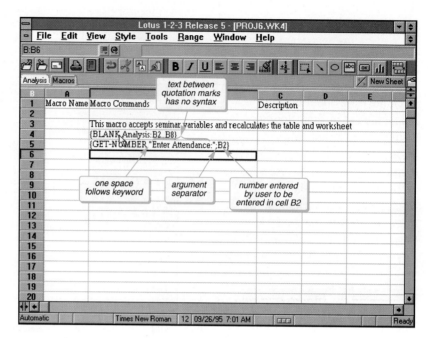

FIGURE 6-45

STEP 4 ▶

Type {GET-NUMBER "Enter Price:";B3} **in cell B6. Type** {GET-NUMBER "Enter Materials Expense:";B5} **in cell B7. Type** {GET-NUMBER "Enter Food Expense:";B6} **in cell B8. Type** {GET-NUMBER "Enter Instructor Expense:";B7} **in cell B9. Type** {GET-NUMBER "Enter Facility Expense:";B8} **in cell B10. Select cell B11.**

The macro commands you typed display in the worksheet (Figure 6-46). Notice the only space outside the quotation marks is located after the keyword, GET-NUMBER, in each macro command.

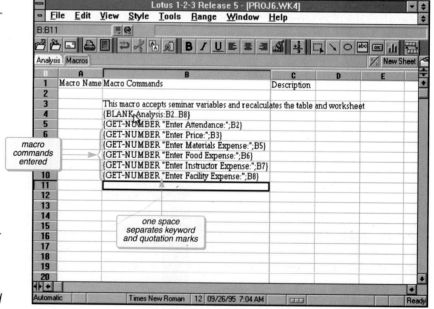

FIGURE 6-46

STEP 5 ▶

Type {TABLE} in cell B11.
Type {QUIT} in cell B12.
**Click the Confirm button or press
the ENTER key.**

*The macro commands you typed
display in the worksheet (Figure
6-47). Notice the commands
have no arguments and
no spaces. The TABLE com-
mand instructs 1-2-3 to
recalculate the 1-variable what-if
table after the new seminar variables are entered. The QUIT command instructs 1-2-3 to stop
performing the macro and returns
control to the user.*

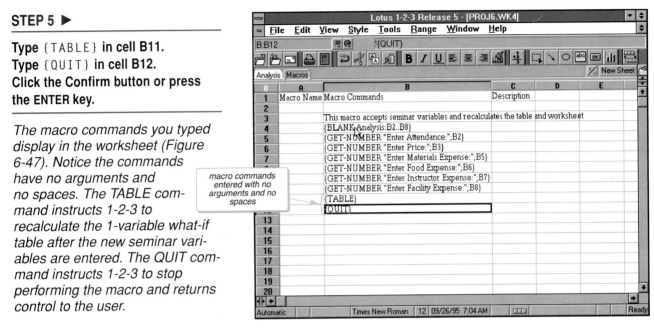

FIGURE 6-47

For a macro to run properly, its syntax must be correct. Be aware of the following rules when typing macro commands.

1. Start the command with an open curly brace and end the command with a
   close curly brace.
2. Type the keyword immediately after the open brace.
3. Spell the keyword correctly.
4. If the command requires arguments, separate the keyword from the first
   argument with one space. If the command includes two or more arguments, separate the arguments from one another with semicolons.
5. Keep the entire macro command in the same cell.

Naming the Macro

After you enter the macro in the worksheet, name the macro by giving it a
range name. For example, the name of the first macro in Figure 6-42 on page L347
is Variables, located in cell A4. Use the Name command to name the macro that
begins in cell B4. To name the macro, perform the following steps.

TO NAME THE MACRO

Step 1: Select cell A4 in the Macros worksheet. Type Variables. Click the
Confirm button or press the ENTER key. Point to the selected cell and
click the right mouse button. Choose the Name command.

Step 2: Ensure that To the right displays in the For cells box. Click the Use
Labels button in the Name dialog box. Choose the OK button.

The worksheet displays as shown in Figure 6-48 on the following page.

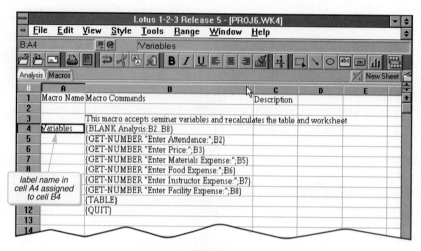

FIGURE 6-48

Notice in the previous steps you named the macro based only on cell B4. When you run the macro named Variables, 1-2-3 executes the command in cell B4 and then continues executing the macro down column B until the command {QUIT} instructs 1-2-3 to stop the macro.

▶ WORKING WITH A MACRO BUTTON

T he next step is to add a macro button to the worksheet. A **macro button** is a button that executes an associated macro when you click the button. Assigning a macro to a button makes it easier to play back the macro.

To create the macro button use the **Draw Button icon** on the set of Smart-Icons. You position and size a macro button in the same way you did a chart in the earlier projects. Finally, you can assign a macro name to the button. Perform the following steps to create the macro button and assign a macro to it.

TO CREATE A MACRO BUTTON AND ASSIGN A MACRO TO THE BUTTON ▼

STEP 1 ▶

Click the Analysis work-sheet tab. Click the Draw Button icon (▣). Position the mouse pointer in the top left corner of cell D15.

The mouse pointer changes to a cross hair (-¦-) and is positioned in the top left corner of cell D15 (Figure 6-49). 1-2-3 displays an instruction in the title bar prompting you to click and drag to draw a macro button.

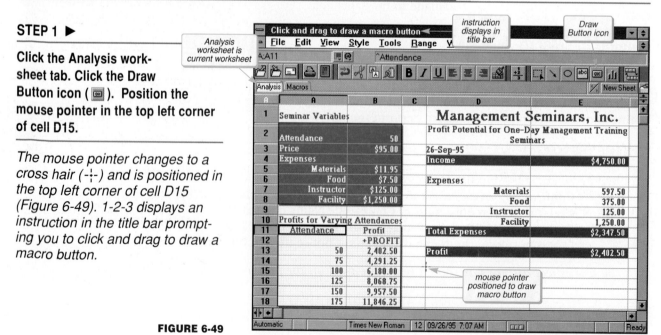

FIGURE 6-49

STEP 2 ▶

Drag the mouse pointer down and to the right to the lower right corner of cell D16. Release the mouse button. When the Assign to Button dialog box displays, point to the Assign macro from drop-down box arrow.

1-2-3 displays the macro button with the default label, Button, centered in the button (Figure 6-50). The Assign to Button dialog box displays. The Button text text box displays the default label that displays in the button. The default button name, Button 1, displays in the selection indicator. The mouse pointer points to the Assign macro from drop-down box arrow. Notice that handles display on the sides of the button indicating the button is selected. You can resize and relocate the macro button on the worksheet after the Assign to Button dialog box is closed.

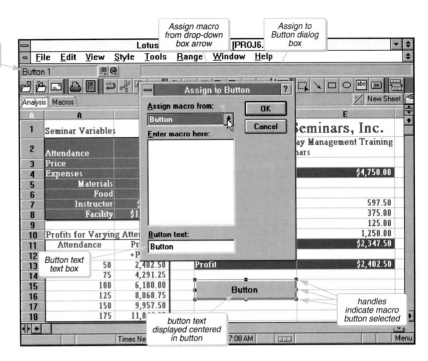

FIGURE 6-50

STEP 3 ▶

Click the Assign macro from drop-down box arrow and select Range from the drop-down list. Use the down scroll arrow to view the range name, VARIABLES, in the Existing named ranges list box. Point to VARIABLES in the Existing named ranges list box.

When you choose Range from the Assign macro from list, 1-2-3 removes the Enter macro here list box and displays the Range text box and the Existing named ranges list box (Figure 6-51). The Existing named ranges list box displays the named ranges in the file. The mouse pointer points to the desired named range.

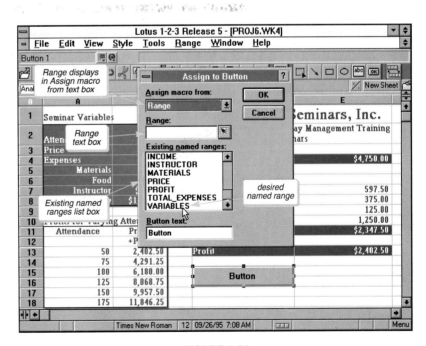

FIGURE 6-51

STEP 4 ▶

Select VARIABLES. Highlight the label, Button, in the Button text text box and type New Seminar Variables. **Point to the OK button in the Assign to Button dialog box.**

1-2-3 enters the range name, VARIABLES, in the Range text box (Figure 6-52). The new label displays in the Button text text box. The mouse pointer points to the OK button in the Assign to Button dialog box.

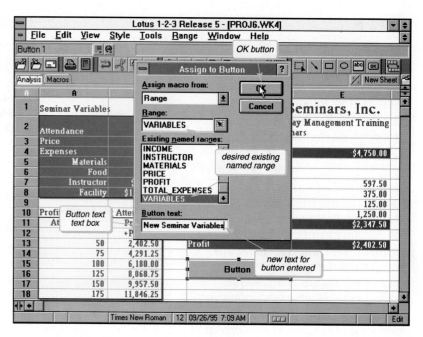

FIGURE 6-52

STEP 5 ▶

Choose the OK button. Select any cell in the worksheet to remove the selection handles.

The macro button with the label, New Seminar Variables, displays in the range D15..D16 of the Analysis worksheet (Figure 6-53). Clicking the macro button will play back the macro commands located in the range B4..B12 in the Macros worksheet.

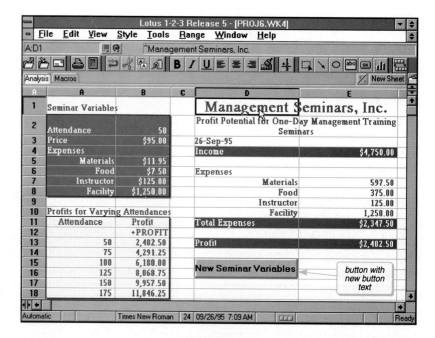

FIGURE 6-53

Once you create a macro button, it remains locked in the same position on the worksheet until you resize or move it.

To resize or move a macro button, you must select the macro button by first holding down the CTRL key and then clicking the macro button. To resize a selected button, drag one of the handles until the button is the desired size. To move a selected button, position the mouse pointer inside the macro button and drag the button to the desired location.

To edit a selected macro button's label, point to the selected button and click the right mouse button. When the quick menu displays, choose the Assign to Button command and make the desired changes in the Button text text box (see Figure 6-52).

To delete a selected macro button from the worksheet, press the DEL key.

The **Draw Button command** is on the Tools menu on the main menu bar. The **Macro Assign to Button command** is on the Tools menu on the main menu bar.

▶ RUNNING A MACRO WITH A BUTTON

hen you run a macro, 1-2-3 performs each task that the macro automates. Perform the following steps to enter new seminar variables: Attendance — 75; Price — $50.00; Materials — $17.50; Food — $8.75; Instructor — $200.00; and Facility — $1,500.00.

TO RUN A MACRO AND ENTER NEW SEMINAR VARIABLES ▼

STEP 1 ▶

Position the mouse pointer over the New Seminar Variables button and click the left mouse button. When the dialog box displays with the prompt message, Enter Attendance:, type 7 5 in the text box. Point to the OK button.

The mouse pointer changes to a hand pointing ( ) when you position the mouse pointer over the New Seminar Variables button. When you click the button, 1-2-3 erases the contents in the range B2..B8 due to the macro command in cell B4 in the Macros worksheet (Figure 6-54). The mouse pointer shape changes to a block arrow. 1-2-3 displays the dialog box with the prompt message, Enter Attendance:, due to the macro command in cell B5 in the Macros worksheet. The value you typed displays in the text box. The status indicator, Cmd, displays in the status bar indicating 1-2-3 is executing a macro command. The mouse pointer points to the OK button.

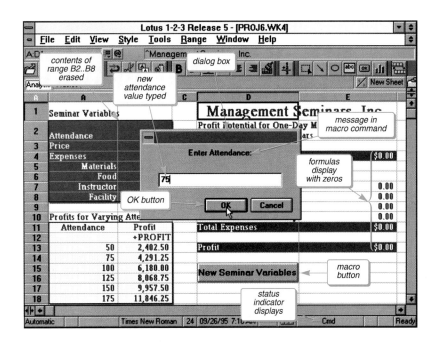

FIGURE 6-54

STEP 2 ▶

Choose the OK button in the dialog box. When 1-2-3 displays the dialog box with the prompt message, Enter Price:, type 50 in the text box. Point to the OK button.

1-2-3 enters the value you typed in Step 1 in cell B2. The dialog box with the prompt message, Enter Price:, displays due to the macro command in cell B6 in the Macros worksheet (Figure 6-55). The value you type displays in the text box. The mouse pointer points to the OK button.

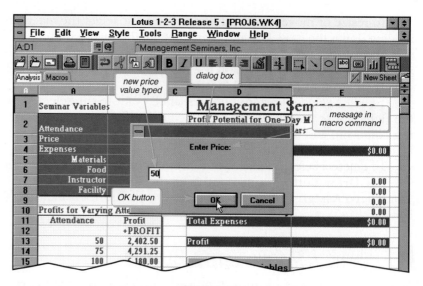

FIGURE 6-55

STEP 3 ▶

Choose the OK button in the dialog box. When 1-2-3 displays the dialog box with the prompt message, Enter Materials Expense:, type 17.50 in the text box. Point to the OK button.

1-2-3 displays the dialog box with the prompt message, Enter Materials Expense:, due to the macro command in cell B7 in the Macros worksheet (Figure 6-56). The value you type displays in the text box. The mouse pointer points to the OK button.

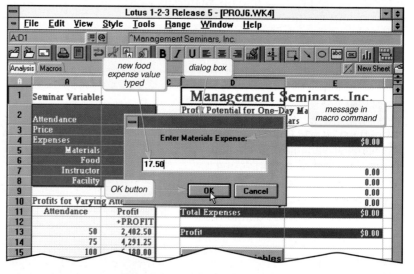

FIGURE 6-56

STEP 4 ▶

Choose the OK button in the dialog box. When 1-2-3 displays the dialog box with the prompt message, Enter Food Expense:, type 8.75 in the text box. Point to the OK button.

1-2-3 displays the dialog box with the prompt message, Enter Food Expense:, due to the macro command in cell B8 in the Macros worksheet (Figure 6-57). The value you typed displays in the text box. The mouse pointer points to the OK button.

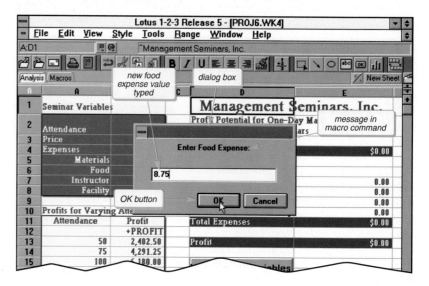

FIGURE 6-57

STEP 5 ▶

Choose the OK button in the dialog box. When 1-2-3 displays the dialog box with the prompt message, Enter Instructor Expense:, type 200 in the text box. Point to the OK button.

1-2-3 displays the dialog box with the prompt message, Enter Instructor Expense:, due to the macro command in cell B9 in the Macros worksheet (Figure 6-58). The value you type displays in the dialog text box. The mouse pointer points to the OK button.

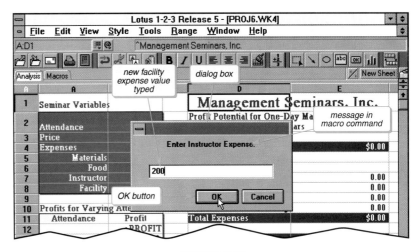

FIGURE 6-58

STEP 6 ▶

Choose the OK button in the dialog box. When 1-2-3 displays the dialog box with the prompt message, Enter Facility Expense:, type 1500 in the text box. Point to the OK button.

1-2-3 displays the dialog box with the prompt message, Enter Facility Expense:, due to the macro command in cell B10 in the Macros worksheet (Figure 6-59). The value you type displays in the text box. The mouse pointer points to the OK button.

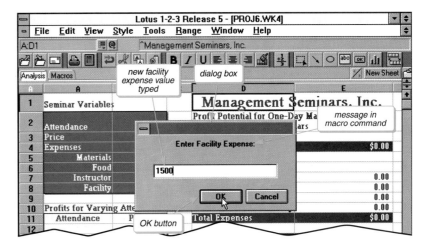

FIGURE 6-59

STEP 7 ▶

Choose the OK button.

1-2-3 recalculates the management seminars section (Figure 6-60). The what-if table is recalculated due to the macro command in cell B11 in the Macros worksheet.

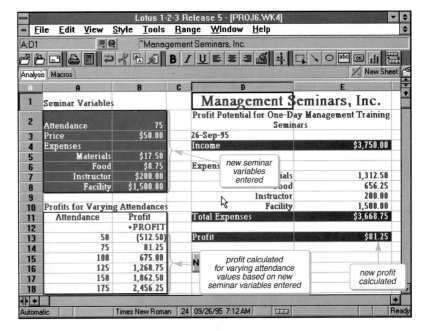

FIGURE 6-60

▶ DOCUMENTING THE MACRO

Now that the macro runs correctly, you should document the macro. To **document a macro,** add a description of the task each macro command performs (see right side of Figure 6-42 on page L339). For example, the description in cell C4 explains the task, {BLANK Analysis:B2..B8}, the macro command performs. Documenting the macro helps you understand the purpose of the macro at a later date. To document the macro in the range C4..C12, perform the following steps.

TO DOCUMENT THE MACRO

Step 1: Click the Macros worksheet tab. Select cell C4. Type `Erases the range B2..B8 in the Analysis worksheet.`.

Step 2: Select cell C5. Type `Accepts attendance and assigns it to cell B2.`. Click the Confirm button or press the ENTER key.

Step 3: Enter the remaining descriptions in the range C6..C12 (see Figure 6-42 on page L347).

The worksheet displays as shown in Figure 6-61.

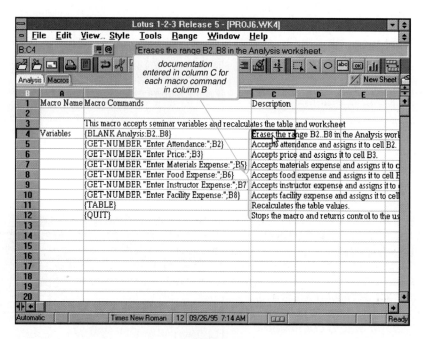

FIGURE 6-61

▶ CREATING A MACRO TO PRINT THE WORKSHEET

The next step is to create the macro in the range B14..B18 (see Figure 6-42 on page L347). This macro selects the ranges D1..F13 and A1..B8 on the Analysis worksheet and prints the ranges. The following sections illustrate entering the macro commands in the Macros worksheet, naming the macro, creating a macro button in the Analysis worksheet, assigning the macro to the macro button, running the macro, and documenting the macro.

TO ENTER THE MACRO COMMANDS IN THE MACROS WORKSHEET

Step 1: Select cell B13. Type `This macro prints the Analysis worksheet.`
Step 2: Type `{SELECT Analysis:D1..E13}` in cell B14.
Step 3: Type `{SELECT-APPEND Analysis:A1..B8}` in cell B15.
Step 4: Type `{PRINT "Selection"}` in cell B16.
Step 5: Type `{SELECT Analysis:A1}` in cell B17.
Step 6: Type `{QUIT}` in cell B18. Click the Confirm button or press the ENTER key.

The second macro displays in the Macros worksheet as shown in Figure 6-62.

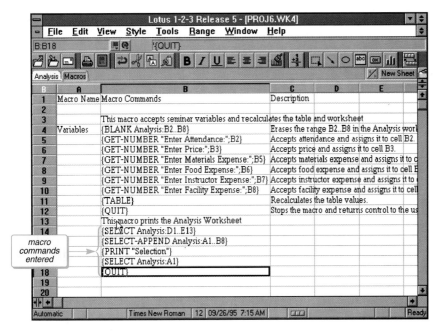

FIGURE 6-62

The {SELECT Analysis:D1..E13} command in Step 2 instructs 1-2-3 to select the range D1..E13 in the Analysis worksheet. The command SELECT-APPEND command in Step 3 instructs 1-2-3 to append the range A1..B8 in the Analysis worksheet to the selection. The command {PRINT "Selection"} in Step 4 instructs 1-2-3 to print the selection. The command {SELECT Analysis:A1} in Step 5 instructs 1-2-3 to select cell A1 in the Analysis worksheet.

The next step is to name the macro. Perform the following steps to name the macro.

TO NAME THE MACRO

Step 1: Select cell A14 in the Macros worksheet. Type `Prints`.
Step 2: Point to the selected cell and click the right mouse button. When the quick menu displays, choose the Name command. When the Name dialog box displays, ensure that To the right is selected in the For cells text box. Then, click the Use Labels button. Choose the OK button.

The worksheet displays as shown in Figure 6-63 on the next page.

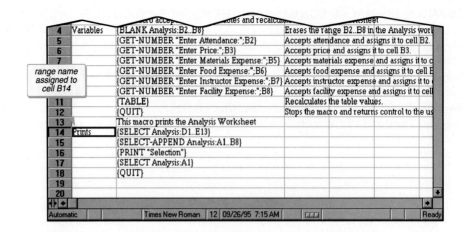

4	Variables	{BLANK Analysis:B2..B8}	Erases the range B2..B8 in the Analysis wor
5		{GET-NUMBER "Enter Attendance:";B2}	Accepts attendance and assigns it to cell B2.
6		{GET-NUMBER "Enter Price:";B3}	Accepts price and assigns it to cell B3.
7		{GET-NUMBER "Enter Materials Expense:";B5}	Accepts materials expense and assigns it to c
8		{GET-NUMBER "Enter Food Expense:";B6}	Accepts food expense and assigns it to cell B
9		{GET-NUMBER "Enter Instructor Expense:";B7}	Accepts instructor expense and assigns it to
10		{GET-NUMBER "Enter Facility Expense:";B8}	Accepts facility expense and assigns it to cell
11		{TABLE}	Recalculates the table values.
12		{QUIT}	Stops the macro and returns control to the us
13		This macro prints the Analysis Worksheet	
14	Prints	{SELECT Analysis:D1..E13}	
15		{SELECT-APPEND Analysis:A1..B8}	
16		{PRINT "Selection"}	
17		{SELECT Analysis:A1}	
18		{QUIT}	
19			
20			

(callout: range name assigned to cell B14)

FIGURE 6-63

The next step is to create a macro button in the Analysis worksheet and assign the Prints macro to the button. Perform the following steps to create the macro button and assign the Prints macro to the button.

TO CREATE THE MACRO BUTTON AND ASSIGN THE PRINTS MACRO TO THE BUTTON

Step 1: Click the Analysis worksheet tab. Click the Draw Button icon on the set of SmartIcons. Drag the range E15..E16.

Step 2: When the Assign to Button dialog box displays, click the Assign macro from drop-down box arrow and select Range from the drop-down list. Use the down scroll arrow in the Existing named ranges list box to view the range name, PRINTS. Select PRINTS. Highlight the label, Button, in the Button text text box and type `Print`. Choose the OK button in the Assign to Button dialog box. Select any cell.

The worksheet displays as shown in Figure 6-64.

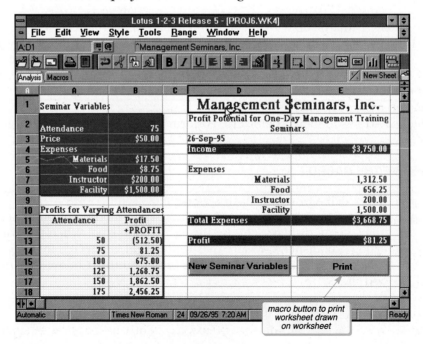

macro button to print worksheet drawn on worksheet

FIGURE 6-64

The next step is to run the macro that selects the nonadjacent ranges in the Analysis worksheet and print the ranges. To run the macro, perform the following step.

TO RUN THE MACRO

Step 1: Click the Print button on the Analysis worksheet.

The printed worksheet displays as shown in Figure 6-65.

Management Seminars, Inc.
Profit Potential for One-Day Management Training Seminars

26-Sep-95

Income	$7,500.00

Expenses

Materials	2,625.00
Food	1,312.50
Instructor	200.00
Facility	1,500.00
Total Expenses	**$5,637.50**

Profit	$1,862.50

Seminar Variables

Attendance	150
Price	$50.00
Expenses	
Materials	$17.50
Food	$8.75
Instructor	$200.00
Facility	$1,500.00

FIGURE 6-65

Notice several important points when selecting a range to print. First, 1-2-3 prints the nonadjacent ranges in the order in which they were selected (see Figure 6-65). The Prints macro instructs 1-2-3 to select range D1..E13 first, and then to append the range A1..B8 to the selection (see the commands in cells B14 and B15 in the Macros worksheet Figure 6-62 on page L359). The first range selected, D1..E13, prints at the top of the page; the second range selected, A1..B8, prints below the first range on the page.

Second, 1-2-3 places a dashed gray outline around the ranges to print (Figure 6-66 on the next page). 1-2-3 has no command to remove the dashed gray outline around the selected ranges. However, you can control the display by using the Set View Preferences command on the View menu. Use the following steps to control the display of the dashed gray outline.

TO CONTROL THE DISPLAY OF THE DASHED GRAY OUTLINE

Step 1: Choose the Set View Preferences command on the View menu.
Step 2: Deselect the X in the Page breaks check box in the Show in current file area by pointing to the X and clicking the left mouse button.
Step 3: Choose the OK button in the Set View Preferences dialog box.

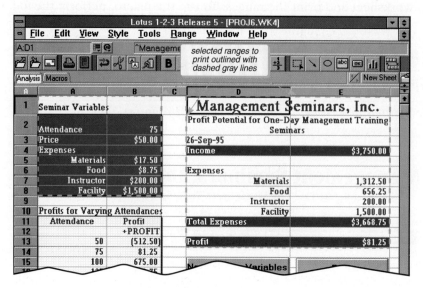

FIGURE 6-66

The last step in creating the Prints macro is to add documentation. Perform the following steps to document the macro.

TO DOCUMENT THE MACRO

Step 1: Click the Macros worksheet tab. Select cell C14. Type `Selects the range D1..E13 in the Analysis worksheet.`.

Step 2: Select cell C15. Type `Appends the range A1..B8 to the selection.`. Click the Confirm button or press the ENTER key.

Step 3: Enter the remaining descriptions in the range C16..C18 (see Figure 6-42 on page L347).

The worksheet displays as shown in Figure 6-67.

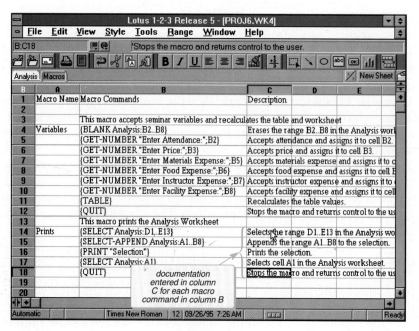

FIGURE 6-67

▶ FORMATTING THE MACROS WORKSHEET

F ormatting the Macros worksheet in Project 6 includes changing the color of the text, changing the background color of cells, aligning the labels, and placing the values in the proper format. When formatting is complete, the worksheet will appear as shown in Figure 6-42 on page L347.

To accomplish the formatting, perform the following steps:

TO FORMAT THE MACROS WORKSHEET

Step 1: Select the range A1..F1. Point to the selected range and click the right mouse button. Choose the Lines & Color command from the quick menu. When the Lines & Color dialog box displays, select the first blue in the top row of the Background color drop-down box. Select white in the top row of the Text color drop-down box. Click the Designer frame drop-down box arrow and select the second designer frame from the left in the top row of the Designer frame drop-down box. Choose the OK button in the Lines & Color dialog box. Click the Bold icon on the set of SmartIcons

Step 2: Click the point-size selector on the status bar. Choose 18 from the pop-up list of font sizes.

Step 3: Select cell A1. Point to the selected cell and click the right mouse button. When the quick menu displays, choose the Alignment command. When the Alignment dialog box displays, select the Wrap text check box. Choose the OK button. Click the Center icon on the set of SmartIcons.

Step 4: Select cell B1. Click the Center icon on the set of SmartIcons.

Step 5: Select cell B3. Press and hold down the CTRL key. Select cells A4, B13, and A14. Release the CTRL key. Click the Bold icon on the set of SmartIcons.

Step 6: Select the ranges B4..F12 and B14..F18. Point to the selected ranges and click the right mouse button. Choose the Lines & Color command from the quick menu. When the Lines & Color dialog box displays, select teal (Color: 118) in the top row of the Background color drop-down box. Select white in the top row of the Text color drop-down box. Choose the OK button. Select any cell.

Step 7: Point to the worksheet tab and click the right mouse button. Choose the Worksheet Defaults command from the quick menu. When the Worksheet Defaults dialog box displays, click the Worksheet tab drop-down box arrow and select teal (Color: 118) in the first row. Choose the OK button.

▶ USING VERSION MANAGER TO ANALYZE DATA

A n alternative to using a data table to analyze worksheet data is to use 1-2-3's Version Manager. **Version Manager** allows you to create and view different sets of data for any named range in a worksheet. Each different set of data you create is called a **version**. You can evaluate the impact that changes in attendance and expenses may have on the profit of a seminar.

For Project 6, you are to create a high and low version for the attendance range in cell B2 and a high and low version for the expenses in the range B5..B18. Once the versions are created, you can view different combinations of attendance and expenses to evaluate the impact on the profit for a seminar. For example, you can view the high attendance projection with the low expenses projection to determine the impact on the profit.

Creating a Version

For Project 6, you are to create two versions of the attendance range. First, you will create a version named Low containing the current value for attendance. Then, you will create a second version of the attendance range named High. This version will contain data that represents a projected high attendance value for a seminar. Perform the following steps to create a version of a named range.

TO CREATE A VERSION OF A NAMED RANGE ▼

STEP 1 ▶

Select cell B2 in the Analysis worksheet. Select the Range menu and point to the Version command.

Cell B2 is selected (Figure 6-68). 1-2-3 displays the Range menu, and the mouse pointer points to the Version command. The data displayed in cell B2 represents a projected low attendance for a one-day management seminar.

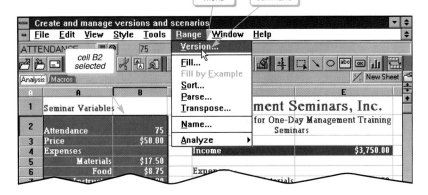

FIGURE 6-68

STEP 2 ▶

Choose the Version command. When the Version Manager window displays, move the window to the lower left corner of the worksheet by dragging the Version Manager's title bar. Verify Tracking is on ( ). Point to the Create button ( ) in the Version Manager window.

When you choose the Version command, 1-2-3 displays the Version Manager window containing the Version Manager (Figure 6-69). If Version Manager Index displays in the title bar, click the To Manager button ( ) in the right corner of the Version Manager Index window. Notice the Version Manager window is the active window. The Named range and With version(s) drop-down boxes are blank indicating no versions

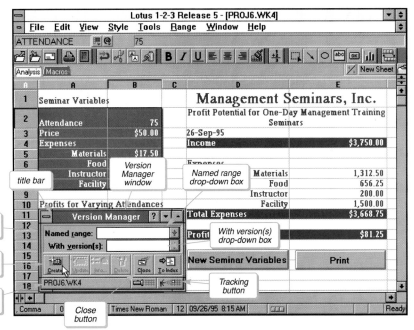

FIGURE 6-69

have been created. A row of buttons displays below the With version(s) drop-down box. The buttons that are dimmed cannot be selected. The Create button is used to create new versions. The Close button ( ) closes the Version Manager window. The current file name, PROJ6.WK4, displays at the bottom of the Version Manager window. The mouse pointer points to the Create button. When tracking is on, the cell pointer is moved to the versioned range when you select the named range in Version Manager.

STEP 3 ▶

Click the Create button. When the Create Version dialog box displays, type Low **in the Version name text box. Position the mouse pointer in the Comment text box and click the left mouse button. Type** Low projection for attendance. **Point to the OK button.**

1-2-3 displays the Create Version dialog box (Figure 6-70). The range name, ATTENDANCE, displays in the Range name text box. This is the name assigned to cell B2 in the worksheet. The default version name, Version1, is replaced with the version name you typed in the Version name text box. The comment for the selected version displays in the Comment text box. The mouse pointer points to the OK button.

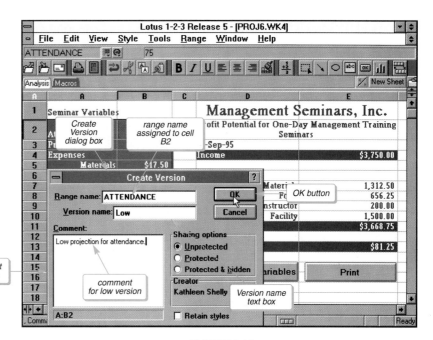

FIGURE 6-70

STEP 4 ▶

Choose the OK button.

1-2-3 displays the Version Manager window (Figure 6-71). The name of the range displays in the Named range drop-down box. The name of the version displays in the With versions(s) drop-down box. A check mark (✓) displays next to the version name indicating this version is currently displayed in the worksheet. Notice the Info button (⊞) and Delete button (🗑) now display. Use the Info button to change the explanatory remarks about a version. The Delete button deletes the selected version from the worksheet.

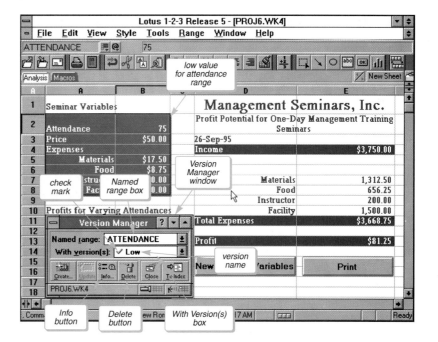

FIGURE 6-71

The next step is to create a second version of the attendance range. This second version represents a projected high value for attendance. To create a second version of the attendance range, you can enter the new data in the range. Then, click the Create button in the Version Manager window. To create a second version of a named range, perform the following steps.

TO CREATE A SECOND VERSION OF A NAMED RANGE ▼

STEP 1 ▶

Select cell B2. Type 150. **Point to the Create button in the Version Manager window.**

When you select cell B2, the 1-2-3 window becomes the active window (Figure 6-72). The new value you typed for attendance displays in cell B2. As you enter data in the range, the check mark next to the version name in the Version Manager window changes to a crossed check mark (✖), the version name, Low, displays in italics, and the Update button (▨) becomes available. These changes indicate new data has been entered in the range since this version was displayed. The Update button is used to change the existing values in the selected version.

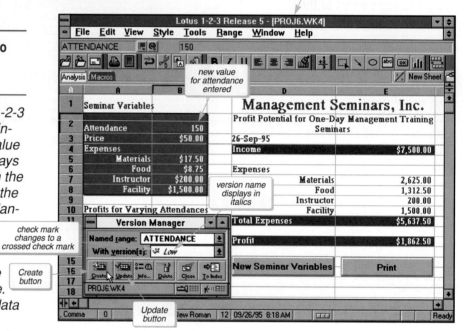

FIGURE 6-72

STEP 2 ▶

Click the Create button in the Version Manager window. When the Create Version dialog box displays, type High **in the Version name text box. Position the mouse pointer in the Comment text box and click the left mouse button. Type** High projection for attendance. **Point to the OK button in the Create Version dialog box.**

1-2-3 displays the Create Version dialog box (Figure 6-73). The range name, ATTENDANCE, displays in the Range name text box. The version name, Low, is replaced with the version name you typed in the Version name text box. The comment for the selected version displays in the Comment text box. The mouse pointer points to the OK button.

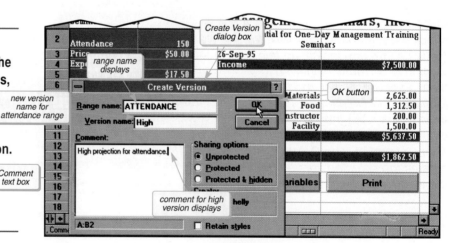

FIGURE 6-73

STEP 3 ▶

Choose the OK button.

1-2-3 displays the Version Manager window (Figure 6-74). The name of the new version displays in the With versions(s) box.

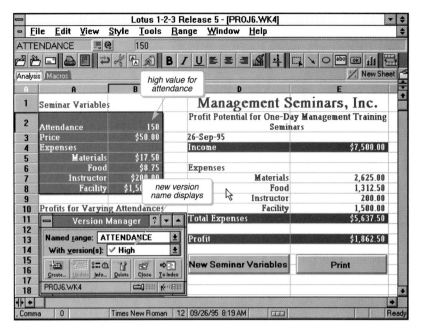

FIGURE 6-74

Notice several important points when working with Version Manager. First, the Version Manager window remains open as you move between the 1-2-3 worksheet and the Version Manager window. A single named range can contain many versions. Version names can be up to 32 characters, are case-sensitive, and may contain spaces or special characters.

Second, you can move, resize, and minimize the Version Manager window as you do any window. You close the window by clicking the Close button.

Finally, 1-2-3 keeps track of the Version Manager window size and position when you close the window. When you choose the Version command from the Range menu again, 1-2-3 opens the Version Manager in that same size and position.

When you save the worksheet, 1-2-3 saves all versions associated with the named ranges.

The next step is to create two versions for the expenses in the range B5..B8. First, you will name the range B5..B8, SEMINAR_EXPENSE. Then, you will create a version named Low representing the lowest projected expenses for the one-day management seminar and a version named High representing the highest projected expenses for the one-day management seminar. The values currently displayed in the range B5..B8 represent the low projected expenses. Perform the steps on the next page to name a range and create two versions of the range.

TO NAME A RANGE AND CREATE TWO VERSIONS OF THE RANGE ▼

STEP 1 ►

Select the range B5..B8 in the Analysis worksheet. Click the Create button in the Version Manager window. When the Create Version dialog box displays, type SEMINAR_EXPENSE in the Range name text box. Highlight Version 1 in the Version name text box. Type Low. Type Low projection for seminar expenses. in the Comment text box. Choose the OK button in the Create Version dialog box.

The range name for the range B5..B8 displays in the Named range box in the Version Manager window (Figure 6-75). The version name you typed displays in the With version(s) box.

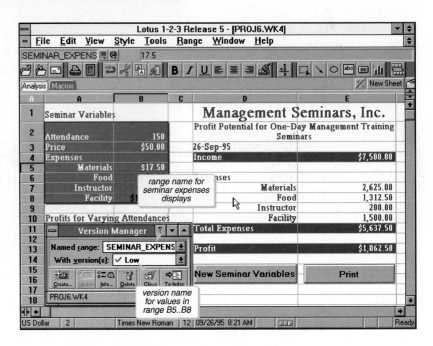

FIGURE 6-75

STEP 2 ►

Select cell B5 in the Analysis worksheet. Type 24.95. Type 12.95 in cell B6. Type 350 in cell B7. Type 2000 in cell B8. Select the range B5..B8. Click the Create button in the Version Manager window. When the Create Version dialog box displays, type High in the Version name text box. Type High projection for seminar expenses. in the Comment text box. Choose the OK button in the Create Version dialog box.

The version name you typed in the Create Version dialog box displays in the With version(s) box (Figure 6-76). 1-2-3 recalculates the worksheet based on these versions. A high projected attendance and high projected seminar expenses will result in a loss of $535.00.

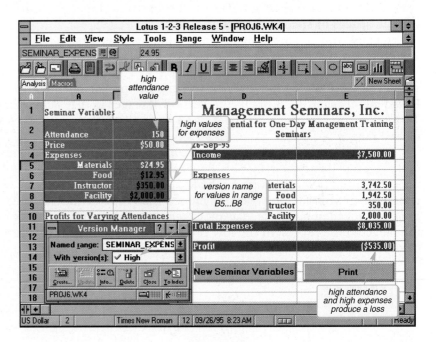

FIGURE 6-76

Displaying Versions

Now that you have created two versions for attendance (High and Low) and two versions for expenses (High and Low), you can display various combinations of versions to evaluate the impact of the changes on profit. For example, What would be the impact of a low attendance and high seminar expenses on profit for a one-day seminar? Another example might be What would be the impact of a high attendance and low seminar expenses on profit for a one-day seminar? Perform the following steps to display a version for each range in the worksheet.

TO DISPLAY A VERSION IN THE WORKSHEET ▼

STEP 1 ▶

Click the Named range drop-down box arrow and select ATTENDANCE. Click the With version(s) drop-down box arrow and select Low.

1-2-3 displays the low version for the attendance range in the worksheet (Figure 6-77). The high version for the expenses range already displays in the worksheet from Step 2 on the previous page. 1-2-3 recalculates the worksheet based on these values. The lowest projected attendance and the highest projected expenses will result in a loss of $1,442.50 for a one-day seminar.

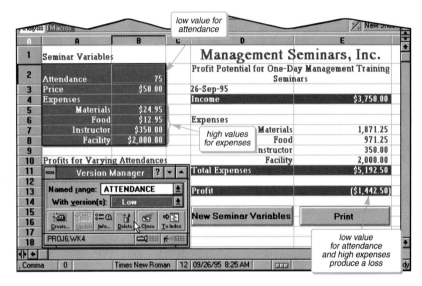

FIGURE 6-77

STEP 2 ▶

Click the With version(s) drop-down box arrow and select High. Click the Named range drop-down box arrow and select SEMINAR_EXPENSE. Click the With version(s) drop-down box arrow and select Low. Point to the Close button in the Version Manager dialog box.

When you select the high version for attendance, 1-2-3 displays the high value in the worksheet (Figure 6-78). When you select the low version for the seminar expenses, 1-2-3 displays the low values in the worksheet. 1-2-3 recalculates the worksheet based on these values. A high projected attendance and low projected seminar expenses will result in a

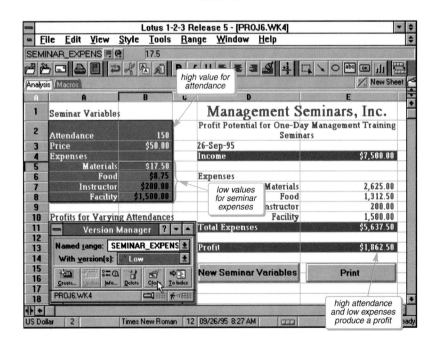

FIGURE 6-78

profit of $1,862.50 for a one-day seminar. The mouse pointer points to the Close button in the Version Manager window.

STEP 3

Click the Close button in the Version Manager window. Press F8 to recalculate the what-if table.

1-2-3 removes the Version Manager window from the screen.

By comparing the profit in Figures 6-76, 6-77, and 6-78 (on the previous pages), you can see the best profit is attained by a high attendance and low expenses.

When you press the F8 function key, 1-2-3 recalculates the what-if table using the new values entered for attendance and expenses.

▶ PROTECTING DATA

When you create a worksheet that you don't want others to change, you can seal the file to prevent changes to cell contents. When you **seal a file**, others can open the file but cannot change the data in the file.

When you create a new worksheet, all the cells are unprotected. **Unprotected cells** are cells whose values you can change at any time versus **protected cells** that you cannot change. If a cell is protected and the user attempts to change its value, 1-2-3 displays a dialog box with a message indicating the cells are protected.

When you seal a file, you can leave specified ranges unprotected. For example, the values in the range B2..B8 and the values in the what-if table in the range B13..B18 in Project 6 must change when the macro buttons are used to enter new seminar variables. The remaining cells in the worksheet should be protected so they cannot be changed. To seal a file and leave specified ranges unprotected, perform the following steps.

TO SEAL A FILE AND LEAVE SPECIFIED RANGES UNPROTECTED ▼

STEP 1 ▶

Select the range B2..B8. Hold down the CTRL key and select the range B13..B18. Release the CTRL key. Select the Style menu and point to the Protection command.

The ranges to remain unprotected are selected (Figure 6-79). 1-2-3 displays the Style menu. The mouse pointer points to the Protection command. The Protection command allows you to unprotect the selected cells so they can be changed after the file is sealed.

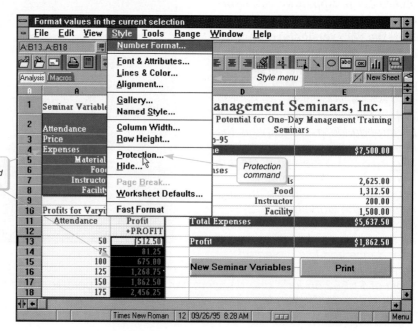

FIGURE 6-79

STEP 2 ▶

Choose the Protection command. When the Protection dialog box displays, select the Keep data unprotected after file is sealed check box and point to the OK button.

1-2-3 displays the Protection dialog box (Figure 6-80). The Keep data unprotected after file is sealed check box is selected. The selected ranges to be unprotected after the file is sealed display in the Range text box. The mouse pointer points to the OK button.

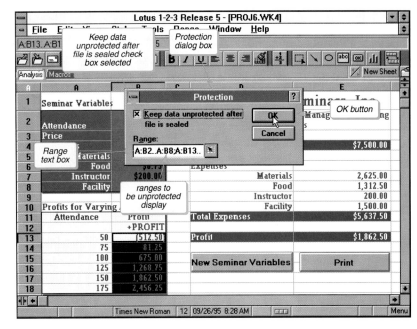

FIGURE 6-80

STEP 3 ▶

Choose the OK button in the Protection dialog box. Select the File menu and point to the Protect command.

The Protection dialog box is removed from screen (Figure 6-81). Notice the status indicator in the status bar displays U when the cell pointer is in an unprotected cell indicating the contents of the cell can be changed. 1-2-3 displays the File menu. The mouse pointer points to the Protect command. The Protect command allows you to seal the file. When a file is sealed, you cannot enter data in ranges that have not been unprotected.

FIGURE 6-81

STEP 4 ▶

Choose the Protect command. When the Protect dialog box displays, select the Seal file check box in the File protection area. Point to the OK button.

1-2-3 displays the Protect dialog box (Figure 6-82). The Seal file check box is selected. The mouse pointer points to the OK button.

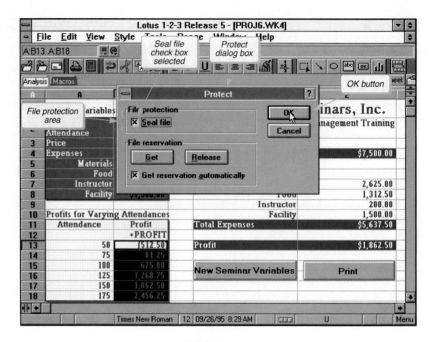

FIGURE 6-82

STEP 5 ▶

Choose the OK button. When the Set Password dialog box displays, point to the OK button.

1-2-3 displays the Set Password dialog box (Figure 6-83). You can enter a password in the Password text box when you want to keep others from changing the worksheet from sealed to unsealed. No password is entered for Project 6. The mouse pointer points to the OK button. Notice the Protect dialog box displays behind the Set Password dialog box.

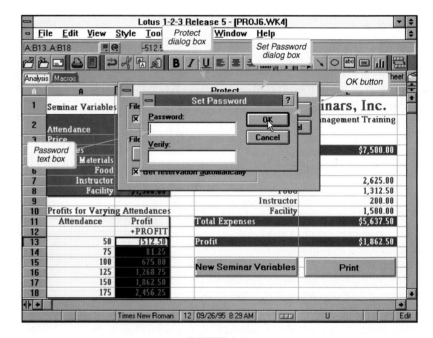

FIGURE 6-83

STEP 6 ▶

Choose the OK button in the Set Password dialog box. Select cell A1.

1-2-3 removes the Set Password dialog box and the Protect dialog box (Figure 6-84). Notice the status indicator displays Pr when the cell pointer is in a protected cell, indicating the contents of the cell cannot be changed.

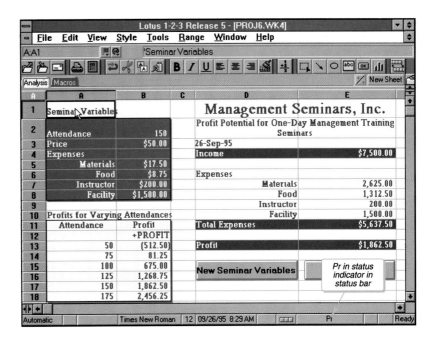

FIGURE 6-84

Using the macro buttons in the Analysis worksheet, you can continue to enter new seminar variables and print the worksheet with the worksheet sealed. If you try to change any protected cell, 1-2-3 displays a dialog box with a message. For example, if you were to attempt to change the row title Attendance in cell A2, 1-2-3 responds by displaying the message shown in Figure 6-85 on the next page. If you want to change any cells in the worksheet, such as titles or formulas, use the following steps to unseal the file.

TO UNSEAL A FILE

Step 1: Choose the Protect command from the File menu.
Step 2: Deselect the Seal file check box by pointing to the check box and clicking the left mouse button. Then, choose the OK button.
Step 3: When 1-2-3 displays the Get Password dialog box, choose the OK button.

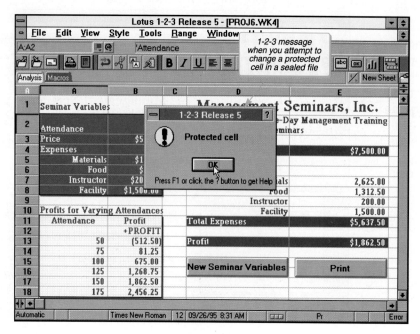

FIGURE 6-85

▶ PROJECT SUMMARY

In Project 6, you learned how to analyze data using Backsolver. You also learned how to analyze data by creating a 1-variable what-if table. By creating macros, you automated worksheet tasks and assigned those macros to macro buttons in the worksheet. Using the steps and techniques presented, you learned how to use Version Manager to enter different sets of data in a range in the worksheet. Finally, you learned how to seal a document so a user can change only the contents of cells that are unprotected.

▶ KEY TERMS AND INDEX

1-variable what-if table *(L338)*
@TODAY function *(L324)*
{BLANK}*(L347)*
{GET-NUMBER}*(L347)*
{PRINT}*(L347)*
{QUIT}*(L347)*
{SELECT-APPEND}*(L347)*
{SELECT}*(L347)*
{TABLE}*(L347)*
Analyze command *(L336)*
arguments *(L348)*
Backsolver *(L336)*
Backsolver command *(L337)*

Calendar category *(L325)*
date number *(L324)*
document a macro *(L358)*
Draw Button command *(L355)*
Draw Button icon *(L352)*
keyword *(L348)*
macro *(L346)*
Macro Assign to Button
   command *(L355)*
macro button *(L352)*
macro command *(L320)*
Name command *(L322)*
navigator *(L327)*

Protect command *(L371)*
protected cells *(L370)*
Protection command *(L370)*
range name *(L322)*
run a macro *(L355)*
seal a file *(L370)*
syntax *(L348)*
unprotected cells *(L370)*
version *(L363)*
Version command *(L364)*
Version Manager *(L363)*
What-if Table command *(L342)*

In Lotus 1-2-3 for Windows, you can accomplish a task in a number of ways. The following table presents a quick reference to each task presented in this project with its available options. The commands listed in the Menu column can be executed using either the keyboard or mouse.

Task	Mouse	Menu	Keyboard Shortcuts
Control the Display of the Dashed Gray Outline		From View menu, choose Set View Preferences	
Create a Macro Button	Click Draw Button icon on set of SmartIcons	From Tools menu, choose Draw, then choose Button	
Create a 1-Variable What-if Data Table		From Range menu, choose Analyze, then choose What-if Table	
Create a Version		From Range menu, choose Version	
Edit a Macro Button	Press CTRL key and click macro button		
Name a Range		From Range menu or quick menu, choose Name	
Seal a File		From File menu, choose Protect	
Unprotect Cells		From Style menu, choose Protection	
Unseal a File		From File menu, choose Protect	
Use Backsolver		From Range menu, choose Analyze, then choose Backsolver	

STUDENT ASSIGNMENTS

STUDENT ASSIGNMENT 1
True/False

Instructions: Circle T if the statement is true or F if the statement is false.

T F   1. To name a range using an adjacent label, you must first select the range that contains the label you want to use to name the range, and then choose the Name command from the quick menu.

T F   2. A range name can contain up to 30 characters.

T F   3. The @TODAY function returns a number that is equal to the number of days since January 1, 1900.

T F   4. If cell B2 is named ATTENDANCE and cell B3 is named PRICE, then the formula +B2*B3 can be written +ATTENDANCE*PRICE.

(continued)

STUDENT ASSIGNMENT 1 (continued)

T F   5. To delete a range name, select the named range in the worksheet and press the DEL key.

T F   6. When you use Backsolver, 1-2-3 works backwards from the result of the formula to find the input value of a variable in the formula.

T F   7. If you select a command from the main menu and an arrowhead displays to the right of the command, 1-2-3 will display a dialog box.

T F   8. A 1-variable what-if table creates a table displaying the results of changing multiple variables in a formula.

T F   9. You can have as many what-if tables in a worksheet as you want.

T F   10. When creating a 1-variable what-if table, the formula to be evaluated must be entered in the first column of the first row of the table range.

T F   11. The F8 function key recalculates a 1-variable what-if table.

T F   12. A macro is made up of a series of commands that tell 1-2-3 what to do to complete a task.

T F   13. The macro command TABLE creates a 1-variable what-if table.

T F   14. You end a macro with the STOP macro command.

T F   15. All macro commands must begin and end with braces ({ }).

T F   16. When executed, the macro command GET-NUMBER causes a dialog box to display.

T F   17. To select a macro button, hold down the ALT key and click the button.

T F   18. Version Manager allows you to create and view different sets of data for any named range in a worksheet.

T F   19. A single named range can contain only one version.

T F   20. Select the cells to unprotect after you seal the file.

STUDENT ASSIGNMENT 2
Multiple Choice

Instructions: Circle the correct response.

1. To name a range using the adjacent label, use the _____ command.
   a. Navigator
   b. @function selector
   c. Name
   d. Range

2. Which one of the following characters is valid to use in a range name?
   a. plus sign (+)
   b. underscore (_)
   c. minus sign (–)
   d. number sign (#)

3. Use the navigator in the edit line to _____.
   a. select a macro command to insert in a worksheet
   b. select an @function to insert in a formula
   c. select a date format to apply to a cell
   d. select a named range to insert in a formula

4. If you know the results you want a formula to return, but you don't know the input values the formula needs to achieve that return value, you can use _____ to solve such a formula.
   a. a 1-variable what-if table
   b. Backsolver
   c. Version Manager
   d. Find

5. To create a table that displays the results of changing a single variable in a formula, use the _____ command.
   a. Analyze What-if Table
   b. Backsolver
   c. Version
   d. Name

6. In a 1-variable what-if table, the formula to be evaluated must be entered in the _____.
   a. second column of the second row of the table range
   b. first column of the first row of the table range
   c. second column of the first row of the table range
   d. in the upper left corner cell of the worksheet

7. To recalculate a 1-variable what-if table after changes are made, use the _____ function key.
   a. F8
   b. F9
   c. F3
   d. F5

8. In a macro, use the _____ macro command to erase the contents of a range.
   a. CLEAR
   b. SPACE
   c. ERASE
   d. BLANK

9. Which of the following is a correct example of a macro command?
   a. {SELECT Analysis:A10..A20}
   b. {PRINT
   c. {GET-NUMBER "Enter Materials Expense:";}
   d. {ERASE Analysis:A1..A50}

10. To allow others to open a file but make no changes to the file, use the _____ command.
    a. Save As
    b. Protection
    c. Protect
    d. Seal

STUDENT ASSIGNMENT 3
Understanding @Functions, Naming Ranges, Data Analysis, and Worksheet Protection

Instructions: Fill in the correct answers.

1: Enter the @function to display the system date in cell D3.

Steps: _____

_____

2: Assign the name EXPENSES to the range B5..B8.

Steps: _____

_____

3: Leave the range B2..B8 unprotected after the file is sealed.

Steps: _____

_____

4: Seal a file.

Steps: _____

_____

5: Make the result of the formula in cell E13 equal to 3200 by changing cell B2.

Steps: _____

_____

STUDENT ASSIGNMENT 4
Understanding 1-2-3 Dialog Boxes

Instructions: Write the command that causes the dialog box to display and allows you to make the indicated changes.

CHANGES	COMMAND
1. Name a range using adjacent labels.	_____
2. Find the input value for a cell that makes the results of a formula equal to a value you specify.	_____
3. Create a 1-variable what-if table.	_____
4. Assign a macro to a macro button.	_____
5. Name a macro.	_____
6. Create different sets of data for a named range.	_____
7. Keep data unprotected after you seal the file.	_____
8. Seal a file.	_____

STUDENT ASSIGNMENT 5
Understanding Macro Commands

Instructions: In the space provided, write the macro command that completes the specified task.

TASK	MACRO COMMAND
1. Erase the contents of the range G35..J50.	_____
2. Select the collection A1..A10; B5..B50.	_____
3. Accept a value from the user and enter it in cell F3 in the worksheet.	_____
4. Recalculate a 1-variable what-if table.	_____
5. Return control to the user.	_____
6. Print the ranges C50..C55; D1..D10.	_____

STUDENT ASSIGNMENT 6
Understanding the Version Manager Window

Instructions: In Figure SA6-6, arrows point to various areas of the Version Manager window. Write a brief description of each area in thespace provided.

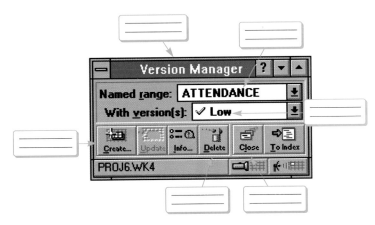

FIGURE SA6-6

COMPUTER LABORATORY EXERCISE 1
Using the Help Menu

Instructions: Perform the following tasks using a personal computer.

1. Start Lotus 1-2-3 Release 5 for Windows.
2. Select the Help menu.
3. Choose How Do I? from the Help menu.
4. Scroll down to the group titled Analyze data.
5. Select Analyze data from the How Do I? topic. Maximize the Help window if necessary.
6. Select Range Version in the group titled Solve what-if problems. Read and print the Range Version topic.
7. In the Range Version topic, scroll down to the group titled Working with Version Manager. Select Version Manager. Read the Range Version Manager topic. Use the mouse pointer to click each part of the Version Manager picture and answer the following questions:
   a. How do you move the Version Manager window?

   _____

   _____

   b. What does the Named range text box list?

   _____

   _____

   c. What does the With version(s) text box list?

   _____

   _____

   d. How do you display the comment for a selected version?

   _____

   _____

   e. How do you change the comment for a selected version?

   _____

   _____

   f. What is highlighting mode? How do you turn on highlighting?

   _____

   _____

8. Choose the Exit command from the File menu in the Help window.

COMPUTER LABORATORY EXERCISE 2
Using Backsolver

Instructions: Start 1-2-3. Open the CLE6-2.WK4 file from the Lotus4 subdirectory on the Student Diskette that accompanies this book. Using the worksheet on your screen and illustrated in Figure CLE6-2, use Backsolver to answer the questions below Figure CLE 6-2.

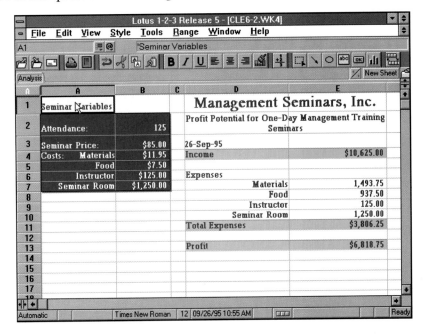

FIGURE CLE6-2

1. What attendance level is necessary to break even? (Break-even is the point at which the income equals the expenses and the profit is zero).

   _____

2. What attendance level is necessary to yield a profit of $12,000?

   _____

3. If 125 are in attendance, what price must be charged to break even?

   _____

4. If 125 are in attendance, what price must be charged to yield a profit of $25,000?

   _____

5. Close the file. Do not save the worksheet you have changed.
6. Follow directions from your instructor for turning in this exercise.
7. Quit 1-2-3.

COMPUTER LABORATORY EXERCISE 3
Creating a 1-Variable What-if Table

Instructions: Start 1-2-3. Open the CLE6-3.WK4 file from the Lotus4 subdirectory on the Student Diskette that accompanies this book. Using the worksheet on your screen and illustrated in Figure CLE6-3a, perform the tasks on this and the next page.

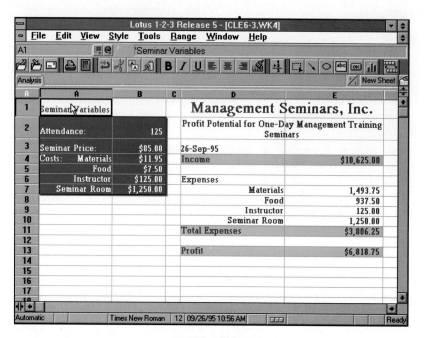

FIGURE CLE6-3a

1. Use the Name command to assign the name in cell D13 to cell E13.
2. Enter the 1-variable what-if table title and column titles in the range A9..A17. Use drag-and-fill to create the sequence of values in the range A12..A17 (Figure CLE6-3b).

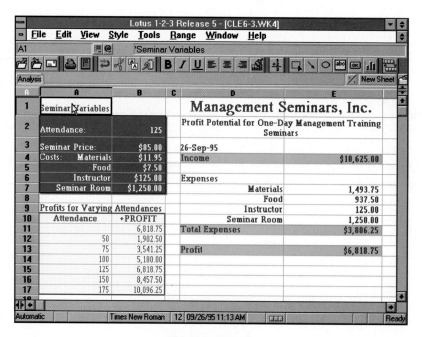

FIGURE CLE6-3b

3. Assign to cell B11 the formula +PROFIT.
4. Create a 1-variable what-if table in the range A11..B17. Use cell B2 as the input cell.
5. Format the 1-variable what-if table as shown in Figure CLE6-3b.
6. Print the worksheet.

COMPUTER LABORATORY ASSIGNMENTS

COMPUTER LABORATORY ASSIGNMENT 1
Analyzing Profit Analysis for a New Product

Purpose: To provide experience using Backsolver, 1-variable what-if tables, macros, and macro buttons.

Problem: Create a worksheet for Pacific Manufacturing to analyze the profit potential for a new product that includes a 1-variable what-if table to calculate the profit for a new product at varying units produced (Figure CLA6-1a). The worksheet will be used by users who know little about computers and spreadsheets. Thus, create two macros (Figure CLA6-1b on the next page) that will guide the user through entering the product variables and printing the worksheet.

FIGURE CLA6-1a

(continued)

COMPUTER LABORATORY ASSIGNMENT 1 (continued)

Instructions: Perform the following tasks.

1. Change the font of the entire worksheet to Times New Roman.
2. Enter the product variables section of the worksheet. Create names for cells B2, B3, B5, B6, and B7.
3. Enter the Pacific Manufacturing section of the worksheet. Assign cell D3 the @TODAY function so the system date displays. Calculate the sales in cell E5 by multiplying the units in cell B2 by the price in cell B3. Calculate the production cost in cell E8 by multiplying the units in cell B2 by the production cost in cell B5. Calculate the materials cost in cell E9 by multiplying the units in cell B2 by the material cost in cell B6. Calculate the marketing cost in cell E10 by entering the value in cell B6. Calculate total costs in cell E11 by adding the production, materials, and marketing costs. Calculate the profit in cell E13 by subtracting the total costs in cell E11 from the sales in cell E5. Create names for cells E5, E11, and E13.
4. Enter the title and column headings in the profits for varying units produced section of the worksheet. Enter the formula, +PROFIT, in cell B11. Use drag-and-fill to create the sequence in the range A12..A19. Create a 1-variable what-if table in the range A11..B19. Use cell B2 as the input cell.
5. Format the worksheet as shown in Figure CLA6-1a on the previous page. The column widths are: A = 14; B = 14; C = 5; D = 21; and E = 18. The row heights are: 1 = 26 and 2 = 17. The title in cell D1 is 24 point.
6. Insert a second worksheet and create the macro in the range B4..B11. Enter the range name in cell A4. Create a name for cell B4 by using the Name command. Create the macro button as shown in the Analysis worksheet. Assign the macro in the range B4..B11 in the Macros worksheet to the macro button.

	A	B	C	D	E	F
1	Macro Name	Macro Commands	Description			
2						
3		This macro accepts product variables and recalculates the table and worksheet.				
4	Variables	{BLANK Analysis:B2..B7}	Erases the range B2..B7 in the Analysis worksheet.			
5		{GET-NUMBER "Enter Units:",B2}	Accepts units and assigns it to cell B2.			
6		{GET-NUMBER "Enter Price:",B3}	Accepts price and assigns it to cell B3.			
7		{GET-NUMBER "Enter Production Costs:",B5}	Accepts production costs and assigns it to cell B5.			
8		{GET-NUMBER "Enter Materials Costs:",B6}	Accepts materials costs and assigns it to cell B6.			
9		{GET-NUMBER "Enter Marketing Cost:",B7}	Accepts marketing costs and assigns it to cell B7.			
10		{TABLE}	Recalculates the 1-variable what-if table.			
11		{QUIT}	Stops the macro and returns control to the user.			
12						
13		This macro prints the Analysis worksheet.				
14	Prints	{SELECT Analysis:D1..E13}	Selects the range D1..E12 in the Analysis worksheet.			
15		{SELECT-APPEND Analysis:A1..B7}	Appends the range A1..B6 to the selection.			
16		{PRINT "Selection"}	Prints the selection.			
17		{SELECT Analysis:A1}	Selects cell A1 in the Analysis worksheet.			
18		{QUIT}	Stops the macro and returns control to the user.			

FIGURE CLA6-1b

7. Create the macro in the range B14..B18. Enter the range name in cell A14. Create a name for cell B14 by using the Name command. Create the macro button as shown in the Analysis worksheet. Assign the macro in the range B14..B18 in the Macros worksheet to the macro button. Document the macros.
8. Unprotect ranges B2..B7 and B12..B19. Seal the file.
9. Save the worksheets using a file name consisting of the initials of your first and last names followed by the assignment number. Example: KS6-1.

10. Use the New Product Variables button to determine the profit using the following data: units – 55,000, price – $9.50, production costs – 2.50, materials costs – 4.25 and marketing costs – $125,000.
11. Use the Print button to print the worksheet.
12. Use Backsolver to answer the following questions:
    a. How many units must be produced to break even using the variables entered in Step 10? (Break-even is the point at which the income equals the expenses and the profit is zero).

    _____

    b. How many units must be produced to yield a profit of $50,000 using the variables entered in Step 10?

    _____

13. Follow directions from your instructor for turning in this assignment.

COMPUTER LABORATORY ASSIGNMENT 2
Creating a Profit and Loss Projection Worksheet

Purpose: To provide experience using Version Manager, range names, macros, and macro buttons.

Problem: Create a profit and loss projection worksheet to evaluate the impact that different versions of Sales and Expenses have on Return on Sales (Figure CLA6-2a). Create a macro that prints each different version analyzed (Figure CLA6-2b).

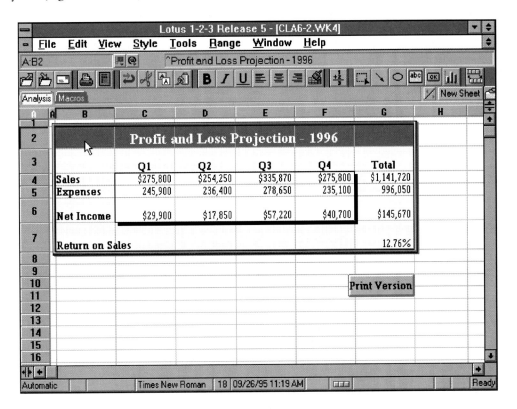

FIGURE CLA6-2a

(continued)

COMPUTER LABORATORY ASSIGNMENT 2 (continued)

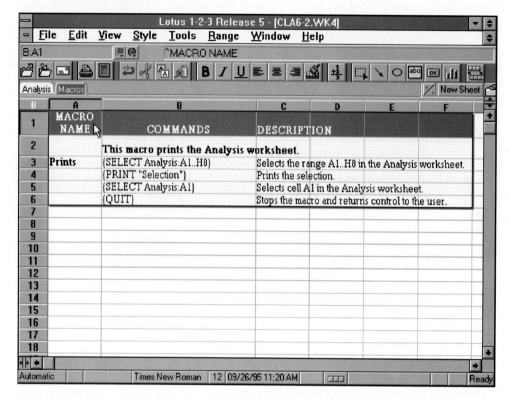

FIGURE CLA6-2b

Instructions: Perform the following tasks.

1. Change the font of the entire worksheet to Times New Roman.
2. Create the worksheet as shown in Figure CLA6-2a on the previous page. Use the values in the No Growth in Sales and No Increase in Expenses table shown below.

▸ **NO GROWTH IN SALES AND NO INCREASE IN EXPENSES**

	Q1	Q2	Q3	Q4
Sales	$275,800	$254,250	$335,870	$275,800
Expenses	245,900	236,400	278,650	235,100

3. Calculate the net income in row 6 by subtracting the expenses in row 5 from the sales in row 4. Calculate the total in column G by summing the values in the respective rows. Calculate the return on sales in cell G7 by dividing the net income in cell G6 by the total sales in cell G4.
4. Use the Name command to name the sales range (C4..F4) and the expense range (C5..F5).
5. Format the worksheet as shown. The column widths are: A = 1; B = 10; C = 10; D = 10; E = 10; F = 10; and G = 10. The row heights are: 1 = 8; 2 = 25; 3 = 28; 6 = 28; and 7 = 33. The title in cell B2 is 18 point.
6. Create the following versions using Version Manager:
   a. Version for no growth in the sales range
   b. Version for no growth in the expense range

7. Enter in the worksheet the values in the Rapid Growth in Sales and Increase in Expenses table shown below.

▸ **RAPID GROWTH IN SALES AND INCREASE IN EXPENSES**

	Q1	Q2	Q3	Q4
Sales	$406,775	$414,425	$424,606	$431,680
Expenses	325,400	275,400	337,500	275,000

8. Create the following versions using Version Manager:
   a. Version for rapid growth in the sales range
   b. Version for an increase in expense range
9. Insert a second worksheet and create the macro as shown in Figure CLA6-2b. Enter the range name in cell A3. Create a name for cell A3 by using the Name command. Create a macro button on the Analysis worksheet and assign the macro to the macro button.
10. Use Version Manager to determine the return on sales for the following combinations of versions. Use the macro button to print each version of the worksheet.

COMBINATION OF VERSIONS	**RETURN ON SALES**
a. No growth in sales and no increase in expenses	_____
b. Rapid growth in sales and no increase in expenses	_____
c. No growth in sales and an increase in expenses	_____
d. Rapid growth in sales and an increase in expenses	_____

11. Document the macro.
12. Save the worksheets using a file name consisting of the initials of your first and last names followed by the assignment number. Example: KS6-2.
13. Follow directions from your instructor for turning in this assignment.

COMPUTER LABORATORY ASSIGNMENT 3
Determining the Monthly Loan Payment

Purpose: To become familiar with using the @PMT function, range names, 1-variable what-if tables, macros, and macro buttons.

Problem: Create a worksheet for Expressway Loan Company that determines the monthly loan payment and includes a 1-variable what-if table that shows the monthly payment for a loan with varying interest rates (Figure CLA6-3a on the next page). The worksheet will be used by users who know little about computers and spreadsheets. Thus, create two macros (Figure CLA6-3b on page L389) that will guide the user through entering the loan data and printing the worksheet.

Instructions: Perform the following tasks.

1. Change the font of the worksheet to Times New Roman.
2. Enter the Loan Data section of the worksheet. Assign cell B2 the @TODAY function. Create names for the range B3..B6.
3. Calculate the monthly payment in cell B6. Hint: use the @PMT function. Assign cell B6 the following formula: @PMT(Principal,Interest/12,Term*12).

COMPUTER LABORATORY ASSIGNMENT 3 (continued)

FIGURE CLA6-3a

4. Enter the payments for the varying interest rates section title in cell D1 and column titles in cells D2 and E2. Assign cell E3 the formula, +MONTHLY_PAYMENT. Use drag-and-fill to create the series in the range D4..D18. Create a 1-variable what-if table in the range D3..E18 using the Analyze What-if Table command on the Range menu. Use cell B4 as the input cell.

5. Format the worksheet as shown. Name the worksheet, Loan-Analysis. The column widths are: A = 15; B = 12; D = 13; and E = 14. The row height is: 1 = 40. The title in cell A1 is 18 point. The title in cell D1 is 18 point. Format the formula in cell E3 to Text. Reduce the point size to 8.

6. Insert a second worksheet and name the worksheet Macros. Create the macro in the range B4..B9. Enter the range name in cell A4. Create a name for cell B4 by using the Name command. Create the macro button as shown in the Loan_Analysis worksheet (New Loan Data). Assign the macro in the range B4..B9 in the Macros worksheet to the macro button.

7. Create the macro in the range B12..B15 in the Macros worksheet. Enter the range name in cell A12. Create a name for cell B12 by using the Name command. Create the macro button as shown in the Loan_Analysis worksheet Print New Loan Data. Assign the macro in the range B12..B15 in the Macros worksheet to the macro button. Document the macros.

8. Unprotect the ranges B3..B5 and D4..E18 in the Loan-Analysis worksheet. Seal the file.

9. Save the worksheets using a file name consisting of the initials of your first and last names followed by the assignment number. Example: KS6-3.

10. Use the macro button to determine the loan payment for the following loan data and print the work-sheet for each data set: (a) principal – 55,000, interest – 9.50%, and term – 8; and (b) principal – 30,000, interest – 10.0%, and term – 3.

11. Follow directions from your instructor for turning in this assignment.

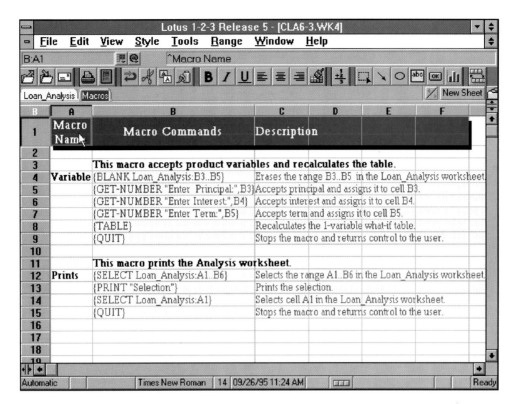

FIGURE CLA6-3b

COMPUTER LABORATORY ASSIGNMENT 4
Determining the Future Value of an Investment

Purpose: To become familiar with using the @FV function, range names, 1-variable what-if tables, macros, Backsolver, and macro buttons.

Problem: Create a future value worksheet that tells a user the future value of an investment based on periodic, constant payments and a constant interest rate.

Instructions: Perform the following steps.

1. Enter the future value data section of the worksheet as shown in Figure CLA6-4 on the next page. Create range names for cells B3, B4, B5, and B6. Calculate the future value. Hint: use the @FV function. Assign cell B6 the following formula: @FV(Payment,Interest,Term).
2. Create a 1-variable what-if table that determines future values of an investment for varying interest rates between 5.00% and 8.50% in increments of .25%.
3. Insert a second worksheet. Create a macro to accept new future value data. Assign the macro to a macro button. Create a macro to print the future value data section and the 1-variable what-if table. Assign the macro to a macro button. Document the macro.
4. Save the worksheet using a file name consisting of the initials of your first and last names followed by the assignment number. Example: KS6-4.

(continued)

COMPUTER LABORATORY ASSIGNMENT 4 (continued)

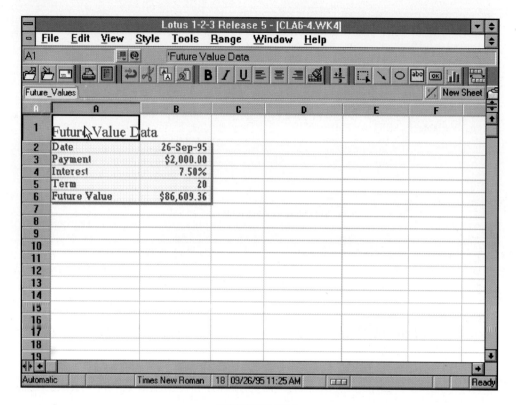

FIGURE CLA6-4

5. Format the worksheet.
6. Follow directions from your instructor for turning in this assignment.

WORKING WITH DATABASE TABLES

OBJECTIVES You will have mastered the material in this project when you can:

▸ Define the elements of a database table
▸ Create a database table
▸ Sort a database table on one sort key or multiple sort keys
▸ Find records that satisfy single criterion
▸ Find records that satisfy multiple criteria
▸ Specify fields in a query table

▸ Create a query table
▸ Change a field name in a query table
▸ Print a query table
▸ Create a crosstab table to summarize data in a database table
▸ Print a crosstab table

▸ INTRODUCTION

I n Projects 1 through 6, you created worksheets using formulas and @functions, created drawn objects on a worksheet and chart, charted data on a worksheet, organized data in multiple worksheets, created macros, and analyzed data. In this project you will learn about the database capabilities of 1-2-3.

Using a database allows you to create, store, sort, and retrieve data. Many people record data such as the names, addresses, and telephone numbers of business associates, records on employment, and records on inventory. These records must be arranged so the data can be easily accessed when required.

A 1-2-3 database, also called a **database table**, describes a collection of related data organized in a manner that allows access, retrieval, and use of that data. 1-2-3 allows you to create a database; add, delete, and change data in the database; sort the data in the database; retrieve the data in the database; and print the data in the database.

▸ PROJECT SEVEN

P roject 7 shows you how to create the database table. This database contains personnel information about employees of Outland Traders. The information for each employee is stored in a record. A **record** contains all the information about one item of the table. For example, the first record in the database table contains all the information about Mary Page.

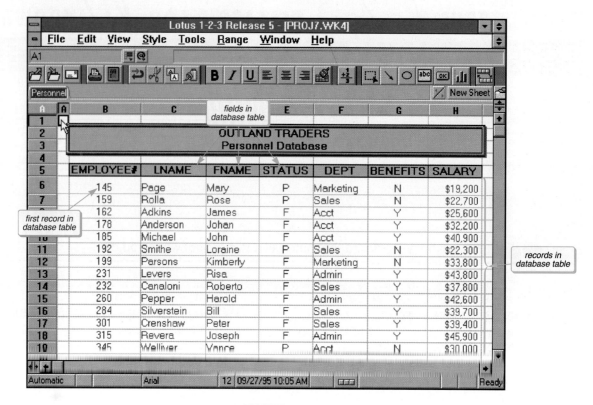

FIGURE 7-1

A record consists of a series of fields. A **field** contains a specific piece of information within a record. For example, in the database table shown in Figure 7-1, the first field is the EMPLOYEE# field, which contains the employee number. The LNAME field contains the last name of each employee.

The remaining fields in each of the records are:

FNAME: First name of each employee.
STATUS: F for full-time; or P for part-time.
DEPT: Department where employee works.
BENEFITS: Y for benefits; N for no benefits.
SALARY: The yearly salary of each employee.

Each of these fields contains information about an employee record. Thus, for record one, the employee's number is 145, the employee's last name is Page, the first name is Mary. Her status is part-time (P). She works in the Marketing department, does not receive benefits (N), and has a yearly salary of $19,200.

▶ STARTING LOTUS 1-2-3 RELEASE 5 FOR WINDOWS

 o start Lotus 1-2-3 Release 5 for Windows, follow the steps you used in previous projects. These steps are reviewed below.

TO START LOTUS 1-2-3 RELEASE 5 FOR WINDOWS

Step 1: From Program Manager, open the Lotus Applications group window.
Step 2: Double-click the Lotus 1-2-3 Release 5 program-item icon.

▶ CREATING A DATABASE TABLE

 o create the database table shown in Figure 7-1, enter the worksheet titles in row 2 and row 3, the field names in row 5, and the records in row 6 through row 19. The database title, OUTLAND TRADERS, entered in row 2, allows room for the designer frame that will be added when formatting the database table.

After you enter all the records in the database table, you will use the Name command on the Range menu to name the database table. The following steps create the database table shown in Figure 7-1 on the previous page and name the database table.

TO CREATE A DATABASE TABLE ▼

STEP 1 ▶

Select cell B2. Type OUTLAND
TRADERS. **Type** Personnel
Database **in cell B3. Select cell B5.**
Type EMPLOYEE#. **Type** LNAME **in**
cell C5, FNAME **in cell D5. Type**
STATUS **in cell E5,** DEPT **in cell F5,**
BENEFITS **in cell G5, and** SALARY
in cell H5. Click the Confirm button
or press the ENTER **key.**

The worksheet title displays in cell B2, and the worksheet subtitle displays in cell B3 (Figure 7-2). The field names display in row 5. The field names identify the category of data in each column.

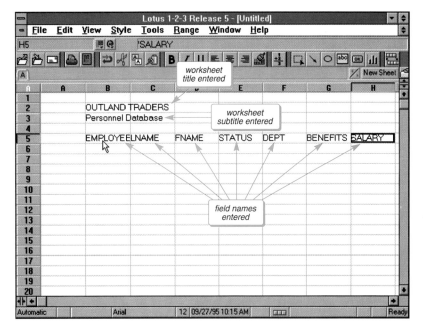

FIGURE 7-2

STEP 2 ▶

Select cell B6. Type 145. **Type** Page **in cell C6,** Mary **in cell D6,** P **in cell E6, Type** Marketing **in cell F6, Type** N **in cell G6, and Type** 19200 **in cell H6. Click the Confirm button or press the ENTER key.**

The data for the first record is entered in row 6 (Figure 7-3). Notice the first record is entered immediately below the field names in row 5.

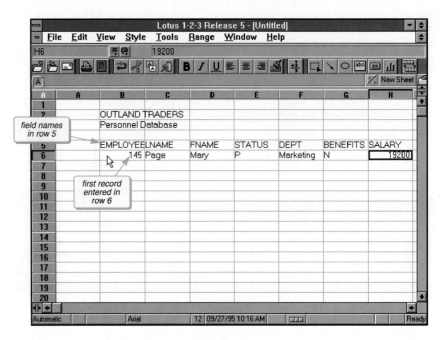

FIGURE 7-3

STEP 3 ▶

Continue entering the records in row 7 through row 19 using the data in Figure 7-1 on page L392.

The database table displays as shown in Figure 7-4. The database table consists of the field names in row 5 and the records in row 6 through row 19. The worksheet titles in row 2 and row 3 are not part of the database table even though they identify the database table.

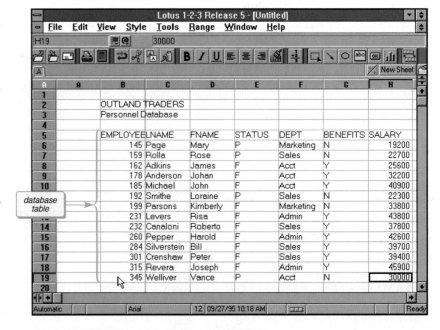

FIGURE 7-4

STEP 4 ▶

Select the range B5..H19. Point to the selected range and click the right mouse button. Choose the Name command from the quick menu. When the Name dialog box displays, type PERSONNEL in the Name text box. Point to the OK button.

The database table range B5..H19 is selected and the Name dialog box displays (Figure 7-5). The name you typed displays in the Name text box. The mouse pointer points to the OK button. The name, PERSONNEL, is assigned to the database table.

STEP 5

Choose the OK button. Select any cell.

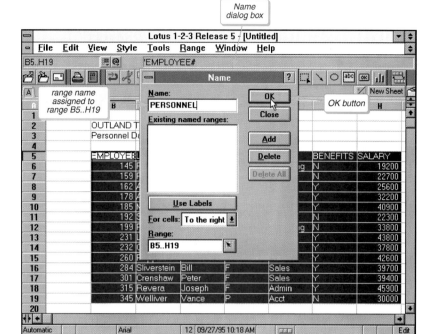

FIGURE 7-5

Be guided by several important rules when you create a database table. First, **field names** must be in one row only; the first row of the database table. Each field name must be unique, contain no spaces, and should not resemble a cell address, such as Q1. Avoid using the following characters in field names: , . : ; – # ! / + *.

Second, enter the data for the first record in the row immediately below the field names. Enter additional records without leaving empty rows.

Third, a 1-2-3 database table must fit on a single worksheet and can contain up to 256 fields and 8,191 records.

▶ FORMATTING THE DATABASE TABLE

T he next step is to name and color the worksheet tab, format the worksheet titles in row 2 and row 3, the field names in row 5, and the actual data in the range B6..H19 (see Figure 7-1 on page L392). The formatting includes: (1) centering the worksheet titles over columns B through H, bolding the titles, and adding color and a designer frame to the range B2..H3; (2) bolding the field names, centering the field names, adding color and a border around each cell in the range B5..H5; (3) displaying the text in the range B6..H19 in blue; (4) changing the widths for columns A, B, C, and G; and (5) formatting the salary values in column H to a currency format with no digits to the right of the decimal point. The following steps format the worksheet titles and the database table (see Figure 7-1 on page L392):

TO FORMAT THE WORKSHEET TITLES AND THE DATABASE TABLE

Step 1: Double-click the worksheet tab and type Personnel. Press the ENTER key. Point to the worksheet tab and click the right mouse button. Choose the Worksheet Defaults command from the quick menu. When the Worksheet Defaults dialog box displays, click the Worksheet tab drop-down arrow and choose burgundy in the top row of the Worksheet tab drop-down box. Choose the OK button.

Step 2: Select the range B2..H3. Point to the selected range and click the right mouse button. Choose the Lines & Color command from the quick menu. When the Lines & Color dialog box displays, click the Background color drop-down box arrow and choose light gray in the top row of the Background color drop-down box. Click the Designer frame drop-down box arrow and choose the last designer frame on the right in the third row from the top in the Designer frame drop-down box. Click the Frame color drop-down box arrow and choose dark gray in the top row of the Frame color drop-down list box. Choose the OK button.

Step 3: Point to the selected range and click the right mouse button. Choose the Alignment command from the quick menu. When the Alignment dialog box displays, select the Center option button and the Across columns check box in the Horizontal area. Choose the OK button. Click the Bold icon on the set of SmartIcons.

Step 4: Select the range B5..H5. Point to the selected range and click the right mouse button. Choose the Lines & Color command from the quick menu. When the Lines & Color dialog box displays, click the Background color drop-down box arrow and choose light gray in the top row of the Background color drop-down box. Select the All check box in the Border area. Choose the OK button. Click the Bold icon on the set of SmartIcons. Click the Center icon on the set of SmartIcons.

Step 5: Select the range B6..H19. Point to the selected range and click the right mouse button. Choose the Font & Attributes command. When the Font & Attributes dialog box displays, click the Color drop-down box arrow and choose the first blue in the top row of the Color drop-down box. Choose the OK button.

Step 6: Select the ranges B6..B19, E6..E19, and G6..G19. Click the Center icon on the set of SmartIcons.

Step 7: Select the range H6..H19. Click the format selector in the status bar and choose the US Dollar format from the pop-up list. Click the decimal selector in the status bar and choose 0 from the pop-up list.

Step 8: Point to the right column border of column A. Drag the column border to the left until the width displayed in the selection indicator is 2Characters. Point to the right column border of column B. Drag the column border to the right until the width displayed in the selection indicator is 12Characters. Point to the right column border of column C. Drag the column border to the right until the width displayed in the selection indicator is 11Characters. Point to the right column border of column G. Drag the column border to the right until the width displayed in the selection indicator is 10Characters.

▶ SAVING THE FILE

 ow that the database table is entered and formatted, you should save the file on disk. To save the file on a diskette in drive A using the file name PROJ7, complete the following steps.

TO SAVE THE FILE

Step 1: Click the Save icon on the set of SmartIcons.
Step 3: When the Save As dialog box displays, type `proj7` in the File name text box.
Step 3: Select drive a: from the Drives drop-down list box.
Step 4: Choose the OK button in the Save As dialog box.

1-2-3 saves the worksheet of the file PROJ7.wk4 in drive A.

▶ SORTING A DATABASE TABLE

T he data in the database table is easier to work with and more meaningful if the records are arranged in sequence on the basis of one or more fields. 1-2-3 allows you to change the order of records by sorting them according to the contents of the fields. **Sorting** means placing the rows of data in a prescribed order. The order can be either **ascending**, meaning the records appear from lowest to highest, or **descending**, meaning the records appear from highest to lowest. Table 7-1 illustrates this concept when sorting the database table on the last name field.

Notice that when the names are in ascending order, they move from the first letter of the alphabet (A) toward the last letter of the alphabet. In descending order, they move from the last of the alphabet to the first letter of the alphabet.

When you sort numbers, ascending order moves from the lowest number to the highest number, while a descending order moves from the highest number to the lowest number.

The database table in Figure 7-1 on page L392 is arranged in ascending order by the employee number field in column B.

▶ **TABLE 7-1**

UNORDERED	ASCENDING ORDER	DESCENDING ORDER
Page	Adkins	Welliver
Rolla	Anderson	Smithe
Adkins	Canaloni	Silverstein
Anderson	Crenshaw	Rolla
Michael	Levers	Revera
Smithe	Michael	Pepper
Parsons	Page	Parsons
Levers	Parsons	Page
Canaloni	Pepper	Michael
Pepper	Revera	Levers
Silverstein	Rolla	Crenshaw
Crenshaw	Silverstein	Canaloni
Revera	Smithe	Anderson
Welliver	Welliver	Adkins

Sorting a Database Table on a Single Sort Key

When you initiate a sorting operation, you must specify the records to be sorted, the field on which to sort, and the sort order. The field you select to sort the records on is called the **sort key**. For example, to sort the database table in alphabetical order according to last name, the range to sort is B6..H19, the field to sort by is cell C6, and the sort order is ascending. Perform the following steps to sort the database table on a single sort key.

TO SORT A DATABASE TABLE ON A SINGLE SORT KEY ▼

STEP 1 ▶

Select the range B6..H19. Select the Range menu and point to the Sort command.

1-2-3 highlights the range of records to sort and displays the Range menu (Figure 7-6). Notice the field names at the top of the database table in row 5 are not included in the selection.

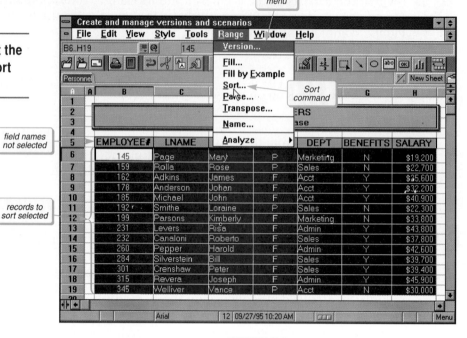

FIGURE 7-6

STEP 2 ▶

Choose the Sort command. When the Sort dialog box displays, point to the range selector in the Sort by area.

1-2-3 displays the Sort dialog box and moves the cell pointer to cell B6 (Figure 7-7). Cell B6 displays in the Sort by text box and the mouse pointer points to the range selector in the Sort by area. The Ascending option button is selected by default. The range to sort displays in the Range text box located at the bottom of the Sort dialog box.

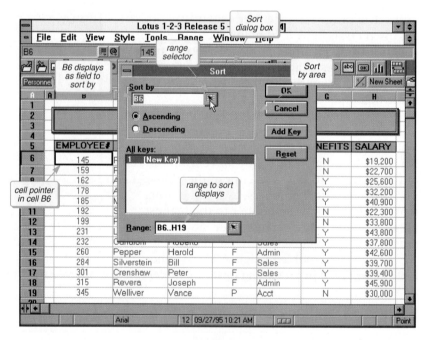

FIGURE 7-7

STEP 3 ▶

Click the range selector. When the Sort dialog box is removed, select cell C6. When the Sort dialog box redisplays, point to the OK button.

When you click the range selector, 1-2-3 removes the Sort dialog box so you can select the field to sort by. 1-2-3 highlights the range C6 (Figure 7-8). The selected field displays in the Sort by text box. The range to sort displays in the Range text box. These selections instruct 1-2-3 to sort range B6..H19 in ascending order by the field located in column C. The mouse pointer points to the OK button.

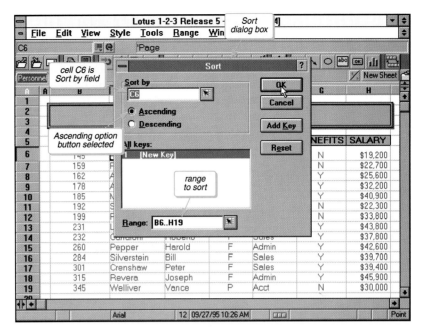

FIGURE 7-8

STEP 4 ▶

Choose the OK button. Select any cell in the worksheet.

1-2-3 sorts the database table in ascending order by last name (Figure 7-9). If you discover a mistake while sorting, click the Undo key to reverse the Sort command.

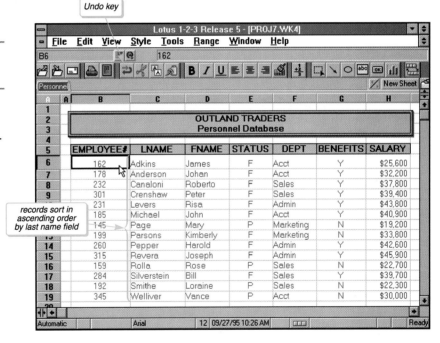

FIGURE 7-9

Exercise caution when sorting a database table. When selecting the range to sort, do not include the field names along with the database records. Including the field names in the sort range will sort the field names along with the database records. When selecting the range to sort, ensure the sort range includes all the rows and columns in the database. If you omit columns, the integrity of the data is destroyed. If you omit rows, the resulting sort order will be inaccurate. If you discover you made a mistake while sorting, click the Undo icon on the set of SmartIcons immediately after the sort operation to reverse the Sort command.

Sorting a Database Table on Multiple Sort Keys

1-2-3 allows you to use up to 255 sort keys at a time. A multiple key sort uses more than one key to sort the records. For example, to sort the database table by department and have the records within each department appear in descending order by salary, you must use two sort keys. The first sort key is a cell from the department field, cell F6, and the second sort key is a cell from the salary field, cell H6. Perform the steps on the next two pages to sort the database table on multiple sort keys.

TO SORT THE DATABASE TABLE ON MULTIPLE SORT KEYS ▼

STEP 1 ▶

Select range B6..H19. Choose the Sort command from the Range menu. When the Sort dialog box displays, click the Reset button (Reset) and point to the range selector in the Sort by area.

1-2-3 highlights the range to sort and displays the Sort dialog box. When you click the Reset button, the previous sort key is cleared (Figure 7-10). 1-2-3 moves the cell pointer to cell B6. The mouse pointer points to the range selector in the Sort by area.

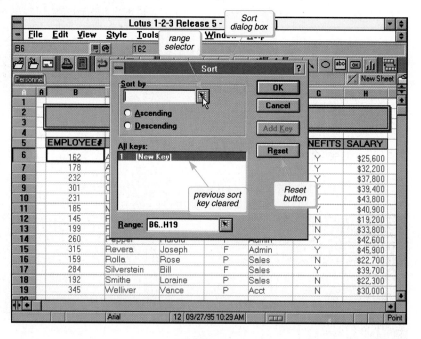

FIGURE 7-10

STEP 2 ▶

Click the range selector and select cell F6. When the Sort dialog box redisplays, ensure that the Ascending option button is selected and click the Add Key button (Add Key). Point to the range selector in the Sort by area.

1-2-3 enters the first sort key in the All keys list box (Figure 7-11). This entry instructs 1-2-3 to sort the database table in ascending order by the field located in column F. The mouse pointer points to the range selector in the Sort by area.

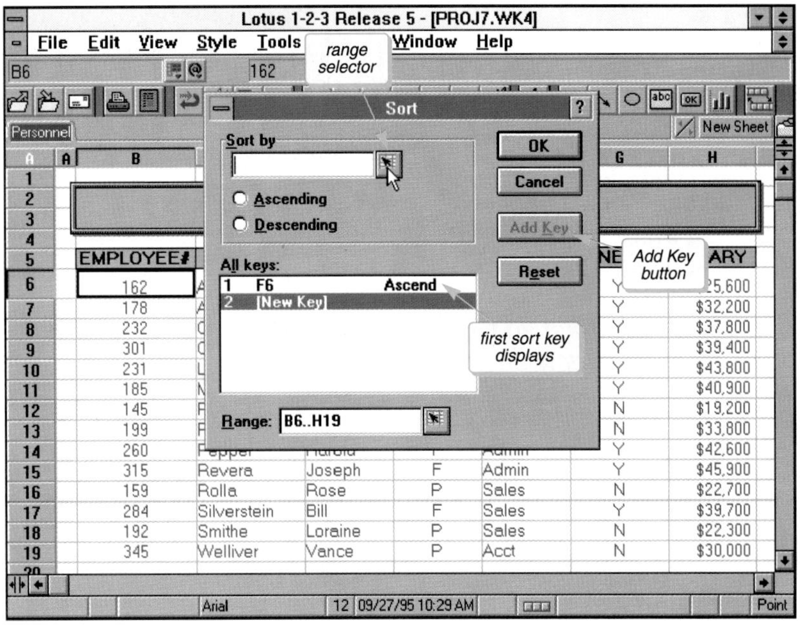

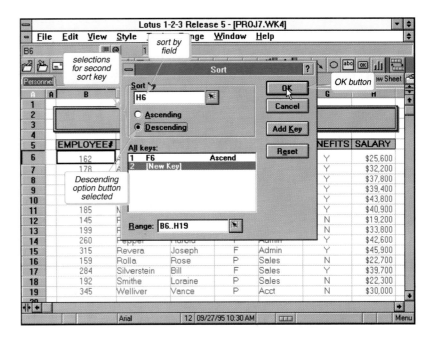

FIGURE 7-11

STEP 3 ▶

Click the range selector and select cell H6. When the Sort dialog box redisplays, select the Descending option button in the Sort by area. Point to the OK button.

Cell H6 displays in the Sort by text box (Figure 7-12). 1-2-3 enters the first sort key information in the All keys list box. The selections in the Sort by area instruct 1-2-3 to sort the field located in column H in descending order. The mouse pointer points to the OK button.

FIGURE 7-12

STEP 4 ▶

Choose the OK button. Select any cell.

1-2-3 sorts the records in the database table by department in ascending order (Figure 7-13). Within each department, the records are sorted by salary, with the highest salary first and the lowest salary last (descending order).

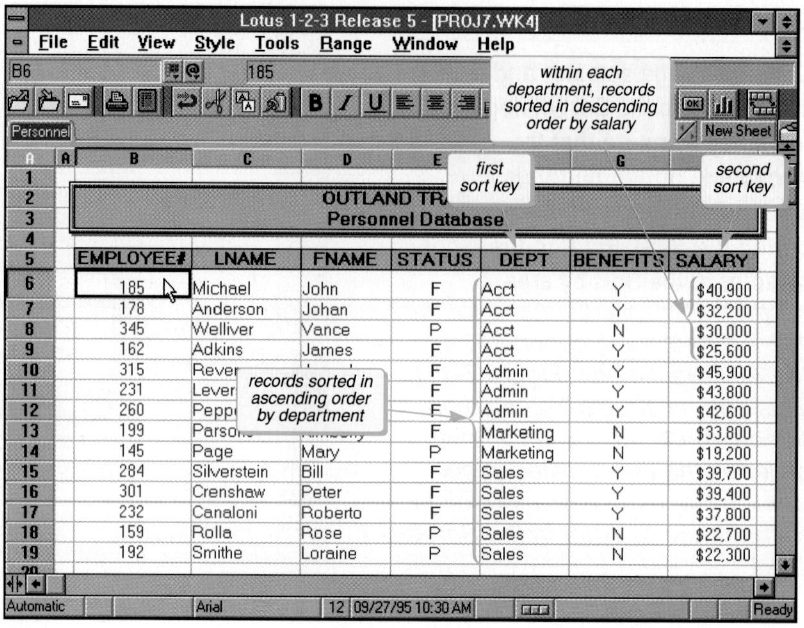

FIGURE 7-13

You can return the database table to its original order at any time by sorting the same range (B6..H19) and using the field that contains the employee numbers (column B).

▶ FINDING RECORDS USING CRITERIA

Once the database table is created, you can use the Database Find Records command on the Tools menu to find records whose fields satisfy certain criteria. **Criteria** tell 1-2-3 which records to find from a database table. The criteria used can vary depending on individual requirements. The following examples illustrate using a single criterion and multiple criteria to find records in the Outland Traders database table.

▶ **TABLE 7-2**

OPERATOR	MEANING
=	Equal
<	Less than
>	Greater than
<=	Less than or equal to
>=	Greater than or equal to
<>	Not equal

Finding Records Using a Single Criterion

To build a single criterion, you specify a field, a logical operator, and a value. A **logical operator** indicates the relationship that is to be made between the field and the value. A list of the logical operators and their meanings are shown in Table 7-2.

The following steps illustrate how to find all records in which the value in the salary field is greater than $40,000 using the criterion: Salary > 40000.

TO FIND RECORDS USING A SINGLE CRITERION ▼

STEP 1 ▶

Click the navigator in the edit line. When the navigator drop-down box displays, point to PERSONNEL.

1-2-3 displays the navigator drop-down box (Figure 7-14). The name assigned to the database table displays in the navigator drop-down box.

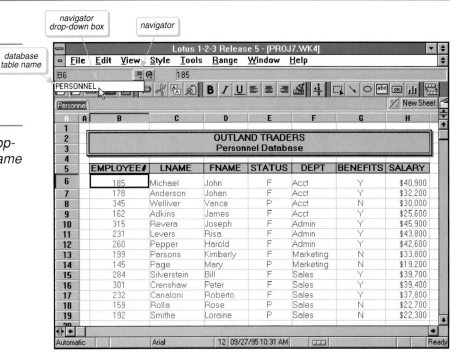

FIGURE 7-14

STEP 2 ▶

Choose PERSONNEL by clicking the left mouse button. Choose the Database command from the Tools menu. When the Database cascading menu displays, point to the Find Records command.

When you select the named range, PERSONNEL, 1-2-3 highlights the database range (Figure 7-15). When you choose the Database command on the Tools menu, 1-2-3 displays a cascading menu. The mouse pointer points to the Find Records command. Notice the selected range includes the field names in row 5 of the database table.

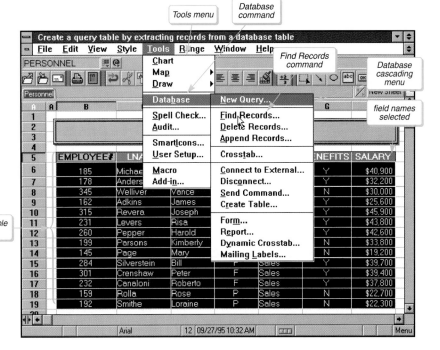

FIGURE 7-15

STEP 3 ▶

Choose the Find Records command. When the Find Records dialog box displays, point to the Field drop-down box arrow.

1-2-3 displays the Find Records dialog box (Figure 7-16). The Field box displays the first field name in row 5 of the database table. The Operator box displays the equal logical operator. The Value box displays the first value in the employee field name for the first record in the database table. The Criteria box displays graphically the criterion selected in the Field box, Operator box, and Value box. The entry, EMPLOYEE#=185, tells 1-2-3 to find all records in which the value in the employee field is equal to 185. The database table range displays in the Find records in database table text box. The mouse pointer points to the Field drop-down box arrow.

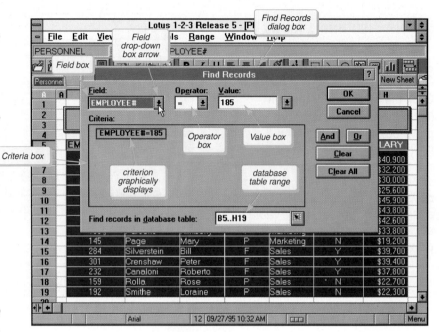

FIGURE 7-16

STEP 4 ▶

Click the Field drop-down box arrow and point to SALARY.

The Field drop-down box displays, and the mouse pointer points to the desired field (Figure 7-17). The Field drop-down box lists all the field names in the selected database table.

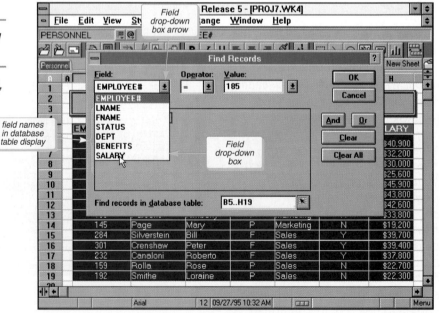

FIGURE 7-17

STEP 5 ▶

Click the left mouse button to select SALARY. Click the Operator drop-down box arrow, and point to the greater than (>) logical operator.

The field name SALARY is entered in the Field box (Figure 7-18). 1-2-3 displays the Operator drop-down box listing the logical operators. The mouse pointer points to the desired logical operator. The Value box displays $40,900 which is the salary value in the first record of the database table. The entry, SALARY= $40,900, in the Criteria box tells 1-2-3 to find all records in the database table in which the value in the SALARY field is equal to $40,900.

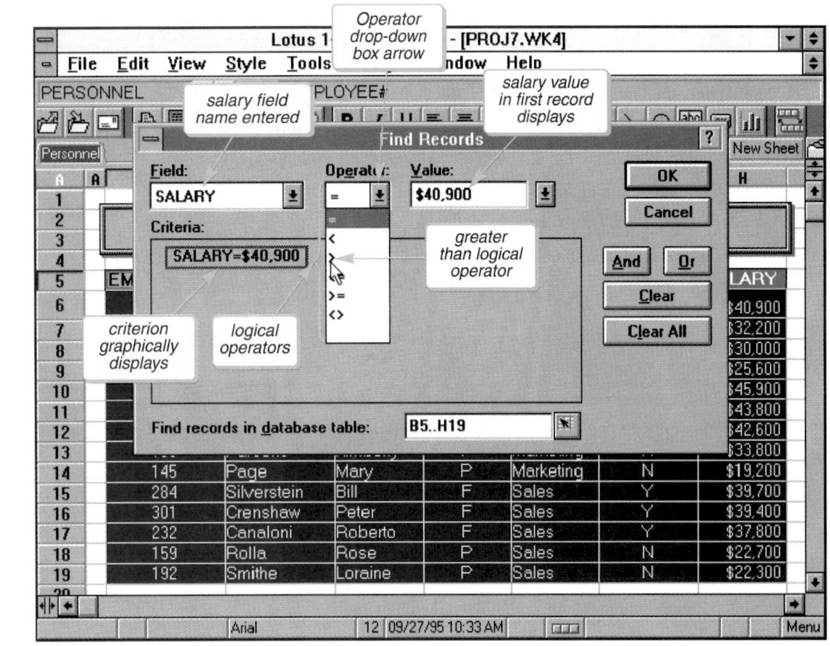

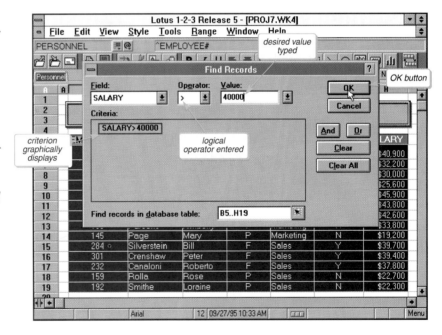

FIGURE 7-18

STEP 6 ▶

Click the left mouse button to select the greater than logical operator. Highlight the value $40,900 in the Value drop-down box and type 40000. Point to the OK button in the Find Records dialog box.

The logical operator you selected displays in the Operator box (Figure 7-19). The value you typed displays in the Value box. The entry, SALARY>40000, tells 1-2-3 to find all records in the database table in which the value in the SALARY field is greater than 40000.

FIGURE 7-19

STEP 7 ►

Choose the OK button in the Find Records dialog box.

1-2-3 highlights a collection of all records in which the SALARY field is greater than 40000 (Figure 7-20).

highlighted records in which the SALARY field is greater than $40,000

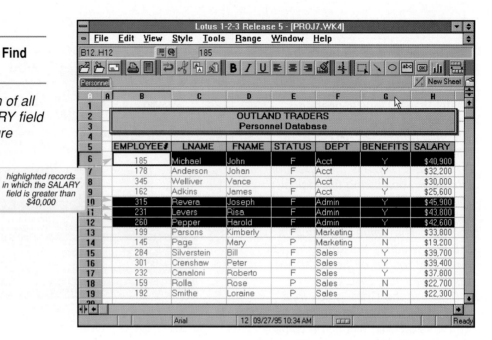

FIGURE 7-20

You can move around and edit the highlighted records using the keyboard as directed in Table 7-3.

▶ **TABLE 7-3**

TASK	KEYS PRESSED
Go to the next cell in a record	ENTER
Go to the previous cell in a record	SHIFT+ENTER
Got to the next record	CTRL+ENTER
Go to the previous record	CTRL+SHIFT+ENTER
Edit data in a record	F2, make your edits, and press ENTER to go to the next cell

To remove the highlighted collection, click any cell in the worksheet or press the ESC key.

In Step 6 on the previous page, you were instructed to type 40000 in the Value box. Be aware that clicking the Value drop-down box arrow displays a drop-down box containing the unique values included in the SALARY field. The actual value you are searching for (40000) may or may not be in the SALARY field. Therefore, you were instructed to type the value in the Value box.

Finding Records Using Multiple Criteria

You have seen how to find records based on a single criterion. You can find records using multiple criteria by using the logical operators And and Or. When the **And logical operator** is used with multiple criteria, both criteria must be true. For example, to find all records of employees who work in the Sales department and have a status of full-time (F) specify the first criterion DEPT = Sales. Then, choose the logical operator And and specify the second criterion, STATUS = F. 1-2-3 will highlight all records that have Sales in the DEPT field and F in the STATUS field. To find records using multiple criteria with the And logical operator, perform the steps on the next two pages.

TO FIND RECORDS USING MULTIPLE CRITERIA WITH THE AND LOGICAL OPERATOR ▼

STEP 1 ▶

Click the navigator in the edit line. When the navigator drop-down box displays, choose PERSONNEL. Choose the Database command from the Tools menu. When the Database cascading menu displays, choose the Find Records command. When the Find Records dialog box displays, click the Field drop-down box arrow and select DEPT. Click the Value drop-down box arrow and point to Sales.

1-2-3 highlights the database table range and displays the Find Records dialog box (Figure 7-21). The field name DEPT displays in the Field box. The logical operator = displays in the Operator box. The values contained in the DEPT field display in the Value drop-down box. The mouse pointer points to the desired value. The database table range displays in the Find records in database table text box. The Criteria box graphically illustrates the criterion currently specified in the Field, Operator, and Value boxes.

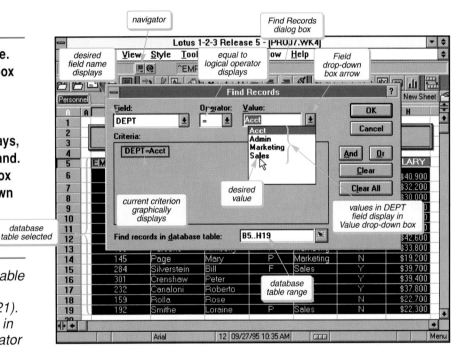

FIGURE 7-21

STEP 2 ▶

Click the left mouse button to select Sales. Point to the And button (And).

The Criteria box illustrates graphically the first criterion selected (Figure 7-22). The mouse button points to the And button.

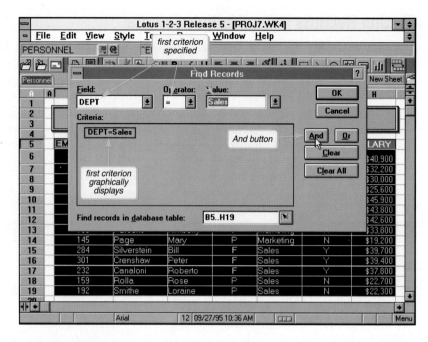

FIGURE 7-22

STEP 3 ▶

Click the left mouse button to choose the And button. Click the Field drop-down box arrow and select STATUS. Verify F displays in the Value box. Point to the OK button.

1-2-3 displays the second criterion you selected (Figure 7-23). 1-2-3 expands the graphic illustration in the Criteria box to include the second criterion. The first criterion displays above the second criterion connected by the word and. Connecting two criteria with the And logical operator requires 1-2-3 to find records that match both criteria. This entry instructs 1-2-3 to find all records in which the DEPT field is equal to Sales and the STATUS field is equal to F.

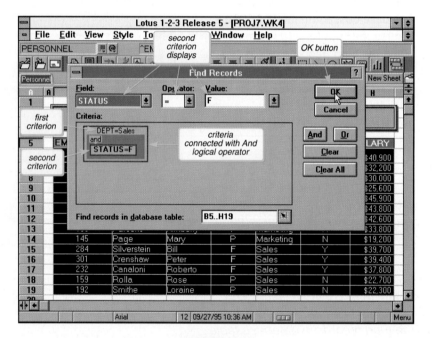

FIGURE 7-23

STEP 4 ▶

Choose the OK button.

1-2-3 highlights a collection of all records in which the DEPT field is equal to Sales and the STATUS field is equal to F (Figure 7-24).

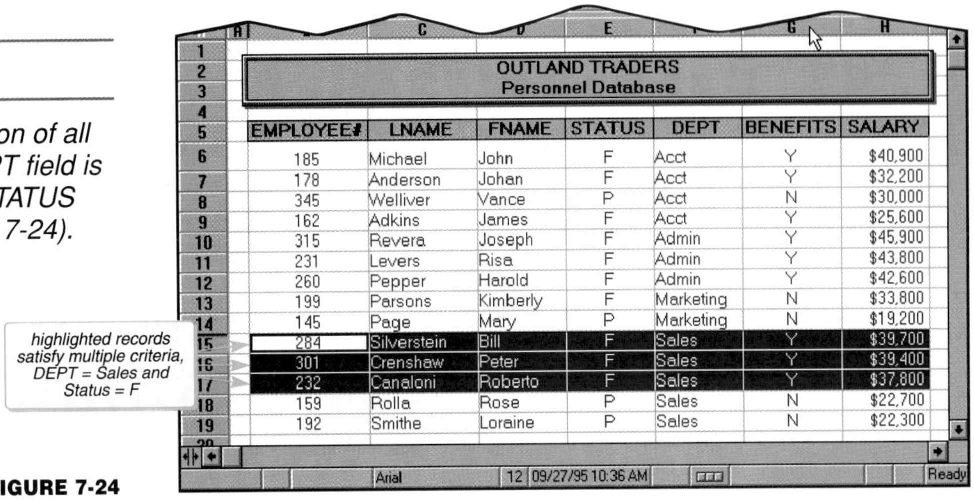

highlighted records satisfy multiple criteria, DEPT = Sales and Status = F

FIGURE 7-24

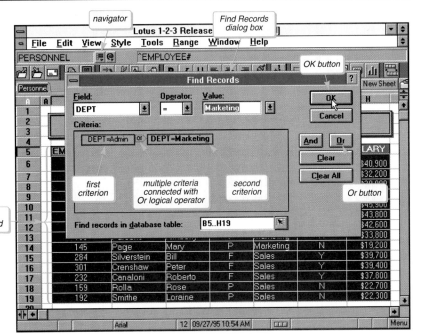

When the **Or logical operator** is used with multiple criteria, if either or both of the criterion stated are true, then the criteria is satisfied. For example, to find all records of employees who work in the Admin department or the Marketing department, specify the first criterion, DEPT = Admin. Then, choose the logical operator Or and specify the second criterion, DEPT = Marketing. 1-2-3 will highlight all records that have Admin in the DEPT field or Marketing in the DEPT field. Perform the following steps to find records using multiple criteria with the Or logical operator.

TO FIND RECORDS USING MULTIPLE CRITERIA WITH THE OR LOGICAL OPERATOR ▼

STEP 1 ▶

Click the navigator in the edit line and choose PERSONNEL. Choose the Database command from the Tools menu. Choose the Find Records command from the Database cascading menu. When the Find Records dialog box displays, select the first criterion, DEPT=Admin. Click the Or button. Select the second criterion, DEPT = Marketing. Point to the OK button.

1-2-3 highlights the database table and displays the Find Records dialog box (Figure 7-25). The Criteria box graphically displays both criteria on the same line connected by the Or logical operator. Connecting two criteria with the Or logical operator requires 1-2-3 to find records that match one criterion or the other.

FIGURE 7-25

STEP 2 ▶

Choose the OK button.

1-2-3 highlights a collection of all records in which the DEPT field is equal to Admin or Marketing (Figure 7-26).

highlighted records satisfy multiple criteria DEPT = Admin or DEPT = Marketing

EMPLOYEE#	LNAME	FNAME	STATUS	DEPT	BENEFITS	SALARY
185	Michael	John	F	Acct	Y	$40,900
178	Anderson	Johan	F	Acct	Y	$32,200
345	Welliver	Vance	P	Acct	N	$30,000
162	Adkins	James	F	Acct	Y	$25,600
315	Revera	Joseph	F	Admin	Y	$45,900
231	Levers	Risa	F	Admin	Y	$43,800
260	Pepper	Harold	F	Admin	Y	$42,600
199	Parsons	Kimberly	F	Marketing	N	$33,800
145	Page	Mary	P	Marketing	N	$19,200
284	Silverstein	Bill	F	Sales	Y	$39,700
301	Crenshaw	Peter	F	Sales	Y	$39,400
232	Canaloni	Roberto	F	Sales	Y	$37,800
159	Rolla	Rose	P	Sales	N	$22,700
192	Smithe	Loraine	P	Sales	N	$22,300

FIGURE 7-26

The difference between the And and Or logical operators is very important. Connecting two criteria with And requires 1-2-3 to find records that satisfy both criteria, whereas using Or requires 1-2-3 to find records that satisfy one criterion or the other.

▶ QUERY TABLES

1-2-3 allows you to extract information from a database table by using the Database **New Query command** on the Tools menu. When you **query** a database table, 1-2-3 finds all the records in the database table that satisfy the criteria you specify. Instead of highlighting those records as it does when the Find Records command is used, 1-2-3 places a copy of the records that satisfy the criteria in a query table. A **query table** is a special workspace separate from the original database table that contains the records that match specific criteria. Once the records are copied to a query table, you can format the query table and print the records.

Creating a Query Table

To create a query table, you must specify the database table to query, the fields and records to display, and the location for the query table. Project 7 illustrates creating a query table that contains all records in which the BENEFITS field is equal to Y. The query table shown in Figure 7-27 contains the fields, LNAME, FNAME, and DEPT. The query table is located on a second worksheet named Query_Table inserted after the Personnel worksheet and lists all employees receiving benefits. To insert a second worksheet and create the query table, perform the steps on the next four pages.

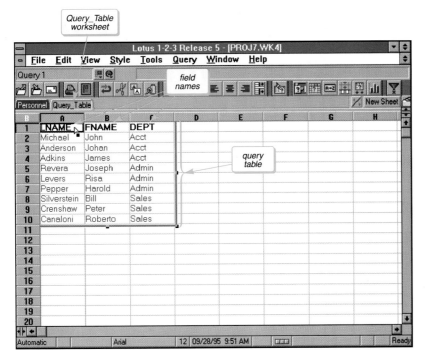

FIGURE 7-27

TO INSERT A SECOND WORKSHEET AND CREATE A QUERY TABLE ▼

STEP 1 ►

Click the New Sheet button. Double-click the worksheet tab for worksheet B, type `Query_Table`, and press the ENTER key. Choose the Database command from the Tools menu. When the Database cascading menu displays, point to the New Query command.

1-2-3 inserts the new worksheet (worksheet B) after the Personnel worksheet (Figure 7-28). The worksheet name you typed displays in the worksheet tab. The cell pointer is located in cell A1 in the Query_Table worksheet. 1-2-3 displays the Tools menu and the Database cascading menu. The mouse pointer points to the New Query command.

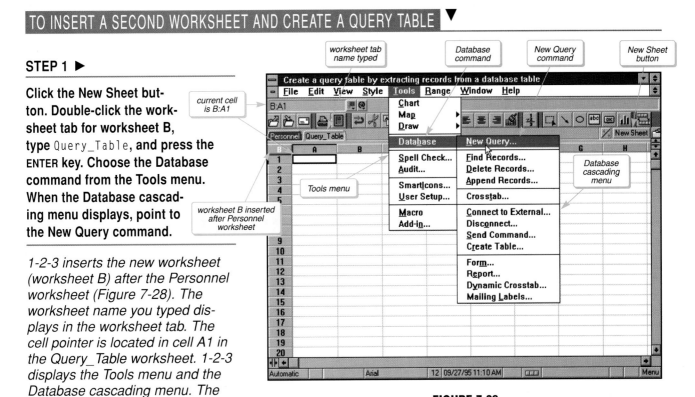

FIGURE 7-28

STEP 2 ►

Choose the New Query command. When the New Query Assistant dialog box displays, point to the Select database table to query range selector.

1-2-3 displays the New Query Assistant dialog box (Figure 7-29). The mouse pointer points to the Select database table to query range selector. The New Query Assistant dialog box contains a numbered list of selections to be made to perform a query.

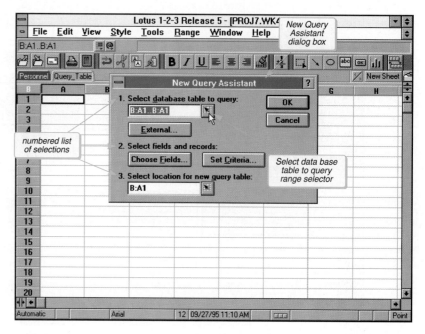

FIGURE 7-29

STEP 3 ►

Click the left mouse button. Click the navigator in the edit line. Choose PERSONNEL in the navigator drop-down box. When the New Query Assistant dialog box redisplays, point to the Choose Fields button (Choose Fields...).

When you click the Select data-base table to query range selector, the New Query Assistant dialog box is tem-porarily removed from the screen. The named range you chose displays in the Select data-base table to query box (Figure 7-30). 1-2-3 highlights the data-base table to query. The mouse pointer points to the Choose Fields button.

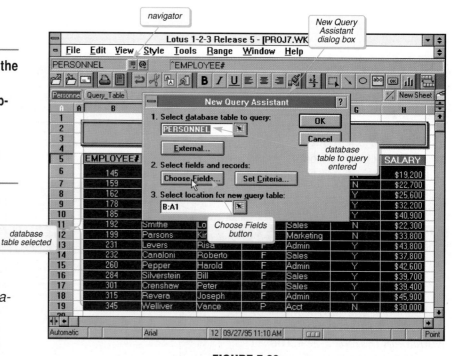

FIGURE 7-30

STEP 4 ▶

Choose the Choose Fields button. When the Choose Fields dialog box displays, verify EMPLOYEE# is highlighted in the Selected fields list box. Press and hold down the CTRL key. Select STATUS, BENEFITS, and SALARY. Release the CTRL key. Point to the Clear button (Clear).

1-2-3 displays the Choose Fields dialog box in front of the New Query Assistant dialog box (Figure 7-31). 1-2-3 highlights the selected fields in the Selected fields list box. The selected fields will not display in the query table. The mouse pointer points to the Clear button. Notice the Add button appears dimmed indicating no additional fields can be added to the query table.

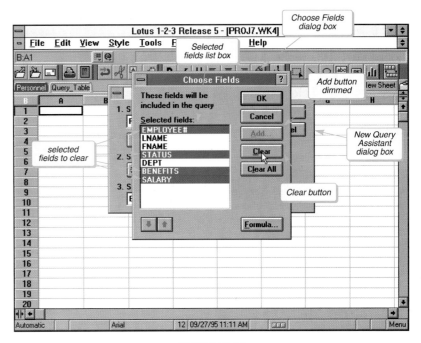

FIGURE 7-31

STEP 5 ▶

Choose the Clear button. Point to the OK button in the Choose Fields dialog box.

1-2-3 clears the selected fields from the Selected fields list box (Figure 7-32). The Add button no longer appears dimmed. The LNAME, FNAME, and DEPT fields will be included in the query table. The mouse pointer points to the OK button.

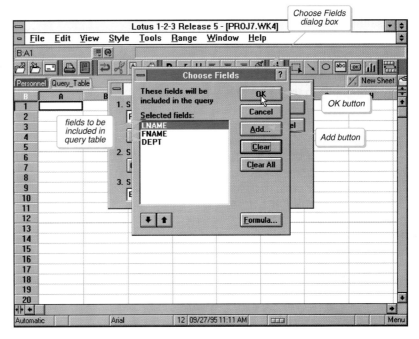

FIGURE 7-32

STEP 6 ▶

Choose the OK button in the Choose Fields dialog box. When the New Query Assistant dialog box displays, point to the Set Criteria button (Set Criteria...).

1-2-3 closes the Choose Fields dialog box (Figure 7-33). The mouse pointer points to the Set Criteria button.

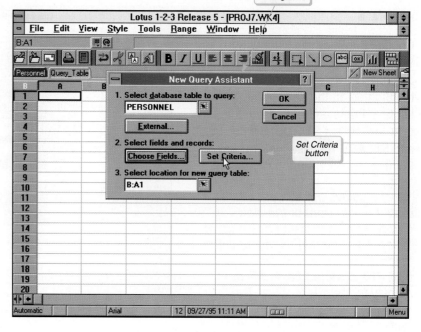

FIGURE 7-33

STEP 7 ▶

Choose the Set Criteria button. When the Set Criteria dialog box displays, click the Field drop-down box arrow and select BENEFITS. Verify Y displays in the Value box. Point to the OK button.

1-2-3 displays the Set Criteria dialog box (Figure 7-34). The criterion you selected graphically displays in the Criteria box. The mouse pointer points to the OK button.

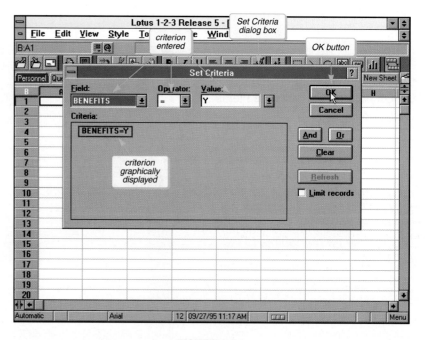

FIGURE 7-34

STEP 8 ▶

Choose the OK button in the Set Criteria dialog box. When the New Query Assistant dialog box displays, ensure the cell address, B:A1, displays in the Select location for new query table text box. Point to the OK button.

1-2-3 closes the Set Criteria dialog box and displays the New Query Assistant dialog box (Figure 7-35). Cell B:A1 in the Select location for new query table text box identifies the top leftmost cell for the query table. The mouse pointer points to the OK button.

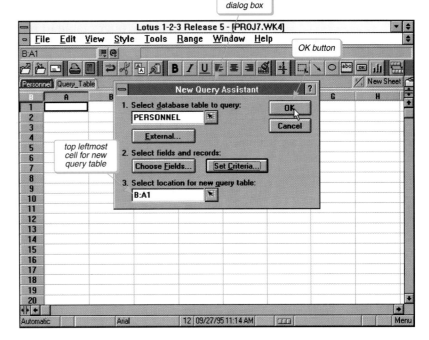

FIGURE 7-35

STEP 9 ▶

Choose the OK button.

1-2-3 searches the Personnel database table for all records in which the BENEFITS field is equal to Y. 1-2-3 copies the records that satisfy the criteria and places the records in the query table located in the Query_Table worksheet (Figure 7-36). The query table includes the field names, LNAME, FNAME, and DEPT, in row 1. These three fields are included in the query table because you specified these fields in Step 5. The query table displays with a heavy gray outline and selection handles. The handles on the outline indicate the query table is selected. When the query table is selected, the Query menu name

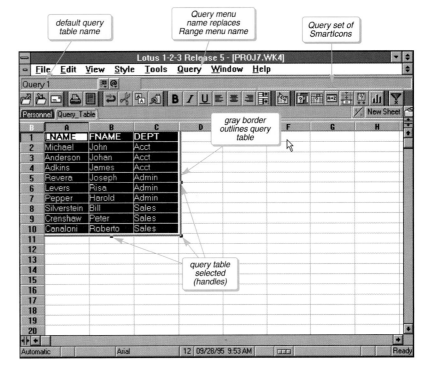

FIGURE 7-36

replaces the Range menu name on the main menu bar. The query set of SmartIcons display below the edit line. 1-2-3 assigns the default name Query 1 to the query table and displays the default name in the selection indicator in the edit line.

Select any cell in the query table to remove the selection.

When you create a query table, it assumes the styles and formats from the original database table. For example, the text in the query table displays in blue and the salary values are formatted with the US Dollar format. The query table did not assume the column widths from the original database table. The column widths in the Query_Table worksheet are the default width of nine characters.

When specifying the fields in the Choose Fields dialog box (Figure 7-32 on page L413), you can use the down and up arrows ( ) below the Selected fields list box to specify the order in which you want the fields to appear in the query table. To change the order of the fields in the query table, select a field in the Selected fields list box and click the up or down arrow below the list box until the field is in the desired position.

Use the Formula button (Formula...) in the Choose Fields dialog box to create a new field based on one or more fields in the database table.

Use the Clear All button (Clear All) to remove all the fields from the Selected fields list box. Use the Add button (Add...) to add a field you previously removed.

To delete a query table, use the following steps:

TO DELETE A QUERY TABLE

Step 1: Position the mouse pointer on the gray border and click the left mouse button.

Step 2: Press the DEL key.

Formatting Query Tables

The next task is to format the query table and add worksheet titles. The formatted worksheet is shown in Figure 7-37. The following requirements complete the formatting:

1. Move the query table.
2. Enter the worksheet titles in row 1 and row 2, add bold, change the color, increase the font, and align the titles across columns.
3. Change the query table field names in cells A4 and B4.
4. Set the widths of column A, column B, and column C to fit the widest entry.

To color the worksheet tab, move the query table, and enter and format the worksheet titles, perform the following steps.

TO COLOR THE WORKSHEET TAB, MOVE THE QUERY TABLE, AND ENTER AND FORMAT THE WORKSHEET TITLES

Step 1: Point to the worksheet tab and click the right mouse button. Choose the Worksheet Defaults command from the quick menu. When the Worksheet Defaults dialog box displays, click the Worksheet tab drop-down arrow and choose dark blue in the top row of the Worksheet tab drop-down box. Choose the OK button.

Step 2: Position the mouse pointer on the gray outline that surrounds the query table and click the left mouse button to select the query table.

Point to the gray outline, click and drag the mouse pointer until the table is positioned over the range A4..C13. Release the mouse button. Point to the selected range and click the right mouse button. When the quick menu displays, choose the Font & Attributes command. When the Font & Attributes dialog box displays, click the Color drop-down box arrow and select the first blue in the top row of the Color drop-down box. Choose the OK button.

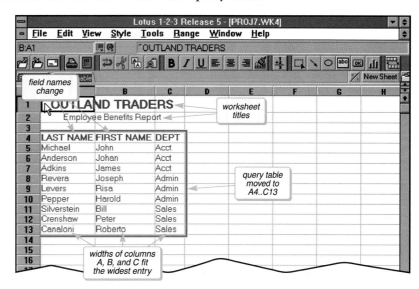

FIGURE 7-37

Step 3: Select cell A1. Type OUTLAND TRADERS and press the ENTER key or click the Confirm button. Click the Bold icon. Click the point size selector on the status bar and choose 18 from the pop-up list of point sizes.

Step 4: Select cell A2. Type Employee Benefits Report and press the ENTER key or click the Confirm button.

Step 5: Select the range A1..C2. Point to the selected range and click the right mouse button. Choose the Font & Attributes command from the quick menu. When the Font & Attributes dialog box displays, click the Color drop-down box arrow and select the first blue color in the top row of the Color drop-down box. Choose the OK button. Point to the selected range and click the right mouse button. Choose the Alignment command from the quick menu. When the Alignment dialog box displays, select the Center option button and the Across columns check box in the Horizontal area. Choose the OK button.

Changing Field Names in a Query Table

Instead of using the field names 1-2-3 copied from the database table, alternative field names can be assigned to the query table. Use the Show Field As command to change the field name in cell A4 to LAST NAME and the field name in cell B4 to FIRST NAME. Once the field names are entered, use the Fit Widest Entry icon (📇) on the query set of SmartIcons to change the column widths of column A and column B. The **Fit Widest Entry icon** adjusts the column width to display the widest entry in the column. To change the field names in the query table and adjust the column widths to fit the widest entry, perform the steps on the next three pages.

TO CHANGE FIELD NAMES IN A QUERY TABLE AND ADJUST COLUMN WIDTHS ▼

STEP 1 ▶

Point to cell A4 and click the right mouse button. When the quick menu displays, point to the Show Field As command.

1-2-3 highlights the LNAME field in the query table (Figure 7-38) and displays the quick menu. The mouse pointer points to the Show Field As command. Notice when a query table is selected, the Query menu replaces the Range menu in the menu bar and the query Smart-Icons display below the edit line.

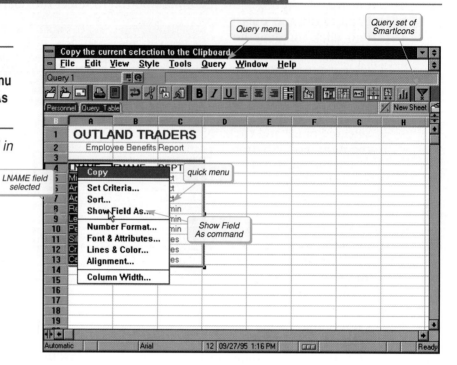

FIGURE 7-38

STEP 2 ▶

Click the left mouse button to choose the Show Field As command. When the Show Field As dialog box displays, type LAST NAME in the Show As text box. Point to the OK button.

1-2-3 displays the Show Field As dialog box (Figure 7-39). LNAME displays in the Field text box because you selected the LNAME field. The new field name you typed displays in the Show As text box. These entries instruct 1-2-3 to show field name LNAME as LAST NAME in the query table. The field name LNAME in the database table does not change.

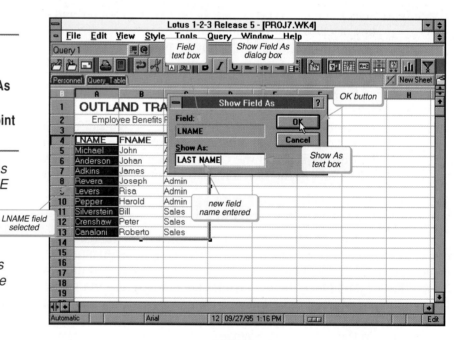

FIGURE 7-39

STEP 3 ▶

Choose the OK button in the Show Field As dialog box. Point to cell B4 and click the right mouse button. When the quick menu displays, choose the Show Field As command. When the Show Field As dialog box displays, type FIRST NAME in the Show As text box. Point to the OK button.

1-2-3 shows the LNAME field name as LAST NAME in cell A4 (Figure 7-40). 1-2-3 highlights the FNAME field and displays the Show Field As dialog box. The name you typed displays in the Show As text box. These entries instruct 1-2-3 to show field name FNAME as FIRST NAME in the query table. The field name FNAME does not change in the database table.

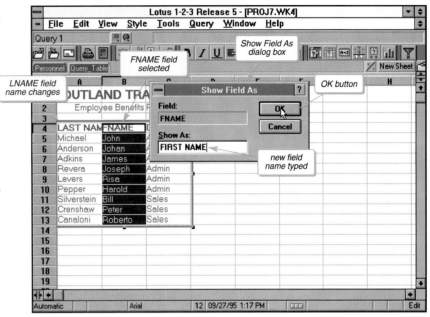

FIGURE 7-40

STEP 4 ▶

Choose the OK button. Select the query table by pointing to the gray outline and clicking the left mouse button. Point to the Fit Widest Entry icon on the query set of SmartIcons.

1-2-3 shows the new field name, FIRST NAME in cell B4 (Figure 7-41). The mouse pointer points to the Fit Widest Entry icon on the query set of SmartIcons.

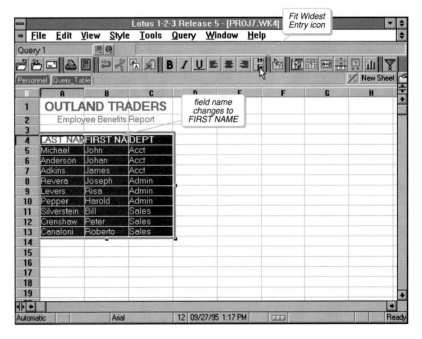

FIGURE 7-41

STEP 5 ►

Click the Fit Widest Entry icon on the query set of SmartIcons.

1-2-3 adjusts the widths of columns A, B, and C to fit the widest entry (Figure 7-42). You can click any cell to remove the selection. Column A width is 11 characters, column B width is 12 characters, and column C width is 6 characters.

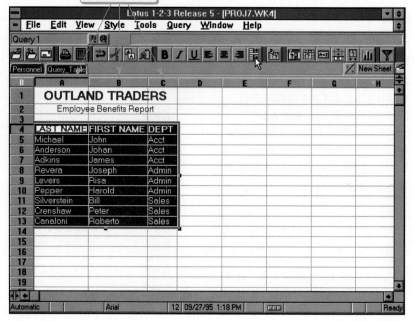

FIGURE 7-42

The Show Fields As command is also on the Query menu on the main menu bar when a query table is selected. The Fit widest entry option is in the Column Width dialog box, which you open by choosing the Column Width command from the Style menu on the main menu bar.

Printing the Query_Table Worksheet

Often your next step will be to print the Query_Table worksheet. To print the worksheet, complete the steps on the next page.

TO PRINT THE QUERY_TABLE WORKSHEET

Step 1: Ensure that the Query_Table worksheet is the current worksheet. Click the Print icon on the set of SmartIcons.

Step 2: Select the Current worksheet option button in the Print area in the Print dialog box.

Step 3: Choose the OK button in the Print dialog box.

1-2-3 produces the printout shown in Figure 7-43. Notice the gray outline around the query table does not print.

FIGURE 7-43

▶ CREATING A CROSSTAB TABLE TO SUMMARIZE DATABASE TABLE INFORMATION

A **crosstab table** is a table in which one field in a database table is summarized based on two other fields in the table. For example, the crosstab table shown in Figure 7-44 shows the total salary by department and status in the PERSONNEL database table.

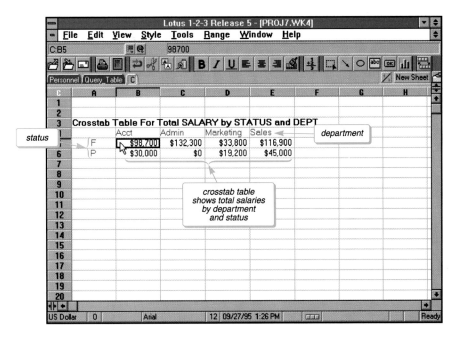

FIGURE 7-44

To create a crosstab table, use the **Crosstab command** on the Tools menu. Select one field to be used as the row headings and one field to be used as the column headings. Then, select the field to summarize and the type of summary to be performed. For example, in the crosstab table shown in Figure 7-44 on the previous page, the STATUS field is selected for the row headings (F and P) and the DEPT field is selected for the column headings (Acct, Admin, Marketing, and Sales). The field (SALARY) is summed for each department by full-time (F) and part-time (P). Continuing with the example, in the accounting department, full-time employees are paid a total salary of $98,700, while part-time employees are paid a total salary of $30,000.

1-2-3 creates a crosstab table and automatically places the table in a new worksheet. 1-2-3 inserts the new worksheet after the current worksheet.

To create the crosstab table shown in Figure 7-44 on the previous page, perform the following steps.

TO CREATE A CROSSTAB TABLE ▼

STEP 1 ►

Ensure the cell pointer is located in the Query_Table worksheet. Choose the Database command from the Tools menu. When the Database cascading menu displays, point to the Crosstab command.

The cell pointer is located in cell A1 in the Query_Table worksheet (Figure 7-45). The Tools menu displays with the Database cascading menu. The mouse pointer points to the Crosstab command.

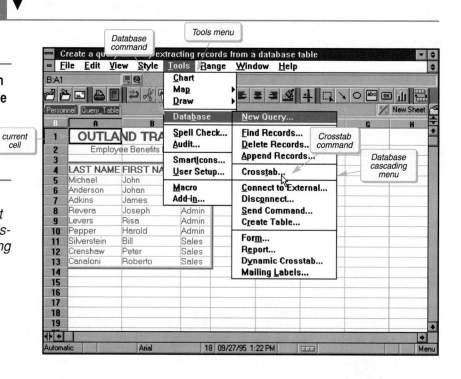

FIGURE 7-45

STEP 2 ▶

Choose the Crosstab command.
When the Crosstab Assistant dialog
box displays, click the Select
database range for crosstab
including column headings range
selector. When the Crosstab
Assistant dialog box is removed,
click the navigator in the edit
line and choose PERSONNEL
from the navigator drop-down box.
When the Crosstab dialog box
redisplays, point to the Continue
button (Continue).

1-2-3 displays the Crosstab Assistant dialog box. When you click the
range selector in the Crosstab
Assistant dialog box, 1-2-3
removes the Crosstab Assistant
dialog box so you can choose
PERSONNEL from the navigator drop-down box. When you choose PERSONNEL 1-2-3 highlights
the database table range B5..H19 (Figure 7-46). The mouse pointer points to the Continue button.

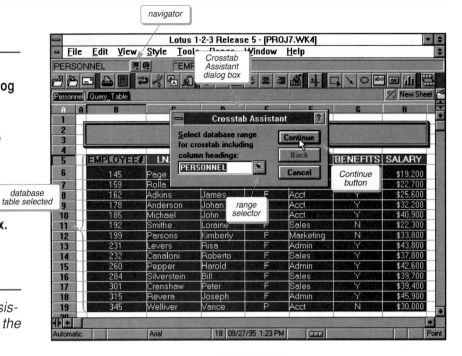

FIGURE 7-46

STEP 3 ▶

Choose the Continue button in the
Crosstab Assistant dialog box.
When the Crosstab Heading Options
dialog box displays, click the Row
headings drop-down box arrow and
select STATUS. Click the Column
headings drop-down box arrow and
select DEPT. Point to the Continue
button.

1-2-3 displays the Crosstab Heading Options dialog box (Figure
7-47). The selection for the row
headings (STATUS) displays in the
Row headings box. The selection
for the column headings (DEPT)
displays in the Column headings
box. The graphic illustration indicates the values in the STATUS
field are to display down the left
side of the crosstab table and the values in the DEPT field are to display across the top of the
crosstab table. The mouse pointer points to the Continue button.

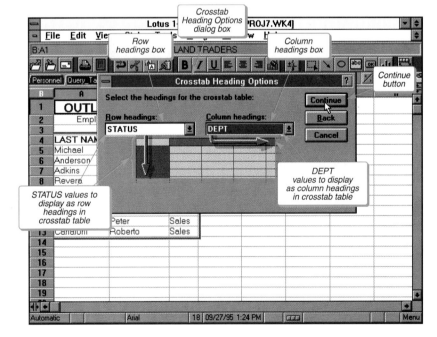

FIGURE 7-47

STEP 4 ►

Choose the Continue button in the Crosstab Heading Options dialog box. When the Crosstab Data Options dialog box displays, point to SALARY in the Summarize field list box and click the left mouse button to select the field to summarize. In the Calculate area, verify the Sum option button is selected. Point to the Continue button.

1-2-3 displays the Crosstab Data Options dialog box (Figure 7-48). The Summarize field list box displays the field names in the selected database table. The field you selected in the Summarize field list box is highlighted. The options in the Calculate area indicate the type of calculation to

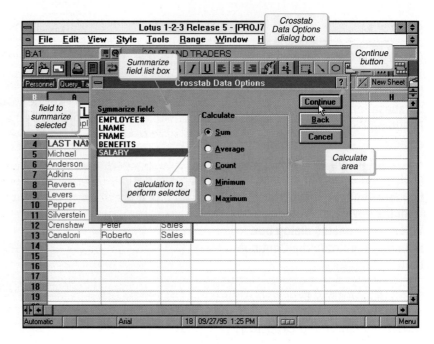

FIGURE 7-48

perform on the selected field in the Summarize field list box. The Sum option button is selected in the Calculate area. These selections instruct 1-2-3 to sum the values in the SALARY field. The mouse pointer points to the Continue button.

STEP 5 ►

Choose the Continue button in the Crosstab Data Options dialog box.

1-2-3 automatically inserts a new worksheet (worksheet C) after the Query_Table worksheet and creates the crosstab table (Figure 7-49). The crosstab table displays the total salary for full-time and part-time employees for each department.

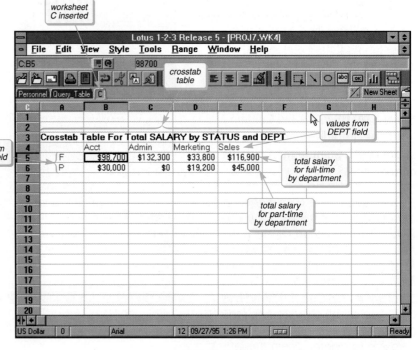

FIGURE 7-49

When you use the Crosstab command to create a crosstab table, you can click the Back button (Back) in the Crosstab Heading Options dialog box and the Crosstab Data Options dialog box to return to the previous dialog box.

The Crosstab Data Options dialog box shown in Figure 7-48 on the previous page offers four additional calculations to perform on a selected field. The Average option calculates the average of the values in a selected field. The Count option counts the nonblank cells in a selected field. The Minimum option finds the minimum value in a selected field. The Maximum option finds the maximum value in a selected field.

The final step is to name the new worksheet tab, enter worksheet titles, and format the crosstab table as shown in Figure 7-50. Perform the following steps to name the new worksheet tab, enter the worksheet titles, and format the crosstab table.

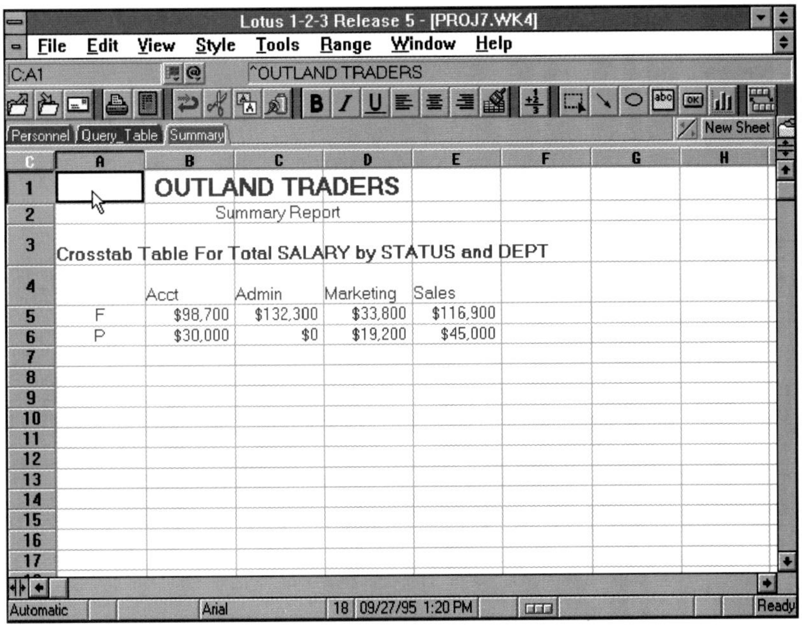

FIGURE 7-50

TO NAME THE WORKSHEET TAB, ENTER THE WORKSHEET TITLES, AND FORMAT THE CROSSTAB TABLE

Step 1: Double-click the worksheet tab (C). Type Summary and press the ENTER key. Point to the worksheet tab and click the right mouse button. Choose the Worksheet Defaults command from the quick menu. When the Worksheet Defaults dialog box displays, click the Worksheet tab drop-down arrow and choose teal in the top row of the Worksheet tab drop-down box. Choose the OK button.

Step 2: Select cell A1. Type OUTLAND TRADERS and press the ENTER key or click the Confirm button. Click the Bold icon. Click the point-size selector on the status bar and choose 18 from the pop-up list of point sizes.

Step 3: Select cell A2. Type Summary Report and press the ENTER key or click the Confirm button.

Step 4: Select the range A1..E2. Point to the selected range and click the right mouse button. Choose the Alignment command from the quick menu. When the Alignment dialog box displays, select the Center option button and the Across columns check box in the Horizontal area. Choose the OK button.

Step 5: Select the range A1..E6. Point to the selected range and click the right mouse button. Choose the Font & Attributes command from the quick menu. When the Font & Attributes dialog box displays, click the Color drop-down box arrow and select the first blue color in the top row of the Color drop-down box. Choose the OK button.

Step 6: Position the mouse pointer on the bottom border between row heading 3 and row heading 4. Drag the border of row heading 3 down until the height for row 3 displays 28 points in the selection indicator in the edit line. Release the left mouse button. Position the mouse pointer on the bottom border between row heading 4 and row heading 5. Drag the border of row heading 4 down until the height for row 4 displays 28 points in the selection indicator in the edit line. Release the left mouse button. Select any cell.

The Summary worksheet with the crosstab table displays as shown in Figure 7-50.

Printing the Summary Worksheet

The Summary worksheet can be printed using the steps presented earlier for printing the Query_Table worksheet. To print the worksheet, complete the following steps.

TO PRINT THE SUMMARY WORKSHEET

Step 1: Ensure the Summary worksheet is the current worksheet. Click the Print icon on the set of SmartIcons.

Step 2: Select the Current worksheet option button in the Print area in the Print dialog box.

Step 3: Choose the OK button in the Print dialog box.

1-2-3 produces the printout shown in Figure 7-51.

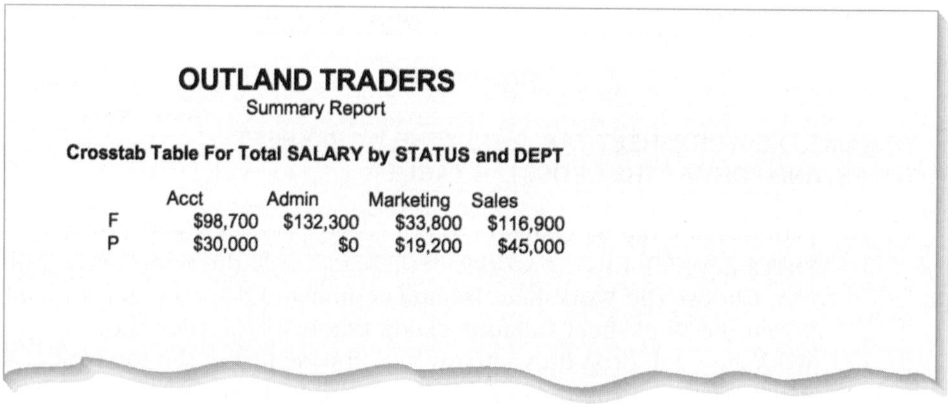

OUTLAND TRADERS
Summary Report

Crosstab Table For Total SALARY by STATUS and DEPT

	Acct	Admin	Marketing	Sales
F	$98,700	$132,300	$33,800	$116,900
P	$30,000	$0	$19,200	$45,000

FIGURE 7-51

▶ PROJECT SUMMARY

Project 7 introduced you to creating a database table. With the steps and techniques presented, you sorted the database table records in ascending and descending order, and you used the Find Records command to locate records based on a single criterion and multiple criteria. Using the New Query command, you learned how to copy records from a database table. Finally, you used the Crosstab command to summarize records in a crosstab table.

▶ KEY TERMS

And logical operator *(L407)*
ascending order *(L397)*
Choose Fields button *(L412)*
Choose Fields dialog box *(L413)*
criteria *(L402)*
Crosstab command *(L422)*
Crosstab Assistant dialog box *(L423)*
Crosstab Data Options dialog box *(L424)*
Crosstab Heading Options dialog box *(L423)*

crosstab table *(L421)*
Database command *(L403)*
database table *(L391)*
descending order *(L397)*
field *(L392)*
field name *(L395)*
Find records command *(L403)*
Find Records dialog box *(L404)*
Fit Widest Entry icon *(L417)*
logical operator *(L402)*
New Query command *(L410)*
New Query Assistant dialog box *(L412)*

Or logical operator *(L409)*
Query *(L410)*
Query menu *(L418)*
Query table *(L410)*
record *(L391)*
Show Field As command *(L418)*
Show Field As dialog box *(L418)*
Sort command *(L398)*
Sort dialog box *(L398)*
sort key *(L397)*
Sorting *(L397)*

Q U I C K   R E F E R E N C E

In Lotus 1-2-3 for Windows, you can accomplish a task in a number of ways. The following table presents a quick reference to each task presented in this project with its available options. The commands listed in the Menu column can be executed using either the keyboard or mouse.

Task	Mouse	Menu	Keyboard Shortcuts
Change a Field Name in a Query Table		From Query menu, choose Show Fields As command	
Create a Crosstab Table		From Tools menu, choose Database, then Crosstab	
Create a Query Table		From Tools menu, choose Database, then New Query	
Find Records		From Tools menu, choose Database, then Find Records	
Fit the Widest Entry	Click Fit Widest Entry icon on query set of SmartIcons	From Style menu, choose ColumnWidth command	
Sort		From Range menu, choose Sort	

STUDENT ASSIGNMENT 1
True/False

Instructions: Circle T if the statement is true or F if the statement is false.

T F 1. A database table describes a collection of related data organized in a manner that allows access, retrieval, and use of that data.

T F 2. Information in a database table is divided into records and characters.

T F 3. A record is the name given to all the information about one item of the database table.

T F 4. You can specify a maximum of twenty fields in a database.

T F 5. When creating a database table, the field names must be in one row only; the first row of the database table.

T F 6. Sorting means placing the rows of data in a prescribed sequence.

T F 7. If you sort last names in ascending sequence, and the names Warren and Arronson are in the list, Warren will be nearer the top of the names than the name Arronson.

T F 8. When sorting a database table, the field names are included in the range to sort.

T F 9. 1-2-3 allows you to use up to 255 sort keys at a time when sorting a database table range.

T F 10. Logical operators indicate the relationship that is to be made between fields and values when using criteria.

T F 11. The criterion SALARY>$30,000 instructs 1-2-3 to find all records in which the salary field is less than $30,000.

T F 12. When the And logical operator is used with multiple criteria, if either or both of the criteria stated are true, then the criteria is satisfied.

T F 13. When the Or logical operator is used with multiple criteria, both criteria must be true for the criteria to be satisfied.

T F 14. When you query a database table, 1-2-3 highlights all the records in the database that satisfy the criteria you specify.

T F 15. A query table is a special workspace separate from the original database table that contains the records that match specific criteria.

T F 16. To move a query table, select the table, position the mouse pointer inside the table, click, and drag the table to the desired location.

T F 17. Once a query table is created it cannot be deleted.

T F 18. To change the field names in a query table, use the Choose Fields command.

T F 19. A crosstab table is one in which one field in a database table is summarized based on two other fields in the table.

T F 20. The Crosstab command on the Tools menu is used to summarize database table information.

STUDENT ASSIGNMENT 2
Multiple Choice

Instructions: Circle the correct response.

1. In a database table, you can enter up to _____ records.
   a. 200
   b. 256
   c. 1,891
   d. 32,000
2. Information in a database table is divided into _____.
   a. records and fields
   b. fields and characters
   c. worksheets and files
   d. fields and files
3. A database table may contain up to _____ fields.
   a. 200
   b. 256
   c. 1,891
   d. 32,000
4. Which of the following lists is sorted in descending order?
   a. 3250, 23433, 13433, 772, 56
   b. Washington, Utah, Texas, South Dakota, California
   c. Jones, Knight, Lemon, Martin, Nero
   d. 5, 6, 7, 8, 9
5. If you make a mistake sorting a database table, immediately use the _____ icon on the set of SmartIcons.
   a. Paste
   b. Copy
   c. Undo
   d. Cut
6. 1-2-3 allows you to use up to _____ sort keys at one time.
   a. 20
   b. 200
   c. 255
   d. 300
7. Use the _____ command to find records whose fields satisfy certain criteria.
   a. New Query
   b. Database
   c. Crosstab
   d. Find Records
8. To indicate the relationship that is to be made between a field and a value when setting up a criterion, use _____.
   a. the TAB key
   b. logical operators
   c. the SPACEBAR
   d. arithmetic operators

(continued)

STUDENT ASSIGNMENT 2 (continued)

9. To create a query table, use the _____ command.
   a. New Query
   b. Find Records
   c. Crosstab
   d. Sort
10. To create a crosstab table, use the _____ command.
   a. New Query
   b. Find Records
   c. Crosstab
   d. Sort

STUDENT ASSIGNMENT 3
Understanding Sorting Using Multiple Sort Keys

Instructions: The database table shown in Figure SA7-3 is sorted using multiple sort keys. Below Figure SA7-3 write the sort keys and sort order of the records illustrated in the Personnel Database table shown in Figure SA7-3.

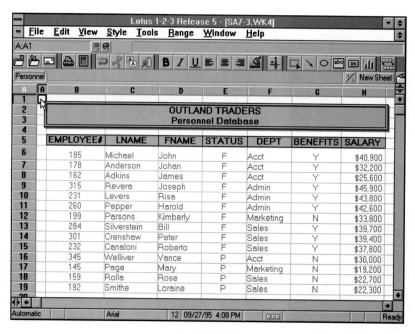

FIGURE SA7-3

SORT KEYS	SORT ORDER
_____	_____
_____	_____
_____	_____

STUDENT ASSIGNMENT 4
Understanding 1-2-3 Dialog Boxes

Instructions: Write the command that causes the dialog box to display and allows you to make the indicated changes.

CHANGES	COMMAND
1. Name the database table range.	_____
2. Sort a database table.	_____
3. Find records.	_____
4. Create a crosstab table.	_____
5. Create a query table.	_____
6. Choose fields to display in a query table.	_____
7. Change the field name in a query table.	_____

STUDENT ASSIGNMENT 5
Understanding the And Logical Operator

Instructions: The Find Records dialog box shown in Figure SA7-5 contains criteria using the And logical operator. Examine the criteria and then examine the database table in Figure 7-1 on page L382. In the space provided below Figure SA7-5, write the employee number of each record that will be highlighted when the OK button is chosen.

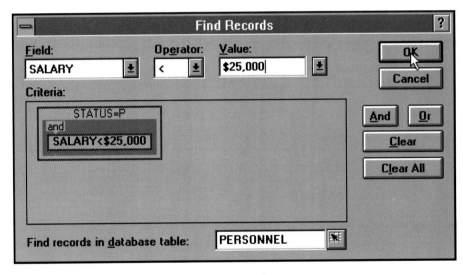

FIGURE SA7-5

Employee numbers: _____

STUDENT ASSIGNMENT 6
Understanding the Or Logical Operator

Instructions: The Find Records dialog box shown in Figure SA7-6 contains criteria using the Or logical operator. Examine the criteria and then examine the database table in Figure 7-1 on page L392. In the space provided below Figure SA7-6, write the employee number of each record that will be highlighted when the OK button is chosen.

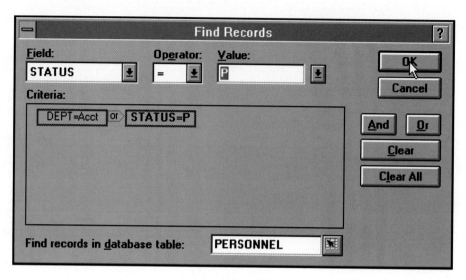

FIGURE SA7-6

Employee numbers: _____

C O M P U T E R   L A B O R A T O R Y   E X E R C I S E S

COMPUTER LABORATORY EXERCISE 1
Using the Help Menu

Instructions: Perform the following tasks using a personal computer.

1. Start Lotus 1-2-3 Release 5 for Windows.
2. Select the Help menu.
3. Choose Contents from the Help menu.
4. Click the Basics icon from the 1-2-3 Release 5 Help Contents topic.
5. Choose Keeping Records in a 1-2-3 Database Table from the Basics topic.
6. Read the Keeping Records in a 1-2-3 Database Table information, print the topic, and answer the following questions:

   a. List the characteristics that all records in a database have in common.

   _____

   _____

   b. What information is entered in the first row of a database table? The second row?

   _____

   _____

c. List two ways you can find specific records in a database table.

_____

_____

d. What are the advantages of the using the New Query command.

_____

_____

7. Exit from the Help window.

COMPUTER LABORATORY EXERCISE 2
Creating a Query Table

Instructions: Start 1-2-3. Open the CLE7-2.WK4 file from the Lotus4 subdirectory on the Student Diskette that accompanies this book. Using the worksheet on the screen and illustrated in Figure CLE7-2, create a query table of all full-time employees whose salary is less than $40,000. Print the query table. Turn in a copy of the printout to your instructor.

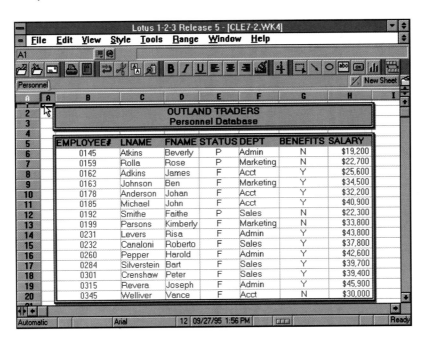

FIGURE CLE7-2

COMPUTER LABORATORY EXERCISE 3
Creating a Crosstab Table

Instructions: Start 1-2-3. Open the CLE7-3.WK4 file from the Lotus4 subdirectory on the Student Diskette that accompanies this book. Using the worksheet on the screen and illustrated in Figure CLE7-3, create a crosstab table that shows the average salary by department and status. Use STATUS as the row heading and DEPT as the column heading. Print the crosstab table. Turn in a copy of the printout to your instructor.

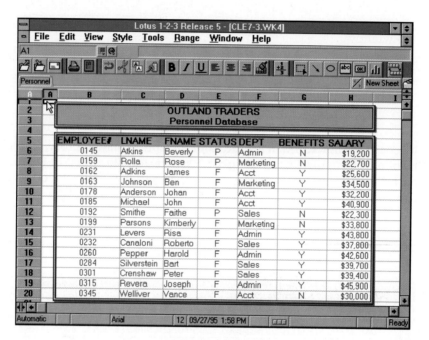

FIGURE CLE7-3

COMPUTER LABORATORY ASSIGNMENTS

COMPUTER LABORATORY ASSIGNMENT 1
Creating and Sorting a Trainers Database Table

Purpose: To provide experience in creating and sorting a database table.

Problem: Create a database table that contains information regarding trainers for Software Training Specialists. The contents of the database table are shown in the table on the next page.

Instructions:

1. Create the database in the format shown in Figure CLA7-1.
2. Format the worksheet as shown. Name the worksheet tab Trainers. The worksheet default font is Times New Roman. The column widths are: A = 2; B = 11; and E = 16. The row heights are: 1 = 22; 2 = 30; 3 = 22; and 4 = 28. The title in row 1 is 18 point and the subtitle in row 2 is 14 point.
3. Use the Name command on the Range menu to name the database table in the range B3..F16.
4. Save the database file on a diskette using a file name consisting of the initials of your first and last names followed by the assignment number. Example: KS7-1.
5. Sort the records in the database table in ascending sequence by last name. Print this sorted version.
6. Sort the database table in ascending order by region and have the records within each region appear in descending order by specialty. Print this sorted version.

7. Do not save the sorted versions of the database table.
8. Follow the directions from your instructor for turning in this assignment.

LNAME	FNAME	REGION	SPECIALTY	RATE
Gerrard	Mark	N	Presentation Graphics	$165
Zappone	Clynton	N	Presentation Graphics	$145
Tropila	Cristine	N	Word Processing	$125
Jacobowitz	Phillip	W	Database	$170
Vaillancourt	Kimberly	S	Database	$150
Christensen	Brian	E	Database	$175
Costa	Mark	E	Spreadsheet	$150
Imagawa	Nilar	W	Presentation Graphics	$155
Napier	Peter	S	Spreadsheet	$125
Ghaffari	Radhika	E	Word Processing	$115
O'Neal	Sussan	E	Spreadsheet	$135
Cole	Kemp	S	Word Processing	$100
Ogunbola	Uli	W	Database	$165

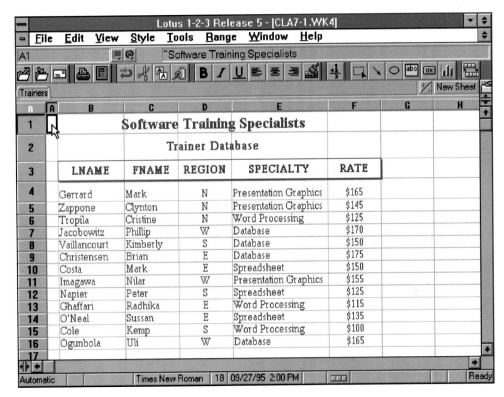

FIGURE CLA7-1

COMPUTER LABORATORY ASSIGNMENT 2
Finding Records, Performing Queries, and
Summarizing Data in the Trainers Database Table

Purpose: To provide experience in finding records, performing queries, and summarizing data in a database table.

Problem: Use the Trainers database created in Computer Laboratory Assignment 1 (Figure CLA7-1 on the previous page) to complete the find and query operations described in Part 1 and Part 2 of this assignment. (Note: If you did not create this database table in Computer Laboratory Assignment 1, your instructor will provide you with the database file.)

Instructions Part 1: Open the file CLA7-1. Use the Database Find Records command on the Tools menu to find the records that pass the criteria for the following tasks. Write down and submit to your instructor the names of the prospective programmers who pass the criteria for tasks a through d.

> a. Find all records that represent trainers whose specialty is database.
> b. Find all records that represent trainers whose specialty is presentation graphics or spreadsheet.
> c. Find all records that represent trainers in the east (REGION = E) whose rate is $150 or less.
> d. Finds all records that represent trainers in the north (REGION = N) whose rate is greater than $130.

Instructions Part 2: Open the file CLA7-1. Use the New Sheet button to insert a new worksheet after the Trainer worksheet. Perform the following tasks.

1. Use the Database New Query command on the Tools menu to create the query table shown in Figure CLA7-2a. The query table contains all trainers in the east (REGION = E) whose specialty is word processing or spreadsheet. Name the worksheet tab Query_Table. Format the query table as shown in Figure CLA7-2a. Print the query table.
2. Use the Database Crosstab command on the Tools menu to create the crosstab table shown in Figure CLA 7-2b. The crosstab table summarizes the Trainers database table by counting the number of trainers by specialty and region. Name the worksheet tab Summary. Format the crosstab table as shown in Figure CLA7-2b. Print the crosstab table.
3. Save the database file on a diskette using a file name consisting of the initials of your first and last names followed by the assignment number. Example: KS7-2.
4. Follow the directions from your instructor for turning in this assignment.

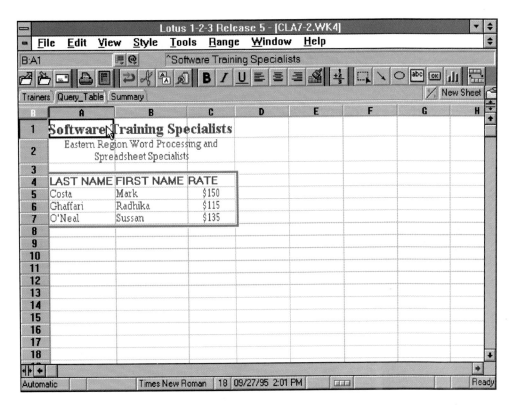

FIGURE CLA7-2a

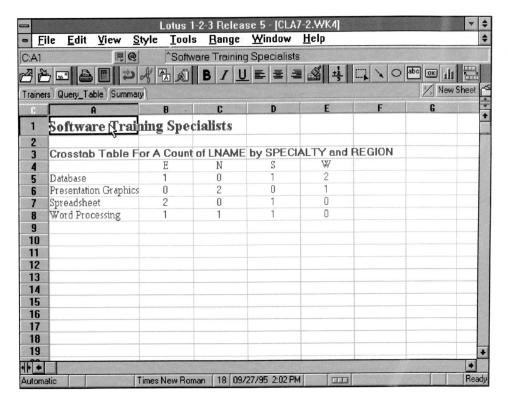

FIGURE CLA7-2b

COMPUTER LABORATORY ASSIGNMENT 3
Creating a Database Table, Using Query Tables, and Summarizing Data

Purpose: To provide experience in creating a database table, using query tables, and summarizing data in a database table.

Problem: Create a database table that contains information regarding donations for State College Foundation. The database table displays as shown in Figure CLA7-3a.

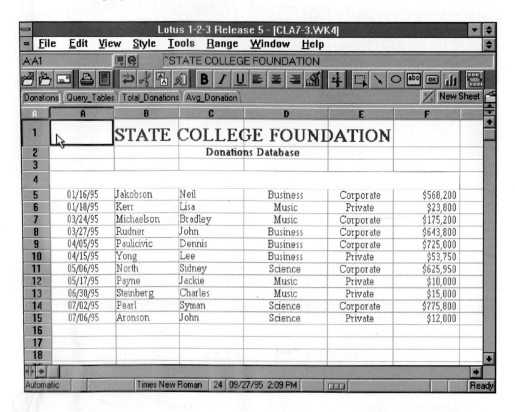

FIGURE CLA7-3a

Instructions:

1. Use the Worksheet Defaults command on the Style menu to change the worksheet default font to Times New Roman and the default worksheet column width to 11.
2. Create the database table in the same format as shown in Figure CLA7-3a. Name the worksheet tab Donations. Change column D to a width of 14 characters. The row heights are: 1 = 30 and 4 = 20. The title in row 1 is 24 point.

3. Save the database table on a diskette. Use a file name consisting of the initials of your first and last names followed by the assignment number. Example: KS7-3.
4. Use the Database New Query command on the Tools menu to create the query table in the range A4..F9 as shown in Figure CLA7-3b. This query table contains all donations from private sources (TYPE = Private).

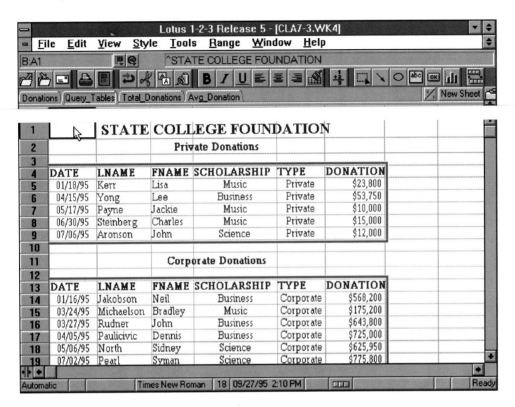

FIGURE CLA7-3b

5. Use the Database New Query command on the Tools menu to create the query table in the range A13..F19 as shown in Figure CLA7-3b. This query table contains all donations from corporate sources (TYPE = Corporate). Name the worksheet tab Query_Tables. Format the query tables as shown in Figure CLA7-3b. Print the query tables.
6. Use the Database Crosstab command on the Tools menu to create the crosstab table shown in Figure CLA 7-3c on the next page. The crosstab table summarizes the donations database table by summing the donations by scholarship and type. Name the worksheet tab Total_Donations. Format the crosstab table as shown in Figure CLA7-3c on the next page. Print the crosstab table.

(continued)

COMPUTER LABORATORY ASSIGNMENT 3 (continued)

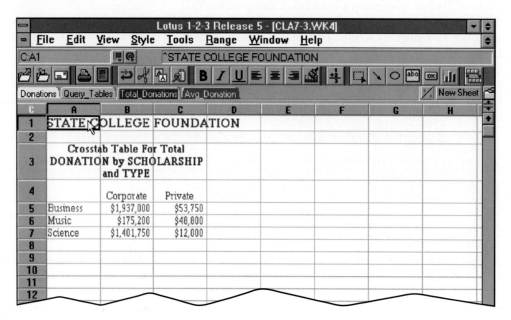

FIGURE CLA7-3c

7. Use the Database Crosstab command on the Tools menu to create the crosstab table shown in Figure CLA 7-3d. The crosstab table calculates the average of donations by scholarship and type. Name the worksheet tab Avg_Donations. Format the crosstab table as shown in Figure CLA7-3d. Print the crosstab table.

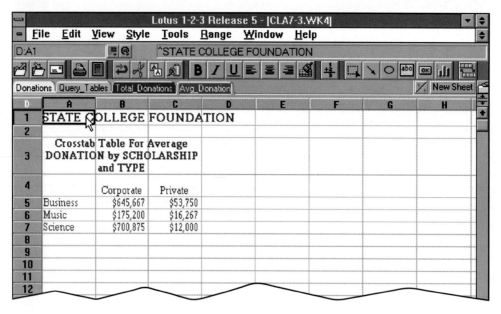

FIGURE CLA7-3d

8. Save the changes made to the file.
9. Follow the directions from your instructor for turning in this assignment.

COMPUTER LABORATORY ASSIGNMENT 4
Creating a Database Table

Purpose: To provide experience in creating a database table.

Problem: Create a database table that contains at least fifteen movies from a nearby video store. The database table should contain the following fields: title, type (comedy, suspense, drama, science fiction), Rating (R, PG, G), and Producer.

Instructions:

1. Create the database table.

3. Format the database table.
4. Save the database table on a diskette. Use a file name consisting of the initials of your first and last names followed by the assignment number. Example: KS7-4.
5. Print the database table.
6. To provide as complete a picture as possible of your list of videos, design and create three different query tables that will answer most of the questions someone may have about your videos.
7. Print the three query tables.
8. Design and create one crosstab table performing a calculation of your choice on the list of videos.
9. Print the crosstab table.
10. Follow the directions from your instructor for turning in this assignment.

*I*NDEX

Absolute cell reference,
  L150-151
 copying and, L152-153
Across columns alignment,
  L86-87
A data range, pie chart, **L238**
Add button, range name and,
  L331
Addition, order of precedence
  and, L68
Add Key button, L401
Add To Dictionary button, L112
Alignment
  Across columns, L86-87
  date, L325
  labels, L14
  multiple worksheets titles, L228
  rotating data within cell and,
    L284
  text in text block, L162
  values, L19
Alignment command
  centering text in cell and, L88
  worksheet title, L86-87
Alignment icons, L93
Always on Top command, Help
  menu, **L46**
Analyze command, L336
Analyze What-if Table command,
  L342-343
And logical operator, **L407**-408,
  L410
Angled rotation, L285
A range, pie chart, **L103**
Arguments, macros and, **L348**
  separator, L350
Arrow, adding to chart, L243,
  L292-293
Ascending sort, **L397**
Asset, **L211**
Attributes, *see* Font attributes
Automatic format, **L67**
Automatic recalculation,
  L191-193
Average of values, L68
Axes, titles, L182, L279

Back button, Crosstab command
  and, L425
Background color, L99-101
  default, L138

line chart, L279
 multiple worksheets, L231
 pie chart, L245
Backsolver, **L336**-338
BACKSPACE key, L43
Balance sheet, **L211**-218
 consolidated, L211, L218-226
Bar chart, **L30**-37, L271
Bins, maps and, **L299**, L303-305
 colors, L303-305
Block, text, *see* Text block
Bold format
 multiple worksheets titles, L228
 text in cell, L88-89
 worksheet title and, L85
Bold icon, L85, L228
Border, **L168**-172
Bottom of cell, line at, L171
Braces ({}), macro commands
  and, L348

Calendar function category, **L325**
Cancel button, **L12**
Candlestick HLCO chart, **L298**
Cell(s), **L9**
 bold text in, L88
 border around, L168-172
 centering text in, L88
 clearing, L44-45
 copying adjacent, in a column,
   L23-24
 copying cell to adjacent, L20-24
 copying down, L22
 copying in multiple columns,
   L75-76
 copying right, L22
 copying using drag-and-drop,
   L145
 current, *see* Current cell
 editing data in, L43-44
 moving insertion point in, L43
 moving using drag-and-drop,
   L147
 naming adjacent, L324
 protecting, L370-374
 rotating data in, L284-285
 selecting, L10-11, L69
Cell address
 formula beginning with, L68
 worksheet letter as part of, L175
Cell pointer, **L9**

Cell protection, L318
Cell reference
 absolute, L150-151
 copying formulas and, L76
 in formula, L68
 relative, L149
 worksheet letter as part of, L175
Cells referenced in a formula,
  changing values in, L191-193
Center-Align icon, **L93**
Centering
 charts, L283
 horizontal, L87
 labels, L65
 multiple worksheet titles, L228
 range of cells, L93
 text in cell, L88-89
 values, L93
 vertical, L87
 worksheet title, L86
Chart(s), **L3**, **L30**-37, **L269**-299
 automatic, L273
 bar, L30-37, L271
 candlestick HLCO, L298
 centering, L283
 clearing, L45
 creating, L271
 data labels, L240-242
 default type, L271
 deleting, L45
 filling entire page, L282
 footnotes below, L239-240
 HLCO, L271, L295-298
 line, L270, L272-283
 location of, L31
 mixed, L270-271, L284-295
 moving, L31
 naming, L274, L280-281
 pie, L102-108
 printing separately from
   worksheet, L115-116
 printing with worksheet data,
   L114
 saving, L282
 selecting, L184
 spell checking, L111
 stacked bar, L176-186
 terminology, L272
 text block and, L211
 types of, L269-271
 whisker HLCO, L295

Chart command, L271, L273
Chart icon, L31-32, L104, L271, L273, L274
Chart legend, **L30, L34**
Chart menu, **L7, L106**
  Headings, L106
  Name, L281
  Ranges, L181, L286-287
  Type, L271
Chart note frame, L245
Chart plot, **L184**
Chart Ranges command, L180
Chart title, L182
  consolidated worksheet, L239
  formatting, L106-108
  line chart, L274
Chart title frame, resizing, L183
Choose Fields button, L412-413, L416
Classic menu, **L48**
Clear command, L44
  styles and, L87
Clearing the data, **L44**
Clearing worksheet, L45
Clear Split command, **L235**
Clipboard, **L220,** L222
Close button
  print preview and, L114
  spell checker and, L112
Close command, L39, L117
Close icon, Print Preview window and, L251
Close the worksheet, **L39**
Collection of ranges, **L75**
Color
  adding to worksheet, L98-102
  background, L99-101
  bin, L303-305
  chart titles, L107
  database tables, L395
  data series, L273
  default settings, L138
  frame, L167
  line charts, L275
  mixed chart, L293-294
  multiple worksheets, L231
  pattern, L166
  pie chart, L245
  query tables and, L417
  range, L101
  stacked bar chart, L185
  text, L100
  worksheet tabs, L232-233
Colors & Legends command, maps and, L304
Column, **L8**
  alignment across, L86-87

copying adjacent cells in, L23-24
copying cells in multiple, L75-76
hiding, L97
plotting data series by, L273
Column letter, **L8**
Column titles, L11, **L14-15,** L66
  formatting, L88-89, L167
Column width, L94-97
  changing, L172
  default, L137
  fitting widest entry and, L417
  multiple worksheets, L230
Column Width command, **L94,** L95-96
Comma format, L90-91
Confirm button, **L12,** L13, L43, L71
Consolidated balance sheet, **L211,** L218-226
Contents box, **L8**
Contents command, help and, **L46**
Context-sensitive help, **L46**
Control menu box, L7
Control panel, **L6,** L7-8
Copy/copying, **L20**
  absolute cell references and, L152-153
  cell to adjacent cells, L20-24
  cells in multiple columns, L75-76
  cells using drag-and-drop, L145
  Copy icon and, L220
  data between worksheets using drag-and-drop, L214-217
  formulas, L153, L157
  Paste icon and, L220
  @SUM function, L20-21, L224
Copy command, L222
Copy Down command, **L23-24,** L76-77
Copy icon, copying data between worksheets using, **L220-222**
Copy Right command, L22, L152-153, L157
Criteria, finding records using, **L402-410**
Crosstab command, **L422-425**
Crosstab table, **L421-426**
Currency format, **L90-91,** L229, L278
Current cell, **L9,** L17
Current worksheet, **L175**
  inserting worksheet before, L218

Custom - 87% command, L165
Cut command, L222
Cut icon, **L44-45, L222**

Data
  clearing, L44
  deleting, L44
  editing, L42-45
  entering, L66-84
  moving to another worksheet, L216-217
  pasting, L220-221
  protecting, L370-374
  rotating in cell, L284
Data analysis, L318-370
  1-variable what-if table and, L338-346
  Backsolver and, L336-338
  Version Manager and, L363-370
Database, **L3**
Database command, finding records and, L403, L407
Database Crosstab command, L422
Database tables, **L391-427**
  creating, L393-395
  crosstab table summarizing, L421-426
  formatting, L395-396
  naming, L393
  querying, L410-420
  sorting, L397-402
Data entry, macros automating, L346-363
Data label, pie chart, L240-242, L245
Data range, pie chart, L238
Data sequence, creating using drag-and-fill, L142-144, L340-341
Data series, **L273,** L286
Date formats, **L67**
Date number, **L324**
Date-time/height-width indicator, column width and row height information, L98
Debugging, **L116**
Decimal, multiplying decimals by, L149
Decimal selector, currency format, L90
Deleting data, **L44**
  chart, L45
  data labels, L242
  grid lines, L278
  range name, L332
  text block, L141

version, L365
DEL key, L44
Descending sort, **L397**
Designer frame, **L164**
color, L167
multiple worksheets, L231
pie chart, L245
stacked bar chart, L186
Destination, **L220**
Dictionaries, spell checker, L108
Disk, saving worksheet on, L25
Division, order of precedence
and, L68
Documenting macro, L358, L362
Dollar format, L90, L229
Dollar sign ($), absolute cell
reference and, L150
Drag-and-drop
copying cells using, **L145**
copying data between work-
sheets using, L214-217
moving cells using, L147
over existing data, L216
Drag-and-fill, creating data
sequence using, **L142**-144,
L340-341
Draw Arrow icon, L292
exploded pie slice and, L243
Draw Button command, **L355**
Draw Button icon, macro button
and, **L352**
Draw Ellipse command, **L293**
Draw Ellipse icon, **L292**
Drawn objects, **L139**
Draw Text command, **L141**
Draw Text icon, L140, L243
Drives, saving worksheet and,
L25-26

Edge area, Line color and, L245
Edit data, **L42**-45
Edit line, **L8**
navigator in, L327
Edit menu
Clear, L44, L87
Copy, L222
Copy Down, L24, L77
Copy Right, L22
Cut, L222
Insert, L218
Paste, L222
Edit mode, **L43**, L78
Edit text block, L141
Ellipse, mixed chart, **L292**
ENTER key, entering formulas
and, **L13**, L43, L71
Error correction, L42-45

Exit command, L40, **L46**, L117
Exiting Lotus 1-2-3, **L39**-40
Exploded pie slice, L242-243
arrow pointing to, L243
Exponentiation, order of
precedence and, L68

F4 (absolute cell reference), L151
Field, **L392**
choosing to query, L412-413
Field names, changing in query
tables, L417-420
File
opening, L40-42
sealing, L370
unsealing, L373
File name, L7
Close, L39, L117
Exit, L40, L46, L117
opening file and, L43
Page Setup, L115, L190,
L248-249
Print Preview, L115
Save, L27
Save As, L27
File name extension, L26
Fill by Example command, **L142**
Filling range, L142-144
Fill page but keep proportions
option, **L283**
Fill pattern, gradient, L164, L166
Finding records, using criteria,
L402-410
Find Records command, L404,
L409
Fit Widest Entry icon, **L417**
Font(s), **L84**, L321
default, L137
Font & Attributes command
chart titles and, L107
column titles, L167
pie chart and, L245
query tables and, L417
row titles, L167
stacked bar chart, L185
text block and, L159
Font attributes, **L84**
text block, L159
Font color, stacked bar chart,
L185
Font size
multiple worksheets, L226
row height and, L97
stacked bar chart, L185
text block, L159
Font style, stacked bar chart,
L185

Footers, **L248**-250
Footnotes, below chart,
L239-240
Format/formatting, **L27**
automatic, L67
chart titles, L106-108
column titles, L88-89, L167
comma, L90-91
crosstab table, L425
currency, L90-91, L229, L278
database tables, L395-396
date, L67
default, L137-138
fonts and, see Font(s)
General, L278
group mode and, L226
labels, L85-90
line chart values, L278
macros worksheet, L363
multiple worksheets, L226-237
percent, L92-93
pie chart, L245
query tables, L416-417
row height and, L97
row titles, L88-89, L167
templates and, L27-30
text, L117
text blocks, L158-167
values, L90-93, L168
what-if table, L345
worksheet, L164-173, L334-335
worksheet titles, L85, L228
Format selector, **L67**, L91
currency, L229
Formula(s), **L67**
Backsolver and, L336-338
beginning with numbers or
special characters, L68
cell reference in, L68
changing values in cells
referenced in, L191-193
copying, L153, L157
debugging, L116
displaying, L116
entering, L67-73
entering in 1-variable what-if
table, L341
moving data between
worksheets and, L217
operators in, L68
order of precedence and, L68
printing, L116-117
range names in, L327-333
resetting to values, L117
Formula button, Choose Fields
dialog box and, L416

Frame, text block, L161. *See also* Designer frame
@function, **L19**
  help and, L326
@Function list, **L81**
@Function menu
  List All, L78, L81
  ROUND, L150, L154-156
  SUM, L224
@function selector, L8, **L77, L325**
Functions, categories, L325-326

General format, **L278**
GET-NUMBER macro, L350
Gradient fill pattern, **L164**, L166
Grid lines, **L9**
  deleting, L278
  HLCO chart, L296-297
  line chart, L276-277
  stacked bar chart, L184-185
Grids command, L184, L277
Grouping worksheets, L227-228
Group mode, **L226**

Handles, chart, **L33**
Headers, **L248**-250
Headings, crosstab, L423
Headings command, L106
  chart title, L105-106
  consolidated worksheet title, L239
Help, L46-47
  @functions, L326
Help icon, L46
Help menu, L46
  Tutorial, L47
Hiding columns, **L97**
HLCO chart, **L271**, L295-298
Horizontal axis, L273
Horizontal centering, L87, L93
Horizontal splitter, **L193**
How Do I? command, **L46**

Icon, **L8**
Info button, version, L365
Insert buttons, **L249**
Insert command, **L218**
Inserting
  footers, L249-250
  worksheet, L173-175, L215
Insertion point, **L12**
  moving in cell, L43
Italics icon, worksheet title and, L85

Keyword, macros and, **L348**

Label(s), **L11**
  alignment of, L14
  balance sheet, L217
  centered, L65
  entering, L11-16, L66-67
  formatting, L85-90
  naming range using adjacent, L322-324, L328
Label mode, L12
Label-prefix character, **L14**
Labels, x-axis, L273
Landscape page orientation, L188
Language dictionary, **L108**
Left-Align icon, **L93**
Left-align labels, L14
Legend, chart, **L30, L34, L176, L273**
  mixed chart, L290-291
  stacked bar chart, L176
Legend, maps, L299
Liabilities, **L211**
  summing, L212
Line chart, **L270**, L272-283
  axes title, L279
  creating, L274
  formatting values, L278
  grid lines, L276-277
  line style and, L275
  printing, L282-283
Line style, line charts, L275
Line width, line charts, L275
Lines & Color command
  background color and, L99-101
  border around cells and, L169
  line chart and, L275, L280
  mixed chart, L294
  multiple worksheets, L231
  pie chart and, L245
  text block and, L165
List, **L77**
List All command, @Function menu, **L78,** L81
Logical operators, **L402**-404
  And, L407-408, L410
  Or, L409-410
Long International Date format, L67
Lotus 1-2-3 Classic menu, **L48**
Lotus 1-2-3 Release 5 for Windows
  exiting, L39-40
  introduction to, L2-3
  starting, L4-6, L65
Lotus 1-2-3 Tutorial, **L47**
Lotus 1-2-3 window, L6-10
Lotus Applications group window, L4-5, L65

Macro(s), L318, **L346**-363
  documenting, L358, L362
  naming, L351-352
  printing in worksheet, L358-362
  running with a button, L355-357
Macro Assign to Button command, **L355**
Macro button, **L352**-355
  printing and, L360-361
Macro command, **L320**, L347-348
  entering, L348-351
  planning, L348
  L363
Main menu, **L7**
Major interval grid lines, L277
Map(s), **L269**, L299-305
Map Colors & Legend command, L303
Map legend, **L299**
Map New Map command, **L300**
Map regions, **L299**
Map title, **L299**, L302
@MAX function, **L81**
Maximize button, L6
Menu(s)
  1-2-3 Classic, L48
  quick, L21
Menu names, L7
@MIN function, **L81**
Minimize button, L7
Mixed chart, **L270**-271, L284-295
  arrow, L292
  color and pattern, L293-294
  creating, L286-288
  ellipse, L292
  legend, L290-291
  plot, L290-291
  style options, L288
  y-axis, L287-289
Mode indicators, **L10**
Mouse
  column width and, L94
  row height and, L97
Mouse pointer, **L9**
Mouse pointer shapes, **L9**
Move data, **L216**-217, **L222**
Moving
  cells using drag-and-drop, L147
  chart, L31
  data to another worksheet, L216-217
  exploded pie slice, L242
  macro button, L355
  map, L301
  text block, L163, L244
  using cut and paste, L222

Multiple columns, copying cells in, L75-76
Multiple operators, **L68**
Multiple Pages icon, print preview and, L251
Multiple worksheets, L173-176, L209-254
  copying data between using drag-and-drop, L214-217
  creating, L212-218
  formatting, L226-227
  grouping, L227-228
  inserting worksheet and, L173-175
  moving data between, L216-217
  page breaks and, L246-248
  printing, L246-253
  print preview, L250-251
  row titles, L228-229
  titles, L228
  viewing, L233-237
Multiplication (*), L70, L154
  decimals by a decimal, L149
  order of precedence and, L68

Name command, L281, **L322**
  database tables, L393
Naming
  adjacent cells, L324
  charts, L274, L280-281
  database tables, L393
  macros, L351-352
  range using adjacent labels, L322-324, L328
  worksheets, L175-176, L218
Navigator, L8
  inserting range names in formulas using, L327
New Query command, **L410**, L412
New Sheet button, L215
  inserting worksheets and, L174
  macros and, L349
Number, beginning formulas with, L68
Number format, default, L138
Number Format command
  comma format and, L92
  currency and, L90
  percent format and, L93

Objects, drawn, L139
1-2-3 Classic menu, **L48**
1-2-3 window, L6-10
1-2-3 worksheet, **L8**
1-variable what-if table, **L338**-346
Online Help, **L46**-47, L326
Open icon, L42

Opening a worksheet file, **L40**-42
Operators, **L68**
Order of precedence, **L68**
Orientation, rotating data and, L284-285
Or logical operator, **L409**-410

Page Break command, L246-248
Page number, printing, L249
Page orientation, printing and, L188-189
Page Setup command, **L115, L248**
  chart filling page and, L282
  footers and, L248-249
  printing in landscape mode, L188-189
  print preview and, L112-113, L114
Pane, **L191**-193
Parentheses ( ), operation contained within, **L68**
Password, L372-373
Paste command, L222
Paste icon, copying data between worksheets using, **L220**-222
Pattern, **L164**
  color, L166
  mixed chart, L293-294
  transparent, L294
Percent change, L77, L80
Percent format, **L92**-93
Perspective view, **L233**
Pie chart, **L102**-108, L237-246
  A data range, L238
  arrow in, L243
  consolidated worksheet and, L237-246
  data labels, L240-242
  exploded slice, L242-243
  footnotes below, L239-240
  formatting, L245
  text block, L243
  titles, L105-106
  X data range, L238
Plot, **L273**, L290-291
Plus sign (+), beginning formulas with, L68, L69, L327
Point mode, L21, L69, **L71**
Point size, **L84**
  row height and, L97
  worksheet title, L86
Portrait page orientation, **L188**
Print/printing
  chart separately from worksheet, L115-116
  chart with worksheet data, L114
  footers, L248-249

  formulas, L116-117
  headers, L248-249
  landscape reports, L188-189
  line chart, L282-283
  macro in worksheet, L358-362
  multiple worksheets, L246-253
  page breaks and, L246-248
  page number, L249
  page orientation and, L188-189
  query tables, L420
  stacked bar chart, L190
  summary worksheet, L426
  worksheet, L37-38
Print icon, **L37,** L115
  multiple worksheets and, L252
Printing Sections of Help, **L46**
PRINT macro, L359
Print Preview, L112-113, L187-188
  multiple worksheets, L250-251
Print Preview command, **L115**
Print Preview window, Page Setup dialog box, L190
Print Topic command, help menu, **L46**
Protected cells, **L370**-374

Query tables, **L410**-420
  changing field names in, L417-420
  creating, L410-416
  formatting, L416-417
  printing, L420
Quick menu, **L21**
QUIT macro, L351

Range(s), **L20**
  border around, L168-172
  centering, L93
  charting, L104, L273
  clearing, L44-45
  collection of, L75
  color, L101
  copying between multiple worksheets, L214
  copying using drag-and-drop, L145
  database table, L395
  entering data sequence in using drag-and-fill, L142-144
  fill, L142-144
  HLCO chart, L295
  moving using drag-and-drop, L147
  naming using adjacent labels, L322-324
  printing, L361
  protecting, L370-374

selecting, L69
selecting noncontiguous, L104
sorting, L397-402
3D, L222-225
versions, L363-370
Range menu, **L7**
  Analyze, L336
  Analyze What-if Table, L342-343
  Fill by Example, L142
  Name, L393
  Sort, L398
  Version, L364
Range names
  adjacent labels and, L328
  deleting, L332
  in formulas, L327-333
  typing, L331
Range selector, sorting and, L399
Ranges command, L181,
  L286-287
Ranges & Titles command, maps
  and, L302
Ready mode, L12
Recalculation
  automatic, L191-193
  what-if table, L344
Record(s), **L391**-392
  finding using criteria, L402-410
  sorting, L397-402
Relative cell reference, **L149**
Relative reference, **L20**
Rename button, charts and, L281
Replace All button, spell checker,
  L112
Replace button, spell check and,
  L110
Reports, landscape, L188-189
Reset button, sorting and, L400
Restore button, L7
Revenue values, L148-149
Right-aligned values, **L19**
Right-Align icon, **L93**
Rotate data within cell, **L284**
@ROUND function, **L149**-152,
  L154-156
Row(s), **L8**
  plotting data series by, L273
Row height, **L97**
  changing, L172
  multiple worksheets, L230
Row number, **L8**
Row titles, L11, L16, L77
  balance sheet, L212
  entering, L142
  formatting, L88-89, L167
  multiple worksheets, L228-229
Row total, summing, L23

Save As command, **L27**
Save command, **L27**
Save icon, L25
Saving
  charts, L282
  worksheet, L25-27, L84, L158
Scrolling
  panes and, L192, L193
  viewing multiple worksheets
    and, L234
Seal a file, **L370**
Search command, help and, L46
2nd Y-Axis command, L289
SELECT-APPEND command, L359
Selecting/selection
  cell, L10-11, L69
  chart, L184
  collection of ranges, L75
  exploded slice, L242
  legend, L290
  map, L301
  noncontiguous ranges, L104
  range, L69
  range to print, L361
  removing, L24
  text block, L158
Selection indicator, **L8**
Sequence, see Data sequence
Set Criteria button, queries and,
  L414
Show Field As command, L418
Skip All button, spell checker,
  L112
Skip button, spell checker and,
  L111
SLASH key, Classic menu and,
  L48
Slices, pie chart, **L102**
  consolidated worksheet,
    L237-239
  exploding, L242-243
SmartIcons, **L8**
SmartIcons selector, L10
SmartSum icon, L19, L77
Sort command, L398
Sorting, **L397**-402
  multiple sort keys, L400-402
  single sort key, L397-399
Sort key(s), **L397**
  multiple, L400-402
  single, L397-399
Source, **L220**
SPACEBAR, blank character and,
  L44
Spell Check command, **L108,**
  L187
Spell checking, L108-112
  charts, L111

Split command, viewing multiple
  worksheets and, L233-235
Splitting window into panes,
  L191-193
Square text block, L243
Stacked bar chart, **L176**-186
  designer frame and, L186
  enhancing, L183-186
  grid lines and, L184-185
  printing, L190
  titles, L182
States, see Map(s)
Status bar, **L6, L10**
Stockholders' equity, **L211**
Stock market chart, L271,
  L295-298
Style(s), removing all, L87
Style menu, **L27, L87**
  Alignment, L87
  Gallery, L27
  Number Format, L90, L92, L93
  Page Break, L246-248
  Worksheet Defaults, L137, L227
Styles, removing all, L87
Style settings, changing, L137-139
Subtitle, consolidated worksheet
  chart, L239
Subtraction, order of precedence
  and, L68
Sum, calculating, L19-20
@SUM function, L19-20, L156
  balance sheet and, L212
  consolidated balance sheet and,
    L222
  copying, L20-21, L224
  @Function menu, L77-78
  list, L77
Summary worksheet, printing,
  L426
Symbols, **L270**
  line charts, L275
Syntax, macro commands, **L348,**
  L351
System date, L324-325

Table
  crosstab, L421-426
  database, see Database tables
  query, L410-420
  what-if, see What-if table
TABLE macro, L351
Table of values, displaying, L179
Templates, formatting, **L27**-30
Text, wrap, L88, L244
Text blocks, **L135, 211**
  aligning text in, L162
  consolidated worksheet chart,
    L238

creating, L139-141
designer frame and, L164-166
editing, L141
font size and attributes, L159
formatting, L158-167
moving, L163, L244
pattern and, L164-166
pie chart, L243
resizing, L160-162
selecting, L158
square, L243
Text color, L100, L138
Text format, L117
3D Bar chart, L178
3D Pie icon, L105
3D (three-dimensional) range,
  L222-225
3D vertical bar chart, L33-34
3D Vertical Bar icon, L33
Tick marks, **L273**
Title bar, L7
@TODAY function, **L324**
Tools menu, **L108**
  Chart, L271, L273
  Database, L403, L407
  Database Crosstab, L422
  Draw Button, L355
  Draw Ellipse, L293
  Draw Text, L141
  Macro Assign to Button, L355
  Map, L300
  Map Colors & Legend, L303
  New Query, L410
  Spell Check, L108, L187
Total increase/decrease in value,
  L77, L80
Transparent pattern, L294
Tutorial, **L47**
Type command, charts, L271

Underlining, multiple worksheets
  and, L231
Undo icon, **L44**
Unprotected cells, **L370**
Unseal file, L373
Update button, version, L366
US dollar currency format, L90,
  L229, L278
Use Labels button, L322
User dictionary, **L108**
Using Help command, **L46**

Value(s), **L11,** L17-19
  alignment, L19
  balance sheet, L217
  centering, L93
  referenced in a formula,
    changing, L191-193

entering, L67-73
formatting, L90-93, L168, L229
formatting line chart, L278
maps, L299
percent change in, L77, L80
resetting formulas to, L117
revenue, L148-149
rounding, L149-152
sequence of, *see* Data sequence
table of, L179
total, L77
total increase/decrease in, L77,
  L80
Value mode, L17, L69
Version, **L363**-370
Version command, L364
Version Manager, **L363**-370
Vertical centering, L87
Vertical scroll bar, panes and,
  L192, L193
Vertical splitter, L191
Viewing entire worksheet,
  L160-161
Viewing multiple worksheets,
  L233-237
View menu, **L233**
  Clear Split, L235
  Custom - 87%, L165
  Split, L233-235
  Zoom Out, L160

What-if analysis, **L134, L191**
What-if table, L320
  1-variable, L338-346
  recalculating, L344
  sequence of values, L340
Whisker HLCO chart, **L295**
Window, splitting into panes,
  L191-193
WK4 filename extension, L26
Work area, **L6,** L8-10
Work on an existing worksheet
  option button, L40
Worksheet(s), **L3, L8**
  building, L2-49
  charting, *see* Chart(s)
  clearing, L45
  closing, L39-40
  color in, L98-102
  consolidated, L218-226
  current, L175, L218
  default display size, L165
  font, L321
  formatting, L164-173, L334-335
  formatting values in, L168
  grouping, L227-228
  inserting, L173-175, L215

inserting worksheet before
  current, L218
macro in separate, L348
multiple, *see* Multiple
  worksheets
naming, L175-176, L218
opening, L40-42
preparation steps, L4, L64-65,
  L136, L211
printing, L37-38
printing chart with, L114
printing macro in, L358-362
printing summary, L426
saving, L25-27, L84, L158
spell checking, L108-112
ungrouping, L228
versions, L363-370
viewing entire, L160-161
Worksheet Defaults command,
  L137
grouping worksheets and, L227
Worksheet style defaults, **L137**
Worksheet tab, **L9**
color of, L232-233
Worksheet titles, L11-14, L65-66
  balance sheet, L212, L217
  formatting, L85, L228
  multiple worksheets, L226
Wrap text, **L88,** L244

X-axis, **L273**
  bar chart, L33, L34-35
  grid lines, L276-277
  stacked bar chart, L176,
    L180-181
  title, L280
X-axis labels, **L273**
X data range, pie chart, **L103,
  L238,** L241

Y-axis, **L31, L273**
  bar chart, L31, L34, L36-37
  General format, L278
  grid lines and, L184-185,
    L276-277, L297
  HLCO chart, L296-297
  line charts, L280
  mixed charts, L284, L287-289
  second, in mixed chart,
    L288-289
  title, L280

Zoom In, print preview and,
  L114
Zoom In icon, L188
Zoom Out, print preview and,
  L114
Zoom Out command, **L160**